An Auditor's Guide to Auditing Financial Statements in the UK

An Auditor's Guide to Auditing Financial Statements in the UK

Steve Collings FCCA

Bloomsbury Professional

LONDON · DUBLIN · EDINBURGH · NEW YORK · NEW DELHI · SYDNEY

BLOOMSBURY PROFESSIONAL

Bloomsbury Publishing Plc

50 Bedford Square, London, WC1B 3DP, UK
1385 Broadway, New York, NY 10018, USA
29 Earlsfort Terrace, Dublin 2, Ireland

BLOOMSBURY and the Diana logo are trademarks of Bloomsbury Publishing Plc

British Library Cataloguing-in-Publication Data

A catalogue record for this book is available from the British Library.

ISBN: PB: 978 1 52652 748 6
       Epdf: 978 1 52652 749 3
       Epub: 978 1 52652 750 9

Typeset by Evolution Design & Digital Ltd (Kent)

Foreword

I regularly hear auditors say that 'auditing isn't getting any easier'. This is true.

The ISAs (UK) are getting increasingly complex. Pressure for better regulatory compliance is increasing from the FRC and professional accountancy bodies. Expectations in terms of audit quality are only heading in one direction. Thankfully, we have Steve Collings to guide us!

I clearly remember the first time that I saw Steve's name in print. After reading an online piece on auditing, I was immediately impressed with his exceptionally clear writing. Shortly afterwards an opportunity presented itself to work with him and I jumped at it and we have been collaborating for many years now.

Steve's books are insightful and practical. His books are so good because he uses plain language to describe how things work and he uses plenty of examples based upon a wide range business types. What I like most is that he never forgets to give enough focus to small and medium-sized audits and the less complex entities that many auditors see every day.

Whatever standard setters might tell us, ISAs are written with large, complex companies in mind. This book does a great job of explaining how the same requirements apply to less complex audits.

There have been some major changes in ISAs (UK) recently. ISA (UK) 315, ISA (UK) 240 and ISA (UK) 540, spring to mind. In my opinion these are very positive revisions and should contribute to improvements in audit quality. However, the way the ISAs (UK) are drafted does not always provide clarity to the typical auditor.

That is why Steve's book is so important. Reading the ISAs (UK) themselves is useful but this book not only explains what is required but *why* it is necessary and *how* to apply it. It is a friend to accompany you on a journey to better understand what good, compliant auditing looks like.

Of course, auditors use standard methodologies, audit programmes and checklists. These of themselves do not guarantee audit quality and ISA (UK) compliance. This book will help auditors improve their knowledge and skills and to become less reliant on standardised paperwork.

I hope that you get as much from Steve's work as I do.

John Selwood
April 2024

Preface

I was standing at my local petrol station filling my car up racking my brains on what words to use for an attention-grabbing opening paragraph and suddenly thought 'Why don't I just use that – standing at the petrol station trying to figure out what words to use?'. This is a book I've wanted to write for a long time because I believe there is a gap in the market for it, so I wanted an attention-grabbing opening paragraph to capture readers' attention. Hopefully, it has worked, and I have grabbed your attention!

Recent data from one of the leading cloud platform providers showed that a worrying 36% of accountants are considering leaving the profession in the next five years (including 30% of under 25s). At the time of writing this Preface, there was already a huge skills shortage in auditing so the results of this survey concerned me because this problem could get worse. So, I decided to see for myself what the main issues real-life auditors faced on a daily basis.

A key feature of this book is the real-life interviews that have been carried out during the early stages of its production. These ranged from telephone interviews to questions and discussions I've had with auditors and accountants in my time on the lecture circuit to bring some context into the theoretical aspects of each chapter. One such interview that took place in the early stages of writing this book and struck a chord with me was with a practitioner who I will refer to as 'Mrs K'.

Mrs K is a sole practitioner with approximately 120 clients with one part-time administration lady, who just happens to be her former mother-in-law. Two of Mrs K's clients are audit clients. I asked Mrs K what she thought the current challenges in the accountancy and auditing profession were at the present time, and her responses were very candid.

She told me that in the last couple of years, she had been prescribed Sertraline – a form of prescribed anti-depressant. She blamed this largely on pressures in her professional life, but also because she was in the process of a divorce.

At around the same time, Mrs K underwent a routine audit monitoring visit from her professional body. Mrs K said it was not necessarily the inspection that accentuated her issues; it was the time spent preparing for the inspection and the sheer level of continuing demands from clients that seemed to be the start of her problems. She admitted that being informed of a monitoring visit did not exactly do her anxiety levels any good.

The results of her audit monitoring visit were, in Mrs K's words '... *surprisingly fine, but there were improvements required.*' I remember thinking that reference to 'surprisingly fine' was strange, because most audit monitoring visits conclude with a satisfactory result but there are usually some recommendations that follow. Mrs K went on to say:

> I started to think that I just wasn't cut out for the profession. I had all sorts going on in my personal life; client requests were simply relentless; the monitoring visit took (what seemed) forever to conclude and I just became completely overwhelmed with the whole situation. I cannot afford to leave the profession so I needed my work to be the one thing that could never be questioned.

From our interview, it became clear to me that it was not necessarily her audit monitoring visit or the satisfactory with limited improvements outcome that was to blame, it was her mindset.

It seemed to me that the reason Mrs K was under so much pressure was, of course, because of occurrences in her personal life and the daily challenges that life as an accountancy practitioner brings, but also, she was striving for 100% perfection, 100% of the time. Anything less than 100% would mean that, in Mrs K's eyes, she would be 'hung out to dry' by her professional body and this compounded her anxiety.

I am not a therapist (by any stretch of the imagination), so how did I know she was feeling like this? Because, I have felt like this myself and it becomes unbelievably draining to the point where you actually feel worthless and an utter waste of space. Some people strive for 100% perfection all the time – anything less and it just simply is not good enough. In auditing, feedback will always be a mix of positive and negative and there will *always* be some recommendations to take on board.

The key is to accept you're never going to have the red carpet rolled out for you because you're such a great auditor – the key is to accept there will always be some room for improvement. Some practitioners may do certain audit procedures one way, whereas a reviewer may have done it another way. It does not necessarily mean the practitioner is wrong. Life is a learning process all the way and that certainly applies in the world of accountancy and audit (which is why we have things like CPD that we have to do).

Since our interview, Mrs K is in a much better place. She has a done a 'root-cause' analysis of what was causing her depression and while the stress from the job did contribute, she realised it was not wholly to blame – her expectations were set a little too high. She is now on a much more positive path.

The 36% who are thinking of leaving the profession in the next five years may benefit from chatting with someone they do not necessarily know. Or, even chatting with someone they do know that has no idea about the accountancy profession, but who can perhaps make you look at things in a different light.

This book is aimed at auditors of all levels and those wishing to enter the auditing profession that may be wondering how certain things are done. It is also useful as an aide mémoire in reminding ourselves why certain procedures are carried out in a specific way and what their objective is. As you will see when you read this Preface, I deliberately go back to basics in many areas of auditing to articulate why things are done in a certain way.

Yes, this book is about auditing and, yes, most authors will claim their book is 'like no other book' and I am unashamed to say that this book is most definitely not like any other auditing book you may have seen or bought. This book goes right into the depths of why auditing has become somewhat problematic over recent years, and we go back to basics to revisit the reasons why certain audit procedures are done in the way they are done.

My aim is that this book will help auditors in their everyday working lives to understand some of the more complex areas of auditing and what regulators and reviewers are looking for during quality management reviews. It also strives to bring some of the positivity back into auditing and to make people realise that auditing is a valuable and rewarding profession. The 'horror stories' you hear/ read about in the professional press are isolated incidents that could well have been avoided. Hopefully this book will help auditors in their work and make the muddy waters less muddy.

Steve Collings FCCA
July 2024

Contents

Foreword	*v*
Preface	*vii*
Table of Examples	*xvii*
Introduction	1
Chapter 1 The Regulatory Framework	11
Introduction	11
Companies Act 2006 requirements	15
Rights and duties of the auditor under CA 2006	23
Anti-Money Laundering Regulations	26
Appointing an auditor	27
Auditor resignation	28
Chapter roundup	34
Pitfalls to avoid	35
Chapter 2 The Role of Regulators and Professional Bodies	37
Introduction	37
UK regulation	39
Transition of the FRC to ARGA	40
Development of ISAs (UK) and ISQMs (UK)	42
Regulation by the professional bodies	47
Auditor's liability for non-compliance with rules and regulations	61
Chapter roundup	65
Pitfalls to avoid	66
Chapter 3 Ethics	67
Introduction	67
Fundamental principles	69
Financial, business, employment and personal relationships	83
Long association with an audit client	93
Fees, remuneration and evaluation policies, gifts and hospitality, litigation	96
Non-audit services	102
Changes to the Ethical Standard	107
Provisions available for audits of small entities	111
Chapter roundup	115
Pitfalls to avoid	116
Chapter 4 Client Acceptance	117
Introduction	117
Advertising for services	118

Contents

Client acceptance and due diligence 121
Anti-money laundering protocol 132
Agreeing the terms of an audit 140
Chapter roundup 148
Pitfalls to avoid 149
Appendix 1 150
Appendix 2 154
Appendix 3 155

Chapter 5 Planning the Audit I: Risk and Understanding 159
Introduction 159
Objective of audit planning 162
Obtaining an understanding of the entity and its environment 166
Risk assessment and the auditor's response 177
Audit risk 188
Risk of material misstatement at the financial statement and
    assertion level 194
Evaluating the client's systems and controls 201
Chapter roundup 203
Pitfalls to avoid 204

Chapter 6 Planning the Audit II: Other Aspects of Planning 205
Introduction 205
Determining materiality 207
Analytical procedures 217
Developing the audit strategy and audit plan 222
Design of audit procedures 230
Fraud 237
Chapter roundup 244
Pitfalls to avoid 245

Chapter 7 Audit Evidence 247
Introduction 247
Audit evidence that responds to assessed risks 248
Sufficient and appropriate audit evidence 251
Obtaining audit evidence 258
Types of audit procedures 269
Corroborating audit evidence 276
Applying professional judgement 277
Risk and audit evidence 277
Audit sampling 278
Directional testing 295
Interim audit 296
Chapter roundup 298
Pitfalls to avoid 298
Appendix 299

Chapter 8 Other Audit Evidence Issues 323
Introduction 323
Using the work of experts 325
Using a service organisation 331
Auditing opening balances 337
Attending the stock count 344
Litigation and claims 351
Segment information 353
External confirmations 354
Considering the work of internal audit 358
Accounting estimates 363
Data analytics 371
Communication with management and those charged with
    governance 376
Reporting deficiencies in internal control 382
Chapter roundup 386
Pitfalls to avoid 387
Appendix 387

Chapter 9 Fraud, Laws and Regulations 393
Introduction 393
Fraud versus error 395
Responsibilities in relation to fraud 400
Professional scepticism 419
Closing the expectations gap 422
Laws and regulations 426
Chapter roundup 433
Pitfalls to avoid 434

Chapter 10 Audit Completion 435
Introduction 435
Evaluation of misstatements 437
Final analytical review 451
Subsequent events 456
Going concern 464
Opening balances, comparative information and corresponding
    figures 478
Chapter roundup 483
Pitfalls to avoid 484

Chapter 11 The Unmodified Auditor's Opinion 485
Introduction 485
Content of the auditor's report 486
The auditor's report 490
Emphasis of Matter paragraphs 495
Other Matter paragraphs 504

Contents

Other information in the auditor's report 505
Material uncertainties related to going concern 510
Key audit matters (KAM) 518
Limiting the auditor's liability 524
Chapter roundup 526
Pitfalls to avoid 527
Appendix 527

Chapter 12 The Modified Auditor's Opinion 533
Introduction 533
Modified audit opinion 536
Material but not pervasive 543
Material and pervasive 544
Reporting a modified audit opinion 547
Qualified 'except for' opinion 547
Adverse opinion 551
Disclaimer of opinion 554
Going concern 558
Chapter roundup 563
Pitfalls to avoid 564

Chapter 13 Group Audits 565
Introduction 565
Objectives of the group auditor 566
Accepting a group audit 568
Planning the group audit 569
Relying on the work of component auditors 578
Communication with the group auditor 581
Auditing the consolidation 583
Evaluating the sufficiency and appropriateness of the audit
   evidence 584
Communicating deficiencies in internal control 586
Expressing an opinion by the component auditor 587
Communication with those charged with governance of the group 587
Support letters 587
International groups 589
Transnational audits 589
Documentation 590
Chapter roundup 593
Pitfalls to avoid 595
Appendix 595

Chapter 14 Quality Management 601
Introduction 601
Monitoring audit quality 603
ISQM (UK) 1 611

ISQM (UK) 2 — 635
Quality management at the engagement level — 641
When the system of quality management fails — 646
Chapter roundup — 647
Pitfalls to avoid — 648

Chapter 15 Other Types of Engagement — 649
Introduction — 649
The framework for assurance engagements — 650
Review engagements — 652
Agreed-upon procedures — 654
Compilation engagements — 656
Due diligence engagements — 659
Social and environmental reporting — 663
Management commentary — 665
Providing assurance on historical financial information — 670
Providing assurance on prospective financial information — 671
Chapter roundup — 674
Pitfalls to avoid — 674

Index — 675

Table of Examples

[All references are to paragraph numbers]

Calculating the average number of employees 1.3

Determining the size of a company 1.4

Audit exemption statement 1.5

Excerpt from an auditor's report . 1.9

Excerpt from the Report of the Directors under CA 2006, s 418 ...... 1.9

Resignation statement with matters to report 1.12

Resignation statement with no matters to report 1.12

Illustrative response to an incoming auditor 1.13

Trivial hospitality 3.29

Provision of a business lunch 3.29

Provision of gift vouchers 3.29

Attendance at regular social gatherings 3.29

Inappropriate advertisement 4.5

Accepting an inappropriate client 4.6

Lack of client resources 4.13

Preconditions for an audit are NOT present 4.22

Understanding the entity 5.6

Understanding the environment a client operates in 5.7

Company is attempting to diversify 5.9

Identification of a risk of material misstatement 5.11

Business risks arising in different settings 5.13

Audit failure 5.14

Business risk and resulting audit risk 5.14

An irrelevant business risk 5.14

Forward foreign currency contract 5.17

Weak system of control over the bank reconciliation process . 5.18

Lack of going concern disclosures 5.22

Determining whether an item is material 6.2

A previously profit-making business sustains a loss 6.4

Determination of financial statement materiality 6.4

Calculation of performance materiality 6.5

Illustration of inverse relationship between materiality and audit risk 6.6

Clearly trivial errors 6.7

Interaction of ratio analysis with the financial statement assertions 6.9

Extracts from an audit strategy document 6.10

Extracts from an audit plan 6.11

Test of control 6.15

Capitalisation of development expenditure 6.16

High level of staff turnover 6.17

Substantive analytical procedures 6.17

Auditing the bank balance 7.6

Related parties 7.6

Auditor's attendance at the year-end stock count 7.9

Staff shortages in the purchase ledger department 7.13

Tests of controls over a sales system 7.14

New finance director appointed prior to the year end 7.15

Proof in total test 7.18

Audit of trade debtors 7.22

Use of sampling 7.23

Attendance at stock count 7.24
Sample size is too low 7.25
Non-sampling risk 7.26
Stratification 7.29
Attribute sampling 7.30
Selecting a sample 7.31
Monetary unit sampling 7.32
Misstatement within the trial
    balance 7.34
Trade debtors 7.34
Revenue and liabilities 7.34
Evaluating the work of an expert   8.7
Payroll function is outsourced 8.9
New audit engagement 8.14
Continuous movement of stock ... 8.25
Auditor's point estimate 8.46
Audit data analytics 8.52
Management and governance 8.54
Deficiencies in a client's system
    of internal control 8.59
Fraudulent financial reporting 9.5
Internal controls relating to fraud 9.11
Illustrative wording for the
    irregularities section of the
    auditor's report 9.16
Demonstrating professional
    scepticism 9.18
Non-compliance with laws and
    regulations 9.23
Reporting to a regulator 9.25
Factual misstatement 10.3
Projected misstatement 10.3
Judgemental misstatement 10.3
Evaluating the effect of identified
    misstatements 10.16
Final analytical procedures 10.17
Non-adjusting event 10.20
Adjusting event 10.21
Non-adjusting event 10.21
Illustrative Material Uncertainty
    Related to Going Concern
    paragraph 10.31

Illustrative disclosure made by
    management 10.32
New auditors appointed after the
    balance sheet date 10.34
Prior year's financial statements
    not audited – reporting in
    the auditor's report 10.36
Reporting by exception 11.8
Incorrect use of an EOM
    paragraph (1) 11.12
Incorrect use of an EOM
    paragraph (2) 11.12
Post-balance sheet event 11.12
Restructuring post-year end 11.14
Illustrative Other Matter
    paragraph 11.15
Inconsistency identified 11.16
Other Information section 11.18
Illustrative KAM section 11.28
Bannerman paragraph wording ... 11.29
Irrecoverable debt 12.7
Auditor discovers a material issue
    in the financial statements ... 12.12
Lack of related party disclosures 12.12
Adverse opinion 12.14
Disclaimer of opinion 12.15
A sole practitioner with two audit
    clients 14.4
Relevant ethical requirements 14.7
Outsourcing a system of quality
    management 14.10
Ensuring the five elements of an
    assurance engagement are
    present 15.2
Illustrative report of factual
    findings 15.5
Illustrative accountant's report on
    financial statements 15.6
Due diligence assignment 15.13
Illustrative assurance report on
    selected key performance
    indicators 15.16

Introduction

In recent years, auditing has been in the headlines and, sadly, not for the right reasons. High profile corporate collapses have led to questions being asked about the role of audit and the accountability of auditors. Not only is this a problem that doesn't seem to be improving, but there have also been lots of reports in the professional press about deficient audit work resulting in sanctions being imposed on firms and individuals.

So, what do I think the problem is and how can we possibly overcome it?

For many years, I have written about auditing and present courses to professionally qualified accountants on auditing and financial reporting subjects. This has given me an insight into some of the reasons why audit firms seem to struggle to 'get things right'. When I analyse the problems there are some common themes:

Now, it's fair to say that nobody in the auditing profession can produce a 100% technically perfect file. Believe me, I've tried and there will always be some negative (but constructive) feedback – that's just the nature of the beast, I'm afraid. What I think is important is to make sure that you act on negative feedback and make sure that the firm's system of quality management is as robust as possible.

I am an audit practitioner myself and have been subject to many file reviews (both independently and via my professional body, ACCA, through its audit monitoring regime) so I know what regulators and reviewers are looking for in a good file. This book aims to share that knowledge to help firms improve their audit work (especially if a file review hasn't yielded the results one hoped for).

WHY HAVE I WRITTEN THIS BOOK AND WHO IS AIMED AT?

For many years regulators such as the Financial Reporting Council (FRC) have been tackling the perennial problem of poor audit quality. I am old enough to remember the 'Clarity Project' which resulted in the International Standards on Auditing (UK) (ISAs (UK)) being revised and redrafted. Fast forward several years and the effects of the Clarity Project appear to have been forgotten about. The ISAs (UK) are complex in many areas and it's fair to say that many smaller audit firms tend to misinterpret the requirements or, in some cases, fail to apply the requirements.

In my view, the ISAs (UK) have been written from a 'think big first' approach rather than a 'think small first' approach. This means that the ISAs (UK) are primarily aimed at very large audits (such as a listed group) and hence are somewhat disproportionate when it comes to the smaller audits.

The FRC have revised some of the ISAs (UK) in recent years, even withdrawing some and creating new ones (for example, the International Standard on Quality Management (ISQMs (UK) which replaced the International Standard on Quality Control (UK)). This hasn't really solved the problem of deficient audit work and when you consider comments from practitioners there is a common theme running through them – the ISAs (UK) are sometimes difficult to understand in several areas which results in problems in interpreting them correctly. This is a problem that I doubt will go away anytime soon unfortunately.

The way in which the ISAs (UK) are developed are based on International Standards on Auditing that are published by the International Auditing and Assurance Standards Board. They are then 'tweaked' to become UK-specific – this results in the ISAs (UK) or 'ISA pluses' as they are often referred to. So, even for a small audit, the auditing standards are based on international requirements.

I am a firm believer of going back to basics to try and understand what it is that an accounting or auditing standard requires. This is a useful tactic (and has certainly helped me in my career as an audit engagement partner) because it makes you question *why* we must do something rather than just simply asking *how* to do something. Remember, as a child you probably repeatedly said '… but why?' to your parents; or you, as a parent, may be going through the same thing with your children now. That's the way my mind works when an issue crops up that means I must look to legislation or regulation to get something right (or at least as right as possible).

So, let me illustrate with an example. Take the concept of 'professional scepticism'. This is something that is frequently complained about by professional bodies and regulators in that practitioners are failing to demonstrate that they have applied a sufficient level of professional scepticism. But what actually is *professional scepticism* and how do you demonstrate you've applied it? In **Chapter 9** I introduce you to a fictional character called Dave. Dave boasts about various things, and you're left questioning the truthfulness of some of his statements. You're being sceptical. In auditing, you exercise professional scepticism by maintaining a questioning mind on stuff like accounting estimates or areas of the financial statements that require significant judgement. What an auditor needs to do then is to **document** what they have done in terms of questioning and challenging management's judgements or estimation techniques. I think for most firms, it's the issue of documentation that proves to be the challenge. My advice – just write it down on an audit working paper.

You can see just by that analogy that if you go back to basics and think about what the ISA (UK) or ISQM (UK) is requiring in a logical manner, you should find you may not be far off the ISA (UK) or the ISQM (UK) objectives. Sometimes, of course, the answer is to ask for help from the technical advisory helpline of your professional body who can steer you in the right direction.

In this book, I've deliberately gone back to basics because that is a good way of laying the foundations for a high-quality audit. I think sometimes we can become so lost in the technical content of professional standards that we forget what it is we are supposed to be doing and why we are supposed to be doing it. Knowing *why* something needs doing rather than just doing a procedure 'parrot fashion' means the work becomes tailored to the client and the objective of the ISA (UK) is met.

For example if I say to an auditor 'the starting point for testing sales is the customer's order and not the sales invoice', the auditor may just carry out that instruction and test, say, 60 sales transactions but not have a clue why they are doing what they are doing. But, if I say, 'the starting point for testing sales is the customer's order and not the sales invoice because the purpose of the test is to check that goods dispatched have been invoiced – ie, we are testing that income is **complete**', this explains *why* that procedure starts at a certain point and the procedure then makes sense. In other words, if the procedure is aimed at testing that goods dispatched have been invoiced, and thus the resulting revenue is complete, what is the point of starting the test using the sales invoice? So, understanding *why* we do something means that when we are using off-the-shelf audit programmes, the audit procedures make sense and we are then able to understand what it is we are doing a bit better.

3

This book is aimed at auditors of all levels including those that aspire to go into the auditing profession. The aim of the book is to revisit the basics of auditing which can be used by auditors as a basis of carrying out a high-quality audit.

The way it is written is different as well. I've deliberately used a chatty style (I'm a Boltonian lad and we're renowned for chatting!). I understand that a lot of books on this subject are written in very formal language, which is absolutely fine, but I didn't want to write this book in that way because of what I want it to achieve; which is to make auditing more understandable so that firms' audit quality improves. I owe a lot of thanks to my publisher, Bloomsbury Professional, for allowing me to write the book in this way. Throughout the book you'll find references to my first car, (which was an Austin Mini that spent the majority of the time in the garage); you'll find a reference to *Meatloaf's* song 'Two out of Three Ain't Bad'; and as I've already mentioned, you'll get to meet Dave who is a colourful character and I think adds some humour to what many accountants find a 'dry' subject. I'd also just like to emphasise that Dave is entirely fictional and is not based on any friends, family members or other associates of mine. So, to all the Daves I know, there can be no 'claims to fame' for that one!

STRUCTURE OF THE BOOK

I've deliberately structured the book so that readers can 'dip' in and out of it. This is not a novel or a book that is likely to be read from cover to cover (although it would be really great if someone did read it from cover to cover), but here's a run-down of how the book is structured:

Chapters 1 to 3

So, in my mind I have a hierarchy which works like this. We start by looking at the regulatory framework that underpins audit work in the UK, including the FRC's Ethical Standard. I've started with the regulatory aspects because essentially regulation and legislation underpin the work of the auditing profession. This is split over the first three chapters:

- Chapter 1: • The Regulatory Framework
- Chapter 2: • The Role of Regulators and Professional Bodies
- Chapter 3: • The Ethical Standard

Chapter 4

To do an audit, you of course must clearly have an audit client – you're not going to get far without one really, are you? There are a lot of rules that deal with client acceptance so in **Chapter 4**, I look at client acceptance and the various protocol that must be followed (eg, professional handover, Anti-Money Laundering Regulations (AMLR) and such like).

Chapters 5 and 6

Once we've gone through the hurdles of client acceptance and AMLR, we then need to look at planning the assignment. I'd say this is probably the 'lion's share' of the audit in that you could probably expect to spend about 40 to 50% of your time on planning. That's why I've split audit planning over two chapters.

Chapters 7 to 9

Once planning is finished, we then move into the detailed audit fieldwork (this is what I call the 'evidence-gathering' stage). **Chapter 7** looks at audit evidence which is one of the most crucial aspects of the audit because it is this evidence that the audit engagement partner uses to formulate their audit opinion, which is the entire objective of the audit. There's also an **Appendix** to **Chapter 7** which outlines various procedures that the auditor can use to obtain audit evidence, but this comes with a strong caveat – it is absolutely not intended to be a comprehensive list of procedures and cannot be used as a substitute for audit firms developing their own procedures. I've just used a list of 'typical' procedures for the various areas of the audit but ones which I think will be helpful.

In **Chapter 8** we look at other issues related to audit evidence such as the use of service organisations and auditing opening balances (as well as other aspects). In **Chapter 9** I cover issues such as fraud and laws and regulations because these are particularly sensitive areas of the audit and auditors are required to exercise extreme caution when it comes to dodgy stuff that comes to the auditor's attention (especially if money laundering is involved). Remember, there are so many rules and regulations that auditors are bound by, that it can be so easy to fall foul of the many pitfalls that exist when it comes to whistleblowing. Never underestimate the need to have a sound understanding of these rules and regulations – especially Anti-Money Laundering Regulations – and keep in mind that your professional body's technical advisory helpline can often be a source of good advice if you come across anything dodgy.

Chapters 10 to 12

These are what I've coined the 'completion chapters'. There are no prizes for guessing what these chapters are about – they cover the completion phase of the audit. In **Chapter 10** I look at specific completion procedures such as subsequent events and going concern. In **Chapters 11** and **12** we explore the auditor's opinions. Remember, the whole point of the audit is for the auditor to express an opinion on whether the financial statements give a true and fair view and have been properly prepared in accordance with accounting standards and company law requirements.

I've split the audit opinions over two chapters. **Chapter 11** looks at the unmodified (often referred to as the 'unqualified') opinion and the various elements that an auditor's report must contain. An unmodified opinion is the best opinion that an organisation can receive. **Chapter 12** looks at the modified (often referred to as the 'qualified') opinion. A qualified opinion is expressed when there is something wrong. Depending on the nature of the matter, the auditor expresses one of three types of modified opinion:

Chapter 12 goes into the detail of which type of modified opinion is needed in certain situations and how the paragraphs must be structured in the auditor's report. This, I think, is one of the most important chapters because one thing an auditor must avoid at all costs is expressing the wrong type of opinion. There can be very serious repercussions for doing this so it's crucial that we understand which type of opinion is most appropriate in the client's specific circumstances.

Chapter 13

Group audits are now a popular thing, too. Indeed in my role as audit engagement partner, I've seen group audits increase a lot, so we look at undertaking a group audit in this chapter. Also, if you are involved in group audits in your role, then it's worth keeping in mind that I wrote a book on group accounts for Bloomsbury Professional called *Group Accounts Under UK GAAP* which is definitely worth a read if you're involved in preparing accounts for groups. I really enjoy both doing and auditing group accounts but one thing you can never under-estimate is the level of complexity that these things bring with them.

Chapter 14

In **Chapter 14** I look at quality management. This is an issue that has been in the headlines a lot recently because of the new ISQMs (UK) on quality management. Quality management underpins audit work and is something that regulators are very keen on, so I've covered these issues in their own chapter.

Chapter 15

And then we get to the final chapter. In **Chapter 15** I sort of digress slightly from audit because here we look at other non-audit engagement work that a practitioner is likely to carry out for their client, for example, due diligence work and accounts preparation assignments. These sorts of engagements may offer some form of assurance, but not as high a level of assurance as an audit. The reports that are issued in non-audit engagement work will also differ quite a lot from an auditor's report, so I take a look at how the wording might look depending on what sort of assignment the practitioner is carrying out for their client.

REAL-LIFE SCENARIOS

As I mentioned in the Preface, while writing this book, I interviewed a lot of people. The people who I spoke to have been heavily anonymised to preserve confidentiality. They include audit practitioners, file reviewers and former file reviewers. In addition, I've also used some 'stories' that I've picked up during my many years on the lecture circuit from auditors who have asked me various questions and have shared some of their experiences with me. When a delegate asks me a question in a lecture I often wonder if they realise just how helpful they are being to me as well as others in the profession as you can use their queries as a basis for learning material.

These real-life scenarios (one of which you have already seen in the Preface) help to bring the theory in each chapter to life. There are some 'horror stories' where practitioners have been hung out to dry by their professional body for not doing what they are supposed to be doing and these have been included to articulate what firms should *not* be doing.

CHAPTER ROUNDUPS

At the end of each chapter is a roundup of what has been examined. This section of the chapters acts as a sort of summary and highlights key points in each section. I often find that chapter roundups can sometimes result in a 'lightbulb moment' where you think 'aaahh, yes, now I get it!'. I used to find that happening a lot when I was a student, especially in papers such as management accounting (which were very much my Achilles heel!).

PITFALLS TO AVOID

It is true that one of the main ways we learn is to make a mistake. That way we know not to do the same thing again. At the end of each chapter is a 'Pitfalls to avoid' section where I offer some friendly advice about what **not** to do.

FRAMEWORKS THAT ARE USED IN THE BOOK

Where references to an accounting framework are mentioned in the book, it is assumed that the entity uses FRS 102 *The Financial Reporting Standard applicable in the UK and Republic of Ireland.* You may also come across FRS 105 *The Financial Reporting Standard applicable to the Micro-entities Regime,* but FRS 105 doesn't crop up a lot because very few micro-entities have their financial statements audited.

I also try to avoid the use of adopted IFRS® Accounting Standards because this book is aimed at auditors of private entities, so I've assumed the main accounting standard that will be used by readers of this book is FRS 102.

ETHICS

Chapter 3 looks at ethics. My focus in **Chapter 3** is on the FRC's Ethical Standard and this has recently been updated so please make sure you're up to speed with the changes that are covered in this chapter. However, as audit firms will be regulated by a professional body, it also looks at some 'generic' ethical issues that are often found in professional bodies' Codes of Ethics. Each professional body is different, but their Codes are often broadly consistent.

USEFUL RESOURCES

As I have mentioned earlier, this book is pitched at quite a basic level as it is intended to form the groundwork for a high-quality audit. There are some other really good resources that firms can use where their audit work is concerned such as:

www.stevecollings.co.uk (I often publish articles on audit-related issues on here)

www.accaglobal.com

www.icaew.org

www.frc.org.uk

ACKNOWLEDGEMENTS

Writing a book is not a one-person or a solitary journey. There are many people involved behind the scenes that help during the writing process and final production process.

My sincerest thanks go to my Commissioning Editors, Dave Wright and Sarah Hastings. Their belief in this book during the proposal stage has resulted in its final publication. Their assistance and feedback during the initial chapter review stage was invaluable. As I have mentioned earlier, this book is written in a different style than one would normally expect a book on auditing to be written so Dave and Sarah's belief in me that this would work is very much appreciated. I also need to thank Dave and Sarah for their patience while I was writing this book as deadlines went slightly off course (due, in the main, to my holidays!)

One of the most important editors that the author of a technical book such as this one can have is the technical editor, whose job is to ensure my technical detail is right. My heartfelt thanks and gratitude go to Diane Nichols BA FCA whose keen eye for detail and suggestions have helped the chapters become even better. Diane is an audit file reviewer herself and so can probably relate to a couple of the real-life scenarios that crop up in this book.

Another person I am always lucky to work with is my copy editor, Claire Banyard. Claire and I have worked on all sorts of projects over the years. I have an immense amount of trust in Claire's work, and she has once again excelled herself in the copy editing of this book.

I must thank everyone who has taken the time to speak to me about their experiences. I cannot name them for obvious reasons, but they know who they are. Without their time I would not have been able to include the unusual 'Real-Life Scenario' feature that this book proudly contains. Your contributions to this book will undeniably help others in the long run.

My good friend and colleague, John Selwood FCA (who I am sure most readers will know) agreed to write the Foreword for this book. John's knowledge of auditing and the way that he can explain a complex issue in the most concise way has always amazed me and I am very lucky to be able to call him a friend. My heartfelt thanks and gratitude go to John for writing the Foreword.

I'd like to extend my thanks to all those at Bloomsbury Professional that have been involved in the marketing of this book, including designing the cover.

All my friends and family are an amazing support network. My friend and co-director, Les Leavitt, always provides a massive amount of support when it comes to projects like this. As an 'interesting fact', where you see references to 'Sunnie Industries' or 'Sunnie Enterprises', the Sunnie is Les's family dog who is just amazing.

Finally, I must thank you, the reader. I hope that it helps you in your dealing with auditing and that it helps with those 'lightbulb' moments. As always, I'm happy to receive comments and suggestions for future editions via the publisher.

BIOGRAPHY

Steve Collings FCCA is a Director of Leavitt Walmsley Associates, a firm of Chartered Certified Accountants based in Warrington and Sale, where Steve trained and qualified. Steve specialises in UK and Ireland accounting standards, International Financial Reporting Standards, auditing and Solicitors' Accounts Rules work.

Steve is the author of several books on UK and Ireland accounting standards, IFRS Accounting Standards and auditing. He has strong links with accountancy professional bodies and has written authoritative material for ACCA members and several articles for various magazine publishers.

Steve has served as a member of the UK and Ireland GAAP Technical Advisory Group at the Financial Reporting Council and currently represents the Northwest of England on the ACCA Practitioners Panel. In addition, Steve is a nationwide lecturer in the UK on financial reporting and auditing topics and, having been trained in international accounting standards, has lectured further afield in Barbados and Singapore.

Steve's work has been recognised by him receiving *Outstanding Contribution to the Accountancy Profession* by the Association of International Accountants and *Accounting Technician of the Year* at the British Accountancy Awards. Steve has also been highly commended by the Association of Accounting Technicians for his work in the accountancy profession.

Chapter 1

The Regulatory Framework

CHAPTER TOPIC LIST

- Introduction (see **1.1**).

- Companies Act 2006 requirements (see **1.2**).

- Rights and duties of the auditor under Companies Act 2006 (see **1.7**).

- Anti-Money Laundering Regulations (see **1.10**).

- Appointing an auditor (see **1.11**).

- Auditor resignation (see **1.12**).

INTRODUCTION

1.1   For many years, the debate about whether the term 'accountant' should be a protected term has raged on and is a very divisive subject. Currently, anyone can call themselves an accountant, but terms such as 'chartered accountant' and 'chartered certified accountant' are reserved titles which can only be used by those eligible to do so by virtue of being professionally qualified.

WHAT ARE WE TRYING TO ACHIEVE?

The starting point to understand anything where accountancy and auditing are concerned is to have a sound grasp of the legislation that governs the applicable issue(s). In this chapter we are focussing our attention on the regulatory framework that governs the auditing profession. Remember, auditing has come under increased focus in the last few years and failing to have a good understanding of the legal and regulatory bits can leave the auditor open to negligence claims or disciplinary action from their professional body.

1.1 *The Regulatory Framework*

Accountancy services, such as the preparation of financial statements and tax work are generally unregulated. However, professional bodies usually have strict rules in place whereby members can only provide such services (known as carrying out 'public practice') when they are permitted to do so through their relevant professional body (ie, by obtaining a practising certificate).

Auditing, on the other hand, is a regulated profession. Auditors provide a valuable service to an organisation and hence regulation is needed to ensure that auditors carry out their work to a high standard. Recent high-profile corporate collapses have shown that failing to carry out high-quality audit work results in significant fines and sanctions being imposed on the auditor individually and the audit firm and, often, this can lead to individuals being banned from carrying out audit work as well as expulsion from membership of their professional body. This essentially means the auditor has wasted years of hard toil in passing their exams to become a qualified accountant.

Regulation of the auditing profession exists in various forms. At the international level, there are several regulatory bodies such as the International Federation of Accountants (IFAC) and the two independent standard setting bodies:

The International Auditing and Assurance Standards Board (IAASB)

International Ethics Standard Board for Accountants (IESBA)

At the international level, these bodies issue standards and guidance which 'trickle down' to national standard setters who issue their own standards and guidance, having regard to international standards.

In the UK, the Companies Act 2006 contains the legal requirements which govern certain aspects of audit practice. For example, company law specifies the thresholds by which a company may claim audit exemption (see **1.3** below) and also provides the rights and duties of an auditor. In addition to company law, the Financial Reporting Council (FRC) issue standards and pronouncements which (while not being law) are mandatory for auditors.

IMPORTANT POINT

The UK has adopted International Standards on Auditing (ISAs) issued by the IAASB which have been amended to become UK-specific. The ISAs have been amended by the FRC to fit the UK's legal, economic and commercial environment and are referred to as ISAs (UK) (or 'ISA pluses').

There are also other regulations which an auditor falls under the scope of. For example, in the UK, Anti-Money Laundering Regulations (AMLR) will apply. In these respects, auditors are required to carry out specific AMLR protocol in adequately identifying the audit client and its shareholders/members and have specific obligations in AMLR to report any suspicions of money laundering to the audit firm's Money Laundering Reporting Officer.

Finally, there are the professional bodies who each have a role to play in assisting with the regulation of auditors, such as the Association of Chartered Certified Accountants (ACCA) and Institute of Chartered Accountants in England and Wales (ICAEW). There are other professional bodies whose members are eligible to carry out audit work, but I've chosen just two to provide some quick examples of who these professional bodies are.

Professional bodies play a vital role in the regulation of auditors. Each professional body has their own specific rules with which members who are auditors must comply. While each professional body in the UK *broadly* requires the same things, their specific regulations may differ in certain areas hence I won't be concentrating on one specific professional body's requirements. What is important to bear in mind at the outset is that they add a further layer to the regulation of auditors.

Professional bodies are responsible for holding audit firms to account where audit work is deemed to be deficient. Periodic inspections of audit firms take place to ensure that the work they are carrying out is of a high standard and sanctions are often placed on firms where audit work is noted to be falling short of the mark. In addition, the FRC also monitor audit firms who carry out audits of public interest entities (PIEs) and listed entities and it is not uncommon to find reports from the FRC criticising PIE auditors for failing to carry out audit work in accordance with the expected standards. Again, such shortfalls can result in heavy sanctions being imposed on the audit firm and its engagement partner(s).

The role of the auditor has come under increasing scrutiny over the last couple of decades and particularly in recent years due, for the most part, to the collapse of some high-profile companies. It would not be unreasonable to say that the catalyst for regulatory change came about when Enron collapsed, back in 2001, closely followed by its auditor, Arthur Andersen (which was one of the 'Big 5' auditing firms at the time).

The move to restore confidence in the audit market is not without its challenges. Regulators around the world have tried to introduce three initiatives:

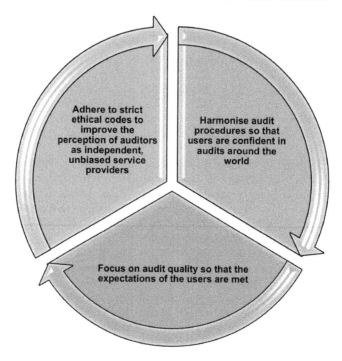

In order to try to achieve these goals, audit firms must follow all regulatory guidance. This is usually (but not exclusively) in the form of:

COMPANIES ACT 2006 REQUIREMENTS

1.2   If you've ever looked at the Companies Act 2006, you can be forgiven if you have tried to run a mile once you've seen the sheer size of it. It can be described as *anything* but a 'light read'. In fact, it has previously been given the accolade of being described as the largest piece of legislation passed by the UK Parliament. I think the other piece of legislation that is equally as 'daunting' is UK tax law (but, thankfully, I'll be leaving that to the tax experts to write a book on!)

Generally, only companies and groups that are medium-sized and large are compelled to have an audit. However, this is not absolute and other types of entity may be required to have an audit, regardless of their size, such as academy schools and some regulated entities.

Micro-entities and small entities, in the main, do not have to have an audit if the shareholders don't wish to have one. This is because company law provides an exemption from having an external audit of their statutory financial statements.

Remember, the way in which the Companies Act 2006 (CA 2006) works is to start off by saying 'all companies must have an audit'. The CA 2006 offers exemptions for certain companies and groups (eg, those that are deemed to be small under the legislation).

Now, just because there is an exemption available in company law that allows, say, a small company to claim audit exemption, that does not necessarily mean that every small company will choose to apply this exemption. In practice, the majority of small companies do claim the exemption, but some small companies do not. This may be because the directors wish to have an audit to increase the credibility of the company's financial statements; or it may be because a financier or the bank have specifically asked the small company to obtain an audit of their financial statements.

Sometimes an audit may be required because the company's legal documents (ie, the Articles of Association) require an audit. A shareholder can also request that the company has an audit if they hold more than 10% of the share capital.

Audit exemption thresholds

1.3   CA 2006 distinguishes between micro-entities, small companies/ groups, medium-sized companies/groups and large companies/groups. The sizes of a company or group is determined having regard to its turnover, balance sheet total and average number of employees.

In UK company law, these thresholds determine whether a company or a group is micro or small. In addition, there are also the audit exemption thresholds which track the company size thresholds.

1.3 The Regulatory Framework

The thresholds which, at the time of writing, were in place are as follows:

Size of company	Turnover	Balance sheet total	Employee headcount
Micro-entity	Not more than £632,000	Not more than £316,000	Not more than ten
Small company	Not more than £10.2 million	Not more than £5.1 million	Not more than 50
Small group	Not more than £10.2 million net; or Not more than £12.2 million gross	Not more than £5.1 million net; or Not more than £6.1 million gross	Not more than 50
Medium-sized company	Not more than £36 million	Not more than £18 million	Not more than 250
Medium-sized group	Not more than £36 million net; or Not more than £43.2 million gross	Not more than £18 million net; or Not more than £21.6 million gross	Not more than 250
Large company	More than £36 million	More than £18 million	250 or more
Large group	More than £36 million net; or More than £43.2 million gross	More than £18 million net; or More than £21.6 million gross	250 or more

Important point

On 18 March 2024, the government announced its first set of planned regulatory changes which are designed to ease the burdens placed on businesses in respect of non-financial reporting.

Legislation in the form of The Companies (Non-financial Reporting) (Amendment) Regulations 2024 is expected to be laid in the summer of 2024 to increase the size thresholds noted above. This aims to cut complexity and burden from legislative reporting requirements.

If the new measures are implemented, the table below outlines the revised thresholds:

Two out of three of:	Micro		Small		Medium		Large	
	Old	**New**	**Old**	**New**	**Old**	**New**	**Old**	**New**
Annual turnover	Not more than £632k	*Not more than £1m*	Not more than £10.2m	*Not more than £15m*	Not more than £36m	*Not more than £54m*	£36m+	*£54m+*
Balance sheet total	Not more than £316k	*Not more than £500k*	Not more than £5.1m	*Not more than £7.5m*	Not more than £18m	*Not more than £27m*	£18m+	*£27m+*
Average number of employees	*Not more than 10*		*Not more than 50*		*Not more than 250*		*251+*	

At the time of writing, the government intends that companies will be able to benefit from these new thresholds for financial years commencing on or after 1 October 2024.

There are some important points to note where references to 'turnover', 'balance sheet total' and 'employee headcount' are concerned:

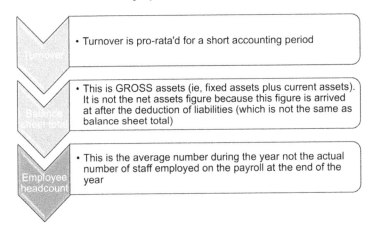

Turnover
• Turnover is pro-rata'd for a short accounting period

Balance sheet total
• This is GROSS assets (ie, fixed assets plus current assets). It is not the net assets figure because this figure is arrived at after the deduction of liabilities (which is not the same as balance sheet total)

Employee headcount
• This is the average number during the year not the actual number of staff employed on the payroll at the end of the year

Example 1.1 – Calculating the average number of employees

Brewster Ltd has an accounting reference date of 31 December. The company has a high turnover of staff due to the nature of its production. The payroll department has provided details of the information held in the payroll records during the year to 31 December 2024 as follows:

Month	Number of employees on the payroll
January	56
February	52
March	58
April	49
May	52
June	52
July	58
August	57
September	56
October	56
November	55
December	<u>58</u>
	<u>659</u>

The average number of employees is 55 (659 / 12 months) and has been rounded up.

The 'two out of three' rule

1.4   Some of you may be old enough to remember the band *Meatloaf*. One of *Meatloaf's* songs was called *'Two out of three ain't bad'*. I have not completely digressed from auditing here, but I think if you have heard or know of that song, it's an easy way of keeping in mind the 'two out of three' rule.

A company can only qualify as a small company if it meets **two out of the above three** criteria for **two consecutive years**. Hence, if the company was small in the prior year, but in the current year turnover just happens to exceed £10.2 million and gross assets exceed £5.1 million, the company will still be small under company law in the current year. If, in the next year, turnover exceeds £10.2 million and gross assets exceed £5.1 million, the company will be classed as medium-sized and hence will not be small. Once a company is medium-sized, it will generally need an audit (unless it can claim exemption under another area of company law, such as CA 2006, s 479A if it is a subsidiary whose parent has guaranteed the liabilities and complied with that area of the law in full).

I suppose you can say therefore, that 'two out of three' ain't bad as it means the company is doing rather well (for those that know the song by *Meatloaf*, I'm guessing it's now playing in your head).

IMPORTANT POINT

The audit exemption thresholds track the small company thresholds (ie if there is an increase in the small company thresholds, the audit exemption thresholds will automatically change), so a company generally must have an audit if it fails to qualify as a small company.

Example 1.2 – Determining the size of a company

Dexter Ltd has been trading for several years and is a standalone company (ie, not a member of a group). Extracts from the financial statements and accounting records of the business show the following:

	2021 £'000	2022 £'000	2023 £'000	2024 £'000
Turnover	11,500	9,800	10,000	10,900
Gross assets	6,700	5,000	5,350	4,980
Employee numbers	63	58	47	46

2021

Assuming, for the purposes of this example, that the company was medium-sized in 2020, the company is still medium-sized in 2021 because it has turnover of more than £10.2 million (£11.5 million) and gross assets of more than £5.1 million (£6.7 million). The average number of employees is higher than 50 (63). Therefore, Dexter Ltd is required to have an audit in 2021.

2022

In 2022, turnover reduces to £9.8 million which is below the £10.2 million threshold. In addition, gross assets also fall below £5.1 million while the average number of employees remains above 50 (58). Two out of the three criteria for small company classification have been met because turnover and gross assets are both below the small company thresholds. However, as the company was classed as medium-sized in the prior year, it is still medium-sized in 2022 (remember, two out of three **for two consecutive years**).

<u>2023</u>

In 2023, turnover again falls below the £10.2 million threshold, but gross assets go over the £5.1 million limit. However, the average number of employees falls below 50 and so the company now meets the two out of three criteria for two consecutive years and therefore becomes small in 2023. The company can now apply the small companies' regime in the preparation of its financial statements and hence claim audit exemption (if the directors wish to claim audit exemption, that is).

<u>2024</u>

In 2024, turnover exceeds £10.2 million, but both gross assets and the average number of employees are below the thresholds, hence the company is still small.

Small and micro-entities

1.5   Small and micro-entities can claim audit exemption and it is fair to say that most small and micro-entities take this exemption up (although there are some small companies that do have an audit, either voluntarily or because one has been requested by a parent company or a bank).

The main reasons for exempting small and micro-entities from the need to have an external audit are:

- The owners and managers of the company are often the same people.

- The advice and value which professional accountants add to a small company is more likely to concern services such as accountancy and tax compliance (other services may also include payroll).

- The impact of misstatements in the financial statements of a small or micro-entity is unlikely to be material in the wider economy.

- Owners may perceive that the cost of the audit fee and disruption of an audit outweigh the benefits.

Where audit exemption is claimed, the directors must make a statement to this effect on the company's balance sheet.

Example 1.3 – Audit exemption statement

The directors of Smallco Ltd have chosen to take up audit exemption for the year ended 31 December 2023. A statement to this effect is shown on the face of the balance sheet as follows:

The company is entitled to exemption from audit under CA 2006, s 477 for the year ended 31 December 2023.

The members have not required the company to obtain an audit of its financial statements for the year ended 31 December 2023 in accordance with CA 2006, s 476.

IMPORTANT POINT

It should be noted that the Economic Crime and Corporate Transparency Act 2023 which was issued in October 2023 will require a company (including dormant companies) which claim audit exemption to make an additional statement which identifies the exemption in company law being taken and confirming that the company qualifies for audit exemption.

At the time of writing, secondary legislation was awaited which dictates the form and content that this statement will make.

Remember, that audit exemption is claimed each year. However, there are also provisions in company law that protect minority shareholders. For example, a shareholder which holds not less than 10% of the share capital can require a small or micro-entity to have an audit.

Also, I think it is worth pointing out again that the audit exemption thresholds track the small companies' thresholds, so the planned increase in the small company thresholds (scheduled for periods commencing on or after 1 October 2024) will mean the audit exemption thresholds will automatically increase at the same time. This means that more companies will fall into the small category and hence be eligible to claim audit exemption. This will clearly be good news for some businesses, but it is important that the entity carefully considers the impact that a new reporting regime will have on stakeholders such as banks and other creditors (ie will they welcome a reduced level of disclosure if an entity drops into the small companies' regime from being a medium-sized entity?)

Over the years, there have been concerns raised by the professional bodies about the fact that a company can have a turnover of up to £10.2 million and not have its financial statements subjected to external scrutiny. To that end, some professional bodies have introduced an 'assurance plus' assignment which, I suppose, you could say acts as a 'mini audit' but is not as rigorous as an actual audit. The aim of this regime is to provide the users of small entities' financial statements with a low level of assurance over the financial statements, although it is not compulsory for a small entity to subject the financial statements to such a check.

Micro-entity audit

1.6   Micro-entities are a subset of the small companies' regime. They were introduced back in 2013 by the EU. Companies in the UK and Republic of Ireland can apply their own financial reporting framework in the form of FRS 105 *The Financial Reporting Standard applicable to the Micro-entities Regime*. FRS 105 has become an increasingly popular standard over the years since its introduction in 2015 and has also proven to be a standard that has been of interest to other jurisdictions that are perhaps looking at adopting a similar regime for their own micro-entities.

Again, a micro-entity need not have an audit, but it can choose to if it wishes. The problem the auditor has when a micro-entity decides to have an audit is the deeming provisions in company law.

So, what do I mean by the 'deeming provisions'?

The micro-entities' legislation states that where the micro-entity prepares its financial statements in accordance with the basic legally required minimum (ie, FRS 105), those financial statements are **presumed** (ie, 'deemed') to give a true and fair view. This means that the directors of the micro-entity do not have to consider any additional disclosure requirements that enable a true and fair view to be given.

IMPORTANT POINT

Consider a micro-entity that chooses to have an audit and there are material uncertainties related to going concern. Now, outside of the micro-entities' regime, standards such as FRS 102 *The Financial Reporting Standard applicable in the UK and Republic of Ireland* would require disclosure of these material uncertainties (if applying FRS 102, Section 1A *Small Entities*, such disclosures would be encouraged, but will become mandatory for small entities in the UK for accounting periods commencing on or after 1 January 2026 following the periodic review of UK and Ireland accounting standards).

A micro-entity preparing its financial statements under FRS 105 is not required to make disclosures in respect of a material uncertainty related to going concern and yet the financial statements would still be presumed to give a true and fair view. However, the auditors may take the view that in the absence of such disclosures, the financial statements would still be misleading (by virtue of the fact that they are **material** uncertainties) and hence, notwithstanding the requirement to report on going concern within the auditor's report, the auditor may determine it appropriate to resign.

Remember, the deeming provisions are contained in the micro-entities' legislation. There are no equivalent provisions in the Small Companies Regulations.

RIGHTS AND DUTIES OF THE AUDITOR UNDER CA 2006

1.7 CA 2006 makes provision for certain minimum rights and duties for an auditor and it is important that the audit client fully understand these rights and duties:

The rights and duties of an auditor are set out in CA 2006 and can be summarised as follows:

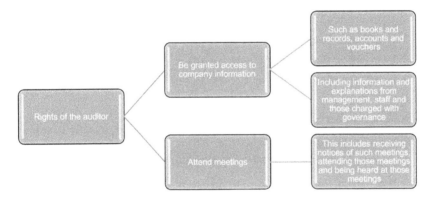

Rights

1.8 The above rights may seem fairly obvious. I mean, at the end of the day, how is an auditor going to audit a company's financial statements if they are not granted full access to books, records and staff who can provide information and explanations? However, in law, the auditor has a right of access at all times to the company's books and records, regardless of the format they are in (ie, manual or electronic). It should also be emphasised that these rights extend to overseas subsidiaries.

These are quite powerful rights (and understandably they need to be). If the auditor is restricted in any way from obtaining information they need to carry out their audit, the repercussions can be serious, such as the expression of a modified (qualified) audit opinion or, in more serious cases, resignation of the auditor, which can make it inherently difficult for the company to find a replacement.

The auditor also has a right of access to individuals within the organisation to assist with providing information to the auditor. This extends beyond management as other individuals within the business may be more suitably experienced to handle certain specific requests (eg, the production director might be better suited to explain the production process when auditing work in progress than, say, the finance director).

IMPORTANT POINT

Misleading the auditor is a criminal offence. A person found guilty of misleading, or withholding information from a company's auditor can receive:

- on conviction on indictment, a prison sentence not exceeding two years or a fine, or both;

- on summary conviction:

  — in England and Wales, a prison sentence not exceeding 12 months or a fine not exceeding the statutory maximum (or both); and

  — in Scotland or Northern Ireland, a prison sentence not exceeding six months or a fine not exceeding the statutory maximum (or both)

The rights in relation to meetings are important because they allow the auditor to communicate with the shareholders. In some cases, this communication may be the only chance the shareholders get to communicate with the auditor, so it is an important right. Remember, it is the shareholders that appoint the auditors (except the first auditor or the need to fill a casual vacancy, which is carried out by the directors) and it is the shareholders to whom the auditor's report is addressed (note: 'shareholders' are also sometimes referred to as 'members').

Duties

1.9   The duties of an auditor largely relate to the provision of an auditor's report to the shareholders/members of the business (or equivalent in a non-limited company). The auditor is obliged to form a conclusion on a range of matters and then report to the shareholders on those conclusions.

Remember, the auditor's report will include the auditor's **opinion** on the financial statements. However, rather than dealing with the auditor's opinion, the area of company law that deals with the auditor's duties deals instead with a number of issues relating to the accounting records that have been maintained by the directors, the information and explanations received by the auditors and the sufficiency of disclosure on various issues.

CA 2006 requires the auditor to form an opinion on the following matters:

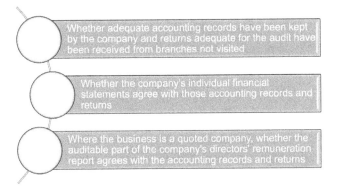

Whether adequate accounting records have been kept by the company and returns adequate for the audit have been received from branches not visited

Whether the company's individual financial statements agree with those accounting records and returns

Where the business is a quoted company, whether the auditable part of the company's directors' remuneration report agrees with the accounting records and returns

In the auditor's report it is not uncommon to see these issues **reported by exception**. Granted, this terminology is somewhat out of date nowadays and used to refer to a point in time when the auditor would only report on them if there was a problem that needed to be flagged up to the shareholders, but reporting 'by exception' is still a common term used in the auditing profession when describing such matters.

Example 1.4 – Excerpt from an auditor's report

The excerpt below is from an auditor's report for a private limited company showing how these issues are reported by exception:

Matters on which we are required to report by exception

In the light of our knowledge and understanding of the company and its environment obtained in the course of the audit, we have not identified material misstatements in the Strategic Report or the Report of the Directors.

We have nothing to report in respect of the following matters where CA 2006 requires us to report to you if, in our opinion:

- adequate accounting records have not been kept, or returns adequate for our audit have not been received from branches not visited by us; or

- the financial statements are not in agreement with the accounting records and returns; or

- certain disclosures of directors' remuneration specified by law are not made; or

- we have not received all the information and explanations we require for our audit.

> **IMPORTANT POINT**
>
> The duties of an auditor are wide-ranging and the powers granted to auditors under CA 2006 should enable their duties to be discharged accordingly.

It should also be noted that the directors must make a statement under CA 2006, s 418 that each of the directors who held office during the period covered by the financial statements have made available all relevant audit information to the auditors and they have taken steps to make themselves aware of any relevant audit information, and ensured that the auditors are made aware of that information.

Example 1.5 – Excerpt from the Report of the Directors under CA 2006, s 418

Statement as to disclosure of information to auditors

So far as the directors are aware, there is no relevant audit information (as defined by CA 2006, s 418) of which the company's auditors are unaware, and each director has taken all the steps that he or she ought to have taken as a director in order to make himself or herself aware of any relevant audit information and to establish that the company's auditors are aware of that information.

ANTI-MONEY LAUNDERING REGULATIONS

1.10   Anti-Money Laundering Regulations (AMLR) are a significant set of regulations that auditors must ensure they comply with as far as possible. At the outset, it is worth noting that I examine AMLR protocol in more detail in **Chapter 4** (see **4.7** and **4.8**).

As a basic introduction, money laundering is the process by which criminals attempt to conceal the true origin and ownership of the proceeds of their criminal activity and essentially profit from their unorthodox practices.

Over the last few years, compliance with AMLR has moved up the ranks of importance for audit firms because the regulations have become more intense. Professional bodies such as ACCA and ICAEW carry out monitoring visits on member firms to ensure that they have sufficient AMLR protocol in place and heavy sanctions (including expulsion from membership) can be dished out by the professional body where a member firm is failing to comply with the protocol. **Chapter 4** looks at some real-life issues where professional bodies have come down heavily on members and expelled them due to non-compliance with AMLR protocol. The government have also clamped down hard over the last couple of years where money laundering is concerned and the accountancy profession is one of the professions that can be said to be at the 'forefront' of policing this (rightly or wrongly).

As I mentioned, **Chapter 4** looks in more detail at the auditor's duties where money laundering is concerned but it is important that staff are trained in all aspects of AMLR and this needs to be carried out at least annually.

IMPORTANT POINT

Remember, there are no *de minimis* concessions where AMLR is concerned hence there is no monetary threshold below which suspicions should not be reported. The obligation to make a Suspicious Activity Report is irrespective of the amount involved, or the seriousness of the suspicion.

APPOINTING AN AUDITOR

1.11 I mentioned earlier in the chapter that it is usually the shareholders (members) of a company that appoint the external auditors. I say 'usually' because a company's *first* auditors are usually appointed by the directors and this is then ratified by the shareholders at the first Annual General Meeting (AGM). In exceptional situations, the Secretary of State can appoint an auditor if no auditors are appointed by the shareholders or directors.

The appointment of an auditor will depend on whether the company is a:

Public company; or
Private company

Public companies must hold an AGM and at each AGM where the financial statements are presented, the auditors are appointed. In a lot of cases, the company's existing auditors are reappointed (provided, of course, they want to be reappointed or CAN be reappointed if there are no ethical issues). The incoming auditors must cease to hold office at the end of the next general meeting where the accounts are discussed (unless they are reappointed).

The auditors of a **private company** are appointed before the end of a 28-day period which starts from:

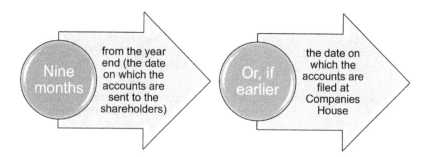

A private company is not required to hold an AGM. Therefore, there are provisions in company law that allow a private company's auditor to be automatically reappointed and this is the case for many private companies. The exception to this rule would be where the company's Articles of Association stipulate that the auditors must be reappointed by way of a vote at a meeting. It is important that the provisions in a company's Articles of Association are carefully checked to see if this provision is in there to avoid the company not properly complying with its Articles.

CA 2006 also makes provision for a shareholder which holds more than 5% of the shares to **object** to automatic reappointment of the auditors, meaning that an annual appointment process will need to be carried out. In practice, this objection is quite rare and, in my experience, has only ever arisen where there have been some issues with the auditors in a previous audit.

In **Chapter 4**, I examine protocol that is involved when an audit client changes auditor. While most of the professional handover protocol for a non-audit assignment is pretty much the same for an audit assignment, there are some other issues that need to be covered (eg, allowing the incoming auditor access to the outgoing auditor's audit working papers).

AUDITOR RESIGNATION

1.12   An auditor can cease to act for a client either by resigning or by removal from office by the client.

Auditors can resign at any time they feel is appropriate simply by notifying the company. Historically, auditors had to provide a copy of their resignation (via a 'statement of reasons' sometimes known as a 'statement of circumstances' – see **1.13** below) to Companies House and while this is the case in certain situations, it is not necessarily the case that the auditor has to lodge a copy of their resignation letter with the Registrar of Companies. An auditor need not lodge a copy of their resignation letter when their reasons for resignation are **exempt reasons**. These exempt reasons are:

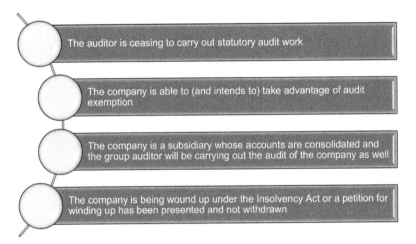

The auditor is ceasing to carry out statutory audit work

The company is able to (and intends to) take advantage of audit exemption

The company is a subsidiary whose accounts are consolidated and the group auditor will be carrying out the audit of the company as well

The company is being wound up under the Insolvency Act or a petition for winding up has been presented and not withdrawn

Auditors can also be removed from office by the shareholders. The shareholders are required to give the company 28 days' notice of their intention to put a resolution in place to remove the auditor, or to appoint another auditor, and this resolution must be presented in a general meeting. The auditor must receive a copy of the resolution and they then have the right to provide a written response and require that it be sent to the shareholders. The shareholders then vote by a simple majority, which is known as an 'ordinary resolution' to remove the auditor.

IMPORTANT POINT

The law is clear that **only** a company's shareholders can vote to remove the auditor. This provides an element of protection to the auditor against the directors picking and choosing who acts as auditor without the approval of the shareholders. In theory, this should act as a deterrent against an intimidation threat made by the directors against the auditor.

REAL-LIFE SCENARIO

Mr D was a partner in a six-partner firm that had an audit client in the food industry. The audit client had a separate external accountant who was responsible for preparing the statutory accounts and doing the tax side of things.

Mr D's audit team encountered significant difficulties in the previous year's audit (which was their first year as auditor). Lots of balance sheet control accounts had imbalances and the financial statements were in a poor state. It took a significant amount of time to complete the audit as the financial statements had to be redrafted by the external accountant about four times. Eventually, the audit was signed off but the accounts were late for filing by about four months.

The following year it was clear that similar problems existed. Nothing that Mr D nor his audit team had suggested in terms of improvements had been implemented by the company or the external accountant. The draft financial statements contained a huge suspense account balance and the external accountant had proposed that this simply be written off to cost of sales.

Mr D quickly concluded that his firm could not carry out this audit without a significant amount of additional work being carried out to correct the financial statements. The external accountant was clearly out of his depth and lacked the ability to prepare statutory financial statements to the standard that were auditable.

Mr D decided that his firm could not carry out the audit because they lacked the resources needed to get the audit signed off and therefore he duly resigned.

This situation demonstrates that the auditor has the right to resign from an audit client at any time. Resignation need not necessarily take place after the financial statements have been approved.

I mentioned earlier that only the shareholders have the ability to remove the auditor. Now, in real life this is often done in conjunction with the directors. Consider a company that has several hundred shareholders in place. Not all these shareholders will be sufficiently informed to make their own decision, and so the directors will be required to assist in helping them make this decision. Shareholders are likely to follow the recommendation to replace the auditor without much discussion or debate.

Some companies apply Corporate Governance principles, which involves appointing an audit committee. One of the objectives of an audit committee is to strengthen the independent position of a company's external auditor by providing an additional channel of communication. Not all companies have an audit committee, and it tends to be the larger ones that do.

Where an audit committee is in place, they will be involved with the appointment and removal of the auditor. Where a company (eg, a small company) does not have such a committee in place, the auditors can find themselves in a difficult position if the directors are influencing the shareholders to vote on a removal from office.

Example 1.6 – Resignation statement with matters to report

Dear Sir

Statement to Tennyson Enterprises Ltd ('the Company') on ceasing to hold office as auditors pursuant to CA 2006, s 519

We resign as Auditor to the above Company. Our reason for resigning is due to difficulties in obtaining sufficient appropriate audit evidence during our audit of the financial statements for the year ended 31 July 2024.

Unless the Company applies to Court, the Company must, within 14 days of receipt of this Statement of Reasons, send a copy of the Statement of Reasons to every person who, under CA 2006, s 423, is entitled to be sent copies of the financial statements.

Yours faithfully

ABC Chartered Accountants

Example 1.7 – Resignation statement with no matters to report

Dear Sirs

Statement to the Directors and Shareholders of Morley Industries Ltd (Registered Number 12345678) on ceasing to hold office as auditors pursuant to CA 2006, s 519

In accordance with CA 2006, s 519, we confirm that there are no matters or circumstances connecting with our ceasing to hold office that we consider should be brought to the attention of the company's shareholders or creditors.

Yours sincerely

ABC Chartered Certified Accountants

IMPORTANT POINT

A point worthy of note (and one which is often forgotten about until it is brought to the auditor's attention) is that if an auditor resigns, or is removed from office, **before the end of their term of office**, they must notify their relevant professional body (eg, ICAEW or ACCA).

Statement of reasons

1.13   When an auditor resigns from office, company law states they have the right to call a shareholders' meeting to discuss their reasons for resigning. This doesn't apply where there are no matters which need to be brought to the attention of shareholders or creditors.

The auditor will need to draft a 'statement of reasons' (sometimes called a 'statement of circumstances') when the auditor resigns from an audit client prior to the end of their term of office. This statement may need to be sent to Companies House unless the reason for the auditor's resignation is covered by an exempt reason (see **1.12** above).

When a statement of reasons is required, it should contain the following information:

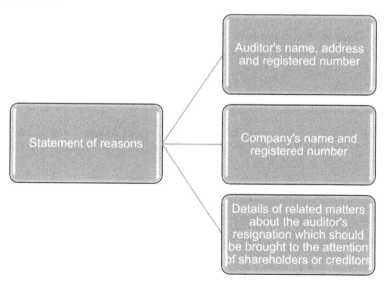

IMPORTANT POINT

The statement of reasons is important because it provides the auditor with a mechanism of explaining to shareholders why they have resigned.

Sometimes the reasons for the resignation will need particular care and attention. For example, where the auditor had suspicions of money laundering or had discovered fraud. In such situations, the auditor will need to comply with other regulation, such as Anti-Money Laundering Regulations (AMLR).

IMPORTANT POINT

Where the auditor has decided to resign because of sinister reasons, it is critical that the auditor takes careful steps where this is concerned. For example, where the auditor chooses to resign because of money laundering or fraud, the auditor must be careful not to 'tip off' the client by explaining their reasons for resignation. It is always advisable to seek advice from the technical advisory department of the relevant professional body, or external legal advice. This is because while fraud or money laundering are issues that *should* be brought to the attention of creditors or shareholders, it cannot be brought to their attention by the auditor because of protocol under AMLR.

When an auditor resigns in such situations, it is likely that an incoming auditor will contact the outgoing auditors to request 'professional clearance'. Again, the outgoing auditor cannot inform the potential incoming auditors of their exact reasons for resignation because this, too, would constitute a breach of the AMLR, which is a criminal offence in its own right.

Many professional bodies have standard text that can be used in dealing with this situation, a copy of which is shown as follows:

Insofar as our ethical and legislative responsibilities allow us to reply, we can confirm that we are not aware of any professional reason why you should not accept the appointment.

This will allow for a reply to be given to the potential incoming firm.

Example 1.8 – Illustrative response to an incoming auditor

Dear Sir/Madam

Sunnie Enterprises Ltd

Thank you for your letter dated 17 September 2024, the contents of which are noted. We know of no reasons, professional or otherwise, which you will need to consider on deciding whether or not to formally accept the appointment as auditors to Sunnie Enterprises Ltd.

Yours faithfully

ABC Chartered Certified Accountants

CHAPTER ROUNDUP

- The auditing profession has come under increasing levels of scrutiny over the last few years due to some high-profile corporate collapses that have brought the auditing profession into question in terms of its reliability and its trustworthiness.

- Auditing standards in the UK are issued by the Financial Reporting Council in the form of International Standards on Auditing (UK) (ISAs (UK)). ISAs (UK) are essentially the auditing standards issued internationally by the International Auditing and Assurance Standards Board, which are then 'tweaked' to become UK-specific.

- Legislation contains the rights and duties of an auditor and also outlines those types of entities that are required to have an audit and those that can claim exemption from audit.

- Audit exemption thresholds are the same as the small companies' thresholds.

- A company qualifies as small (and hence may be able to claim audit exemption) when it meets two out of the three small companies' criteria for two consecutive years.

- Auditors have a right of access to books and records and also have a right to attend meetings.

- The auditing profession is subject to the requirements of the Anti-Money Laundering Regulations; hence an auditor must ensure they are up to speed with developments in this important legislation.

- Appointing an auditor is quite a straightforward process but there are provisions in law that govern the appointment of an auditor to a private company and a public company.

- Auditors can resign at any time and can also be removed by the shareholders. Again, there is protocol that must be followed by an outgoing auditor, including drafting a statement of reasons and, in certain situations, lodging a copy of this statement to Companies House as well as notifying the relevant professional body.

PITFALLS TO AVOID

- Failing to understand the audit exemption thresholds correctly (eg, misinterpreting 'balance sheet total' as being net assets, rather than total assets).

- Not complying with Anti-Money Laundering Regulations properly (eg, failing to obtain appropriate identification for the new audit client).

- Not notifying the relevant professional body where the auditor is removed from office (or resigns) before the end of their term.

Chapter 2

The Role of Regulators and Professional Bodies

CHAPTER TOPIC LIST

● Introduction (see **2.1**).

● UK regulation (see **2.2**).

● Transition of the FRC to ARGA (see **2.3**).

● Development of ISAs (UK) and ISQMs (UK) (see **2.4**).

● Regulation by the professional bodies (see **2.9**).

● Auditor's liability for non-compliance with rules and regulations (see **2.13**).

INTRODUCTION

2.1　　The debate on whether the term 'accountant' should be protected has been raging on for years, and I suspect it is one of those issues that will continue raging on for years to come (a bit like the old amortisation vs non-amortisation of goodwill that has been debated for years by the International Accounting Standards Board® (incidentally, they have agreed, for now at least, on a non-amortisation approach but do remember that under UK and Ireland GAAP goodwill must be amortised). The debate on protecting the term 'accountant' is a divisive one and I'd rather not open up the proverbial 'can of worms' but it is an issue that is relevant to this chapter in terms of who can and cannot do audit work.

As we know, anyone can call themselves an accountant. They cannot, however, call themselves a Chartered Accountant or a Chartered Certified Accountant without having obtained membership of the relevant professional body.

Auditing, on the other hand, is a regulated activity. Only those holding 'statutory auditor' status (which is often referred to as 'registered auditor' status or 'responsible individual' (RI) status) can sign auditors' reports in the

2.1   *The Role of Regulators and Professional Bodies*

UK. It isn't unknown for accountants without auditor status to sign auditors' reports but this is a definite no-no if you want to avoid heavy sanctions being imposed on you by your professional body (sanctions including expulsion from membership). You've spent years studying, investing blood, sweat and tears to become a qualified professional, so why would you risk all that by doing things you're not supposed to?

WHAT ARE WE TRYING TO ACHIEVE?

In this chapter I examine the role that regulators and professional bodies play in the auditing profession. A regulated activity, such as auditing, must be overseen properly and the mechanism by which this is done must be clearly understood by those in the profession. Auditors must have a sound understanding of who they are regulated by and what standards are expected of them. This chapter aims to address those issues.

I think the best way to start this chapter is to examine the hierarchy:

At the top of the hierarchy is the IAASB. They issue International Standards on Auditing (ISAs) and are a subsidiary of the International Federation of Accountants (IFAC). IFAC is simply a grouping of accountancy bodies and hence has no legal standing in individual countries. Countries therefore need to have arrangements in place for regulating their own auditing profession and implementing auditing standards. The IAASB is responsible for developing and promoting ISAs and International Standards on Quality Management (ISQMs). Key principles of the ISAs include the following:

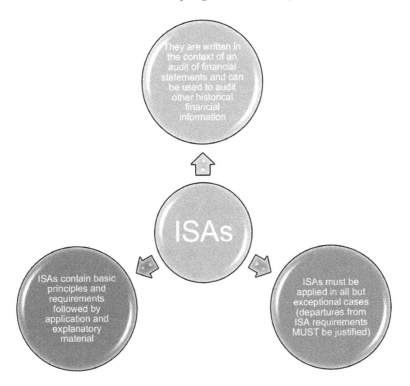

Underneath the IAASB sits the IESBA. The IESBA is responsible for issuing ethical standards which both accountants and auditors must comply with. Most professional bodies' Codes of Ethics and Conduct have their 'roots' embedded in the IESBA's Code of Ethics.

Then we come to the UK. Of course, we all know that the Financial Reporting Council (FRC) regulates the accountancy and auditing profession, and they are responsible for developing and maintaining accounting and auditing standards for use in the UK (the FRC is also responsible for issuing accounting standards for use in the Republic of Ireland as well).

UK REGULATION

2.2 In the UK, the FRC are the 'Competent Authority' for audit. This seems a bit of a strange title to give to the FRC, but the title is borne out of the Audit Directive. Article 2(1) of the Audit Directive states that:

'competent authorities' means the authorities designated by law that are in charge of the regulation and/or oversight of statutory auditors and audit firms or specific aspects thereof; the reference to 'competent authority' in a specific Article means a reference to the authority responsible for the functions referred to in that Article.[1]

Generally, the FRC oversees the audit work of public interest entities (PIEs) and listed entities. Audits of non-PIEs and non-listed entities are generally overseen by the professional bodies, such as ACCA and ICAEW (see **2.9** below for how the professional bodies regulate the audit work of member firms).

The FRC is responsible for issuing and maintaining ISAs (UK) and other regulations, such as Practice Notes and Bulletins. The FRC have also issued the Ethical Standard which must be followed by auditors in the UK (**Chapter 3** examines the Ethical Standard in more detail).

In relation to audit, the FRC carries out other duties, such as:

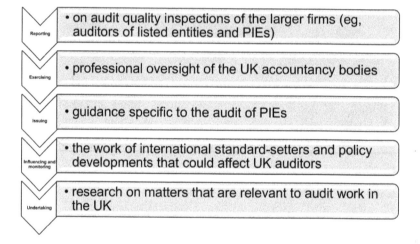

Reporting • on audit quality inspections of the larger firms (eg, auditors of listed entities and PIEs)

Exercising • professional oversight of the UK accountancy bodies

Issuing • guidance specific to the audit of PIEs

Influencing and monitoring • the work of international standard-setters and policy developments that could affect UK auditors

Undertaking • research on matters that are relevant to audit work in the UK

TRANSITION OF THE FRC TO ARGA

2.3   There has been much in the professional press about the FRC transitioning to the **Audit, Reporting and Governance Authority** (ARGA). This followed recommendations by Sir Donald Brydon CBE who carried out an independent review of the auditing profession and who was very critical of the way in which the FRC operates. The intention is that ARGA will have a new mandate, a new clarity of mission, new leadership and new powers.

A separate review of the FRC was carried out by Sir John Kingman following the Brydon review who was specifically tasked with evaluating the FRC

---

1 Audit Directive (2014/56/EU) and Audit Regulation (537/2014/EU), Article 2(1).

following the collapse of Carillion and other high-profile companies. The Kingman review supports the findings of the Brydon review and was intended to be a 'root and branch' review which included:

- Consideration of the governance of the FRC.

- Whether the FRC is sufficiently independent from those whom it regulates.

- Whether there are appropriate safeguards that offer protection against conflicts of interest.

- The powers of the FRC and whether these powers should be extended.

- The resources and capacity at the FRC.

The findings from this review did not make for pleasant reading and were pretty scathing. It stated that the role of the FRC is confused and has an apparently little-known role in investigating complaints raised relating to its remit by whistle-blowers.

In addition, it is well-known that the quality of audits performed by auditors of PIEs and listed entities is often criticised by the FRC. The Kingman report stated that 81% of FTSE 350 audits in 2016 required only limited improvement, meaning that 19% were significantly below standard which is not a ringing endorsement of a high-quality and competitive audit market. The report went on to say that the FRC is far too passive in demanding improvements and monitoring subsequent performance. This means the FRC has not been entirely effective in preventing poor quality audits.

As you can see, not a great set of feedback, to say the least and that's before we even consider the final 'kick when you're down' comment that the FRC is a *'ramshackle house'* which *'leaks and creaks, sometimes badly'*. It then goes on to say that it is *'... time to build a new house.'* I must admit to 'wincing' somewhat when I read that feedback.

Much work has been done by the FRC to address the recommendations of the Kingman review and this work started pretty quickly following receipt of the report. However, a lot of the recommendations required Parliament to delegate powers to the new regulator via Statutory Instruments and this, of course, is not something that can be done overnight.

So, where are we now in terms of the transition to ARGA?

The FRC issued a three-year plan to form ARGA in 2022 and obviously the COVID-19 pandemic had a detrimental impact on the progress that could be made on this transition. However, the transition to ARGA has effectively been put on the 'back burner' as the Audit Bill was not covered in the King's speech in October 2023 and (at the time of writing) there is likely to be a general election before the next King's speech. This was a disappointing turn of events because a lot of work had been done behind the scenes to prepare for the eventual transition to ARGA. I say it has been put on the back burner because it is not the case that the transition to ARGA has been scrapped – it will eventually happen, but it's not likely to happen until 2026 or 2027 (and there is no certainty that it will happen then, so don't hold me to ransom with those dates).

Following the King's speech, the FRC issued a policy update on 7 November 2023. This update confirmed that the FRC will only take forward a small number of proposals out of the 18 proposals that it set out in the consultation and will stop development of the remainder. The proposals it will take forward are:

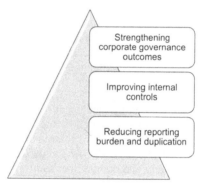

So to wrap this section up, it's a case of wait and see what happens in the next couple of years. However, notwithstanding the delay in transitioning to the new regulator, what is important is that audit quality improves and confidence in the auditing profession is restored.

DEVELOPMENT OF ISAS (UK) AND ISQMS (UK)

2.4   For an ISA (UK) or an ISQM (UK) to be issued, a lengthy process of discussion and debate takes place. Remember, they are not just issued 'on a whim' and behind the scenes at the FRC a considerable amount of work is carried out before an ISA (UK) or ISQM (UK) sees the light of day.

Once an ISA (UK) or ISQM (UK) is issued, that is not the end of the story. Standards must be carefully monitored to ensure they remain proportionate and up to date. This can often result in amendments to a standard.

New standards, or amendments to existing standards, are consulted upon via a public consultation. This generally (but not always) starts with an initial consultation, or 'request for views'. This may lead into the development of an Exposure Draft for which a public consultation is announced and enables stakeholders to feedback to the FRC on their proposals. Once the comment period has closed, this feedback is analysed and usually results in the new or amended standard being published.

ISQMs (UK)

2.5   In July 2021, the FRC issued two quality management standards:

- ISQM (UK) 1 *Quality Management for Firms that Perform Audits and Reviews of Financial Statements, Or Other Assurance Or Related Services Engagements*; and

- ISQM (UK) 2 *Engagement Quality Reviews*.

These ISQMs (UK) do not just apply to audit engagements, they also apply to other types of engagements that are carried out by auditors (eg, reviews of interim financial information). These ISQMs (UK) are applied at firm-wide level because there is a specific ISA (UK) that deals with quality management at the audit engagement level, being ISA (UK) 220 *Quality Management for an Audit of Financial Statements* (revised at the same time as the new ISQMs (UK) were issued). I examine these two quality management standards and ISA (UK) 220 in more detail in **Chapter 14**.

ISAs (UK)

2.6   These are the 'backbone' for the performance of an audit. Essentially, ISAs (UK) are the main source of regulation and guidance for auditors and are applied in audits of historical financial information.

If you look carefully at the structure of the ISAs (UK), you will see that they are numbered according to a codification system which groups them in, effectively, a logical 'flow' of an audit as follows:

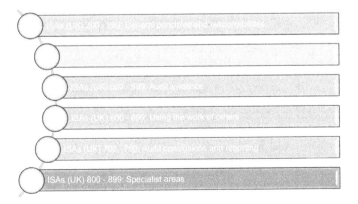

2.6   *The Role of Regulators and Professional Bodies*

At the time of writing, the following UK auditing standards were in extant:

Quality management standards	
ISQM (UK) 1	Quality Management for Firms that Perform Audits and Reviews of Financial Statements, Or Other Assurance Or Related Services Engagements
ISQM (UK) 2	Engagement Quality Reviews

ISA (UK) standards	
ISA (UK) 200	Overall Objectives of the Independent Auditor and the Conduct of an Audit in Accordance With International Standards on Auditing (UK)
ISA (UK) 210	Agreeing the Terms of Audit Engagements
ISA (UK) 220	Quality Management for an Audit of Financial Statements
ISA (UK) 230	Audit Documentation
ISA (UK) 240	The Auditor's Responsibilities Relating to Fraud in an Audit of Financial Statements
ISA (UK) 250, Section A	Consideration of Laws and Regulations in an Audit of Financial Statements
ISA (UK) 250, Section B	The Auditor's Statutory Right and Duty to Report to Regulators of Public Interest Entities and Regulators of Other Entities in the Financial Sector
ISA (UK) 260	Communication With Those Charged With Governance
ISA (UK) 265	Communicating Deficiencies in Internal Control to Those Charged With Governance and Management
ISA (UK) 300	Planning an Audit of Financial Statements
ISA (UK) 315	Identifying and Assessing the Risks of Material Misstatement
ISA (UK) 320	Materiality in Planning and Performing an Audit
ISA (UK) 330	The Auditor's Responses to Assessed Risks
ISA (UK) 402	Audit Considerations Relating to an Entity Using a Service Organisation
ISA (UK) 450	Evaluation of Misstatements Identified During the Audit
ISA (UK) 500	Audit Evidence
ISA (UK) 501	Audit Evidence – Specific Considerations for Selected Items
ISA (UK) 505	External Confirmations
ISA (UK) 510	Initial Audit Engagements – Opening Balances
ISA (UK) 520	Analytical Procedures
ISA (UK) 530	Audit Sampling
ISA (UK) 540	Auditing Accounting Estimates and Related Disclosures

ISA (UK) 550	Related Parties
ISA (UK) 560	Subsequent Events
ISA (UK) 570	Going Concern
ISA (UK) 580	Written Representations
ISA (UK) 600	Special Considerations – Audits of Group Financial Statements (Including the Work of Component Auditors)
ISA (UK) 610	Using the Work of Internal Auditors
ISA (UK) 620	Using the Work of an Auditor's Expert
ISA (UK) 700	Forming an Opinion and Reporting on Financial Statements
ISA (UK) 701	Communicating Key Audit Matters in the Independent Auditor's Report
ISA (UK) 705	Modifications to the Opinion in the Independent Auditor's Report
ISA (UK) 706	Emphasis of Matter Paragraphs and Other Matter Paragraphs in the Independent Auditor's Report
ISA (UK) 710	Comparative Information – Corresponding Figures and Comparative Financial Statements
ISA (UK) 720	The Auditor's Responsibilities Relating to Other Information
ISA (UK) 800	Special Considerations – Audits of Financial Statements Prepared in Accordance with Special Purpose Frameworks
ISA (UK) 805	Special Considerations – Audits of Single Financial Statements and Specific Elements, Accounts or Items of a Financial Statement

When you look at each ISA (UK) in isolation, you'll see that they are very detailed documents (some more than others). This is because each ISA (UK) is structured in a uniform way as follows:

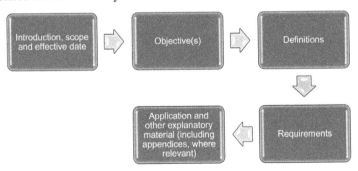

IMPORTANT POINT

It's really important to understand certain terminology contained in the ISAs (UK) and ISQMs (UK) because some auditors have been known

45

to misinterpret the requirements. Where a standard says '... the auditor shall' this means that a requirement is **mandatory**. There is no option but to apply that particular requirement. However, if the auditor considers it necessary to depart from the requirement of an ISA (UK) or ISQM (UK) the departure must be fully justified and documented.

Remember, the requirements of the ISAs (UK) only need to be applied to matters which are **material** to the financial statements.

As you can see from the above, the ISAs (UK) also contain application and explanatory material. This is included in the ISAs (UK) as a means of communicating the rationale behind the requirements. This application and explanatory material are not mandatory, but it must be read and understood by the auditor otherwise there is a risk that the audit procedures applied may not comply with the ISA (UK) requirements.

Practice Notes and Bulletins

2.7   The FRC is responsible for issuing Practice Notes and Bulletins in addition to the ISAs (UK) and ISQMs (UK). A Practice Note is intended to help auditors apply ISAs (UK) to specific circumstances and industries. Bulletins are published to provide auditors with guidance on new or emerging issues.

Of course, anything issued by a regulator is an important publication and Practice Notes and Bulletins are no exception. However, it is worth noting that Practice Notes and Bulletins are persuasive rather than prescriptive; but are indicative of good practice.

Practice Notes (PNs) that are currently in extant are as follows:

PN 10 (Revised)	The Audit of Public Sector Financial Statements is now issued by the Public Audit Forum, which has been designated by the FRC to issue a Statement of Recommended Practice
PN 11 (Revised)	The audit of charities in the United Kingdom
PN 14	The audit of housing associations in the United Kingdom
PN 15 (Revised)	The Audit of Occupational Pension Schemes in the United Kingdom
PN 19 (Revised)	The Audit of Banks and Building Societies in the United Kingdom
PN 20 (Revised)	The audit of Insurers in the United Kingdom
PN 23	Special Considerations in Auditing Financial Statements

Bulletins that are currently in extant are as follows:

2021	Illustrative Auditor's Reports on United Kingdom Private Sector Financial Statements
2020	Illustrative Auditor's Reports on United Kingdom Private Sector Financial Statements
2020	Miscellaneous Reports by Auditors Required by The United Kingdom Companies Act 2006
2020	Auditor's Reports on Revised Accounts and Reports in The United Kingdom
2017	The Auditor's Association with Preliminary Announcements made in accordance with UK Listing Rules
2009/4	Developments in Corporate Governance Affecting the Responsibilities of Auditors of UK Companies
2006/5	The Combined Code on Corporate Governance: Requirements of Auditors under the Listing Rules of The Financial Services Authority and the Irish Stock Exchange

Other publications by the FRC

2.8   There are other publications which may be relevant to auditors that have been issued by the FRC as follows:

The Ethical Standard	The Ethical Standard must be applied in the audit of financial statements and other public interest assurance engagements in both the private and public sectors. It was last revised in January 2024 and the latest revised Ethical Standard is effective from 15 December 2024.
Glossary of Terms (auditing and ethics)	Provides defined terms used in the ISAs (UK), ISQMs (UK) and the Ethical Standard
Scope and Authority of Audit and Assurance Pronouncements	Outlines the nature of the standards and guidance issued by the FRC and their status
Staff Guidance Notes	Notes that are intended to support practitioners when they make judgments on the application of standards
Discussion papers and consultation documents	These are issued on a periodic basis to help the regulator consider improvements to standards and guidance

REGULATION BY THE PROFESSIONAL BODIES

2.9   As I mentioned at the start of this chapter, anyone can call themselves an accountant, but not everyone can call themselves a Chartered Accountant or Chartered Certified Accountant as these titles are reserved to those qualified members of either the ICAEW or ACCA.

An auditor's report can **only** be signed by a **statutory auditor**. The statutory auditor must be a member of a Recognised Supervisory Body (RSB). In the UK, there are currently four RSBs for the purposes of statutory audit work:

These professional bodies are also known as **Recognised Qualifying Bodies** (RQB). In addition, the Association of International Accountants (AIA) is a RQB, but is not a RSB because it does not supervise its members for the purpose of carrying out statutory audit work. The role of the RQB is to determine who becomes a qualified accountant and ultimately who is then eligible to sign auditors' reports in the UK.

IMPORTANT POINT

It is important to understand your professional body's (bodies) rules on practising. Holding yourself out to be in public practice (eg, preparing financial statements and tax returns) is not permissible unless you have a practising certificate. This means that, even though you may be a qualified accountant, you must still obtain a practising certificate, and this may need further post-qualification experience. The specific requirements for each professional body are beyond this discussion as each body is different. Unfortunately, lots of people fall foul of the rules, sometimes (but not always) unintentionally.

As the holder of an auditing practising certificate is a 'responsible individual' (RI), there are various checks on the legal, financial integrity and reliability of the individual that must be carried out prior to responsible individual (RI) status being issued.

The rules on practising as an auditor must also be clearly understood. For example, ACCA members must have an auditing practising certificate **in addition to** their general practising certificate in order to be able to sign auditors' reports. Auditing practising certificates are issued following the satisfactory completion of a specific period of post-qualification experience which must be documented and signed off by a relevant supervisor. Certain 'elements' of the audit process must be achieved before an auditing practising certificate can be issued. In order to ensure compliance with the requirements, it is important to understand the relevant professional body's requirements and if in doubt, ask them. It is always better to be safe than sorry where these issues are concerned. If you are caught practising without the relevant practising certificate(s), you could find yourself excluded from membership.

While audit engagement team members may not necessarily have a practising certificate, this does not stop them carrying out audit work. It just means they cannot sign the auditor's report in the capacity of senior statutory auditor.

RSBs are supervised by the FRC and must be able to demonstrate that they have complied with company law requirements. For example, RSBs must be able to demonstrate that they have adequate rules and practices designed to ensure that members who are appointed as statutory auditors:

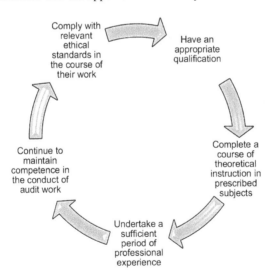

- Comply with relevant ethical standards in the course of their work
- Have an appropriate qualification
- Complete a course of theoretical instruction in prescribed subjects
- Undertake a sufficient period of professional experience
- Continue to maintain competence in the conduct of audit work

There are certain individuals who are **prohibited** from acting as a statutory auditor by the CA 2006 as follows:

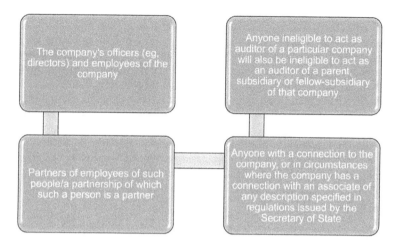

As you can see so far from this section, there are a lot of hurdles to jump over before getting to statutory auditor status. However, once statutory auditor status is awarded to the individual, they are subject to very rigorous rules and regulations from their professional body (and the FRC) which they must ensure they comply with. Remember, ignorance is no form of defence.

Professional body regulation

2.10   Of course, the first port of call is getting through the examinations; qualifying as a member of your professional body; completing relevant post-qualification experience; documenting that experience; and obtaining a practising certificate and the audit qualification.

Over the years, there have been many individuals that have been caught short of the rules on practising by professional bodies. What I mean by that is that they have engaged in public practice work (preparing accounts, tax returns and such like) without the necessary practising certificate.

REAL-LIFE SCENARIO

[Note, this real-life scenario was not derived from an interview, it is a published disciplinary notice].

Mr N was admitted as an ACCA member in 2009 and became a fellow member in 2014. Mr N had never held an ACCA practising certificate. This means that Mr N could not hold himself out to be in public practice, which includes signing or producing any accounts or report or certificate

---

or tax return concerning any person's financial affairs in circumstances where reliance is likely to be placed on such by any other person. It also includes holding oneself out as being available to undertake such activities or allowing oneself to be known as an 'Accountant' or 'Chartered Certified Accountant'. It also prohibits a member from being a director of a firm which carries on public practice or holding rights in such a firm which puts the member in the position of principal.

Mr N was appointed as a director of a firm in April 2010 and his occupation was listed as 'Accountant'. Mr N had a shareholding equal to or greater than 50%. A Google search on the firm revealed a website describing it as an 'independent accountancy and tax consulting firm.'

The problem with this was twofold. First of all, Mr N had no practising certificate from ACCA. ACCA does not allow members or fellow members to hold themselves out to be in practice without such a practising certificate. Secondly, Mr N had confirmed on his CPD declarations that he had not engaged in public practice, which was clearly inaccurate.

ACCA contacted Mr N notifying him that it had come to their attention that Mr N appeared to be practising without a practising certificate and outlined the matters that were the subject of the investigation. Mr N's reply was that none of his businesses provide services which fall within the definition of a public practice and, specifically, that the firm he was director/shareholder of only provides some bookkeeping, payroll and healthcare consultancy services. He then went on to state that none of the businesses in which he was director or majority shareholder would be offering any services that are deemed to be public practice.

Mr N had clearly not understood that ACCA's regulations prohibited him from referring to himself as 'accountant' as this effectively results in Mr N holding himself out to be in public practice. Mr N confirmed that he would change his occupation at Companies House, which he duly did. He also confirmed to ACCA that he had removed all material that could be construed as advertising himself or his firm as engaging in public practice.

Mr N further went on to state that while he had initially set up his firm to supply payroll and bookkeeping services to small businesses, the firm had become overwhelmed with enquiries from new bookkeeping clients, some of which requested the preparation of accounts. This really did stray into murky waters.

Mr N then went on to state that any accounts that had been delivered to Companies House which were signed by his firm as the accountants, should have been signed by another firm. He said that he presumed this mistake arose because the software used had the name of his firm as the accountants.

Mr N provided a further response to the investigation admitting his oversights. In respect of declaring he was not engaged in public practice on his CPD declaration, Mr N stated that he thought that this will fall away as the business had come into his possession unintentionally.

On 22 July 2022, ACCA took into account Mr N's mitigating factors but considered that his conduct had been carried on for a number of years and as this was repeated, it was deemed to be an aggravating factor.

Mr N was excluded from membership and was ordered to pay costs of £11,325.

As you can see, the sanctions for carrying out work for the general public without the appropriate practising certificates are serious. Essentially, members (and student members) who do this are bringing the profession into disrepute because if they make a mistake, there is generally no recourse via Professional Indemnity Insurers. There are good reasons why professional bodies have rigorous rules in place where public practice is concerned and those that choose not to abide by them can expect to be sanctioned accordingly.

REAL-LIFE SCENARIO

[*Note, this real-life scenario was not derived from an interview, it is taken from a question asked on a public accountancy forum*].

Person Q was a member of an accountancy body that is not a RSB. They had a licence to carry out accounts and tax work for their clients and were studying towards their Chartered Accountancy qualification. The person's question was whether they were allowed to do this.

The fact that they had got a licence from another professional body does not mean they can engage in public practice work if they are also a student member of a RSB (eg, ACCA or ICAEW). Remember, they must comply with the requirements of the other professional body which has not issued their licence. If the rules of the chartered professional body prohibit student members from engaging in public practice without a practising certificate, the fact that the person already holds a licence from another professional body becomes irrelevant. If they want to continue engaging in public practice, they must resign their registration with the Chartered Accountancy body.

Once statutory auditor status has been achieved, you can sign auditors' reports. Hooray! However, with this comes a **lot** of responsibility. Do not underestimate the level of responsibility placed on your shoulders, and it is not just confined to making sure an audit runs smoothly.

I've already mentioned that the FRC regulate auditors which carry out audit work for PIEs and listed entities. I'm not going to go into the detail of how this regulation works because it is beyond the scope of this book. However, for non-PIE and non-listed entities, audit regulation is generally carried out by the RSBs.

RSBs require their members to carry out audit work in accordance with prescribed standards, regulations and legislation. RSBs monitor the work of member firms through audit 'monitoring visits'. I suppose you could say that a monitoring visit is the auditor's equivalent of an OFSTED inspection.

Audit monitoring visits are carried out periodically. For ACCA members this tends to be on a six- to eight-year cycle, depending on risk. ICAEW members are no more than six years apart, but visits can be carried out more regularly, especially where the audit firm deals with more 'high risk' audits or has had issues at past visits.

Now, I can only speak from my experience of going through a monitoring visit from my professional body, ACCA; other professional bodies may be slightly different, but generally the following happens (the below assumes the outcome of the monitoring visit is 'satisfactory'):

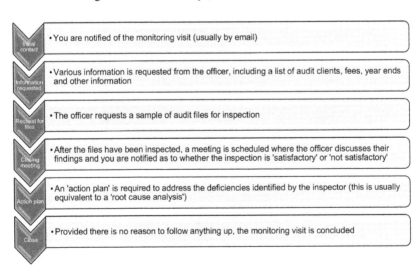

• You are notified of the monitoring visit (usually by email)

• Various information is requested from the officer, including a list of audit clients, fees, year ends and other information

• The officer requests a sample of audit files for inspection

• After the files have been inspected, a meeting is scheduled where the officer discusses their findings and you are notified as to whether the inspection is 'satisfactory' or 'not satisfactory'

• An 'action plan' is required to address the deficiencies identified by the inspector (this is usually equivalent to a 'root cause analysis')

• Provided there is no reason to follow anything up, the monitoring visit is concluded

There are additional aspects to a monitoring visit, but these will all depend on what the firm does and the number of audits etc. The visit will also look at other aspects of the firm, such as CPD records, 'Fit and Proper' forms, the firm's own accounts, client and office bank accounts, Professional Indemnity Insurance coverage and such like.

The objective of these visits is to make sure that the firm is carrying out its audit work in accordance with professional standards, regulations and legislation. Many firms will receive a satisfactory outcome with only limited improvements required in their audit work. For others, however, this will not be the case where problems have been identified during the visit.

Where the professional body deems audit work to be deficient, or significantly deficient, the firm can expect an 'unsatisfactory' outcome. Of course, an unsatisfactory outcome is probably the worst thing that an audit practitioner can be on the receiving end of and it may cause stomachs to sink. I'm fortunate that I've not been in this position, but I know practitioners that have and the advice I have given to them is to keep calm but most of all **co-operate** with the inspector. Do not bury your head in the sand because the problem will not go away and 'head in the sand syndrome' will only make things worse.

Over the years, I have met several practitioners on the lecturing circuit whose monitoring visits haven't gone according to plan. There are many reasons why a monitoring visit may end up with an unsatisfactory outcome, but the most common reasons seem to include:

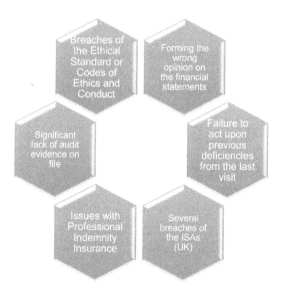

During every monitoring visit, there will always be deficiencies noted on any audit file. Look, even I (as the author of an auditing text) get deficiencies during my file reviews. I remember my last monitoring visit, not so long ago, and I knew the inspector was reviewing a sample of my audit files during a specific week and that the closing meeting was on the Friday of that week. On the Thursday night, I felt exactly the same as I did the night before I was about to receive my results for my professional exams. Knots in the stomach; the perennial 'what if I've done this wrong?' question; and the voice of the inspector saying [in that 'echo' type sound you hear on the TV] *'this is an unsatisfactory outcome.'* I have no qualms in admitting that I am a natural 'over-thinker' to start off with so I know exactly how anxiety levels can shoot through the skies when a monitoring visit is taking place. So, when the inspector opened the closing meeting by saying it was a satisfactory outcome, the sense of sheer relief was exactly as it was when I saw that magical 50% pass on the Advanced Financial Management exam paper that I sat as my final, final ACCA exam (I absolutely despised Advanced Financial Management, by the way).

Like I say, every audit file will have some deficiencies (or improvements needed) on it. As long as those deficiencies are not **significant** deficiencies, then the outcome of the visit should be fine. It's very difficult to make a list of deficiencies that, individually or collectively, would tip a visit into unsatisfactory territory. I think you would at least be looking at major areas of the audit that do not have sufficient appropriate audit evidence to support the conclusion.

REAL-LIFE SCENARIO

Mr T was an audit engagement partner with two audit clients in his sole trader practice. He received notification of an audit monitoring visit from his professional body, and this went ahead as planned. The visit was conducted face-to-face as this was well before the COVID-19 pandemic threw everything into chaos.

In the closing meeting, the inspector confirmed that the visit was unsatisfactory. The reasons cited were as follows:

- On File 1, work had not been carried out to support the estimate of construction contract revenue (which was a significantly material amount). Work had been limited to ensuring the bookkeeping entries were correct.

- On File 1, there was insufficient audit evidence to support most of the material areas of the financial statements. In some cases, the inspector had noted that the work on each area of the file was

---

nothing more than that expected for an accounts preparation file with a summarising lead schedule.

- On File 2, the written representation letter was dated six weeks after the date of the auditor's report, rendering it of no real value.

- On File 2, no subsequent events review had been carried out. The audit programme had been annotated as 'No subsequent events have arisen' without any audit work to support this conclusion.

- On File 2, the going concern review was limited to a period of 12 months from the balance sheet date; rather than 12 months from the date of approval of the financial statements.

- On File 2, no analytical procedures had been carried out at completion to enable Mr T to form a conclusion as to whether the financial statements are consistent with his knowledge and understanding of the client in compliance with ISA (UK) 520 *Analytical Procedures*.

Mr T acknowledged that his knowledge of the ISAs (UK) was lacking as he had been unable to attend update courses due to time constraints and pressures of practice work. Unfortunately, these excuses were not acceptable, and the practitioner was subject to a further follow-up visit, the cost of which was to be borne by Mr T. In the meantime, all audit work had to be subject to a pre-issuance ('hot') review by a training provider at Mr T's cost.

Professional Indemnity Insurance

2.11   I think a common reason why practitioners run into problems with regulators is when they do not have Professional Indemnity Insurance (PII) or when their PII coverage is insufficient. Different professional bodies have different rules on levels of PII and what needs to be covered, so it is always worth making sure your firm is compliant with the requirements.

Remember, PII exists to indemnify clients from loss if the firm makes a mistake or acts negligently so that the client is no worse off than they would have been if the mistake or negligence had not arisen.

During the course of any monitoring visit, you can expect the professional body to request sight of PII documentation to not only ensure that the firm has PII, but that this PII is adequate and complies with specific requirements.

Not having PII, in my opinion, is unforgivable – it's the same as not having car insurance. It's one of those insurances that you know you must have, so not having it in place deserves a wrap on the knuckles from the regulators.

Continuing Professional Development

2.12   Understandably, professional bodies mandate their members to keep up to date. This rule applies regardless of whether, or not, the member holds a practising certificate. Keeping up to date is done through continuing professional development (CPD).

Take, for example, tax. I don't specialise in tax, but I do know that it changes frequently and that it is often cited that the UK is one of the most complex tax systems in the world. A member of a professional body that works in tax will need to stay up to date with changes so that they can advise their clients or company directors correctly.

Remember, the professional examinations do not equip us with indefinite knowledge. We need CPD to keep the knowledge that professional examinations do equip us with up to date.

Professional bodies usually require a minimum number of hours of CPD each year. For example, ACCA requires a minimum of 40 hours and 21 of these hours must be **verifiable**. CPD is 'verifiable' when:

It should be noted that professional bodies require an annual CPD declaration each year whereby the member confirms that they have complied with the professional body's CPD requirements. There are significant sanctions (including expulsion from membership) where the member provides a false declaration.

In addition, professional bodies carry out random monitoring checks on members' CPD. This usually involves the professional body requesting copies of the member's CPD records (or requesting access to their online portal, where applicable) and reviewing the CPD carried out during a specific CPD year.

During the course of any CPD monitoring visit, the member may be asked to supply evidence of their learning (ie, verifiable CPD). For example, sending in copies of certificates that a training provider may provide following successful completion of a CPD course.

A professional accountant may also be a member of two professional bodies. Invariably, the CPD requirements of both professional bodies will need to be followed, although some professional bodies may accept that complying with the other professional body requirements may meet their requirements.

Usually, CPD activities are established at the start of each CPD year. Whatever activities are decided upon, the member must ensure that they are relevant to their role within the firm.

In addition, auditors that are engagement partners responsible for audits of financial statements must comply with the requirements of International Education Standard (IES) 8 *Professional Competence for Engagement Partners Responsible for Audits of Financial Statements (Revised)* (www.ifac. org/_flysystem/azure-private/publications/files/IAESB-IES-8-Professional-competence-for-engagement-partners.pdf). IES 8 (Revised) prescribes the professional competence that professional accountants are required to develop and maintain when carrying out the role of audit engagement partner.

Both ACCA and the ICAEW require the auditor to:

- Consider the IES 8 learning outcomes when planning CPD.

- Identify which learning outcomes you will focus on during the year and build these into your wider CPD plan.

- Select these learning outcomes and record the date on which each learning outcome was selected.

- Undertake relevant learning activities.

- Complete a CPD record for each learning activity undertaken.

- Cross-reference your CPD record to the IES 8 checklist.

IMPORTANT POINT

ICAEW have introduced a new CPD regime for their members off the back of a request by the Irish Auditing and Accounting Supervisory Authority (IAASA) and the FRC requesting more rigorous regulation around CPD and record-keeping by audit staff and principals. The new CPD rules came into effect on 1 November 2023.

There are three categories under the new regime: Category 1, 2 and 3. Members that work in practice but do not perform any of the specified roles for category 1 or 2 will fall into category 3.

Examples of roles that would result in **category 1** classification include:

- Acting as responsible individual/key audit partner/engagement partner or spending 30% or more of your professional time on:
  - — audits of public interest entities (PIEs);
  - — major local audits;
  - — audits of central government departments or devolved administrations; or
  - — CASS audits.

  It should be noted that each of these categories are assessed individually and not in the aggregate.

- Leading, managing, or spending 30% or more of your professional time on delivery of internal audit or assurance services to PIEs, a major local audit entity or central government departments or devolved administrations.

- Working in an audit regulatory role, including monitoring and enforcement, within an accountancy professional body, a training organisation, or an oversight body.

- Being an insolvency practitioner who is authorised to take on insolvency appointment.

- Providing direct or indirect tax services to large companies, listed or international companies or groups, or high net-worth individuals.

- Spending 30% or more of your professional time providing ESG assurance services to PIEs, local bodies where the audit is a major local audit, central government departments and devolved administrations.

Examples of roles that would result in **category 2** classification include:

- Acting as responsible individual/key audit partner/engagement partner or spending 30% or more of your professional time on large company audits.

- Acting as engagement partner or spending 30% or more of your professional time on the audit of public sector bodies (excluding those in the category 1 classification).

- Spending 30% or more of your professional time working on performance or value for money audits of public sector bodies.

- Leading, managing, or spending 30% or more of your professional time on the delivery of internal audit or assurance services to large companies or public sector bodies (excluding those in the category 1 classification).

- Being an insolvency practitioner who holds non-appointment taking insolvency licences.

- Spending more than 30% of your time on:

    — insolvency or restructuring engagements which are not related to insolvency appointments;

    — forensic accounting work; or

    — ISAE 3000 *Assurance Engagements Other than Audits or Reviews of Historical Financial Information* or ISRS 4400 *Agreed-upon Procedures* work on behalf of a recipient of a grant from a public sector body as defined by ONS (these categories are assessed individually, not in the aggregate).

- Undertaking probate work.

- Undertaking DPB (Investment Business or Consumer Credit) licensed activities.

- Provision of corporate finance advice to individuals, public sector bodies or businesses.

- Provision of direct or indirect tax services to individuals or entities outside the category 1 classification.

- Spending less than 30% individually, but more than 40% collectively on:

    — PIE audit engagements;

    — major local audits;

    — audits of central government departments or devolved administrations;

    — CASS audits;

    — large company audits; or

    — audits or performance of value for money audits of public sector bodies.

The CPD requirements for ICAEW members in practice are shown in the following table:

Category	Total hours	Verifiable hours
1	40	30
2	30	20
3	20	10

AUDITOR'S LIABILITY FOR NON-COMPLIANCE WITH RULES AND REGULATIONS

2.13   It is fair to say that the majority of firms try, as far as possible, to comply with rules and regulations, including those issued by their relevant professional body. However, it is important to consider the auditor's liability if they do face a legal claim – for example, due to negligent audit work.

I've mentioned a couple of times in these introductory chapters the high-profile corporate collapses that have resulted in 'shocks' to the business world and these have resulted in audit firms and their [former] partners receiving heavy fines, expulsions from membership of the accountancy profession and bans from practising audit work.

A criminal offence can arise when a law is broken, and an auditor is no exception to this rule. If an auditor breaches the CA 2006 (or other legislation, such as the Charities Act 2011), a criminal offence arises. Civil offences will include breaches of contract and the law of tort, under which the auditor can be sued for negligence.

Auditors can be prosecuted for either knowingly or recklessly issuing an inappropriate audit opinion (eg, expressing an unmodified opinion when the opinion should be modified). The term 'knowingly or recklessly' is derived from the CA 2006 and gave rise to some contention when it first appeared in the legislation.

The contention that arose was that some auditors could be deemed to be committing a criminal offence for negligence or honest mistakes because there was no definition of the term 'recklessly'. The government considers 'recklessness' to be a high hurdle and it must be demonstrated that the auditor knew they were taking unreasonable risks in their actions. One of the MPs involved in drafting the legislation said that a person who is merely negligent will not be guilty of this offence, even if the negligence is gross.

The term **duty of care** is bandied around the profession a lot. But who does the auditor owe a duty of care to?

Well, an auditor automatically owes a duty of care to the parties to whom they are issuing their report. For example, an auditor will owe a duty of care to the company's shareholders (members) because their auditor's report is addressed to those shareholders (members). However, the law is unclear about the extent of the auditor's duty of care beyond the shareholders and this is where case law becomes important. I'll go through a couple of well-known cases later on in the chapter to help illustrate what I am talking about in this respect.

The other issue concerns a breach of a duty of care. Remember, the auditor must exercise reasonable care and due skill when carrying out their work. Again, though, the term 'reasonable care and due skill' is not defined in the ISAs (UK), legislation or other guidance and the level of reasonable care and due skill will, of course, depend on the nature, size and complexity of the audit client.

A way in which the auditor exercises reasonable care and due skill is to carry out the audit in accordance with the ISAs (UK) and other professional standards, legislation and guidance. However, there are certain 'caveats' that need to be borne in mind here. Even if the auditor carries out their work in accordance with ISAs (UK), this is no guarantee that the financial statements are 100% accurate, or that the auditor has discovered every misstatement. This is the reason why an auditor can only ever express **reasonable assurance** in their auditor's report. Reasonable assurance is a high level of assurance but is not maximum or absolute assurance that the financial statements are perfect. This is one of the inherent limitations of an audit because the auditor does not test every single transaction and may need to rely on certain management representations.

REAL-LIFE SCENARIO

Kingston Cotton Mill (1896)

Of course, 1896 was a very long time ago now but this case does actually help to articulate the 'reasonable skill and care' concept.

Kingston Cotton Mills collapsed in 1894 after a fraud was discovered because the manager had deliberately overstated the stock valuation over the previous four years (which, of course, resulted in an inflated profit figure). The auditors had failed to discover this as they had simply relied on representations from management in the form of a certificate which described the value of the stock in the accounts as being 'per manager's certificate'.

The impact of this fraud was that eventually the company was unable to pay its debts (clearly because the profits were not cash-backed). A subsequent investigation discovered the grossly over-valued stock.

In considering the issue of the auditor's duty of care, Mr Justice Lopes said:

> It is the duty of an auditor to bring to bear on the work he has to perform that skill, care, and caution which a reasonably competent, careful, and cautious auditor would use. What is reasonable care, skill and caution must depend on the particular circumstances of each case. An auditor

---

is bound to be a detective, or, as was said, to approach his work with suspicion, or with a foregone conclusion that there is something wrong. He is a watchdog, but not a bloodhound. He is justified in believing tried servants of the company in whom confidence is placed by the company. He is entitled to assume that they are honest and rely upon their representations, provided he takes reasonable care.

Auditors must not be made liable for not tracking out ingenious and carefully laid schemes of fraud, when there is nothing to arouse their suspicion ... So, to hold would make the position of an auditor intolerable.

Here, Mr Justice Lopes is stating that the auditor cannot be expected to discover a fraud if there is nothing to indicate that a fraud is taking place (ie, there are no fraud risk factors).

Today, we have ISA (UK) 240 *The Auditor's Responsibilities Relating to Fraud in an Audit of Financial Statements*. ISA (UK) 240 emphasises the auditor's duty to exercise 'professional scepticism' despite the standard's focus being on fraud. The reality is that, even today, some auditors simply accept records, documents and management explanations at face value. This could mean that auditors are neither watchdogs nor bloodhounds and even more care needs to be exercised by the auditor to avoid legal claims being brought against them.

REAL-LIFE SCENARIO

Thomas Gerrard & Son (1968)

This case demonstrates the importance of professional scepticism. The managing director of the company falsified the closing stock value to manipulate the profits so as to allow the payment of dividends to the shareholders. This was done by including non-existent stock in the final valuation as well as creating fictitious invoices. These acts were discovered by the auditor but nothing was done about them.

The auditor's defence in the case was that they were not responsible for counting the year-end stock. They claimed their responsibility was to verify the figure in the financial statements and rely on assurances provided by a responsible individual at the company and nothing else.

In the previous case (Kingston Cotton Mill), Mr Justice Lopes had stated that the auditor '... is justified in believing tried servants of the company in whom confidence is placed by the company.'

However, reliance on 'believing tried servants of the company' did not work in the Thomas Gerrard & Son case because the auditors had already discovered what was going on, so they should have investigated the matter further. Had this been done, the fraud would have been revealed and so the outcome of the case was that the auditors were found guilty of negligent auditing (ie, there had been a breach of duty of care).

The case of Thomas Gerrard & Son emphasises the importance of corroborating assertions by management and challenging management's assumptions (ie, exercising professional scepticism which is examined in more detail in **Chapter 9**).

The judge in the Thomas Gerrard & Son case also noted that '... the standards of reasonable care and skill are, upon the expert evidence, more exacting than those which prevailed in 1896.' This comment indicates that developments in the profession do impact on the evaluation of duty of care, and that more is expected of auditors now than was the case in 1896.

The next 'Real-life scenario' deals with to whom the duty of care is owed. Remember, that to be found guilty of negligence, it must be proven that there was a breach of duty of care, and that the duty of care is owed to the Plaintiff. The connection between the audit firm and the Plaintiff is a crucial issue: this is sometimes called 'proximity'.

REAL-LIFE SCENARIO

ADT Ltd v BDO Binder Hamlyn (1996)

BDO Binder Hamlyn were the auditors of the Britannia Security Group ('Britannia') which was acquired by ADT in 1990 for £105 million. Subsequent investigations revealed that the company was only worth £40 million, and the financial statements were misleading. ADT sued BDO for damages, claiming a breach of a duty of care.

In this case, the decision went in favour of the Plaintiff and not BDO. This was because the judge ruled that 'proximity' had been created by the BDO partner saying that he 'stood by' the financial statements in a meeting with ADT prior to the takeover. BDO were aware that ADT were looking to acquire Britannia and hence the assurances provided to ADT created a relationship between ADT and BDO.

Unfortunately for the audit firm, there was insufficient insurance to pay the damages and costs and the partners of the firm became personally liable for

£34 million. As a result of this case, the BDO Binder Hamlyn partnership was broken up; some offices merged with Stoy Hayward, and staff of other offices were either made redundant or offered positions in other firms.

CHAPTER ROUNDUP

- The ISAs (UK) are based on ISAs issued by the IAASB and are tweaked to become the ISAs (UK). These tweaks are to ensure they are proportionate for use in the UK.

- In the UK, the FRC is responsible for developing and maintaining auditing standards, quality management standards and other guidance for use by auditors.

- The FRC also inspect the work of audit firms that audit public interest entities and listed entities to ensure their standards are being maintained.

- The FRC will eventually transition to ARGA, but at the time of writing, this transition has been delayed.

- Developing and maintaining auditing standards involves a rigorous process including various consultations.

- Each ISA (UK) is structured in a specific way starting with the introduction and ending with the application and explanatory material.

- Professional bodies also have an important role to play in regulating the auditing profession and will inspect the work of auditors of private entities to ensure that they are meeting the required standards.

- There are four **Recognised Supervisory Bodies** and five **Recognised Qualifying Bodies**.

- Monitoring visits conducted by professional bodies involve rigorous processes to ensure standards are being maintained. These visits result in one of two outcomes: satisfactory or unsatisfactory. The range of sanctions for unsatisfactory outcomes varies depending on the deficiencies noted but can involve follow-up visits through to expulsion from membership and heavy fines.

- All professional firms are required to hold Professional Indemnity Insurance and all professional accountants and auditors must undertake CPD.

- Auditors can be prosecuted for criminal offences (eg, a breach of company law) or civil offences (eg, a breach of contract).

PITFALLS TO AVOID

- Holding yourself out to be in practice without a practising certificate (this is a huge no-no and there is little, if any, form of defence).

- Failing to understand the practising requirements of your professional body.

- Assuming holding a licence/practising certificate of one professional body means you automatically meet the requirements of another professional body of which you are a member. Remember, each professional body has their own requirements so you need to ensure a sound understanding to avoid any breaches of regulations that could involve disciplinary action being taken against you.

- Failing to co-operate with a professional body's monitoring protocol.

- Failing to respond to correspondence from your professional body on a timely basis (or by any deadlines imposed by the relevant body).

Chapter 3

Ethics

CHAPTER TOPIC LIST

- Introduction (see **3.1**).

- Fundamental principles (see **3.2**).

- Financial, business, employment and personal relationships (see **3.9**).

- Long association with an audit client (see **3.21**).

- Fees, remuneration and evaluation policies, gifts and hospitality, litigation (see **3.25**).

- Non-audit services (see **3.31**).

- Changes to the Ethical Standard (see **3.34**).

- Provisions Available for Audits of Small Entities (see **3.43**).

INTRODUCTION

3.1 Ethics. An issue that is perhaps the 'lifeblood' of a professional accountant. From a very early age, we are taught to be well-behaved, respect our elders, say 'please' and 'thank you' and generally make our parents proud. Going into adulthood, these traits should hopefully stay with the majority of us but, unfortunately, they don't stay with everyone and the same is true for ethics in a professional setting.

WHAT ARE WE TRYING TO ACHIEVE?

You should view professional ethics as the 'lifeblood' of both the auditing and accountancy professions. Professional ethics strengthens the credibility of accountants and auditors and so it's vital that auditors and accountants have a sound understanding of them. Remember, the Ethical Standard issued by the Financial Reporting Council is updated on a periodic basis,

---

so it's important to keep abreast of developments to ensure you are not left behind. In this chapter we look at some of the fundamental principles and the threats that can arise in the world of audit to make sure we can make the right decisions if such situations present themselves.

As trainee accountants, we are taught to be professional, act with professional courtesy, be technically competent and observe client confidentiality. All traits which, to most professional accountants, are second nature. This applies equally to auditors (especially auditors). All auditors are required to act in the public interest and uphold fundamental principles and integrity.

When someone becomes a student member, and then a full member, of a professional accountancy body, they will be subject to a *Code of Ethics*. This *Code of Ethics* might be called something else, such as a *Code of Ethics and Conduct* but, generally, each professional body's *Code of Ethics* is broadly consistent. In addition, there is also the Ethical Standard which is issued by the Financial Reporting Council (FRC) which sets out the ethical requirements for audit engagements.

These Codes and the FRC's Ethical Standard usually apply a principles-based approach. When we refer to a 'principles-based' approach (as opposed to a rules-based one), it means that the framework will rely on the professional accountant's professional judgement to a certain extent, although there are some rules contained in the Codes and the Ethical Standard which must be adhered to. Any breaches of Codes or the Ethical Standard can result in heavy sanctions being imposed by professional bodies and regulators, which can include expulsion from membership of the relevant professional body, loss of an auditing practising certificate and, ultimately, loss of the person's job.

In particular, where an auditor acts for public interest entities (PIEs), care must be taken to ensure a thorough understanding of the FRC's Ethical Standard because this contains specific rules when acting for PIEs.

IMPORTANT POINT

The underpinning rule in auditing is that the auditor must be and be seen to be independent and objective in their dealings with an audit client. As you will see as we progress through this chapter, many Codes and the Ethical Standard relate to independence, which is a key characteristic of sound ethical behaviour. However, there are other traits which are equally as important, such as integrity and confidentiality.

Another important point to emphasise is that a professional body's Code does not *just* apply to audit engagements. They apply to other types of engagements that are performed for clients. It should also be noted that Codes apply also to professional accountants that are in business (ie, work for organisations other than professional accountancy firms). Therefore, if you are a qualified accountant, you will be subject to ethical standards.

FUNDAMENTAL PRINCIPLES

3.2 There are five fundamental principles which must be applied at all times by auditors:

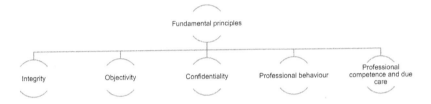

Integrity

This means being trustworthy, straightforward, honest, fair and candid in all business relationships. When an auditor acts with integrity, it is said to enable trust in the auditing profession to be maintained.

Objectivity

This means acting and making decisions and judgements impartially, fairly and on merit. There should be no discrimination, bias, or compromise due to commercial or personal self-interest, conflicts of interest or undue influence of others.

Confidentiality

Auditors must respect the confidentiality of information which they acquire as a result of the services they provide to the client. In general, any professional accountant must not disclose information to third parties without the client's specific authority. There are, however, exceptions to this rule where, for example, there is a public interest or specific legal duty to disclose information (such as where the auditor has suspicions of money laundering). Other exceptions relate to where a professional body is carrying out a monitoring visit and requests to see the audit file or where disclosure of information may also be needed when an auditor is defending themselves in a disciplinary or negligence claim.

3.2 Ethics

Professional behaviour

All professional accountants (including auditors) are expected to behave in a professional manner at all times. This means they must comply with all relevant laws and regulations and avoid any actions which bring the accountancy and auditing professions into disrepute. This applies to personal lives as well (eg, the use of social media provides an opportunity for such discreditable behaviour and professional bodies have taken action to fine and censure their members for inappropriate comments on social media which discredit the profession).

REAL-LIFE SCENARIO

In 2016, a professionally qualified accountant (who will be referred to as Mr F) attended a dinner in his capacity as president. During the dinner, Mr F consumed a large amount of alcohol and witnesses reported that he was 'almost unable to stand'. Despite being twice over the legal alcohol limited for driving, Mr F still go into his car to drive home.

Én route, Mr F hit a 16-year-old cyclist on his way home from work at his local restaurant. The collision destroyed the bike and the victim suffered a multitude of life-changing injuries, including a broken skull, a fractured spine, neurological and cognitive impairments and paralysis down his right side. Mr F left the 16-year-old injured on the road and drove more than 130 miles to his mother's house in Birmingham.

The 16-year-old was later found by two members of the public. He was taken to hospital where he was to stay for nine months undergoing neurosurgery and the removal of part of his skull.

Mr F initially denied any involvement in the accident. However, the 16-year-old's hair particles were found on the car's shattered windscreen.

Mr F received a three-year prison sentence on 10 April 2017. However, Mr F's professional body concluded that exclusion from membership was an 'appropriate and proportionate sanction'. Mr F did not attend the disciplinary hearing as he was in prison but he had tried to resign before the hearing concluded, which was meaningless and the disciplinary report noted '*The only process for dealing with members who commit offences of this nature is to bring disciplinary proceedings before this tribunal.*'

The tribunal found that even though this sad and appalling case had happened outside a professional setting, it had brought discredit on both the professional body concerned and the profession as a whole.

In addition to Mr F's exclusion from membership, costs of £5,274 were reduced to £2,500 to reflect the length of the hearing. These costs had to have been paid within a year of Mr F's release from prison, otherwise the professional body would pursue recovery through the court system.

As you can see from the above, occurrences outside a professional capacity can have ramifications for an individual. It is therefore important to think about the 'cause and effect' of actions, especially given the widespread use of social media nowadays.

Professional bodies and regulators do not expect professional accountants to become recluses and not engage in social activities (such as attending a birthday party) or 'letting your hair down' and enjoying yourself. It is about just ensuring that you behave accordingly and don't end up in a prison cell or in court on a criminal charge.

Professional competence and due care

Professional accountants must always maintain professional knowledge and skill at a level which will ensure the client receives a professional service. For example, a firm offering tax services must ensure that all staff providing this service are up to date with the latest developments in tax legislation to ensure that the client pays/receives the right amount of tax.

The table below provides some examples of how the fundamental principles can be breached:

Example	Fundamental principle breached
An auditor carried out an audit of a client in which they owned shares. This means that they have a financial interest in the audit client. The auditor may therefore fail to be objective when carrying out the audit.	Objectivity
An auditor signed an unmodified (unqualified) auditor's report without carrying out an appropriate amount of audit work under the ISAs (UK).	Integrity and professional competence and due care
An auditor lost the audit working papers file for a client which contained sensitive client information.	Confidentiality
An auditor carried out a poor-quality audit on a charity because they were unaware of changes in the Charities Statement of Recommended Practice and FRS 102 *The Financial Reporting Standard applicable in the UK and Republic of Ireland*.	Professional competence and due care

Example	Fundamental principle breached
An auditor was found guilty of misconduct because they had posted several allegations on social media about another firm.	Professional behaviour.
A professionally qualified accountant was found guilty of misconduct because they had posted several defamatory statements on social media about another accountant.	Professional behaviour.

Nowadays, professions such as auditing and accounting are heavily regulated, especially since the large-scale corporate collapses that have happened in recent years. Breaches of a code of ethics can involve:

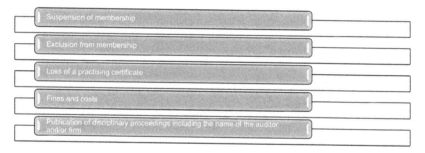

Identifying and responding to ethical threats

3.3   Threats to independence, objectivity and integrity arise frequently and there are a myriad of reasons why they arise. When an ethical threat arises, it is not necessarily the case that the firm's only course of action is to resign – indeed many firms identify ethical threats to independence and can continue acting for the client for several years. It is about ensuring that **safeguards** are put in place to mitigate the threat to an acceptable level. These safeguards should, of course, be documented on the file together with the reasons why they are deemed to be appropriate.

There are six threats to objectivity which the FRC have identified in their Ethical Standard:

Self-interest threat

A self-interest threat arises when an auditor has a financial or other interest in a client that could impact on their work. Consider a situation where an auditor owns shares in the audit client. There is a risk that the auditor would 'turn a blind eye' to anything that could impact on an unmodified audit opinion because this could then have a detrimental effect on things like the company's credit-rating, insurance premiums and ability to secure additional funding. (Basically, when it comes to the auditor having *any* financial interest whatsoever in the client, my advice is always to say 'no' or to get rid of the financial interest before acting as auditor. It is not worth the hassle.)

Examples of other self-interest threats include:

● Fee dependency

● Gifts and hospitality

● Business and personal relationships

● Employment relationships

● Overdue audit fees

● Contingent fees (always a 'no no')

● Litigation with a client

Self-review threat

This is a common threat that most smaller firms can expect to see in practice. A self-review threat arises when the audit firm has provided a non-audit service to the audit client – for example, preparation of the statutory financial statements from a trial balance or calculating the client's liability to corporation tax because they would then be auditing that work. The auditor may place too much reliance on the fact that the firm has been involved in these aspects of the work and hence may fail to apply professional scepticism. This can ultimately lead to poor-quality audit work and a lack of integrity.

Examples of other self-review threats include:

● Valuation services (be *really* careful with these because they cannot be provided if they are material to the financial statements)

● A client's staff joins the audit firm

Remember as well that the external auditor **cannot** perform internal audit services.

Familiarity threat

This is sometimes called a 'trust threat'. It arises when the auditor fails to challenge the audit client or relies on representations from them. This is cited a lot in regulatory reports where auditors fail to challenge management on areas that involve a lot of judgements and estimates. A familiarity threat can also arise when the auditor has a family member or a personal friend working at the audit client. Again, a familiarity threat can cloud the auditor's judgement and they may fail to apply professional scepticism. Familiarity appears to have been one of the issues in some high-profile cases, such as the audit of BHS, for which PwC received a £6.5m fine and the partner involved was banned from auditing for 15 years.

Examples of other familiarity threats include:

- Long association with the audit client

- Movement of staff between the firm and the client

- Gifts and hospitality

Intimidation threat

This does not mean physical intimidation, thankfully! An intimidation threat arises when the auditor's actions are impacted by threats or fear. For example, if the client suggests that the auditor will not be reappointed if they express a modified audit opinion; or if they include (say) a Material Uncertainty Related to Going Concern paragraph in the auditor's report. This would mean that the auditor will try to appease the client for fear of losing the audit.

Examples of other intimidation threats include:

- Fee dependency

- Personal relationships

- The audit engagement partner leaves to join the client

- Litigation with a client

Advocacy threat

An advocacy threat arises when the audit firm is seen to be supporting or promoting the audit client. Typically scenarios may include the audit firm representing the audit client in a HM Revenue and Customs investigation or in a court case. The problem with advocacy threats is that they result in the auditor's position being so closely aligned to that of management that it is difficult for the auditor to act in an impartial manner.

Another example of an advocacy threat would be negotiating on behalf of an audit client.

Management threat

Decisions which could be seen as 'management decisions' should not be made by an auditor as this creates a management threat.

Examples of management threats include:

● Deciding on the best candidate to fill the finance director's role

● Deciding on dividend policies

● Decisions relating to tax planning strategies

● Authorising transactions

● Taking responsibility for the preparation and fair presentation of financial statements in accordance with the applicable financial reporting framework

Responding to ethical threats

3.4 As I mentioned earlier, lots of audit firms will identify threats to independence, objectivity and integrity when dealing with audit clients – especially smaller audit firms. The important thing is dealing with the threat appropriately and making sure that the measures implemented by the firm in mitigating the applicable threat to an acceptable level is documented in the audit working papers.

There may be occasions when, for example, the threat cannot be minimised to an acceptable level and the audit firm must either resign or decline the engagement.

REAL-LIFE SCENARIO

Mr P is a director in a three-partner firm of accountants that carries out audit work. He is responsible for overseeing the production of monthly management accounts for a client, Entity A Ltd. Over recent years, Entity A has seen its revenue and profitability increase significantly and Mr P's role has developed into that of a non-executive finance director.

The audit is overseen by another partner, Mr Q. Mr Q has no involvement in the accounts production cycle of the business and both Mr Q and his team only carry out the audit work. The safeguard applied in this respect is, of course, separate teams both of whom have no cross-over between each other. This maintains Mr Q's independence, objectivity and integrity.

In 2021, Mr P was approached by the board of Entity A with an offer of a small amount of equity in the business as a means of rewarding Mr P for his efforts over the last couple of years. Mr P decided to take this offer up (which was set up by way of an Employee Ownership Trust).

In this situation, Mr Q has nothing whatsoever to do with the arrangement and, on the face of it, it would seem plausible that the audit could continue to be carried out by the firm given that Mr Q does not have a financial interest and things could pretty much continue as normal. However, that is not necessarily the case.

Mr P is a director of the audit firm and hence could unduly influence the audit, especially as Mr P will have a financial interest in Entity A. The Ethical Standard at paragraph 2.3 states that each partner in the audit firm and any persons closely associated with a partner in the firm, must not hold any financial interest, other than an immaterial indirect financial interest.

Remember, the FRC's Ethical Standard has a 'third-party test' which means you have to consider what a third-party would conclude if they were asked *'Would you consider the auditor or audit firm to be independent in this situation, even after the applicable safeguards have been put in place?'* It is highly likely that any third-party would say the audit firm is **not** independent where a fellow director or partner has a financial interest in the audit client.

Of course, if there are no threats, or a threat is clearly insignificant, no responses or safeguards are needed. However, I would always advise that where an auditor concludes that a threat is 'clearly insignificant' then the reasons for that conclusion should be documented on the audit file for clarity and completeness.

The process that an audit firm will go through when dealing with threats to ethical principles will generally involve the following (including communicating to the audit client):

The table below provides some scenarios and potential safeguards that audit firms could use when they identify a threat to independence:

Self-review and management threats	Safeguard(s)
The finance director has requested that the audit firm carries out the year-end tax computation and completes the company tax return. This creates a self-review threat and it may result in the audit engagement team placing too much reliance on the fact that the firm has been involved in this work and therefore be reluctant to point out any errors. There could also be judgements involved in preparing tax computations which is akin to the audit firm taking on a management role.	Use separate teams (ie, the audit engagement team must not be involved in any aspects of the tax computation work and vice versa). The firm must not be involved in any role that involves a management decision. Source data, underlying assumptions and any subsequent adjustments must be carried out by the audit client. If the entity is a public interest or listed entity, the audit firm must decline this work.
The finance director has asked the audit manager to carry out a valuation of its investment portfolio. The investments are significantly material to the financial statements. These sorts of valuations involve making significant estimates and judgements which, again, could result in the audit firm making a management decision. As the investment portfolio will also be subject to audit, a self-review threat arises as well.	Decline the valuation work and suggest another independent third-party because valuations which involve a significant degree of subjectivity should not be provided. If the client is a public interest or listed entity, valuation services which are material to the financial statements (regardless of subjectivity) cannot be provided.
Self-interest threat	**Safeguard(s)**
During the gathering of information on a potential new audit client, you discover that the audit engagement partner has a minority holding in the shares of the potential client. Owning a beneficial interest in an audit client creates a self-interest threat (which I discussed earlier). The audit engagement partner would clearly want to maximise their return on the investment and hence may overlook adjustments that could potentially affect the value of that investment.	Immediate disposal of the interest by the audit engagement partner. If the audit engagement partner refuses to dispose of the interest in the potential client, the firm should decline the offer to act as auditor.
An audit client's fee for the prior year's audit is still outstanding and the planning work on the current year is about to commence. Overdue fees could be viewed as a loan or, if the fees remain unpaid, it could be perceived that the audit has been performed for free. Both of these situations are prohibited.	Request that the client pays the prior year's audit fee immediately before commencing any work on the current year's audit.

Familiarity threat	Safeguard(s)
The audit engagement partner has been involved in the audit of a standalone limited company (which is not a public interest entity) for 11 years. Long association with an audit client increases the risk that the audit engagement team will be too trusting and familiar with the client, hence less sceptical and may fail to challenge certain judgements and/or estimates.	Rotate the audit engagement partner. Ensure independent engagement quality reviews are conducted on a cyclical basis (ie, pre-issuance (hot) or post-issuance (cold) reviews). Where the audit engagement partner is retained on the audit, ensure the documentation explains how the safeguard has reduced the threat to an acceptable level.
The finance director is married to the audit manager. There is overlap with a couple of threats here. In this situation a familiarity threat, a self-review threat and an intimidation threat arises. This is because the finance director is in a position to exert significant influence over the financial statements. This type of threat can also arise if a partner or a member of staff of the firm has a family or personal relationship with someone at the audit client that can exert significant influence over the financial statements (even if that individual is not a member of the audit engagement team).	Remove the individual from the audit engagement team. Ensure the team is structured in such a way that the individual does not deal with any matters which are the responsibility of the relation/friend.

Intimidation threat	Safeguard(s)
The finance director has informed the client that under no circumstances can an audit opinion be modified due to a loan application being lodged with the bank. The bank has requested a copy of the audited financial statements once approved to assist in their lending decision. This is pressure from the client to express a specific opinion. As the bank wish to see a copy of the audited financial statements to assist in a lending decision, there is a risk that the financial statements have been deliberately manipulated to ensure the best possible financial performance and position.	Inform the audit client that the opinion is based on the audit evidence obtained and if any misstatements are discovered that are material (individually or in the aggregate), they must be corrected if an unmodified opinion is to be expressed. If the client continues to exercise undue influence over the audit, the audit engagement partner may choose to resign.

Advocacy threat	Safeguard(s)
The finance director has asked the audit engagement partner to attend a meeting with the bank to negotiate a ten-year loan to assist with the company's expansion plans. These sorts of negotiations would give rise to the firm 'taking sides' with the client and would mean the auditor is not acting independently.	The audit engagement partner must decline the request to meet with the bank.

The above scenarios are 'typical' scenarios which may present themselves, but there may be others which create an ethical threat. Remember, whenever an ethical threat to independence, objectivity or integrity arises, the auditor must **always** apply safeguards to reduce the threat to an acceptable level. If the application of safeguards doesn't do the trick (ie, fails to reduce the threat to an acceptable level), the auditor must resign or decline the engagement. It may also be the case that the auditor deems it necessary to seek third-party advice on how to handle the threat (eg, by discussing the situation with the firm's professional body or with a third-party technical specialist).

Documenting the safeguards on the audit file

3.5   I've mentioned this already in this chapter, but it is something that regulators are becoming increasingly keen on. When the audit engagement partner determines a particular safeguard is appropriate in the circumstances, they must ensure the audit working papers contain documentation concerning the safeguard (ie, the threat that has arisen and the appropriate safeguard(s) that are to be put in place). This is usually found in the planning section of an audit working papers file.

In addition, it is also important that the auditor ensures the documentation explains **how** those safeguards reduce the threat to an acceptable level. Remember, it is not necessarily just about putting safeguards in place – the important part is ensuring those safeguards are effective.

IMPORTANT POINT

Breaches of the FRC's Ethical Standard are reportable to the 'competent authority'. In the UK, the 'competent authority' is the FRC. The FRC have also delegated powers to professional bodies (known as 'responsible supervisory bodies') who can receive reports of breaches of the Ethical Standard from auditors of unlisted/non-public interest entities. This is known as 'self-reporting' and must be carried out on a bi-annual basis. Such breaches must also be notified to those charged with governance of the entity.

In addition, the FRC's Ethical Standard requires the audit firm to appoint an Ethics Partner. The Ethics Partner is responsible for ensuring the audit firm complies with relevant ethical requirements. Among other things, the Ethics Partner has a responsibility to ensure that the firm has adequate policies and procedures in place that ensure compliance with ethical regulations and that these are effectively communicated within the firm. Ordinarily, these policies and procedures are contained within the firm's system of quality management which must comply with ISQM (UK) 1 *Quality Control for Firms that Perform Audits or Reviews of Financial Statements, or Other Assurance or Related Services Engagements.*

I mentioned in the 'Important point' box above that breaches of the FRC's Ethical Standard are reportable. Now, it's important to emphasise that inadvertent breaches of the Ethical Standard would not necessarily call into question the firm's ability to provide an audit or other assurance opinion, provided that:

- the firm has got policies and procedures in place that require all partners, staff and others to promptly report any breach to the audit engagement partner or ethics partner, as appropriate;

- that the engagement or ethics partner notifies the relevant partner, member of staff or other covered person in a timely manner that the matter giving rise to the breach must be remedied as quickly as possible (note – the engagement or ethics partner must also make sure that such remedial action is taken);

- safeguards, where appropriate, are applied;

- the actions that have been taken and the rationale for those actions are documented; and

- where the breach relates to the provision of non-audit services to a public interest entity, the engagement partner reports in accordance with the requirements of ISA (UK) 700 *Forming an Opinion and Reporting on Financial Statements*, para 45-1(d).

IMPORTANT POINT

The FRC's Ethical Standard refers to 'inadvertent breaches' but does not define the term. Hence, professional judgement will need to be applied by the ethics partner and/or the audit engagement partner in determining whether a breach is inadvertent or not.

Use of other firms in the engagement

3.6   An audit firm may use another firm (including a network firm) during an audit engagement. It is important to remember that it is the responsibility of the **lead firm** to be satisfied that another firm involved in the engagement is independent of each entity in the engagement. The audit engagement partner must also obtain sufficient appropriate audit evidence that other firms and third-party firms are independent. In situations when the audit engagement partner is unable to obtain such evidence or obtains evidence suggesting that a firm is not independent, the engagement team must not use the work of that other firm.

Where the entity is a public interest entity, or listed entity, the audit engagement partner must establish that the client has communicated its policy on the use of firms to supply non-audit or additional services to its affiliates and must obtain confirmation that the other firms involved in the engagement will comply with this policy.

Overall conclusion

3.7   At the end of the engagement, when forming the opinion that is to be expressed on the financial statements, the audit engagement partner must reach an overall conclusion that any threats to integrity, objectivity or independence have been appropriately addressed in accordance with the Ethical Standard.

IMPORTANT POINT

This conclusion is drawn on both an individual and cumulative basis and **must** be formed **before** the auditor's report is signed.

The audit engagement partner must consult with the firm's ethics partner or ethics function if they are unable to conclude that any individual threat(s) to integrity or objectivity (including any which could impair independence), or that all such threats viewed on a cumulative basis, have been eliminated or reduced to an acceptable level.

Where the audit engagement partner is unable to make such a conclusion, the partner must not report and the firm must either resign from the engagement or withdraw accordingly. The exception to this rule would be where law or regulation prohibits resignation or withdrawal.

Documentation

3.8   As I mentioned earlier on in the chapter, the audit working papers must contain documentation about threats to independence together with the safeguards that have been applied to minimise those threats and the reasons why those safeguards are appropriate. The audit engagement partner must also ensure that their consideration of the firm's integrity, objectivity and independence is also appropriately documented.

The Ethical Standard also requires the audit engagement partner (before accepting or continuing an audit engagement) to assess and document the following:

3.8 *Ethics*

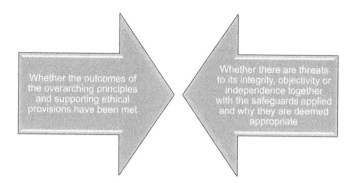

There are a few more documentation requirements where the audit client is a public interest entity. For such entities, the audit engagement partner is required to assess and document the following:

(a)   whether it complies with the requirements of Regulations 79 and 80 of The Statutory Auditors and Third Country Auditors (Amendment) (EU Exit) Regulations 2019 (SI 2019/177);

(b)   whether the conditions of Regulation 91 of The Statutory Auditors and Third Country Auditors (Amendment) (EU Exit) Regulations 2019 (SI 2019/177) are complied with; and

(c)   the integrity of the members of the supervisory, administrative and management bodies of the public interest entity.

IMPORTANT POINT

Audit firms often receive criticism from reviewers for not having sufficient documentation on file which details the threats identified and the safeguards that have been put in place together with why those safeguards are deemed appropriate. In practice, many smaller firms provide non-audit services to their clients (eg, payroll and taxation services) and these will create a self-review threat at the very least.

Firms should take care to fully review their assessment of threats and safeguards each year. A safeguard which was originally considered appropriate a few years ago, and which is based on a third-party test perspective, may not now be considered appropriate. This is because the perspective of what is considered acceptable changes over time, even where specific standards or laws do not change. Of course, where the standards do change, then a fresh analysis against the new requirements must be carried out.

FINANCIAL, BUSINESS, EMPLOYMENT AND PERSONAL RELATIONSHIPS

3.9   The FRC's Ethical Standard deals with financial, business, employment and personal relationships in Section 2.

A financial interest in an audit client will arise when any member of the engagement team has an interest in, say, the shares of the business. Such an interest is said to be a 'direct' interest where the team member owns shares in the client or a 'direct beneficial interest' which would be an interest that is held through an intermediary controlled by the person holding the interest. Financial interests can also be held 'indirectly' where the interest is held through, say, an investment trust or pension scheme.

Understandably, the Ethical Standard is strict on its approach to these types of interest because they can clearly impact on independence. The Ethical Standard prohibits any of the team members (including the audit engagement partner and any partner) from having a financial interest in an audit client. Where any such interest is held (and the person does not wish to dispose of the interest), that person must be removed from the audit engagement team.

IMPORTANT POINT

The easiest solution where financial interests are concerned is for the firm to ensure that neither partners nor staff (or any persons closely associated with them, as far as is known) holds such an interest. In practice, if such interests are held in an audit or other assurance client, it becomes a difficult issue.

Financial interests held as trustee

3.10   When a direct or indirect financial interest is held in a trustee capacity, a self-interest threat may be created. This is because the existence of the trustee interest could influence the outcome or conduct of the engagement, or the trust may influence the actions of the entity. Again, it is advisable to avoid these situations by ensuring no member of the team has a financial interest in a trustee capacity.

The Ethical Standard states that such a trustee interest must **not** be held when:

3.11 *Ethics*

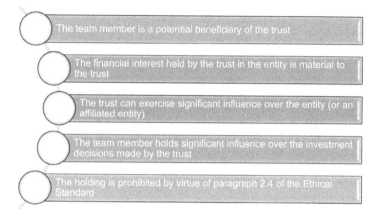

- The team member is a potential beneficiary of the trust
- The financial interest held by the trust in the entity is material to the trust
- The trust can exercise significant influence over the entity (or an affiliated entity)
- The team member holds significant influence over the investment decisions made by the trust
- The holding is prohibited by virtue of paragraph 2.4 of the Ethical Standard

The Ethical Standard clarifies that a trustee interest should also not be held in the case of a 'living will' or power of attorney, where the person holding that interest is, or may be, a potential beneficiary of the estate to which it relates, or where that person is able to influence the investment decisions of the estate.

IMPORTANT POINT

The holding of such prohibited trustee interests has been identified by regulators as an area where breaches of the Ethical Standard are sometimes found. This can have repercussions for the firm and the individual.

REAL-LIFE SCENARIO

An audit engagement partner was the executor of a client's estate. The estate of the deceased included shares in an audit client.

Although as executor, the audit engagement partner had no benefit interest, the firm still received a significant fine for the breach. The important point to emphasise is that anything related to a financial interest is generally entering into 'murky waters' and should be avoided.

Financial interest held by firm pension schemes

3.11   Where the firm's pension scheme has a financial interest in an audit client (or their affiliates) and the firm can influence the investment decisions of the trustees, this is viewed as a self-interest threat. The Ethical Standard views this threat as being so great that no safeguards can eliminate it, or reduce it to an acceptably low level. In these situations there is no alternative but to either decline the engagement or resign from it immediately.

Loans and guarantees

3.12   Again, as with financial interests, loans and guarantees are generally a 'no-no'. Even overdue fees can be viewed, in some situations, as being some form of loan to the client and hence care needs to be taken in that respect.

The Ethical Standard prohibits loans and guarantees being made to an audit client because of the self-interest and intimidation threats that arise. In such cases, no safeguards are available that could reduce these sorts of threats to an acceptably low level.

A similar preclusion exists in the reverse situation (ie, where a client may make a loan to an audit firm or guarantee its liabilities). Of course, these situations are uncommon but the Ethical Standard does identify three exceptions to this prohibition:

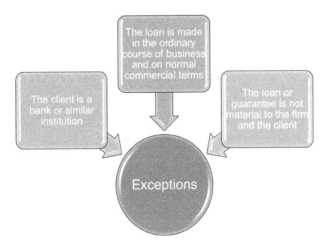

Business relationships

3.13   The Ethical Standard says that a business relationship involves two parties having a common commercial interest. Because of this commercial interest, a self-interest, advocacy or intimidation threat arises.

Consider a situation where a publisher and an audit firm worked together to publish technical guidance for accountancy firms. The firm could not then be the auditor of the publisher. Remember, this is all about maintaining independence so care must be taken to ensure compliance with the Ethical Standard.

The Ethical Standard does identify a couple of exceptions where business relationships are concerned:

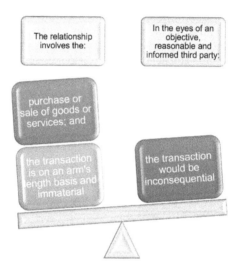

If there is any doubt as to whether a relationship would be inconsequential in the eyes of an objective, reasonable and informed third party, then the relationship is deemed not to be inconsequential.

Employment relationships

3.14   Again, the Ethical Standard generally prohibits key audit partners who are directly involved with the audit assignment and any closely associated persons from having an employment relationship with an audit client, or an affiliate of an audit client.

Conversely, a firm is unable to admit a partner to the firm's partnership, or employ a person in a position as key audit partner (or other covered position), or a person who is also employed by an audit client (or an affiliate of the audit client).

Partners or staff of the audit firm are generally prohibited from accepting secondments to an audit client, or affiliates of the audit client. In this respect, however, there are exceptions to this rule as follows:

Partners and engagement team members joining an audit client

3.15   In practice, staff come and go in the same way as for any organisation. However, when an audit partner or member of the audit engagement team leaves the firm to join a client, care must be taken by the audit firm because this could create a threat to independence. The Ethical Standard deals with the issue and states that when a former partner in the firm joins a client, the firm must act swiftly and certainly before any work is done by the firm in respect of that client. The reason for this is to ensure that no significant connections remain between the firm and the individual. The other alternative for the audit firm would be to resign.

Audit firms must have policies and procedures in place that require an individual which is, or was at any time over the previous year (two years in respect of a partner), directly involved:

(a)   for all such audit engagements:

   (i)   senior members of the engagement team to inform the firm of any situation which may involve their potential employment with an audit client; and

   (ii)   other members of the engagement team to inform the firm of any circumstance which involves their probable employment with an audit client; and

   (iii)   all partners within the firm to notify the firm of any situation which involves their potential employment with an audit client; and

   (iv)   any other employee of the firm, including other people whose services can be used by the firm and where such a person is a senior statutory auditor, to notify the firm of any situation that involves their probable employment with an audit client;

(b)   anyone who has informed the firm of employment with an audit client is to be removed from the audit engagement team; and

(c)   a review of the work carried out by the resigning or former engagement team member must be conducted in the current and (if appropriate), the most recent engagement.

IMPORTANT POINT

The Statutory Auditors and Third Country Auditors Regulations 2016 (SI 2016/649) does not allow a person who is appointed as a statutory auditor, or key audit partner for an audit client, to take up:

- any key management position;

- membership of the entity's audit committee;

- a role on a body within the entity that performs equivalent functions to that of an audit committee; and

- any other position of director or on a management body or other committee or membership of that body or committee,

before the end of:

- two years for a public interest entity; or

- one year for other entities.

The two-year/one-year clock starts ticking from the day on which the person ceased to be the statutory auditor or key audit partner.

When a partner, or another person who holds statutory auditor status, accepts an appointment as a director (including a non-executive director role), a member of the client's audit committee or a body that performs a similar function to that of an audit committee, or accepts a role involving a key management position and has previously been an audit partner or member of the engagement team:

- in the case of a partner, at any time during the two years prior to the appointment; or

- in the case of another person, at any time during the year prior to the appointment,

the firm must resign from the audit where possible under applicable law and regulation and must not accept another engagement for that particular client until:

- in the case of a partner, a two-year period has elapsed; or
- in the case of another person, a one-year period has elapsed.

Again, the two-year/one-year clock starts ticking from the **sooner** of:

- the person ceasing to be a covered person;
- the timescale lapsing; or
- the person ceasing employment with the client.

You often see the phrase 'where law or regulation prohibits the auditor resigning or declining such an engagement' (or words to that effect). In practice, it is uncommon for law or regulation to prohibit an auditor resigning or declining an engagement, particularly when independence or objectivity are compromised. However, where law or regulation does prohibit the auditor resigning, the firm must consider alternative safeguards that can be applied to reduce the threats to integrity or objectivity.

When a person that is either a partner or another person holding statutory auditor status (or was a former member of the audit engagement team) joins the entity as a director, a member of the client's audit committee or equivalent body or joins in a key management position, within two years of ceasing to be a covered person in the audit firm, the firm must ensure that no significant connections remain between the firm and the individual. Consideration must also be given as to whether the composition of the audit engagement team remains appropriate and, where necessary, this must be changed accordingly.

When a former partner of the firm, or another person who held statutory auditor status, has joined the client as a director, a member of the audit committee or equivalent body or in a key management position, the firm cannot accept engagement as auditor if that person had been a covered person for any engagement involving any partner of the firm who would be a member of the engagement team, or would carry out the engagement quality review for the client if it were to be accepted:

- in the case of a partner, within two years prior to acceptance of the engagement; or
- in the case of another person, within one year prior to acceptance of the engagement.

These rules can be very confusing and it may be advisable to take third-party professional advice where audit partners and staff join or leave an audit client to make sure that there are no breaches of the Ethical Standard in this respect.

REAL-LIFE SCENARIO

In 2018, Grant Thornton, several partners, and a retired partner were given fines and variously excluded from ICAEW or given severe reprimands by the FRC for breaching the above requirements. In brief, the facts of the situation were that a retired partner continued to act for the firm in a consultancy capacity, but also took up audit committee position within two clients of Grant Thornton.

This was in clear breach of the requirements set out above, and demonstrates the care which must be taken to ensure that a former partner (or other members of staff) fully sever their relationships with the firm if they wish to take up positions with audit clients of their former firm.

Even where such relationships end, there must be a cooling-off period before continuing with an audit where threats to independence have been created by staff or partners moving to the audit client in senior roles, including non-executive roles. Terms in partnership agreements and in contracts of employment should specify that cooling-off periods must be complied with in order to avoid the firm from having to resign from an audit due to an individual who was a partner in, or employee of, the audit firm joining an audit client before the cooling-off period has expired.

Client staff joining the audit firm

3.16   Sometimes staff from an audit client may join the firm. Again, care must be taken here because if a former employee of a client joins the firm and that person was in a position to exert significant influence over the preparation of the financial statements, that individual must be excluded from any role in which they would be a covered person for a period of two years following the date they left the audit client.

Family member is employed by the audit client

3.17   If the audit engagement partner, another partner or a member of the audit engagement team becomes aware that someone closely associated with them, or a close family member who is not closely associated with them, is employed by the audit client and that particular person is in a position that allows them to exercise influence over the accounting records or financial statements, that partner or member of the audit engagement team must:

(a)   be excluded from any role in which they are a covered person; or

(b)   in the case of a close family member of a covered person or any close member of the family of any partner in the firm, inform the audit engagement partner so that he/she can take appropriate action.

IMPORTANT POINT

When applying the above rule, it must be remembered that a partner in a senior management position will almost **always** meet the definition of a covered person. This is because they are regarded as being able to influence the conduct or outcome of the audit.

It will not be possible to undertake the audit of the client where a close family member or person that is closely associated with a partner of the audit firm (or other person in a management role) works and that person is in a position to exercise influence over the accounting records. Examples of such individuals would be the finance director, financial controller or a person responsible for the preparation of the statutory financial statements.

Governance roles

3.18   I think by now you get the theme of where relationships other than auditor are concerned – they are generally a 'no no'.

The same thing goes for governance roles. The Ethical Standard prohibits the audit firm, partner or staff member of the firm to accept appointment with an audit client in the capacity of:

(a)   an officer or member of the board of directors;

(b)   a member of any sub-committee of the board; or

(c)   in such a position within the client that holds directly or indirectly more than 20% of the voting rights in an audit client, or in an entity which the audit client holds directly or indirectly more than 20% of the voting rights.

Where a covered person becomes aware that someone closely associated with them (or a close family member that is not a person closely associated with them) holds any of the positions in (a) to (c) above, the firm must take appropriate action to ensure that the relevant person does not assume a role in which they could be a covered person.

Where there are no safeguards that can be applied in such a situation, the audit firm must withdraw from the engagement.

Family and other personal relationships

3.19   The audit firm must ensure that there are procedures in place which require any partners and professional staff members to notify the firm of any family and other personal relationships which could threaten integrity and objectivity or compromise independence. These procedures must also require that the relevant audit engagement partners are informed, on a timely basis, of such information.

The audit engagement partner must then assess the threats to integrity and objectivity and consider whether independence could be impaired. Appropriate safeguards must then be applied to minimise any threats to an acceptable level (or mitigate them in their entirety).

External consultants involved in an audit engagement

3.20   The use of external consultants on an audit engagement is not unusual. Where the use of an external consultant is considered appropriate, the audit engagement partner is responsible for:

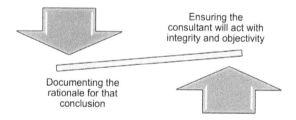

The audit engagement partner must also obtain information from the external consultant concerning the existence of any connection which they may have with the entity, including:

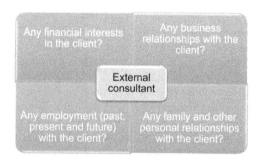

LONG ASSOCIATION WITH AN AUDIT CLIENT

3.21   Many audit firms act for a long time for an audit client and this is certainly not uncommon. However, the risk with long association is that it can give rise to a familiarity threat which, if not reduced to an acceptable level, can impact on independence and objectivity. The familiarity threat arising from long association with an audit client can be reduced by putting in appropriate safeguards, such as:

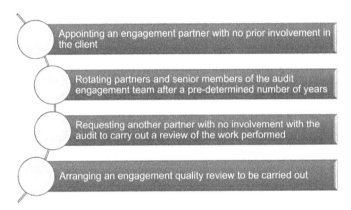

Appointing an engagement partner with no prior involvement in the client

Rotating partners and senior members of the audit engagement team after a pre-determined number of years

Requesting another partner with no involvement with the audit to carry out a review of the work performed

Arranging an engagement quality review to be carried out

REAL-LIFE SCENARIO

Mr C is the audit engagement partner of Entity A that operates in the chemical processing industry. He has acted as audit engagement partner for a period of 12 years and so there is a familiarity threat due to the long association.

In this situation, the audit firm must carefully consider whether it is probable (ie, more likely than not) that an objective, reasonable and informed third party would conclude that the integrity, objectivity or independence of the firm are compromised. This is done on an annual basis.

Mr C's audit firm put a safeguard in place to maintain independence by having an external quality review by an independent reviewer. While Mr C is the audit engagement partner, these are carried out on a cyclical basis (ie, one year a pre-issuance/hot review will be done and the next year a post-issuance/cold review will be done).

Mr C has also ensured that the reasons why he continues to be involved in the audit are documented. Typical reasons may include the client is low risk and not a public interest entity, the external quality reviewer is independent and the file is reviewed each year.

In addition, Mr C has also ensured compliance with the FRC Ethical Standard by ensuring that the facts are communicated to those charged with governance of the entity.

Public interest entities and long association

3.22 CA 2006, ss 491 and 491A prescribe the relevant period that key audit partners can act for an audit client. Where a public interest entity (PIE) is concerned, key audit partners who are responsible for carrying out the statutory audit must **not** act for more than five years. The firm must ensure that it does not accept or continue an audit engagement which would breach these requirements.

Key audit partners responsible for a statutory audit of a PIE must cease their participation in the audit **not later than** five years from the date of their appointment.

Following the partner's removal from the audit, they will not be permitted to participate in the audit of the PIE until a period of five years has elapsed from the date they ceased to be involved.

In the case of a listed audit client, the firm must implement policies and procedures to ensure that in respect of a recurring engagement:

No-one acts as engagement partner in excess of five years (including time spent on an audit engagement that has moved between firms)

Anyone that has acted as engagement partner for five years must not participate in the engagement until a further period of five years has elapsed

Once rotated, the engagement partner cannot have significant or frequent interaction with senior management or those charged with governance until the cooling-off period has elapsed

When an audit client becomes a PIE or listed entity, the length of time that the audit engagement partner has served the entity in the capacity as engagement partner is taken into consideration when calculating the period prior to the engagement partner being rotated off the audit.

When the audit engagement partner has already served for four or more years, that partner can continue to serve as the engagement partner for not more than two years after the entity becomes a PIE or other listed entity. Where this is the case and the audit engagement partner continues to act for no more than two years, this fact and the reasons for it, must be disclosed to the entity's shareholders as soon as possible as well as in each of the additional years the audit engagement partner continues to be involved in the audit.

In the rare situation that the audit firm is unwilling to make this disclosure to the shareholders, the engagement partner is not permitted to be involved in the audit of the PIE or other listed entity.

If there are circumstances where the audit committee of a PIE or other listed entity decide that a degree of flexibility over the timing of rotation is necessary to safeguard the quality of the audit (and the firm agrees), the audit engagement partner may continue in the role for a maximum of two further years, so that no longer than seven years is spent in the position of engagement partner. This must also be disclosed to the entity's shareholders.

Engagement quality reviews and other key partners involved in the audit

3.23 The Ethical Standard (para 3.17) requires the firm to establish an appropriate gradual rotation mechanism concerning the most senior personnel involved in the audit for public interest entities. This includes at least those who have statutory auditor status. This gradual rotation method must be applied in phases on the basis of individuals as opposed to the engagement team as a whole.

IMPORTANT POINT

For audits of PIEs, the audit firm must be able to demonstrate to the FRC that such a mechanism is being effectively applied and that it has been adapted to suit the scale and complexity of the activity of the audit firm.

Remember, in the case of a PIE or other listed entity, nobody is permitted to act in the capacity of engagement quality reviewer or a key partner in the audit engagement for a period longer than seven years. Also, where an engagement quality reviewer or a key partner involved in the engagement becomes the audit engagement partner, the **combined** period of service in these positions must not exceed seven years. Where the engagement quality reviewer has acted for a period of seven years (either continuously or in combination), they are not permitted to participate in the engagement until a further five years have elapsed.

Where roles have been combined, anyone who has acted in the capacity of engagement quality reviewer, key partner or the audit engagement partner for a PIE or listed entity for a period of seven years (whether continuously or in combination), they are not permitted to be involved in the audit until a five-year period has elapsed.

These policies and procedures must include any time spent participating in an engagement where an audit engagement has moved between firms.

Other partners and staff in senior positions

3.24 For PIEs and listed entities, it is the responsibility of the engagement partner to review the safeguards the firm has put in place to address threats to independence and objectivity where partners and staff have been involved in the audit in a senior capacity for a continuous period longer than seven years and must discuss these situations with the engagement quality reviewer. Where any problems or issues remain unresolved, they must be referred to the ethics function or ethics partner.

FEES, REMUNERATION AND EVALUATION POLICIES, GIFTS AND HOSPITALITY, LITIGATION

Fees

3.25 Carrying out an audit is expensive and there is a risk that the audit could become loss-making for the firm. Audit firms are under increasing amounts of pressure to ensure audit quality is as high as possible which means spending more time and incurring more costs. However, it is a fact of life that many audit clients view the costs of an audit as a 'distressed' cost – in other words, some audit clients view the audit as being a cost of compliance with the requirements of the law with little benefit in return. To that end, a lot of companies look unfavourably at increases in the annual audit fee.

The cost of an audit must, of course, be recovered by the audit firm as far as possible and firms must ensure that they charge a fee which is representative of the level of skill and expertise required to enable a high-quality audit to be carried out and which complies with the ISAs (UK) and other regulatory or legislative requirements.

IMPORTANT POINT

When it comes to determining the level of fee to be charged for an audit, the firm must ensure that it does not end up having a 'contingent fee'. A contingent fee is one in which the audit fee is calculated on a pre-determined basis relating to the outcome or result of a transaction, or other event, or the result of the work performed. For example, if an audit fee is to be based on a client's profit before tax figure, this would be a contingent fee.

The FRC's Ethical Standard is clear on contingent fees. They are not allowed because the self-interest threat created cannot be reduced to an acceptable level through the use of safeguards.

The Ethical Standard revised in January 2024 does not contain the definition of 'contingent fee'. In any event, a contingent fee basis is still strictly prohibited.

Fee dependency

3.26   A self-interest threat may arise when the audit firm is dependent, or is perceived to be dependent, on a particular audit client for their fees. The point is when an audit firm depends on the income from a particular client, their behaviour will be affected. For example, the audit firm is less likely to challenge the judgements used by management in preparing the financial statements and ultimately will be reluctant to issue a modified (qualified) audit opinion for fear of losing the client and the income from performing the audit.

This situation also creates an intimidation threat because the client could threaten the audit firm with removal from office, knowing that the audit firm is reliant on performing the audit for income.

For this reason, the Ethical Standard has limits on the amount of income generated by one client. Where it is expected that the total fees for services receivable from a public interest entity (PIE) will regularly exceed 10% of the annual fee income of the firm, the firm must not act for the client. For non-PIEs this benchmark is increased to 15%.

For PIEs where the fees generated from one client are 5–10% of the audit firm's annual income, the situation must be closely monitored, disclosed to the Ethics Partner and to those charged with governance and safeguards (such as enhanced audit quality reviews) implemented. Where the recurring fees received from a non-PIE are 10–15% of the firm's annual income, a similar response is necessary.

IMPORTANT POINT

It is important that the audit firm regularly reviews its audit fee income to ensure that it does not breach these thresholds. Any such breaches may result in the firm being sanctioned by its professional body or by the FRC. During the course of any routine audit monitoring inspection by a professional body, they are likely to ask for a list of current audit clients and will also ask for details of the last fee charged to check that there are no breaches of the Ethical Standard in this respect.

Overdue fees

3.27   Fees from professional services, including audit fees, that become overdue (and which cannot be regarded as trivial) can give rise to a self-interest threat. In such cases, the audit engagement partner, in conjunction with the firm's ethics partner/function, must decide whether the firm can accept or continue an engagement or whether it is necessary to resign. If the fees in respect of the prior year's services are still outstanding, it is important that the audit engagement partner understands the nature of any disagreement or issue relating to the overdue fee.

A self-interest threat created by an overdue fee is also accentuated by the fact that the audit engagement partner may be under pressure not to express a modified audit opinion, or to include a Material Uncertainty Related to Going Concern paragraph in the auditor's report because this may further delay or preclude payment of the audit fee; whereas an unmodified opinion will improve the prospects of the firm securing payment. There is also a risk that an overdue fee may be perceived as a loan to the client, hence care must be taken where overdue fees are concerned. The letter of engagement issued to the audit client should contain clear clauses outlining when fees will be raised and the terms of payment for such fees.

It may also be the case that the reason for an overdue audit fee is because the client is in financial distress. Where this is the case, the audit engagement partner must consider whether the entity will be able to resolve the financial difficulties and must also consider the threats to independence, integrity and objectivity if the firm were to remain appointed as auditor. This must then be judged against the situation if the firm were to resign in terms of how likely it would be that the client would secure another audit firm to carry out the work.

The Ethical Standard requires that where the firm does not resign, appropriate safeguards must be implemented. For example, a review by a partner with relevant expertise that is not involved in the audit. The Ethics Partner must also be notified of the facts concerning the fees that are overdue.

In practice, the best policy is to always encourage prompt payment of fees, perhaps making use of a monthly payment plan for those entities who are likely to struggle to pay on time. In addition, no further work on the current year's audit should be started until the previous year's audit fee is fully settled.

Remuneration and evaluation policies

3.28 An audit firm must have adequate remuneration policies in place, including profit-sharing policies, which provide sufficient performance incentives to secure engagement quality.

IMPORTANT POINT

Any non-audit or additional services provided by the audit firm must not form part of the performance evaluation and remuneration of any covered person that is involved in, or able to, influence the audit engagement.

The policies and procedures in place must ensure that each of the following is **true** concerning each audit client:

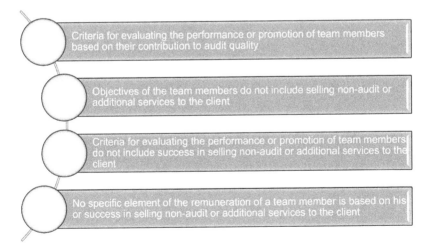

Criteria for evaluating the performance or promotion of team members based on their contribution to audit quality

Objectives of the team members do not include selling non-audit or additional services to the client

Criteria for evaluating the performance or promotion of team members do not include success in selling non-audit or additional services to the client

No specific element of the remuneration of a team member is based on his or success in selling non-audit or additional services to the client

It is important for remuneration and promotion policies for audit team members to reflect the above factors. However, it is equally important that these are seen to be implemented throughout appraisal and promotion meetings and in documentation of these meetings.

3.29 *Ethics*

Gifts and hospitality

3.29   The general rule is that gifts and hospitality cannot be accepted by an audit engagement partner or team. The exception to this rule would be in situations where an objective, reasonable and informed third party would construe the value to be trivial or inconsequential (ie, the third-party test).

Example 3.1 – Trivial hospitality

The audit engagement team is attending Kobe Industries Ltd for two weeks to carry out the detailed audit fieldwork. During the course of that two weeks, the managing director's personal assistant regularly provides the audit team with tea, coffee and biscuits.

The provision of tea, coffee and biscuits (even on a daily basis) is unlikely to cause an ethical threat to integrity, independence and objectivity and therefore it would be acceptable for the audit engagement team to accept these refreshments.

Example 3.2 – Provision of a business lunch

The financial statements of Wrigley Enterprises Ltd for the year ended 31 October 2024 have just been approved and the auditor's report thereon signed by the partner. The CEO of Wrigley Enterprises Ltd has offered to take the audit engagement partner out for a business lunch at the company's expense.

Again, the provision of a business lunch in this scenario is unlikely to cause any ethical issues. This is also accentuated by the fact that the business lunch has taken place after the financial statements have been approved and the auditor's report signed. It would be acceptable for the audit engagement partner to accompany the CEO for lunch.

Example 3.3 – Provision of gift vouchers

The audit of Luna Industries Ltd completed on 10 December 2024 after a number of problems were found in the client's internal controls that caused some misstatements in the financial statements, all of which were corrected prior to the auditor's report being signed.

To thank the team for their efforts, the finance director has sent the audit engagement partner £300 worth of Amazon vouchers to be split among the four team members.

Each audit team member would receive £75 (£300 / 4) worth of vouchers. This is likely to cause an ethical issue and hence the audit engagement partner/team members should politely decline the gift. Christmas gifts from an audit client are unlikely to cause any ethical issues where they are very small (eg, gifts where the value is less than £25).

Example 3.4 – Attendance at regular social gatherings

Stella is the audit engagement partner of Doug & Co LLP and has attended a number of lunch/dinner engagements with the managing director of Bert Enterprises Ltd. In addition, the managing director has invited Stella and her husband to his son's wedding next year.

Attending regular lunches/dinners would indicate a familiarity threat. This is accentuated by the fact that the audit engagement partner and her husband have both been invited to the managing director's son's wedding. Safeguards should be put in place to minimise this threat to an acceptable level or rotate Stella off the audit.

An audit firm's policy on gifts and hospitality will generally be more effective if it provides guidance on the types of situation where independence may be threatened as opposed to having just a rules-based policy based on specific monetary amounts. For instance, a policy that says no gifts or hospitality can be received is unlikely to be workable, as it essentially means the audit team refusing the offer of tea or coffee and other items which are clearly inconsequential. Conversely, a policy which says that everything under £25 is acceptable, might miss the fact that either numerous gifts of this value are received or that a friendship is developing that may impact independence.

IMPORTANT POINT

If gifts or hospitality are accepted more than once, the **cumulative effect** must be considered in terms of its value. Even low value gifts and hospitality can threaten independence if they indicate a familiarity risk.

Litigation

3.30   Unfortunately, the audit firm and an audit client may have a dispute which could escalate to threatened and/or actual litigation. In practice, these situations are thankfully quite rare.

Litigation between an audit firm and an audit client can create a self-interest, advocacy and intimidation threat on the grounds that the firm's interest will be the achievement of an outcome to the dispute or litigation which is favourable to itself. In situations where the audit firm can foresee that such a threat may arise (thus compromising independence), the firm must inform the client of its intention to resign.

Immediate resignation, however, is not necessary in circumstances where an objective, reasonable and informed third party would not regard it as being in the interests of shareholders (or equivalent) or otherwise contrary to the public interest.

The Ethical Standard, at paragraph 4.46 cites two examples which can illustrate this requirement:

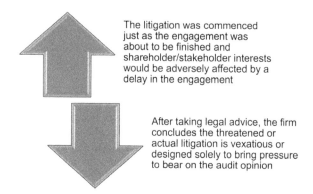

The litigation was commenced just as the engagement was about to be finished and shareholder/stakeholder interests would be adversely affected by a delay in the engagement

After taking legal advice, the firm concludes the threatened or actual litigation is vexatious or designed solely to bring pressure to bear on the audit opinion

NON-AUDIT SERVICES

3.31   A seemingly controversial issue is whether an audit firm should provide their audit clients with non-audit or other services. On the one hand, it may seem sensible that the audit firm should also perform other work for the audit client as they have the knowledge and experience of the client's business as well as a working relationship with key members of staff. In addition, businesses tend to prefer to just deal with one firm rather than having to liaise with different firms who are providing different services to the company. Hence, there can be benefits in terms of consistency when one firm provides a range of services to the client. On the other hand, though, is the issue of independence.

Until a few years ago, it was quite common for an audit firm to perform other engagements for their audit clients. In 2016, the Financial Director Audit Fees Survey found that PwC charged their client, GlaxoSmithKline £15.6 million for their audit, £4 million for 'audit-related services' and £13.6 million for non-audit services. In the same year, Ernst & Young charged £300,000 for the audit of Greene King, but earned a lot more for non-audit work, with £1.3 million being charged for services relating to a significant acquisition by the company.

Understandably, when an audit firm provides other engagements, there is an impact on independence.

IMPORTANT POINT

The threats to independence in respect of the provision of non-audit services to **public interest entities** are such that the regulations now prohibit the provision of such services by audit firms, with the exception of a very small number of audit-related services and those required by specific regulations. The approach to non-audit/additional services provided to public interest entities is dealt with in Section 5B of the Ethical Standard which provides a 'whitelist' of permitted non-audit/additional services that can be performed. This is beyond the scope of this book.

For non-public interest entities, many firms provide non-audit services to an audit client such as payroll, tax compliance/advisory and accounts preparation services. When this happens, the audit firm must ensure that there are policies and procedures in place that ensure independence is maintained when it comes to audit services. To that end, the audit engagement partner must:

(a) identify and assess the significance of any related threats to the integrity and objectivity of the audit firm and consider whether independence would be compromised by providing the non-audit service;

(b) identify and assess the effectiveness of safeguards that may be available which should be designed to either eliminate the threat or (at the very least) reduce it to a level where independence is not compromised; and

(c) consider whether it is probable that an objective, reasonable and informed third party, having regard to the threats and safeguards, would conclude that the proposed non-audit work would not impair integrity or objectivity and compromise independence.

If (c) would result in independence being compromised, the audit firm should either decline the non-audit work or resign from the audit as appropriate.

IMPORTANT POINT

In practice, it can be hard for the audit team to not assume that the work done by another person within the firm is accurate. The audit team must,

---

therefore, take utmost care to ensure that they obtain sufficient appropriate audit evidence to confirm that a particular figure or disclosure is materially correct, regardless of who prepared the information.

Documentation on audit files can often provide a give-away that independence has been compromised. Statements such as 'prepared by the accounts prep team/tax team' with no further evidence that the work is correct immediately indicates that independence safeguards have not operated effectively.

Communication with those charged with governance

3.32   Transparency is a key element in addressing issues raised by the provision of non-audit services to an audit client.

For public interest entities and listed entities (including those entities that are seeking a listing), the audit committee must be properly informed about the issues concerning the provision of non-audit services. This is necessary to ensure that they comply with the provisions of the Corporate Governance Code relating to reviewing and monitoring the external auditor's independence and objectivity and developing a policy on the use of the external auditor to supply non-audit services.

The Ethical Standard at paragraph 5.31 recognises that communication with those charged with governance concerning the impact on integrity, objectivity and independence is likely to be facilitated if disclosure of non-audit/ additional services **distinguishes** between audit-related and non-audit-related work. Appendix A of the Ethical Standard provides an illustrative template for communicating information on audit and non-audit services provided to a group, which helps to ensure that disclosures are adequate and appropriate as follows:

Appendix A: Illustrative template for communicating information on audit and non-audit services provided to the group

	Current year £m	Prior year £m
Audit of company	X	X
Audit of subsidiaries	X	X

Total audit	X	X
Audit-related assurance services[1]	X	X
Other assurance services [2] [3]	X	X
Total assurance services	X	X
Tax compliance services (i.e. related to assistance with corporate tax returns)	X	X
Tax advisory services	X	X
Services relating to taxation	X	X
Internal audit services	X	X
Services related to corporate finance transactions not covered above	X	X
Other non-audit services not covered above	X	X
Total other non-audit services	X	X
Total non-audit services	X	X
Total fees	X	X
Occupational pension scheme audits	X	X
Non-audit services in respect of the audited entity provided to a third party[4]	X	X

Disclosures required under UK company law[5] are indicated by those categories in **bold type** above. Further information can be provided by companies if desired.

1 This will, and will only, include those services which are identified as audit-related services in the Ethical Standard, para 5.38 (Ethical Standard, January 2024).
2 This will not include any tax or internal audit services.
3 The definition of an assurance engagement is provided in the Glossary of Terms.
4 For the purposes of the Ethical Standard, 'non-audit services' include services provided to another entity in respect of the audited entity, for example, where the audit firm provides transaction-related services, in respect of an audited entity's financial information, to a prospective acquirer of the audited entity (see the Ethical Standard, para 5.7).
5 The Companies (Disclosure of Auditor Remuneration and Liability Limitation Agreements) (Amendment) Regulations 2011 (SI 2011/2198).

For clarity, the term 'audit-related services' includes the following examples:

- Reporting required by law or regulation to be provided by an auditor.

- Reviews of interim financial information.

- Reporting on regulatory returns.

- Reporting to a regulator on client assets.

- Reporting on government grants.

- Reporting on internal financial controls when required by law or regulation.

- Extended audit work that is authorised by those charged with governance performed on financial information[6] and/or financial controls where this work is integrated with the audit work and is performed on the same principal terms and conditions.

Documentation

3.33 The audit engagement partner must ensure that they adequately document any decision to provide non-audit services to an audit client. This documentation must include:

The threats identified

The safeguards applied and the reasons they are appropriate

Communication with those charged with governance

IMPORTANT POINT

It is important that the threats and safeguards are considered each year, because over time either the rules, or the perspective of the reasonable and informed third party may change.

---

6 This does not include accounting services.

CHANGES TO THE ETHICAL STANDARD

3.34   On 15 January 2024, the FRC issued an updated Ethical Standard. This updated version followed a consultation draft issued in August 2023. There are three main points that the revised Ethical Standard addresses:

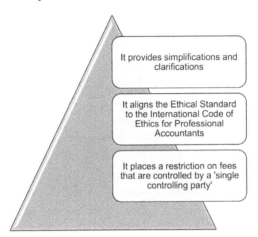

The revisions to the Ethical Standard remove references to the old ISQC (UK) 1 and update certain terminology to be consistent with the new standards (eg, changing references to 'quality control' to 'quality management').

Other Entities of Public Interest (OEPI) category

3.35   In the original consultation draft, the FRC proposed to remove the OEPI category. There was widespread support throughout the profession for this (but only once a final statutory definition became effective). Many also wanted the new definition of a 'public interest entity' to be simpler and aligned to the definitions in law, the Ethical Standard and the IESBA Code.

The FRC does have the power to amend or withdraw the OEPI category but will not do so until a new statutory definition is introduced. The FRC acknowledged that once details of any new statutory definition are known, it is highly likely that it will amend or withdraw the OEPI category given the unanimous nature of stakeholder feedback during the consultation.

Breach reporting

3.36   There was a lot of concern when the consultation draft was issued because the proposals in the draft required any breaches, which the firm's policies and procedures failed to prevent or detect, to be treated as 'not inadvertent'. In other words, if a breach arose which was completely unintentional, it would have been considered a deliberate breach.

Thankfully, these proposals were dropped and, instead, the previous requirement to use professional judgement to determine whether, or not, a breach is inadvertent has been carried over into the revised Ethical Standard. The FRC acknowledged that introducing this new requirement would have driven inconsistent reporting behaviours.

However, care must be taken to ensure a sound understanding of the requirement to report breaches (either to the FRC for listed and public interest entities; or to the relevant supervisory body for unlisted and non-public interest entities) because there are specific requirements in this respect. The revised Ethical Standard requires firms to report all breaches to the Competent Authority on a biannual basis. Where a breach relates to a specific engagement(s), the Ethical Standard requires the breach to be reported to those charged with governance in a timely manner (paragraph 1.23).

In addition, paragraph 1.24 of the Ethical Standard requires the firm to report individual breaches outside of the biannual timetable where the Competent Authority would reasonably expect notice. This may be due to the nature or seriousness of the breach, including, for example, where the firm may need to consider resigning from the engagement.

The Ethical Standard requires the engagement partner (and ethics partner, where there is one) to consider the perspective of an **objective, reasonable and informed third-party test** (see below) on whether it is necessary to resign from an engagement or, alternatively, what safeguards could be put in place.

Objective, reasonable and informed third-party (ORITP) test

3.37   As noted above, the revised Ethical Standard includes requirements for audit and assurance practitioners to consider threats to independence from the perspective of an ORITP. The FRC has published guidance on how this may be applied in practice because it has observed that some firms have struggled to apply this test. In other words, would the third-party deem the threat to be so serious the firm should resign or not accept the engagement, as the case may be; or would they deem the threat to be mitigated to an acceptable level through the use of appropriate safeguards?

Paragraph I14 of the Ethical Standard talks about the 'third-party test' and states that such a person is informed about the respective roles and responsibilities of an auditor (or reporting accountant, as applicable), those charged with governance and management of an entity, and is not another practitioner.

The perspective offered by an informed investor, shareholder or other public interest stakeholder best supports an effective evaluation required by the third-party test, with diversity of thought being an important consideration.

The guidance suggests the following measures to enhance ORITP judgements:

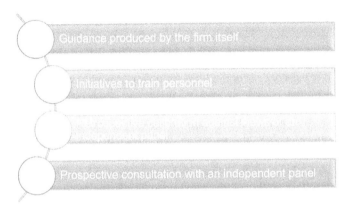

Guidance produced by the firm itself

Initiatives to train personnel

Prospective consultation with an independent panel

Application of prohibitions to different categories of entity

3.38 Section 2 of the Ethical Standard sets out the prohibitions and requirements in respect of personal financial independence for engagement teams and other staff in audit firms. These are combined requirements of the Ethical Standard and those set out in law. The dual source of these prohibitions made the material in the Ethical Standard difficult to understand leading to difficulties in implementation. The FRC have redrafted paragraphs 2.3 and 2.4 of the Ethical Standard to make the requirements more succinct.

Partner staff and rotation

3.39 A table has been included in paragraph 3.22 of the Ethical Standard setting out the rotation rules for various partners on an audit engagement. In addition, further guidance has been included (from previously published material) setting out circumstances such as maternity/paternity leave and sickness absence which may be relevant to those rotation rules.

Fees

3.40 There have been some significant changes made to the Ethical Standard in respect of fees received by the firm. It is well-known that prior to the revisions to the Ethical Standard, where total fees for services from a public interest entity, or other listed entity, and its subsidiaries exceeded 10% of total fee income, the firm must resign or not stand for reappointment.

Where the fees are from a **collection of entities** which have the same beneficial owner or controlling party, which is not a corporate entity, this will also contribute towards the 10% limit. This is something that audit firms will need to be careful of to ensure they do not breach this threshold, especially when they act for a very large group. Keep in mind that the Ethical Standard looks wider (than simply at a group of companies) for other entities that are connected in substance if not in legal form. For example, common ownership that is not a group is now caught when previously it was not.

During the consultation, some concerns were raised from smaller firms that if they were to breach the aggregate fee threshold, they would be caught in a downward spiral which would result in them having to withdraw from engagements which would then have a knock-on effect on their fee income. This could also bring other engagements above fee limits.

The FRC pressed ahead with the fee income proposals anyway and said that they will continue to engage with those practitioners that raised concerns.

Most audit firms (especially the larger ones) will already have systems of internal controls in place to protect against these fee limits. However, given that the FRC has made changes to the Ethical Standard in this respect, it may be the case that there have been some firms that have not had such systems and controls in place resulting in breaches of the fee thresholds given that the changes were triggered through audit inspection and enforcement cases.

Non-audit and additional services

3.41   Changes to Section 5 of the Ethical Standard are aimed to align more closely with changes to the International Ethics Standards Board for Accountants (IESBA) Code. This is in line with the FRC's commitment to have an Ethical Standard which is as stringent as the IESBA's. This also helps UK firms who comply with the IESBA Code as part of their membership commitment to the international Forum of Firms, or because the Code forms the basis of the Ethical Code of UK Professional Accountancy Bodies. Additional changes have been made to reflect FRC inspection or enforcement findings as follows:

- IT services to reflect stricter IESBA Code restrictions on audit firms providing hosting services to audited entities.

• Enhanced tax service prohibitions that can be provided to the majority shareholders of unlisted entities, in response to supervision and inspection findings.

• Recruitment and remuneration services, reflecting more explicit IESBA Code prohibitions where audit firms provide more related services.

• Corporate finance services where IESBA have introduced extended prohibitions relating to the provision of advice on audited entities on debt and financial instruments.

Financial interests of individuals

3.42 As I have already mentioned a couple of times in this chapter, it is generally much easier for anyone in the audit firm *not* to have a financial interest in an audit client. This is because there is clearly a threat to independence where a member of staff or a partner has such an interest. The revised Ethical Standard strengthens the rules in this area.

As well as disposing of the financial interest (or partially disposing of it) and not being involved in the audit engagement, the Ethical Standard then states that where the breach arises from a material prohibited financial interest or a prohibited transaction in a financial instrument, that individual must be excluded from **any** role which means they are operating in the same office or business unit as the audit engagement partner. In addition, the Ethical Standard at paragraph 2.9 requires the firm to not accept, or must withdraw from, the engagement.

This effectively means that the person holding the financial interest would be required to change office or department. Hence, it is much easier to ensure that nobody involved in audit work has any financial interest in an audit client.

PROVISIONS AVAILABLE FOR AUDITS OF SMALL ENTITIES

3.43 The Ethical Standard, Section 6 contains the provisions available for audits of small entities. This section provides alternative provisions and/or exemptions for auditors of small entities which are not public interest entities. For clarity, a 'small' entity is one which meets two out of the following three thresholds for two consecutive years:

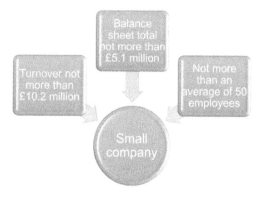

IMPORTANT POINT

Remember, those thresholds are planned to increase if the government presses ahead with legislative changes. As a reminder, the thresholds are likely to increase to £15 million turnover, £7.5 million balance sheet total and not more than an average of 50 employees.

At the time of writing, the government intends that companies will be able to benefit from these new thresholds for financial years commencing on or after 1 October 2024. However, this date is tentative.

The provisions that are available allow auditors of small entities to apply alternative provisions to threats which arise from the provision of tax or accounting services. However, the auditor is required to disclose in the auditor's report the fact that the firm has applied the FRC's Ethical Standard – Provisions Available for Audits of Small Entities.

IMPORTANT POINT

It is helpful to note that the Provisions Available for Audits of Small Entities contains both alternative provisions *and* exemptions. In respect of the former no disclosure is required in the auditor's report or financial statements, but where safeguards are not adopted in relation to a self-review threat there must be informed management and the cycle of cold file reviews is extended.

Where the exemptions in the Ethical Standard are taken, disclosure of this fact must be provided in the auditor's report. In addition, the audit engagement partner must also ensure that either the financial statements, or the auditor's report, discloses the type of non-audit services provided to the client (or the fact that a former engagement partner, or other person personally approved as a statutory auditor, has joined the audit client).

An illustrative example of such a disclosure is shown below:

FRC Ethical Standard – Provisions Available for Audits of Small Entities

The audit firm has taken advantage of the exemption relating to Management Threat – Non-audit Services provided in paragraph 6.11 of the FRC Ethical Standard in respect of a self-review threat. The audit firm has been involved in the preparation of the entity's tax computation for the year ended 31 March 2024 and has calculated the deferred tax liability for the year then ended.

The Provisions Available for Audits of Small Entities provide the following alternative provisions:

Economic dependence

3.44   When a small entity is being audited, the audit firm need not comply with paragraph 4.31 of the Ethical Standard (which relates to the 10% of fees triggering the requirement for an engagement quality review). Hence, an independent quality review is not required where fees are expected to regularly exceed 10% of the income of the firm/relevant part of the firm.

Where there is a risk of fee dependence, the audit engagement partner must disclose the expectation that fees will amount to between 10% and 15% of the firm's annual fee income to the Ethics Partner and to those charged with governance of the entity.

Non-audit services

3.45   The firm need not apply safeguards to address a self-review threat but **only** on the basis that the small entity has **informed management**,[7] and the audit firm performs appropriate reviews of audit work performed in line with requirements for audit quality management. Remember, it is important

---

7 This is defined as a 'Member of management (or senior employee) of the entity relevant to the engagement who has the authority and capability to make independent management judgments and decisions in relation to non-audit/additional services on the basis of information provided by the firm.'

to emphasise that it is management that must accept responsibility for any decisions taken.

IMPORTANT POINT

Firms should document in the audit file whom they regard as informed management. This helps to identify when a reassessment may be needed due to staff changes and helps to show regulators that the matter has been carefully considered.

It must also be clear that more post-issuance (cold) reviews for quality management purposes are to be carried out than would otherwise be the case for audits where non-audit services have been provided. These reviews should particularly check that there is evidence that informed management have made the judgements and decisions needed in relation to the presentation and disclosure in the financial statements.

Exemptions

3.46   The Provisions Available for Audits of Small Entities provide the following exemptions:

Management threat – non-audit services

3.47   An audit firm does not need to comply with the prohibitions in Part B of the Ethical Standard which prohibit the audit firm assuming the role of management, provided that:

(a)   the firm discusses objectivity and independence issues related to non-audit services provided with those charged with governance and also confirms that management accepts responsibility for any decisions that may be taken; and

(b)   it discloses the fact that it has applied the Provisions Available for Audits of Small Entities in the auditor's report and, either in the auditor's report or in the financial statements, discloses the type of non-audit service provided to the client per paragraph 6.15 of the Ethical Standard.

Advocacy threat – non-audit services

3.48   An audit firm need not comply with paragraph 5.79 of the Ethical Standard (tax services that involve the firm acting as advocate) and paragraph 5.106(b) (restructuring services that involve the firm acting as advocate). The audit firm must disclose the fact that it has applied the Provisions Available for Audits of Small Entities and disclose the types of non-audit services provided in either the auditor's report or in the financial statements per paragraph 6.15 of the Ethical Standard.

Partners and other persons approved as statutory auditor joining an audited entity

3.49   Where the audit firm applies the Provisions Available for Audits of Small Entities it is exempt from the cooling-off period requirements. However, the audit firm must:

(a)   take appropriate steps to determine that there is no significant threat to the audit team's integrity, objectivity and independence; and

(b)   disclose the fact that it has applied the Provisions Available for Audits of Small Entities and the fact that a former engagement partner, or other person personally approved as a statutory auditor, has joined the audit client per paragraph 6.15 of the Ethical Standard.

Disclosure requirements when applying the Provisions Available for Audits of Small Entities

3.50   Where the audit firm has taken advantage of the exemptions in the Provisions Available for Audits of Small Entities in respect of:

the audit engagement partner must ensure that:

●   The auditor's report discloses this fact.

●   Either the financial statements, or the auditor's report, discloses the type of non-audit services provided to the audited entity or the fact that a former engagement partner, or other person personally approved as a statutory auditor, has joined the audit client.

CHAPTER ROUNDUP

●   Ethics are a fundamental aspect of auditing and auditors must demonstrate compliance with the Ethical Standard issued by the FRC as well as the relevant Code issued by the member's professional body.

- There are five fundamental principles: integrity, objectivity, confidentiality, professional behaviour and professional competence and due care.

- Audit firms must identify any threats to independence and then put in appropriate safeguards to mitigate the threat(s) entirely or to reduce it/them to an acceptable level.

- The Ethical Standard covers various ethical requirements including financial, business, employment and personal relationships; non-audit services; and fees, remuneration and evaluation policies, gifts and hospitality and litigation.

- There have been changes made to the Ethical Standard in 2024 to ensure it remains up to date and proportionate.

- Section 6 of the Ethical Standard deals with the Provisions Available for Audits of Small Entities.

PITFALLS TO AVOID

- Designing, providing or implementing IT systems for an audit client that have significant reliance placed on them by the auditor. The Ethical Standard, paragraph 5.50 only allows such systems to be designed, provided or implemented by the audit firm if they are not important to any significant part of the accounting system or to the production of the financial statements that are to be audited and where appropriate safeguards can be applied. Such a breach would arise, for example, if the audit firm implements XERO or another accounting system for an audit client.

- Failing to ensure compliance with the Ethical Standard – remember any breaches are reportable.

- Failing to ensure that adequate safeguards are put in place where a threat to integrity, objectivity and independence is identified.

- Not documenting the safeguard(s) that have been put in place as well as the reasons why that safeguard is appropriate in the circumstances.

- Not making necessary disclosures in the auditor's report where the audit firm is relying on the Provisions Available for Audits of Small Entities.

Chapter 4

Client Acceptance

CHAPTER TOPIC LIST

- Introduction (see **4.1**).

- Advertising for services (see **4.2**).

- Client acceptance and due diligence (see **4.6**).

- Anti-money laundering protocol (see **4.20**).

- Agreeing the terms of an audit (see **4.22**).

INTRODUCTION

4.1   It is a fact of life that clients (audit and non-audit clients) will come and go in practice. Some may stay with the firm for several years until such time as they retire, or their business naturally ends; others may stay for only a short while.

Professional firms must have adequate procedures in place to deal with client acceptance (and disengagement). There are some important rules that must be complied with where client acceptance is concerned, and certain protocol must also be adhered to when a client leaves and a new firm is appointed.

Audit firms have specific factors to consider when taking on a new audit client. Among other things, these include ensuring the firm has adequate resources to service the client; appropriate technical knowledge; the timescale required to complete the audit in accordance with International Standards on Auditing (UK) (ISAs (UK)) and other professional standards as well as ensuring the fee charged for the audit is commensurate with the level of skills, knowledge and time needed to carry out a high-quality audit.

IMPORTANT POINT

Audit work has become extremely competitive over the last decade or so, with many firms trying (as far as possible) to quote the lowest fee possible to win the audit. This is not a good strategy because doing this can result in the audit becoming loss-making or, even worse, the audit firm may try to 'cut corners' to keep the audit within budget. Remember, quotations for audit work must be realistic and reflect the level of time needed for the appropriate audit team to carry out the work in accordance with the ISAs (UK) and other regulations or professional standards.

Client acceptance and continuance is not a one-off task. Once an audit client has been accepted, the audit engagement partner must ensure they consider (at a very early stage in the audit) whether they can continue with the engagement. Remember, 'stuff happens' and it may be the case that something went wrong in the previous year's audit that, on reflection, may sway the audit engagement partner into concluding that the firm can no longer act for the audit client. In real life, audit firms will give plenty of notice to an audit client that they do not wish to be reappointed; or they may simply resign at the earliest convenience.

WHAT ARE WE TRYING TO ACHIEVE?

This chapter examines the on-boarding process for audit clients and the important factors that audit firms must consider prior to accepting a new audit client. The audit firm also has important factors to consider for recurring engagements and whether to continue acting for an existing client. This chapter aims to ensure compliance with key protocol, including certain regulations such as anti-money laundering regulations.

In most cases, the audit engagement will continue from one year to the next, subject, of course, to ethical considerations such as long association and having appropriate safeguards in place to reduce the threat to independence, objectivity and integrity, which I have examined in **Chapter 3**. The audit engagement partner must carefully consider whether the firm can continue to act in the current year's audit – for example, has the firm got enough resources to enable the audit to be carried out to a high standard? To that end, it's important to remember that continuation of client relationships is something the audit firm considers each year on every engagement.

ADVERTISING FOR SERVICES

4.2   In a lot of cases, a potential audit client may contact the audit firm because of a recommendation by a third party, ie a 'referral'. The referral may be due to the firm's reputation, knowledge or specialism in a specific sector. Referrals are one of the main ways in which a firm will take on clients.

There are, however, other methods by which a firm attracts clients:

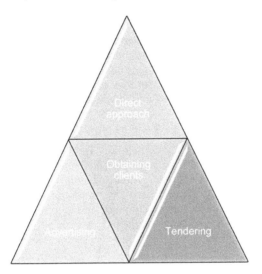

Direct approach

4.3   I have already mentioned this briefly in the opening paragraph in this section. This is where an audit client will directly approach the audit firm to request that they provide a quotation for services. As I mentioned above, this can often be because the audit firm has been recommended by a third party; or it could be down to a simple 'Google' search.

Tendering

4.4   Tendering is another way in which a firm can win audit clients and has become an effective way for organisations to appoint a suitable auditor, particularly as audit has become more competitive. Specific sectors, such as academy schools, will usually invite a number of audit firms to tender for audit services and the successful auditor will usually be chosen after a 'beauty parade' – ie, where each firm is invited to present to the officials of the entity looking to appoint auditors.

Advertising

4.5   Advertising is another way in which audit firms can attract clients. This can be done in a number of ways, but care needs to be taken.

4.5 *Client Acceptance*

IMPORTANT POINT

Professional bodies have strict rules that must be complied with where advertising professional services is concerned. Professional bodies do not allow audit firms to make disparaging comments about other firms and any promotional material that the firm uses must contain factual statements, which can be corroborated, to avoid prospective clients being misled.

ACCA's Rulebook deals with obtaining professional work and states:

> Promotional material may contain any factual statement the truth of which a member is able to justify, but it should not make unflattering references to, or unflattering comparisons with, the services of others. Members are also reminded that any promotional activity should be carried out in accordance with any relevant legislation and should not amount to harassment of the recipient.[1]

Example 4.1 – Inappropriate advertisement

Doug & Co LLP is a small audit firm consisting of three partners and 25 members of staff. In recent months, a number of clients have left the firm due to retirement, death and some have been taken over by larger organisations.

In a recent partners' meeting, the partners decided they need to ramp up their advertising through various community magazines and on social media. The senior partner has drawn up the following advertisement:

DOUG & CO – THE BEST FIRM IN THE TOWN (BY FAR)

We can guarantee we are better than your current accountants! We have the best experts in the profession who can ensure that you will pay less tax than you currently do. Our professional approach to dealing with clients goes much further than other local firms and we will ensure a partner-led service no matter what size of business or sector.

Call us now for a free, no obligation quotation.

This advertisement is not appropriate for a number of reasons:

---

1 ACCA Factsheet *Obtaining professional work.*

- No firm can guarantee that they are better than another firm. This is impossible to measure and is disparaging to other firms in the local area.

- A firm cannot guarantee that a client will pay less tax than it already does. Each client has different tax positions, different income streams, different structures and different tax rules which apply. It may not be possible to pay less tax given the client's specific circumstances so making this claim is unethical at least and illegal at worst. It is also inappropriate to claim that the firm has the 'best experts in the profession' as how can the firm corroborate that claim?

- Stating that the firm's '… professional approach to dealing with clients goes much further than other local firms' implies that other firms in the area are not professional. This, in itself, is unprofessional on the part of Doug & Co.

- The firm claims to be able to offer a partner-led service '… no matter what size of business or sector'. Again, this is misleading, because a three-partner firm with 25 members of staff will be restricted in the types of clients it can take on. For example, it would be unlikely to be able to service a large, multinational public interest entity; or the client could operate in a sector which the firm does not, in fact, have any experience.

This advertisement is likely to breach professional body rules and should be rewritten prior to it being released in magazines or on social media.

CLIENT ACCEPTANCE AND DUE DILIGENCE

4.6   Once the audit firm has been told it has been successful in being appointed as auditor, there are a number of steps that must be taken prior to bringing the client on board. A firm cannot simply agree to be auditor without going through various protocol because otherwise there is a risk that the firm takes on an inappropriate client; or the client may not fit within the firm-wide Anti-Money Laundering (AML) risk assessment.

IMPORTANT POINT

Professional bodies have become increasingly concerned about firms that do not follow correct protocol when it comes to accepting clients. This applies to all clients, and not just to audit clients. There are a couple of 'real-life scenarios' coming up in this section that highlight the importance of not carrying out proper pre-acceptance screening correctly. It would be reckless for a firm to 'bypass' proper client screening because not only do regulators view this unfavourably, but it is also a breach of legislation.

4.6 *Client Acceptance*

Professional firms generally take on clients based on risk profile. A firm's risk assessment will be primarily borne out of how big the firm is, how many staff they have, the firm's specialisms and the laws and regulations to which it is subject to, etc. Remember, that neither the ISAs (UK) nor the CA 2006 specifies an 'acceptable' level of risk – this is very much an entity-specific issue. Professional bodies and regulators will expect firms to only take on clients that they are competent to act for and have the staff that have the necessary skill sets to service the client and to carry out work in accordance with professional standards and legislation.

Example 4.2 – Accepting an inappropriate client

Bella Enterprises Ltd has approached Sophia & Co LLP to act as auditors for the forthcoming year ending 31 March 2025. Bella Enterprises is an entity that specialises in investment management for entities such as pension schemes, hedge funds and offshore investments. Sophia & Co do not act for any other clients in this complex sector.

Sophia & Co have three partners who are quite excited at the prospect of acting for this client because not only will it bring an element of 'kudos' (as the potential client is very well known in the country), but it will also enable them to gain experience in this highly specialised sector.

Bella Enterprises is a specialised entity that has many complex accounting policies, including hedge accounting and a large portfolio of investments that are measured at fair value through profit and loss at each balance sheet date. Such a client will, therefore, need an audit team assigned to it that has the specialist knowledge and experience to carry out this audit in accordance with the ISAs (UK) and other regulatory requirements. The partners of Sophia & Co recognise that currently their four auditors do not have this experience or knowledge but have found a three-hour course run by a reputable training course provider on 'Acting for investment management companies – a refresher for partners and managers' that will be taking place in two weeks' time. All four audit staff have been enrolled on this course.

In addition to enrolling the audit staff on a three-hour refresher course, the audit partner who would be looking after this client (if the firm is successful) has downloaded some information from the internet about acting for such clients. The partners are comfortable that this strategy is sufficient enough to justify acting for the client.

In this example, Sophia & Co clearly lack the expertise and knowledge to carry out this audit properly. The firm acts for no other clients in such a specialist sector and the staff cannot be expected to gain the requisite knowledge just by attending a three-hour course which is designed to be a 'refresher' course (a 'refresher' course being aimed at delegates who already have the knowledge but just need to 'refresh' that knowledge or be briefed on technical updates). Downloading information from the internet is also inappropriate because this information could be technically out-of-date, inappropriate or not correct at all.

While the partners are excited at the prospect of acting for such a client, their approach to all this is reckless. The firm does not have the ability to service the client properly and will be in breach of professional ethics (specifically acting with 'professional competence and due care' – see **Chapter 3**, specifically **3.2**). A lack of specialist knowledge means the audit engagement team will not properly understand the client's complex accounting policies, transactions and other areas of risk. This means that audit risk, at the outset, would be very high. (Remember, audit risk is the risk that the client expresses an incorrect opinion on the financial statements).

Professional ethics

4.7   As well as carefully considering whether a new client fits the firm's risk assessment, the following factors also kick in, too:

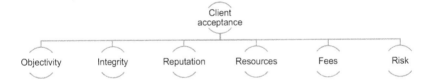

Objectivity

4.8   The firm must be able to demonstrate that it can be both *independent* and *objective*. These are critical traits because a lack of independence and objectivity can not only cloud the judgement of the auditor, but it can also lead them to forming the wrong opinion on the financial statements and/or missing a material misstatement (which could include missing a fraud).

Integrity

4.9   The firm must consider whether management have integrity. A professional firm cannot act for a client whose management lack integrity, such as running a business badly or carrying out illegal acts. A business that changes its auditors on a frequent basis can be a sign that management lack integrity.

Reputation

4.10   I suppose you could interlink 'reputation' with 'integrity'. If the client has a bad reputation or has received a large amount of adverse publicity, this could be enough to sway the audit firm into declining acceptance on the grounds that it would not want to be associated with a client with a bad reputation. Indeed, in today's modern auditing environment and increased regulation, the audit firm would have to have some pretty robust reasons for deciding to act for a client with a bad reputation.

Resources

4.11   I touched on this earlier in the chapter when I mentioned the importance of ensuring the firm has adequate resources in place to be able to service the client in accordance with professional standards. This does not just include ensuring that staff have the requisite skills (although this is clearly an important issue); but it also means considering whether the audit firm has staff available at a time when the client wishes the audit to be carried out. Remember, some audit firms have busy periods where the availability of audit staff is limited. For example, if an audit firm has several academy school clients, then audit staff availability will be limited in the months of September to December, so this is also a crucial factor to consider.

Fees

4.12   The fee must be proportionate to the levels of skill and time required to carry out the audit in accordance with the ISAs (UK), the firm's quality management procedures and other appropriate regulatory requirements. The act of 'low-balling', where an audit firm deliberately tries to undercut other prospective auditors to secure the audit is a reckless strategy because this can then lead to poor quality audit work as a result of 'cutting corners' to keep the audit within budget. In addition, the firm may also want to carry out a credit check on the client to ensure that their fees can be paid within the specified credit period.

Risk

4.13   Risk is of paramount importance when it comes to accepting audit clients. For example, some audit firms refuse to accept clients that deal in cash. Firms are required to establish a level of risk and to ensure that they only accept clients that fit within this level. Remember, there is no 'one-size-fits-all' where risk is concerned – it will very much be down to firm specifics.

Example 4.3 – Lack of client resources

Fraya & Co LLP has been approached by Morris Enterprises Ltd to act as auditors for the forthcoming year ending 30 September 2025. The tender invitation contains a provision that the successful auditor must be able to attend the company to carry out the audit during the last week of October 2025 with a view to signing the financial statements off by the end of November. This is because Morris Enterprises Ltd is restructuring its operations and this involves the sale of one of its subsidiaries and the acquisition of another subsidiary. Both transactions must complete by the end of December which is why the financial statements for the year ended 30 September 2025 must be signed off by the end of November.

Fraya & Co has 18 staff working in the audit department. There are a number of other audits that will be in operation during October and November, utilising 11 audit team members. In addition, the last week of October is school half-term and five team members will be on holiday. This leaves two members of staff available to carry out the audit of the new client, if Fraya & Co is successful in its tender.

Based on this current situation, Fraya & Co will not have sufficient resources available to carry out the audit for Morris Enterprises Ltd in time for the deadline. As this is a first-year audit, there is additional work involved, such as obtaining an understanding of the client, reviewing the predecessor auditor's working papers file for evidence concerning opening balances, understanding the transactions, accounting policies and systems of the client as well as devising specific procedures which address the risks inherent with a new client (to reduce detection risk).

Conversely, it may be the case that two members of staff may be sufficient to carry out the audit of Morris Enterprises depending on the size and complexity of the client. However, in light of the fact that Morris Enterprises Ltd is the parent of a group, this is unlikely to be the case.

In this situation, it would be more than likely that Fraya & Co would have to decline the engagement on the grounds they have insufficient resources available to carry out the audit in accordance with ISAs (UK) and other regulatory requirements.

IMPORTANT POINT

The acceptance factors noted above are included as quality management issues under ISQM (UK) 1 *Quality Management for Firms that Perform*

125

Audits or Reviews of Financial Statements, or Other Assurance or Related Services Engagements. Specifically, ISQM (UK) 1, para 30 requires the audit firm to establish the following quality objectives that address acceptance and continuance of client relationships and specific engagements:

(a) Judgements concerning whether to accept or continue a client relationship which are based on:

    (i) information obtained relating to the nature and circumstances of the engagement as well as the integrity and ethical values of the client which is sufficient to support these judgements; and

    (ii) the firm's ability to carry out the engagement in accordance with professional standards and applicable legal and regulatory requirements.

(b) Processes which ensure that the financial and operational policies of the firm do not lead to inappropriate judgements concerning acceptance or continuation of client relationships or a specific engagement.

The requirement in (a) focuses on integrity and ethical values which means the auditor must obtain information from the client in connection with these matters and then evaluate them to reach a conclusion on them. There are a variety of ways in which the auditor can obtain this information, such as:

● Discussion with the client.

● Discussion with lawyers (with the client's permission, of course).

● Discussion with other professional services firms engaged by the client.

Background information on the client can also be obtained through a simple internet search and any applicable databases.

In (b), the focus is on the firm itself in that it does not allow the firm to prioritise its own income and profit over other client acceptance considerations. While an audit firm will need to make a profit (hence the reason why an appropriate fee must be negotiated with the client), the overriding consideration in ISQM (UK) 1 is the provision of a high-quality audit.

The audit fee

4.14   The audit profession has suffered from bad publicity over the last few years due to high-profile corporate collapses that have brought into question the value of audit. It is fair to say that businesses at the smaller end of the scale (ie, businesses in the small and medium-sized entities' (SME) category) view the audit fee as a 'necessary evil' and one that provides the company with very little benefit.

REAL-LIFE SCENARIO

One practitioner that I spoke to is a partner in a six-partner firm. Among other questions I posed, I asked what he thought that clients thought of the audit process. His response was certainly very interesting…

The practitioner said that most of his audit clients view the audit fee in the same light as paying their car insurance. In other words, it's something they 'must' pay because the law says that they must have an audit and hence must pay for the privilege of that audit. The practitioner told me that none of his audit clients see any benefit of paying for an audit and view it as nothing more than a compliance exercise.

The real-life scenario above is quite a sad situation and is reflective of where the audit profession has ultimately ended up. This is probably one of the reasons why the act of 'low-balling' has become more prevalent over the last decade or so, with audit firms competing to keep as many audits as possible (in some cases) and audit clients trying to drive down the audit fee as far as possible.

There are clear benefits to having an audit (despite what may appear in the professional press), but how can we convince prospective clients of those benefits?

Some of the benefits that should immediately spring to mind include the following:

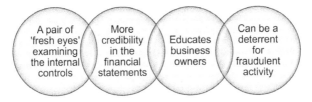

A pair of 'fresh eyes' examining the internal controls | More credibility in the financial statements | Educates business owners | Can be a deterrent for fraudulent activity

4.14 *Client Acceptance*

A **fresh pair of eyes** examining the client's system of internal control can provide invaluable advice on how those internal controls can be improved upon. For example, if the auditor detects a lack of segregation of duties in the payroll department, the advice provided by the auditor can help to improve that weakness, which can serve to prevent and detect fraudulent activity.

The **credibility** of financial information is said to be improved when financial statements are audited because they have been subject to a more rigorous inspection that a set of financial statements which have not been audited.

Educating business owners is a key feature of an audit because it can help the directors become more accountable to the shareholders (although the directors and the shareholders might be the same body of individuals). However, the rigorous nature of the audit means that business owners should want to implement systems and controls that provide accurate financial information and protect the company's assets from theft or fraud.

Audits being a **deterrent for fraudulent activity** is also another benefit of the auditing process. If the finance staff know that the auditors will be carrying rigorous tests on the accounting systems, it should make them stop and think before embarking on a fraudulent activity.

IMPORTANT POINT

Unfortunately, in this day and age, most audit appointments are based on which audit firm can offer the lowest fee. That is something which the auditing profession will struggle to remedy as it is essentially embedded in clients' mindsets, rather than it being something the auditing profession can control. Firms should carefully think twice before low-balling fees. In today's modern auditing profession it is unlikely that a high-quality audit could be carried out for much less than £10,000 – and even that is assuming the client has a sound system of internal control and the financial statements are prepared to a good standard. Where an audit firm is charging something in the region of £3,000 to £5,000, the first question that is asked is 'how good is the audit work on this audit?' Some file reviewers have commented that the level of the audit fee accrual is often a good (preliminary) indicator of how bad the audit file is.

The act of low-balling often results in sample sizes being too small; corners being cut; and the ISAs (UK) not being adequately followed because the audit engagement team is trying to keep the audit within budget. A small budget often results in poor quality audit work and low team morale. Poor quality audit work results in higher audit risk.

There are usually two ways in which a professional firm determines its fees:

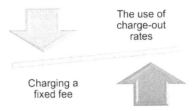

The use of
charge-out
rates

Charging a
fixed fee

I think it is fair to say that the use of charge-out rates is quite an 'oldy worldy' way of arriving at an audit fee. The use of a charge-out rate, of course, uses an hourly rate for audit staff multiplied by the estimated time it is expected to complete the audit. The clear benefit of this fee structure is that it is easy for the client to understand how the fee has been arrived at; but the principal disadvantage is that it can be difficult to predict how long the audit will take – especially if the audit engagement team experiences problems on the audit during the fieldwork stage. The use of a charge-out rate can also result in a fee that the client is dissatisfied with.

Nowadays, most audit firms tend to charge a fixed fee. The clear advantage of this method is that it is preferable for the audit client because they know how much the audit will cost. The principal disadvantage is that if the audit takes longer than anticipated, the firm will not make as much of a profit on the job as anticipated; or, at worst, it becomes loss-making.

Whichever method the audit firm adopts in arriving at an audit fee, it is important that it reflects the time, level of skill and work that will be performed for that fee. In addition, details of any agreed fees, charge-out rates and expenses should be included in the engagement letter so that the audit firm and the client are completely clear as to the levels of fees and expenses to be charged.

Professional handover

4.15   Professional handover is a protocol that all firms must go through. It's worth saying that professional handover either goes smoothly or not.

The professional handover stage comes after the initial pre-acceptance protocol. So, when the firm has assessed the client in terms of how it fits into the firm's risk as well as the other factors that I examined in **4.7–4.13** above, if the firm decides it's good to go, the professional handover stage kicks in.

Professional handover is often referred to as 'professional clearance' in practice. It is arguable whether professional 'clearance' is an appropriate term to use nowadays because a firm does not need 'clearance' to act for a client. Professional bodies often refer to the stage as a 'change in professional appointment'. It is at this stage that the audit firm must make a decision, based on the information they receive from the outgoing audit firm, as to whether (or not) to act for the client.

All UK-based audit firms are regulated by a professional body and while the handover process usually follows (broadly) the same protocol across all the professional bodies, it is worth revisiting that protocol on a regular basis to gauge an understanding of any changes that may have been made to the process; or to even check that the audit firm is complying with the process itself.

As audit firms are regulated by a professional body, the handover process will usually be straightforward as most firms tend not to want intervention by a professional body for failing to comply with their obligations. Only in rare situations do you come across a firm that has failed to co-operate with an incoming auditor and a complaint has been submitted to the relevant professional body.

There are four steps to the handover process:

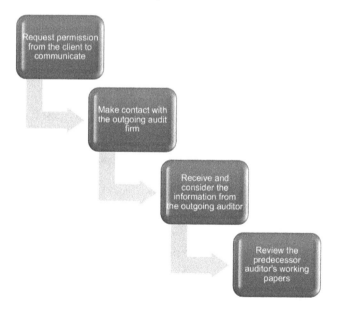

Request permission from the client to communicate

4.16   This is an essential step because if the client does not provide this permission, the outgoing auditor will still be bound by client confidentiality rules and hence will not be able to liaise with the incoming auditor. If the client refuses to grant this permission, the incoming auditor has no alternative but to decline the engagement. In practice, the vast majority of permission requests are granted.

Make contact with the outgoing firm

4.17   After permission has been granted, the incoming firm will make contact with the outgoing firm. The incoming auditor will ask for all relevant information that should be considered by them in deciding whether, or not, to accept appointment as auditor. 'Relevant information' might include fee disputes or breaches of laws or regulations (however, it is important to bear in mind that the outgoing auditor will be subject to anti-money laundering regulations and so may not be able to discuss anything in respect of money laundering which could constitute tipping off).

Where a response is not received, the incoming auditor must try to get a response by other means such as by telephone. Should a response still not be forthcoming, the incoming auditor must seek advice from their professional body as to the way to proceed. In practice, most outgoing audit firms send responses fairly quickly but some firms have been known to issue a notice to the outgoing firm that if a response is not received within, say, seven working days, it will be assumed that the outgoing audit firm has no objection. However, advice in this respect should be sought from the relevant professional body as they may have their own rules on what must happen in such cases.

If handover information (such as the prior year's trial balance and accounts and various working papers) are not received due to a non-response by the outgoing audit firm, this creates an immediate problem for the incoming audit firm because they won't have enough information to audit the opening balances. In a worst case scenario, this could give rise to the auditor issuing a modified audit opinion because of a limitation of scope (insufficient evidence).

Receive and consider the information from the outgoing auditor

4.18   In most cases, a response to a professional handover request is received. On receipt, the incoming auditor will assess if there are any professional or ethical reasons as to why they should not accept appointment.

Review the predecessor auditor's working papers

4.19   For companies based in the UK, the incoming auditor has the right to request access to the predecessor auditor's working papers file under Audit Regulation 3.09. It is important to note that this is not an inspection as to the quality of the previous year's audit; the purpose of reviewing the previous year's working papers file is to obtain evidence over opening balances. The outgoing auditor is compelled to allow this under company law but does not have to do so for certain clients (such as pension schemes). If the auditor concludes that there is insufficient evidence to conclude on the opening balances, the audit plan will need to include work on those opening balances.

Once the audit evidence for the opening balances has been obtained, the audit firm is good to go with the current year's audit.

Appendix 2 provides an illustrative letter which an incoming auditor sends to the outgoing audit firm to request access to their working papers file. Appendix 3 provides an illustrative response.

IMPORTANT POINT

As you can see, there is an awful lot involved in engaging a new client (especially an audit client). It is important, therefore, that the firm understands the professional handover protocol properly so that everything is carried out correctly and in line with the relevant professional body's rules. Many firms have a checklist that they use to on-board a new client and these can be very useful in making sure that nothing is missed during the on-boarding process.

ANTI-MONEY LAUNDERING PROTOCOL

4.20   At the outset, I think it is important to emphasise that this section is not intended to be a comprehensive overview of the anti-money laundering (AML) protocol that all professional firms are obliged to follow under the Anti-Money Laundering Regulations (AMLR). It is intended to be a brief overview of the process that professional firms generally must follow in order to ensure that they are complying, as far as possible, with the Regulations. In complex or contentious situations, it is important that the firm seeks legal or professional third-party advice to ensure compliance with the AMLR.

But what exactly is 'money laundering'? To put it in its broadest terms, money laundering is the process by which criminals attempt to conceal the true origin and ownership of the proceeds from their criminal activity. 'Criminal property' includes:

*   Proceeds from tax evasion

*   Benefits obtained through bribery and corruption

- Benefits obtained, or income received, via the operation of a criminal cartel

- Benefits arising from a failure to comply with regulation

There are three stages to money laundering which are summarised as follows:

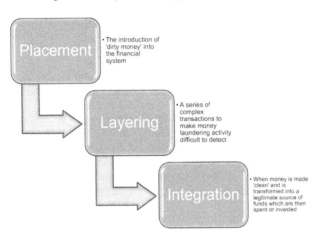

- Placement — • The introduction of 'dirty money' into the financial system
- Layering — • A series of complex transactions to make money laundering activity difficult to detect
- Integration — • When money is made 'clean' and is transformed into a legitimate source of funds which are then spent or invested

Legislation is set out in The Proceeds of Crime Act 2002 which creates three categories of criminal offence:

(1) Offences directly relating to money laundering activity – it is an offence to conceal, disguise, convert, transfer, or remove criminal property from England, Wales, Scotland or Northern Ireland. Concealing or disguising criminal property includes concealing or disguising its nature, source, location, disposition, movement or ownership, or any rights connected with it.

(2) Failure to report – individuals that operate in a regulated sector (such as auditing) may be guilty of an offence to disclose knowledge or suspicion of money laundering where they know or suspect, or have reasonable grounds for knowing or suspecting, that another person is engaged in laundering the proceeds of crime. Disclosure is made to the Money Laundering Reporting Officer who then decides whether a Suspicious Activity Report is to be submitted to the National Crime Agency.

(3) Tipping off – the criminal offence of tipping off arises when a professional accountant makes a disclosure which is likely to prejudice an investigation into money laundering activity. Where the auditor comes across indications of money laundering, the professional accountant must tread carefully to ensure they do not tip off the client.

One of the most important parts of client acceptance and continuance is that of Customer Due Diligence (CDD). All clients must be subject to some form of CDD and while the protocol is onerous, any non-compliance will result in the audit firm being sanctioned by their professional body.

To sum up the process, the audit firm will generally:

- Carry out searches on the audit client at Companies House (or other public registry) to identify who the beneficial owners are and to check the People with Significant Control Register to ensure this is accurate.

- Obtain identification of the company, such as obtaining certificates of incorporation and other incorporation material.

- Obtain identification of the beneficial owners. For UK AMLR, this will usually be directors and shareholders that own more than 25% of the business. The identification must comprise at least photographic identification (such as a passport or driving licence) to identify the person is the person who the firm is dealing with; and proof of residency by obtaining a **recent** utility bill, such as a council tax bill.

- Carry out electronic searches on the client, such as a credit check (although this is not mandatory, but it is a means of efficiently carrying out the requisite search).

At the time of writing, I noticed that there are some companies advertising software that handles the AML protocol. Depending on the success of these programs, this is something that could hugely benefit the accountancy and auditing profession if it enables compliance with the AMLR.

REAL-LIFE SCENARIO

In February 2023, an accountant was excluded from ACCA following a long-winded investigation into the accountant's money laundering processes.

ACCA attempted to contact the accountant to organise a monitoring visit to assess the firm's compliance with AMLR. The accountant falsely told the inspector that his AML policy was created in October 2018.

ACCA's money laundering monitoring visits are estimated to complete within 15 working days. However, in this case, the next few weeks were spent trying to gain a response from the ACCA member. Ignoring correspondence from professional bodies is reckless and is not a strategy that will end well.

Eventually, ACCA tracked down the accountant and the accountant sent in some documents. ACCA then asked for some additional documentation, including the firm's (original) AML policy that was created in 2018 and procedures document. The accountant confirmed that this document had not been subject to any subsequent changes as there were none required.

ACCA pointed out during the disciplinary tribunal that the AML policy document could not have been created in October 2018 because it replicated ACCA's Technical Factsheet on AML policy and procedures which had only been published in February 2020. This led to the accountant admitting he had been dishonest when he informed ACCA that the AML policy had been in place since October 2018.

This was only one issue that was not in the accountant's favour. Not only had the accountant been dishonest, but ACCA concluded there was a lack of evidence of:

• a firm-wide risk assessment;

• AML training for relevant staff; and

• the firm's criteria for different risk ratings.

In respect of the final bullet point, the firm had assessed some of their clients as 'medium-risk' when they should have, in fact, been assessed as high-risk.

There were other things found to be lacking during the monitoring visit including a 'yes/no' template that did not provide an assessment of the risks faced by the firm, or actions to take to mitigate those risks. In addition, it was also found that the template was not tailored to the firm's AML processes and lacked any details of the firm's day-to-day processes (although it did include some processes – the problem was, these were not relevant to the firm). Other issues found included a failure to complete the name of the nominated officer for the firm and not providing details of the topics covered in the staff AML training manual (as well as whether the staff had even received the required training).

ACCA gave the practitioner chance to follow-up on the actions contained in the report of the monitoring visit, but the practitioner failed to do this or make contact with ACCA.

What was the upshot of all this? Understandably, the member was excluded from ACCA and he received an order to pay costs of £6,000 due to his dishonesty and AML breaches.

REAL-LIFE SCENARIO

In another AML case, a sole practitioner was excluded from ACCA because he did not comply with AMLR on the basis that he did not think any of his small clients were a major risk.

This case also proved to be long-winded and protracted, although some of this was due to ACCA giving the practitioner several opportunities to remedy non-compliance with AMLR.

Despite these chances, the practitioner maintained that he was a 'small operator' and that all his clients are 'low risk'. The practitioner also informed ACCA that he simply did not have the time, the money, or the ability to attend to a role that will only be suitable for much bigger practices. As you can imagine, this sort of response does not go down well with a professional body.

In this case, the practitioner had not completed a firm-wide risk assessment and, with the exception of terms and conditions, the practitioner also admitted not having any AML policies in place.

When asked about AML training, the practitioner admitted to ACCA that he had attended a webinar or seminar 'some time ago' and had last completed AML training about three or four years prior to the routine ACCA monitoring visit.

The practitioner confirmed that as all his clients come to his firm via referrals, he relied on an informal process. The practitioner would only take on clients if he felt comfortable, but he did not carry out a new client form for each client, nor did he use any electronic verification as part of his on-boarding process. The practitioner went on to say that if he were to carry out AML procedures, this would make his clients leave and that he has not encountered any problems with his previous clients.

In terms of failing to address the breaches already discovered, the practitioner confirmed during the investigation that he had failed to do this and blamed his lack of response on the 'stress and anxiety' of having to 'adhere to ACCA requirements'. He then went on to ask the investigating officer 'Are you doing this to every practitioner or only the ones caught out?'

The practitioner maintained his stance in that he found the AMLR too comprehensive for a sole practitioner and his son had found a policy set by ICAEW for 'small operators' and concluded that he now had 'a policy tailored for my practice.'

Eventually, ACCA ran out of patience and referred the practitioner to the disciplinary committee. The practitioner called this course of action 'harsh' and refused to defend himself, stating 'Whatever I did was not enough, although a fellow certified accountant, a chartered accountant, and a lawyer said it was good enough. I AM A SMALL OPERATOR. I have nothing to add to my policies and procedures, firm-wide risk assessment, and [customer due diligence]. I am not your model AML operator.'

His defiance did not stop there. In his letter to the disciplinary committee, the practitioner said that as a 'lone practitioner', what ACCA requires from AML compliance is 'far-fetched and totally unreasonable.' He then went on to say that ACCA has thrown on him compliance that they would expect from 'multi-national, multi-partner, multi-hundred employee practices.'

The practitioner claimed that he was very busy and cannot spend time reading emails and other literature. He then ended his letter by complaining that ACCA did not provide the help he needed when he 'cried for it' and 'did not even bother to reply to me'. He went on to say:

I have attended to all feasible requirements of ACCA and beyond. I may differ in opinion, but I abided by their recommendations. ACCA should devise varied policies suitable for difference practices (courses for horses). You simply do not expect landlocked countries to produce submarines.

As you can imagine, the sanctions for all of this were heavy. ACCA's disciplinary committee concluded that the practitioner had demonstrated a complete lack of insight and understanding regarding AMLR, which the committee clearly considered was serious. There was also a concern by the committee that the practitioner would fail to take the required steps to address this non-compliance.

The committee's comments about the practitioner were also less-than-rosy. They described the practitioner's lack of co-operation with the investigation as serious misconduct and fundamentally incompatible with membership of ACCA.

ACCA excluded the practitioner from membership and ordered him to pay costs of £8,400.

As you can see from the above cases, it is important that audit firms comply with AMLR and any non-compliance can result in substantial sanctions, including exclusion from membership. Professional bodies expect a certain minimum standard of compliance with laws and regulations, so it is not sufficient just to say 'Those rules don't apply to me as I am a small firm.'

It may be the case that the audit firm determines it necessary to carry out 'enhanced due diligence' on a client. This will, of course, depend on the level of risk associated with the client and enhanced due diligence is generally carried out on clients that are considered to be higher risk.

IMPORTANT POINT

Professional bodies carry out anti-money laundering monitoring visits on professional firms to ensure they are complying with their obligations under the legislation. There are many specific details to AMLR, which are beyond the scope of this book. However, audit firms must ensure that:

- Staff are fully trained in all aspects of anti-money laundering, in particular on how to identify potential money laundering transactions. Staff should also be trained in how to report suspicions of money laundering. Staff must also be trained in the offence of tipping off so that they know how to avoid this breach during the course of their work.

- The firm has appointed a Money Laundering Reporting Officer (MLRO). The MLRO must have a suitable level of seniority and experience and there must be alternative arrangements made when the MLRO is unavailable. The primary objective of the MLRO is to receive money laundering reports from staff members and make a judgement call as to whether a Suspicious Activity Report is to be lodged with the National Crime Agency.

- Client identification processes are in place which comply with the requirements of AMLR, such as obtaining official documents to verify identity, proof of residential address, evidence that a company exists and electronic checks on entities and individuals.

- A full audit trail of transactions is maintained for a period of at least five years and ensure that the audit firm has controls in place to ensure these records are not inadvertently destroyed. Client verification records must be retained throughout the period of the client relationship and for five years following the termination of the client relationship.

- Where the audit firm handles money on behalf of the client, the firm must ensure there are controls in place to ensure the firm itself does not inadvertently become a party to money laundering.

An audit firm commits an offence if they fail to ensure there are adequate AML processes in place and professional bodies have been known to impose heavy sanctions on firms where this is found to be the case and where the issues are not remedied (see the 'Real-life scenarios' above).

Audit firms are required to report all suspicions of money laundering to the money laundering reporting officer. Remember, there are no *de minimis* levels and so all suspicions must be reported. It is then down to the MLRO to make a judgement call as to whether a Suspicious Activity Report is lodged with the National Crime Agency.

IMPORTANT POINT

Auditors are bound by client confidentiality rules meaning they cannot divulge confidential information to third parties without consent from the client. Where the AMLR are concerned, an auditor will not be in breach of any professional duty of confidence where they report money laundering suspicions to the National Crime Agency. Clearly, the audit firm will need information to substantiate their suspicions (which can sometimes be difficult) but in any event the firm must not tip off the client that they have (or are about to) lodge a Suspicious Activity Report.

AMLR 2017

4.21   On 26 June 2017, new AMLR came into effect in the UK in the form of the Fourth Anti-Money Laundering Directive. These new AMLR brought about some changes from the previous protocol as follows:

- **Firm-wide risk assessment** – The 2017 Regulations set out a more prescriptive approach to firm-wide risk assessments and these must be in writing. There is no 'one-size-fits-all' where the firm-wide risk assessment is concerned and the risk assessment itself will depend on the nature and circumstances of the firm. The most important aspect of the firm-wide risk assessment is that the audit firm must properly identify and assess the risk of money laundering or terrorist financing to which the firm is exposed and document that assessment.

- **Officer responsible for compliance** – A money laundering compliance principle (MLCP) must be appointed who is on the board of directors or equivalent management body of the audit firm. Alternatively, the MLCP can be a member of senior management. Sole practitioners with no employees are exempt from this requirement.

- **Screening relevant employees** – Audit firms have an obligation to assess the skills, knowledge, conduct and integrity of employees involved in identifying, mitigating, preventing or detecting money laundering and terrorist financing. Audit staff must receive regular training in how to recognise and deal with transactions and other activities that may indicate money laundering is taking place. In practice, this training can be delivered by the staff member carrying out an online course which requires a minimum pass mark.

● **Independent audit function** – The firm should have an independent audit function to assess the adequacy and effectiveness of the firm's AML policies, controls and procedures. Sole practitioners with no employees are exempt from this requirement.

● **Policies, controls and procedures** – The audit firm must have written policies, controls and procedures in place which deal with money laundering and terrorist financing. These policies, controls and procedures should be approved by senior management who should evidence their approval.

● **Enhanced due diligence** – Enhanced due diligence is required where:

— there is a high risk of money laundering or terrorist financing;

— where the client or customer operates in a high-risk country;

— the client is a politically exposed person (PEP), or a family member or known close associate of a PEP;

— the client has provided false or stolen identification documentation or information on establishing a relationship; or

— the auditor identifies that the client has entered into complex and unusually large transactions or there is an unusual pattern of transactions with no apparent legal or economic purpose.

● **Politically exposed persons (PEP)** – The audit firm must have procedures in place that identify whether a client, or the beneficial owner of a client, is a PEP or a family member or known close associate of a PEP.

Compliance with AMLR can be an onerous task in practice and it is important that firms demonstrate as far as possible that they are complying with the rules to avoid any sanctions being imposed on them by a professional body or other regulator. It is often worth investing in a third-party review of the firm's AMLR protocol to assess where improvements can be made and that all staff are aware of their responsibilities under the Regulations. These reviews can prove to be valuable and help the audit firm to overcome any difficulties with AMLR in a timely manner.

AGREEING THE TERMS OF AN AUDIT

4.22   So, we have finally got to the stage where we have carried out all our pre-on-boarding processes, identified the client for AMLR purposes and have received responses from the previous audit firm (where applicable). The next step is to agree the terms of the audit engagement.

This is where the provisions of ISA (UK) 210 *Agreeing the Terms of Audit Engagements* kick in and it is important that the auditor has a sound understanding of the provisions in ISA (UK) 210. Remember, the auditor is contracting with the audit client to carry out services and it is crucial that both parties understand exactly what is expected from them.

To that end, the auditor must ensure that the **preconditions** for the audit are present. There are two stages to this process:

Stage 1

Determine whether the financial reporting framework to be applied in the preparation of the financial statements is acceptable. An acceptable financial reporting framework would be UK and Ireland GAAP (UK and Ireland accounting standards in the form of FRS 102 *The Financial Reporting Standard applicable in the UK and Republic of Ireland* or UK-adopted IFRS).

The auditor must also evaluate whether law or regulation prescribes the applicable financial reporting framework, considering the purpose of the financial statements, and the nature of the reporting entity (for example, whether the client is a listed client or a public sector entity).

Stage 2

Obtain the agreement of management that it acknowledges and understands its responsibilities for the following:

(a)   preparing the financial statements in accordance with the applicable financial reporting framework;

(b)   that the entity has a sound system of internal control which enables the preparation of financial statements which are free from material misstatement; and

(c)   that the client will provide the auditor with access to information relevant for the audit and access to staff within the entity from which the auditor can obtain sufficient appropriate audit evidence.

In most cases, the preconditions for an audit will be present because it is rare that the financial reporting framework adopted by a client (particularly in the UK) is unacceptable and management are generally willing to confirm their responsibilities for the preparation of financial statements that are free from material misstatement. Most audit clients want the audit to run smoothly.

However, in the rare situation that the auditor cannot confirm that the preconditions for an audit are present, the auditor must discuss the situation with management. If the preconditions for the audit are **not** present, the auditor must not accept the engagement (unless they are compelled to accept the engagement under law or regulation, which is rare).

Example 4.4 – Preconditions for an audit are NOT present

The audit engagement partner of Jett & Co LLP has recently taken on a new client, Wilson Industries Ltd, a client that manufactures chemicals for use in the forensic science industry. The first audit of this new client will take place for the year ending 31 July 2024. Today's date is 13 May 2024.

Due to illness, the audit manager attended an initial pre-planning meeting with Kirsty Ratchford, the finance director of Wilson Industries. The audit engagement partner has reviewed the minutes of this meeting and was concerned to see the following note of a comment from Kirsty:

> You will be attending our premises at which will be our busiest time but we have no alternative because we will urgently need the audit completing very soon after the year end as the directors wish to approach the bank for a working capital loan and carry out a share issue to help fund our expansion plans. I have read the draft engagement letter and it refers to you having access to all staff within the company to obtain audit evidence. I am afraid this will not be possible because the staff will not have any time to deal with auditors. You must only deal with myself when obtaining your audit evidence.

The audit engagement partner contacted Kirsty upon reading this comment and informed her that it is a specific requirement of ISA (UK) 210 that unrestricted access to other staff members is granted so the audit team can obtain sufficient appropriate audit evidence. Kirsty's stance did not move, and she was adamant that no access to other staff members within Wilson Industries would be granted.

The first thing to note is that is unusual for a finance director to refuse unrestricted access to staff members. This is because there are aspects of the business, such as production, sales, purchasing and manufacturing/warehouse which may be better dealt with by others in the organisation rather than finance staff. For example, it would be unusual for the finance director to have a deep understanding of how various chemicals are manufactured or other production processes which the audit team may need to review when carrying out tests of control, stock pricing etc. Such processes would be best looked at with a production manager or director.

If Kirsty Ratchford continues to refuse unrestricted access to others within the business from which to obtain audit evidence, the audit engagement partner must not accept the audit because the preconditions outlined in ISA (UK) 210 are not present. The only exception to this would be where the audit firm is required to continue with the engagement because they are required to do so by law or regulation.

REAL-LIFE SCENARIO

Mr P is a partner in 24-partner firm and was approached by a large local business to act as auditor.

Mr P downloaded a copy of the latest financial statements for his prospective client from Companies House. The audit opinion on these financial statements had been disclaimed on the grounds of insufficient audit evidence being available and an inability to obtain written representations from the client. The predecessor auditor's resignation letter (which had also been lodged with Companies House) had confirmed they had resigned because of a pervasive inability to obtain sufficient appropriate audit evidence on the financial statements.

Mr P said that initially he was concerned because of the inability for the audit firm to obtain sufficient appropriate audit evidence. The predecessor auditor was a much larger firm than Mr P's and is well-known around the area.

Written representations are an important source of audit evidence as they complement other forms of audit evidence which the audit engagement tea has obtained. On their own, however, they are insufficient forms of audit evidence because they are internally generated. However, ISA (UK) 580 *Written Representations* does require the auditor to obtain written representations for certain areas of the financial statements.

Mr P declined to even tender for this audit, and he was right to do so. If the previous year's financial statements have had an audit opinion disclaimed, then it is highly likely the current year's financial statements would also be. ISA (UK) 210 states that if management, or those charged with governance, impose a limitation on the scope of the auditor's work in terms of a **proposed** audit engagement, such that the auditor believes the limitation will result in the auditor disclaiming an opinion on the financial statements, the auditor cannot accept such an engagement. The exception to this would be where law or regulation would compel the auditor to accept the engagement (which is rare in practice).

Any audit opinion that has been disclaimed should ring (very loud) alarm bells to a prospective auditor. An auditor will only every modify their audit opinion as a last resort, and a disclaimer of opinion is probably the worst outcome of any audit.

The letter of engagement

4.23 ISA (UK) 210 requires the auditor to set out the terms of the audit engagement in an appropriate form to management and those charged with governance. This 'form' is usually an engagement letter addressed to the directors and accepted by them and essentially forms a contract between the audit firm and the audit client. To that end, it's imperative that all parties clearly understand the terms on which the audit firm will act and the responsibilities of both the audit firm and the client.

Professional bodies and regulators require letters of engagement to be in place for all audit assignments (even non-audit work). If a letter of engagement is not in place, there can be problems further down the line in the event of a dispute between the client and the firm. Failing to have a letter of engagement in place can also mean the firm runs into difficulty with their professional body or regulator who will expect an up-to-date engagement letter to be in place. Sanctions imposed by professional bodies can include 'follow up' visits to ensure that deficiencies have been remedied and controls implemented that will prevent their recurrence to more serious sanctions including expulsion from membership and withdrawal of the firm's auditing practising certificates for serious issues.

The purpose of the audit engagement letter is to confirm the acceptance of the engagement by both the audit firm and the client and to minimise the risk of misunderstanding between the auditor and the client by clearly setting out the responsibilities of both parties.

The engagement letter must be in place (ie, agreed and signed by both parties) prior to audit work commencing.

Once the audit engagement letter has been agreed and it is in place it does not necessarily have to be re-issued each year. ISA (UK) 210 does require the firm to carry out a review of the letter of engagement each year to ensure it remains appropriate. Things that may trigger the need for a new letter might include:

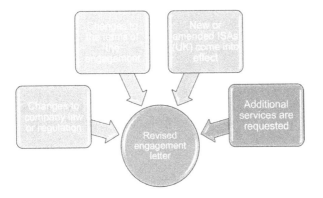

IMPORTANT POINT

ISA (UK) 210 does specifically require the auditor to consider reminding the client of the existing terms and conditions of the audit engagement for continuing engagements. It is often worthwhile documenting that this has been done on the audit file so that any reviewer can see this provision in ISA (UK) 210 has been complied with.

Where additional services are requested and these are non-audit services which an audit firm is permitted to carry out without breaching any ethical rules, it is usual practice for the firm to issue a separate engagement letter which outline the provision of those services. It would be unusual for an audit engagement letter to include non-audit-related services. In practice many methodologies and templates have one covering letter to which are added individual schedules for the services (audit; financial statement preparation; taxation; payroll etc).

Content of the engagement letter for new engagements

4.24   While ISA (UK) 210 sets out the minimum requirements where the terms of an audit engagement is concerned, its requirements are not conclusive. Remember, all audits are different and certain matters may need to be included in an engagement letter that may not necessarily be outlined in the ISA (UK). This is why it is important that each engagement letter is prepared **specifically** for that audit engagement.

IMPORTANT POINT

The final sentence of the preceding paragraph cannot be over-emphasised. Professional bodies frequently complain that engagement letters are in place for audit engagements, but that they are either out-of-date, contain inappropriate or irrelevant terms and there is no evidence that they have been reviewed to assess if the client needs reminding of the engagement's terms.

Nowadays, many firms subscribe to professional bodies or other reputable sources for engagement letter 'templates'. These are often a really good starting point for drafting an engagement letter but should be used with a degree of caution. As I mentioned earlier in this section, every audit is different and a 'template' engagement letter may not necessarily contain the relevant terms needed for a specific engagement. This is where tailoring will be required to ensure the engagement letter captures all relevant issues and omits any superfluous or irrelevant ones.

With that in mind, the content of an audit engagement letter should include the following:

- The objective and scope of the audit
- The responsibilities of the auditor
- The responsibilities of management
- The identification of the applicable financial reporting framework (eg, FRS 102)
- Reference to the expected form and content of any reports to be issued
- Reference to professional standards, regulations and legislation that apply to the audit
- Limitations of an audit
- An expectation that management will provide written representations
- Basis on which the fees are to be calculated
- Agreement of management to notify the auditor of subsequent events
- Agreement of management to provide draft financial statements in time to allow for the audit to be completed before any agreed or imposed deadline (this is especially important where the audit has to be completed in a very short timescale – such as for an academy school)
- Form and timing of any other communications during the audit
- Complaints procedures

The Appendix to this chapter contains an illustrative audit engagement letter. Its content is not comprehensive and is included purely for illustrative purposes only.

The engagement letter and continuing engagements

4.25   It is unusual for an audit client to change its auditors on a regular basis – indeed, frequent changes of auditor will usually raise questions as to why the client sees the need to change audit firms on a regular basis.

In practice, most audit clients tend to stay with the same audit firm for several years – subject, of course, to compliance with ethical rules and threats such as long association which must be managed accordingly by appropriate safeguards. Entities such as public interest entities (PIE) are subject to very strict ethical rules, particularly where long association and partner rotation are concerned and it is important to have a sound understanding of these rules if the firm acts for any PIE clients.

I mentioned in **4.24** that for recurring engagements, ISA (UK) 210 requires the auditor to consider whether there is a need to remind the client of the terms of the engagement letter. This is not the only consideration that needs to be looked at when the next audit comes around.

Once the auditor has signed their auditor's report, they have no further responsibility for those financial statements (subject to being notified of any subsequent events which may require the auditor to carry out further audit procedures which are discussed in **Chapter 10**).

On completion of the audit, the auditor will then revisit the acceptance procedures and review the documentation on file to ensure it remains appropriate for the next audit as well as considering whether it would be appropriate to continue as auditor (if re-appointed) next year. This is important because the auditor could have come across issues during the course of the audit that has just been signed off that mean the firm no longer wishes to be continue acting for the client. For example, the integrity of management may have been called into question, or the auditor may have struggled in getting audit evidence. In some more serious cases, the auditor could have been asked to do something (or agree to something) which would be against their professional body's *Code of Conduct* or other ethical rules. In such situations, it is likely the auditor will consider resigning.

For the most part, the majority of audit clients will remain on the firm's portfolio.

There are certain procedures that the firm is required to carry out for continuing engagements to comply with laws and regulations. For example:

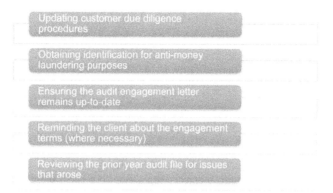

Remember, when considering whether to continue acting for a client, or not, the audit firm will consider all information at their disposal (including their experience of the client during the previous audit) as well as considering the firm's levels of acceptable risk.

CHAPTER ROUNDUP

• Client acceptance and continuance is not a one-off exercise. Once a client has been accepted onto the firm's portfolio, protocol is such that the firm must have procedures in place to monitor the client and conclude whether, or not, the firm wishes to continue with a professional engagement.

• A firm usually attracts clients through direct approach, advertising or tendering.

• Advertising for services is permitted, but care must be taken to ensure that any advertisements are not disparaging against competing firms and that they comply with professional body requirements as professional bodies have strict rules governing advertisements.

• Audit firms must only accept clients that fit into the firm's risk assessment and which they have the necessary skills, experience and technical competence to do work for.

• Professional ethics must be carefully considered when accepting an audit client including objectivity, integrity, reputation, resources, fees and levels of risk.

• Audit fees must be proportionate to the levels of skill, experience and resources needed to complete the audit in accordance with professional standards.

• The act of 'low-balling' is actively discouraged because this can result in work becoming deficient in an attempt to keep the audit within budget.

- Fees may be charged on a fixed-fee basis or by way of charge-out rates, with the former being the most popular nowadays.

- Professional handover protocol requires the incoming audit firm to liaise with the outgoing auditors to request various information and access to the predecessor auditor's working papers file to obtain evidence on opening balances.

- The firm must have sufficient anti-money laundering procedures in place to comply with Anti-Money Laundering Regulations.

- There are three stages to money laundering: placement; layering; and integration.

- The terms of an audit agreement should be in writing and comply with the provisions laid down in ISA (UK) 210. Other client-specific terms may also be needed.

- The engagement letter need not be reissued each year; but it must be reviewed on an annual basis to ensure it remains appropriate and to consider whether the client needs to be reminded of the terms of the engagement.

PITFALLS TO AVOID

- Engaging an audit client that the firm has no experience or technical competence in dealing with.

- Failing to agree the terms of the engagement in an engagement letter.

- Not changing the terms of the engagement when required by law or regulation.

- Failing to have adequate anti-money laundering protocol in place.

- Failing to consider the 'bigger picture' when deciding whether the firm should accept appointment for a recurring engagement.

- Not tailoring 'template' engagement letters to be client specific.

APPENDIX 1: ILLUSTRATIVE ENGAGEMENT LETTER

As noted, this illustrative engagement letter has been included for reference purposes only and should not be treated as being a comprehensive engagement letter. Where necessary, auditors should ensure they obtain professional advice in connection with engagement letters to ensure they issue engagement terms that are relevant to the individual circumstances.

Auditor & Co LLP
Audit House
County Street
Anytown
AB1 2CD

29 April 2024

The Board of Directors
Dudson Enterprises Ltd
Nice Street
Brilltown
DE1 2EE

Dear Directors

This letter, together with the attached terms of business dated 29 April 2024, set out the basis on which we are to act as auditors to your company. This letter also sets out both yours and our responsibilities.

You have requested that we carry out an audit of the financial statements for the year ended 31 March 2024.

We are pleased to confirm our acceptance and our understanding of this audit engagement by means of this letter. Our audit will be conducted with the objective of our expressing an opinion on the financial statements.

1. Responsibilities of management

Our audit will be conducted on the basis that management acknowledge and understand that they are responsible for:

(a)   The preparation and fair presentation of the financial statements in accordance with FRS 102 *The Financial Reporting Standard applicable in the UK and Republic of Ireland.*

(b)   Such internal control as management determines is necessary to enable the preparation of financial statements that are free from material misstatement, whether due to fraud or error.

(c)   Providing the auditor with:

(i)   unrestricted access to all information of which management is aware that is relevant to the preparation of the financial statements, such as accounting records, documentation and other matters;

(ii)   additional information that we may request from management for the purposes of the audit; and

(iii)   unrestricted access to persons within the entity from whom we determine it necessary to obtain audit evidence.

As part of our audit procedures, we will request written confirmation from management in the form of representations made to us in connection with the audit.

2.   Responsibilities of the auditor

We will conduct our audit in accordance with International Standards on Auditing (UK) (ISAs (UK)). Those standards require that we comply with ethical requirements issued by the Financial Reporting Council and our professional body and plan and perform the audit to obtain reasonable assurance about whether the financial statements are free from material misstatement. An audit involves performing procedures to obtain audit evidence about the amounts and disclosures in the financial statements. The procedures selected depend on the auditor's judgement, including the assessment of the risks of material misstatement of the financial statements, whether due to fraud or error. An audit also includes an evaluation of the appropriateness of accounting policies selected, and the reasonableness of accounting estimates made by management, as well as evaluating the overall presentation of the financial statements.

Due to the inherent limitations of an audit, together with the inherent limitations of internal control, there is an unavoidable risk that some material misstatements may not be detected, even though the audit is properly planned and performed in accordance with the ISAs (UK).

In making our risk assessments, we consider internal control relevant to Dudson Enterprises Limited's preparation of the financial statements in order to design audit procedures that are appropriate in the circumstances, but not for the purpose of expressing an opinion on the effectiveness of Dudson Enterprise's system of internal control. We will communicate to you, in writing, about any significant deficiencies in internal control relevant to the audit of the financial statements that we have identified during the course of the audit.

3.   Form of our report

We will report to the shareholders of Dudson Enterprises Ltd as a body whether, in our opinion, the financial statements present fairly, in all material respects, the financial position of Dudson Enterprises Ltd as at 31 March, and its financial performance and cash flows for the year then ended in accordance with FRS 102. The form and content of our report may need to be amended in light of our audit findings.

4. Fees

Our fees will be based on the time required by the individuals assigned to the engagement, plus VAT and out-of-pocket expenses. Individual hourly charge-out rates vary depending on the degree of responsibility involved and the skill and experience required.

5. Limitation of liability

To the fullest extent permitted by law, we will not be responsible for any losses, where you or others supply incorrect or incomplete information, or fail to supply any appropriate information or where you fail to act on our advice or respond promptly to communications from us.

Our work is not, unless there is a legal or regulatory requirement, to be made available to third parties without our written consent and we will accept no responsibility to third parties for any aspect of our professional services or work that is made available to them.

6. Confirmation of the terms and conditions of the audit engagement

We would be grateful if you could please sign and return the attached copy of this engagement letter to indicate your acknowledgement of, and agreement with, the arrangements for our audit of the financial statements including our respective responsibilities.

If this letter and the attached terms of business are not in accordance with your understanding of our terms of appointment, please contact the audit engagement partner immediately.

Yours sincerely

Auditor & Co LLP

We understand and agree to the terms and conditions of this letter of engagement and agree to be bound by them.

………………………………………………………………………………...

For and on behalf of the board of directors of Dudson Enterprises Ltd

Date

The above engagement letter contains some specific elements that are worthy of explanation:

Element in the engagement letter	Why it is important
It is addressed to the directors of Dudson Enterprises Ltd.	The auditor's report will be addressed to the shareholders (members) of Dudson Enterprises Ltd, but the directors will sign the engagement letter on behalf of the shareholders.
Responsibilities of management and responsibilities of the auditor.	These paragraphs set out the expectations of each party to reduce the expectations gap and to ensure that each party clearly understands what is expected of them throughout the duration of the professional relationship. In addition, the auditor's responsibilities will include the scope of the audit which is the basis on which the auditor will form their opinion.
The responsibilities of the auditor confirm they will obtain reasonable assurance about whether the financial statements are free from material misstatement, whether caused by fraud or error.	The expression of reasonable (as opposed to 'maximum') assurance is one of the limitations of an audit. The auditor does not strive for maximum assurance as this is not practical due to time constraints and audit evidence is persuasive rather than conclusive. The auditor will provide reasonable assurance in the auditor's report which is a high level of assurance but is not a 100% guarantee that the financial statements are completely accurate, regardless of what the users may think.
The auditor will report to the shareholders of Dudson Enterprises Ltd as a body.	This defines who the intended users of the auditor's report are and therefore who can place reliance on it.
Confirmation of agreement to the terms.	Both the client and the auditor must sign and retain a copy of the engagement letter to confirm their understanding and agreement to the terms of the audit engagement letter which is essentially a contract between the parties.

APPENDIX 2: ILLUSTRATIVE LETTER REQUESTING ACCESS TO PREDECESSOR AUDITOR'S WORKING PAPERS FILE

Dear Sirs

Provision of Information pursuant to audit regulation 3.09 relating to the audit of Revere Ltd

This firm was duly appointed as statutory auditor (as defined by Section 1210 of the Companies Act 2006 ('the Act')) on 12 October 2024 to Revere Ltd ('the Company').

Pursuant to paragraph 9(3) of Schedule 10 to the Companies Act 2006 and Audit Regulation 3.09, [and in accordance with Technical Release AAF 01/09 issued by the Institute of Chartered Accountants in England and Wales[2]], we request for the purposes of our audit work, access to the following audit working papers and information:

- Audit working papers in respect of your auditor's report on the financial statements of the Company relating to the year ended 31 December 2023.

We may also request explanations from you in connection with our consideration of the above information, and on the same basis.

We look forward to receiving your confirmation letter in response to this request, which should be addressed for the attention of Martyn Greaves.

Yours faithfully

ABC Chartered Accountants

---

2 This will be required if the audit firm is regulated by ICAEW.

APPENDIX 3: ILLUSTRATIVE RESPONSE TO INCOMING AUDITOR'S REQUEST FOR ACCESS TO AUDIT WORKING PAPERS FILE

Dear Sirs

Provision of Information pursuant to Audit Regulation 3.09 relating to the audit of Revere Ltd

We refer to your letter dated 30 October 2024 following your appointment as statutory auditor to Revere Ltd.

We confirm we will provide access to the information requested, namely:

- The working papers in respect of our auditor's report on the financial statements of Revere Ltd for the year ended 31 December 2023.

We understand that you may also request explanations from us in connection with your consideration of the above information, and on the same basis.

In accordance with the guidance under Audit Regulation 3.09 [and Technical Release AAF 01/08 issued by the Institute of Chartered Accountants in England and Wales] this letter sets out the basis on which the information and explanations (if any) are to be provided. Should you request or we provide any supplementary information to that set out above, such provision will be made on the same basis.

The access is provided to you:

(a)   solely in your capacity as duly appointed statutory auditor (as defined by Section 1210 of the Companies Act 2006 ('the Act'); and

(b)   solely because we are required to give you access to information pursuant to paragraph 9(3) of Schedule 10 to the Act and Audit Regulation 3.09.

The provision of access does not, and will not, alter any responsibility that we may have accepted or assumed to the Company members as a body, in accordance with the statutory requirements for audit, for our audit work, for our auditor's report or for the opinions we have formed in the course of our work as auditors.

To the fullest extent permitted by law we do not accept or assume responsibility to you or to anyone else:

(a)   as a result of the access given;

(b)   or the information to which we provide access;

155

(c)   for any explanation given to you; or

(d)   in respect of any audit work you may undertake, any audit you may complete and any auditor's report you may issue, or any audit opinion you may give.

Where access is provided to audit working papers, those papers were not created or prepared for, and should not be treated as suitable for, any purpose other than the statutory audit that was the subject of our auditor's report. The statutory audit was planned and undertaken solely for the purpose of forming and giving the audit opinion required by the relevant statutory provision to the persons contemplated by that statutory provision. The statutory audit was not planned or undertaken, and the working papers were not created prepared, in contemplation of your appointment as statutory auditor or for the purpose of assisting you in carrying out your appointment as statutory auditor.

Neither you, nor anyone else should rely on the information to which access is provided, or any explanations given in relation to that information. The information cannot in any way serve as a substitute for the enquiries and procedures that you should undertake and the judgements that you must make for any purpose in connection with the audit for which you are solely responsible as the auditor.

If notwithstanding this letter, you rely on the information for any purpose and to any degree, you will do so entirely at your own risk.

Thank you for your confirmation that you will meet the reasonable costs that we will incur in giving access. We estimate these costs will not exceed £X.

In accordance with the guidance issued under Audit Regulation 3.09:

(a)   you should refuse to accept an additional engagement, such as to act as an expert witness or to review the quality of our audit work, where the engagement would involve the use of the information obtained by you under the Regulation;

(b)   you should not comment on the quality of our audit work unless required to do so by a legal or professional obligation; and

(c)   the information should not be disclosed beyond persons who have a need to access the information where to do so is a necessary part of your audit work, nor should the information be disclosed to a third party including the Company (although this does not prevent you discussing the information with the Company where to do so is a necessary part of your audit work, or providing information to any third party if that is required of you by a legal or professional obligation).

In the event that access to information involves your having access to any intellectual property of ours or any material in which we have copyright, we do not grant permission to you to use or exploit that intellectual property or copyright and you must respect the same at all times.

When in this letter we refer to ourselves, we include our partners, directors, members, employees and agents. This letter is for the benefit of all those referred to in the previous sentence and each of them may rely on and enforce in their own right all of the terms in this letter.

Yours faithfully

ABC Chartered Accountants

Chapter 5

Planning the Audit I: Risk and Understanding

CHAPTER TOPIC LIST

- Introduction (see **5.1**).

- Objective of audit planning (see **5.2**).

- Obtaining an understanding of the entity and its environment (see **5.4**).

- Risk assessment and the auditor's response (see **5.10**).

- Audit risk (see **5.15**).

- Risk of material misstatement at the financial statement and assertion level (see **5.20**).

- Evaluating the client's systems and controls (see **5.24**).

INTRODUCTION

5.1   Audit planning is one of the most critical aspects of the audit. Without a thorough audit planning process, the auditor effectively 'goes in blind' and the audit can ultimately become negligent, or, at worst, chaotic (two words no auditor in the world wants associated with their audit work).

In practice, it probably wouldn't be too far off if I said that around 40–50% of the audit should involve audit planning from initial discussions with the client, through to development of the audit strategy and the audit plan to revisiting the planning areas during the course of the detailed audit fieldwork to ensure all aspects of the planning remain appropriate.

So, as you'll see from just these opening paragraphs, there is a lot to audit planning; but … provided it is carried out in a systematic and orderly manner, it need not be a case of moving heaven and earth.

5.1 *Planning the Audit I: Risk and Understanding*

This chapter is a 'companion' chapter to **Chapter 6** 'Planning the Audit II: Other Aspects of Planning' which looks at:

- Materiality

- Analytical procedures

- Developing the audit strategy and audit plan

- Design of audit procedures

- Fraud (which is also covered in more detail in **Chapter 9**)

WHAT ARE WE TRYING TO ACHIEVE?

Not only are we trying to comply with the International Standards on Auditing (UK) (ISAs (UK)) where audit planning is concerned, but we are also trying to ensure that a high-quality audit is carried out. In order to do this, we must identify the risks of material misstatement and ensure that adequate audit procedures are applied which respond to those assessed risks.

Audit planning is primarily dealt with in the ISAs (UK) in the 300 series as follows:

- ISA (UK) 300 *Planning an Audit of Financial Statements*

- ISA (UK) 315 *Identifying and Assessing the Risks of Material Misstatement*

- ISA (UK) 320 *Materiality in Planning and Performing an Audit*

- ISA (UK) 330 *The Auditor's Responses to Assessed Risks*

I think one of the most important points to emphasise at the outset where audit planning is concerned is that it must not be seen as a 'tick-box exercise' whereby the auditor merely works through the steps on an audit programme in a mechanical ('parrot') fashion. Audit planning does not, and cannot, work like this. Every audit is different and will require different levels of risk assessment, planned audit procedures, documentation and discussions with the audit client. If we were to carry out planning in the same way that we follow instructions when building flat-pack furniture, we could miss some crucial aspects that are relevant to that particular audit client, which may not be relevant to other audit clients.

There are generally four stages to an audit which can be summarised as follows:

Step 1: The risk assessment stage

At this stage the auditor will:

(a)   obtain an understanding of the audit client, the nature of the entity and the environment in which it operates; and

(b)   identify the risks and carefully consider whether these risks could cause a material misstatement in the financial statements.

Step 2: The risk response stage

At this stage the auditor will:

(a)   identify appropriate responses to the risks identified in **Step 1**;

(b)   devise tests of control (see **Chapter 6**); and

(c)   devise substantive procedures (see **Chapter 6**).

Step 3: The audit fieldwork stage

This is the stage where the auditor will gather **sufficient** and **appropriate** audit evidence (see **Chapter 6** and **Chapter 7**) to support the amounts and disclosures in the financial statements. This is often referred to as the 'evidence-gathering' stage.

Step 4: The reporting stage

This is the culmination of the entire audit process. This is the stage where the audit engagement partner reviews the audit evidence and forms a conclusion as to whether the financial statements give a true and fair view (or present fairly, in all material respects). It is at this stage that the audit engagement partner will issue their report in accordance with ISA (UK) 700 *Forming an Opinion and Reporting on Financial Statements.*

The report of the auditor is examined in **Chapter 11** and **Chapter 12**.

OBJECTIVE OF AUDIT PLANNING

5.2   This book deliberately avoids vast amounts of citations from the ISAs (UK) to set out exactly what the ISAs (UK) are trying to achieve. However, the objective of ISA (UK) 300 is straightforward to understand. It states that:

> The objective of the auditor is to plan the audit so that it will be performed in an effective manner.[1]

Despite the fact that there are many reports of audit firms being sanctioned for carrying out negligent audit work, the fact is that no auditor ever *intentionally* sets out with the objective of carrying out a bad audit. (Hopefully) the vast majority of auditors hope to conduct a high-quality audit, even if the wheels do eventually fall off shortly after the process has begun.

IMPORTANT POINT

Audit is a regulated profession in the UK (unlike accountancy). Audit is therefore monitored by professional bodies, such as ACCA and the Financial Reporting Council[2]. The objective of these monitoring exercises is to make sure that audit firms are carrying out audit work in accordance with professional standards, legislation and regulation. Significantly deficient audit work carries sanctions ranging from follow-up visits to make sure the audit firm has improved its work to withdrawal of the firm's (and audit engagement partner's) practising certificates.

When an audit fails, or when things go badly wrong in an audit, it can usually (but not always) be down to the following factors:

- The auditor has not carried out a thorough programme of planning and has missed some significant aspects of the audit.

- The audit client has failed to co-operate with the auditor.

- The auditor does not understand the requirements of the ISAs (UK) (which is primarily why this book was written).

---

1 ISA (UK) 300, para 4.
2 At the time of writing, the Financial Reporting Council is expected to eventually transition to the Audit, Reporting and Governance Authority.

- The auditor fails to correctly understand the requirements of accounting standards and misses an incorrect accounting treatment that has resulted in a material misstatement of the financial statements.

The above list is not exhaustive and an audit can go wrong for a variety of reasons.

REAL-LIFE SCENARIO

A three-partner firm has six audit clients all of whom are private limited companies. There are no complex clients, such as groups, so all straightforward audits.

One of the audit files went for cold file review and was judged as containing 'significant deficiencies'. The audit engagement partner told me that she was 'astonished' at the outcome and fundamentally disagreed with the reviewer.

Seemingly, most of the deficiencies were with audit planning; although some deficiencies were noted in other areas of the audit file. The planning deficiencies seemed to arise from the following issues:

- **No evidence of an audit planning meeting.** The engagement partner told me there had been a meeting, but it had not been documented. If the meeting is not documented, the reviewer can only conclude that it had not taken place.

- **Planned reliance on internal controls when there was a note on the file that the previous year's audit revealed weaknesses in those controls.** At the planning stage, the planned approach would ordinarily be substantive (due to the weaknesses in controls identified in the prior year). Planned reliance on weak controls is a strange approach to take and increases audit risk considerably. The controls should be reassessed in the current year to see if the recommendations by the auditor in the prior year have been implemented and so whether it may be appropriate to test them.

- **No planning stage analytical review.** ISA (UK) 315 *Identifying and Assessing the Risks of Material Misstatement* specifically requires analytical review procedures to be applied at the planning stage as risk assessment procedures (ie, to identify potential sources of misstatement).

- **No evidence of a pre-planning meeting with the client.** Such a meeting helps the auditor to understand any changes in the controls or business of the client, whether any fraud has been discovered during the year, changes in management structure, changes in

---

163

> the accounting function and changes to any accounting policies, amongst other things.
>
> It is difficult to see how the audit engagement partner could 'fundamentally disagree' with the file reviewer when there is clear evidence that the requirements of the ISAs (UK) in the 300 series have not been correctly applied. If procedures *have* been carried out, but just not placed on file, then the reviewer will take this into consideration prior to finalising their cold file review report (if the evidence is subsequently sent to the reviewer, that is). If the audit evidence is not on file within the 60 days allowed by ISA (UK) 230 *Audit Documentation*, then it is not part of the audit file/ evidence to support the audit opinion.

So, back to the objective of audit planning …

All audits must be carried out to the same standard and hence it is crucial that the auditor complies with **all** aspects of the ISAs (UK). The auditor cannot 'choose' which parts of an ISA (UK) they will apply when auditing the client. This is because if an ISA (UK) applies to a client, the entire provisions of the ISA (UK) must be complied with.

> IMPORTANT POINT
>
> Remember, if any aspect of an ISA (UK) is departed from, there must be justifiable reasons for this. These reasons must be thoroughly documented on the audit file and cannot just be annotated with 'N/A' ('not applicable'). In more difficult or contentious cases, it will always be advisable to seek the advice from your professional body's technical advisory or ethics department, or an independent specialist.

In **5.1** above, we summarised the audit process which primarily consists of four parts from planning through to reporting. The audit planning process can be viewed using a diagrammatic approach as follows:

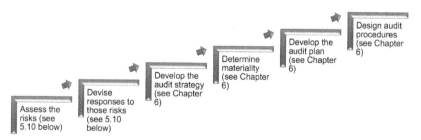

Preliminary planning activities

5.3   The table below provides examples of some **preliminary** risk assessment procedures the auditor may carry out at the planning stage of the audit to help to articulate the reasoning behind why we must carry out audit planning:

Activity at the planning stage	Why would this be needed?
Understand the client	Understanding the client (and the environment in which it operates) is crucial so as to identify key areas of risk which must be evaluated, including the risk of management override of internal controls. If the auditor does not thoroughly understand their client, how can the audit be carried out effectively?
Identify related parties	There may be a higher risk of material misstatement where transactions with related parties have taken place (for example, fraud). Fraud is examined further in Chapters 6 and 9. The audit of related parties is examined in the appendix to Chapter 7.
Identify fraud risk factors	ISA (UK) 240 *The Auditor's Responsibilities Relating to Fraud in an Audit of Financial Statements* requires the auditor to consider the susceptibility of the financial statements to material misstatement due to fraud, including management override of internal controls. Fraud risk factors may also require specific audit procedures being applied.
Identify risks to the entity's going concern ability	The going concern presumption is fundamental to the preparation of the financial statements. The auditor is required to assess management's assertion that the entity is a going concern (although keep in mind that it is not the auditor's responsibility to carry out the going concern assessment – this is management's responsibility). Going concern is examined in Chapter 10.
Review corporate governance compliance (where applicable)	A lack of sound corporate governance, or a disregard of corporate governance principles, will give rise to a higher risk of material misstatement in the financial statements.
Understand the entity's system of internal control	The auditor is required to understand the control environment of the client in accordance with ISA (UK) 315. A lack of proper internal controls (such as segregation of duties and review processes) creates a higher risk of material misstatement in the financial statements. A sound internal control structure may allow the auditor to reduce the level of detailed testing of transactions (substantive procedures), provided that the controls have operated effectively during the reporting period.

Activity at the planning stage	Why would this be needed?
Understand the IT environment	ISA (UK) 315 (Revised July 2020) places more emphasis on developing an understanding of the client's IT environment and general IT controls. Where, for example, the client's accounting system is complex, this creates a higher risk of material misstatement in the financial statements. In addition, most entities use IT, hence gaining an understanding of how efficient and reliable the IT system is will enable the auditor to conclude on any preliminary risks arising at the planning stage.
Review significant account balances and accounting estimates	The larger the account balance, the greater the possibility that it contains a material misstatement. The auditor also considers the risk associated with the account balance and the sensitivity of the associated disclosure information. Significant accounting estimates will also need audit procedures in line with ISA (UK) 540 *Auditing Accounting Estimates and Related Disclosures.*
Review significant classes of transactions	The auditor must review significant classes of transactions which generate the amounts recorded in the significant account balances as well as the process of including material disclosures in the notes to the financial statements. The purpose of this review is to identify potential risks of material misstatement.
Review the year-end closing process	Closing procedures are the processes adopted by the client when closing the accounting system for the accounting period (or year end). If closing procedures are weak, there is a higher risk of material misstatement due to incorrect cut-off or misstated closing balances.

By now, it should be clear why a thorough programme of audit planning is needed. The auditor is primarily concerned with **reducing audit risk** which is the risk that they form an inappropriate opinion on the financial statements (audit risk is examined further in **5.15**). In order to reduce this risk, the auditor must first identify the risks of material misstatement and then devise audit procedures that are specifically responsive to those risks.

OBTAINING AN UNDERSTANDING OF THE ENTITY AND ITS ENVIRONMENT

5.4   To identify the risks of material misstatement in the financial statements, the auditor must obtain a thorough understanding of the client. To all intents and purposes, this may seem pretty obvious to most auditors, but it is surprising the number of audit firms that are criticised because they display a fundamental lack of understanding of an audit client when it comes to a file review. In other cases, while the auditor does appear to have a sound understanding of the client and the environment in which it operates, this understanding is not adequately documented; the 'classic' reason for this is because this understanding is in the head of the audit engagement partner and hasn't found its way onto the audit documentation.

Remember, obtaining an understanding of the entity and its environment is a critical aspect of ISA (UK) 315. According to this ISA (UK), the objective of the auditor is to identify and assess the risks of material misstatement, whether due to fraud or error, at the **financial statement** and **assertion** levels, thereby providing a basis for designing and implementing responses to the assessed risks of material misstatement.

FINANCIAL STATEMENT AND ASSERTION LEVELS

The audit process refers to 'financial statement level' and 'assertion level' a lot. The *financial statement level* refers to the financial statements as a whole; whereas the *assertion level* refers to the individual transactions, balances and disclosures (eg, the **valuation** assertion and the **completeness** assertion). For completeness, ISA (UK) 315 defines 'assertions' as:

> Representations, explicit or otherwise, with respect to the recognition, measurement, presentation and disclosure of information in the financial statements which are inherent in management representing that the financial statements are prepared in accordance with the applicable financial reporting framework. Assertions are used by the auditor to consider the different types of potential misstatements that may occur when identifying, assessing and responding to the risks of material misstatement.[3]

A risk of material misstatement at the **financial statement level** would be a risk that affects all areas of the accounts ('all pervasive') such as adopting the going concern basis of accounting inappropriately. A risk at the **assertion level** would be where the audit client may have incorrectly capitalised expenditure that should be recognised as repairs and maintenance expenditure (hence the **valuation** of property, plant and equipment is overstated).

Financial statement and assertion levels are examined further in **5.20** below.

Acquiring an understanding of the entity and the environment in which it operates is crucial because it impacts the auditor's risk assessment. Remember, from the risk assessment process comes the specific audit

---

3 ISA (UK) 315, para 12(a).

procedures that the auditor will apply which respond to those risks. If the auditor fails to gain a sufficient understanding of the entity and the environment in which it operates, together with the client's system of internal control, they will be unable to carry out a thorough risk assessment. So, what does this mean for the audit? Well, essentially it will increase audit risk and the whole point of the planning process is to devise audit procedures that reduce this risk to an acceptable level.

Sources of information to obtain an understanding of the entity

5.5 In practice, there are many sources of information the auditor can go to for the purposes of obtaining an understanding of the audit client's entity and the environment in which it operates. The diagram below provides a summary of the most common sources, but please bear in mind that this is not a comprehensive list of sources – remember, each audit is different!

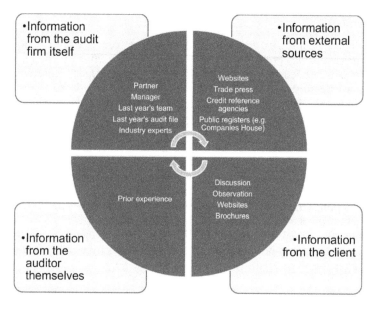

Obtaining an understanding of the entity itself

5.6 The auditor is required to obtain an understanding of the *nature* of the entity. This will generally include:

(a) **The entity's operations**: such as whether it is a chemical manufacturer or a pension scheme.

(b)   **Its ownership and governance structure**: such as who the shareholders are, or who the parent company is and how the management board is structured.

(c)   **The types of investment the audit client makes**: such as investments in subsidiaries, associates, joint ventures or investments in other commodities (such as in shares or precious metals).

(d)   **The way the entity is structured and financed**: such as the number of branches or sites the business operates from and whether it relies on bank borrowings or whether the directors/shareholders provide finance to support the business (or whether there is a mixture of both).

The Appendix to ISA (UK) 315 provides some good examples of matters which the auditor may consider when obtaining an understanding of the activities of the entity. I know I have already said I want to keep citations from the ISAs (UK) as few and far between as possible, but, in my view, the examples provided by ISA (UK) 315 are great, so I've reproduced them as follows:

(a)   Business operations such as:

- Nature of revenue sources, products or services, and markets, including involvement in electronic commerce such as internet sales and marketing activities.

- Conduct of operations (for example, stages and methods of production, or activities exposed to environmental risks).

- Alliances, joint ventures and outsourcing activities.

- Geographic dispersion and industry segmentation.

- Location of production facilities, warehouses, and offices, and location and quantities of inventories.

- Key customers and important suppliers of goods and services, employment arrangements (including the existence of union contracts, pension and other post-employment benefits, stock option or incentive bonus arrangements, and government regulation related to employment matters).

- Research and development activities and expenditures.

- Transactions with related parties.

(b)   Investments and investment activities such as:

- Planned or recently executed acquisitions or divestitures.

- Investments and dispositions of securities and loans.

- Capital investment activities.

169

- Investments in non-consolidated entities, including non-controlled partnerships, joint ventures and non-controlled special-purpose entities.

(c) Financing and financing activities such as:

- Ownership structure of major subsidiaries and associated entities, including consolidated and non-consolidated structures.

- Debt structure and related terms, including off-balance sheet financing arrangements and leasing agreements.

- Beneficial owners (for example, local, foreign, business reputation and experience) and related parties.

- Use of derivative financial instruments.[4]

Of course, the above is merely guidance and not every source listed above will apply to every audit, but it aims to give the auditor a good idea as to what the ISA (UK) is looking for when it comes to obtaining an understanding of the entity and its business model.

Example 5.1 – Understanding the entity

Greaves Industries Ltd is in the technology sector and operates from five sites. It has been established for many years and has always been successful, achieving high profits and paying a high level of dividends to its shareholders. Eight months ago, the company recruited a new finance director, Stefan Ratchford, who overhauled the finance department and introduced a new bespoke accounting system.

During initial discussions with Stefan, it was brought to the auditor's attention that new entrants to the market have become a threat to the client because of their competitive pricing structures. The audit firm has acted for Greaves Industries for four years and the auditor is aware that currently Greaves has a significant market share, hence the emergence of these competitors could impact on that share and could ultimately affect the entity's going concern status.

The auditor will need to understand how these threats impact on the entity so that appropriate audit procedures can be devised to address these risks – for example, performing additional procedures over going concern.

---

4 ISA (UK) 315, Appendix 1, para 5.

These additional risks may have had an impact already on Greaves Industries' financial performance during the year. It is important that the auditor develops a sound understanding of how these additional risks *could* impact the financial statements. For example, management may manipulate the revenue figure in the financial statements to achieve a higher profit to secure any additional financing requirements which the company may be applying for.

In addition, the auditor will also need to look at the entity's business operations in its entirety. The company operates from five sites and so the audit engagement team will need an understanding of how each site operates and the controls that are present at each site.

The new finance director has also overhauled the finance department and implemented a new accounting system. The auditor must carry out a thorough review of how the finance department is now structured, identifying any new processes and changes to previous processes as well as reviewing and testing new and existing controls.

As the accounting system has been changed during the year, the auditor must also:

* carefully document the new system and consider general IT controls;

* devise procedures to ensure transactions and balances from the old to the new system have been transferred correctly;

* review any parallel running of the old and new accounting system to ensure the new system works correctly; and

* devise procedures to test controls over the new system to ensure their operating effectiveness.

The example above demonstrates why it is important not to simply 'carry over' planning from one year to the next because significant changes may have arisen from the prior year which could impact on the current year. In the example above, several changes have taken place which are likely to influence the audit procedures that will be devised:

* A new finance director has been recruited in the year. The finance director will need time to get used to the transactions and accounting systems of the client, hence this gives rise to an additional risk of material misstatement.

* A new structure has been put in place within the finance department, which will invariably bring with it new policies and procedures.

- A new accounting system has been introduced which the audit firm may not have worked with before (especially as it is bespoke).

- Additional competitors have emerged into the market which may threaten the client's ability to continue as a going concern.

The table below also outlines other risk assessment procedures the auditor must carry out to obtain an understanding of the business at entity level:

Factor the auditor needs an understanding of:	Comment:
Other aspects of the entity and the environment in which it operates	This will include: • The organisational structure, ownership and governance and the entity's business model • The extent to which the business model integrates the use of IT • Industry, regulatory and other external factors • How the entity assesses the financial performance of the business (both internally and externally)
Applicable financial reporting framework	To ensure that the applicable financial reporting framework is suitable (remember, this is also a *precondition* of the audit so the framework used must be appropriate). Typical frameworks used include FRS 102 *The Financial Reporting Standard applicable in the UK and Republic of Ireland* and IFRS® Accounting Standards (UK-adopted IFRS).
The entity's accounting policies	To ensure that they are appropriate in the entity's specific situations and that they have been consistently applied in the preparation of the financial statements. Any changes in accounting policies need to be carefully assessed in terms of whether: • the change results in the financial statements providing reliable and more relevant information; and • the change has been retrospectively applied correctly in accordance with the applicable financial reporting framework.
Inherent risk factors (ie, the risk of material misstatement before the auditor considers any related controls) (see **5.17** below)	These need to be considered in terms of the degree to which they will result in a material misstatement.

Obtaining an understanding of the environment (industry) in which the client operates

5.7   Of course, obtaining an understanding of the entity and its system of internal control is crucially important when carrying out the planning of the audit. But the auditor needs to go further than this and consider the environment in which the client operates. When we talk about the 'environment', we are essentially referring to the 'industry' in which the client operates.

Some clients will operate in heavily regulated industries, such as a financial institution (who will be subject to regulation by the Financial Conduct Authority). Hence, obtaining an understanding of the entity at industry level will require a much wider understanding of the business.

The starting point here could be ISA (UK) 315, para A68 which provides four useful matters the auditor may consider about a client's industry:

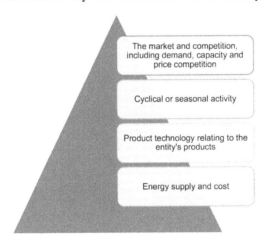

The market and competition, including demand, capacity and price competition

Cyclical or seasonal activity

Product technology relating to the entity's products

Energy supply and cost

Example 5.2 – Understanding the environment a client operates in

Currie Computers Ltd manufactures laptop and desktop computers for sale to corporate customers and retailers. It has produced two distinctive types of computer for five years now, being the 'FastPace' and 'HighTech' brands. These brands became very popular but in the last two years, competitors have emerged in the market which have been able to manufacture faster, lighter and more powerful computers resulting in Currie Computers losing some of its market share.

The company prepares its financial statements under FRS 102 *The Financial Reporting Standard applicable in the UK and Republic of Ireland*.

Currie Computers manufactures computers which become obsolete very quickly. The risk here is that if the company does not keep up with the pace of change in its industry, it will effectively 'get left behind' in the marketplace which would impact on the company's ability to continue as a going concern. It may have stocks (inventory) which have become obsolete and that it can no longer sell at list price, and so its stock could be overstated.

This is not the only issue which the auditor must consider …

This **inherent risk** (see **5.17** below) must also be taken into account when the auditor is devising audit procedures over the company's inventory and work in progress (both of which are likely to be material balances in the year-end financial statements). The reason for this is that there may well be some inventory which is slow-moving or has become obsolete due to technological advancements. Currie Computers would be required to value its inventory at the lower of cost and estimated selling price less costs to complete and sell to comply with the requirements of FRS 102, Section 13 *Inventories*. If any inventory has a selling price below cost, there is a risk that inventory and work in progress is overstated in the financial statements.

Regulatory factors

5.8 Linked to risks at the industry level are regulatory factors which the auditor must also consider. This is because the industry which an audit client operates in may give rise to specific risks of material misstatement that arise from the nature of the business or the degree of regulation.

For example, long-term construction contracts may involve significant estimates of revenues and expenses which give rise to the risk of material misstatement. FRS 102, Section 23 *Revenue from Contracts with Customers* prescribes the accounting treatment for revenue recognition and the section was completely redrafted as part of the FRC's periodic review of UK and Ireland GAAP (in FRS 102 (January 2022), Section 23 is called *Revenue*). FRS 102, Section 23 inherently requires significant management judgement where revenue from contracts is concerned. For the auditor, this is an area of the financial statements which may be particularly prone to material misstatement, hence the auditor must devise specific procedures at the planning stage to address this risk.

IMPORTANT POINT

Revenue is an element of the financial statements which is singled out by ISA (UK) 240. **Chapter 9** examines this issue in more detail, and it is important that auditors clearly understand the reasons *why* revenue is singled out and what they must do to ensure they comply with the requirements of the ISAs (UK).

Other regulatory factors which the auditor must take into consideration may include the following:

- The regulatory framework for a regulated industry – for example requirements where the entity is regulated by the Financial Conduct Authority or one of the charity regulators.

- Legislation and regulation that significantly affects the entity's operations – for example, employment law legislation, National Minimum Wage Act and Health and Safety legislation.

- Tax law.

- Government policies which may affect the conduct of the entity's business – for example, fiscal policies, financial incentives (such as government aid programmes), tariffs or trade restriction policies.

- Environmental requirements affecting the industry and the entity's business – for example, where a chemical company may be subject to effluent limits.

Economic challenges

5.9   It would be fair to say that the world has been in a state of chaos over recent years. First due to the global pandemic, then the Ukrainian war impacted businesses and then inflation started to increase at a significant pace resulting in an increase in interest rates as well as a general increase in costs that a business incurs. These crises will, of course, impact on the economy and this has been seen since the global pandemic hit the UK in 2019/20.

To gain an understanding of the client, the auditor must assess how changes in the economy may affect it. This includes an assessment of economic upturns and downturns, the impact of changes in interest rates and foreign exchange currency fluctuations. Here, the auditor is concerned with how susceptible the audit client is to these changes and its ability to 'ride the storm' through economic pressures.

REAL-LIFE SCENARIO

During times of economic challenge, professional bodies will often issue guidance to audit firms (via factsheets or articles in the professional body's magazine) about areas that should be 'of focus' to audit firms. Such areas may include:

- **Asset impairment** – the carrying values of assets may be impaired due to economic challenges.

- **Going concern** – during times of economic challenge, the ability to continue as a going concern for the foreseeable future may be called into question so more procedures over the going concern status of the entity would be required.

- **Fair values** – where certain elements of the financial statements are measured at fair value, specific audit procedures should be applied to ensure that fair values have not been manipulated to achieve a desired outcome.

- **Increases in interest rates** – this could affect items such as a defined benefit pension plan which has previously been in a deficit position but because of interest rate increases, is now a surplus (ie, defined benefit plan assets exceed defined benefit plan obligations). Defined benefit plan assets can only be recognised on the balance sheet if they are recoverable through a cash refund from the pension scheme or by way of reduced contributions. Where a defined benefit plan asset is recognised, specific audit procedures to address why this has happened must be devised.

- **Deferred tax assets** – these can arise through unutilised tax losses which an entity could sustain in times of economic challenge. FRS 102, Section 29 *Income Tax* only permits a deferred tax asset to be recognised on the balance sheet when it is capable of recovery. If there is no evidence that the deferred tax asset is capable of recovery, it cannot be recognised on balance sheet. Hence, auditors must pay particular attention to any deferred tax assets that have been recognised in the period under review.

Those are just a few examples of how audit firms have responded to challenges arising from the COVID-19 pandemic and the subsequent inflation issues seen in the UK. Professional bodies carrying out monitoring visits in times of recession or economic challenge are likely to devote more attention to these areas to see how the audit firm has addressed them.

When the economy is good, companies are generally under pressure to perform well, or at the very least, better than their competitors. In addition, shareholders may expect to see an improvement in profits. Hence, the focus of the auditor's attention in such economic situations may be the overstatement of revenue and the understatement of expenses, because the inherent risk (see **5.17** below) may be that management will wish to meet shareholders' expectations and report a healthy profit and a strong financial position.

When the economy is poor, management may purposefully understate profits by maximising write-offs since a fall in profits can be easily explained as a downturn in the economy. Here, the auditor's focus could be on the risk of understated revenues and overstated expenses.

Example 5.3 – Company is attempting to diversify

Due to a decline in demand for its products, Westhead Enterprises Ltd is seeking to diversify its operations into a new sector. Before it can enter its chosen market, the company needs access to additional finance in the sum of £1.5 million. The bank has stated that the audited financial statements for the year ended 31 December 2023 are needed before any lending decisions will be made.

The inherent risk in this situation is that the company may try to artificially inflate revenues to report a better profit. This could involve the inappropriate capitalising of expenditure (to boost the balance sheet) or the reversal of prior year provisions.

The auditor must factor this into the risk assessment and devise specific procedures which address this risk. For example, extended cut-off testing on revenues and additional procedures over additions to property, plant and equipment, recalculation of provisions and detailed reviews of journal entries together with adjustments at, or towards, the year end.

RISK ASSESSMENT AND THE AUDITOR'S RESPONSE

5.10   Risk assessment is one of the most important aspects of audit planning. At this stage, the auditor looks at general *business risks* and the *risks of material misstatement* of the financial statements whether due to fraud or error. 'Business risks' are generally those risks which are external to the entity; for example, if the client operates in an industry that is in decline, this could mean there are potential going concern issues.

The auditor will also consider how the financial statements themselves could be at a risk of material misstatement, including carrying out an assessment as to whether a material misstatement could arise because of fraud or error.

The outcome of this risk assessment process will ultimately influence the audit strategy (the document which explains how the auditor will tackle the audit), which, in turn, influences the audit plan (the document that contains all the planned audit procedures, such as after-date cash receipts testing and purchase invoice sampling).

5.10 *Planning the Audit I: Risk and Understanding*

It is at the risk assessment phase that the auditor must obtain a thorough understanding of the audit client, the client's system of internal control, the accounting system, corporate governance issues and the means by which the financial statements are prepared from the client's accounting records and financial reporting system. In addition, the auditor must understand the entity's related parties, transactions with those related parties and the risk that the audit client may not have disclosed all related parties to the auditor.

Throughout all this, it will be necessary for the auditor to carefully document their understanding of the client's IT system. Most audit clients will have some form of IT system in place which generates the financial statements. Remember, ISA (UK) 315 (Revised July 2020) requires the auditor to assess the overall adequacy of the IT system, including the controls in place over the system itself (for example, access rights and how often passwords are changed), as well as how information flows from the IT system into the financial statements.

IMPORTANT POINT

File reviewers have criticised audit files for failing to adequately consider the client's general IT controls which is a specific requirement of ISA (UK) 315 (Revised). I think it is important, at the outset, to clarify that these requirements do not mean the auditor has to become an IT specialist or an IT auditor. In many cases, consideration of the client's general IT controls will just mean applying common sense and thinking about the direction of travel that ISA (UK) 315 (Revised) wants us to go. Some audit methodologies offer IT controls checklists to assist with the process.

For now, let us go back to day-to-day normal life. Most people can access their online bank accounts using their smartphone, laptop, tablet computer or PC (in other words, they do not have to telephone the bank or go into the branch to discuss activity on their account). When logging into the online banking system, they will be prompted to input a username and password and perhaps some memorable information. There may also be a two-way authentication in place where a code is sent by the online banking system to the person's alternative trusted device.

All these are general IT controls to prevent fraudsters from gaining access to the online banking system.

In a company, general IT controls include the use of passwords, access rights and backup processes. They can also extend to programs such as spreadsheets. So, consider a client that has a computerised accounting system and certain information is exported from the accounting system into an Excel spreadsheet. The spreadsheet is then worked on and certain

---

information is then input into the accounting system. The auditor needs to consider the controls in place over the exportation process from the accounting system into the spreadsheet – ie, are there any? If so, what? When it comes to auditing the spreadsheet, the auditor must audit just that – they cannot audit a PDF document of the spreadsheet because the formulae will not be displayed. These are all important considerations that the auditor needs to think carefully about at the planning stage.

So, when it comes to general IT controls, while some clients may have complex systems, some may not and a lot of what ISA (UK) 315 (Revised) needs us to think about is borne purely out of common sense.

The risk assessment phase will generally involve the following:

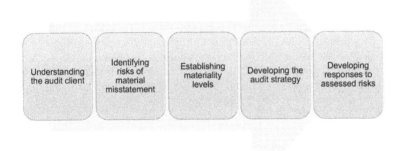

| Understanding the audit client | Identifying risks of material misstatement | Establishing materiality levels | Developing the audit strategy | Developing responses to assessed risks |

Risk assessment phase

5.11   ISA (UK) 300 *Planning an Audit of Financial Statements* requires the auditor to plan the audit to **reduce audit risk**.

IMPORTANT POINT

Audit risk is the risk that the auditor forms an incorrect opinion on the financial statements – ie, they express an unmodified (unqualified) opinion when, in fact, the financial statements contain a material misstatement so should have expressed a modified (qualified) opinion. The auditor's ultimate goal is to reduce audit risk to an acceptably low level at all times.

The risk of material misstatement is the risk that the financial statements contain a material misstatement **before** the audit starts. This is made up of **inherent risk** and **detection risk** (see **5.16**).

Audit risk and detection risk are considered in **5.16**. However, as a brief overview, audit risk is a function of the risk of material misstatement *and* **detection risk**. Detection risk is the only risk that is under the control of the auditor and is the risk that the audit procedures carried out by the auditor will not detect a misstatement that exists, and which could be material either individually or when combined with other misstatements.

Example 5.4 – Identification of a risk of material misstatement

Sofia is the audit manager of Warrington & Co Accountancy Services Ltd and is planning the audit of an existing client, Wolves Ltd, for the year ended 31 March 2024. Wolves Ltd prepares its financial statements under FRS 102. Sofia has been made aware that the client is looking to secure a bank loan to provide working capital to fund a new project which will help the company expand quite rapidly. The financial controller has told Sofia that the company will need to produce financial statements that show a moderately high level of profit and net assets. The bank will decide on the loan once the audited financial statements have been supplied.

The draft financial statements show substantial additions to intangible assets arising from an internal development project that was completed in the year to 31 March 2024. In addition, the finance director has reviewed the depreciation methods in the year and extended the useful lives of plant and machinery from five years to ten years. This has resulted in a much lower depreciation charge in the draft financial statements when compared to the 2023 results.

There is a risk of material misstatement of intangible assets. Sofia will need to devise specific audit procedures that address the risk that intangible assets are overstated because research expenditure cannot be capitalised under FRS 102, para 18.8E. This will involve devising procedures to ensure that only development costs have been capitalised in accordance with the company's stated accounting policy and that those development costs meet the recognition criteria in FRS 102, para 18.8H. It is likely that Sofia will carry out more substantive testing on this area (ie, tests which specifically check for overstatement).

In addition, Sofia will need to discuss with management the rationale for extending the useful lives of plant and machinery. The risk here is that management have deliberately extended the useful lives of plant and machinery with the intention of reducing the depreciation charges for the year knowing that a reduced depreciation charge will result in an increased level of profitability and net book value of fixed assets.

Sofia must exercise professional scepticism (see **Chapter 9**) which will enable her to maintain a questioning mind when carrying out audit procedures over intangible assets and depreciation charges. Sofia must bear in mind that management have already stated that they want to report a high level of profitability and net assets given that the company is going to be applying for a bank loan shortly after the auditor's report has been signed.

Provided Sofia carries out a thorough programme of planning and the audit procedures are devised in such a way that they are responsive to the assessed levels of risk, Sofia should be able to obtain sufficient appropriate audit evidence to identify any material misstatement in intangible assets or property, plant and equipment.

Responses to assessed risks

5.12   Once the auditor has identified the risks of material misstatement, responses to those risks are then required. At the planning stage of the audit, the response does not have to be a detailed audit procedure; rather, it is the approach that the audit engagement team will take to address the risk and the detailed audit procedures will follow during the audit fieldwork stage.

The auditor will also determine whether **tests of controls** could be effective in addition to **substantive procedures**. Tests of controls and substantive procedures are considered in **Chapter 6**. However, as a basic overview, tests of controls test the operating effectiveness of the client's controls in preventing, detecting or correcting misstatements at the assertion level. Substantive procedures aim to detect misstatements at the assertion level.

The risk and response phase may involve detailed testing of internal controls, transactions and balances. When the auditor plans to rely on the client's system of internal control, tests of those controls must be carried out.

IMPORTANT POINT

Keep in mind that tests of controls are not designed to detect material misstatements. This is because the auditor uses **substantive procedures** (also known as 'tests of detail' as well as 'substantive analytical procedures') to gather audit evidence to determine whether the financial statements give a true and fair view (or present fairly, in all material

---

respects). In addition, tests of control do not focus on the monetary amount in the financial statements – they focus on the controls that effectively generate the financial reports.

The table below provides some examples of risks that may be identified during the planning stage of an audit, together with an appropriate auditor's response:

Audit risk identified	Auditor's response
New entrants to the market have resulted in a small number of customers switching to a more competitively priced supplier. There is a risk that if the business loses customers, revenue, profitability, and cash flows will be affected and hence there could be a negative impact on the entity's ability to continue as a going concern.	Discuss with the directors how the threat by the new market entrants is being managed and whether the lost customers have been replaced. Review the cash flow forecast, budgets and current order levels to ascertain if there is a threat to the entity's ability to continue as a going concern.
A new bonus scheme has been introduced in the year to boost sales and profitability. There is a risk that revenue is being overstated by the salespersons, wishing to achieve their targets by accelerating revenue recognition.	Detailed cut-off procedures to be carried out on revenue recognition to ensure that revenue is recognised in the correct accounting period, and tests to ensure that fictitious revenue is not being recorded.
The time spent on the audit in the prior year was increased by 50% due to several deficiencies in the client's system of internal control. If these deficiencies have not been addressed by management, there may be a risk that misstatements will be present in the current year's financial statements.	Discuss with management whether recommendations to improve internal controls in the prior year's audit have been implemented and, if so, devise procedures to test those controls. The audit team must apply professional scepticism throughout the course of the audit and extend detailed substantive procedures over high-risk areas of the financial statements.
A new accounting system has been introduced in the year which can now prepare more useful financial reports. If the opening balances from the old accounting system have not been transferred correctly, the closing figures will not be correct hence a misstatement will be present in the financial statements.	Document the new accounting system in full and carry out detailed substantive procedures to assess if the closing figures in the old system have been correctly transferred to the new system.

Audit risk identified	Auditor's response
The company wishes to apply for a listing on the London Stock Exchange (LSE) and the board of directors and shareholders are excited about this possibility. There is a risk that the financial statements may be manipulated to show a desired level of profit and/or financial position.	The audit team must maintain professional scepticism, keeping in mind that there is a higher risk of material misstatement due to the company applying for a listing to the LSE.

Business risk

5.13   The term 'business risk' is defined in ISA (UK) 315 as:

A risk resulting from significant conditions, events, circumstances, actions or inactions that could adversely affect the entity's ability to achieve its objectives and execute its strategies, or from the setting of inappropriate objectives and strategies. [5]

To successfully identify risks of material misstatement, the auditor should use a **business risk approach**. This involves:

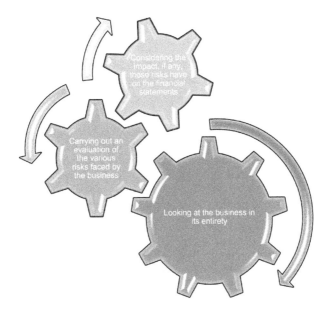

5 ISA (UK) 315, para 12(b).

All businesses will face risks in their normal course of operations, so the auditor must obtain a sound understanding of the business and the environment in which it operates. Business risks generally arise from external factors, such as:

- **Political factors** – due to changes in government policy, tax rates and changes in governments at home and abroad. This may affect companies that operate globally where, in some countries, the political climate may be volatile.

- **Economic factors** – due to changes in the economic situations of the country in which the client operates such as levels of inflation or interest rates (as we have seen in the UK during 2022/23), and recession which could impact on levels of employment. The auditor must consider the risks applicable in all the countries that the client operates.

- **Legislative factors** – changes in law and regulations may result in restrictions to operations or the prohibition of operations (for example, if the government bans a certain product that is manufactured by the client). Changes in environmental legislation may give rise to additional costs having to be incurred by the client to clean up operations.

- **Compliance factors** – risks of material misstatement may arise due to non-compliance with tax legislation or other laws and regulations. However, other legislation such as employment law may be breached by the entity, which could result in material misstatement (for example, the failure to recognise a provision for liabilities due to non-compliance with laws and regulations). **Chapter 9** examines laws and regulations in more detail.

- **Physical factors** – natural disasters such as a fire or flood may affect the client's ability to continue as a going concern.

- **Financial factors** – credit risk (the risk of non-payment by customers), foreign exchange risk (the risk caused by trading in foreign currencies or the translation risk on the conversion of assets held in foreign currencies in overseas subsidiaries to the entity's presentation currency) and interest rate risk (the risk to business financing caused by movements in interest rates) are all beyond the control of the client. Such factors can have a detrimental impact on the results of the entity (some previously profitable entities may end up reporting current year losses).

- **Technological risk** – some clients manufacture and/or sell goods which have a relatively short shelf life due to technical obsolescence (for example, laptop computers). If a business fails to spot opportunities or developments in emerging technologies, it may well find itself being overtaken by its competitors. This could have a detrimental impact on going concern.

- **Market risk** – factors such as increased competition, price wars and development of new products can cause a risk to the client's business.

This chapter has gone into a lot of detail so far on understanding the entity and the environment in which it operates. This is one of the most important tasks in audit planning. Understanding the entity's objectives, strategy and business model helps the auditor to understand the entity at a strategic level and to understand the business risks that the entity takes and faces. An understanding of the business risks that have an effect on the financial statements will help the auditor in identifying risks of material misstatement, since most business risks will eventually have financial consequences and, therefore, an effect on the financial statements.

Example 5.5 – Business risks arising in different settings

Freya Accountancy Services Ltd has two audit clients that sells shoes to the general public. The client may rely on the use of IT in different ways:

(a)   One client sells shoes from a physical store and uses an advanced stock and point of sale system to record the sale of shoes.

(b)   The other client sells shoes online as well and all sales transactions are processed in an IT environment, including initiation of the transaction via the website.

For both entities, the business risks arising from a significantly different business model would be substantially different, notwithstanding the fact that both sell shoes.

Not all aspects of the business model are relevant to the auditor's understanding. Business risks are generally broader than the risks of material misstatement in the financial statements, although business risks include the latter. The auditor does not have a responsibility to understand or identify all business risks because not all business risks give rise to risks of material misstatement.

Business failure versus audit failure

5.14   All businesses, large and small, are at risk of collapse. A business generally fails when it has run out of cash and goes into liquidation or bankruptcy. Business failure is not the same as audit failure (see below). Even the most profitable of businesses can fail – for example, due to over-trading. The term 'over-trading' refers to situations when a seemingly profitable business runs out of cash and hence cannot meet its obligations and has no resources to fund day-to-day working capital requirements. This can happen, for example, when a company is expanding rapidly and must pay its suppliers more quickly than it collects cash from its customers.

Audit failure arises when an auditor's report incorrectly states that the entity's financial statements give a true and fair view when they actually contain material errors or false statements. Until the audit failure has been investigated, it is generally unknown whether the audit failure has arisen through negligence or wrongdoing.

Example 5.6 – Audit failure

The auditor's report for Warriors Ltd for the year ended 31 December 2023 contains an unqualified audit opinion. However, it was later discovered that in order to secure additional bank finance, the directors had deliberately overstated the company's assets by £2.5m. This is called 'fraudulent financial reporting' and is examined further in **Chapter 9**.

Investigations concluded that the audit firm did not sufficiently consider and address some of the known facts that should have raised serious concerns about the valuation of Warriors' assets. A review of the audit of tangible and intangible assets by an unconnected third-party confirmed that there were significant failings in the audit of this area. Audit procedures were limited to merely checking the casts in the company's fixed assets register and agreeing the depreciation charge per the fixed assets register to the profit and loss account. Other procedures to verify the existence and rights and obligations assertions had not been completed.

This is an example of an audit failure. The associated risks had not been properly considered and addressed and there was a failure to audit the assets of the company properly.

An audit failure can be catastrophic for an audit firm. It can lead to heavy fines being levied by regulators and professional bodies and the firm can be banned from practising in audit.

Audit failures usually arise because of a combination of:

● poor planning and execution of the audit;

● deploying staff on the audit assignment who have little, or no, experience;

● failing to carry out sufficient audit procedures to cover the financial statement assertions (see **5.20**); and

● significantly short audit completion deadlines resulting in a failure to carry out the audit in accordance with the ISAs (UK).

In the event of a business failure, users of the financial statements may claim that the auditor has been negligent when carrying out their audit (if this claim is subsequently proven, then this becomes an audit failure). Auditors will evaluate the potential for business failure in an engagement to determine whether the level of audit risk is at an acceptably low level.

All businesses will face some business risks and the auditor must be able to identify the relevant business risks in order to reduce audit risk.

Example 5.7 – Business risk and resulting audit risk

Wanderers Ltd is a business that has a high level of credit risk (credit risk being the risk that customers will fail to pay their debts when they fall due). Credit risk is a **business risk** which goes to increase **audit risk** because it concerns the valuation of trade debtors (receivables).

Here, the auditor must devise audit procedures to cover valuation of trade debtors in Wanderers' balance sheet to ensure they are not overstated. As credit risk is high, there is a wider scope for irrecoverable debts and hence the auditor must be satisfied that year-end trade debtors and profit are valid. For example, the auditor could extend post-year-end cash receipts testing and discuss with the directors the possibility of additional irrecoverable debts.

If the auditor carries out inadequate or insufficient audit procedures over Wanderers' trade debtors and one, or more, debtors cease to trade and are unable to pay the company, this is likely to give rise to an audit failure since the auditor's procedures did not detect the problem and this could result in the auditor being sued for negligence.

Example 5.8 – An irrelevant business risk

City Ltd has a year end of 31 December 2023. The audit of the financial statements commenced in March 2024 and the auditor's report is due to be signed on 10 April 2024. The company is planning to launch a new product in November 2024 and research activities commenced in March 2024. Strategic risk is a business risk (it is the risk resulting from future strategies and plans). However, this strategic risk does not have an impact on the audit of the financial statements for the year ended 31 December 2023. Hence, not all business risks are relevant to an audit.

AUDIT RISK

5.15 I have mentioned 'audit risk' a number of times throughout this chapter and it is the risk that the auditor forms the wrong opinion on the financial statements (ie, expresses an unmodified opinion when the opinion should be modified). Audit risk is fundamental to the audit process because auditors cannot check every transaction that makes up the client's financial statements because to do so would take a disproportionate length of time and would be extremely costly. Hence, the audit is carried out using a risk-based approach. Traditionally, a risk-based approach minimises the chances of the auditor expressing the wrong opinion in the auditor's report. Audits carried out in accordance with the ISAs (UK) take a risk-based approach and this helps to ensure that the work is carried out using the most effective audit procedures based on the auditor's risk assessment.

Auditors must focus their attention on those areas of the financial statements that are more likely to be prone to material errors as this increases the risk of material misstatement.

The audit risk model and its components

5.16 It is important to understand the traditional audit risk model and its components which are as follows:

The audit risk model is:

Audit risk = Inherent risk × Control risk × Detection risk

Inherent risk

5.17 Inherent risk is the risk that an assertion about a class of transaction, account balance or disclosure could be material, either individually or in the aggregate, **BEFORE** the auditor considers any related controls, and the higher the inherent risk then potentially higher the risk of material misstatement.

Inherent risk is, therefore, the risk of a material misstatement in the financial statements because of the nature of the entity, or the item itself. Examples of how inherent risk can arise are as follows:

Inherent risk	Why it is an inherent risk
The entity has a significant portfolio of complex financial instruments that are measured at fair value through profit or loss.	FRS 102, Section 12 *Other Financial Instruments Issues* is a complex section of FRS 102 and the inherent risk is that the accounting standard may not be understood properly by the preparer of the financial statements, resulting in a material misstatement.
The entity manufactures inventory which becomes obsolete quickly.	The inherent risk is that this inventory will not be valued properly at the lower of cost and estimated selling price less costs to complete and sell in accordance with FRS 102, Section 13 *Inventories*.
An accounting estimate is subject to significant estimation uncertainty.	As the accounting estimate is subject to significant estimation uncertainty, this creates a significant risk, meaning that it is likely to be on the upper end of the spectrum of inherent risk.

Example 5.9 – Forward foreign currency contract

Sunnie Enterprises Ltd prepares its financial statements under FRS 102 and has a year end of 31 March 2024. During discussions with the finance director of Sunnie Enterprises Ltd, it was noted that the client had entered into a forward foreign currency contract to buy $300,000 at a contracted rate of $1:£1.50 on 31 March 2025. The finance director has stated that this is the first time the company has entered into such an arrangement with its bank, and she is unsure how to deal with the transactions, stating:

I was unsure about what to do with the forward foreign currency contract as I have never dealt with these before; nor have any of the other finance staff. We have recognised the forward foreign currency contract on the balance sheet and have accounted for the forward foreign currency contract at fair value through profit or loss.

Forward foreign currency contracts are accounted for under FRS 102, Section 12 *Other Financial Instruments Issues*. This section of FRS 102 is complex, and the inherent risk is that the forward foreign currency contract will not be accounted for correctly, resulting in a misstatement in the financial statements.

The definition of 'inherent risk' refers to misstatements which arise **before** the auditor considers any related controls the entity may have over that risk. It may be the case that a client does account for such a transaction correctly, but the auditor must factor this inherent risk in when carrying out their risk assessment at the planning stage and devise suitable audit procedures to reduce the risk of material misstatement to an acceptable level.

In this example, the company has correctly accounted for the forward foreign currency contract.

Business risk and inherent risk will impact the audit because neither risk can be eliminated in totality and neither risk is under the control of the auditor. Remember, business risk relates to the financial statements and affects overall audit risk. Inherent risk is included in the ISAs (UK) and the audit risk model.

The table below summarises the differences between business risk and inherent risk:

Business risk	Inherent risk
The uncertainty of the business making a profit or making a loss. Business risk is concerned with the occurrence of an event which will have a detrimental impact on the business as a whole.	The risk that the financial statements are materially misstated before the auditor considers any related controls and is a function of the audit risk model.
Business risk should be reviewed continuously by management.	Inherent risk is only assessed at the time of the audit.
Business risks are identified by management.	Inherent risk is identified by the auditor.

Control risk

5.18   Control risk is the risk that a misstatement due to fraud or error may occur in an assertion that could be material (either individually or in the aggregate with other misstatements) which will not be prevented, or detected and corrected, on a timely basis by the entity's system of internal control.

Essentially, what we are saying here is that if the client has a weak system of internal control, then that system is unlikely to prevent, detect and correct, on a timely basis a misstatement which could be material. Conversely, the entity's system of internal control may be sound (it won't be perfect because no system of internal control can be); hence, we should expect the system to prevent, detect and correct, on a timely basis a misstatement which could be material.

Control risk may be assessed as high by the auditor when the entity's system of internal control may be ineffective. It may be deemed low risk where the auditor concludes the system of internal control is sound.

Example 5.10 – Weak system of control over the bank reconciliation process

Emery Ltd has prepared its draft financial statements for the year ended 30 April 2024 under FRS 102. The finance director has informed the audit manager that the year-end bank reconciliation contained some small differences that have been written off at the year end. In addition, while the year-end bank reconciliation had been carried out, the previous six had not due to staff shortages in the finance department.

The preparation of the bank reconciliation is an important control. There is the possibility that the small differences that have been written off could actually be large differences that net off to a small amount (particularly as the previous six had not been carried out at all). The auditor should request that the year-end bank reconciliation be prepared correctly, and any reconciling items should be investigated.

It is unlikely that the auditor will place any reliance on the controls over the bank reconciliation process as these have clearly not operated effectively during the year. A more substantive audit approach will, therefore, be devised.

Control risk is influenced by a number of factors, such as:

- The attitude of the directors, management and those charged with governance of an entity towards internal control. If management and those charged with governance have little regard for the entity's system of internal control, control risk becomes higher as the controls in place are likely to be ineffective, or certain direct controls may not exist.

- The overall internal control environment and the capabilities of staff who maintain and operate them.

- The level of supervision within the business.

- The integrity of staff, management and those charged with governance.

IMPORTANT POINT

For the identified risks of material misstatement at the assertion level, the auditor is required to carry out a **separate** assessment of inherent risk and control risk. This separate assessment is needed so the auditor can respond appropriately to the assessed risks of material misstatement at the assertion level.

It should also be borne in mind that ISA (UK) 315, para 34 states that inherent risk and control risk are the same where the auditor chooses not to test controls.

Detection risk

5.19 Detection risk refers to the risk that the audit procedures will not detect a misstatement that exists and that could be material (either individually or in aggregate with other misstatements).

The important thing to bear in mind where detection risk is concerned is that it is the **only** risk in the audit risk model that is under the control of the auditor and is **not** part of the risk of material misstatement. There are two elements to detection risk:

Audit sampling is considered in more detail in **Chapter 7**. However, as a brief overview of sampling and non-sampling risk, we will look at each individual risk in turn:

Sampling risk is the risk that the auditor's conclusion based on a sample is different from the conclusion that would be reached if the auditor had tested the entire population rather than just a sample.

REAL-LIFE SCENARIO

Ms P is a freelance file reviewer and carries out reviews of audit firms' work on both a hot review basis and a cold review basis.

During the audit of one firm's file, Ms P noticed that the value of trade debtors was significantly material to the financial statements. The audit firm had not carried out a debtors' circularisation on the grounds that they considered such a procedure to be a weak procedure and previous circularisations resulted in a low response rate.

Extended after-date cash testing had been carried out by the audit firm as a means of verifying the valuation assertion. However, only 20 debtors had been sampled. Ms P had counted that there were, in fact, 176 trade debtors owing the client money at the year end and the sample of 20 only equated to some 16% of the total trade debtors balance.

The problem here is twofold. Firstly, the audit firm has not carried out a **representative** sample of the population. The sample size itself is only 11.4% of the total population.

Secondly, there is still a risk of material misstatement given that 156 trade debtors have not had the valuation assertion tested.

Ms P noted that the audit firm had obtained a written representation from the client over trade debtors. This would be an inappropriate form of audit evidence in any event because written representations should only be obtained for those areas where other forms of audit evidence are scarce (which, for trade debtors, is not the case) or where the auditor is relying on management's judgement (again, this is not the case for trade debtors).

Ms P correctly concluded that **insufficient** audit evidence had been obtained over trade debtors and this, in itself, could increase audit risk.

In **Chapter 8** I examine data analytics. Data analytics have become increasingly popular over recent years and one of the main advantages to data analytics is that they can reduce sampling risk (in some cases, they can eliminate it completely) because entire populations comprising of large amounts of data can be analysed much quicker than doing the analysis manually. However, as I mention in **Chapter 8**, while data analytics are great at doing analysis work, they cannot draw conclusions, which is where the auditor will need to do some work.

Non-sampling risk is the risk that the auditor's conclusion is inappropriate for any other reason. For example, the application of inappropriate audit procedures or the misinterpretation of audit evidence.

Detection risk is, therefore, the residual risk after the auditor takes into account inherent risk and control risk and the overall risk which the auditor is willing to accept.

IMPORTANT POINT

There is an inverse relationship between **detection risk** and **control risk**. The auditor could conclude that the risk of material misstatement is low, which means the auditor's assessment that the financial statements contain a material misstatement is low. In turn, this also means that the auditor is seeking to place reliance on the entity's system of internal control. If the risk of material misstatement is low, then detection risk becomes high. This is because the auditor is seeking to place more reliance on the entity's system of internal control and therefore will do less substantive testing. Conversely, if the auditor concludes that the entity's system of internal control cannot be relied upon and hence deems the risk of material misstatement to be high, detection risk becomes low because the auditor will undertake more detailed substantive testing.

Remember, if inherent risk or control risk **increase**, the auditor must carry out more rigorous audit procedures to keep audit risk to an acceptable level (which is the auditor's ultimate goal).

RISK OF MATERIAL MISSTATEMENT AT THE FINANCIAL STATEMENT AND ASSERTION LEVEL

5.20   When we talk about financial statement **assertions**, we are referring to the claims made by an entity's management about the financial statements.

To put it differently, management may 'assert' that they own certain fixed assets by capitalising them on the balance sheet. The auditor will therefore test the **rights and obligations** assertion by tracing the asset to a purchase invoice and checking that the invoice is in the name of the client. For land and buildings, the auditor would test rights and obligations by tracing ownership to title deeds. Hence, assertions are claims by management via the information in the financial statements.

Risks of material misstatement at the **financial statement level** are those risks which can cause the financial statements *as a whole* to be materially misstated, for example due to fraud (fraud is examined in more detail in **Chapter 9**). Fraud risk factors must be considered by the auditor as these can lead to a material misstatement at the financial statement level. However, just because the auditor concludes a fraud risk factor is present, this does not necessarily mean that a fraud has occurred – it just means there is a higher risk of fraud occurring due to the risk factor present. Examples of fraud risk factors include:

- incentives, pressures and opportunities;

- fraudulent financial reporting;

- weak internal controls (eg, a lack of segregation of duties);

- risk of management override of internal controls;

- toleration of petty theft;

- corruption; and

- dissatisfied employees.

In addition to the risk of material misstatement at the financial statement level, there is a risk of material misstatement at the **assertion level**. As noted earlier, financial statement 'assertions' are claims by management about the financial statements. Risks of material misstatement at the assertion level are sub-divided into **inherent risk** and **control risk** which are discussed in **5.17** and **5.18** above.

The auditor uses risk assessment procedures to assess the risks of material misstatement. Risk assessment procedures will usually involve inquiries of management and other relevant individuals, analytical procedures (see **Chapter 6**), observation and inquiry. The auditor's risk assessment will then be used to influence the audit procedures they devise when developing the audit plan.

Misstatements at the financial statement level and assertion level can be summarised as follows:

Misstatements at:	
The financial statement level	**The assertion level**
Risk of material misstatement affects the financial statements as a whole – in other words, many assertions are affected	Consists of inherent risk and control risk
Risk of material misstatement at the financial statement level may be due to fraud	Inherent risk is the risk of misstatement before considering any related controls
	Control risk is the risk that the misstatement will not be prevented or detected and corrected by the client's system of internal control

Financial statement assertions

5.21   The financial statement assertions themselves are categorised as follows:

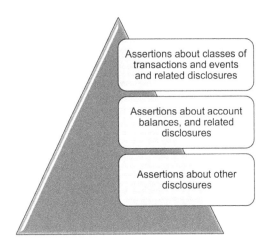

Assertions about classes of transactions and events and related disclosures

According to ISA (UK) 315, there are six assertions related to classes of transactions and events, and related disclosures as follows:

Occurrence	Transactions and events that have been recorded or disclosed, have occurred, and such transactions and events pertain to the entity.
Completeness	All transactions and events that should have been recorded have been recorded, and all related disclosures that should have been included in the financial statements have been included.
Accuracy	Amounts and other data relating to recorded transactions and events have been recorded appropriately, and related disclosures have been appropriately measured and described.
Cut-off	Transactions and events have been recorded in the correct accounting period.
Classification	Transactions and events have been recorded in the proper accounts.
Presentation	Transactions and events are appropriately aggregated or disaggregated and clearly described, and related disclosures are relevant and understandable in the context of the applicable financial reporting framework.

Assertions about account balances and related disclosures

According to ISA (UK) 315, there are six assertions about account balances and related disclosures as follows:

Existence	Assets, liabilities and equity interest exist.
Rights and obligations	The entity holds or controls the rights to assets, and liabilities are the obligations of the entity.
Completeness	All assets, liabilities and equity interests that should have been recorded have been recorded, and all related disclosures that should have been included in the financial statements have been included.
Accuracy, valuation and allocation	Assets, liabilities and equity interests have been included in the financial statements at appropriate amounts and any resulting valuation or allocation adjustments have been appropriately recorded, and related disclosures have been appropriately measured and described.
Classification	Assets, liabilities and equity interests have been recorded in the proper accounts.
Presentation	Assets, liabilities and equity interests are appropriately aggregated or disaggregated and clearly described, and related disclosures are relevant and understandable in the context of the requirements of the applicable financial reporting framework.

Assertions about disclosures

ISA (UK) 315 states that the assertions described above, adapted as appropriate, may also be used by the auditor in considering the different types of potential misstatements that may occur in disclosures not directly related to recorded classes of transactions, events or account balances.

When testing assertions concerning disclosures, the auditor will invariably use a disclosure checklist to ensure the disclosures are complete and conform to the relevant accounting standard (eg, FRS 102) as well as the requirements of company law.

IMPORTANT POINT

It is important that the auditor ensures that any disclosure checklist they use is up to date for any developments or changes in accounting standards or company law that impact on disclosures. This is especially the case for audits of financial statements for accounting periods commencing on or after 1 January 2026 when the amendments arising from the FRC's periodic review take mandatory effect, which gives rise to additional and amended disclosure requirements.

Financial statement level

5.22 The auditor is required to assess the risk of material misstatement, whether due to fraud or error at **both** the financial statement and the assertion level (see **5.23** below for the assertion level).

The financial statements of an entity consist of transaction and account balances.

Transactions include:

- Sales
- Purchases
- Expenses
- Payroll costs

Account balances include:

- Assets
- Liabilities

- Equity

The risk of material misstatement at the **financial statement level** requires the auditor to consider whether there are any figures in the financial statements that could be materially misstated and potentially affect many assertions. ISA (UK) 315 acknowledges that risks of this nature are not necessarily risks identifiable with specific assertions at the class of transactions, account balance or disclosure level (for example, risks due to management override of internal controls). Rather, they represent circumstances that can increase the risk of material misstatement at the assertion level.

Risks at the financial statement level may arise due to poor oversight by management over the preparation of the financial statements, or a general lack of management competence. Such risks can have a more pervasive effect on the financial statements, which will need an overall response by the auditor.

Example 5.11 – Lack of going concern disclosures

The audit of the draft financial statements of Currie Industries Ltd for the year ended 31 December 2024 is nearing completion. The company has sustained a loss for the year amounting to £1.2m (2023: profit of £2.6m). This loss has arisen due to new entrants in the market being more competitive and several 'price wars' happening during the year.

During the audit, the auditor has concluded that there is a material uncertainty related to going concern that has not been adequately disclosed. There have not been any other material misstatements noted within the financial statements.

Here, the auditor has concluded that the monetary amounts in the financial statements are not materially misstated (hence the assertions themselves are fine). However, the financial statements do not contain adequate disclosures concerning the material uncertainties related to going concern. Hence, if adequate disclosures are not included in the financial statements by management, the auditor will need to determine the impact on the wording of the audit opinion because a material misstatement exists even though it is not directly related to the figures in the financial statements.

IMPORTANT POINT

Identifying and assessing the risks of material misstatement at the financial statement level means ensuring that the financial statements **as a whole** give a true and fair view (or present fairly, in all material respects). Hence, the assertions themselves may be fine, but the financial statements as a whole do not present a true and fair view (or present fairly, in all material respects).

Assertion level

5.23   Risks of material misstatement at the **assertion level** for classes of transactions, account balances and disclosures must be considered by the auditor because this leads the auditor to determining the nature, timing and extent of further audit procedures which are necessary to obtain sufficient and appropriate audit evidence.

At the assertion level, the auditor is concerned with obtaining audit evidence to support the individual assertions applicable to the relevant area being audited.

The table below illustrates how the assertions work for various classes of balances and the procedures involved to test those assertions (note, this list is not exhaustive):

Area	Assertions to test	Procedure
Fixed assets	Completeness, classification and presentation	Obtain the fixed assets register, cast and agree the totals to the financial statements
Fixed assets	Existence	Select a sample of assets from the fixed assets register and physically inspect them to ensure they are properly included
Fixed assets	Valuation	Inspect assets for any signs of impairment
Fixed assets	Rights and obligations	Inspect supplier invoices or title deeds for properties to ensure they are in the name of the client
Stock	Completeness and presentation	Trace items counted at the stock count to the final stock valuation to ensure any errors identified at the counting stage have been corrected
Stock	Valuation	Inspect the ageing of stock to identify any old or slow-moving items which may require writing down to estimated selling price
Stock	Completeness and existence	Trace goods dispatched immediately prior to the year end to the nominal ledger to ensure they are not included in stock and revenue has been recorded

Area	Assertions to test	Procedure
Debtors	Accuracy and presentation	Obtain the trade debtors listing, cast the list and agree it to the financial statements
Debtors	Completeness and existence	Agree the sales ledger control account to the list of trade debtor balances
Debtors	Valuation and allocation	Inspect the aged debtors list to identify any slow-moving balances to assess whether a provision for bad debts is required (or needs to be increased)
Debtors	Existence	Select a sample of year-end trade debtor balances and agree back to goods dispatched notes and sales orders
Creditors	Completeness, classification and presentation	Obtain a list of trade creditors, cast the list and agree the list with the nominal ledger and financial statements
Creditors	Existence, completeness, obligations and valuation	Obtain supplier statements and reconcile these to the purchase ledger balance and investigate any significant differences
Revenue	Cut-off	Inspect a sample of goods dispatched notes before and after the year end and ensure they have been recorded in the correct accounting period
Revenue	Accuracy	Recalculate discounts and VAT/other sales taxes applied for a sample of sales invoices
Revenue	Completeness	Select a sample of customer orders and agree these to dispatch notes and sales invoices through to inclusion in the sales day book
Purchases	Cut-off	Inspect goods received notes before and after the year end and ensure they have been recorded in the correct accounting period
Purchases	Accuracy	Recalculate discounts and VAT/sales taxes applied for a sample of purchase invoices
Purchases	Completeness	Select a sample of purchase orders and agree these with goods received notes and purchase invoices through to inclusion in the purchases day book
Payroll	Accuracy	Cast the monthly payroll listings to verify the accuracy of the payroll expense
Payroll	Completeness and presentation	Agree the total payroll expense per the payroll system with the nominal ledger and financial statements

Area	Assertions to test	Procedure
Payroll	Occurrence	Agree the total net pay per the payroll records with the bank transfer listing of payments and cash book

EVALUATING THE CLIENT'S SYSTEMS AND CONTROLS

5.24 When it comes to evaluating the client's systems and controls, the auditor must first identify what controls the client has. So, for example, in a manufacturing company it may be the case that production staff are required to work overtime at busy periods during the year. Overtime worked must be authorised by a responsible official before details are sent to the payroll department for subsequent payment to the employee. This is a control that is in place to prevent payments being made to employees that have not been worked. The auditor may wish to test this control by reviewing overtime worked reports to ensure there is evidence they have been reviewed prior to being sent to payroll.

Remember, all businesses will have some sort of control system in place and those controls (regardless of how sophisticated, or otherwise, they are) will aim to prevent fraud and/or error arising.

ISA (UK) 315 *Identifying and Assessing the Risks of Material Misstatement* requires the auditor to identify the following:

● Controls that address a risk that is deemed to be a **significant** risk.

● Controls over journal entries which should include non-standard journal entries which record one-off (ie, non-recurring or unusual) transactions or adjustments in the nominal ledger.

● Controls which the auditor is planning to test the operating effectiveness to establish the nature, timing and extent of substantive procedures. Remember, this should also include controls which address risks for which substantive procedures alone do not provide sufficient appropriate audit evidence.

● Any other controls which the auditor considers appropriate in the client's circumstances which address risks at the assertion level.

Remember, ISA (UK) 315 (Revised July 2020) places a lot more emphasis on IT and controls over IT systems than previous editions of the ISA (UK). So, once the auditor has identified controls that address risks of material misstatement at the assertion level, the auditor must then identify:

- The IT applications (as well as other aspects of the client's IT environment) which are subject to risks arising from the use of IT.

- In respect of the IT **applications**, consider the related risks arising from the use of IT and the entity's general IT controls that address those risks.

Once the auditor has identified those risks, ISA (UK) 315 requires the auditor to evaluate whether the control is designed effectively (ie, whether it will address the risk of material misstatement at the assertion level) and determine whether the control has been implemented by performing audit procedures over the control. These procedures may include reviewing reports that confirm the control has been operating effectively as well as inquiring with relevant personnel (note, the auditor cannot just inquire of the entity's personnel about the control – ISA (UK) 315, para 26 is specific that other audit procedures are **in addition to** inquiry of the entity's personnel).

All this sounds quite in-depth, which it is, because it is about identifying how 'risky' the client's system of control is when it comes to misstatements arising in the financial statements (including the client's IT system). The auditor cannot just document how a system and relevant controls operate; they also need to consider whether those controls have been properly designed and whether they are operating in the manner intended.

When evaluating the design of a control, the auditor must consider whether the control (individually or in combination with other controls) is capable of effectively preventing, or detecting and correcting, material misstatements. This is where some thought should be devoted because the auditor must consider the **design** of the control **before** looking at how the control has been implemented. Remember, a badly designed control may represent a significant deficiency in internal control.

IMPORTANT POINT

Evaluating the implementation of a control means considering whether the control exists and whether it is being used within the business. If a control has been designed, but there is no evidence of it actually operating, then the control is clearly ineffective, and no reliance should be placed on it.

Understanding the design and implementation of controls is necessary regardless of whether, or not, the auditor wishes to place any reliance on internal controls. If the auditor intends to place reliance on internal controls, they must perform **tests of control**. Keep in mind that tests of control intend to obtain audit evidence which demonstrates that internal controls are sufficiently robust.

To summarise the evaluation of controls, the following diagram may help:

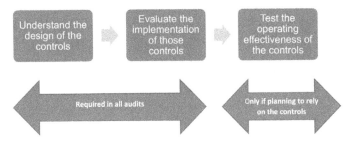

The means by which the auditor evaluates and tests systems and controls are considered in **Chapter 6** (see the Section titled 'Types of Audit Procedures') which focuses on how auditors obtain audit evidence.

IMPORTANT POINT

A training company has recently stated that controls testing is often done incorrectly. For example, stating 'disclosures are checked as part of the audit' is documented as the control as to how management ensure disclosures are complete and accurate. Similarly, there have also been instances of audit testing being given as the control.

Keep in mind that any procedure performed by the auditor is not a valid internal control and documenting them as such should be avoided. There is also a misunderstanding of the distinction between a test of control and a walkthrough test. A walkthrough test would usually involve observing a staff member performing a function (eg, raising a sales invoice) to ensure the auditor has understood the system and that the reference to the system in the planning notes are a fair reflection of the system and a control is being implemented.

CHAPTER ROUNDUP

- Audit planning is dealt with primarily in the ISAs (UK) in the 300 series.

- There are generally four stages to an audit (risk assessment, risk responses, audit fieldwork and reporting).

- The auditor must carry out a thorough programme of planning to ensure that all assessed risks have been properly dealt with and the necessary audit procedures to reduce audit risk have been planned.

- Obtaining an understanding of the entity, its system of controls and risks is crucial in carrying out audit work and there are various sources of information the auditor will look to in developing this understanding.

- The audit is carried out using a risk-based approach. The auditor will develop auditor responses to the assessed risks which will then be formulated into an audit strategy and an audit plan.

- Audit risk is the risk that the auditor will form an incorrect opinion on the financial statements and the auditor will be striving to reduce audit risk to as low a level as possible (although there will always be some audit risk due to the inherent limitations of an audit).

- Inherent risk and control risk must be assessed separately. Detection risk is the only risk in the audit risk model that is under the control of the auditor.

- Risk of material misstatement can arise at both the financial statement level (ie, the financial statements as a whole) or at the assertion level (ie, within individual transactions, balances and disclosures).

- Evaluating the client's system of internal control is necessary to not only identify which controls are present, but to also identify if any reliance can potentially be placed on those controls.

PITFALLS TO AVOID

- Failing to carry out a thorough programme of planning as this will mean the auditor 'goes in blind' and will not have undertaken a proper risk assessment.

- Placing too much reliance on a client's system of internal control and not carrying out substantive procedures (remember, substantive procedures must be carried out as well).

- The audit engagement partner not being involved in the audit planning. The audit engagement partner should review the planning (if they have not done it themselves) to ensure it is complete, appropriate and identifies all the relevant risks.

- Not considering the client's use of IT at the planning stage. This contravenes ISA (UK) 315 as most clients will now have some form of IT system in place that influences the financial reporting process.

Chapter 6

Planning the Audit II: Other Aspects of Planning

CHAPTER TOPIC LIST

• Introduction (see **6.1**).

• Determining materiality (see **6.2**).

• Analytical procedures (see **6.8**).

• Developing the audit strategy and audit plan (see **6.10**).

• Design of audit procedures (see **6.14**).

• Fraud (see **6.18**).

INTRODUCTION

6.1   In **Chapter 5**, I examined the initial stages of audit planning, being risk assessment and understanding the client. In that chapter I explain that audit planning is much more than understanding the structure of the client and its governance. Not only is about understanding the business in which the client operates, but it's also about the risks attached to the business (both **business risks** which are generally external factors affecting the business and **audit risk** which is the risk that the auditor forms an incorrect opinion on the client's financial statements).

WHAT ARE WE TRYING TO ACHIEVE?

Remember, as I mentioned in **Chapter 5**, audits nowadays are carried out using a risk-based approach so risk can be seen as *the* central theme. The auditor is ultimately trying to devise appropriate procedures at the planning stage that reduce audit risk to an acceptably low level. This will mean a thorough degree of planning is needed.

If you haven't reviewed **Chapter 5** prior to looking at this chapter, I would strongly advise that you do so because in this chapter I examine the planning activities that are generally carried out by the auditor **post**-risk assessment (**Chapter 5** looks at the whole issue of risk assessment in a lot of detail). If you have read **Chapter 5**, the next phase will be to reflect the auditor's assessment of risk when:

- Determining materiality (both financial statement materiality and performance materiality).

- Performing analytical review at the planning stage of the audit (which is a mandatory requirement).

- Designing audit procedures (ie, tests of control and substantive procedures).

- Developing the audit strategy and the audit plan.

- Selecting audit samples.

- Establishing the types of audit procedure that could be applied during the evidence-gathering stage of the audit.

- Assessing the risk of fraud at the planning stage (note, fraud is also examined in **Chapter 9**).

IMPORTANT POINT

As I examined in **Chapter 5**, audit risk is the risk that the auditor forms an incorrect opinion on the financial statements (in other words, the auditor 'makes the wrong decision'). It is this risk the auditor is most keen to reduce as far as possible. The auditor cannot eradicate audit risk in its entirety due to the inherent limitations of an audit, such as:

- The financial statements will include subjective estimates and other matters of judgement.

- Internal controls may be relied upon which have their own inherent limitations.

- Management representations may have to be relied upon as the only source of audit evidence in some areas, such as those involving management judgement.

- Audit evidence is generally persuasive rather than conclusive.

- The auditor carries out the audit using sampling – ie, they do not test all transactions and balances as this would be impractical.

While audit risk can never be eradicated, the auditor must reduce the risk as far as possible through the design of audit procedures which specifically

---

respond to the assessed levels of risk. If the procedures fail to respond to the assessed levels of risk, audit risk will increase.

At the planning stage of the audit, the audit engagement team will have a team meeting to discuss, amongst other things, the susceptibility of the financial statements to material misstatement, whether caused by fraud or error. This is a vital meeting and must involve the audit engagement team and be overseen by the audit engagement partner. It should be an exchange of ideas. If any team members cannot be present at the meeting, they must be brought up to speed with developments as quickly as possible, so they are kept fully informed and understand their role within the team and those matters that the team need to be alert to.

The meeting itself is not just about who will do what during the audit. During the meeting, the audit engagement team will also discuss:

● The outcome of any initial discussions with the client (pre-planning discussions).

● Changes to the client's business, system of internal control or accounting systems, and related parties.

● Areas of the financial statements that appear to be a source of misstatement.

● Respective responsibilities of each team member.

● Fraud aspects (see **6.18** below and **Chapter 9**).

The purpose of this team meeting is primarily to share knowledge so that everyone is 'on the same page' and knows exactly what is expected of them. Team members may also be reminded of other specific responsibilities during that meeting (such as compliance with the firm's system of quality management and anti-money laundering requirements).

DETERMINING MATERIALITY

6.2   Determining materiality involves auditor judgement and over the years there have been many debates as to the 'correct' way to calculate materiality – although there is no set method prescribed in ISA (UK) 320 *Materiality in Planning and Performing an Audit*.

An easy way to think of materiality is that it is a way of deciding whether something in the financial statements (eg, a balance, transaction or disclosure) is important enough for it to have an effect on the decision-making process of the users. So if the balance, transaction or disclosure was incorrect or missing, would that error or omission change how the user views the financial statements if it were not incorrect or missing? That basically sums up how materiality works in practice.

To understand how materiality works in audit, we can go right back to the whole point of an audit. The overall objective of the auditor is to determine whether, or not, based on the audit evidence obtained, the financial statements give a true and fair view (or present fairly, in all material respects). If something is materially incorrect or missing in the financial statements, the auditor simply cannot say that the financial statements give a true and fair view.

In this way, you can think of materiality as a way for the auditor to **prioritise** the elements of the financial statements that need to be given more attention. Hence, it is a primary way in which the auditor manages audit risk. In essence, the more material an element of the financial statements, the more audit attention it will require to ensure the auditor draws the right conclusion on that element. A basic example can often shed some light on what materiality is trying to achieve:

Example 6.1 – Determining whether an item is material

Sunnie Pet Stores Ltd operates a chain of pet shops across the south of the UK. Extracts from the audited financial statements for the year ended 31 October 2023 show the following information:

	31.10.2023 **£**	**31.10.2022** **£**
Property, plant and equipment	2,105,223	2,104,964
Trade debtors	165,748	153,001
Cash at bank	121,223	118,743
Sundry creditors	203	–

Just by looking at the information above, sundry creditors are only £203 and last year the balance was nil. If this balance were omitted in 2023, it is unlikely that the user would think anything of it. However, if the sundry creditors should have been £550,203 then it is likely that omission of the figure, which would have a significant impact on the balance sheet, would impact on a user's view of the financial statements.

This example illustrates that the auditor is less likely to devote hours of audit work on the sundry creditor balance but is more likely to devote more attention to the riskier areas of the financial statements (such as the valuation of trade debtors).

Similarly, if the auditor calculates an expense difference of £10,000 then this could be material if the total expense in profit or loss is £40,000 but may not be material if the total expense is £400,000.

As mentioned earlier, materiality is a wholly judgemental issue and decisions concerning the methodology used to arrive at materiality levels and amount are made in light of the client's individual circumstances. Materiality is also affected by the size or nature of a misstatement (or a combination of both).

IMPORTANT POINT

Financial reporting frameworks, such as FRS 102 *The Financial Reporting Standard applicable in the UK and Republic of Ireland* have their own definitions and application requirements where materiality is concerned.

In March 2024, the FRC issued the amendments to FRS 102 arising from the periodic review. These amendments are effective for accounting periods commencing on or after 1 January 2026. Earlier adoption is permissible provided all the amendments are applied at the same time.

The FRC have amended the definition of 'material' in FRS 102 and the revised definition is as follows:

> Information is material if omitting, misstating or obscuring it could reasonably be expected to influence decisions that the users of the **general purpose financial statements** make on the basis of those financial statements, which provide financial information about a specific reporting entity.

Material classes of transactions, account balances and disclosures

6.3   ISA (UK) 320 refers to *'material classes of transactions, account balances and disclosures'*. The ISA (UK) requires the auditor to determine materiality for the financial statements **as a whole** (often referred to as 'financial statement materiality'). However, the ISA (UK) also requires the auditor to determine a lower level of materiality for particular classes of transactions, account balances or disclosures for which a misstatement that is less than financial statement materiality could influence the decisions of the users. Again, this will require professional judgement by the auditor and, in practice, can often be more complicated than it initially sounds.

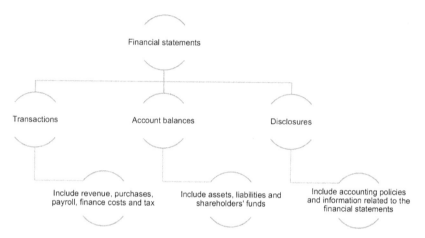

When looking at ISA (UK) 320's reference to 'class of transaction and account balance', the reference is essentially 'dividing' the financial statements into their component parts as can be seen in the diagram above. Expenditure will include 'cost of sales', 'administrative expenses' and 'distribution costs'. A 'class' of account balance may be 'non-current (fixed) assets', 'current assets', 'current liabilities' or 'non-current liabilities'.

The auditor's primary concern is that of **material** transactions, account balances and disclosures. The objective here is for the auditor to obtain sufficient appropriate audit evidence that those transactions, account balances and disclosures are not materially misstated. The auditor is less concerned about immaterial transactions, account balances and disclosures – BUT the auditor cannot forget about them in their entirety. Why? Because an immaterial transaction, account balance or disclosure *may* become material if there are any revisions to materiality levels during the course of the audit or may become material when they are aggregated with other misstatements that the auditor identifies during the evidence-gathering stage of the audit.

IMPORTANT POINT

Materiality is not just calculated at the planning stage and then forgotten about. It must be kept under constant review by the auditor during the **entire** audit process. During the course of the audit, 'things' might happen

---

or be discovered that could mean the planning side of the audit may need to change. For example, unexpected transactions or errors may be discovered meaning the auditor may have to extend their substantive audit procedures beyond what they were initially planning to carry out. Where such issues present themselves, it is likely the auditor will **decrease** materiality to cater for the additional risks.

Whenever there are changes to the audit plan or materiality levels these changes (together with the reasons for those changes) must be documented.

Materiality for the financial statements as a whole

6.4 The first thing to understand is that materiality is two-fold in nature. Materiality is based on **quantitative** aspects (so is concerned with the monetary values – ie, material by **size**) but also **qualitative** aspects (so is also concerned with other areas of the financial statements, such as material related party transaction disclosure notes or directors' remuneration disclosures – ie, issues in the financial statements that are material by **nature**). So, not only is the auditor concerned with monetary aspects of the financial statements; they must also be concerned with non-monetary aspects as well.

There are some issues which could affect the financial statements and are considered to be material by nature, such as:

● Disclosures about a material uncertainty related to going concern.

● Material related party transactions that have not been adequately disclosed.

● Disclosures concerning transactions with directors.

● Contingent liability disclosures which, if omitted, may impact on the usefulness of the financial statements.

● Misstatements which, if adjusted, would cause a profit to turn into a loss.

● Misstatements which, if adjusted, would cause net assets to turn into net liabilities.

During the audit, the auditor may come across immaterial misstatements (eg, an under-accrual for electricity or a slight mistake in the calculation of the depreciation charges). These immaterial misstatements cannot be ignored completely (unless they are trivial (see **6.7** below) – in which case there is no need to collate). Why? Because, when aggregated they could, for example, turn a reported profit into a loss and so may become material by nature.

When it comes to determining the materiality level for the financial statements as a whole, ISA (UK) 320 does not prescribe a calculation. Some auditors find this rather unhelpful, but the reason that the standard does not set out the calculation is because materiality is purely down to the auditor's professional judgement. Remember as well, that what may be material in one entity might not be material in another entity. What ISA (UK) 320 does, however, offer is percentage 'benchmarks' which can be used as a 'starting point' for determining materiality levels. For example:

- ½ to 1% of revenue

- 5 to 10% of profit before tax

- 1 to 2% of total assets (non-current assets plus current assets)

IMPORTANT POINT

The important point to bear in mind where these benchmarks are concerned is that they are **not** prescriptive. Different audit firms may use different benchmarks or different thresholds based on the **risk assessment** for each client. The important point to emphasise is that the auditor should document the reasons for their conclusions where materiality is concerned, and averaging amounts from different benchmarks would not tend to be used.

For profit-orientated businesses, a benchmark based on profit before tax is commonly used (as this figure is the one most likely susceptible to change because of misstatements that are corrected).

Example 6.2 – A previously profit-making business sustains a loss

Churchill Industries Ltd has been in business since 1951 and has always been profit-making. However, the draft financial statements for the year ended 31 December 2023 show a loss before tax amounting to £1,250,333 versus a profit in the previous year of £846,337. For the last four years, the auditor has always assessed financial statement materiality based on profit before tax. However, as the current year draft financial statements show a loss, the auditor has concluded that this is no longer an appropriate benchmark.

In this situation, the auditor could decide to use a different benchmark, such as gross profit or revenue. The auditor may also try to establish the 'driver' of the loss for the current year (if, for example, it has arisen because of a one-off event) and remove this to arrive at a normalised profit figure.

Whatever benchmark the auditor uses, it is important they document the rationale behind their conclusion.

Example 6.3 – Determination of financial statement materiality

The draft financial statements of Wolves Ltd for the year ended 31 December 2023 show the following information:

	31.12.2023 DRAFT £'000
Revenue	12,600
Profit before tax	2,150
Non-current assets	35,433
Current assets	18,268

Financial statement materiality has been determined as being £107,500 (profit before tax of £2,150,000 × 5%). The auditor has concluded that financial statement materiality based on profit before tax is appropriate based on the risk of it being susceptible to change due to audit errors discovered.

During the course of the audit, the audit senior discovers an error of £0.2m which represents capitalised research expenditure which should be recognised in profit or loss.

This misstatement represents 9.3% (£0.2/£2,150) of profit before tax and hence is material as it exceeds the 5% threshold. If the benchmark had been based on, say, total assets, the misstatement would not be material. This demonstrates the importance of exercising careful professional judgement when determining the relevant benchmark(s) for materiality.

In this scenario, management should be requested to correct the misstatement to avoid a modified audit opinion being issued for a material misstatement.

Performance materiality

6.5   Performance materiality is the amount set by the auditor which **must be less than financial statement materiality** and is primarily used by the auditor for designing and performing audit procedures (ie, it is the level at which transactions and balances are tested). Hence, if performance materiality for trade debtors is £40,000, then all individual trade debtor balances that are over £40,000 are included in the sample.

IMPORTANT POINT

Performance materiality aims to reduce the risk that the auditor will not identify misstatements which become material when aggregated.

Example 6.4 – Calculation of performance materiality

The audit engagement team is planning the audit of Harper Ltd for the year ended 31 August 2023. The audit senior has calculated financial statement materiality to be £86,000 and the general level of performance materiality has been calculated at 75% of this (ie, £64,500). The audit senior has identified work in progress and development expenditure as having a high risk of material misstatement, hence a specific level of performance materiality must be applied to these areas.

The audit engagement partner has suggested that 50% of the financial statement materiality level be used in these high-risk areas. Therefore, when auditing work in progress and development expenditure, a performance materiality of £43,000 (£86,000 × 50%) will be applied.

Depending on the level of risk of material misstatement, the auditor could apply a higher or lower percentage to this 'haircut' of the financial statement materiality to give performance materiality or even use a different calculation. This will be down to professional judgement and that judgement should be carefully documented to explain the rationale behind the final decision.

In the example above, specific performance materiality is £43,000. If the auditor had not used this specific performance materiality and then discovered a misstatement of, say, £70,000 in the work in progress valuation, the auditor may have concluded that the misstatement is immaterial when measured against the financial statement materiality of £86,000. However, the auditor may not have detected further misstatements which, when added to the £70,000 misstatement, could have resulted in material misstatement. By using performance materiality, the misstatement of £70,000 becomes material and hence the auditor would need to request management correct the misstatement. This reduces the risk of the auditor expressing an incorrect opinion on the financial statements (ie, reduces audit risk).

IMPORTANT POINT

It is worth noting that ICAEW guidance suggests a performance materiality of 75% of materiality for low-risk audit areas and 50% of materiality for those considered to be higher risk. In the thematic review carried out by the Financial Reporting Council *Audit Quality Thematic Review – Materiality* issued in December 2017, this review shows the percentage reduction in financial statement materiality to arrive at performance materiality is usually between 20% and 60%. First year audits may use a lower level of materiality to mitigate the risks of auditing an unfamiliar set of accounts.

As with financial statement materiality levels, performance materiality levels are revised during the audit, where necessary. A reduced level of performance materiality would be appropriate when facts come to light which the auditor was not previously aware of and which increases the risk of material misstatement (for example, an undisclosed related party).

REAL-LIFE FOCUS

Mrs K is the audit engagement partner in a two-partner firm. She submitted an audit file for a post-issuance review (also known as a 'cold file review') to a reputable third party.

The file reviewer criticised Mrs K's method of calculating materiality. Mrs K calculated materiality using the 'averaging method'. This method typically takes revenue, a measure of profit and total assets, applies the relevant percentage and then divides the sum by three to arrive at an average materiality level. It was this average amount that Mrs K used as financial statement materiality.

ISA (UK) 320 does not make any mention of the averaging method in arriving at a materiality level. Equally, it does not say that the method cannot be used. However, the use of the averaging method does not necessarily focus specifically on assessed risks and tends not to be liked by regulators. The auditor should consider which figures are most important for the client and how the different levels will interact with each other.

Materiality and audit risk

6.6 Audit risk is the risk that the auditor expresses an incorrect opinion on the accounts. There is an inverse relationship between materiality and the level of audit risk. Hence, the higher the assessed level of audit risk, the lower the level of materiality and vice versa. Another way of thinking about this is that if the auditor wishes to reduce audit risk, they should reduce the materiality level (ie, more balances, transactions and disclosures will become material) and sample sizes will become larger.

Example 6.5 – Illustration of inverse relationship between materiality and audit risk

The audit of Breary Industries Ltd is currently underway. During the audit of the payroll cycle, the auditor discovers a significant weakness in the controls. There is no segregation of duties and no authorisation procedures in place. In the last five months of the year, there have been significant changes made to the payroll to correct errors and many staff have become disgruntled.

In this situation, there is a high level of audit risk relating to payroll transactions. If the auditor reduces audit risk by reducing materiality levels over the payroll cycle, there is a much higher chance that the auditor will detect more misstatements because they are performing more substantive procedures over the payroll. In this situation, the auditor is using materiality as a means of reducing their audit risk.

The example of Breary Industries Ltd highlights that materiality does not remain 'set' or 'fixed' during the course of an audit. Matters may well come to light during the evidence-gathering phase that require materiality levels to be changed (either upwards or downwards depending on the issues identified). Where issues such as fraud risk factors, weaknesses in controls or management override of internal controls are concerned, the auditor is likely to decrease materiality and carry out additional substantive procedures.

Trivial error

6.7   As well as documenting the levels of financial statement and performance materiality, the auditor should also document the level below which a misstatement would be treated as 'clearly trivial'.

ISA (UK) 450 *Evaluation of Misstatements Identified During the Audit* clarifies at paragraph A2 that 'clearly trivial' is not the same as 'not material'. Essentially, a clearly trivial misstatement will be one that is much smaller than an immaterial misstatement and will also be clearly inconsequential when taken both individually and in the aggregate with other misstatements.

IMPORTANT POINT

ISA (UK) 450, paragraph 5 requires the auditor to accumulate misstatements identified during the audit, except those that are clearly trivial. When there is any doubt as to whether a misstatement(s) is clearly trivial, the auditor must consider it **not** clearly trivial.

Example 6.6 – Clearly trivial errors

Financial statement materiality for the audit of Tennyson Industries Ltd for the year ended 31 December 2023 has been calculated at £65,000. Tolerable error rate is 5%.

In this situation, an error can be classed as clearly trivial if it is less than £3,250 (£65,000 × 5%). However, this will require professional judgement and may be set lower depending on the auditor's risk assessment.

As with financial statement and performance materiality levels, it is important that the rationale for arriving at a clearly trivial error level is documented on the file so that reviewers can understand how the amounts have been arrived at.

ANALYTICAL PROCEDURES

6.8   ISA (UK) 315 *Identifying and Assessing the Risks of Material Misstatement* requires analytical procedures to be applied at the planning stage of the audit as risk assessment procedures. There is a separate ISA (UK) for analytical procedures, being ISA (UK) 520 *Analytical Procedures*, however, ISA (UK) 520 is for analytical review as a substantive procedure during the audit. Analytical procedures must also be applied towards the end of the audit (ie, at the completion phase) to enable the auditor to form an overall conclusion on the financial statements. Analytical procedures at the completion phase of the audit are dealt with in **Chapter 10**.

At the planning stage of the audit, analytical procedures are used as risk assessment procedures. This enables the auditor to obtain an understanding of the business and its environment to help reduce the risk of material misstatement in the financial statements. This then serves to enable the auditor to devise the nature, timing and extent of audit procedures which then feeds into the development of the audit strategy and subsequent audit plan (see **6.10**).

Put simply, analytical procedures aim to see if there are **plausible** and **expected** relationships between financial and non-financial data. When we talk about 'financial data', we are, of course, talking about the data in the client's financial statements. So, for example, if the client takes out a new bank loan in the year, the auditor would expect to see an increase in finance costs (interest payable and similar expenses) in profit or loss. If such an increase has not happened, this may indicate that costs are understated and there is a risk of material misstatement.

'Non-financial data' could involve considering how the company goes about achieving its objectives, such as marketing, staffing requirements, opening branches in new locations and the client's overall position in the industry in which it operates.

Analytical procedures are a powerful tool for the auditor. They can indicate potential sources of misstatement at the planning stage of the audit, for which the auditor will devise specific audit procedures to see what is going on.

The general process involved in performing analytical procedures is summarised as follows:

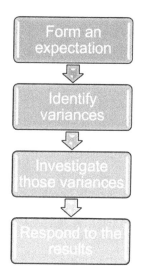

These steps are examined in further detail in **6.17** below. However, keep in mind that at the planning stage, the auditor is not obtaining audit evidence. Analytical procedures at the planning stage will help the auditor to identify inconsistencies, unusual transactions or events and unusual or unexpected relationships which may point to risks of material misstatement.

There are three common types of analytical procedure that the auditor may carry out during the risk assessment stage of the audit:

Trend analysis	The auditor will compare a current year figure to the prior year to see if the two figures are consistent or if one is significantly higher than the other. In addition, the auditor may also compare actual figures to budgeted figures or compare the client's figures to another company in the same industry to see if they are comparable. Where there are significant fluctuations, the auditor will devise procedures to investigate why those fluctuations have occurred.
Ratio analysis	This is probably the most well-known type of analytical procedure used in practice and there are some key financial ratios discussed later in this section. The auditor will calculate various ratios (eg, gross profit margins) to identify potential sources of misstatement. Remember, though, a ratio on its own is meaningless – you will need at least the current year and prior year ratios for comparability purposes.
Reasonableness	This is where the auditor asks themselves *'Does what I am seeing make sense based on other facts?'* So, for example, if I know the company depreciates its computer equipment on a three-year straight-line basis, and cost is £48,000, then would it be reasonable to see a depreciation expense for computer equipment of £4,000? Well, no, because £48,000 / 3 years is £16,000 so you would have to go beyond the figures to find out why the depreciation expense is only £4,000. Has the client made a mistake? Has there been another issue that has caused the depreciation charge to be lower than expected (such as a change in depreciation rate, method or residual value?)

Nowadays, automated techniques such as data analytics and audit software can be used to carry out analytical procedures and these will generally result in a much more efficient use of the auditor's time.

Key ratios

6.9   As noted above, there are some key ratios that are used by auditors at the risk assessment stage of the audit that can indicate **potential** sources of misstatement. They are split between profitability, efficiency, liquidity and return ratios:

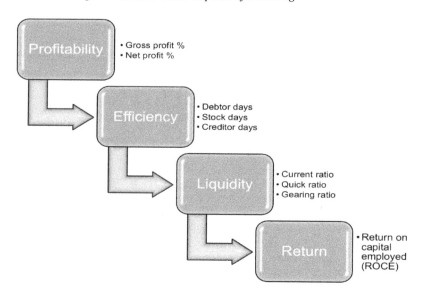

Type and ratio	Ratio calculation	What it tells the auditor
Profitability: Gross margin Profitability: Net margin	Gross profit / Revenue Profit before tax / Revenue	Auditors would generally expect the relationship between costs and revenue to stay relatively stable if they expect that business performance has not significantly changed since the prior year. Issues which may affect these ratios include: • Changes in selling price/sales mix • Discounts received • Economies of scale • Better marketing • Increase in energy costs • Increase in payroll costs • Supply chain issues
Efficiency: Debtor days Efficiency: Stock days Efficiency: Creditor days	Trade debtors / Revenue × 365 Stock / Cost of sales × 365 Trade creditors / Purchases × 365	These ratios show how long, on average, the entity takes to collect cash from customers and hold inventory as well as how long it takes to pay suppliers. Companies should strive to reduce trade debtor days and inventory days to an acceptable level and increase creditor days (within acceptable limits) because this can maximise cash flow

Type and ratio	Ratio calculation	What it tells the auditor
Liquidity: Current ratio Liquidity: Quick ratio Liquidity: Gearing ratio	Current assets / Current liabilities (Current assets – Stock) / Current liabilities Borrowings / Share capital + Reserves	These ratios indicate how able a company is to meet its short-term liabilities. As a result they are key indicators that the auditor uses when assessing going concern
Return: Return on capital employed (ROCE)	Profit before interest and tax / (Share capital + Reserves + Borrowings)	Any changes in gearing or ROCE may indicate a change in the financing structure of the business. It can also indicate changes in the overall performance of the business. These are potentially important ratios for identifying material changes to the entity's balance sheet and for obtaining an overall picture of the annual performance of the business

As noted earlier, ratio analysis is one of the most common types of analytical procedure carried out by auditors. They are helpful because they can 'pinpoint' where specific problems may lie. For example, the gross margin for the current year has been calculated at 40%. In the prior year it was 29%. The first question the auditor will ask is *'Why has the increase happened?'* It may be absolutely the case that the company's gross profit margin has increased by 11% from the prior year, but the auditor cannot just take this at face value. Such a disproportionate increase in gross profit margin could have happened due to:

- Cut-off errors on sales – ie, sales for the succeeding financial year have been recognised in the current year due to a cut-off error.

- Cut-off errors on cost of sales – ie, direct costs for the current year have been recognised in the succeeding year due to a cut-off error or under-accrual.

- Stock valuation – closing stock or work in progress may be overstated due to errors in the stock valuation or cut-off problems.

- Posting errors – sales invoices could have been duplicated or input into the system at an overstated value.

> **IMPORTANT POINT**
>
> As you can see, analytical procedures used as risk assessment procedures at the planning stage do not necessarily identify material misstatements.

Instead, they indicate potential sources of misstatement which the auditor should devise specific procedures to address.

Example 6.7 – Interaction of ratio analysis with the financial statement assertions

The audit senior of Summer & Co Auditors is carrying out the planning of an existing client, Currie Industries Ltd. Preliminary analytical review procedures have indicated that trade debtor days have increased from 35 days in 2022 to 62 days in 2023 (trade debtor days indicate how quickly Currie Industries is collecting cash in from trade debtors).

An increase in trade debtor days to this extent indicates that they may be overvalued. Remember, that a key assertion over trade debtors is the **valuation** assertion (ie, trade debtors are carried in the balance sheet at an appropriate amount). This means that the auditor will be primarily concerned with the **recoverability** of trade debtors – particularly those which may be overdue for payment and will focus on testing trade debtors for overstatement.

DEVELOPING THE AUDIT STRATEGY AND AUDIT PLAN

6.10   ISA (UK) 300 *Planning an Audit of Financial Statements* requires the auditor to:

- Establish the overall audit strategy; and

- Develop an audit plan.

So, the first part we will look at is establishing the overall audit **strategy**. This essentially is the auditor devising the way in which the audit will be tackled. It is considered to be a high-level approach. Once the audit strategy has been developed, the auditor then develops the detailed **audit plan**. The audit plan can be seen as the procedures that will be adopted in each area of the audit that will obtain the audit evidence needed.

The diagram below summarises the approach to developing an audit strategy:

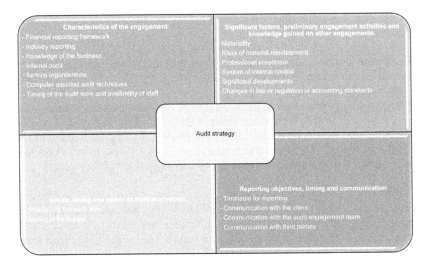

Developing a sound audit strategy should result in sufficient and appropriate resources being deployed on the engagement. Whilst the composition of the audit engagement team is a very important consideration, it also involves matters such as the following:

● How will the team be managed and supervised? How many audit managers and audit partners are (or need to be) involved?

● What is the timing of resource allocation? When will the interim and final audits be performed? Is there sufficient time set aside for review of the work?

● When will specialists be needed and when will their work be required for evaluation?

● Will resources be required in remote locations, or at specific times (such as to attend the stock count)?

Characteristics of the engagement

This is essentially the scope of the audit. It may just be the financial statements that need to be audited, or it could include other information, such as published reports. The audit may involve a simple standalone company whose financial statements need to be audited, or it could be a multi-national group with locations overseas. Hence, some engagements have specific characteristics which means the audit may have a wider scope than others the firm is engaged on.

There may be additional requirements to consider as well, such as whether the client is a listed company (therefore, regard must be had to the Listing Rules) or whether there are other industry-specific or other regulatory reporting requirements.

Significant factors, preliminary engagement activities, and knowledge gained on other engagements

Here, the auditor must bear in mind the results of other planning activities that have been performed, such as the determination of materiality, the results of risk assessments and preliminary analytical procedures. The assessment of the client's system of internal control is also particularly significant in this respect because this will determine the overall audit strategy that is developed.

The results of prior year audits can be very significant in determining the audit strategy. For example, if significant problems were encountered during the audit of the previous year, the reasons for those problems must be carefully considered for the current year audit. Conversely, the audit engagement team engaged on the prior year's audit may have assessed the client's system of internal control as being robust. While it would not be possible to rely on the controls again, the previous evaluation will have some bearing on the amount of work on controls that may be needed in the current year.

Nature, timing and extent of resources

The main issue here is to ensure that the audit strategy is developed in such a way that it results in the formation of an audit engagement team that possesses the necessary skills and resources to perform a high-quality audit. The tasks must also be allocated appropriately within the team. High-risk and more complex areas of the audit must be dealt with by more senior and experienced team members.

Timing is also a key feature of the audit strategy. If the audit is time-pressured due to a tight deadline (as is often the case with clients such as academy schools), then more resources will need to be allocated to ensure the work can be completed and reviewed in time to meet the necessary deadline.

The audit strategy must also consider how the resources are managed, directed and supervised, such as when team meetings and briefings are to be held; and how and when the partner and manager reviews are to take place. In addition, consideration must also be given as to how and when the engagement quality review will take place (if required).

Reporting objectives, timing and communications

There should be a clear timeline developed as to when reporting objectives are to be achieved. This is particularly important if there are tight deadlines by other regulatory bodies (such as the Financial Conduct Authority or Charity

Commission). Communications with the client should be developed in terms of updating the client and holding the audit clearance meeting where the financial statements and auditor's report may be signed off.

Example 6.8 – Extracts from an audit strategy document

The audit is to be carried out in accordance with International Standards on Auditing (UK). The sampling methodology is to be based on the prior year audit approach in accordance with the firm's methodology and we will aim for a 95% assurance level.

Overview of the audit

The audit will concentrate on:

- Carrying out risk assessment procedures.

- Testing assets and expenses for overstatement and liabilities and income for understatement.

- Documenting and evaluating the client's system of internal control.

- Obtaining audit evidence to support the relevant assertions.

- Forming a conclusion on the material areas of the financial statements and minimising audit risk to the maximum extent possible.

Key dates

The following milestones are relevant:

Audit fieldwork to commence	20 April 2024
Issue of draft report for management comments	12 May 2024
Final report to be issued for management comments	19 May 2024
Present audit findings to management	24 May 2024
Approval of the financial statements	25 May 2024

A review of the audit work will be performed by the audit senior and audit manager on a daily basis as each task is completed.

System of internal control

Management have asserted to us that they are committed to the design, implementation and maintenance of sound internal controls which will prevent, detect and correct, on a timely basis, misstatements. Internal control reviews are carried out internally on a quarterly basis and throughout the reporting period all controls have been subject to some internal review for operating effectiveness.

Stock count

The client's stock count will be taking place on 31 March 2024. Stock is located in three warehouses which are local to the audit firm. Each warehouse will be counted by members of staff from the finance department. Four auditors will be required to attend the stock count to ensure management's instructions are being carried out and the stock count reduces the risk of material misstatement of the final stock valuation to an acceptable level.

Financial reporting framework

The financial reporting framework to be used is FRS 102 *The Financial Reporting Standard applicable in the UK and Republic of Ireland.*

Materiality levels (based on forecast financial statements)

Financial statement materiality   £85,000

Performance materiality   £55,000

Fraud

Management and those charged with governance have responsibility for the design and implementation of internal controls which prevent and/or detect fraud and/or error and to ensure regulatory compliance. The audit team is to be informed by management of any fraud or material misstatement.

Management representations

ISA (UK) 580 *Written Representations* requires us to obtain representations from management and, where applicable, those charged with governance on material areas of the financial statements. We will require these written representations to be provided to us before we can sign the auditor's report.

Results of prior year audit

The prior year auditor's opinion was unqualified. The auditor's report included an Emphasis of Matter paragraph in respect of the entity's restructuring exercise which was deemed to be a material subsequent event.

Audit plan

6.11   Once the audit strategy has been developed, the detailed audit plan is produced. This can be thought of as a series of audit procedures which the auditor will apply over the various areas of the financial statements to obtain sufficient appropriate audit evidence. In other words, the audit plan contains the specific procedures to be carried out to implement the audit strategy and complete the audit.

IMPORTANT POINT

At all times, the auditor must ensure that the audit plan is developed with its prime objective in mind which is to **reduce audit risk to an acceptably low level**.

The establishment of the overall audit strategy and the detailed audit plan are not necessarily discrete or sequential but are closely interrelated since changes in one may result in consequential changes to the other. Hence, it may not necessarily be the case that the audit strategy is developed and then the audit plan. In practice, it is generally the case that the two are developed together.

ISA (UK) 300 requires the audit plan to describe:

● The nature, timing and extent of planned risk assessment procedures.

● The nature, timing and extent of planned further audit procedures at the assertion level, including:

— what audit procedures are to be carried out;

— who will carry those procedures out;

— how much work should be done (sample sizes, etc); and

— when the work should be done (eg, at interim or final audit).

● Any other planned audit procedures so that the engagement complies with the ISAs (UK).

ISA (UK) 300 also requires the auditor to plan the nature, timing and extent of direction and supervision of audit engagement team members together with a review of their work. This is to ensure that the requirements of ISA (UK) 220 *Quality Management for an Audit of Financial Statements* are fulfilled.

The amount of detail that is included in an audit plan will vary depending on the size and complexity of the audited entity as well as the assessed risks of material misstatement.

Example 6.9 – Extracts from an audit plan

Typically, an audit plan will include sections dealing with business understanding, risk assessment procedures, planned audit procedures and other mandatory audit procedures. Some examples are provided below (note – this is not a complete audit plan):

Procedures to obtain a business understanding

- Review of the entity's governance and management structure
- Confirmation of the applicable financial reporting framework
- Documentation of systems and controls
- Preliminary analytical review on the latest available management accounts

Risk assessment procedures

- Inquiries with management regarding financial and operating issues
- Discussion with internal audit with respect to their recent activities
- Analytical procedures on financial and non-financial information
- Review of information obtained in prior years (eg, past misstatements)

Planned audit procedures

- Circularisation of trade debtors
- Attendance at the year-end stock count
- Physical verification of a sample of additions to non-current assets
- Substantive analytical procedures on expenses included in operating profit

Other mandatory procedures

- Final analytical procedures
- Going concern review
- Subsequent events review
- Obtaining written representations from management and, where applicable, those charged with governance

Changes to the audit strategy and audit plan

6.12   Planning is viewed as a 'continual and iterative process' and so the audit strategy and audit plan are not 'fixed' once the planning phase of the audit is complete. They can both be seen as 'live' documents and must be updated and changed, as necessary, as the audit progresses. This could be, for example, due to unexpected events or changes in conditions. In addition, the auditor may decide that they wish to modify the overall audit strategy and audit plan because the risk assessment has changed.

Changes to the audit strategy and audit plan will often arise if information comes to the auditor's attention that differs significantly from the information available when the auditor initially planned the procedures (for example, an unidentified related party or a condition is identified that creates doubt over the entity's ability to continue as a going concern). Any changes to the audit strategy and/or audit plan must be carefully documented together with the reasons for the changes.

Planning the audit of disclosures

6.13   At the planning stage, the auditor must consider how they will carry out audit procedures over the disclosure notes contained in the financial statements. Remember, it is easy to become immersed in the audit of transactions and balances in the primary financial statements (profit and loss account, balance sheet, statement of changes in equity, cash flow statement and such like) and forget to devote appropriate planning to the audit of disclosures.

ISA (UK) 300 *Planning an Audit of Financial Statements* emphasises the importance of disclosures within the financial statements and requires the auditor to ensure there are sufficient resources available to audit those disclosures.

The audit of disclosures can be a problematic area for auditors, especially where disclosures are complex. For example, if the client has very complex disclosure notes (such as those relating to complex financial instruments or defined benefit pension plans).

Auditors will also need to factor in time to consider any related changes to disclosure requirements. For example, as the periodic review of UK and Ireland GAAP has now been finalised, amendments to the standards were issued on 27 March 2024. These amendments include additional disclosure requirements in certain areas (eg, FRS 102, Section 19 *Business Combinations and Goodwill*). The auditor must ensure they have adequate resources, such as an up-to-date disclosure checklist to verify the adequacy of the client's disclosures once the periodic review amendments are applied in the entity's financial statements.

IMPORTANT POINT

If the disclosure checklist is out of date, this will increase audit risk because there may be a material disclosure that is inadequate or is missing which may render an unmodified audit opinion incorrect.

REAL-LIFE FOCUS

Ms T is the audit engagement partner of a five-partner firm and was subjected to an audit monitoring visit by her professional body. The professional body reviewer selected three audit files for review.

In all three files, the reviewer was unable to locate a disclosure checklist. The response by Ms T was that her software is up-to-date and is capable of generating all the required disclosures, so the firm does not use a disclosure checklist.

Ms T's response would not be what the reviewer wants to hear. Audit clients tend to be medium-sized and large companies and groups and hence there will usually be inherent complexities attached to them. The disclosure notes are a critical feature of the financial statements and hence the most common way of auditing the adequacy and completeness of the disclosures is to use a disclosure checklist.

While a disclosure checklist does not necessarily have to be completed every year (if there have been no significant changes to the client's circumstances, it may be deemed appropriate to review last year's disclosure checklist or have a policy of completing a disclosure checklist every other audit if there have been no significant changes), simply not having one at all is reckless.

Due to other issues noted in Ms T's audit files, the firm was put on mandatory hot review and a subsequent follow-up visit from the professional body. This meant that all audit files had to be reviewed by a third party prior to the auditor's report being signed, with all deficiencies noted in the review being resolved. Only when the professional body was satisfied that audit standards were up to scratch would the firm have been released from these sanctions.

DESIGN OF AUDIT PROCEDURES

6.14   As noted above, at the planning stage of the audit, the auditor will design an audit plan which essentially documents the procedures that the auditor will adopt during the evidence-gathering stage to obtain sufficient appropriate audit evidence. Remember, this audit plan is not absolute and may change during the course of the audit if the auditor comes across transactions, events or conditions which suggest a change in audit approach is appropriate.

It is important to bear in mind that when developing the audit plan, the auditor is primarily interested in keeping audit risk down to an absolute minimum. To that end, the auditor designs responses to address the risks of material misstatement that have been identified at the planning and risk assessment stage.

Audit evidence primarily comes from two sources:

● Tests of controls; and

● Substantive procedures.

Substantive procedures are then sub-divided into:

● Tests of detail; and

● Analytical procedures.

Tests of control

6.15 Part of the audit risk model is **control risk**. The client's system of internal control is a vital component of the audit risk model because the system is the means by which the entity attempts to prevent, detect and correct (on a timely basis) a misstatement in the financial statements. Sound controls are necessary to safeguard the assets of the business (for example, by restricting access to high-value stock to only authorised employees).

All business will have some degree of internal control present. However, to be able to rely on the client's system of internal control, the auditor will need to:

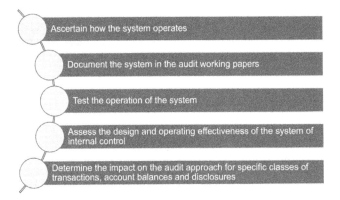

Ascertain how the system operates

Document the system in the audit working papers

Test the operation of the system

Assess the design and operating effectiveness of the system of internal control

Determine the impact on the audit approach for specific classes of transactions, account balances and disclosures

If the entity's system of internal control is deemed to be sound, it is less likely that the financial statements will contain material misstatements (although this cannot be absolute due to inherent risks, such as management override of internal control). Auditors may carry out **tests of control** to determine if controls have operated throughout the period. The design of these tests of control will be completed at the planning stage of the audit.

On the other hand, if the control environment is deemed to be weak or ineffective, auditors will not place reliance on the control environment. It would be a waste of audit resources to do so and so in such instances, a more substantive approach will be undertaken (see **6.16** and **6.17**).

Examples of tests of control include:

- Reviewing purchase invoices for evidence of authorisation by a responsible official.

- Reviewing payroll records for evidence that overtime payments have been authorised.

- Inspecting board minutes for approval of capital expenditure requirements or a restructuring.

- Reviewing a sample of month-end bank reconciliations to ensure they have been approved by a responsible official and for evidence that any reconciling items have been checked.

Example 6.10 – Test of control

During the audit of property, plant and equipment (tangible fixed assets), Sandeep, the audit senior reviewed a purchase invoice from a supplier amounting to £25,000. The objective of this test was to ensure that items of capital expenditure have been appropriately authorised during the year in line with the client's 'Delegation of Authority' document.

The fact that the invoice being tested is for £25,000 is irrelevant because it is the control over the capital expenditure cycle that is being tested (ie making sure the capital expenditure has been authorised).

IMPORTANT POINT

It is important to bear in mind that a test of control does **not** focus on the monetary amounts in the financial statements. As you can see from the example above, the focus of the test of control over the capital expenditure cycle was ascertaining whether the expenditure had been authorised in line with the client's Delegation of Authority document. This test did not test anything in the financial statements.

A test of control can, however, provide **indirect** evidence over the financial statements. This is because the auditor can assume that if the controls are operating effectively, there is less risk of material misstatement in the financial statements.

The auditor must also bear in mind that when planning to place reliance on a client's system of internal control, no system can be said to be 100% effective; as mentioned earlier, that is one of the inherent limitations of an audit. In addition, management override of internal control is viewed as a **significant risk** per ISA (UK) 240 *The Auditor's Responsibilities Relating to Fraud in an Audit of Financial Statements*.

Substantive procedure: Tests of detail

6.16   Tests of detail are used by auditors to gather sufficient appropriate audit evidence that the balances, disclosures and underlying transactions contained in the client's financial statements are correct. For example, the auditor may trace an addition to fixed assets to a purchase invoice to test the **rights and obligations** assertion (this is done by ensuring the invoice is in the name of the company, which proves the company owns the asset). In addition, the **value and allocation** assertion can be tested by ensuring that the item is capitalised at an appropriate value in line with FRS 102, Section 17 *Property, Plant and Equipment*.

Example 6.11 – Capitalisation of development expenditure

The audit senior is auditing the development expenditure in the draft financial statements of Dwyer Ltd (a new audit client for the firm) for the year ended 31 December 2023. During the year, the company has capitalised a material amount of development expenditure and the audit engagement partner has flagged this area of the financial statements as a high-risk area. This risk classification has been done on the grounds that the prior year's auditor's report was qualified 'except for' as the client had incorrectly capitalised research expenditure, in contravention of FRS 102, Section 18 *Intangible Assets other than Goodwill* and the directors refused to correct the material misstatement.

The key assertion for development costs is **existence**. Development costs can only be capitalised under FRS 102 (as an accounting policy choice) if they meet the recognition criteria. The following are the principal tests of detail the auditor could apply over the intangible assets of Dwyer Ltd:

- Obtain a breakdown of costs capitalised during the year, cast the schedule for mathematical accuracy and agree the amount included in the financial statements (verifies **valuation**).

- For a sample of costs, agree to invoices or timesheets (verifies **valuation**).

- Obtain the board minutes, inspect them for evidence of any discussions relating to the intended use or sale of the asset (verifies **existence**).

- Obtain details of the project(s) and assess compliance with FRS 102, Section 18 (verifies **existence**).

- Obtain the project plans and other documentation to evaluate compliance with FRS 102, Section 18 (verifies **existence**).

- Obtain budgets and review to confirm financial feasibility (verifies **existence**).

For other intangible assets, the auditor may:

- Inspect purchase invoices for purchased intangible assets (verifies **existence**, **rights and obligations** and **valuation**).

- Inspect any valuer's reports and agree the amount stated with the amount in the general ledger (verifies **valuation**).

Substantive procedure: Substantive analytical procedures

6.17 Remember, analytical procedures (see **6.8** above) are used to identify trends and to understand relationships between sets of data. They are a great tool for the auditor as they can indicate potential sources of misstatement.

Analytical procedures must be applied at the planning stage as risk assessment procedures to comply with the requirements of ISA (UK) 315.

Substantive analytical procedures can also be used during the evidence-gathering stage to gather sufficient appropriate audit evidence which is where ISA (UK) 520 *Analytical Procedures* kicks in. Caution is advised where the auditor plans to do this. All too often, firms are criticised for over-reliance on substantive analytical procedures that are essentially irrelevant because they are based on information that would not give rise to analytical procedures being appropriate.

Example 6.12 – High level of staff turnover

'Proof in total' is a reasonableness test that is a substantive analytical procedure which is often used when auditing payroll. The auditor will create an expectation of payroll costs during the year by taking last year's payroll expense from profit or loss, inflating this number for pay increases during the year and changes in staff numbers.

If there are high levels of staff turnover, or inconsistent staff numbers or pay rates during the year, a proof in total test is likely to be unreliable because it will invariably determine an expected figure that bears little resemblance to the figure in the profit or loss account. Hence, a more effective substantive procedure, such as recalculation or reperformance of the payroll expense may be more effective.

There are four steps that must be taken when devising substantive analytical procedures, which you may sometimes see as 'predict, compare and judge'.

Step 1: Develop an independent expectation

The development of an appropriately precise and objective expectation is fundamental when using substantive analytical procedures. An 'expectation' is a prediction of a recorded amount or ratio and can be a specific number, a percentage, a direction or an approximation.

IMPORTANT POINT

Keep in mind that whenever the auditor uses substantive analytical procedures, they must always have an expectation to work with in order to identify plausible relationships.

Step 2: Define a significant difference or threshold

The auditor should always consider the amount of difference from the expectation they are willing to accept without having to perform further audit procedures. This is often referred to as 'tolerable error' or a 'threshold' and may be defined as a numerical value or as a percentage of the items being tested.

Establishing a threshold is important to ensure effective use of substantive analytical procedures. It is also particularly important that the threshold does not exceed **performance materiality**.

IMPORTANT POINT

The threshold must be sufficiently small to enable the auditor to identify misstatements which could be material, either individually or when aggregated.

Step 3: Calculate the difference

This is where the auditor compares the expected value with the recorded amounts and identifies the difference, if any. The calculation of the difference should be done after consideration of an expectation and a threshold.

IMPORTANT POINT

When the auditor is using substantive analytical procedures, it would be inappropriate to first calculate the difference from the prior year balances and then allow the results to influence the expected difference and acceptable threshold.

Step 4: Investigate any significant differences and draw conclusions

The final step is the investigation of significant differences and the auditor's conclusions thereon. Differences indicate an increased likelihood of misstatements and must be investigated.

IMPORTANT POINT

The auditor must obtain explanations/corroboratory reasons for the *full* difference, not just the amount of the difference which exceeds the tolerable threshold. Remember, any unexplained difference may indicate an increased risk of material misstatement.

Substantive analytical procedures are useful for assessing several assertions at once, because the auditor is effectively auditing a whole account balance or class of transactions to assess if it is reasonable. The objective of substantive analytical procedures is to identify unusual items which can then be investigated further to ensure that a misstatement in the balance does not exist.

Example 6.13 – Substantive analytical procedures

The audit of Greaves Industries Ltd for the year ended 31 December 2023 is at the planning stage. The audit engagement partner has stated that the audit approach must be a combination of tests of controls and substantive procedures, which must include substantive analytical procedures. The audit engagement partner has identified various risks at the planning stage, including:

- a fall in the demand for the company's products;

- a risk of material misstatement in the year-end stock valuation should the stock count not be properly co-ordinated;

- a change in the company's accounting system, which proved to be problematic;

- incorrect capitalisation of research expenditure in the prior year, which could still be material in the current year, hence a potential modification of the auditor's opinion;

- additional research expenditure which may have been capitalised in the current year in contravention of FRS 102, Section 18 *Intangible Assets other than Goodwill*; and

- outsourcing of the payroll function.

Substantive analytical procedures which could be used in the audit of Greaves Industries Ltd include:

- Calculation of gross profit margins and investigating any significant differences.

- Calculating the change in percentage of purchases during the year and assessing if the change is in line with the change in sales.

- Performing a proof in total of the depreciation/amortisation charges to assess their reasonableness.

- Performing a proof in total of wages and salaries, incorporating joiners and leavers and the annual pay increase. Compare this to the actual payroll charge in the profit and loss account and investigate any significant differences.

FRAUD

6.18   Fraud – a subject that can send shivers down many accountants' and auditors' spines. Nobody likes to talk about fraud and experiencing fraud (whether it is personal or within a business) is a particularly unpleasant experience. I examine fraud in much more detail in **Chapter 9**, but for now we need to consider the auditor's responsibilities at the planning stage where fraud is concerned.

This book deliberately avoids citing major parts of an ISA (UK), but the definition of 'fraud' according to ISA (UK) 240 *The Auditor's Responsibilities Relating to Fraud in an Audit of Financial Statements* is quite straightforward to understand. It defines 'fraud' as:

An intentional act by one or more individuals among management, those charged with governance, employees, or third parties, involving the use of deception to obtain an unjust or illegal advantage.[1]

This definition is quite broad and includes both management and those charged with governance, which acknowledges that fraud can be, and often is, conducted by senior people within the organisation.

Generally, fraud committed by a member of management or those charged with governance of the entity arises through overriding the system of internal control. The senior status of the person within the organisation allows management override to take place, because subordinates will generally not question their intentions. ISA (UK) 240 recognises that management override of internal control is a significant risk and hence the auditor must devise procedures at the planning stage which respond to this risk.

The auditor's risk assessment procedures for fraud

6.19   The auditor is required to consider fraud risk factors when carrying out their risk assessment at the planning stage of the audit. Unfortunately, there is no exhaustive list available to auditors that provides definitive indicators that a fraud is present at an audit client. ISA (UK) 200 *Overall Objectives of the Independent Auditor and the Conduct of an Audit in Accordance with International Standards on Auditing (UK)* defines 'professional scepticism' and ISA (UK) 240 requires the auditor to maintain professional scepticism throughout the audit. Maintaining a questioning mind and not relying on the past integrity and honesty of management and, where applicable, those charged with governance, will help the auditor to identify indicators of fraud. I examine typical fraud risk factors in **Chapter 9**.

Discussion among the engagement team

ISA (UK) 240 requires that there is a discussion among the audit engagement team focussing on fraud. Engagement team members may discuss matters including management incentives to commit fraud, factors relating to the business environment and how frauds **could** be perpetrated. This discussion must involve the audit engagement partner and should be an exchange of ideas. It should take place regardless of the past experience of the client and the level of trust the auditor may have in the integrity of management and those charged with governance. The discussion can also be particularly useful for more junior members of the audit team because they can learn from the insights of more experienced team members.

---

1 ISA (UK) 240, para 12(a).

IMPORTANT POINT

Remember, the discussion should be about how fraud **could** arise at the client, even if there has been no past history of frauds. For example:

● Fictitious suppliers being set up on the purchase ledger

● Ghost employees being set up on the payroll

● Controls becoming ineffective during the year

● Aggressive accounting policies or a large number of changes in accounting policies

● Ineffective monitoring of assets such as cash or computer equipment

● Weak passwords on critical programs, such as the online banking system

---

When planning the audit, planning procedures (such as preliminary analytical review) may indicate the possibility of fraud. For example, if a company's operating profit margin unexpectedly reduces due to increased payroll costs, this could be due to a ghost employee fraud.

It is fundamental that the auditor obtains a good level of business understanding when planning the audit. Knowledge of the business environment may lead the auditor to conclude that there are specific circumstances which increase the risk of fraud. For example, if the company is facing financial difficulties, there will be pressure on management to present a good picture of the company's financial performance and position, which creates a motivation for fraudulent financial reporting.

Revenue

ISA (UK) 240 singles out one area of the financial statements that the auditor must consider, which is revenue. The presumption that there are fraud risks in revenue recognition can be rebutted, but it is not usually a good idea to rebut this presumption because it can lead the auditor ignoring a risky area that is susceptible to fraud.

Revenue is at risk of deliberate over or understatement. Overstatement could occur, for example, if revenue is deliberately recognised too early, perhaps to boost poor performance or to maximise a bonus based on revenue growth. Conversely, if may be understated to reduce profits, perhaps to reduce tax payable. Where the business is cash-based, revenue may be more susceptible to manipulation. I examine fraud and revenue recognition in more detail in **Chapter 9** (see **9.15**).

Responding to the assessed risks of material misstatement due to fraud

6.20   Assessing the risks of material misstatement in the financial statements due to fraud is one side of a two-pronged fork. The second step involves the auditor considering how the assessed risks impacts the audit plan. Remember, the audit plan is the document that essentially sets out the procedures the auditor will undertake during the audit.

There are many factors the auditor must consider when responding to the assessed risks of material misstatement. For example:

- An entity with little regard to a sound system of internal control may be more likely to have several fraud risk factors.

- If management appear to come across as aggressive, this could indicate they have something to hide.

- Economic pressure may increase fraud risk – especially if the entity is expected to report a certain level of profit or net assets to shareholders or other interested parties.

- The audit client may be suffering financial distress which could heighten the risk of fraudulent financial reporting (especially if they are considering approaching the bank or another financier for funding).

Clearly the above list of factors is not comprehensive, and each audit will present its own fraud risks. Remember, though, when the auditor discovers a fraud risk **factor**, this does not necessarily mean a fraud has been committed; it merely means the risk of fraud is higher **because of** the fraud risk factor. In this case, the auditor will more than likely apply more substantive procedures rather than rely on controls.

Responses to the assessed risks of fraud will generally mean the auditor will assign more senior and experienced personnel to the audit engagement – especially on those areas where the auditor has identified risks of material misstatement due to fraud. This is not necessarily the only 'tool' in the auditor's metaphoric toolbox. The auditor can apply unpredictable audit procedures, such as a 'surprise' cash count or a non-routine inspection of fixed assets.

IMPORTANT POINT

An important part of the auditor's risk assessment where fraud is concerned is considering the system of internal control; specifically, the risk of management override of controls. The auditor must bear in mind that management is in a unique position to be able to carry out fraudulent

---

financial reporting and override controls. In **Chapter 9**, I examine the 'fraud triangle' (see **9.6**); one of the three elements of the fraud triangle is 'opportunity' and management have this opportunity available to them. Management fraud can be covered up through the use of inappropriate or unauthorised journals and it is for this reason the auditor must carry out a careful review of journal entries.

At the planning stage of the audit, there are some (non-comprehensive) factors which auditors should look out for when devising responses to fraud risks. They include the following:

- Financial distress of a client as this provides a motive for management to manipulate the financial statements to show a better profit (or a reduced loss), higher assets and less liabilities.

- Management has the power to override internal controls and hence can make adjustments to the financial statements by way of journal entry in the accounting system (and in many cases, without authorisation).

- Reversals of impairment losses may indicate a fraud risk factor because such reversals are unusual. Reasons such as '… *we are using a new model to determine recoverable amount*' are often invalid.

- Several small adjustments throughout the year could accumulate into a large impact on profit or loss and reported net assets or liabilities.

- In a group, intercompany transactions can be used as a mechanism for moving transactions around the group that may indicate a fraud risk factor.

- Large, round-sum items that are frequently posted by journal could indicate a fraud risk factor.

- Management may have an idea of the auditor's method of calculating materiality and could 'pre-empt' the auditor's materiality threshold. Where the auditor suspects malpractice within the accounting records, it would be appropriate to use a different method of calculating materiality levels.

IMPORTANT POINT

The auditor is required to devise appropriate responses to the assessed risks of material misstatement due to fraud and this, to all intents and purposes, will be down to the auditor's professional judgement. However, ISA (UK) 240, para 33 does require the auditor to carry out the following procedures as a minimum, regardless of the auditor's assessment as to the risk of management override of controls:

(a) Testing the appropriateness of manual or automated journal entries and other adjustments that have been made when preparing the financial statements. This includes consolidation adjustments as well when the parent is preparing the consolidated financial statements. These tests must include:

   (i) inquiries of individuals within the organisation with differing levels of responsibility who are involved in the financial reporting process concerning any inappropriate or unusual activity relating to journal entries and other adjustments;

   (ii) testing the appropriateness of journal entries and other adjustments made at the balance sheet date; and

   (iii) considering the need to test the appropriateness of journal entries and other adjustments made throughout the reporting period.

(b) Reviewing accounting estimates (such as revenue in a construction contract) for evidence of management bias. If the auditor discovers such bias, they must consider whether this represents a risk of material misstatement due to fraud. In addition, the auditor must also:

   (i) evaluate the judgements and decisions made by management when arriving at the accounting estimate to determine whether this indicates a possible bias which may represent a risk of material misstatement due to fraud. If it does, the auditor must re-evaluate the accounting estimates as a whole; and

   (ii) carry out a retrospective review of management judgements and assumptions which relate to significant accounting estimates in the prior year.

(c) Where the auditor comes across significant transactions that are outside the normal course of business, or that otherwise appear to be unusual or inconsistent with the auditor's understanding of the business and the environment in which it operates, the auditor must evaluate whether the business rationale (or lack thereof) suggests the transactions may have been entered into to engage in fraud (either fraudulent financial reporting or misappropriation of the entity's assets).

Fraud and related parties

6.21 There is an interaction with fraud and ISA (UK) 550 *Related Parties*. At the planning stage of the audit, it is important that the audit engagement team discuss the susceptibility of the financial statements to material misstatement due to fraud in respect of transactions with related parties. But why?

ISA (UK) 550 recognises that the nature of related party relationships and transactions can, in some cases, give rise to a higher risk of material misstatement in the financial statements than transactions with unrelated parties. For example:

- Related parties may operate through a complex structure (such as a complex group structure) and such transactions could be inherently complex.

- IT systems may be ineffective at identifying transactions with related parties and identifying balances outstanding at the reporting date with such parties.

- Related party transactions may not necessarily be conducted on an arm's length basis. In some cases, related party transactions may be undertaken without a price being charged.

ISA (UK) 550 acknowledges that it is important the auditor obtains an understanding of the entity and its related parties and transactions with those related parties. This understanding is essential for the auditor to consider whether there are any fraud risk factors associated with the entity's related parties. Remember, the key issue here is that fraud committed through related parties is more easily carried out than other types of fraud.

To that end, there must be evidence of a discussion among the engagement team that they have considered the susceptibility of the financial statements to fraud among related parties.

REAL-LIFE FOCUS

Professional bodies frequently criticise audit files for a failure to demonstrate that a discussion among the engagement team has taken place concerning fraud. In some cases, the audit file will simply state that fraud is not expected and in many cases, it is not apparent from the file that a discussion concerning fraud in respect of related parties has taken place at all.

Holding a team discussion as to *how* fraud *could* arise, not only in general, but also with related parties, demonstrates the exercising of professional scepticism. Remember, regulators and professional bodies place a lot of emphasis on professional scepticism and reports are frequently critical of auditors that fail to demonstrate they have exercised professional scepticism.

CHAPTER ROUNDUP

- The planning phase of the audit is made up of several stages including documenting systems and controls, designing audit procedures, calculating materiality and considering fraud.

- Financial statement and performance materiality must be calculated at the planning stage and revised during the audit, if necessary. Materiality is a wholly judgemental issue and is primarily based on risk.

- Analytical procedures must be applied at two stages of the audit (planning and completion). Analytical procedures may be used during the evidence-gathering stage if appropriate. Analytical procedures can be based on financial and non-financial data.

- At the planning stage, the audit strategy is developed which is a document that explains how the audit will be tackled. Following the audit strategy, the detailed audit plan will be produced (although, in a lot of cases, issues dealt with in the audit strategy can also feed into development of the audit plan at the same time).

- The audit strategy and audit plan must be changed during the course of the audit if previously unknown issues come to light. Materiality levels must also be considered. Any changes to the audit plan and materiality must be sufficiently documented in the working papers.

- Audit procedures developed by the auditor will consist of tests of controls and substantive procedures. Substantive procedures are sub-divided into tests of details and analytical procedures.

- At an early stage in the audit planning, the audit engagement team must consider the susceptibility of the financial statements to material misstatement due to fraud.

- Fraud can arise generally through management override of internal controls or employee manipulation of weaknesses in controls.

- Fraud encompasses both fraudulent financial reporting and misappropriation of assets.

- The audit engagement team must discuss how the financial statements could contain material misstatement due to fraud among related parties (as well as fraud in general).

PITFALLS TO AVOID

- Failing to document the discussion among the engagement team at the planning stage in respect of the susceptibility of the financial statements to material misstatement due to fraud.

- Forgetting to calculate performance materiality.

- Seeking to place reliance on weak internal controls.

- Failing to understand the key differences between a test of control and a substantive procedure.

- Relying on the previous experience and past integrity and honesty of management where fraud is concerned.

Chapter 7

Audit Evidence

CHAPTER TOPIC LIST

- Introduction (see **7.1**).

- Audit evidence that responds to assessed risks (see **7.2**).

- Sufficient and appropriate audit evidence (see **7.5**).

- Obtaining audit evidence (see **7.10**).

- Types of audit procedures (see **7.17**).

- Corroborating audit evidence (see **7.20**).

- Applying professional judgement (see **7.21**).

- Risk and audit evidence (see **7.22**).

- Audit sampling (see **7.23**).

- Directional testing (see **7.33**).

- Interim audit (see **7.38**).

INTRODUCTION

7.1   While every stage of the audit process is important, the evidence-gathering stage is probably *the* most important. It is the audit evidence obtained during the course of the assignment that the audit engagement partner will base their opinion on and is obtained through the audit procedures applied through the audit plan.

The primary objective of the auditor is to obtain audit evidence that is **sufficient** and **appropriate**. I'll examine what 'sufficient' and 'appropriate' mean later in the chapter but, for now, it is important to remember that audit evidence will provide the auditor with information about whether (or not, as the case may be) the financial statements are free from material misstatement, whether caused by fraud or error; and whether (or not, as the case may be) that the financial statements have been prepared in accordance with the applicable financial reporting framework (such as FRS 102 *The Financial Reporting Standard applicable in the UK and Republic of Ireland*).

WHAT ARE WE TRYING TO ACHIEVE?

The auditor must ensure that they obtain sufficient appropriate audit evidence on which to base their audit opinion. This is achieved by applying various audit procedures to generate and/or gather this evidence.

In **Chapters 5** and **6**, I examined the procedures that are involved in audit planning. During the planning phase of the audit, the auditor must develop a thorough understanding of the client, the environment in which it operates and the nature of the client's system of internal control. This understanding essentially drives the development of the audit strategy and the audit plan. The audit plan contains the detailed audit procedures the auditor will perform to generate the audit evidence.

AUDIT EVIDENCE THAT RESPONDS TO ASSESSED RISKS

7.2   ISA (UK) 330 *The Auditor's Responses to Assessed Risks* provides guidance to the auditor on how to design audit procedures. The ISA (UK) requires the auditor to obtain sufficient appropriate audit evidence (see **7.10** below) concerning the assessed risks of material misstatement. This is done by designing and implementing **responses** to those assessed risks.

There are two levels at which the auditor must respond to assessed levels of risk:

Responding to risks at the financial statement level

7.3   These are also known as 'overall responses'. They are responses to risks that potentially pervade the whole financial statements (ie, they are not specific to a particular transaction or balance). The auditor's risk assessment may suggest many different factors that create risks at the financial statement level and may include the following (note the list below is not comprehensive):

● **Going concern difficulties**

Going concern difficulties may increase the risk of management bias. For example, management may wish to overstate profit (or understate losses) or overstate assets and understate liabilities to present a more promising picture in the financial statements.

● **Lack of management competence**

Where management lack competence in the financial reporting process, there is a higher risk that the financial statements could be prepared incorrectly, particularly where there may be complex transactions (such as a defined benefit pension plan or complex financial instruments measured at fair value).

● **Risk of management override of internal controls**

I have covered this quite a lot in **Chapters 5** and **6** and the risk of management override of internal controls is always considered a significant risk. If controls can be easily overridden (for example if there is a lack of segregation of duties), this can result in the financial statements containing material misstatements (some of which may be down to fraud).

● **Exceptional items**

Exceptional items are items which are not expected to reoccur in the future (such as a major restructuring). These unusual transactions are at risk of incorrect accounting treatments or a lack of disclosure.

You can see from the above points that these examples all could lead to misstatements in many areas of the financial statements, rather than just specific transactions or balances.

The auditor's responses to risks identified at the financial statement level may vary, but would typically include the following:

Professional scepticism

Emphasising the need for the audit engagement team to maintain professional scepticism at all times (especially where fraud risks are identified)

Assigning more experienced members

The auditor would use more experienced team members (or assign experts) for more complex areas of the financial statements or where subjectivity is needed

Unpredictability

The auditor is likely to use more unpredictable testing, particularly in riskier areas

Additional supervision

The auditor may increase the amount of supervision to ensure high levels of risk have been identified and adequately dealt with in the audit

Nature, timing and extent of procedures

The auditor may decide to perform more substantive procedures rather than relying on tests of control

Responding to risks at the assertion level

7.4   Again, ISA (UK) 330 requires the auditor to respond to the assessed risks of material misstatement arising at the financial statement **assertion** level.

Financial statement **assertions** are basically claims made by management in the financial statements. **Chapter 5** covers the financial statement assertions in **5.21** and they are split as follows:

- Assertions about classes of transactions, events and related disclosures;

- Assertions about account balances and related disclosures; and

- Assertions about disclosures.

Head back to **Chapter 5** if you need to refresh your knowledge on the financial statement assertions because they are a very important part of the audit.

For example, if the financial statements record a freehold building in the balance sheet, management are asserting that they have the **right** to include this building in the financial statements (through the **rights and obligations** assertion) by way of capitalising the building on the balance sheet.

Responses to this assertion will be the auditor checking title deeds to ensure that the company does, in fact, own the building. If the title deeds do show that the company owns the building, the auditor can be satisfied that the freehold building is correctly capitalised on the balance sheet.

ISA (UK) 330 says that the auditor must design and perform further audit procedures '*... whose nature, timing and extent are responsive to the assessed risks of material misstatement at the assertion level.*'[1]

I think it's important to examine what the ISA (UK) means when it refers to the 'nature, timing and extent'.

The **nature** of a procedures relates to its purpose and its type. The *purpose* of a procedure relates to whether the procedure is a test of control or a substantive procedure (see **Chapters 5** and **6**). The *type* of procedure relates to what the procedure actually involves; for example, it could be an observation test, an inspection or a reperformance etc. I'll take a look in more detail about these types of procedures later in the chapter.

The **timing** of an audit procedure refers to when the auditor will perform it. For example, an audit procedure may be carried out at the interim stage (such as a debtors' circularisation) or at the completion stage (such as the going concern assessment).

The **extent** of an audit procedure relates to the amount of work that will be carried out. For example, if the auditor determines that an audit procedure must be extended, they will typically increase the sample size to ensure correct conclusions can be drawn from the audit procedure.

SUFFICIENT AND APPROPRIATE AUDIT EVIDENCE

7.5   ISA (UK) 500 *Audit Evidence* requires the auditor to design and perform audit procedures which will result in the auditor obtaining **sufficient appropriate** audit evidence to draw conclusions on which the auditor's opinion will be based.

The two emboldened phrases are 'sufficient' and 'appropriate'. But what is sufficient appropriate audit evidence and how does the auditor know when they have sufficient appropriate audit evidence?

---

1 ISA (UK) 330, para 6 (excerpt).

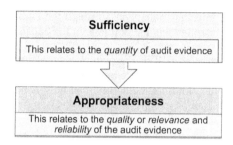

IMPORTANT POINT

Auditors and audit clients must bear in mind that audit evidence would be **persuasive** rather than conclusive. This is one of the inherent limitations of an audit because the auditor does not test everything in the financial statements. They use sampling techniques primarily to obtain audit evidence (see **7.23**).

Obtaining audit evidence is a **cumulative** process and the auditor can obtain audit evidence from many different sources, including:

• The accounting records themselves (nominal ledger, journal entries and supporting documentation).

• Minutes of meetings.

• External confirmations from third parties.

• Analysts' reports.

• Comparable information concerning competitors.

• Controls manuals.

• Information from prior year audits.

• Evidence generated by the auditor through observation, inquiry, inspection and such like.

Sufficient audit evidence

7.6   The audit opinion must be based on the audit evidence obtained during the audit. To that end there needs to be 'enough' audit evidence to support the conclusion. The auditor can think of the audit file as a book which aims to tell the story of how the audit opinion was arrived at. Clearly, arriving at the conclusion for each audit area is going to involve professional judgement. When determining whether audit evidence is sufficient, the auditor must consider:

(a)   the risk of material misstatement;

(b)   the materiality of the item;

(c)   the client's system of internal control;

(d)   whether tests of control have revealed operating weaknesses;

(e)   the auditor's knowledge and experience of the client;

(f)   the size of the population being tested;

(g)   the size of the sample selected to test; and

(h)   the reliability of the evidence obtained.

Example 7.1 – Auditing the bank balance

Ebony Watson is the audit semi-senior of Carcassonne & Co Accountancy Services. She is auditing the cash at bank figure in the balance sheet of Toulouse Limited for the year ended 30 April 2024. Due to the risk assessment, the audit manager concluded that a bank audit letter (sometimes referred to as a 'bank confirmation letter' or 'bank letter') is necessary this year, which has been received. The balance on the bank audit letter has been agreed to the year-end bank statement and the semi-senior has stated that in her opinion this is sufficient.

While a bank audit letter is a good source of audit evidence (because it is externally generated and sent directly to the auditor), it is *insufficient* to provide assurance regarding the **completeness** and final **valuation** of bank balances. There may well be timing differences resulting in a difference between the balance per the bank statement/bank audit letter and the cash book balance per the trial balance.

Ebony should also obtain year-end bank reconciliations for all bank accounts and review these by tracing any reconciling items to after-date cash payments/receipts, checking casts on the bank reconciliation and reperforming the year-end bank reconciliation.

In combination, this work (in addition to the bank audit letter) will provide sufficient audit evidence over the bank balances recorded in Toulouse's balance sheet.

Example 7.2 – Related parties

The draft financial statements of Catalan Limited for the year ended 30 April 2024 show no disclosures in respect of related party transactions. The audit-semi senior, Kelly, has held a discussion with the finance director who has confirmed there were no related parties and has agreed to provide a written representation to that effect. Kelly has concluded that this is sufficient audit evidence.

Written representations and inquiries are weak forms of audit evidence which would not constitute sufficient audit evidence on their own and are generally used when there is limited (or no) audit evidence available which would not be the case for related parties. While 'inquiry' is a valid audit procedure under ISA (UK) 500, on its own it is a weak form of audit procedure because it generates internal responses from the client. Inquiry should, therefore, serve to complement other forms of audit procedure.

ISA (UK) 580 *Written Representations* also confirms that written representations, on their own, are necessary audit evidence, but do not provide sufficient appropriate audit evidence on their own about any of the matters with which they deal.

Both inquiry and written representations in respect of a subjective (and usually material) area such as related parties would be insufficient to conclude there have been no related party transactions during the year. Kelly would need to carry out further procedures, such as:

- Reviewing accounting records for evidence of transactions with related parties.

- Inspecting board minutes or evidence of any undisclosed related parties or transactions with those related parties.

- Discussing the schedule of related parties with the finance director to ensure completeness.

- Carrying out searches on the directors via the public record (such as Companies House) to identify any other entities in which the directors have an interest and reviewing accounting records to identify any transactions with those companies.

- Reviewing the bank audit letter (if obtained) for evidence of any related parties.

- Reviewing the prior year's audit file to identify any related parties and establishing whether there have been any transactions with those related parties in the year.

IMPORTANT POINT

It is important that the auditor bears in mind that where a subjective area of the financial statements is concerned (such as in the example above in connection with related parties), audit risk is increased. Audit risk is the risk that the auditor forms an incorrect opinion on the financial statements. This is because if sufficient appropriate audit evidence is not obtained, the auditor may express an unqualified (unmodified) opinion incorrectly as further audit procedures may contradict the response by management or the written representation.

Appropriate audit evidence

7.7   Appropriate audit evidence is sub-divided into two components:

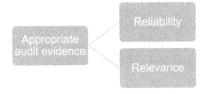

Reliability

7.8   Auditors should always try, wherever possible, to obtain audit evidence from the most trustworthy and dependable source possible. Audit evidence is generally considered to be more reliable when it is:

(a)   Obtained from an independent and external source.

(b)   Generated internally by the client, but is subject to an effective system of internal control.

(c)   Obtained directly by the auditor.

(d)   Is provided in documentary form, rather than orally.

(e)   Is an original document (not a photocopy or a scanned document).

The more reliable the audit evidence which the auditor can collate as part of their audit procedures, the less of it they will need.

IMPORTANT POINT

Keep in mind that if the audit evidence is unreliable, it will never be appropriate, no matter how much of it the auditor gathers.

Relevance

7.9 To be relevant, audit evidence must address the objective or purpose of an audit procedure.

Example 7.3 – Auditor's attendance at the year-end stock count

Three members of the audit engagement team have attended Revere Ltd's year-end stock count (see also **Chapter 8**, at **8.21**). The procedures involve selecting items that have already been counted and tracing them from the count sheets to the physical stock and vice versa.

- Selecting items from the count sheets to the physical stock confirms the **existence** of the stock at the count date.

- Selecting items from the physical stock to the count sheets confirms the **completeness** of the stock at the count date.

As you can see, while the procedures look (on the face of it) to be similar in nature, their purpose (and hence **relevance**) is to test different assertions (existence and completeness) concerning the year-end stock valuation.

- **Real-life focus**

In December 2022, ACCA issued their *Audit monitoring reviews – quarterly update*. These quarterly updates identify the most common issues that ACCA's compliance team identify during audit monitoring reviews.

The December 2022 report identifies **completeness** and **valuation** testing as an area of weakness where ISA (UK) 500 is concerned. The report highlights the following specific issues:

- **No attendance at stocktake and no (or poor) alternative procedures to test existence of stock**

As noted in the example above, the auditor's attendance at stock count enables the auditor to obtain audit evidence concerning the existence (as well as the completeness) of stock held at the balance sheet date. If the auditor does not attend the stock count, there will be no evidence supporting the means by which stock was valued at the year end and may constitute a limitation of scope (resulting in a qualified opinion) if alternative procedures cannot be applied.

● **Not appropriately assessing stock obsolescence**

Most financial reporting frameworks (including FRS 102 *The Financial Reporting Standard applicable in the UK and Republic of Ireland*) require stock to be valued at the lower of cost and estimated selling price less costs to complete and sell (or 'net realisable value'). If stock is slow-moving, damaged or obsolete then estimated selling price could be lower than cost and hence a write-down to estimated selling price may be needed in order to avoid stock being overvalued in the year-end financial statements.

If the auditor fails to appropriately assess stock for obsolescence, there may be a material overstatement in the final valuation.

● **Accepting third-party evidence via the client**

As noted above, external audit evidence is generally more reliable. Third-party evidence should be sent directly to the auditor rather than the client. If it is sent directly to the client, there is a risk that this evidence can be tampered with.

● **Income and creditor testing not done outside of the accounting records to test for what's not there**

Income and creditors are primarily tested for **completeness (understatement)**. So, for income, the auditor is primarily concerned with goods and/or services that have been provided to customers that have not been invoiced (ie, income is tested directly for understatement – see 'Directional testing' in **7.33** below). Creditors are also tested directly for understatement to identify any creditors that may not have been provided for in the financial statements (ie, goods and/or services received by the year end which have not been invoiced).

If testing is not started from outside of the accounting records, the completeness assertion is not adequately covered so the auditor must ensure that the correct starting point (ie, the *source* of the transaction) is used such as a customer order for a sale or a goods received note for a creditor.

● **Recoverability of trade debtors and amounts owed from related parties not sufficiently reviewed**

The primary test for trade debtors (including amounts owed from related parties) is that of **valuation**. Remember, assets are tested directly for

overstatement and the risk that concerns the auditor is that trade debtors may be included in current assets which may be irrecoverable (ie, they should be written off as a bad debt). This also applies to amounts owed from related parties.

For related parties, the principal audit risk is that they are not disclosed adequately and hence audit procedures must adequately address this risk.

- **Valuation of properties and title to properties at/after the year end not considered**

Again, properties in the balance sheet must have the **valuation** assertion covered adequately to ensure they are carried in the balance sheet at a reasonable value (especially where the properties may be measured under the revaluation model). Remember as well, the auditor is also primarily concerned with the **rights and obligations** assertion so any capitalised properties must be agreed to title deeds to ensure they are in the name of the company and hence qualify for recognition on the balance sheet.

IMPORTANT POINT

Sufficiency and appropriateness should not be considered in isolation. For example, the more reliable the source of evidence, a lesser quantity of evidence may need to be gathered.

For example, if the auditor is obtaining evidence in relation to a lease that has been entered into during the year, the auditor should obtain an original signed copy of that lease. This would be construed as being a reliable source of evidence and limited further procedures will need to be performed.

However, if the client presents the auditor with a scanned copy of the lease (or cannot produce the lease in any form at all), further audit procedures will likely need to be carried out.

OBTAINING AUDIT EVIDENCE

7.10　Usually the procedures adopted by the auditor are set out in audit programmes which essentially contain the procedures to be undertaken by the audit engagement team to generate the audit evidence to support amounts and disclosures in the financial statements.

IMPORTANT POINT

While 'off-the-shelf' audit programmes are a useful tool in the auditing process, certain audit procedures will need to be tailored to the client's individual circumstances. Hence, over-reliance on an audit programme should be avoided.

There are generally two types of audit programme that are used in modern auditing:

Standardised audit programmes	Tailored audit programmes
Standardised audit programmes are a pre-prepared set of audit instructions that can be used on any audit. There should be a caveat here that they will need to be tailored (as they won't come with pre-prepared tailoring) to the entity being audited. The main benefit of using standardised audit programmes is that they are comprehensive and hence should reduce the risk that audit procedures are missed or carried out inadequately.	These are specifically tailored to reflect the circumstances of the entity being audited. They reflect the entity's size, complexity and specific risk factors. Tailored audit programmes are the most favoured because: ● they contain audit procedures which respond to the auditor's specific risk assessment and hence should reduce audit risk; ● they can prevent over-auditing because unnecessary procedures will not be included in the audit programme; and ● they will match the exact systems and controls in place at the audit client which increases audit efficiency.

REAL-LIFE FOCUS

Mr P is a sole practitioner with two audit clients. Following a cold file review, the reviewer indicated a number of deficiencies in the audit file for a client that operates in the building construction industry. Notably, the reviewer stated:

● Audit work on contract balances at the year end was insufficient. Specifically, there was a lack of audit evidence to support recoverability.

● Income completeness testing was incorrectly carried out because it did not start from outside the accounting system, but started from sales invoices.

● There was little audit evidence to support the stage of completion of work in progress at the year end.

- There was no indication on file that the surveyor used in assessing the stage of completion of work in progress at the year end was technically competent, independent of the entity and had the necessary expertise to carry out the assessment.

There was a lack of tailoring of the revenue recognition section of the audit programme. Construction contract accounting is renowned for having its inherent complexities and this audit file did not adequately cover the accounting treatment of contracts in progress at the year end.

I discussed this issue with the practitioner who said that he relies on standardised audit programmes and he goes through each step on the programme. While this may be the case, what did become apparent was that Mr P did not tailor those programmes so that they adequately covered contract balances at the year end and the stage of completion of construction contracts.

In addition, it is surprising that despite Mr P claiming he had followed every step of the audit programme, that the programme did not have any procedures that dealt with the use of an expert. ISA (UK) 620 *Using the Work of an Auditor's Expert* includes procedures that must be applied by the auditor even when relying on the work of management's expert. To that end, Mr P should have carried out the following procedures:

- Obtained an understanding of the field of expertise of the expert.

- Considered the competence, capabilities and objectivity of the expert.

- Evaluated the adequacy of the expert's work.

This situation highlights the importance of not relying too heavily on standardised audit programmes because they will invariably need tailoring so that the procedures are specific to the client.

Tests of controls and substantive procedures

7.11   In **Chapter 6**, I examined tests of controls and substantive procedures which are the two main sources from which audit evidence is obtained. Remember, substantive procedures are then sub-divided into tests of detail and substantive analytical procedures.

ISA (UK) 330 *The Auditor's Responses to Assessed Risks* requires the auditor to check the operating effectiveness of the client's system of internal control. While ISA (UK) 330 requires this, there is a caveat within the ISA

(UK) that the auditor is only required to obtain sufficient appropriate audit evidence concerning the operating effectiveness of controls **only if** there is an expectation that those controls have operated effectively during the year. It would be a waste of time to test ineffective controls because they will not have operated effectively during the year. In that situation, the auditor would carry out more substantive procedures and discuss the deficiencies in the client's system of internal control with management.

In rare situations, the auditor may have to carry out tests of controls because the use of substantive procedures alone cannot provide sufficient appropriate audit evidence. Remember, substantive procedures aim to detect misstatements at the financial statement assertion level. ISA (UK) 330 cites an example of an entity which conducts its business using IT and no documentation of transactions is produced or maintained (other than through the IT system itself). In this case, it would not be possible to carry out substantive procedures such as inspection of documents, hence tests of controls on the IT system would be used instead to provide audit evidence.

IMPORTANT POINT

Tests of controls are different from obtaining an initial understanding of the controls in place and evaluating their design and implementation. This is where some practitioners trip up. The same types of audit procedures will often be used to obtain an understanding of the controls and evaluate those controls so the auditor may decide it is more efficient to test the operating effectiveness of the controls at the same time as evaluating their design and determining that they have been implemented.

When documenting the design of a control, the auditor will carry out a test to ensure it has operated effectively during the year. For example, the systems notes may indicate that bank reconciliations are carried out monthly and are reviewed by the finance director. This is where the auditor is documenting the system in place. A test of control would be reviewing the bank reconciliations for evidence that the finance director has reviewed them (eg, reviewing the bank reconciliations for evidence of the finance director's signature).

Nature and extent of tests of controls

7.12   The nature of tests of controls refers to the type of procedure that is carried out. It is important to bear in mind that ISA (UK) 330 clarifies that **inquiry** alone is insufficient to obtain audit evidence concerning the operating effectiveness of controls. This is because inquiry is internally generated, and the auditor must obtain other forms of evidence to complement the results of inquiries. Additional procedures may include the inspection of documentation relevant to the particular control being tested.

The extent of controls testing will be driven by the consideration of several matters, including the extent of planned reliance on the client's system of internal control by the auditor. Other factors that come into play will be the expected rate of deviation from a control which has operated and the consistency of application of controls during the period under audit.

Using prior year evidence

7.13   In real-life, a client's system of internal control is unlikely to change substantially from one year to the next. Therefore, it may not be efficient to test the controls in exactly the same way year on year. However, the auditor must bear in mind that just because the design of an internal control may not have changed, its operating effectiveness could vary year on year.

Example 7.4 – Staff shortages in the purchase ledger department

Dufty Ltd has been audited by Walker & Co Auditors for the last six years. Controls in the finance department have always been assessed as operating effectively. Part of the month-end routine of Dufty Ltd is to carry out supplier statement reconciliations to ensure the balance on the client's supplier statement is fully reconciled to Dufty's purchase ledger. Any reconciling items are investigated promptly.

However, in the year to 31 March 2024, the purchase ledger department has been under-resourced, and the company has struggled to recruit an additional purchase ledger clerk. Consequently, supplier statement reconciliations have not been carried out for the last six months of the financial year.

In this situation, the design of the control has not changed, but its operating effectiveness has. The client has not carried out supplier statement reconciliations for the last six months of the financial year and hence this means the auditor will not rely on that control because it has not operated effectively. Additional substantive procedures over the year-end trade creditors balance will have to be carried out to ensure the completeness assertion is adequately covered.

While some work on controls must be carried out each year, ISA (UK) 330 takes a pragmatic approach and does not require full tests of controls to be carried out each year. Instead, the auditor will make inquiries about whether significant changes in those controls have occurred since the last audit. Depending on the outcome of this discussion:

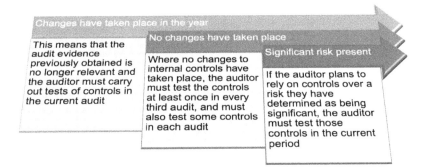

Changes have taken place in the year

This means that the audit evidence previously obtained is no longer relevant and the auditor must carry out tests of controls in the current audit

No changes have taken place

Where no changes to internal controls have taken place, the auditor must test the controls at least once in every third audit, and must also test some controls in each audit

Significant risk present

If the auditor plans to rely on controls over a risk they have determined as being significant, the auditor must test those controls in the current period

Evaluating the results of tests of control

7.14 When testing controls, the auditor obtains evidence relating to the operating effectiveness of a control procedure as opposed to generating audit evidence over a specific transaction (the latter being the purpose of substantive testing). Having tested a control, if the results indicate that the control is not operating effectively (or has not been operating effectively during the period under audit), the auditor must ask themselves the following questions:

(a) Is the deficiency an isolated incident, or is it systematic and indicative of a wider control failure?

(b) What is the reason for the control deficiency?

(c) Did the control fail at one particular time, or throughout the year under audit?

(d) Should we extend the controls testing so it includes a wider sample?

(e) If we are not extending the controls testing, should further substantive testing be performed? (The latter would normally be the most appropriate response in this situation).

It is not unusual for an auditor to discover control deficiencies or failings during tests of controls. Remember, no system of internal control can be said to be perfect because every control system will have inherent risks (such as management override, or it may even have become outdated). Control deficiencies can also arise due to staff leaving the business, hence certain controls may go unperformed or human error may create deficiencies in internal control. ISA (UK) 330 recognises these factors and suggests that the auditor compare the detected rate of deviation to an expected rate of deviation to assess whether, or not, the control can be relied upon.

Where deficiencies in internal controls are detected, it is likely that there will have to be consequential amendments made to the audit strategy and audit plan. This is particularly the case where the auditor concludes that a control (or multiple controls) that have been tested cannot be relied upon and hence more substantive procedures will need to be applied.

In addition to this, ISA (UK) 265 *Communicating Deficiencies in Internal Control to Those Charged with Governance and Management* will also kick in. I examine the provisions in this ISA (UK) in **Chapter 8** (see **8.59**).

Example 7.5 – Tests of controls over a sales system

Mamo Ltd is a plant hire company with a 31 March 2024 year end. It provides services to several hundred corporate customers, many of which receive a discount based on levels of sales. Discounts must be authorised by the sales director who evidences her review by way of signature on the company's sales order documentation.

When checking a sample of 50 orders, the audit senior noted that four lots of sales order documentation had no evidence of authorisation from the sales director.

In this situation, the auditor senior should:

- discuss the results of the testing with the sales director to understand the reasons behind the control failure for four out of the 50 orders sampled; and

- consider extending the sample further to determine if the four instances of the control deficiency were isolated or not.

If further testing reveals that the control failure was relatively isolated and only occurred at a specific point in time (eg, while the sales director was on holiday), the control can be relied upon to some extent to reduce the levels of substantive testing.

However, if the additional controls testing reveals that the control failure is not isolated, further substantive procedures should be carried out and the control failure notified to management or those charged with governance in accordance with ISA (UK) 265.

Substantive procedures

7.15   I examined substantive procedures in detail in **Chapter 6**, but I do believe it's worth recapping on these issues because they are important. Remember that substantive procedures are used to detect misstatement in the figures and disclosures in the financial statements. There are two types of substantive procedure:

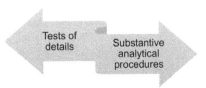

Tests of details involve the auditor obtaining audit evidence over the individual amounts that make up the classes of transactions, account balances or disclosures in the financial statements. Essentially, they provide assurance over a particular transaction, balance or disclosure and may include:

Tests of detail can be arduous and time-consuming to carry out but are viewed as essential audit procedures. Their main benefit is that they can be reliable as sources of audit evidence because they are performed by the auditor. They also provide specific evidence over particular balances, so can provide assurance over high-risk transactions and balances.

On the flip side, the main drawback to tests of details is the fact that they are often performed on a sampling basis. This means that they are subject to **sampling risk**.

IMPORTANT POINT

'Sampling risk' is the possibility that the auditor's conclusion based on a sample is different from that reached had they tested the entire population.

The auditor could conclude that a material misstatement in the sample exists, when it does not; or that a material misstatement does not exist, when it does. Auditors try to manage sampling risk by increasing their sample size when appropriate.

Substantive analytical procedures are carried out by the auditor as a means of obtaining audit evidence through analysing the relationships between financial and non-financial information to evaluate the reasonableness of financial information. ISA (UK) 520 *Analytical Procedures* applies in the evidence-gathering stage.

Examples of substantive analytical procedures may include the following:

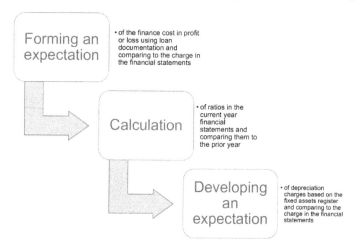

Forming an expectation
• of the finance cost in profit or loss using loan documentation and comparing to the charge in the financial statements

Calculation
• of ratios in the current year financial statements and comparing them to the prior year

Developing an expectation
• of depreciation charges based on the fixed assets register and comparing to the charge in the financial statements

IMPORTANT POINT

The auditor must bear in mind that ISA (UK) 330, para 18 requires that, regardless of the assessed risks of material misstatement, the auditor must design and perform substantive procedures for each material class of transactions, account balance and disclosure. In addition, ISA (UK) 330, para 20 states that the auditor **must** perform substantive procedures related to the financial statement closing process, in relation to:

● Agreeing or reconciling the financial statements with the underlying supporting documentation. This includes agreeing or reconciling information in associated disclosures irrespective of whether that information is obtained from within or outside of the nominal and/or subsidiary ledgers.

> ● Examining material journal entries and other adjustments made during the course of preparing the financial statements.

The nature and extent of substantive procedures performed will depend on the nature and complexity of the client's financial reporting process, accounting system, system of internal control as well as associated risks of material misstatement.

Example 7.6 – New finance director appointed prior to the year end

Fraya Enterprises Ltd has been in business for over 30 years as a manufacturer of flat-pack garden furniture. The company has a 31 December 2023 year end. On 29 October 2023, a new finance director, Joe Philbin, was appointed. Joe has previously worked in banking and insurance companies and has been involved in the oversight of the production of the draft financial statements for Fraya Enterprises.

In this scenario, the auditor is likely to conclude that there is a relative high risk of material misstatement due to Joe's lack of experience in both the financial statement closing process and the entity in which Fraya Enterprises operates. The auditor is likely to increase substantive testing in this area.

Remember, it is not just about the numbers in the financial statements (although these are clearly a very important aspect of them). The auditor must also perform substantive procedures to evaluate whether the **overall presentation** of the financial statements, including related disclosures, accords with the applicable financial reporting framework. This means the auditor must assess the adequacy of issues such as the classification and description of financial information, the terminology that is used and the amount of detail provided.

How much is 'enough' in terms of substantive procedures?

7.16   There is definitely no quantitative amount in the ISAs (UK) which states how much is enough in terms of substantive procedures. This is all down to the auditor's professional judgement. The auditor may decide to use just tests of detail, or a combination of tests of detail and substantive analytical procedures.

Quite often, the auditor will plan to carry out substantive analytical procedures before performing test of detail because the results of substantive analytical procedures can impact on the nature and extent of detailed testing. Substantive analytical procedures may direct the auditor's attention to areas of increased risk and hence more tests of detail will be needed in those areas; conversely, the assurance obtained from effective substantive analytical procedures can serve to reduce the amount of tests of detail the auditor may perform.

Substantive analytical procedures are quick to perform, and they will usually provide the auditor with reliable (auditor-generated) audit evidence. However, the auditor must bear in mind that substantive analytical procedures can only be used where there is an expectation that a relationship exists among the data in question. It is the presence of this relationship that provides audit evidence as to the completeness, accuracy and occurrence of transactions. Therefore, in such cases, substantive analytical procedures can respond to risks at the assertion level.

IMPORTANT POINT

The extent of audit procedures, whether tests of controls or substantive procedures, must always be linked to materiality and audit risk. Generally, the lower the level of materiality and the higher the level of audit risk assessed, the more extensive the audit procedures will need to be. This will usually give rise to an increase in sample sizes as well.

It is common to use substantive analytical procedures in combination with tests of detail on the same assertion because this increases the persuasiveness of the audit evidence obtained. However, the auditor must also bear in mind that it may not be possible to use substantive analytical procedures alone to provide sufficient audit evidence.

To summarise, substantive procedures (either tests of detail or substantive analytical procedures) must be carried out on the following:

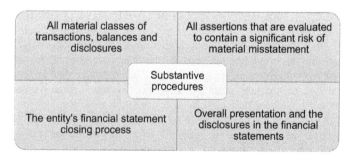

TYPES OF AUDIT PROCEDURES

7.17   So far, we've looked quite extensively at the way in which the auditor generates audit evidence through tests of controls and substantive procedures. That is not, however, the end of the story. There are certain procedures which the auditor carries out to gather audit evidence and ISA (UK) 500 *Audit Evidence* recognises seven types of procedure which the auditor can apply to get hold of that evidence:

- Inspection
- Observation
- External confirmation
- Recalculation
- Reperformance
- Analytical procedures
- Inquiry

The table below examines these procedures in further detail:

Type of audit procedure	Examples of audit evidence obtained
Inspection of records or documents This may involve the inspection of internal or external records or documents in paper or digital format. For example, inspecting a share certificate, inspecting books and records, inspecting contracts, invoices, minutes of meetings and correspondence.	• Can provide evidence over the **rights and obligations** assertion, such as inspection of title deeds for a property or inspection of an invoice for ownership of an asset. • Can provide evidence that a control is operating effectively, such as a timesheet being authorised or that an invoice is correctly authorised. • Can provide evidence over cut-offs, such as the date on a goods dispatched note and an invoice. • Can confirm the value of a sale or purchase.
Inspection of assets Typically this is the physical verification of fixed assets, such as properties and plant and machinery. It can also be applied to other assets, such as inspection of stock during a stock count.	• Provides evidence over the **existence assertion**, such as physically inspecting a machine in the warehouse from the fixed assets register.

Type of audit procedure	Examples of audit evidence obtained
Inspection of assets – *contd*	• Provides evidence over the **valuation** assertion such as inspecting an asset for evidence of any indicators of impairment.
	• Inspecting tangible fixed assets may also help to provide evidence for other balances. For example, inspecting assets used in research and development could provide evidence over the recognition of intangible development assets.
Observation Observing a process or procedure being performed by others. This is usually performed as a test of control. However, it is important to note that observation can be limited in terms of its appropriateness because it only provides evidence that a control is operating properly at the time of the observation. The fact that the auditor is present may have an influence over the operation of the control.	• Can provide evidence that a control is operating correctly. For example, there is sufficient segregation of duties in the payroll department. • Can provide evidence that the year-end stock count is being conducted properly by the auditor attending the count and ensuring management's instructions are properly adhered to.
External confirmation This involves obtaining a direct response from an external third party (usually in writing) and is dealt with specifically in ISA (UK) 505 *External Confirmations*.	• Circularisation of trade debtors or trade creditors, where customers/suppliers are asked to confirm the year-end balance owed to/from the company can provide evidence over the **existence** and **completeness** of debtors and creditors.
	• Obtaining a bank confirmation letter can provide evidence over the **completeness** of bank balances at the year end.
	• Obtaining confirmation from the entity's lawyers concerning litigation at the year end provides evidence over the **completeness** of provisions or contingent liability disclosures.
	• Confirmation of stock held by third parties can provide evidence over the **existence** and **completeness** of stock at the year end.

Type of audit procedure	Examples of audit evidence obtained
Recalculation This involves checking the arithmetical accuracy of documents, records or the client's calculations.	• Recalculating values on a sample of sales invoices can provide evidence over the **accuracy** of sales transactions. • Recalculation of foreign currency translation can provide evidence over the **completeness** and **accuracy** of foreign currency transactions. • Recalculating payroll information can provide evidence over the **accuracy** of the payroll expense. • Recalculating depreciation calculations can provide evidence over the **accuracy** of the depreciation expense and **valuation** of the fixed assets in the balance sheet. • Recalculating the trial balance and financial statements themselves can provide evidence over the **accuracy** and **completeness** of the financial statements.
Reperformance This is where the auditor reperforms a process or control which was originally executed by the company and is often performed as a test of control.	• Reperforming a bank reconciliation at the year end can provide evidence over the **valuation** of the company's bank balances at the year end. • Reperforming the Pay As You Earn and National Insurance control account can provide evidence over the **completeness** of the year-end accrual. • Reperforming the ageing of the trade debtors can provide evidence over the **completeness** and **valuation** of trade debtors.
Analytical procedures This involves the auditor evaluating financial information through the analysis of plausible relationships among both financial and non-financial data. ISA (UK) 520 *Analytical Procedures* provides further guidance to auditors.	• Comparing this year's payroll expense to the prior year and investigating any significant differences can provide evidence over the **completeness** and **accuracy** of the payroll expense.

271

Type of audit procedure	Examples of audit evidence obtained
Analytical procedures – *contd*	• Comparing the current year's gross profit margin to the prior year can provide evidence over the **occurrence, accuracy** and **completeness** of revenue and cost of sales.
Inquiry This involves the auditor seeking information from those internal (and external) to the business. It can range from formal written enquiries to informal verbal conversations. It should be emphasised that evaluating responses to an inquiry is an important part of the inquiry process. Inquiry is often a limited procedure and is insufficient on its own as audit evidence and is generally performed in addition to other audit procedures. The results of inquiry procedures will often need to be corroborated in some other way through other audit procedures.	• Making inquiries of the sales director to ascertain the procedure for opening credit accounts; or inquiring of management as to the entity's system of internal control can form part of a test of control. • Discussing the **valuation** of trade debtors with the credit controller can provide evidence of the **completeness** of a bad debt provision. • Making inquiries with the company's law firm concerning a legal claim against the company can provide evidence over the **completeness** of a provision for liabilities or the **completeness** of contingent liability disclosures. • Inquiries can also corroborate the results of analytical procedures.

Using analytical procedures

7.18   Remember, analytical procedures can feature a lot in an audit and I examined these in connection with the planning phase of the audit in **Chapter 6** (see **6.8**). Specifically, ISA (UK) 315 requires them to be applied at the planning stage of the audit as risk assessment procedures and at the end of the audit to enable the auditor to form an overall conclusion on the financial statements. They can also be used during the audit as a source of audit evidence – but only in certain situations and when appropriate.

Substantive analytical procedures can be used during the audit fieldwork stage because they are used to identify trends and understand relationships between sets of data. This is where the provisions of ISA (UK) 520 kick in.

IMPORTANT POINT

Analytical procedures will not necessarily detect specific misstatements (this is what tests of details are used for). They will, however, identify possible sources of misstatement. Hence, it is important that the auditor understands that analytical procedures cannot be used on their own to generate sufficient appropriate audit evidence; instead, they must be used in conjunction with other forms of audit procedures (such as inquiry or reperformance).

When we think of analytical procedures, it's not unusual to think 'ratio analysis'. Analytical procedures go beyond simply calculating various ratios and comparing them (although ratio analysis is clearly an important procedure because it can point to the source of a misstatement). Other analytical procedures can include:

Trend analysis	Proof in total test
Analysing changes in an account over time or calculating an expected balance and then comparing it to the actual balance	The creation of an expectation of a figure (usually payroll) by taking the payroll charge in the prior year and increasing this for pay rises, bonuses and changes in staff numbers

Example 7.7 – Proof in total test

Grace is the audit senior of Wolves & Co and is auditing Crabtree Technology Ltd for the year ended 31 December 2024. Crabtree Technology runs a chain of ten shops across the country that repairs laptops and mobile phones. Grace knows from the prior year's financial statements that the total revenue for the previous year was £5.4 million and that there were ten stores in operation during 2023.

From initial discussions with the directors, Grace understands that two new shops were opened on 1 July 2025. She also knows from obtaining an understanding of the business that customer demand has been strong this year and there is an expectation that sales will increase by 10% for the year ended 31 December 2024.

Grace is able to form an expectation of turnover in the year-end financial statements as follows:

Step 1

Sales for the year ended 31 December 2023 were £5.4m which was generated by ten shops, so an average revenue of £540,000 per shop.

Step 2

Assuming that sales per shop increase by 10% due to the increase in customer demand, each shop will now generate £594,000.

Step 3

During 2024 there were ten shops open for the whole year and two for six months of the year. Hence, assuming that all shops generate the same average revenue, the expected revenue for the year would be £6,354,000.

In **Chapter 6** (see **6.8**) I explain that the general process involved in performing analytical procedures is as follows:

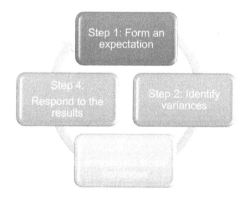

To use substantive analytical procedures properly, the auditor must create an expectation. Hence, the use of analytical procedures would be inappropriate in a business which has experienced a significant restructuring during the year or has diversified into several new areas because the business would be too different to conduct a sensible comparison. In the example of Crabtree Technology above, opening two additional shops during the year would probably not be considered too significant a change to make the analytical procedure (the proof in total test) unreliable as a source of audit evidence.

Remember, the suitability of substantive analytical procedures depends on four issues:

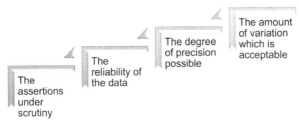

The
assertions
under
scrutiny

The
reliability of
the data

The degree
of precision
possible

The amount
of variation
which is
acceptable

The assertions under scrutiny

The assertions under scrutiny should be suitable for the assertions which are being tested. For example, analytical procedures would be unsuitable for testing the existence of work in progress. However, they would be suitable for assessing whether any write-down to estimated selling prices less costs to complete and sell for stock may be required by using the stock holding period ratio.

The use of analytical procedures is appropriate for those balances which are likely to be predictable over time because the auditor will need to analyse the relationships between those sets of data. This is the reason why it is important to only use substantive analytical procedures in specific situations as they are not always appropriate.

The reliability of the data

In a business where controls over the financial information are weak, the risk of material misstatement is higher. In this situation, the use of analytical procedures is generally not a suitable basis for assessment.

The degree of precision possible

Analytical procedures are viewed as a high-level approach when testing a balance. If the auditor needs to test a balance (or multiple balances) with a high level of precision, analytical procedures are unlikely to detect misstatements. A degree of precision will be involved if the auditor is to disaggregate the balance being tested. For example, if the auditor were to disaggregate turnover into products/divisions/regions. By disaggregating a balance, the auditor will be applying analytical procedures over a smaller balance and therefore the procedures are likely to be more effective.

The amount of variation which is acceptable

The auditor needs to create an expectation to compare against the actual amount recorded in the financial statements. If the level of variation from actual is higher than the level of variation which the auditor is willing to accept, the auditor will need to carry out further audit procedures to ensure the balance in the financial statements is not materially misstated.

Data analytics in analytical procedures

7.19   Data analytics have certainly moved up the ranks of popularity over recent years. This is because auditors can use their client's accounting information (sourced from reputable packages such as SAGE or XERO) which feed into the auditor's data analytics software to perform powerful data analytics and produce useful data visualisation. The clear benefit of this is that it is quick because performing analytical procedures manually can be time-consuming and the auditor is particularly interested in increasing audit efficiency. Data analytics are examined in more detail in **Chapter 8** so this section will just give a brief overview.

Audit data analytics can be used to perform several aspects of analytical review, such as ratio analysis, trend and common-size analysis, industry comparison and identification of anomalies as well as highlighted variances that may need additional auditor attention.

Using data analytics to perform analytical procedures is not just efficient, but it can also enhance the auditor's ability to detect risks of material misstatement. This is because it allows the auditor to sort and filter large amounts of data quickly and easily, hence variances or anomalies that may not have been identified from performing high-level analytical procedures can be spotted.

A typical example could be analysing sales trends. Data analytics can be used to analyse sales trends by day, by specific location, by individual customer, or by product. The results are presented in a user-friendly way which helps the auditor interpret the information better. Prior to using data analytics, the auditor could have performed this granular level of analysis, but it would have been time-consuming so the auditor may not have bothered due to the effort involved. Now that this detailed analysis can be performed in seconds, auditors can include it in their planning much easily.

CORROBORATING AUDIT EVIDENCE

7.20   Where audit evidence is obtained from various sources and that audit evidence is consistent, it provides corroboratory evidence. This goes to improve the reliability of the audit evidence obtained. For example, consider an audit client that is facing a potential legal claim brought against the company by a customer for breach of contract. The auditor has obtained a written representation from the directors stating that the claim is unlikely to lead to a cash outflow.

On its own, the written representation is very weak evidence because it is generated by the client. The auditor should consider obtaining further audit evidence from an independent source, such as the law firm, that the claim is unlikely to be successful. In this case, the two sources of audit evidence are consistent and corroborate each other, hence the evidence when **combined** is deemed to be reliable.

APPLYING PROFESSIONAL JUDGEMENT

7.21   ISA (UK) 200 *Overall Objectives of the Independent Auditor and the Conduct of an Audit in Accordance with International Standards on Auditing (UK)* requires the auditor to draw a conclusion as to whether they have obtained sufficient appropriate audit evidence. This is going to require professional judgement to decide whether there is sufficient *and* appropriate audit evidence on file to support the auditor's opinion.

There's no 'one-size-fits-all' where this is concerned, and it will be down to the auditor to make the decision as to whether there is sufficient appropriate audit evidence on file that supports the opinion. Remember, the audit file should 'tell a story', with the ending being the audit opinion (the client will 'live happily ever after' (well, at least for a year) if they get an unmodified audit opinion).

In forming their conclusion as to whether sufficient appropriate audit evidence has been obtained, or not, the auditor must review the audit working papers to ensure that the audit engagement team has done enough work and that work has been adequately supervised and reviewed during the evidence-gathering phase. In some cases, the audit engagement partner may decide that more work must be carried out on a certain area of the financial statements because there is not enough audit evidence on file to support the conclusions drawn. This decision will be based on matters such as the assessed levels of risk of material misstatement, the nature of the audit procedures performed and the timeliness of financial reporting.

RISK AND AUDIT EVIDENCE

7.22   ISA (UK) 330 *The Auditor's Responses to Assessed Risks* flags up a link between the auditor's assessment of risk and the persuasiveness of audit evidence obtained. Remember, audit evidence will **always** be persuasive and never conclusive. The correlation here is that the higher the assessment of risk, the more persuasive the audit evidence should be. To obtain more persuasive audit evidence, the auditor can:

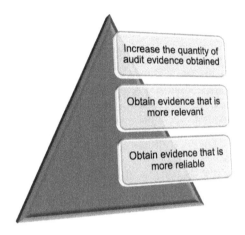

Example 7.8 – Audit of trade debtors

Prior to the commencement of the audit fieldwork stage of Balham Industries Ltd, Jeanette, the audit senior carried out a trade debtors' circularisation. 18 of the 20 circularisation letters received back indicated differences which, in turn, indicates a higher risk than had been previously identified at the initial planning stage.

Jeanette could respond to this increased risk in several ways to improve the persuasiveness of audit evidence, such as:

● Extend the sample of trade debtors that have been circularised.

● Extend other audit procedures which are relevant and reliable, such as after-date cash receipts testing.

AUDIT SAMPLING

7.23 There is a specific ISA (UK) which is dedicated to audit sampling, ISA (UK) 530 *Audit Sampling*. The definition of 'audit sampling' in ISA (UK) 530 is easy to understand and is as follows:

> The application of audit procedures to less than 100% of items within a population of audit relevance such that all sampling units have a chance of selection in order to provide the auditor with a reasonable basis on which to draw conclusions about the entire population.[2]

2 ISA (UK) 530, para 5(a).

What this definition tells us is that the auditor selects items from an entire balance to test. I suppose you could view 'audit sampling' like a buffet (it does sound like a strange analogy but let me articulate). When you go to a party and there's a buffet on offer, you don't eat the whole thing (well you may have a good go!). Instead, you choose a selection of food. If you like everything that's on offer, you generally only choose your favourite foods, but because you like everything, every item stands an equal chance of being selected. That basically sums up audit sampling in the most basic of ways.

When you see the word 'population', this refers to the entire set of data from which the auditor selects their sample. Remember, the sample selected is the one which the auditor will draw conclusions about. It will usually be impractical for the auditor to test every item in the population because of the costs involved and time constraints. This is recognised as one of the inherent limitations of an audit.

Example 7.9 – Use of sampling

Sunnie Industries Ltd has approximately 750 credit accounts through its sales ledger. The entity raises approximately 3,000 sales invoices per month.

3,000 sales invoices multiplied by 12 months is equivalent to 36,000 sales invoices each year. It would be impractical for the auditor to test every single sales invoice during the year because this would not only be expensive, but it would also take a significant amount of time to complete. For this reason, the auditor selects a sample of sales invoices from the population and tests that sample.

If errors are noted in the sample, the auditor will extend the sample (ie, increase it) to decide whether the error(s) is/are isolated, or if the error(s) is/are indicative of further problems which may need to be discussed with management and/ or those charged with governance. Errors in the sample will also give rise to potential adjustments being made to the financial statements if the errors are material both in isolation and in the aggregate.

IMPORTANT POINT

Remember, the audit will only ever provide **reasonable** assurance (not **absolute** assurance) that the financial statements are free from material misstatement, whether caused by fraud or error. Hence, the auditor is not certifying that the financial statements are 100% accurate because the auditor is not verifying 100% of the transactions that are included in the financial statements.

Sampling risk within tests of controls

7.24   You will have gathered by this stage in the book that risk features a lot in auditing, and we discussed risk in **Chapter 6**. Audit risk is the risk that the auditor expresses the wrong opinion on the financial statements and is made up of inherent risk, control risk and detection risk. Detection risk is the only risk that is under the control of the auditor.

Sampling risk is a component of detection risk. It is worth clarifying that detection risk is the risk that the auditor will fail to detect a misstatement that exists in an assertion which could be material (either individually or when aggregated with other misstatements). The following are the types of erroneous conclusions that can be drawn by the auditor where sampling risk is concerned:

- **Tests of controls**: The auditor may incorrectly conclude that the client's internal controls are <u>more</u> effective than they actually are.

- **Tests of details**: The auditor may incorrectly conclude that a material misstatement does not exist, when in fact it <u>does</u>.

The auditor is concerned about drawing these incorrect conclusions because they affect the effectiveness of the audit and are likely to lead to an inappropriate opinion being formed.

- **Tests of controls**: The auditor may incorrectly conclude that the client's internal controls are <u>less</u> effective than they actually are.

- **Tests of details**: The auditor may incorrectly conclude that a material misstatement exists, when in fact it <u>does not</u>.

The auditor is concerned about drawing these incorrect conclusions because they would affect audit efficiency as they would usually lead to additional work being carried out to establish that initial conclusions were incorrect.

As discussed earlier, tests of controls are designed to evaluate the operating effectiveness of controls in preventing or detecting and correcting a material misstatement on a timely basis.

The risk to auditors where tests of controls are concerned is that controls are either more or less effective than they actually are because the rate of errors in the sample is not the same as the actual rate of errors in the population.

Sampling risk affects tests of controls because the wrong conclusion over the operating effectiveness of the client's internal control system could lead the auditor to relying too heavily on controls, hence failing to detect a material misstatement, and thus expressing the wrong audit opinion. Conversely, the auditor could place less reliance on the client's internal controls which results in more substantive procedures having to be applied. This results in audit inefficiencies due to more work having to be performed, which increases costs.

Example 7.10 – Attendance at stock count

During the initial audit planning meeting with Miggle Industries Ltd, the audit engagement partner was told by Samina Rai, the finance director, that all staff involved in the year-end stock count are provided with detailed instructions drawn up by her and the company's production director, Josh Johnson. Samina confirmed that at each warehouse there will be a number of teams counting the stock in different numbered sections which has been mapped. Each team will comprise two individuals: one will count the inventory and the other will record the inventory on the sequentially numbered stock count sheets.

The audit engagement team will be attending each warehouse on 31 December 2024 to carry out a sample of test counts: from stock count sheets to stock (testing the **existence** assertion) and from the physical stock to the stock count sheets (testing the **completeness** assertion). As each section of the warehouse has been counted, it will be crossed out on the floor plan to indicate that counting in that area is complete. This will also prevent double-counting or missing out items of stock.

In this scenario, the sampling risk is the risk that the auditor's sample from the entire stock count is not representative of the population (the population, of course, being the entire stock). This can arise because the auditor's sample is inadequate (ie, it is too small). To reduce sampling risk, the auditor must increase the size of the sample selected. However, the auditor may consider that increasing the sample size may not be necessary as Miggle Industries has a number of controls in place over the stock count as follows:

- Detailed instructions are provided to counting staff by management.

- Each section of the warehouse has been numbered on the warehouse floor plan.

- Teams are comprised of two individuals – one counting and one recording.

- Sequentially numbered stock counting sheets are being used.

Sampling risk can lead the auditor to erroneously concluding that the above controls are more effective than they actually are. This means that the auditor's sample of stock counting will be lower than would otherwise be the case (as they are placing reliance on the effectiveness of the controls) and is more likely to lead to an inappropriate audit opinion being expressed as those items of stock which have not been sampled may contain a material misstatement due to the incorrect conclusion over controls over the stock count.

Conversely, sampling risk can lead the auditor to erroneously conclude that the above controls are less effective than they actually are. This results in the auditor increasing sample sizes than would otherwise have been the case which creates additional work (and costs) and hence reduces audit efficiency.

Sampling risk within substantive procedures

7.25 As discussed earlier, substantive procedures are those procedures that detect misstatement at the assertion level. Tests of detail, which are one type of substantive procedure, are often performed on a sampling basis.

Remember that sampling risk is the risk that the auditor's sample from a population is not representative. If the sample is too small, the sampling risk is that the auditor fails to detect a material misstatement (detection risk). On the flip side, if the auditor has concluded that a material misstatement exists and hence requires a large sample to be tested, the auditor is carrying out more substantive procedures than is necessary. This increases time spent on the audit.

Example 7.11 – Sample size is too low

During the audit of trade debtors, the audit senior selected a sample of 20 debtor balances. The population (ie the total amount of trade debtors) was £1.5 million and the sample selected totalled £82,500.

In this scenario, the sample is too low because it only represents 5.5% (£82,500 / £1.5 million) of total trade debtor balances. There is a risk that those trade debtor balances which remain untested if the sample is not increased will contain a material misstatement. This increases detection and audit risk and hence the auditor should increase their sample accordingly so that it is representative of the population.

Non-sampling risk

7.26 Non-sampling risk is the risk that the auditor reaches an incorrect conclusion for any other reason that is not related to sampling risk. This could happen because the auditor carries out inappropriate audit procedures or fails to recognise a misstatement or deviation from the entity's system of internal control. Non-sampling risk can also arise by the auditor misinterpreting the audit evidence obtained.

Example 7.12 – Non-sampling risk

Olive Cahill is the auditor supervisor of ABC & Co Accountancy Services and is attending the stock count of an existing client, Wrigley Industries Ltd, with a team of four other audit engagement team members. The stock count is being carried out as at the year end of 31 December 2024.

During December 2024, a significant problem arose in the company's stock control system. A junior member of the warehouse team incorrectly input the selling prices of goods as opposed to their cost prices into the stock control system. This resulted in overstated stock valuations for approximately 20% of the company's products.

Theo Holmes (the production director) carries out monthly reviews of the prices input into the stock system to ensure they are cost prices, so the stock valuation complies with FRS 102 *The Financial Reporting Standard applicable in the UK and Republic of Ireland*, Section 13 *Inventories* 'lower of cost and estimated selling price less costs to complete and sell' principles. However, in December 2024, Theo was absent due to illness and could not carry out the checks – nor did any other responsible official. Olive has fully documented the controls over the client's stock cycle, including the checks carried out by Theo, but has not been made aware of the control deviation that took place in December 2024. Olive has also not asked Theo about any problems arising in the system during the year.

The issue here is that further inputting errors could have been made by the junior member of staff. A failure to recognise a misstatement or deviation is a non-sampling risk. Hence, Olive could conclude that controls over the stock cycle have been operating effectively enough during the year to reduce the risk of material misstatement when, in fact, there has been a deviation from the internal control which should result in more substantive procedures being applied.

Statistical and non-statistical sampling

7.27 *Statistical sampling* includes a random selection of items to form a sample and the use of probability theory (a mathematical procedure) to evaluate the sample results.

Statistical sampling will require the use of mathematical procedures and it also requires the auditor to exercise professional judgement (for example, determining what constitutes a misstatement or deviation and what the performance materiality level is). In practice, a certain level of mathematical competence is required if valid conclusions are to be drawn from the sample evidence.

The table below outlines the advantages and disadvantages of statistical sampling:

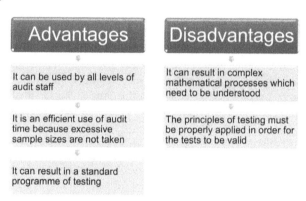

Advantages	Disadvantages
It can be used by all levels of audit staff	It can result in complex mathematical processes which need to be understood
It is an efficient use of audit time because excessive sample sizes are not taken	The principles of testing must be properly applied in order for the tests to be valid
It can result in a standard programme of testing	

Non-statistical sampling means selecting an appropriate sample sized based on the auditor's judgement of what is desirable. In contrast to statistical sampling, no time is spent on complex mathematical procedures and no specialist knowledge of statistics is required.

Sampling techniques

7.28 There are a variety of sampling techniques (both statistical and non-statistical) which the auditor can use in devising a sample of a population to perform audit procedures over. Bear in mind that most methodologies have sampling forms that can be used to ensure a consistent approach. The technique used will ultimately be at the discretion of the auditor's professional judgement and there are various factors which must be carefully considered because not every technique will be appropriate in the circumstances.

The principal methods identified by ISA (UK) 530 are as follows:

- **Random selection**

This can be achieved through the use of random number generators or tables.

- **Systematic selection**

This is where the number of sampling units in the population is divided by the sample size to give a sampling interval. For example, every 20th sales invoice. While the starting point may be determined on a haphazard basis, the sample is more likely to be truly random if it is determined by the use of a computerised random number generator or by way of random number tables. It is important when auditors are using this sampling technique that they ensure that the sampling units within the population are not structured in a way that the sampling interval corresponds with a particular pattern in the population.

- **Monetary unit sampling**

This is a type of value-weighted selection in which sample size, selection and evaluation results in a conclusion in monetary amounts. This technique selects items based on monetary values (usually focussing on higher value items) and can be particularly useful in overstatement tests (eg, debtor recoverability).

- **Haphazard selection**

When the auditor adopts a haphazard technique, it is not a structured technique. When no structured technique is followed, the auditor would nonetheless avoid any conscious bias or predictability (for example, avoiding difficult to locate items, or always avoiding items on the first or last page of a nominal ledger account). This ensures that all items in the population stand an equal chance of selection. ISA (UK) 530 acknowledges that haphazard selection is inappropriate when using statistical sampling.

- **Block selection**

This involves selecting a block of contiguous (ie, next to each other) items from a population and is often used when testing cut-off. ISA (UK) 530 clarifies that such a technique would rarely be appropriate when the auditor intends to draw valid inferences about the entire population based on the sample.

Stratification

7.29 Stratification is the process of breaking down a population into smaller sub-populations. Each sub-population is a group of sampling units which have similar characteristics.

Example 7.13 – Stratification

Naylor Enterprises Ltd has a large sales ledger which is made up of customers in the UK, Ireland, Asia, America and Poland. The auditor has concluded that because the client supplies the majority of its goods to overseas customers, overseas trade debtors are high risk because they could be translated at the year end at inappropriate foreign exchange rates. The auditor divides the population (the population being the trade debtors) into stratas (layers) as follows:

	Number of items in stratum	Value of stratum	Test size
Above £1m	9	£25m	9
£750,000 – £1m	28	£21m	20
£250,000 – £750,000	40	£40m	30
£50,000 – £250,000	95	£80m	60
£10,000 – £50,000	120	£60m	60
£0 – £10,000	200	£15m	20

The sample chosen is weighted towards the higher value items because they are most material. If one transaction in excess of £1m contains a misstatement, it may be material to the financial statements whereas an error totalling £50,000 may not.

When non-statistical methods (such as haphazard and block selection) are used, the auditor must use professional judgement to select the items to be tested. This increases the risk of auditor bias, but it does support the risk-based approach whereby the auditor focuses on those areas of the financial statements which are more susceptible to material misstatement.

Attribute sampling

7.30 Attribute sampling is a technique used by auditors to test controls. To sum it up in a nutshell, it provides the auditor with results which are based on two possible *attributes*:

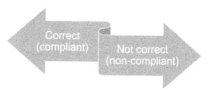

Correct (compliant)

Not correct (non-compliant)

Example 7.14 – Attribute sampling

Savelio Enterprises Ltd has a policy that every purchase invoice over £5,000 must be authorised by a director. In this situation, every purchase invoice over £5,000 will either be authorised or it won't be authorised.

The audit junior has extracted a sample from the purchases day book report showing all supplier invoices over £5,000. There are 150 invoices in the sample, and six out of the 150 invoices are not authorised by a director. This gives a population error rate of 4% (6/150 × 100).

The audit file contains the following details:

- Tolerable error is 7%
- Expected error is 5%
- Sampling risk is 2%
- Confidence level is 98% (confidence level plus sampling risk should always equal 100%)
- Population error rate is 4%

Remember, the audit junior is only looking at a sample of invoices – not the entire population. Notwithstanding the fact that the 4% population error rate is less than the tolerable error of 7%, the auditor cannot conclude that the sample is sufficient. When using attribute sampling, the auditor must add the sampling risk of 2% to the population error of 4%. When combined, these two figures are referred to as the **upper deviation rate**.

The upper deviation rate is 6% which is below tolerable error of 7% and hence the auditor can place reliance on the control.

Factors to consider when using sampling

7.31 Sampling is a 'fine art' in fairness and there are various factors which the auditor must consider when selecting a sample to test. Some (non-exhaustive) factors are as follows:

Purpose of the procedure

What is the overall objective of the test? What contribution does the test make to the overall assessment of the financial statements presenting a true and fair view?

Combination of procedures being performed

Are tests of control being carried out and can they contribute towards audit evidence? What other audit procedures are being carried out over the area being audited?

Nature of the audit evidence sought

Is external, third-party audit evidence available? Can auditor-generated evidence be obtained?

Possible misstatement conditions

Is the area being audited at a higher risk of material misstatement, or are controls over the area weak or non-existent?

Example 7.15 – Selecting a sample

Olive Industries Ltd has approximately 400 sales ledger accounts in its computerised accounting system and the majority of these sales ledger accounts are expected to owe the company money at the year end 31 March 2024. The audit engagement partner has decided that a trade debtors' circularisation will not be carried out this year due to the low response rate received in the prior year's audit and the fact that they are generally viewed as a weak form of audit evidence.

The audit engagement partner has requested extended post-year-end cash receipts testing be performed to support the assertions of valuation and existence.

Given the number of sales ledger accounts in operation, it is highly likely that the trade debtors balance at the year end will be material. The audit engagement partner has requested **extended** post-year-end cash receipts testing. Hence, the auditor must consider:

The purpose of the procedure	Which is to provide reasonable assurance that the trade debtors amount in the balance sheet does not contain material misstatement and the valuation of trade debtors is appropriate.
The combination of the procedures that are being performed	Extended post-year-end cash receipts testing will be performed in **addition** to other audit procedures to support the trade debtors amount (such as agreeing the sales ledger control account to the list of trade debtors and selecting a sample of year-end balances and agreeing them back to goods dispatched notes and the sales order).
The nature of the audit evidence sought	The extended post-year-end cash receipts testing will confirm (or otherwise) that the trade debtors exist at the year end and that they are appropriately valued as they will be traced to monies received after the balance sheet date.
Possible misstatement conditions	The auditor must consider the possibility that some debtor balances may not be recoverable (particularly if they cannot be traced back to post-year-end cash receipts). Hence an additional bad debt provision may be necessary to avoid overstated trade debtors and profit.

REAL-LIFE SCENARIO

Mrs Y is a sole practitioner with two audit clients. During her last audit monitoring visit, the reviewer had concerns over the way in which Mrs Y selects a sample. Throughout all material areas, Mrs Y had used a sample size of 20 (for example, 20 purchase invoices, 20 sales invoices, 20 members of staff on the payroll, 20 petty cash receipts and so on). The reviewer commented that there was no formal structure to the sampling and the approach used in the audit did not reflect the assessment of risk of material misstatement.

Mrs Y's audit file was graded as requiring improvement in almost all areas of the audit.

The most important factor to consider when determining the sample size is the risk of material misstatement. The higher the auditor's assessment of the risk of material misstatement, the larger the sample size must be. Keep in mind that the auditor's assessment of the risk of material misstatement is affected by **inherent risk** and **control risk**.

Mrs Y had not carried out tests of control as she prefers to do a wholly substantive audit. This can (and often does) reduce audit efficiency. However, that aside, if the auditor does not perform tests of controls, the auditor's risk assessment cannot be reduced for the effective operation of internal controls with respect to the particular assertion. In two material areas of the audit, Mrs Y had placed reliance on the client's system of internal control, without performing any tests over those controls.

In order to reduce audit risk to an acceptably low level, Mrs Y would need a low detection risk and will place more reliance on substantive procedures. The more audit evidence that is obtained from tests of details (that is, the lower the detection risk), the larger the sample size will need to be. On the flip side, if Mrs Y were to rely on other substantive procedures (tests of details and/or substantive analytical procedures) to reduce detection risk to an acceptable level, the less assurance she would need from sampling and, therefore, the smaller the sample size can be.

Using standard sample sizes of 20 across all material areas of the audit can be, and often is, a risky strategy, particularly where there are obvious risks (such as the use of significant estimates or complex calculations are involved to arrive at the balance in the financial statements).

IMPORTANT POINT

Sampling is a focus area for regulators and there has also been a debate on sampling and the use of caps. The FRC has previously indicated that it is not keen on the use of sample size caps, but this view is not rooted in ISA (UK) 530 *Audit Sampling* which requires a sample size sufficient to reduce sampling risk to an acceptably low level. In addition, the FRC also published a thematic review in November 2023. Some high-level observations noted by the FRC during the thematic review are as follows:

- Audit sampling for tests of details and controls is still widespread despite the increasing use of Audit Data Analytics.

- Most firms' methodologies are based on similar statistical models with firms building on these with their own guidance and preferences. This has led to substantial variation in the firms' final methodologies.

- This variation does not indicate one approach is better, but stakeholders, such as audit committees, need to be aware of these variances to understand how the firms obtain audit evidence.

- When applying these methodologies in practice, professional judgement is key, with significant professional judgements made throughout the use of audit sampling. Judgement is needed to use firms' sample size calculators, including to assess inherent risk and determine the contribution of evidence from other procedures. The extent of firms' guidance to support these judgements is variable.

- Previous Audit Quality Review findings, and the FRC's sample review of ongoing audit inspections, indicate sufficient evidencing of the key professional judgements made when determining sample sizes. Evidencing these key judgements is vital.

Monetary unit sampling

7.32 Monetary unit sampling is a method of sampling which uses the currency unit value as opposed to the items as the sampling population.

This method should be used with caution. It is generally applied to large variance populations (such as debtors or stock and work in progress) where the individual members are of varying size. Monetary unit sampling takes into consideration:

- The size of the population;

- The level of tolerable misstatement which is related to performance materiality; and

- The level of assurance required.

Example 7.16 – Monetary unit sampling

Kate is the audit senior auditing the trade debtors of Howard Enterprises Ltd which shows a total trade debtor balance (the population) of £750,000. Kate's sample size is 120. The sampling interval is £6,250 (£750,000 / 120).

Extracts from the sales ledger are as follows:

Debtor's name	Balance (£)	Cumulative (£)	Selected
Ratchford Group Ltd	10,250	10,250	Yes
Greaves Industries Ltd	600	10,850	No
Breary Holdings Ltd	1,300	12,150	No
Philbin Components Ltd	4,050	16,200	Yes
Leavitt Shelving Ltd	2,820	19,020	Yes
And so on…			
	750,000	750,000	

If Kate starts at £0:

- The first balance, Ratchford Group, has within it the first sampling interval of £6,250, so this is selected.

- The next £12,500 (£6,250 + £6,250) arrives in the balance belonging to Philbin Components Ltd.

- Finally (in the list above), the sampling interval has reached £18,750 (£6,250 + £6,250 + £6,250) which is in the balance belonging to Leavitt Shelving Ltd, and so on.

The sample is essentially based on random sampling because the starting point for sampling can be random, although the amount that Kate starts off with does not necessarily have to be zero. This will be left to the professional judgement of the auditor.

When using monetary unit sampling, the larger balances have a greater chance of being selected, which can be useful.

DIRECTIONAL TESTING

7.33 Nowadays, most firms use an audit methodology that provides audit programmes which set out various procedures to cover the relevant assertions and tend to adopt directional testing. The concept of 'directional testing' was developed in the 1980s and can be useful and efficient because, being based on the principles of double-entry bookkeeping, it tests debits for **overstatement** and credits for **understatement**.

Note: The term 'directional testing' is frequently used in the wrong context because the majority of audit tests (tests of control and substantive procedures) necessarily have a 'direction' which is determined by the purpose of the test. Simply testing for, say, completeness and existence of certain transactions and balances without considering the other financial statement assertions does not constitute directional testing as either an audit methodology or an audit strategy.

Directional testing is still consistent with current best practices which is reflected in the ISAs (UK), such as:

- ISA (UK) 300 *Planning an Audit of Financial Statements* which requires the auditor to plan and perform the audit in an effective manner.

- ISA (UK) 315 *Identifying and Assessing the Risk of Material Misstatement* which requires the auditor to gain an understanding of transactions relevant to the entity.

- ISA (UK) 320 *Materiality in Planning and Performing an Audit* which requires the auditor to consider materiality (eg, in determining the extent of audit procedures).

- ISA (UK) 330 *The Auditor's Responses to Assessed Risk* which requires an assessment of inherent risk relating to financial statement assertions about transactions and balances.

The use of directional testing

7.34 The concept of directional testing has its roots placed in the basic bookkeeping principle that every debit has a corresponding credit. If the trial balance balances (which it invariably does these days due to computerised bookkeeping), there could still be a misstatement of balances.

Example 7.17 – Misstatement within the trial balance

An auditor discovers the client's trade debtors are overstated by £19,000, this must mean that:

- another asset is understated by £19,000 (ie, if cash received has not been recorded); or

- liabilities are overstated by £19,000 (eg, if the bank account is overdrawn and cash is not recorded); or

- the bad debt provision and charge in the profit and loss account is understated; or

- revenue is overstated by £19,000 (for example, due to incorrect cut-off procedures or invalid or incorrect invoices being processed via the sales ledger); or

- some other combination amounting to £19,000.

Directional testing works by testing debits in the trial balance for **overstatement** and credits in the trial balance for **understatement**. Therefore, by testing debits for overstatement, the matching credits will be tested indirectly for overstatement. By testing credits for understatement, the matching debits will be tested indirectly for understatement. Direct and indirect tests are often referred to as *primary* and *corollary* tests respectively. The primary tests interlock so as to give complete audit coverage.

Some auditors may ask if it is possible to use directional testing the other way around – ie, test debits for understatement and credits for overstatement. This is permissible, but the 'rule of thumb' is that is applied in the former – ie, debits are tested for overstatement and credits for understatement for the reasons outlined below:

● It addresses some of the more common errors that may arise in the balance sheet such as understating a liability due to oversight or deliberately overstating an asset, such as failing to recognise a bad debt provision.

● It helps to identify irregularities because a theft will often result in an overstatement of an asset or an expense – eg, the theft of cash may be accounted for by writing it off to an expense account or other asset account.

● It is more difficult for revenue/income to be overstated and it will be detected, where material, indirectly. For example, if a sales ledger clerk has overstated revenue by raising fictitious invoices, the debit (eg, cash or a debtor) will be overstated which will be tested directly.

● A primary test for overstatement starts with the end result, ie, the monetary amount stated in the financial statements. The direction of testing is backwards to its source to confirm the occurrence and valuation of recorded transactions and the existence, valuation and rights to the asset.

● The primary test for understatement starts at the source of the transaction (eg, goods dispatched notes) and traces transactions forward to the financial statements. These tests are aimed at ensuring the completeness and valuation of recorded transactions and balances.

Example 7.18 – Trade debtors

The audit objective for trade debtors is to ensure they are not overstated. Amounts due from customers will be overstated if, for example:

● cash received has not been posted to the customer's account; or

● a sales invoice is overstated or posted twice or raised incorrectly; or

● a credit note due has not been raised; or

● a bad debt has not been written off.

The auditor will direct their substantive procedures towards ensuring such errors have not happened. Therefore, a sample of customers are selected from the trade debtors list and are asked to confirm their balances through a debtors' circularisation procedure with all discrepancies being investigated. For any non-responses, the auditor will test the make-up of the balance to supporting invoices, goods dispatched notes and/or customer orders. After date cash received is matched against amounts due at the year end to verify the valuation of trade debtors.

Example 7.19 – Revenue and liabilities

The audit objective for revenue (sales) is to ensure that the figure is not understated in the financial statements. Revenue could be understated if, for example:

- goods have been dispatched but not invoiced; or

- receipts from cash sales have not been recorded; or

- sales invoices are under-valued; or

- sales invoices raised have not been recorded in the sales ledger or revenue nominal account; or

- cut-off is incorrect.

When starting at the goods dispatched notes as the source of the sale, the auditor could ensure (through performing a walkthrough test) that goods cannot be dispatched without a document being raised (ie, a sales invoice, or at least a goods dispatched note). This is to establish the completeness of the population from which a sample of documents can be selected to trace through the accounting system. It is also possible to start the substantive tests over revenue from the customer's order. Where orders do exist, this is the preferred starting point because it is 'outside' of the accounting system.

The audit objective for liabilities is to ensure they are not understated. For trade creditors, testing from the source document means starting with goods received. However, if this is not documented, for example on goods received notes, purchase invoices can provide the most complete population from which transactions can be tested. When a sample is selected from the other side of the entry (in this example purchases are debits, but the actual test is a test for understated creditors), it is called the 'reciprocal population'.

For trade creditors, material understatement is usually likely to arise in respect of the largest suppliers who will have been identified in the testing of purchases for overstatement. Balances from supplier statements (if available) can be used to test for understatement. Note, that just selecting a creditor from the ledger and vouching this to invoices and goods received notes will not test adequately for understatement. What you are concerned about is whether the entity has a liability that **is not recorded**. Therefore, you must start from a population of items either external to the entity (such as statements from suppliers) or earlier in the workflow (such as goods received as mentioned above)

Stock

7.35   Stock appears in both the balance sheet and the profit and loss account and hence is tested for both overstatement and understatement. When the auditor attends the year-end stock count, they will test stock from the count sheets to the physical stock (testing for **existence**) and from the physical stock to the count sheets (testing for **completeness**). For directional testing purposes, testing from the physical stock to the count sheets also tests that the amounts are recorded.

Testing the balance sheet in both directions

7.36   By conducting direct tests on assets and liabilities in both directions, complete audit coverage can be achieved (although careful consideration must be given to audit-related costs by doing this). Testing liabilities for overstatement is straightforward because suppliers' accounts can be selected from the trade creditors list and traced back to supporting invoices, goods received notes, etc. When the auditor considers testing assets for understatement, they should consider *how* this could arise. For example, trade debtors will be understated if cash credited to a sales ledger account has not been posted; or, if a credit note has been incorrectly raised. It will, therefore, be credit entries in the asset accounts that are tested for their validity.

Testing the profit and loss account in both directions

7.37   Again, testing the profit and loss account in both directions will achieve complete audit coverage (but consideration must be given to audit-related costs by doing this).

Testing income for overstatement requires that recorded sales are substantively tested for occurrence. To test an expense for understatement will involve identification of its source and verification of its completeness. For purchases, this will usually involve tracing goods received notes through the accounting system. However, for many expenses such as rent, rates, depreciation and payroll costs, completeness may be established through analytical procedures (eg, a proof in total test).

INTERIM AUDIT

7.38   At an interim audit, audit procedures are performed *during* the client's financial year, rather than after the year end. For example, if the client has a December year end, interim audit procedures could be carried out in September or October. In practice, interim audits tend to be carried out on larger entities or when there is a very tight reporting timetable (ie, the audit has to be completed very shortly after the year end, perhaps due to group reporting requirements) because they can be costly to carry out.

The main advantage to an interim audit is for the auditor to carry out audit procedures during the year and the evidence obtained in the interim audit can be used at the final audit.

Typically, the auditor will carry out tests of controls during the interim audit. This will allow the auditor to identify risks of material misstatement at an early stage. Substantive procedures may also be carried out during the course of an interim audit, such as:

Interim audits may not be useful for all clients and there are a number of factors which should be considered, some of which are listed in the table below (note, the factors below are not intended to be a comprehensive list):

Factor	Matters to consider
Control environment	If the auditor is planning to rely on controls, it is sensible to perform an initial assessment and possibly some tests on those controls as early as possible to determine whether reliance can be placed on the operating effectiveness of them.
Risk assessment	For specific balances and transactions that are considered high risk, it may be more efficient to leave the detailed audit work until the final audit so that procedures are focussed on detailed testing of the balance that is included in the financial statements.
Nature of the specific risk	There are some risks which can only be audited at, or after, the year end. For example, risks related to cut-off, or the stage of completion of work in progress.

Factor	Matters to consider
Logistical issues	It will usually be preferable for the audit firm to perform work at the interim stage because it allows more flexibility in the allocation of work to members of the audit engagement team. This can spread the work which may be a better use of audit resources.
Availability of information	Some audit clients may have limited information available at an interim date. For example, a smaller audit client may not produce management accounts at each month end. This can restrict the work that the auditor may choose to carry out prior to the year end.

IMPORTANT POINT

When the auditor carries out tests of control at an interim period, ISA (UK) 330 *The Auditor's Responses to Assessed Risks* requires the auditor to obtain sufficient appropriate audit evidence relating to any significant changes to those controls subsequent to the interim audit (where applicable). In addition, the auditor must also determine what additional audit evidence should be obtained for the period subsequent to the interim audit and the balance sheet date.

This is an important issue, because it could be the case that controls have become ineffective since the interim audit. Factors which should be considered are:

(a)   The specific controls that were tested at the interim audit together with any significant changes to them.

(b)   The length of the interim period.

(c)   The extent to which the auditor intends to reduce further substantive procedures due to reliance being placed on the controls.

(d)   The significance of the assessed level of risk of material misstatement.

Where the auditor has carried out substantive procedures at an interim date, ISA (UK) 330 also requires:

(a)   substantive procedures, combined with tests of controls, for the intervening period; or

(b)   if the auditor determines that it is sufficient, further substantive procedures only, that provide a reasonable basis for extending the audit conclusions from the interim date to the balance sheet date.

CHAPTER ROUNDUP

- Audit evidence must be obtained in respect of risks at the financial statement level and risks at the assertion level.

- Audit evidence must be both **sufficient** and **appropriate**. Sufficiency relates to the quantity of audit evidence; whereas appropriateness relates to the quality or relevance and reliability of audit evidence.

- Tests will usually be set out on audit programmes, some of which may be standardised or tailored. Tailored audit programmes are always preferable and will reflect the levels of risk assessed at the planning stage.

- Audit procedures consist of tests of controls and substantive procedures. Substantive procedures involve tests of detail and substantive analytical procedures.

- Professional judgement must be applied in determining whether sufficient and appropriate audit evidence has been obtained. This will involve a careful review of the audit evidence in order to ensure that it supports the conclusions drawn in each area.

- Audit evidence is generally persuasive and not conclusive. The higher the assessment of risk, the more persuasive the audit evidence must be.

- Auditors may apply sampling techniques when selecting items in a population, rather than selecting the whole population to test. This is one of the inherent limitations of an audit. Sampling risk should be minimised as far as possible (and may be nowadays with the use of Audit Data Analytics).

- Sampling may involve statistical and non-statistical methods.

- Directional testing is a concept that was developed in the 1980s but is now embedded into many audit methodologies.

- Interim audits are usually carried out for larger audit clients or for audits with tight reporting deadlines and can save time at the final audit if they are planned and executed properly.

PITFALLS TO AVOID

- Failing to ensure audit evidence is sufficient and appropriate.

- Not documenting how sample sizes have been arrived at and placing too much reliance on a set number of transactions to test throughout the entire audit.

- Using analytical procedures inappropriately.

- Placing reliance on internal controls which are ineffective or have failed during the period.

- Not minimising sampling risk as far as possible, particularly where deviations in the sample are noted.

- Failing to ensure a proper review of audit work (and the evidence obtained) is carried out as review processes can indicate further procedures are necessary.

APPENDIX: AUDIT PROCEDURES

Please note the following audit procedures are not designed to be comprehensive procedures. They are designed to be an indicative illustration of the **typical** audit procedures that may be carried out by the auditor to generate sufficient appropriate audit evidence.

Related parties

At the **risk assessment** stage, the auditor should:

- Discuss among the engagement team the susceptibility of the financial statements to material misstatement due to related parties or transactions with them.

- Inquire of management as to:

    — the identity of related parties, including any changes from the prior year;

    — the nature of the relationship between the entity and its related parties;

    — whether any transactions have arisen between the entity and its related parties during the reporting period;

    — the controls that are in place governing related parties and transactions with them (including approval of related party transactions); and

    — what controls are in place to approve significant transactions and arrangements outside the ordinary course of business.

- Apply professional scepticism at all times throughout the course of the audit, recognising the possibility that there may be related parties, or related party transactions, which the auditor is unaware of.

- When significant transactions, outside the ordinary course of business, are discovered, discuss with management the rationale behind them and whether related parties could be involved.

- At all times share additional information obtained in connection with related parties with the rest of the audit engagement team.

During the **audit fieldwork** stage, the auditor should:

- Inquire of management as to whether transactions with related parties have taken place. If so, agree a sample of transactions with supporting documentation, ascertaining whether transactions have been carried out at market rates.

- Review the prior year's working papers file for details of related parties.

- Review information held at Companies House (or other public registries) for evidence of directors' involvement in any other entities.

- Review accounting records for any large or unusual transactions or balances, particularly around the balance sheet date.

- Review confirmations of loan balances – in particular, if any guarantors are related parties.

- Agree amounts disclosed in the financial statements (transactions and balances) to the accounting records and investigate any significant differences.

- Review investment transactions, such as a purchase or sale in a joint venture or associate.

- Review the entity's tax returns for any information supplied to HM Revenue and Customs (or equivalent tax authority) for evidence of the existence of any additional related parties.

- Review invoices and correspondence from lawyers/regulatory bodies for indicators of the existence of related parties or related party transactions.

- Inspect the bank audit letter (bank confirmation letter) for evidence of any related party transactions.

IMPORTANT POINT

If the auditor suspects there are additional related parties which have not been disclosed by management, they must determine whether the information giving rise to the suspicion confirms there are related parties which were previously unknown to the auditor.

Related parties are discovered which were previously unknown to the auditor

Where the auditor identifies related parties which have not been disclosed by management, the auditor should:

● Inform the rest of the audit team as quickly as possible.

● Request that management identify all transactions with those related parties.

● Inquire of management as to why the system of internal control did not identify the related parties.

● Carry out substantive procedures over the related parties by:

— making enquiries of third parties, such as lawyers, who may have knowledge of the related party relationship;

— analysing accounting records for transactions with related parties; and

— verifying the terms and conditions of transactions by looking at related contracts.

● Revisit the risk assessment over related parties and consider its appropriateness in light of the findings.

● If the non-disclosure of related parties to the auditor appears to be intentional (and hence a fraud risk factor), consider the implications for the audit as additional procedures will be necessary.

Related party transactions outside the ordinary course of business

If the auditor identifies related party transactions which are outside the ordinary course of business, the auditor should:

● Inspect contracts and agreements to evaluate:

— the business rationale (or lack thereof) and whether this gives rise to a fraud risk factor;

— whether the terms of the transactions are consistent with management's explanations; and

— whether the transactions have been accounted for and correctly disclosed.

Related party transactions conducted at market rates

Where management have made an assertion that all related party transactions were conducted on an arm's length basis (ie, at market rates), the auditor should:

- Obtain sufficient appropriate audit evidence that this assertion is correct by reviewing the terms of any contract, paying particular attention to:

  — prices charged;

  — terms of credit granted;

  — specific charges; and

  — any contingencies.

Written representations

The auditor must obtain a written representation from management and, where appropriate, those charged with governance that:

- they have disclosed to the auditor the identity of the entity's related parties and all the related party relationships and transactions of which they are aware; and

- they have appropriately accounted for and disclosed such relationships and transactions in accordance with the applicable financial reporting framework (eg, FRS 102 *The Financial Reporting Standard applicable in the UK and Republic of Ireland*, Section 33 *Related Party Disclosures*).

Intangible fixed assets

For intangible assets other than development costs:

- Inspect purchase documentation for purchased intangible assets and agree the amounts capitalised are appropriate (verifies **existence**, **rights and obligations** and **valuation**).

- Inspect any valuer's report and agree the amount on the report with the amount included in the nominal ledger and financial statements (verifies **valuation**).

- Agree the opening balances of intangible assets (cost and amortisation) with the prior year's working papers file and ensure they have been brought forward correctly (verifies **valuation** and **completeness**).

- Carry out an assessment of the intangible assets to identify if any are showing indicators of impairment (verifies **valuation**).

Amortisation

The procedures which the auditor would apply over amortisation are similar to those of depreciation of property, plant and equipment (see next section).

Development costs

Audit procedures for development costs include the following:

- Obtain a schedule of development costs capitalised during the period, cast the schedule and agree the amount to the financial statements (verifies **valuation**).

- Discuss details of the project with management and evaluate compliance with the applicable financial reporting framework (eg, FRS 102, Section 18 *Intangible Assets other than Goodwill*) to ensure that only development costs are capitalised (research costs are always expensed) (verifies **existence**).

- Inspect the project's plans and other documentation to assess compliance with the applicable financial reporting framework.

- Inspect the entity's budgets to confirm the project is financially viable, as this is one of the criteria of FRS 102, Section 18 (verifies **existence**).

- Inspect board minutes for discussions relating to the intended sale or use of the asset (verifies **existence**).

- For a sample of costs, agree them to purchase invoices or labour costs to payroll records (verifies **valuation**).

- Agree the opening balances of development costs (cost and amortisation) with the prior year's working papers file and ensure they have been brought forward correctly (verifies **valuation** and **completeness**).

Property, plant and equipment (PPE)

- Obtain the fixed assets register, cast the register and agree the totals with the financial statements and ensure cost and accumulated depreciation have been correctly brought forward from the prior year (verifies **completeness**, **classification** and **presentation**).

- Select a sample of assets from the fixed assets register and physically inspect them, ensuring they are in working order and not showing indicators of impairment such as damage (verifies **existence** and **valuation**).

- Select a sample of physical assets and inspect the fixed assets register to ensure they have been included (verifies **completeness**).

- For assets that have been revalued during the reporting period, inspect the valuation report and agree the revalued amount with the nominal ledger and the financial statements and ensure that all assets in the same asset class have been revalued (verifies **valuation**).

- Select a sample of additions and agree the cost with the supplier invoice (verifies **valuation**).

- Select a sample of additions and agree the supplier invoice is in the name of the company (verifies **rights and obligations**).

- For properties, inspect title deeds and ensure they are in the name of the company (verifies **rights and obligations**).

- Obtain a schedule of additions to fixed assets during the period and confirm that they are capital in nature rather than repairs and renewals expense (verifies **existence**).

- For assets that have been self-constructed by the client, obtain a schedule of costs that have been incurred, cast the schedule to check mathematical accuracy and agree a sample of costs with supporting documentation (eg, labour costs to payroll records and material costs to supplier invoices) (verifies **valuation**).

- For disposals, agree sales proceeds to supporting documentation such as sales invoices (verifies **accuracy** [of profit or loss on disposal]).

- For a sample of disposals, recalculate the profit or loss on disposal and agree to the gain or loss on disposal per the profit and loss account (verifies **accuracy** [of profit or loss on disposal]).

Tests of control: PPE

- Review board minutes for evidence of authorisation of capital expenditure by the directors.

- Inspect purchase orders for capital expenditure for evidence of a signature of a responsible individual.

- Inspect the reconciliation of the fixed assets register and evidence of approval by a responsible official to ensure the reconciliation has been performed correctly.

- Inspect insurance policies and compare this with the value of tangible fixed assets to ensure the value of the company's fixed assets is sufficiently covered.

- Inspect management accounts/revenue expenditure schedules for evidence of review to ensure that capital items are not incorrectly written off to profit or loss (ie, as overhead expenditure).

● For a sample of disposals of tangible fixed assets, review board minutes to ensure that such disposals have been formally approved by the board prior to the disposal taking place.

Audit procedures: depreciation

● For a sample of fixed assets, recalculate the depreciation charge for the year and agree to the fixed assets register (verifies **valuation and allocation**).

● Inspect the financial statement disclosures with respect to the accounting policies for depreciation and agree that these policies have been consistently applied (verifies **presentation**).

● For assets that have been revalued during the year, recalculate the depreciation charge based on the revalued amount and agree the charge to the profit and loss account (verifies **valuation and allocation**).

● Review the profit and loss on disposal of fixed assets to assess the reasonableness of the depreciation policies (note – if depreciation policies are reasonable, there should be no significant profits or losses on disposal) (verifies **valuation**).

● Perform a proof in total calculation for the depreciation charge for each category of tangible fixed asset and discuss any significant fluctuations with management (this is an **analytical procedure** which verifies **completeness** and **valuation**).

● Inspect budgets for the next few years to assess the appropriateness of the useful economic lives in comparison with the asset replacement cycle (verifies **valuation**).

Stock and work in progress

● Attend the year-end stock count **during** the counting process to observe the stock count being carried out (verifies **existence** and **completeness**).

● Trace items counted during the stock count and check against the final stock valuation; check to confirm that any errors identified during the count have been corrected (verifies **completeness** and **presentation**).

● Obtain schedule of stock disaggregated into raw materials, finished goods and work in progress. Cast the list to ensure it is mathematically correct and agree the final total with the financial statements (verifies **completeness** and **classification**).

● For a sample of stock, agree cost to purchase invoices (verifies **valuation**).

● For a sample of stock items, inspect post-year-end sales invoices to determine if estimated selling price less costs to complete and sell is determinable. Compare estimated selling price less costs to complete and sell with cost to determine if stock is valued at the **lower** of cost and estimated selling price less costs to complete and sell (verifies **valuation**).

• Consider using data analytics or computer-assisted audit techniques to age the inventory items in order to identify any slow-moving stock which may need an allowance and discuss these with management (verifies **valuation**).

• Trace goods received immediately prior to the balance sheet date and agree these with year-end trade creditors and stock records (verifies **completeness** and **existence**).

• Trace goods dispatched immediately prior to the balance sheet date to ensure these goods are not in stock at the balance sheet date (they should be included in turnover and debtors) (verifies **completeness** and **existence**).

• Agree the valuation of raw materials with invoices and price lists (verifies **valuation**).

• Confirm with management that an appropriate basis of valuation is being used (verifies **valuation**).

• Agree labour costs with payroll records (verifies **valuation**).

• Review standard labour costs in light of actual costs and production (verifies **valuation**).

• Reconcile labour hours with time records (verifies **valuation** and **completeness**).

• Compare actual manufacturing overhead costs with budgeted or standard manufacturing overhead costs (verifies **valuation** and **completeness**).

Analytical procedures over stock valuation

Analytical procedures over the stock valuation at the balance sheet date include:

• Calculating stock days or stock turnover ratio and comparing this to the prior year to determine if the company is holding stock longer than the prior year, which may indicate the need for an allowance to write stock down to estimated selling price less costs to complete and sell (verifies **valuation**).

• Calculate the gross profit margin and compare this to the prior year and investigate any significant fluctuations which may highlight an error in the closing stock valuation (verifies **valuation**).

Stock held by third parties

If stock is held by third parties:

- Obtain external confirmation from the third party concerning the quantity and condition of the goods (verifies **rights and obligations**).

- Where the stock held by a third party is material, attend the third-party's stock count (verifies **existence** and **completeness**).

- Obtain a report from the third-party's auditors over the system of internal control at the third party to ensure these are operating effectively.

Stock in transit

For stock in transit:

- Review transfer documentation to ensure that stock quantities and costs are adequately reflected in the stock valuation.

- Review goods received notes after the balance sheet date to ensure that the goods were genuinely in transit.

Attendance at stock count

Prior to attending the stock count:

- Obtain a copy of the counting instructions issued to the counting staff to understand how the count will be carried out and assess the effectiveness of the counting process.

- Obtain the prior year's working papers file and review the counting process and audit evidence acquired during last year's counting process to identify any issues which may need to be taken into account this year.

- Establish the location(s) of the stock and whether any third parties are holding stock on behalf of the client. If third parties are holding stock that is material, consider how sufficient and appropriate audit evidence will be obtained.

- Consider circularising third-party warehouses requesting confirmation of stock balances held at the balance sheet date, together with quantities and condition of the stock.

- Consider the need to utilise the services of any experts which may need to assist in valuing stock being counted.

During the inventory count:

IMPORTANT POINT

As noted above, the auditor should attend the stock count **during** the actual counting process because one of the primary objectives of attending the stock count is to ensure that management's instructions are being adhered to. The auditor must carry out tests of control and substantive procedures during the stock counting process to gather sufficient appropriate audit evidence that the stock counting process reduces the risk of material misstatement in the final stock valuation.

Tests of control usually carried out by the auditor include the following:

- Ensure that staff who are normally employed in the warehouse are not involved in the stock counting process (this is to ensure that there is adequate segregation of duties because if the warehouse staff were involved in the counting process, not only would they not be independent, but if there was any fraud being committed, they would be in a position to cover the discrepancies up).

- Ensure that once a section of stock has been counted it is flagged as counted to avoid double-counting or not counting at all.

- Ensure that there are no movements of stock during the counting process.

- Where movement of stock cannot stop (eg, because the client operates 24 hours a day, seven days a week), ensure items requiring dispatch are moved to a different location from the other stock. Also ensure that any deliveries of goods are made to a different location while the count is taking place. A separate count can then be performed on these segregated items, which can be added to the warehouse count.

- Ensure that count sheets which record the stock and quantities run in numerical sequence.

- Ensure there are at least two people in each counting team performing the count (one counting and the other recording).

- Ensure that damaged and/or obsolete items of stock are segregated from other stock to enable it to be valued appropriately.

- Ensure that count sheets do not show expected quantities of goods (to prevent staff avoiding physically counting the stock).

Substantive procedures which the auditor would normally carry out during the stock counting process include the following:

- Select a sample of stock from the stock counting sheets to the physical stock in the warehouse and highlight these once counted for subsequent checking with the final stock valuation (verifies **existence**).

- Select a sample of stock from the physical stock in the warehouse to the stock counting sheets and highlight these once counted for subsequent checking with the final stock valuation (verifies **completeness**).

- For goods held on behalf of third parties, discuss with management the process for ensuring these are not included in stock and ensure they are not included in the stock count (verifies **rights and obligations**).

- Obtain details of the last deliveries into the warehouse immediately prior to, or at, the balance sheet date, and retain a record of these deliveries so that during the final audit procedures the auditor can ensure that no further adjustments have been made which may misstate the final stock valuation (verifies **completeness** and **existence**).

- Attend the stock count at third-party warehouses where stock balances are material and carry out test counts and inspect the condition of the stock (verifies **completeness** and **existence**).

- Inspect stock being counted for evidence of any damage or obsolescence which may indicate the need to write down stock to estimated selling price less costs to complete and sell (verifies **valuation**).

Perpetual stock counts

Perpetual stock counts are also known as 'continuous counting systems'. A perpetual stock counting system means that all lines of stock are counted on a regular basis (eg, monthly) throughout the accounting period, so that by the balance sheet date all lines of stock have been counted.

Where the client uses a perpetual stock counting system:

- Attend at least one stock count to ensure that there are adequate controls in place during the counting process.

- Inspect the number of exceptions raised as a result of the count. Where significant variations arise, this may indicate that the stock valuation at the balance sheet date is unreliable and hence a full stock count at the balance sheet date may need to be carried out.

- Carry out additional tests to verify cut-off, valuation and rights and obligations, even where the perpetual stock counting process is deemed to be reliable.

- Inspect goods received notes and goods dispatched notes immediately pre- and post-year end to verify cut off is correct.

- Carry out an estimated selling price test to ensure that goods are being sold in excess of cost (if estimated selling price less costs to complete and sell is lower than cost, this indicates impairment of stock).

- Calculate stock holding days and compare with the prior year to identify if there is any slow-moving stock which may need an allowance to bring its valuation down to estimated selling price less costs to complete and sell.

Revenue, debtors and prepayments

For revenue (turnover/sales), the auditor should:

- Inspect a sample of goods dispatched notes (GDNs) before and after the year end and ensure they have been recorded in the correct period (verifies **cut-off**).

- Recalculate any sales discounts and VAT applied for a representative sample of sales invoices (verifies **accuracy**).

- Select a sample of GDNs and agree these with the sales invoice and follow through to inclusion in the accounting records (verifies **completeness**).

- Inspect post-year-end credit notes, trace to the GDN and invoice and if the credit note related to a pre-year-end sale, ensure the sale has been reversed (verifies **occurrence**).

- Recalculate amounts of contract liability at the balance sheet date and agree this amount with the balance sheet position (verifies **completeness** [of revenue and liabilities] and **accuracy**).

- For a sample of service revenue invoices, agree service revenue has been recognised when contractual obligations to the customer have been fulfilled and any remaining obligations are recognised as a contract liability (verifies **occurrence** and **completeness**).

Analytical procedures over revenue

Analytical procedures can also be applied over revenue as follows:

- Compare current year revenue against the prior year and investigate any significant fluctuations.

- Compare revenue with the entity's budget/forecast and investigate any significant fluctuations.

- Compare revenue against industry averages or benchmarks and investigate any significant fluctuations.

- Calculate the gross profit margin (gross profit/sales × 100) and compare to the prior year and investigate any significant fluctuations.

Tests of control over revenue

Tests of control which the auditor may carry out over revenue include the following:

- For a sample of trade debtors, carry out a review of credit limits to ensure they are appropriate and operate correctly.

- Ensure the sales process does not allow customers to exceed their credit limits by entering a fictitious sales order into the system which will take the customer over their credit limit. The system should reject the order.

- Ensure the sales system only accepts sales orders which can be fulfilled (goods not dispatched promptly can result in a loss of customer goodwill). Attempt to enter an order for goods which are out of stock – the system should reject the order.

- Inspect GDNs for evidence of being matched to invoices to ensure that the invoice is raised from the GDN and not the original order.

- Inspect a sample of sales invoices for evidence of approval by a responsible official prior to it being sent to the customer.

- Obtain a copy of the entity's price list which is currently in use and for a sample of invoices ensure that correct prices have been used.

- Enquire of management as to who has the authority to amend standing data in the sales system (eg, customer discounts or credit limits). Attempt to input a change of standing data using the user ID of an employee not authorised to make such changes, ensuring the system does not allow the change to be made.

- With the client's permission, attempt to process an invoice with a sales discount without authorisation from a responsible official. The system should reject the invoice.

- For sales orders where discounts are given, review the order for evidence of a signature approving the discount by a responsible official.

Debtors and prepayments

For debtors, the auditor should:

- Obtain a trade debtors listing, cast the list and agree the total with the financial statements (verifies **valuation** and **presentation**).

311

- Agree the sales ledger control account to the list of trade debtors at the balance sheet date (verifies **completeness** and **existence**).

- Inspect post-year-end cash receipts and follow through to pre-year-end trade debtor balances (verifies **valuation, rights and obligations** and **existence**).

- Select a sample of year-end trade debtor balances and agree back to supporting documentation such as GDNs and sales orders (verifies **existence**).

- Select a sample of GDNs immediately pre- and post-year end and follow through to the sales invoice to ensure that the sale has been recorded in the correct accounting period (verifies **completeness, existence** and **cut-off** of revenue).

- Perform a trade debtors' circularisation by selecting a representative sample of trade debtors and sending a letter on the client's letterhead asking the customers for confirmation of the balance on their purchase ledger at the balance sheet date (verifies **rights and obligations** and **existence**).

- Review the valuation of trade debtors to ensure that an appropriate allowance has been made for doubtful debts. Discuss the aged debtors list with credit control to assess if any further allowance is required (verifies **valuation**).

- Inspect any customer correspondence to assess if there are any material disputed items which may need to be written off (verifies **existence, valuation** and **rights and obligations**).

- Inspect the trade debtors listing for any credit balances to assess whether these need to be reallocated to creditors (verifies **existence** and **completeness** [of liabilities] and **classification**).

Analytical procedures over trade debtors

An analytical procedure which can be applied when auditing trade debtors is the calculation of trade debtor days (trade debtors / sales × 365) for the current year, comparing to the prior year and investigating any significant fluctuations (verifies **completeness** and **valuation**).

Prepayments

Procedures to test prepayments include the following:

- Inspect the cash book and bank statements to ensure that the payment has been made (verifies **existence**).

312

- Inspect invoices to ensure that the payment relates to a good or service that has not yet been delivered or rendered (verifies **existence**).

- Inspect the trade creditors listing to identify any debit balances and assess whether these debit balances relate to on-account payments (verifies **classification** and **existence** [of prepayments]).

- Recalculate the amount prepaid to confirm mathematical accuracy (verifies **valuation**).

Analytical procedures over prepayments

Analytical procedures can be applied over prepayments by comparing the current year's prepayments with the prior year and identifying those which may require further testing (eg, items which were not prepaid last year or have not been prepaid this year) (verifies **existence**, **valuation** and **completeness**).

Cash at bank and in hand

- Obtain the bank reconciliations for all accounts and cast the bank reconciliations to ensure mathematical accuracy. Agree the balance per the cash book with the trial balance and financial statements (verifies **accuracy, valuation and allocation**).

- Obtain a bank confirmation letter from the bank and agree the balance on the bank confirmation letter with the year-end bank reconciliation (verifies **accuracy, valuation and allocation**).

- Agree the balance per the cash book with the year-end reconciliation (verifies **accuracy, valuation and allocation**).

- Agree the balance per the bank statement on the bank reconciliation with an original bank statement and bank confirmation letter (verifies **accuracy, valuation and allocation**).

- Trace all outstanding payments on the bank reconciliation to a post-year-end bank statement and note the date the payment clears (verifies **accuracy, valuation and allocation** and **completeness**).

- Trace all outstanding lodgements to the pre-year-end cash book and post-year-end bank statements (verifies **accuracy, valuation and allocation** and **existence**).

- Examine old unpresented cheques to determine whether these should be written back into the purchase ledger if they are no longer valid to be presented (verifies **accuracy, valuation and allocation** and **completeness**).

- Inspect the bank confirmation letter for details of security pledged by the company or any legal right of set-off of overdrafts against positive bank balances which may require disclosure in the financial statements (verifies **presentation** and **rights and obligations**).

- Review the cash book for any large or unusual items, particularly around the balance sheet date, as this may indicate window dressing (verifies **completeness** and **existence**).

- If cash on hand at the balance sheet date is material, attend the year-end cash count to ascertain that the closing balance on hand at the balance sheet date is accurate (verifies **completeness** and **valuation and allocation**).

Tests of controls over cash at bank and in hand

Tests of controls over cash at bank and in hand may include the following:

- Review a sample of bank reconciliations for evidence of review by a responsible official.

- Enquire of management who have access to the online banking system and attempt to log into the bank system using an unauthorised staff member's login details. The system should reject access.

- Inspect petty cash requisitions to ensure they are authorised by a responsible official.

- Review the payments cycle to assess whether supporting documentation is presented (eg, an invoice) before a payment is authorised.

- If cash on hand at the balance sheet date is material, attend the year-end cash count to ascertain that the closing balance at the year end is accurate.

- Observe whether the entity's staff are following instructions for the cash count as this will help to ensure the count is complete and accurate.

- Perform test counts to ensure procedures and internal controls are working properly.

Purchases, expenses, creditors and accruals

Purchases

- Inspect goods received notes (GRNs) immediately pre- and post-year end and ensure they have been recorded in the correct accounting period (verifies **cut-off**).

- Select a sample of purchase orders and agree these with GRNs and purchase invoices and follow through to inclusion in the purchase ledger (verifies **completeness**).

- Recalculate the values, including discounts, on a sample of large purchase invoices (verifies **accuracy**).

- Recalculate VAT on a sample of purchase invoices (verifies **accuracy**).

Analytical procedures over cost of sales

Analytical procedures can be applied over the entity's cost of sales in profit and loss by calculating the gross profit margin for the current year and comparing it with the prior year. Any unusual fluctuations in gross profit margin should be investigated. Such fluctuations can occur if:

- The entity's purchases figure is incomplete – an understated purchases figure would usually give rise to a higher gross profit margin in the current year, whereas an overstated purchases figure would increase cost of sales and hence the gross profit margin would be lower than the prior year.

- The entity's closing inventory is misstated – an understated stock valuation would give rise to a lower gross profit margin, whereas an overstated stock valuation would give rise to a higher gross profit margin.

Tests of control

Tests of control over purchases which the auditor may perform include the following:

- Inspect a sample of purchase orders to ensure that they are generated by the central purchasing department rather than by individuals within the organisation.

- Inspect a sample of purchase orders for evidence of authorisation by a responsible individual (eg, the purchasing manager or purchasing director) to ensure that only necessary goods and/or services are ordered.

- For a sample of purchase orders, inspect the order and written confirmation from the supplier to ensure all and only necessary goods and services are received.

- Observe the ordering process to ensure that the purchase order clerk checks the stock levels prior to ordering. This ensures that only necessary goods/services are ordered.

- Inspect a sample of purchase orders for evidence that orders have been authorised by responsible officials prior to the order being placed. In addition, observe a sample of purchase orders being processed to ensure that they have been authorised prior to the purchasing department placing the order.

- Review the entity's procedures to ensure correct cut-offs over purchases and for a sample of purchases immediately pre- and post-year end, carry out a review to ensure controls have operated effectively.

- For a sample of purchase orders, carry out a sequence check of order numbers for completeness.

- Review the entity's purchasing policy, such as tendering processes and obtaining quotations, to ensure the company is obtaining value for money.

Expenses

- Obtain a schedule of accruals at the balance sheet date, inspect the dates on GRNs to ensure they have been included within expenses in the correct accounting period and that goods received post-year end are not included (verifies **cut-off**).

- For a sample of expense accounts in the nominal ledger, agree the entries in the nominal ledger with purchase invoices (verifies **accuracy** and **completeness**).

- Inspect unmatched GRNs not yet invoiced and if they relate to the current year, agree with the schedule of accruals (verifies **completeness**).

- For GRNs immediately pre- and post-year end, ensure they have been recorded in the correct accounting period (verifies **cut-off**).

- Recalculate discounts for a sample of large purchases (verifies **accuracy**).

Analytical procedures: expenses

Analytical procedures can be used to identify possible sources of misstatement in an entity's expenses as follows:

- Compare expenses for each category within the same category in the prior year and investigate any significant fluctuations (verifies **accuracy**, **completeness** and **occurrence**).

- Compare expenses against budgets and investigate any significant fluctuations (verifies **accuracy** and **completeness**).

- Calculate the operating profit margin and compare with the prior year and investigate any significant variances (verifies **accuracy**, **completeness** and **occurrence**).

- Calculate the gross profit margin and compare with the prior year to identify any potential misstatement of purchases and overhead expenses. For example, if the gross profit margin has significantly reduced in the current year but operating margin has significantly increased, this may indicate that overhead expenditure has been included in cost of sales (verifies **accuracy**, **completeness** and **occurrence**).

Creditors and accruals

- Obtain a list of trade creditors, cast the list to ensure mathematical accuracy and agree the total of the purchase ledger control account in the nominal ledger and the financial statements (verifies **completeness**, **classification** and **presentation**).

- Reconcile the total of the creditors listing with the purchase ledger control account (verifies **completeness**).

- Inspect payments made by the entity post-year end and where they relate to the current year, agree them with invoices on the purchase ledger or schedule of accruals (verifies **completeness**).

- Inquire of management as to any unrecorded liabilities (verifies **completeness**).

- Select a sample of trade creditor balances and perform a trade creditors' circularisation. Follow-up any non-replies and any reconciling items between balances confirmed and trade creditors' balances per the purchase ledger (verifies **completeness** and **existence**).

- Obtain supplier statement reconciliations and agree these with the balance on the purchase ledger at the balance sheet date and investigate any reconciling items (verifies **existence**, **completeness**, **obligations** and **valuation**).

- Review invoices received post-year end and if any relate to the current year, agree them to the schedule of accruals (verifies **completeness**).

- Select a sample of GRNs immediately pre- and post-year end and ensure those received pre-year end are included in the trade creditors balance and those received post-year end are excluded (verifies **completeness** [of trade creditors] and **cut-off** [of purchases]).

- Inspect the purchase ledger for any debit balances and for material amounts discuss with management and consider whether reclassification as a debtor is appropriate (verifies **classification** and **completeness** [of debtors]).

- Obtain a schedule of accruals, cast the schedule to ensure mathematical accuracy and agree the total with the nominal ledger and financial statements (verifies **completeness** and **classification**).

- Inspect invoices received post-year end and compare with the list of accruals to ensure the accrual at the balance sheet date is reasonable (verifies **valuation**).

Analytical procedures: creditors and accruals

- Compare total creditors and accruals with the prior year and investigate any significant fluctuations (verifies **completeness** and **valuation**).

- Calculate trade creditors days and compare with the prior year and investigate any significant fluctuations (verifies **completeness** and **valuation**).

Taxation

- Review the calculation of the corporation tax provision to ensure correct tax rates and ensure the computation is mathematically correct (verifies **occurrence**, **completeness**, **accuracy** and **cut-off**).

- Review current tax liabilities and assets in respect of corporation tax computations that have yet to be agreed (verifies **occurrence**, **completeness**, **accuracy** and **cut-off**).

- Review correspondence with HM Revenue and Customs/other tax authorities to identify any amounts that may need providing for (verifies **occurrence**, **completeness**, **accuracy** and **cut-off**).

- Consider whether provisions for interest on overdue tax or penalties are necessary (verifies **occurrence**, **completeness**, **accuracy** and **cut-off**).

- Review the tax reconciliation and control account ensuring appropriate allocation of the income/expense (verifies **occurrence**, **completeness**, **accuracy** and **cut-off**).

Deferred tax

- Ensure the rates of tax used in the calculation of deferred tax are those enacted or substantively enacted at the balance sheet date and which will apply to the reversal of the timing differences (verifies **occurrence**, **completeness**, **accuracy** and **cut-off**).

- Ensure permanent differences have been eliminated (verifies **occurrence**, **completeness**, **accuracy** and **cut-off**).

- Where a deferred tax asset has been recognised, consider evidence to support recoverability (such as a review of budgets/forecasts and any contracts that indicate the existence of future taxable profits) (verifies **occurrence**, **completeness**, **accuracy** and **cut-off**).

- Ensure the correct allocation of deferred tax between profit and loss/ other comprehensive income/gains and losses and reserves is reasonable (verifies **presentation**).

Provisions and contingencies

- Obtain a breakdown of provisions, cast the schedule and agree the total with the nominal ledger and financial statements (verifies **valuation and allocation**).

- Discuss the schedule of provisions with the directors and/or inspect relevant supporting documentation to confirm that the entity does have a present obligation as a result of a past event at the balance sheet date (verifies **rights and obligations**).

- Inquire of the directors, or inspect board minutes, to ascertain if payment is probable (verifies **existence**).

- Where necessary, recalculate components of the provision and agree the calculation to supporting documentation (verifies **valuation** and **completeness**).

- Obtain the post-year end cash book, review the cash book for any payments made in respect of the provision in the next accounting period and agree such payments with the bank statements; compare the payments made with the provision to assess whether the provision is reasonable (verifies **valuation**).

- With the client's permission, obtain confirmation from the lawyers as to the likely outcome of the case and how probable it is that payment will be made. Alternatively, inspect correspondence from the lawyers regarding the issue to confirm whether a provision should be recognised and if the amount provided for is reasonable (verifies **existence**, **rights and obligations** and **completeness**).

- Review the financial statement disclosures in respect of the provision or contingency and confirm they are compliant with the financial reporting framework (eg, FRS 102, Section 21 *Provisions and Contingencies*).

- For reimbursement assets, agree the debtor to written confirmation that the receipt is virtually certain and agree the receipt to the post-year end cash book and bank statement (verifies **valuation**).

- Perform a review of the legal expenses account in the nominal ledger to identify any items which may indicate the need for a provision at the balance sheet date (verifies **existence**).

- Obtain a written representation from management that they believe the provision is appropriately valued and is complete (verifies **valuation** and **completeness**).

Capital and reserves

For **share capital**:

- Agree share capital and nominal value of share capital with underlying shareholder agreements/statutory documents (verifies **existence** and **completeness**).

- Agree the prior year amounts of share capital have been correctly brought forward to the current year (verifies **completeness**).

- For shares issued during the year, agree the proceeds from the share issue with the cash book and bank statements (verifies **existence** and **completeness**).

- For shares called up but not yet paid, agree that these have been correctly disclosed as 'Called-up share capital not paid' (verifies **presentation**).

- For shares issued at a premium, ensure the proceeds have been correctly recorded in share premium (verifies **presentation**).

- Inspect board minutes to verify the issue of share capital during the year (verifies **existence**).

For **reserves**:

- Agree prior year reserves have been correctly brought forward into the current year and reconcile all movements (verifies **completeness**).

- Agree movements in reserves to supporting documentation – for example, agree movements on the revaluation reserve to a valuation report (verifies **accuracy** and **completeness**).

For **dividends**:

- Inspect board minutes for evidence that the dividend has been declared at, or prior to, the reporting date (verifies **rights and obligations**).

- Check the legality of any dividends (ie, sufficient distributable reserves).

- Recalculate the dividend based on the announced dividend per share and agree the amount to the financial statements (verifies **accuracy** and **completeness** [of liabilities]).

- Agree the dividend with the post-year-end cash book and bank statement (verifies **completeness**).

- Review the financial statement disclosures in respect of the dividend and ensure compliance with accounting standards and local legislation (verifies **presentation**).

Payroll

- Agree the total wages and salaries charge per the payroll system to the trial balance/nominal ledger and financial statements (verifies **completeness** and **presentation**).

- Obtain the monthly payroll reports and cast them to verify the accuracy of the payroll reports (verifies **accuracy**).

- For a sample of employees, recalculate the gross and net pay and agree with payroll records (verifies **accuracy**).

- Select a sample of joiners and leavers and agree their start/leave date with the first/last payroll run (verifies **accuracy**).

- For a sample of employees, reperform the calculation of payroll taxes and confirm that these have been included in the payroll expense for the year (verifies **accuracy**).

- For a sample of monthly payrolls, agree the total net pay per the payroll records with the bank transfer listing of payments and agree to the cash book (verifies **occurrence**).

- Agree the year-end payroll tax liability to the payroll records (eg, P32) and trace to the payment made after the balance sheet date (verifies **occurrence** and **completeness** [of liabilities]).

- For a sample of employees, agree individual wages and salaries with human resources records and records of hours worked per timesheets (verifies **accuracy**).

Tests of control: payroll

- Review a sample of timesheets, especially where overtime has been worked, to ensure they have been authorised by a responsible official prior to being sent to payroll.

- Review the log of amendments to payroll standing data to ensure that changes have been authorised by a responsible official.

- For bonuses to staff and directors, review board minutes for approval of the bonus.

- Observe the clocking-in/out process to ensure that it is adequately supervised.

- Review the payroll process to ensure there is sufficient segregation of duties in place (eg, one person processing and another individual reviewing the payroll prior to it being finalised).

- Review joiner and leaver forms to ensure they have been correctly completed and authorised by a responsible official.

Analytical procedures: payroll

- Perform a proof in total test by taking last year's payroll expense, incorporating joiners and leavers and the annual pay increase. Compare this expectation with the actual payroll expense and investigate any significant fluctuations (verifies **completeness** and **accuracy**).

- Compare the current year's payroll expense with the prior year and identify any unusual fluctuations (verifies **completeness** and **accuracy**).

Directors' remuneration

- Obtain a schedule of directors' remuneration split among wages and salaries, bonuses, benefits, pension contributions and other remuneration and agree to the financial statement disclosures (verifies **completeness**).

- Agree directors' wages/salaries with payroll records and human resources records (verifies **completeness**, **accuracy** and **occurrence**).

- Agree a sample of directors' wages/salaries with bank statements and/or the bank transfer listing and cash book (verifies **occurrence**).

- Inspect board minutes for discussion and approval of directors' bonuses or other additional remuneration (verifies **accuracy** and **occurrence**).

- Obtain a written representation from the directors that they have disclosed directors' remuneration to the auditor (verifies **completeness**).

Chapter 8

Other Audit Evidence Issues

CHAPTER TOPIC LIST

- Introduction (see **8.1**).
- Using the work of experts (see **8.2**)
- Using a service organisation (see **8.8**)
- Auditing opening balances (see **8.14**)
- Attending the stock count (see **8.21**)
- Litigation and claims (see **8.26**)
- Segment information (see **8.29**)
- External confirmations (see **8.30**)
- Considering the work of internal audit (see **8.34**)
- Accounting estimates (see **8.38**)
- Data analytics (see **8.51**)
- Communication with management and those charged with governance (see **8.54**)
- Reporting deficiencies in internal control (see **8.59**)

INTRODUCTION

8.1   In **Chapter 7**, I explored the issue of audit evidence where I mention that this is probably *the* most important area of the audit. When I say *'the most important area'* I have to add a caveat in that all areas of the audit are obviously important, but it is the audit evidence stage that 'tells the story' which determines whether the organisation 'lives happily ever after' (or at least lives happily until the next audit to see if this happiness can continue).'

I think one issue that often gets forgotten about during an audit (especially a complex one) is *why* we are doing the audit in the first place. Remember, the end goal is for the auditor to express an opinion on the financial statements as to whether they give a true and fair view (or present fairly, in all material respects). This opinion is then communicated to the shareholders and users of the financial statements through the auditor's report.

WHAT ARE WE TRYING TO ACHIEVE?

This chapter considers some areas of the audit which may be specific to an audit client and for which audit evidence will need to be obtained. We need to understand what sort of audit evidence needs to be obtained in these areas and consider how we communicate certain issues to management and/or those charged with governance.

At the risk of repeating myself from other chapters as well, I must emphasise that audit evidence is persuasive in nature. It cannot be conclusive. This is on the basis that the auditor can only ever give reasonable assurance at best that the financial statements are free from material misstatement, whether caused by fraud or error. Maximum assurance is not an option, despite this being a common belief as part of the 'expectations gap'.

Chapter 7 goes into a lot of detail on how the auditor obtains the audit evidence they need to support the amounts and disclosures in the financial statements. The **Appendix** to **Chapter 7** then outlines the typical procedures an auditor may adopt when gathering this evidence (although the procedures in the **Appendix** to **Chapter 7** are not conclusive, so just be aware of that).

There are some other issues that are linked to the evidence-gathering stage that we must consider as follows:

- Using the work of an expert

- Service organisations

- Auditing opening balances

- Attending the stock (inventory) count

- Audit work in respect of litigation and claims

- Audit work in respect of segment information

- The use of external confirmations in the audit

- Considering the work of internal audit

- Accounting estimates and their related disclosures

- Data analytics

- Communication with management and those charged with governance
- Reporting deficiencies in internal control

This chapter aims to be a 'companion chapter' to **Chapter 7**, but the issues discussed in this chapter are generally considered to be 'less common' than those examined in the previous chapter.

USING THE WORK OF EXPERTS

8.2   I think it is fair to say that auditors cannot be experts in every aspect of their client's business and sometimes the auditor will need to rely on the use of experts to assist in generating audit evidence. Consider, for example, a defined benefit pension plan (often called a 'final salary scheme'). These sorts of plans are very complex to account for and rely on a whole host of complex estimates and calculations that are carried out by an actuary. Auditors cannot possibly understand how every figure in the defined benefit plan has been arrived at (especially when it comes to actuarial estimates) and this is where the auditor must place some faith in an expert (the expert being the actuary).

ISA (UK) 620 *Using the Work of an Auditor's Expert* provides the auditor with guidance when an individual or an organisation is used to provide (or help in providing) audit evidence. This ISA (UK) states that where expertise in a field, other than accounting or auditing, is necessary to obtain sufficient appropriate audit evidence, the auditor must determine whether to use the work of an expert (either engaged by management or by the auditor him/ herself).

IMPORTANT POINT

Remember, simply using the work of an expert is not enough to provide sufficient appropriate audit evidence. The auditor will have to do some work as well in ensuring that the work performed by the expert is suitable as audit evidence.

It is also worth emphasising that where the auditor does engage the services of an expert, nothing in respect of that work relieves the auditor of any responsibilities for the audit opinion. The auditor cannot state in their report '… but we engaged the services of XYZ Ltd to corroborate the valuation of…' because to do so would devalue the audit opinion. The only exception to this rule would be where law or regulation compels the auditor to refer to the use of an expert in their report, which is very rare in practice.

There are generally two types of expert that are used in an audit:

ISA (UK) 620 sets out the definitions of these experts. In terms of an auditor's expert, this is an individual or an organisation with expertise in a field, other than accounting or auditing, whose work in that particular field will help the auditor in obtaining sufficient appropriate audit evidence. An auditor's expert can be used from within the firm (such as an expert working in the firm that specialises in valuing complex financial instruments); or an external expert.

In terms of a 'management's expert', this, again, is an individual or an organisation that has expertise in a field, other than accounting or auditing, whose work in that particular field will help the entity prepare its financial statements.

The focus of this section will be on the use of an auditor's expert.

The need for an auditor's expert will usually be determined at an early stage in the audit – such as at the planning and risk assessment stage. Given the in-depth nature of planning, it would be highly unusual for an auditor to conclude they need the use of an expert during the evidence-gathering (fieldwork) stage.

There are a number of stages that involve the use of an auditor's expert:

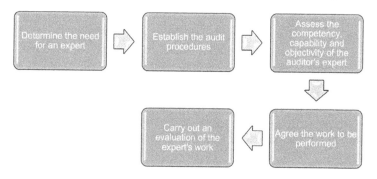

Determine the need for an auditor's expert

8.3   As I mentioned earlier in this section, it will usually be clear to the auditor at the planning and risk assessment stage if the auditor will require the use of an expert to assist in obtaining sufficient appropriate audit evidence. For example, the client may have a material amount of complex financial instruments that need a specialist's input in terms of their valuation.

Establish the audit procedures

8.4   ISA (UK) 620 states that the nature, timing and extent of audit procedures where the work of an expert is concerned will vary depending on the specific circumstances of the engagement. Factors which ISA (UK) 620 states the auditor must consider are as follows:

(a)   The nature of the matter to which the work of the expert relates.

(b)   The risk of material misstatement in respect of the matter to which the expert's work relates.

(c)   The significance of the work of the expert in the context of the engagement.

(d)   The auditor's knowledge and experience with regard to any previous work the auditor's expert has performed.

(e)   Whether the expert is subject to the audit firm's system of quality management policies and procedures (ie, ISQM (UK) 1 *Quality Management for Firms that Perform Auditors or Reviews of Financial Statements, or other Assurance or Related Services Engagements.*)

The audit procedures that will be performed need to be conducive to the complexity and subjectivity of the item(s) as well as how material the item(s) is/are to the financial statements. It is important to appreciate that in this respect there is no 'one-size-fits-all' approach that can be taken.

Assess the competency, capability and objectivity of the auditor's expert

8.5   The first thing to emphasise where this is concerned is that the auditor's expert must be independent. This is to ensure that the work carried out by the expert will not be biased or their judgement clouded by virtue of the fact that they could be connected or not independent.

'Competence' refers to the nature and level of expertise of the expert; whereas 'capability' refers to the expert's ability to exercise that competence in the performance of their duties on the audit engagement.

> **IMPORTANT POINT**
>
> It is important to emphasise that competence and capability are not the same thing. An auditor's expert may be competent to perform the valuation of a building, for example, but they may not have the capability to value it in accordance with UK and Ireland GAAP.

Agree the work to be performed

8.6   As with other professional work, the auditor's expert will need to agree the scope of their work and reporting responsibilities. This will usually take the form of an engagement letter or other formal agreement. As with the letter of engagement between the auditor and their client, the engagement letter between the expert and the auditor essentially forms a contract between the two parties to minimise any misunderstanding.

ISA (UK) 620 provides guidance on the content of the engagement letter between the auditor and the expert. Typical clauses will include:

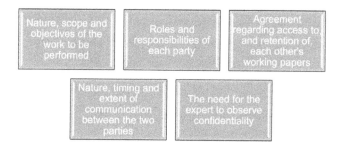

Both the audit firm and the expert must sign the letter of engagement to acknowledge their understanding of the terms before any work is carried out.

Carry out an evaluation of the expert's work

8.7   The final stage in the process is for the auditor to carry out an evaluation of the expert's work. This is so the auditor can determine whether, or not, the work is appropriate for the purposes of the audit.

In carrying out this evaluation, the auditor is required to consider the following:

• The relevance and reasonableness of the expert's findings and/or their conclusion. When reviewing this, the auditor must also assess the consistency of the findings/conclusion with other audit evidence. This is to ensure there is no contradiction with other forms of audit evidence.

● Where the expert has used significant assumptions and methods during the course of their work, evaluate the reasonableness of those assumptions and methods in light of the client's circumstances.

● Where the expert's work has involved the use of source data which is significant to the expert's work, consider the relevance, completeness and accuracy of that source data.

In practice, the use of an expert will be carefully considered prior to engaging them. To that end, it is likely that in most cases the work will be appropriate for the purposes of the audit. However, there could be circumstances when the auditor determines the work of the expert is inadequate for the purposes of the audit. Examples of such situations could be where the basis of the work carried out by the expert is inconsistent for the purposes of financial reporting (eg, under FRS 102) or the auditor discovers the expert is not wholly independent of the client.

When these situations present themselves, the auditor must tread carefully. The auditor and the expert could agree on further work to be performed that would resolve the situation. Conversely, the auditor may decide that they need to extend their audit procedures to address the situation.

IMPORTANT POINT

Remember, this is not just about the use of an auditor's expert. ISA (UK) 620 recognises that management could appoint their own expert. Where management have used an expert (such as a property valuer), the auditor must evaluate the work carried out by the management's expert in the same way as they would if it was an auditor's expert. This is important because it may be that the expert is not, in fact, independent of the client and hence is a risk that must be addressed through this sort of evaluation.

Example 8.1 – Evaluating the work of an expert

Dwyer Enterprises Ltd is a rental property company with a year end of 31 May 2025. The company has a portfolio of 45 rental properties within a 30-mile radius which it rents out to third parties. All investment properties are measured at fair value through profit or loss in accordance with FRS 102, Section 16 *Investment Property*. For the year ended 31 May 2025, the directors of Dwyer

Enterprises decided to appoint a new valuation agent to carry out the year-end investment property valuation.

The draft valuation report prepared for the directors suggests that the portfolio of properties has increased in value by some £1.5 million. Internet searches carried out by the audit firm, Kasiano & Co LLP, revealed that properties in the location of the investment properties have, in fact, decreased by approximately 24% due to a strained economic environment.

The audit senior, Sam, is not happy with the valuation because there is a significant contradiction between the valuation and actual property prices in the area.

Sam continued to research the valuation agent and found that the agent's managing partner is the wife of the financial controller of Dwyer Enterprises.

In this situation, the auditor cannot place reliance on the valuation report because the valuer is clearly not independent of the entity. In addition, it is unlikely that the audit firm will ask the valuation agent to carry out any additional work on the grounds of their lack of independence. It may be appropriate for the audit firm to engage the services of an auditor's expert to corroborate the valuation of the investment properties or carry out a separate valuation exercise (although clearly there will be costs associated with this).

If the client is unwilling to obtain a further valuation, it is likely that the auditor will need to modify their audit opinion accordingly on the grounds of insufficient audit evidence.

The example above shows how the auditor has demonstrated professional scepticism and has not simply relied on the work of the valuation agent. If the audit senior had not carried out this evaluation of the expert, the lack of independence would not have been discovered.

In practice, it is common to rely on the work of the expert where this can be justified. Where reliance is being placed, it is important that the auditor does not make any reference to the work of the expert in the auditor's report. Why? Well, to do so would imply the auditor is shifting some of their responsibility in the area that has been worked on by the expert – this has the risk of devaluing the auditor's report. The only exception to making reference to the work of the expert in the auditor's report is where such reference is required by law or regulation and in practice this is rare.

IMPORTANT POINT

Even if law or regulation requires the auditor to make reference to the work of an expert in the auditor's report, the report must indicate that such reference does not reduce the auditor's responsibility for the auditor's opinion.

USING A SERVICE ORGANISATION

8.8   The use of service organisations is common when it comes to auditing. Many clients outsource some of their day-to-day functions to a third party, such as payroll to an accountancy firm or specialist payroll bureau. Other outsourcing functions could be internal audit or bookkeeping. Whenever a business outsources a particular function to a third party, this party is known as a 'service organisation'.

The use of a service organisation in an audit is dealt with in ISA (UK) 402 *Audit Considerations Relating to an Entity Using a Service Organisation*. I think it's important to understand the reasons why a client may outsource a particular function to a third party by looking at both the advantages and disadvantages from the perspective of the auditor:

Advantage	Disadvantage
The service organisation will invariably be independent of the entity and hence this can increase the reliability of the audit evidence obtained.	Laws and regulations may cause difficulties in the auditor obtaining relevant information due to legislation such as General Data Protection Regulation or other local legislation.
The service organisation will be a specialist in the particular area (eg, an actuarial firm will be a specialist in valuing defined benefit pension schemes) hence there is usually increased reliability in the data.	It may prove difficult to carry out tests of control at the service organisation due to confidentiality or practicality reasons.
Control risk can be reduced and the auditor will usually be able to place reliance on the reports that are produced by the service organisation.	If there are any difficulties in obtaining information from the service provider, this could give rise to a limitation of scope (insufficient audit evidence) meaning there is a higher risk the auditor will modify their audit opinion accordingly.

When an audit client uses a service organisation, ISA (UK) 420 prescribes the objective of the auditor:

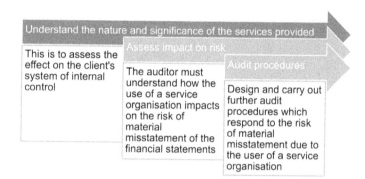

Understand the nature and significance of the services provided

8.9   It goes without saying that the auditor must gain a sound understanding of the nature and significance of the services provided by the service organisation. This is absolutely necessary when the services provided have a material impact on the financial statements of the client (for example, if the outsourced service is payroll, for example, which is likely to be material to the financial statements). As a minimum, the auditor must obtain an understanding of:

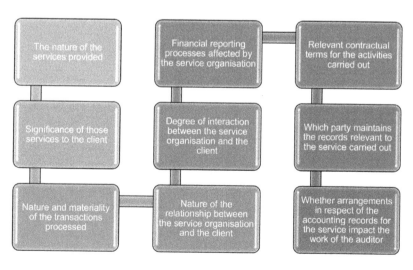

> **IMPORTANT POINT**
>
> Remember, the critical part of understanding the nature and significance of the services provided is so the auditor can assess any risk of material misstatement that may creep into the financial statement preparation process. This is particularly the case if any aspect of the outsourced area has been problematic in the year (or if there were problems identified on the initial outsourcing of the service).

Example 8.2 – Payroll function is outsourced

Sunnie Ltd manufactures replica sportswear such as football and rugby shirts and has a year end of 31 May 2025. During the year, the company decided to outsource its payroll function to Paul's Payroll Services so that the finance department can spend more time on the production of management information. Payroll is one of the company's highest costs and is material to the financial statements.

The audit engagement partner has had an initial pre-planning meeting with Chris Naylor, the client's finance director, who confirmed that the transition to the new payroll provider was smooth and no problems have been encountered during the year.

While Paul's Payroll Services is simply providing a payroll service, the auditor is required to:

● Establish the materiality of the transactions to the client.

● Determine the level of interaction between Paul's Payroll Services and Sunnie Ltd.

● Gain a sound understanding of the relationship between Paul's Payroll Services and Sunnie Ltd, including the terms of the contract. This will be important when it comes to determining whether Paul's Payroll Services is independent of Sunnie Ltd and the respective responsibilities of both parties (including which party is to maintain the payroll records and how easy it will be for the auditor to access those documents for the purposes of obtaining sufficient appropriate audit evidence).

When it comes to gaining access to the accounting records over the outsourced service, it is likely that the client will have a copy of these (especially over key areas of a function, such as payroll). The auditor is required to evaluate the impact of this arrangement on the audit because there may be initial difficulties that present themselves that must be overcome. In the UK, company law requires the entity to maintain adequate accounting records which enable the business to assess its financial performance and position with reasonable accuracy. If a service organisation maintains all, or part, of the client's accounting records, this could impact on the audit as the auditor may not be able to easily assess the state of the records.

Sources of information

8.10   One of the important factors the auditor must consider is the impact the service organisation has on the client's system of internal control. This is necessary in order for the auditor to understand the control risk that is associated with the outsourced function. For example, if the client outsources their payroll function, the auditor will need to understand what checks are carried out by the client prior to posting the payroll figures into the accounting system (ie, has the payroll been correctly calculated, is the associated PAYE and national insurance liability correct and what, if any, fraud risk factors are present?) This will lead the auditor into carrying out an appropriate risk assessment to identify the susceptibility of the financial statements to material misstatement.

Remember, just because a client might outsource a function to a third party, this does not reduce the risk of material misstatement at the assertion level. There may well be inherent problems in the source records provided to the service organisation which could lead to a misstatement in the financial statements.

When it comes to the sources of information the auditor can use in respect of the service organisation, ISA (UK) 402 provides four such sources:

A **type 1** report provides a description of the design of controls present at the service organisation. In practice it will also include a report by the service organisation's auditor which provides an opinion on the description of the system and the suitability of the controls. The auditor is less likely to place reliance on the service organisation's controls if the service organisation's auditor has modified their report in any way. Appendix 1 provides an illustrative type 1 report.

A **type 2** report is a report on the description, design and operating effectiveness of controls at the service organisation. It will contain a report prepared by the service organisation's management as well as a report by the service organisation's auditor which provides an opinion on:

(a)   The description of the system.

(b)   The suitability of the controls.

(c)   The effectiveness of the controls.

(d)   A description of the tests of controls carried out by the auditor.

Contacting the service organisation directly can be an effective way of obtaining information, particularly on aspects such as controls over the area subject to the service organisation's work.

Visiting the service organisation can enable the auditor to carry out tests of controls at the service organisation. In practice, this type of procedure is less common due to practicality reasons, but can be a valuable exercise if it can be carried out.

Using another audit firm to carry out procedures can also enable tests of controls to be carried at the service organisation if the service organisation agrees to such procedures. There will, of course, be costs associated with using another audit firm to carry out such work which may need to be cleared by the audit client first.

Responding to assessed risks

8.11   As we have seen throughout this book so far, risk plays a vital part in an audit. During the planning phase of the audit (specifically at the risk assessment phase), the auditor will consider whether, or not, to place reliance on the client's system of internal control. Remember, if the auditor is planning to rely on controls, this can serve to reduce the level of detailed substantive testing the auditor performs and thus increase audit efficiencies which allows the auditor to devote more time in focussing on higher risk areas.

If the auditor is planning to rely on the client's system of internal controls (or at least some element(s) of the system), there must be an expectation that controls have been operating effectively. Hence, the auditor could:

•   Obtain a type 2 report, where one is available.

•   Perform tests of controls at the service organisation, bearing in mind the limitations and practicability of doing this.

•   Use another auditor to carry out tests of controls at the service organisation, again bearing in mind the limitations that may be present, such as the service organisation refusing such requests.

IMPORTANT POINT

The three methods described above can be time-consuming and the client's permission will, of course, be needed. It should also be borne in mind that the service organisation is under no obligation to allow access to the client's auditor to carry out tests of controls at the service organisation.

It is important to bear in mind that the auditor must obtain audit evidence concerning the controls present at the service organisation **before** they place reliance on them.

When the auditor is in receipt of a type 2 report, that is not the end of the story. It does not just get put onto the audit file – other audit procedures must be applied. The first thing the auditor must do is to consider whether the type 2 report provides sufficient appropriate audit evidence over the client's system of internal control. There are certain other issues which the auditor must consider, such as:

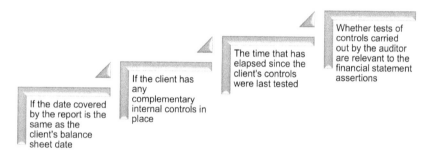

If the date covered by the report is the same as the client's balance sheet date

If the client has any complementary internal controls in place

The time that has elapsed since the client's controls were last tested

Whether tests of controls carried out by the auditor are relevant to the financial statement assertions

---

IMPORTANT POINT

In terms of the date covered by the report, this is an important consideration. The client's balance sheet date and the service organisation's balance sheet date may not be the same. In such cases, the auditor may need to consider obtaining a 'bridging letter/report' which covers the intervening period. If this is not done, there could well be issues within the service organisation's system of internal control that are not brought to the attention of the auditor.

There may be an occasion that crops up whereby the auditor believes that the type 2 report does *not* provide sufficient appropriate audit evidence. For example, the report may not contain a description of the service auditor's tests of controls and conclusions drawn from those tests. In such an instance, the client auditor could perform the work necessary to obtain the necessary audit evidence concerning the controls. For example:

- discussion with the service auditor concerning the scope and results of the service auditor's work;

- request that the service auditor performs additional procedures; or

- the client auditor, or another audit firm, performs additional procedures.

Fraud and non-compliance with laws and regulations

8.712   During the course of their work, the auditor must make inquiries of the client as to whether the service organisation has reported any frauds to them, or if they are aware of any such frauds. Enquiries must also be made as to whether the service organisation has reported any non-compliance with laws and regulations. The purpose of these enquiries is to make sure that that any such reports are properly reflected in the client's financial statements, so they help the auditor to determine whether any additional audit procedures are necessary.

Service organisations and the auditor's report

8.13   Remember, the client auditor cannot make any reference at all to the work of a service organisation's auditor in the auditor's report where the audit opinion is unqualified. The only exception to this rule would be where law or regulation specifically require such reference (which is rare in practice) and even then, the client auditor's report must indicate that the reference does not diminish the auditor's responsibilities for the opinion. None of this responsibility can be shifted to a third party.

AUDITING OPENING BALANCES

8.14   As accountants and auditors it is obvious what opening balances are and how they arrive in the current year's financial statements. The closing balance sheet of the prior year rolls forward into the current year and those are the opening balances of the current year.

Life, however, is not straightforward and the auditor cannot just simply assume that opening balances are correct. This is particularly the case with new engagements.

In this section of the chapter, we need to focus our minds on two specific scenarios:

Let's start this section by looking at the starting point for auditors. This is in the form of ISA (UK) 510 *Initial Audit Engagements – Opening Balances*. This ISA (UK) provides guidance to the auditor on obtaining sufficient appropriate audit evidence concerning the client's opening balances.

The title contains the word 'initial' so you can be forgiven for thinking that this applies simply to new engagements. This is not the case. ISA (UK) 510 also applies to continuing engagements as well, so don't let the title of the ISA (UK) fool you into thinking there is no specific guidance on recurring engagements.

In the UK, company law makes provision to enable an incoming auditor to be provided with access to the outgoing auditor's audit file to obtain the evidence they need to support opening balances. If you think about this logically, the incoming auditor cannot just accept that opening balances are free from material misstatement – they must obtain sufficient appropriate audit evidence about this and the way to do this is to be granted access to the predecessor auditor's working papers file.

The incoming auditor will write to the predecessor auditor formally to request access and this is usually granted. If the outgoing auditor refuses such access, the incoming auditor must carefully consider the reasons for such refusal (including considering raising the issue with the outgoing auditor's professional body such as the ICAEW or ACCA). It is uncommon for an outgoing auditor not to allow access to their working papers. If they do, the incoming auditor may need to:

- Review the audit firm's acceptance and continuance and risk assessment procedures and carry out more audit work on opening balances.

- Discuss the issue with the client's management with a view to obtaining audit evidence concerning opening balances, in particular requesting support to address the situation.

If other barriers which are perceived as unreasonable arise (ie, the outgoing auditor simply refuses to provide access without any valid reasons), the incoming auditor may need to notify the outgoing auditor's professional body. These circumstances are, thankfully, very rare in practice.

For the purposes of this area, it is worthwhile diving straight into an example:

338

Example 8.3 – New audit engagement

Today's date is 10 June 2024. Gil Enterprises Limited has just appointed a new audit firm, Dudson Accountants and Auditors. Dudson will carry out the audit of the financial statements for the year ending 31 July 2024. The audit manager, Ryan Ashton, has received professional clearance from the outgoing audit firm and has been granted permission to access the outgoing auditor's audit file for the year ended 31 July 2023.

As Dudson did not carry out the prior year's audit, they will need to carry out additional audit procedures to generate sufficient appropriate audit evidence. Specifically, Ryan will need to:

- Determine if the opening balances have been brought forward correctly from the prior year or, where appropriate, restated.

- Determine if Gil Enterprises' opening balances correctly reflect the application of appropriate accounting policies.

- Review the predecessor auditor's working papers file to obtain evidence concerning the opening balances (note – this is not to be viewed as a review on the quality of the audit work carried out by the previous firm).

- Evaluate whether audit procedures to be carried out in the current year (or any interim audit procedures already performed) provide evidence relevant to the opening balances.

- Perform client-specific audit procedures to obtain audit evidence concerning opening balances.

For some balances that have rolled over into the current year's balance sheet, it is likely that current year audit procedures can provide some evidence over them. For example, audit work on trade debtors will provide the auditor with some audit evidence about the existence, completeness and valuation of the opening balances of trade debtors. For other areas, such as stock and work in progress, it is likely that specific procedures will be needed for opening balances.

For other balances, such as loan balances, the auditor can inspect (or obtain) confirmations to confirm the accuracy of the opening balances.

IMPORTANT POINT

If the audit client's prior year's financial statements have been audited by another firm of auditors, the natural assumption is that some comfort can be taken from this. However, it is important to bear in mind that when reviewing the predecessor auditor's working papers, the incoming auditor must consider the competence and objectivity of the predecessor audit firm as part of their evaluation of whether the working providers do provide sufficient appropriate audit evidence.

Prior year auditor expressed a modified audit opinion

8.15 Where the outgoing auditor has expressed a modified (qualified) audit opinion on the previous year's financial statements and that modification remains relevant and material to the current year's financial statements (such as non-attendance at the year-end stock count), the incoming auditor must also modify their audit opinion as well.

Client requires an audit for the first time

8.16 It may be the case that an existing client breaches the audit exemption thresholds and requires an audit for the first time. If the comparative financial statements have not been audited (for example, because the client was able to take advantage of audit exemption in the prior year), the auditor must ensure that the auditor's report discloses that the comparatives were not audited. This can be achieved by using an Other Matter paragraph as demonstrated in the illustration below:

ILLUSTRATION – AUDITOR'S REPORT EXTRACT FOR A FIRST-YEAR AUDIT

Other matters which we are required to address

Without qualifying our opinion, we draw your attention to note 2 'Basis of Preparation of the Financial Statements' and the fact that the company's comparative financial statements were unaudited. For the year ended 31 December 2023, the company qualified as small and the directors took advantage of the exemption in CA 2006, s 477 and did not require the company to have its financial statements for the year then ended audited.

The auditor must ensure that they are not aware of any possible material misstatement in those opening figures. If the auditor is unable to obtain sufficient appropriate audit evidence that the opening balances are free from material misstatement, the audit opinion must be modified on the basis that the comparative financial statements may not be comparable.

Key audit matters (KAM)

8.17   Only auditors of listed entities are mandatorily required to include a KAM section in the auditor's report to comply with ISA (UK) 701 *Communicating Key Audit Matters in the Independent Auditor's Report.* Where the auditor encounters difficulty in obtaining sufficient appropriate audit evidence that the opening balances do not contain material misstatement, this is likely to be a KAM and should be referred to as such in the auditor's report.

Opening balances contain misstatements

8.18   A typical scenario where opening balances may contain misstatement is when the predecessor auditor issued a modified audit opinion on the previous year's figures which then impacts on opening balances. For example, where the predecessor auditor did not attend the year-end stock count.

When the auditor concludes that the opening balances contain misstatements which could be material to the current year's financial statements, they must devise audit procedures which respond to that risk assessment.

REAL-LIFE SCENARIO

Ms B was an audit engagement partner in a 12-partner firm. A few years ago the firm engaged a new client that had been audited by another mid-sized firm. Professional handover protocol was correctly followed and access to the predecessor's audit working papers file was granted.

During the review of the predecessor's audit file, the audit manager noted several loan agreements which related to a significant balance in 'sundry debtors'. These sundry debtors were loans to companies which were also related parties. Details of these loans had not been disclosed in the financial statements as related party transactions.

Upon investigation, it turned out that the companies had, in fact, been dissolved several years ago and so the loans were not recoverable. They should have been written off approximately five years ago but had been 'rolled over'. The auditor's report on these financial statements had always contained an unqualified opinion.

The client maintained that the loans were, in fact, recoverable, because they knew the former directors of these dissolved companies personally. The client refused to write the sundry debtors off.

In this situation, Ms B's audit manager had discovered a material misstatement in the opening balances which remained uncorrected.

ISA (UK) 450 *Evaluation of Misstatements Identified During the Audit* would also require the auditor to communicate these misstatements to the appropriate level of management and those charged with governance. A modified audit opinion was also expressed by Ms B's audit firm but what this did flag up was the fact that the predecessor audit firm had expressed the wrong opinion on the previous years' financial statements. As the loan balances were clearly material, they should have been written off to avoid a modified audit opinion.

In this real-life scenario, the incoming audit firm was correct to express a modified opinion because the financial statements contain overstated debtors and understated bad debt expenses. A qualified 'except for' opinion was expressed because the misstatement was material but not pervasive. However, the type of modification will depend on whether the misstatements are material but not pervasive (resulting in a qualified 'except for' opinion) or material *and* pervasive (resulting in an adverse opinion or a disclaimer of opinion). **Chapter 12** examines modified audit opinions in more detail.

Consistency of accounting policies

8.19   ISA (UK) 510 requires the auditor to consider whether the client's accounting policies have also been consistently applied in relation to opening balances. This is just one part of the process. The auditor must also consider whether the client's accounting policies are compliant with the applicable financial reporting framework (eg, FRS 102) as well.

REAL-LIFE SCENARIO

Mr L is the audit engagement partner of a six-partner firm with several audit clients. The firm engaged a new client with six branches across the UK. The client prepares its financial statements under FRS 102. The client owned all the properties occupied by the head office and the branches. The client's accounting policy in respect of these properties was the revaluation model which requires revaluations to be carried out with sufficient regularity to ensure the carrying amount of the properties does not differ materially from fair value at the balance sheet date.

On reviewing the predecessor auditor's working papers file, it was noted that a revaluation exercise had been carried out by the client using a valuation agent. The revaluation exercise resulted in four properties being increased in value, but the value of the remaining two properties had barely increased or decreased. The revaluation gain was credited to profit and loss.

Mr L recognised that this accounting treatment was incorrect because FRS 102, Section 17 *Property, Plant and Equipment* would require the revaluation gain to be accumulated within the revaluation reserve in the equity section of the balance sheet (ie, as other comprehensive income). This is because the revaluation model in FRS 102, Section 17 applies the Alternative Accounting Rules in company law and not the Fair Value Accounting Rules. Consequently, the previous year's financial statements were materially incorrect as profit was materially overstated and the revaluation reserve materially understated. In addition, the predecessor auditor had not realised the client had omitted to account for deferred tax.

Clearly, the client's accounting policies had not been applied in accordance with FRS 102. The auditor's opinion on the financial statements had been unmodified so this called into question the review process by the audit engagement partner who should have spotted that the revaluation had been incorrectly treated in the financial statements.

The opening balances therefore contained a material misstatement. Mr L informed the client that they would need to carry out a restatement of the previous year's financial statements to correct the material error in accordance with FRS 102, Section 10 *Accounting Policies, Estimates and Errors*. This was the correct course of action.

Current auditor audited the previous year's financial statements

8.20   In respect of recurring audit engagements, the auditor's work may be limited to checking that the opening balances from the prior year have been correctly brought forward into the current year and that may be sufficient because the auditor will have sufficient appropriate audit evidence on closing balances in the prior year. In addition, the auditor will be required to ensure the client's accounting policies have been consistently applied to opening balances and that they comply with the applicable financial reporting framework.

As you can see from this particular section, there are a lot of issues to consider where opening balances are concerned. For new engagements, audit evidence must be obtained to support the opening balances (do not just rely on a previous year's unmodified opinion). For recurring engagements, do not forget to consider whether accounting policies have been consistently applied on opening balances as discussions with file reviewers indicate that this is frequently spotted during file reviews.

ATTENDING THE STOCK COUNT

8.21   Attending a client's year-end stock count is dealt with in ISA (UK) 501 *Audit Evidence – Specific Considerations for Selected Items*. The idea of the auditor attending the stock count is to gather audit evidence to cover the following assertions:

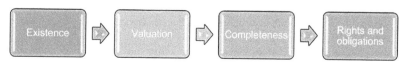

The important point to emphasise is that the auditor attends the stock count **during** the count where stock (and work in progress) is material to the financial statements. In addition, the auditor will need to carry out audit procedures on the final stock records to determine whether those records accurately reflect the count results. Auditing the final stock records is usually carried out when the final audit is being done, but for now we will concentrate on attending the stock count while it is in progress.

IMPORTANT POINT

It is not the auditor's responsibility to carry out the stock count. The auditor's responsibility is to evaluate management's instructions and procedures for the count; observe the performance of the count; inspect the stock and work in progress and perform test counts.

There are three stages to the stock count which the auditor must consider:

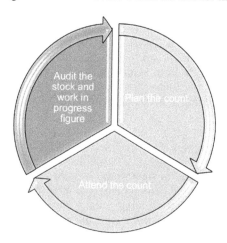

Planning the count

8.22   Before the auditor attends the stock count, they must carry out an element of planning. This normally includes:

- Performing analytical procedures and discussing any significant variances with management.

- Discussing stocktaking arrangements and procedures with management.

- Familiarising themselves with the nature of the stock, volume, identification of high-value items and the general accounting method of stock value (eg, first-in first-out or average cost).

- Considering the location of the stock.

- Considering the quantity and nature of work in progress, quantity of stocks held by third parties and whether an auditor's expert may be required.

- Considering the system of internal control relating to stock to identify potentially problematic areas (eg, problems in relation to cut-off).

- Considering whether any internal audit function exists and establishing the extent to which reliance can be placed on internal audit.

- Reviewing the results of previous stock counts.

- Reviewing the prior year's audit working papers file.

IMPORTANT POINT

Remember, the auditor must attend the stock count if the value of stock at the balance sheet date is (likely to be) material to the financial statements. Primarily the attendance at stock count is an observation test (a test of control) to observe whether the procedures adopted by management are likely to reduce the risk of material misstatement in the final stock valuation. It is also a substantive test as the auditor will check existence and completeness of stock via test counts. To that end, the auditor is required to obtain sufficient and appropriate audit evidence concerning the **existence** and **condition** of the stock, in addition to other audit procedures, unless physical attendance at the stock count is impracticable. Reasons for impracticability are rare and geographical location is not a valid reason – if the client is located far away from the auditor's base, the auditor must make alternative arrangements (for example, asking another audit firm to attend the stock count).

Attending the stock count

8.23 Once the auditor has carried out some planning on how they are going to tackle the stock count, the next step is to attend it. It is important that the stock count is attended whilst counting is still in progress. Whilst this may seem a little disruptive (and it often can be), the whole point of attending the count is so the auditor can determine whether management's instructions will reduce the risk of material misstatement in the final stock valuation and whether the counting teams are complying with those instructions. It is a test of control – the auditor is not focussing on the final stock valuation because that hasn't been established at this stage – instead they are focussing on the procedures in place and whether they are working as they should.

In addition, the auditor must also ensure that:

- Count 'teams' are in place – ie, one person counts the stock whilst another person records the quantities on 'rough' count sheets.

- No movements of stock take place during the count.

- Sequentially numbered count sheets and a sequence check is carried out of these stock sheets once count is complete (to ensure completeness of the sheets).

- Count sheets show the description of the goods, but do not show the quantities expected to be counted.

- Damaged and/or obsolete items are separately identified so they can be valued appropriately (ie, at the lower of cost or estimated selling price less costs to complete and sell).

Normally, the auditor will use an audit programme to undertake this work but should not approach the stock count as a 'tick box' exercise. In addition, the auditor should also carry out some substantive procedures such as:

- Selecting a sample of items from the stock count sheets and physically inspecting the items in the warehouse (this verifies **existence**).

- Selecting a sample of physical items from the warehouse and tracing to the count sheets to ensure that they are recorded accurately (this verifies **completeness**).

- Enquiring of management whether goods held on behalf of third parties are segregated and recorded separately (this verifies **rights and obligations**).

- Inspecting the stock being counted for evidence of damage or obsolescence that may affect estimated selling price (this verifies **valuation**).

- Recording details of the last deliveries prior to the year end. This information will be used during the final audit to ensure that no further amendments have been made thereby overstating or understating stock (this verifies **completeness** and **existence**).

- Obtaining copies of stock counting sheets at the end of the count, ready for checking against the final stock valuation after the count (this verifies **completeness** and **existence**).

- Attending the stock count at third-party warehouses (this verifies **completeness** and **existence**).

IMPORTANT POINT

The timing of the stock count is a critical factor to consider. For example, the client may have a balance sheet date of 31 December but the year-end stock count may not be undertaken on this particular day (it may be carried out before or after 31 December) and therefore additional procedures may need to be carried out by the auditor, such as roll-back or roll-forward procedures.

The auditor must consider the controls in place over the counting process. For example, whether the teams carrying out the count are objective and have the necessary experience; what controls the client has over the stock and the susceptibility of stock to theft or deterioration; the degree of fluctuation in stock levels and whether there are any inherent difficulties when it comes to estimates included in the final stock valuation.

Sources of evidence relating to the **existence** of stock are:

- Relating to the reliability of accounting records upon which the final stock valuation is based

- These include the counting procedures and the effectiveness of the count

- Substantive procedures would include physical inspections of the stock and the two-way counts carried out by the auditor

Where the entity does not maintain detailed stock records, the quantification of stock is likely to be based on a full, physical count at the balance sheet date, or at least very close to the balance sheet date. Evidence to satisfy the existence assertion is therefore greater when the stock count is carried out at the year end, or at a date very close to the year end. This could well provide sufficient and appropriate audit evidence; however, the auditor must also be satisfied that the records of stock movement are also reliable in the intervening periods.

Audit the stock and work in progress figure

8.24   The auditor is required to carry out certain procedures after the stock count and these procedures are usually carried out during the detailed audit fieldwork on the financial statements. They usually include the following:

Procedure	Relevant assertion(s) tested
Tracing the items counted during the stock count to the final stock listing to ensure it is the same as the one used at the year end and to ensure that any errors identified during the counting process have been rectified.	Completeness
Casting the list to ensure arithmetical accuracy and agree the total valuation to the financial statements and relevant disclosures.	Completeness and classification
Inspecting purchase invoices for a sample of stock items to agree their cost.	Valuation
Inspecting purchase invoices to ensure the goods are in the name of the client.	Rights and obligations
Inspecting post-year-end sales invoices for a sample of stock items to determine if estimated selling price is reasonable. This will also assist in determining if inventory is held at the lower of cost and estimated selling price less costs to complete and sell.	Valuation
Inspecting the ageing of the stock to identify any old or slow-moving items that may require an allowance and discussing these with management.	Valuation
Recalculating work in progress and finished goods valuations using payroll records for labour costs and utility bills for overhead absorption.	Valuation
Tracing the goods received immediately prior to the year end to creditors and stock balances.	Completeness and existence
Tracing goods dispatched immediately prior to the year end to the nominal ledger to ensure the items are not included in stock and sales (and debtors where relevant) have been recorded.	Completeness and existence

Procedure	Relevant assertion(s) tested
Calculating stock turnover days and comparing this to the prior year to assess whether stock is being held longer and therefore requires a provision to bring the value down to the lower of cost and estimated selling price less costs to complete and sell. This is an analytical procedure.	Valuation
Calculating gross profit margins and comparing this to the prior year. The auditor should investigate any significant differences which may highlight an error in cost of sales and/or closing stock. This is an analytical procedure.	Valuation

The above procedures are not designed to be comprehensive and further (client-specific) procedures will invariably be necessary. They do, however, illustrate some of the typical audit procedures necessary to obtain sufficient appropriate audit evidence over the final stock valuation.

Stock held at third parties

8.25   Where a third party holds stock on behalf of the client, the auditor should obtain external confirmation from the third party concerning the quantity and condition of the goods to confirm the **rights and obligations** assertion. Remember, guidance is also provided in ISA (UK) 505 *External Confirmations* which was last revised in October 2023 and is examined in **8.30** below.

If the goods held by the third party are material, the auditor should attend the stock count to verify the **existence** of the stock. In addition, the auditor may also obtain a report from the third party's auditor confirming the reliability of the system of internal control at the third party (a type 1 or a type 2 report).

REAL-LIFE SCENARIO

Entity A was a do-it-yourself retailer operating from two branches. The auditor was based 180 miles away in the south of the country but belonged to a network so was able to source another local firm to attend the year-end stock count which was held on 31 January.

During the counting process, the auditor noted that warehouse staff were also involved in the count. This demonstrates a weakness in controls because they are actively involved in the day-to-day administration of

---

the stock and hence if there was any fraud being committed, it would be concealed. Ideally, warehouse staff or other staff who have close contact on a daily basis to the client's stock should not be involved in the counting process.

However, more serious was the fact that during the final audit of the stock valuation, the auditor noted that several stock sheets were missing (in fact more than half). A lot of the stock that had been counted by the third-party audit firm had been counted on the stock sheets that were missing.

The client auditor was told by the client that the stock sheets may have been shredded inadvertently once the final quantities had been amended on the year-end stock valuation.

In this situation, the auditor had no audit evidence concerning the **existence** and condition of the inventory at the reporting date. Hence, a qualified opinion was deemed necessary due to the limitation on scope. The audit opinion was qualified 'except for', which would also have a consequential impact on the next year's financial statements due to the closing stock in the year the limitation arose becoming the opening stock in profit and loss.

Attending the year-end stock count is an important exercise for the auditor and provides valuable audit evidence in terms of the final valuation. Where stock is material, the auditor must maintain professional scepticism bearing in mind how easy it is to manipulate this figure. It is also important to remember that the auditor must carry out a thorough programme of planning prior to attending the stock count to identify those risks of material misstatement that may creep into the final stock valuation.

Example 8.4 – Continuous movement of stock

Olive Industries Ltd operates 24 hours a day, seven days a week with production staff working night and day shifts to ensure continuous production. The directors have confirmed that production cannot be stopped during the stock counting process because this will negatively impact the business and customer orders may not be fulfilled on time.

Josh Drinkwater has recently joined Sunnie & Co Accountants and Auditors as a trainee auditor and is attending the year-end stock count which is to be held on 31 January 2025. He is unsure as to how the stock count will be possible if production is not stopped, commenting that stock values will constantly change. He is concerned that the stock balance at the balance sheet date will contain a material misstatement.

Ideally, during the counting process, movements of stock should be stopped to enable the count to be conducted without it being affected by goods in and goods out. However, for some entities such as Olive Industries Ltd, it is not practicable to do this.

Management should ensure that they move the items requiring dispatch to a different location from that being counted prior to the count being carried out. Any deliveries of goods should be made to a different location while the count is being undertaken. A separate count can then be performed on the items delivered or produced during the count, which can then be added to the warehouse items counted.

Ensuring such controls are in place will ensure that the completeness and existence assertions can be verified and that cut-offs for purchases and sales can also be tested effectively.

LITIGATION AND CLAIMS

8.26   It is not unusual for an entity to be dealing with litigation and claims. This can happen for a variety of reasons, such as breach of contract, dissatisfied customers and injury. Whatever the circumstances giving reason to litigation and/or claims, the auditor must devise procedures to ensure they adequately cover them during the course of the audit.

ISA (UK) 501 requires the auditor to design and perform audit procedures to identify litigation and claims that involve the entity and which may give rise to a material misstatement.

I cover the principles of directional testing in **Chapter 7** where I discuss that the auditor primarily tests assets for overstatement and liabilities for understatement, thus indirectly testing the other side for under and overstatement accordingly. Where litigation and claims are concerned, the auditor is primarily concerned with ensuring that liabilities are not understated (ie, that provisions for litigation and claims have been properly recognised when they meet the recognition criteria in FRS 102, Section 21 *Provisions and Contingencies*) and/or that disclosures are complete (for example a contingent liability disclosure).

The procedures which the auditor may carry out when testing litigation and claims are varied and will take account of the risk assessment. However, primarily the auditor will:

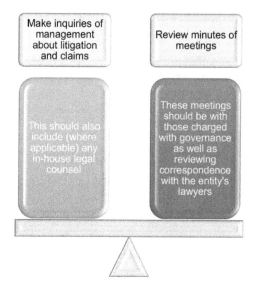

If the auditor concludes there *is* a risk of material misstatement arising from litigation and claims, or if audit procedures have revealed the presence of litigation and claims, the auditor should enter into dialogue with the entity's legal advisers. ISA (UK) 501 prescribes the process and requires the auditor to enter into this dialogue through a letter of inquiry. This letter must be prepared by management or those charged with governance but be sent to the lawyers **by the auditor** (in a similar way to how a trade debtors' circularisation is done).

In situations where law, regulation or even the lawyer's professional body, prohibits the lawyer from communicating directly with the auditor, the auditor must carry out alternative audit procedures to obtain sufficient appropriate audit evidence that litigation and claims have been adequately dealt with in the financial statements.

Management or lawyer refusal

8.27   If management (or those charged with governance) refuse to grant permission to the auditor to communicate or meet with the lawyer(s) or the lawyer(s) refuses to respond to the letter of inquiry (or is prohibited from responding) and the auditor is unable to obtain sufficient appropriate audit evidence by performing alternative audit procedures, the auditor must modify the audit opinion accordingly. This will be done having regard to the provisions in ISA (UK) 705 *Modifications to the Opinion in the Independent Auditor's Report.*

Written representation

8.28 ISA (UK) 501 requires the auditor to request management and, where appropriate, those charged with governance to provide a written representation stating that all known litigation and claims (both actual and possible) have been disclosed to the auditor and properly reflected in the financial statements either by way of recognition of an amount(s) and/or disclosed in accordance with the applicable financial reporting framework.

Remember, the auditor cannot just simply ask for a written representation. The written representation (which will be drafted in accordance with ISA (UK) 580 *Written Representations*) will serve to complement other forms of audit evidence gathered during the audit in connection with litigation and claims.

SEGMENT INFORMATION

8.29 So what exactly do we mean by segment information? Putting our financial reporting hats on for a moment, when a business has several different classes of business or operates from more than one geographical location, simply disclosing a single figure for profit and for revenue is not *really* that useful to the users of the accounts. If meaningful comparisons are to be made, the user will need further detail on performance and sales within the business.

Consider a supermarket. Nowadays, you can buy all sorts of things from a supermarket – from fruit and veg through to televisions and audio equipment and it can even arrange a loan if you like! If the supermarket's financial statements don't disclose the revenues and other meaningful information from the various different types of revenue streams, the user will not be being given the complete picture.

In the UK, you may see a breakdown of a company's sales between geographical region or by class of business. This is what we mean by 'segment information'.

ISA (UK) 501 requires the auditor to obtain sufficient appropriate audit evidence concerning both the presentation and disclosure of segment information in the financial statements. Where such information is material, it often won't be enough to just simply use a disclosure checklist; the auditor will have to carry out additional procedures which will usually involve:

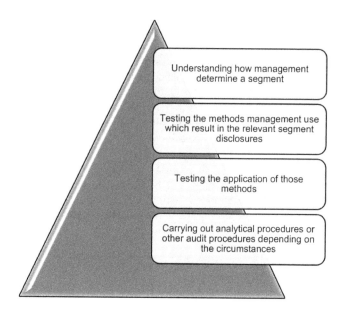

Understanding how management determine a segment

Testing the methods management use which result in the relevant segment disclosures

Testing the application of those methods

Carrying out analytical procedures or other audit procedures depending on the circumstances

EXTERNAL CONFIRMATIONS

8.30 External confirmations are often a good source of audit evidence because, as their name suggests, they come from external sources. ISA (UK) 505 *External Confirmations* provides the guidance to auditors on obtaining external confirmations and using those confirmations as audit evidence.

IMPORTANT POINT

I think it is important to flag up that the FRC recently issued a revised edition of ISA (UK) 505 off the back of recent enforcement findings as well as making sure that the ISA (UK) reflects modern approaches to obtaining confirmations (ie, a lot of communication is sent electronically nowadays rather than through the postal system).

Prior to the revisions, ISA (UK) 505 did acknowledge that external confirmations can be obtained electronically. However, the revised version now confirms that external confirmations can be obtained through directly accessing information held by third parties through web portals or software interfaces. Effectively, ISA (UK) 505 is now reflective of modern ways of obtaining such information.

'Negative confirmation requests' are where the confirming party responds to the auditor only if the confirming party disagrees with the information

---

provided in the request. Negative confirmation requests have been withdrawn from ISA (UK) 505 (Revised) on the grounds that auditors have inappropriately relied on negative confirmations, for example where a response was unlikely ever to be received (even if there were relevant matters). The FRC also considered negative confirmation requests to be a less persuasive form of audit evidence compared to positive confirmation requests.

The FRC have also included additional material in ISA (UK) 505 (Revised) to ensure that auditors design confirmations to obtain sufficient appropriate audit evidence in relation to **all** assertions identified in conjunction with ISA (UK) 330 *The Auditor's Responses to Assessed Risks*.

ISA (UK) 505 also contains enhanced requirements in respect of the auditor's responsibilities when investigating exceptions. The FRC have done this on the grounds that it has come across instances where auditors are failing to consider risk when confirmations are not as expected.

The enhanced requirements direct auditors to consider if exceptions are indicative of fraud or a deficiency in the entity's system of internal control and provide guidance on how follow-up procedures will allow the auditor to obtain sufficient appropriate audit evidence.

As you can see from the above, ISA (UK) 505 (Revised) has been modernised to reflect the ways in which auditors carry out their work in today's modern auditing environment.

Examples of external confirmations include:

Bank audit letters confirming bank balances, loan balances and secured debt

Trade debtors' circularisation letters

Trade creditors' circularisation letters

REAL-LIFE SCENARIO

Mr H is a file reviewer who conducts pre- and post-issuance ('hot' and 'cold') file reviews. During the examination of an audit file, Mr H noted that the audit firm had carried out a positive trade debtors' circularisation which involves a letter from the client to the debtor asking them to confirm the balance on their purchase ledger (or otherwise provide a reconciliation of any difference). A sample of 20 debtors (out of 189) was selected and 14 of those debtors replied positively (ie, they agreed with the balance cited in the letter).

No further audit work was performed on trade debtors on the basis that the auditor had concluded that as the majority of trade debtors had replied positively to the circularisation letter, the auditor could take comfort that the trade debtors' figure in the balance sheet was correct.

This conclusion is fundamentally flawed and was noted as a significant deficiency by the file reviewer.

Trade debtors' circularisation letters are a form of audit evidence but they are considered a weak form of audit evidence on their own because they do not verify the **valuation** assertion. In other words, they confirm that a debt exists (ie, the **existence** assertion) but they do not indicate whether the balance will actually be received. Trade debtors' circularisation letters should, therefore, complement other forms of audit evidence such as after-date cash receipts testing.

In addition, the sample selected was very low and would not be considered representative of the population. Only 11% (20/189 × 100) of the total trade debtors were selected for circularisation and only 7% (14/189 × 100) actually replied. The rest of the sample should have been followed up by alternative means, such as proof of delivery, vouching to invoices for existence and, as already noted, to after-date cash received to test recoverability.

It should also be borne in mind that trade debtors' circularisations can be unreliable. Some circularisations can come back in agreement, but that may not necessarily be correct and further audit procedures should be carried out to ensure that the trade debtor's balance is, in fact, accurate.

Carrying out a confirmation request

8.31   It is important to emphasise that ISA (UK) 505 requires the **auditor** to maintain control over the circularisation process. To that end, the auditor must:

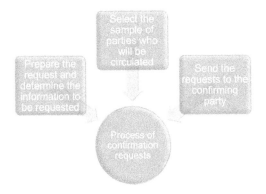

Carrying out this process correctly should enhance the **reliability** of external confirmations because they are prepared by the auditor (on the client's letterhead), sent out by the auditor and received back to the auditor's office. If a confirmation request is sent back to the audit client, it could be 'doctored'.

I mentioned earlier that ISA (UK) 505 had been revised to modernise the standard. Remember, there is a risk with electronic communications as well. For example, it may be difficult to verify the sender of the confirmation. The auditor can reduce these risks by having a secure electronic communication environment, such as a secure portal where confirmation requests can be uploaded by the sender.

Client refuses to agree to a confirmation request

8.32   Prior to writing to any of the customers, the auditor must obtain permission from the client. So, what happens if the client refuses to allow the auditor to carry out an external confirmation request? Well, the first thing to do is to ask the client the reasons for such a refusal. In practice, it is unusual for a client not to agree to a confirmation request and alarm bells should ring where the client does refuse such a request.

A client that refuses to agree to a confirmation request is effectively imposing a limitation of the scope on the auditor's work. Whatever reasons the client gives for refusing such a request, the auditor must ensure they corroborate those reasons because it may be the case that management are refusing permission to send a confirmation request in an attempt to conceal a fraud or error. Where the auditor suspects that the refusal is a fraud risk factor, they must revise the risk of material misstatement.

Remember, any refusal may have an impact on the audit opinion. It is likely that such a refusal may constitute a modified audit opinion because of the

357

scope limitation. Where a client is informed of this risk, it is usually sufficient to change the client's mind and grant permission for the auditor to carry out the confirmation request.

Evaluating the results of the external confirmation

8.33   Once the confirmation request has come back from the third party, it does not just get put on the audit file. The auditor must do something with that confirmation in the form of evaluating the results to determine whether sufficient appropriate audit evidence has been obtained. The auditor does this through looking at:

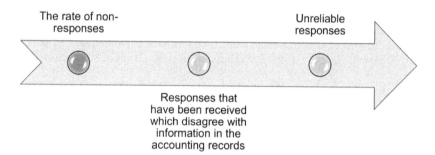

The rate of non-responses

Unreliable responses

Responses that have been received which disagree with information in the accounting records

It could well be the case that the auditor concludes that the external confirmation does **not** give rise to sufficient appropriate audit evidence. In such an instance, the auditor must devise alternative audit procedures to satisfy the relevant assertion.

CONSIDERING THE WORK OF INTERNAL AUDIT

8.34   Internal audit is part of a company's system of internal control and can provide helpful audit evidence to the external auditor. Guidance on using the work of internal audit is provided in the form of ISA (UK) 610 *Using the Work of Internal Auditors*.

IMPORTANT POINT

It is important to emphasise that the external auditor cannot use a client's internal audit function to provide **direct assistance** to them. The term 'direct assistance' is defined as:

> The use of internal auditors to perform audit procedures under the direction, supervision and review of the external auditor.[1]
>
> Why does the ISA (UK) prohibit external auditors from doing this as surely it would save time and costs? Well, internal audit (IA) is not independent of the client because they are a function of the client's internal control system (but they must be independent from the operations they evaluate so they can provide an unbiased and objective view). That is not to say the auditor cannot rely on some of the work/functions carried out by IA; it's just that IA cannot carry out audit procedures that would normally be carried out by the external auditor – for example, carrying out audit sampling for the external auditors.

Many businesses, especially those that apply corporate governance principles and some academy schools, have an IA function. This can be helpful to the external auditor because they can choose to rely on some of the work performed by IA **provided** that it is relevant to the scope of the external audit and is of a high quality.

I mentioned earlier in this section that one of the primary objectives of IA is to monitor the effectiveness of the entity's system of internal control. Remember, 'control risk' is the risk that a material misstatement in the financial statements will not be prevented or detected and corrected on a timely basis by the entity's system of internal control. An efficient IA function may reduce control risk.

It is often helpful to understand the notable differences between the work of the external auditor and the work of the internal auditor. Some of these differences are set out in the table below:

External audit	Internal audit
Objective The main objective of the external auditor is to provide an opinion on whether the financial statements give a true and fair view (or present fairly, in all material respects).	The main objective of internal audit is to improve the entity's operations by reviewing the efficiency and effectiveness of the system of internal control.
Reporting External auditors report to the shareholders. External auditors' reports are included in the annual report and financial statements and are publicly available.	Internal audit reports are not publicly available and are only intended to be seen by the addressee of the report (usually the directors, the audit committee and those charged with governance).

1 ISA (UK) 610, para 14(b).

External audit	Internal audit
Scope of work The external auditor's work is limited to verifying the truth and fairness of the financial statements.	The internal auditor may have a wide remit which is determined by the requirements of management or those charged with governance. Usually (but not in every case), the internal auditor's work will focus on internal controls and how those controls may be improved upon (though internal audit would not implement controls as otherwise they would then be reviewing controls they have devised).
Relationship External auditors are appointed by the shareholders and are therefore independent of the client.	Internal auditors are appointed by management and are usually employees. However, in some cases the internal audit function can be outsourced which can increase independence.

Typical assignments that may be carried out by internal audit include the following:

In terms of the relationship internal audit has with the external auditors, this would all depend on whether the internal audit function is relevant to the external audit. Even if it is relevant, there is nothing to require the external auditor from using the work of internal audit and hence in these situations, ISA (UK) 610 would not apply to the external audit. Remember, it is down to the external auditor to decide on whether, or not, to use the work of the client's internal audit function and this decision will usually be based on risk assessment and the overall effectiveness of the internal audit function itself.

Where the external auditor chooses to use the work of the internal audit function, the external auditor still remains wholly responsible for the audit opinion on the financial statements. Where the work of internal audit is being used, the auditor is required:

(a)   to determine whether the work of the internal audit function can be used and, if so, in which areas and to what extent; and

(b)   to determine whether the work of internal audit is adequate for the purposes of the external audit.

Eagle-eyed auditors will probably think I have missed an objective out in ISA (UK) 610, para 13(c). However, this paragraph requires the auditor to consider whether internal auditors will be used to provide direct assistance. Remember, ISA (UK) 610 prohibits internal audit (or internal auditors) from providing direct assistance to the external auditor, hence why I did not cite it as an objective.

Using the work of internal audit

8.35   Of course, in the world of audit, nothing is ever as simple as just using the work of the client's internal audit function. No, first of all the external auditor must evaluate the work of internal audit and this is a three-pronged attack:

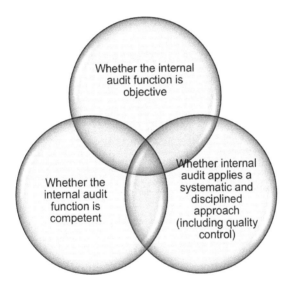

Assuming the external auditor concludes that they can use the work of internal audit, care must be taken in determining how much reliance to place on that work. Remember, it is likely the auditor will also have to carry out some of their own procedures which is where the risk assessment procedures will kick in. ISA (UK) 610 suggests that where the assessed risks of material misstatement are higher, the more persuasive the audit evidence will need to be. In other words, the auditor will need to obtain their own audit evidence rather than just relying on the work of internal audit for those areas of the audit which are considered at higher risk of material misstatement.

The external auditor will also need to discuss and co-ordinate with the internal audit function. The external auditor cannot ask the internal auditor to perform specific tasks for them (remember, direct assistance in ISA (UK) 610 is prohibited). Hence, the external auditor will need to carefully consider matters which will need to be discussed as well as the timing of work, the type of work to be performed and how it will be documented. To that end, it is important that there is effective communication between the external and internal auditors.

Reviewing the work of internal audit

8.36   Sufficient time must be set aside for the external auditor to review the work of internal audit. The key consideration by the external auditor during the review process is whether, or not, the work carried out by internal audit is high quality and whether it has been carried out in an objective manner. The review process will typically involve:

Ascertaining

If the work carried out by internal audit has been properly planned, performed, supervised, reviewed and documented

Determining

Whether sufficient appropriate audit evidence has been obtained

Considering

If the conclusions reached are appropriate in the circumstances

Concluding

Whether the reports prepared by internal audit are consistent with the work performed

Documentation

8.37   When the external auditor uses the work of the client's internal audit function, ISA (UK) 610 requires certain documentation to be prepared as follows:

(a)   The auditor's evaluation of:

    (i)   whether internal audit's organisational status and relevant policies and procedures supports the objectivity of the internal auditors;

(ii)   the level of competence of internal audit; and

(iii)   whether a systematic and disciplined approach is applied by internal audit.

(b)   The nature and extent of the work used as well as the basis for that decision.

(c)   The audit procedures that have been carried out by the external auditor to evaluate the adequacy of the work used.

ACCOUNTING ESTIMATES

8.38   You could safely say that pretty much every set of financial statements contains an accounting estimate in some shape or form. For example, the useful lives of property, plant and equipment is an estimate on which the depreciation expense is based. This is a fact of life in accountancy and audit and while some accounting estimates may be inconsequential (or 'clearly trivial'), others may not. Accounting estimates are included in complex areas such as the valuation of financial instruments and defined benefit pension plans. This is where the auditor must carefully devise audit procedures to address risks of material misstatement – and this is a tricky job in itself.

The problem with accounting estimates is that they can be difficult to audit because they involve subjectivity. An estimate cannot be 100% accurate (because otherwise it wouldn't be an estimate) and they may lack supporting evidence. To further compound the complexities surrounding accounting estimates, they may also be made in areas which the auditor does not have specialist knowledge of (such financial instruments) and hence the use of experts will be required which I looked at in **8.2** above.

ISA (UK) 540 *Auditing Accounting Estimates and Related Disclosures* is the ISA (UK) that provides guidance to the auditor when it comes to dealing with accounting estimates and their related disclosures in the financial statements. The objective of the auditor according to ISA (UK) 540 is to obtain sufficient appropriate audit evidence about whether accounting estimates and related disclosures are reasonable and in line with the requirements of the financial reporting framework (eg, FRS 102). The ISA (UK) also requires the auditor to obtain an understanding of *how* management identifies transactions, events or conditions that give rise to the need for an accounting estimate.

Risk assessment process for accounting estimates

8.39   What auditors will find in ISA (UK) 540 is what is known as the 'spectrum of inherent risk'. This is a concept that is also found in ISA (UK)

315 *Identifying and Assessing the Risks of Material Misstatement* hence there is overlap between ISA (UK) 540 and ISA (UK) 315. Both these ISAs (UK) share the spectrum of inherent risk, which is not a new concept in the world of auditing and most modern audit methodologies include such a spectrum, albeit on a 'low', 'moderate' or 'high' scale.

One of the important risks that the auditor must bear in mind where accounting estimates are concerned is the risk of management bias. Management has the capability (and sometimes the incentive) to manipulate an accounting estimate to achieve a desired result – this 'desired result' is usually how much profit needs to be reported.

When carrying out the inherent risk assessment in relation to accounting estimates, the auditor must consider three areas:

Estimation uncertainty

8.40   Estimation uncertainty may be affected by a specified method within a financial reporting framework (such as FRS 102). It can also be affected by assumptions that are highly susceptible to change or where the data is unobservable. Unobservable data may, for example, be used when valuing a decommissioning liability that was taken on as part of a business combination. The valuation is based on the company's own estimates of future cash flows taken at present value.

Complexity

8.41   Some estimates may need to be arrived at by individuals who have specialist skills and knowledge over the area giving rise to the estimate. In some cases, the estimate may need to be calculated by models or algorithms which may be highly complex. Conversely, other estimates may not be so complex (such as the useful economic life of an item of property, plant and equipment or a provision for liabilities).

Subjectivity

8.42   Subjectivity includes the risk of management bias. The auditor must keep in mind that certain estimates are not subject to prescribed approaches, hence management are given free rein to apply their own approach. This increases the risk of management bias and therefore results in increased subjectivity. There may also be instances where there is a lack of external data to support the accounting estimate and hence it is based solely on professional judgement and management's experience.

Interaction with audit planning and risk assessment

8.43 As always, there is a degree of interaction with planning. As we know, the auditor is required to obtain an understanding of the client and the environment in which it operates. This includes matters related to accounting estimates. The table below outlines some factors which the auditor should consider:

Matter	What needs to be understood
Events and conditions giving rise to estimates	Whether there are any new types of balances and transactions that involve estimates or changes in terms and conditions
Requirements of the financial reporting framework	Changes to the applicable financial reporting framework (eg, FRS 102) or legislation may give rise to the need for new or additional accounting estimates. This is particularly the case given the FRC's recent finalisation of the periodic review of UK and Ireland GAAP which brought in some significant changes in key areas of the financial statements (eg, leasing and revenue recognition)
Governance and oversight	Consideration of whether management have the appropriate skills to develop models or methods which are involved in arriving at accounting estimates
IT system	The role the IT system plays in dealing with accounting estimates, such as the methods and assumptions used and the input data
Outcome of previous estimates	Whether these have an impact on the estimation process (eg, if they were inaccurate in the prior year, they could be inaccurate in the current year)
Use of specialist skills	Whether specialist skills and knowledge are required to perform risk assessment and audit procedures. This includes considering whether a management or auditor's expert will be required

IMPORTANT POINT

When it comes to assessing risks, it's important to keep in mind that ISA (UK) 540 requires a **separate** assessment of inherent risk and control risk (similar to ISA (UK) 315) when it comes to assessing the risk of material misstatement at the financial statement assertion level.

The auditor must also document controls over the accounting estimates and check they have been implemented correctly. It may also be the case that the auditor concludes that substantive procedures alone cannot provide sufficient appropriate audit evidence (for example, if an estimate is generated through a complex system with inputs and outputs that cannot be observed directly) and so a decision to test controls may be made.

Responses to assessed risks in respect of accounting estimates

8.44   When responding to the assessed risks of material misstatement where accounting estimates are concerned, there are three approaches which can be used by the auditor:

Subsequent events

8.45   This can be an efficient means of verifying the accuracy of an accounting estimate (especially where a significant amount of management judgement has been applied). The auditor can look at events that have happened after the balance sheet date to determine how reliable the accounting estimate turned out to be. Clearly, this cannot be done for every accounting estimate as some estimates will relate to events or conditions that occur over a long timescale, but for some it could well be an effective way of ensuring an accounting estimate is not materially misstated.

Develop an auditor's point estimate

8.46 This approach is often used when management's point estimate cannot be relied upon, for example when:

● prior year audit evidence shows that management's method is ineffective;

● controls over accounting estimates are poorly designed or not implemented;

● there are appropriate alternative assumptions or evidence sources which can be used;

● post-date evidence has not been properly considered by management or contradicts management's point estimate; or

● management has not considered the level of estimation uncertainty.

It's probably more useful to look at an example where the development of an auditor's point estimate is concerned:

Example 8.5 – Auditor's point estimate

Holmes Homes Ltd is a private rental property business which rents properties out to individuals and families in the north of England. It is run by three directors, none of whom have experience in valuing properties. All properties owned by the company meet the definition of 'investment property' in FRS 102 *The Financial Reporting Standard applicable in the UK and Republic of Ireland* and are accounted for under Section 16 *Investment Property* at fair value through profit or loss. Holmes Homes Ltd is not a member of a group and hence the accounting policy option of measuring intra-group investment property under the cost model does not apply.

The year-end carrying amount of the investment properties is significantly material to the financial statements and has been derived at using a model which takes into consideration local price indices, rental yields and occupancy rates. There is no evidence available post-year end to back up the valuations and given the directors inexperience and lack of professional qualifications in valuing investment property, the auditor has deemed this area of the financial statements to be at significantly high risk of material misstatement.

To mitigate this risk, the audit engagement partner has decided to engage the services of a local firm of chartered surveyors, Sunnie & Co LLP, which specialises in domestic property valuations and has offices nationwide. Terms, including the scope of work and respective responsibilities, have been agreed in the form of an engagement letter.

The chartered surveyor has been instructed to carry out an appraisal of a small sample of properties within each town in order to determine the fair value.

Once this valuation work has been carried out by the surveyor, the auditor can extrapolate the surveyor's findings across the rest of the properties to determine whether management's estimate is reasonable or whether it is misstated.

Test how management has arrived at the accounting estimate

8.47   The auditor will usually use this method in the following circumstances:

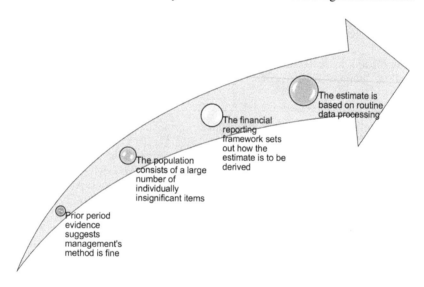

Now, as is always the case, there are some complexities thrown into the mix for good measure, too (after all, this is auditing!) The auditor must carefully consider whether there is any presence of bias indicators. Accounting estimates provide a range of opportunities for the client to manipulate the financial statements to achieve a desired outcome, so the auditor must ensure they maintain professional scepticism and question what **could** go wrong where the accounting estimates are concerned.

ISA (UK) 540 is specific in the procedures it requires. In particular, the auditor must address the following:

- Whether the method selected by management is appropriate in the context of the financial reporting framework used by the client. Also, if there have been changes in the method used to arrive at accounting estimates, are those methods appropriate?

- Whether judgements made in selecting the method give rise to potential indicators of management bias.

- Whether the calculations used are consistent with the method adopted by management and whether they are, of course, mathematically correct.

- Where complex modelling is involved, whether judgements have been consistently applied and whether:

  — the design of the model meets the measurement objectives of the financial reporting framework and is appropriate in the circumstances (including whether any changes from the prior period are also appropriate); and

  — whether adjustments to the output of the model are consistent with the measurement objective of the financial reporting framework and are appropriate in the circumstances.

- Whether the integrity of the significant assumptions and the underlying data has been maintained when management have applied the chosen method.

Remember, this is all about making sure the estimate is **reasonable** in the circumstances. When the auditor maintains an adequate level of professional scepticism, it will allow them to challenge the assumptions used and be alert to evidence of bias.

Now, it is not *just* the estimate itself that we are concerned with (although it is a major concern of the auditor). What is also important to understand is whether the data underpinning the estimate is appropriate, relevant and reliable as well as considering whether it has been properly understood or interpreted by management. If the underpinning data is unreliable (or the controls over that data are weak) or management have failed to understand or interpret the data correctly, the accounting estimate will be at risk of material misstatement and therefore the auditor must devise alternative audit procedures that address these risks.

Other audit procedures for accounting estimates

8.48   In a book like this one, it is difficult to be prescriptive as to what procedures are necessary in every circumstance because life is just not that simple (especially life in auditing). However, there are some 'typical' audit procedures that are usually applied over accounting estimates, such as:

- Reviewing the judgement and decisions made by management when determining the accounting estimate as this is likely to indicate any potential management bias.

- Comparing accounting estimates in the current year versus the prior year to identify if any significant fluctuations exist which need further audit procedures.

- Reviewing the disclosures made in the financial statements concerning the accounting estimates (such as determining whether disclosures of a provision comply with FRS 102, Section 21 *Provisions and Contingencies*).

- Obtaining a written representation from management and, where appropriate, those charged with governance, as to whether they believe significant assumptions used in making accounting estimates are reasonable.

Evaluating and concluding on accounting estimates

8.49   At the end of the process of auditing accounting estimates, ISA (UK) 540 requires the auditor to evaluate (based on the audit evidence obtained) whether the accounting estimates are reasonable. Audit procedures may have identified misstatements in the accounting estimates (which have been discovered through procedures such as subsequent events reviews or developing an auditor's point estimate) that may need correction to avoid the need for a modified audit opinion.

In addition, financial reporting frameworks, such as FRS 102, require management to clearly differentiate between:

- Judgements; and

- Sources of estimation uncertainty.

The auditor must carefully consider whether the client's disclosures comply with the requirements of the applicable financial reporting framework. This is to ensure that a true and fair view is given in the financial statements.

IMPORTANT POINT

A written management (or from those charged with governance if different) representation point must be obtained about whether the methods, significant assumptions and the data used in arriving at accounting estimates and the related disclosures are appropriate to achieve recognition, measurement or disclosure that complies with the

---

applicable financial reporting framework. In addition, ISA (UK) 540 also requires the auditor to consider the need to obtain representations concerning specific accounting estimates, including the methods, assumptions or data used.

Remember, ISA (UK) 580 *Written Representations* contains an Appendix 1 which identifies paragraphs in other ISAs (UK) requiring subject-matter specific written representations. The Appendix requires a representation in respect of ISA (UK) 540, para 37.

Documentation

8.50   As with most of the ISAs (UK), there is a lot of documentation that will be required on file where accounting estimates are concerned. This is necessary to demonstrate that the auditor has responded to the risks of material misstatement where accounting estimates are concerned.

IMPORTANT POINT

ISA (UK) 540 makes a point of discussing how the auditor should document their use of professional scepticism when auditing accounting estimates. For example, how the auditor has addressed indicators of possible management bias. This is an issue which is commonly forgotten about, and should be borne in mind when completing audit work on accounting estimates. It is often worthwhile flagging this point up in the planning meeting so that whichever member(s) of the audit engagement team are responsible for the audit of accounting estimates understand they will need to document how they have applied professional scepticism (not just document that they have applied it).

DATA ANALYTICS

8.51   In the last couple of years, the phrase 'data analytics' has been bandied around the auditing profession more and more. However, it is actually a technique that has been around for a long time. In general terms, the use of data analytics can allow the analysis of complete sets of data to identify unusual fluctuations and trends which the auditor may need to investigate. It can assist with analytical review. Data analytics can also provide the auditor with evidence regarding a specific area of the financial statements.

Advantages and challenges of data analytics

8.52 Auditors have used computer-assisted audit techniques (CAATs) for years and the increasing use of technology (certainly over the last 20 years) means the auditor can quickly analyse entire populations of data as opposed to using sampling because CAATs are effectively quicker at doing the analysis work for obvious reasons. Audit tests that used to take hours (or even days) to perform can now be carried out in a matter of seconds and can eliminate sampling risk. Inherently, this will provide the auditor with more persuasive audit evidence, especially when entire populations are examined and the efficiency of the audit increases. All this sounds ideal, doesn't it?

Clearly, one of the main advantages of data analytics is the fact that the auditor can use them at a very early stage of the audit to identify potentially problematic areas, especially those where inordinate fluctuations have been noted. As mentioned earlier, data analytics can increase audit efficiencies allowing the auditor to spend more time focussing on those areas of the financial statements which are at heightened risk of material misstatement. Data analytics can also be used as part of a continuous auditing approach, rather than having audit procedures concentrated on year-end balances and transactions.

Another advantage of data analytics is that they can uncover more anomalies within the financial statements or the client's system of internal control than traditional audit procedures can. This, in turn, means the auditor can communicate more issues to those charged with governance which may be of interest to them.

There are, however, some disadvantages to data analytics. For example, their use can be restricted if the client's data is of poor quality, or the data cannot be converted into the same format which is used by the software driving the data analytics.

Another disadvantage is that data analytics will involve training audit staff in how to use them. This will involve additional costs being incurred and if the audit firm is small, the costs of this training may outweigh the benefits.

FINANCIAL REPORTING COUNCIL (FRC) THEMATIC
REVIEW INTO DATA ANALYTICS

In January 2017, the FRC issued a thematic review into the use of data analytics in the audit of financial statements. In this thematic review, the FRC look at a sample of firms' policies and procedures in respect of a specific area or aspect of the audit or firm-wide procedures so they can make comparison to identify good practice and areas of common weakness.

Thematic reviews are narrow in scope and allow the FRC to focus in one specific area in greater depth, which cannot be done when they review an audit of a public interest entity.

The FRC reviewed the use of data analytics at the six largest UK audit firms. They found that data analytics is most commonly used to:

- Provide an analysis of all transactions within a population, stratify that population and identify outliers which the auditor must examine further.

- Reperform calculations relevant to the financial statements.

- Match transactions as they are processed through the relevant cycle.

- Assist in the segregation of duties testing.

- Compare entity data to data that has been obtained externally.

- Manipulate data to assess the impact of different assumptions.

The thematic review identified positive contributions to audit quality, including:

- Deepening the auditor's understanding of the entity.

- Facilitating the focus of audit testing to those areas of high risk by stratifying large populations.

- Strengthening the exercise of professional scepticism.

- Improving consistency and central oversight in group audits.

- Enabling the auditor to perform tests on large or complex datasets where a manual approach may be impractical.

- General improvements to audit efficiencies.

- Identifying instances of fraud.

- Enhancing communications with audit committees.

Typical areas of the financial statements where data analytics are used in practice include:

- Selecting and testing journal entries.

- Nominal ledger analysis.

- Revenue analytics.

- Process analytics.

- Valuation of financial instruments including derivatives.

- Impairment modelling.

- Tracing individual revenue transactions to debtors and after-date cash received.

- Recalculation of stock ageing.

- Recalculation of debtors ageing.

- Tracing supplier income to agreements and cash received.

- Recalculation of fund management fees based on the value of assets under management.

The FRC's thematic review clarifies that data analytics are not used in isolation, but they form part of a body of audit evidence. To that end, the FRC recommend that audit firms:

- Consider whether a data analytic is a 'good tool' for the client's specific environment. The thematic review identifies one audit where an analytic was designed on the basis that the entity posts granular journals but the entity, in fact, posts large batch journals. This analytic would therefore produce a number of anomalies in the output and hence significant follow-up work was required.

- Ensure that all relevant assertions are covered for the balance which is being tested. The FRC identified one audit where the completeness assertion for revenue was not addressed and one audit where the classification assertion was relevant, but also not addressed.

- Assess whether audit testing in other areas needs to be 'flexed' to provide the necessary supporting evidence for the use of data analytics. The FRC identified four audit firms that used data analytics in various ways to provide assurance over revenue by tracing sales transactions through to debtors and cash. This technique may then rely on testing of debtors and cash to provide substantive audit evidence for revenue. The FRC observed one such audit where the cash procedures were inappropriately performed on a sample basis and the bank account used for sales receipts was omitted from the sample.

Example 8.6 – Audit data analytics

Darren Heyes is the audit senior of Mallard & Co Accountancy Services who has been assigned to the audit of Hummingbird Industries Ltd for the year ended 31 December 2024. Darren has used the firm's data analytics software to interrogate the journal entries that have been entered into the accounting system during the year. The software presents this report for Darren:

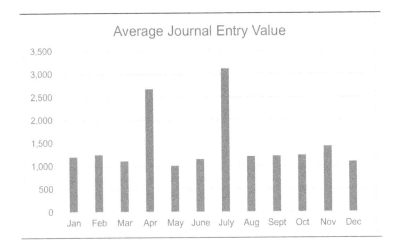

Average Journal Entry Value

This report shows Darren that in April and July there are unusually high average values for the journals that have been posted to the client's nominal ledger. Darren must devise audit procedures to find out the reason why this has happened. Perhaps there may be genuine business reasons, such as an exceptional item or bonus payments made via the payroll. Conversely, there could be a problem with the accounting records.

If Darren had not used data analytics, it would have taken him a lot longer to determine the trends and possibly the unusual value of journals in the months of April and July would not have been identified.

Use of data analytics for audit sampling

8.53 Modern audit sampling will often utilise data analytics due to the efficiencies that they bring to the audit (the audit test can cover the whole population, which can potentially eliminate sampling risk). It can be argued, therefore, that data analytics can improve the quality and efficiency of audit evidence.

The auditor must bear in mind that the results of data analysis will need to be carefully evaluated and this will involve time and skill. For example, when the auditor is testing an entire population using data analytics, the results are likely to highlight many more anomalies or exceptions (which are referred to as 'outliers') than if the test had been performed using traditional audit sampling. The auditor will need to be able to decide which of these outliers need further investigation. This will usually involve setting a threshold in terms of the number, or perhaps the monetary value, of outliers to look at in more detail and then devise procedures to corroborate them.

COMMUNICATION WITH MANAGEMENT AND THOSE CHARGED WITH GOVERNANCE

8.54   Effective communication during the audit is a critical process and the auditor is required to assess the effectiveness of the **two-way** communication between the auditor and the client. If there is ineffective communication between the auditor and the client, it is likely that audit evidence will be insufficient and/or inappropriate, audit procedures may end up incomplete and there may be gaps in the auditor's understanding of the client and the environment in which it operates.

There are two specific ISAs (UK) that are devoted to communication aspects:

- ISA (UK) 260 *Communication with Those Charged with Governance*

- ISA (UK) 265 *Communicating Deficiencies in Internal Control to Those Charged with Governance and Management*

So, we have two parties to consider where communication is concerned:

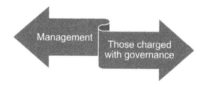

ISA (UK) 260 states that 'management' is the person(s) with executive responsibility for the conduct of the organisation's operations. This might also include some, or all, of those charged with governance (see below). For example, in a smaller organisation, management might also include the shareholders even though they are really two distinct bodies of individuals.

ISA (UK) 260 states that 'those charged with governance' includes people or an organisation(s) that has responsibility for overseeing the strategic direction of the business and obligations in respect of the accountability of the entity.

To a certain extent, this is common sense, but what the auditor must also understand is that those charged with governance also have a responsibility to oversee the financial reporting process and will also include the board of directors as a whole (including both executive and non-executive directors and the audit committee, if one exists).

I mentioned earlier that in a smaller organisation, management and those charged with governance may be the same body of individuals. However, this is not always the case. Management will clearly include the executive directors, but it would not normally include any non-executive directors.

As different audit clients have different structures, the auditor will need to determine at a very early stage in the audit (usually at the pre-planning stage) the appropriate person(s) to communicate with. Organisations that are 'public interest entities' will often have an audit committee whom the auditor should primarily communicate with. Where an audit committee does not exist, the auditor will usually communicate with the body that performs an equivalent function.

Example 8.7 – Management and governance

Client 1

Doug Ltd is an electronic goods retailer with 35 branches across the UK. Its head office is located in Nottingham and it has 11 directors and approximately 28 shareholders. There is a very small audit committee in place.

The directors of Doug Ltd will be responsible for running the company in the best interests of the shareholders. Those charged with governance will include the audit committee to whom the external auditor will discuss any significant deficiencies in internal control (as well as the directors, if the auditor deems this appropriate).

Client 2

Bert Ltd is a clothing retailer operating from two stores in a city centre. The company is owned by two shareholders, Chris and Kate, who are both married and own 50% of the ordinary shares each. Both Chris and Kate are also the directors of Bert Ltd and are active in the day-to-day running of the business.

In this case, Chris and Kate will act as both management and those charged with governance. There is no other person involved in a governance role.

Any matters that need to be communicated to management need not be communicated twice (ie, once to Chris and Kate as management and then again to them as those charged with governance). However, the auditor must be satisfied that communicating with those individuals with management responsibilities adequately informs all of those with whom the auditor would also communicate with in their governance capacity.

Communication with management and those charged with governance starts at an early stage in the audit. Take, for example, the letter of engagement. This communicates the respective responsibilities of the auditor, management and, where applicable, those charged with governance. The auditor will then hold a discussion with management and those charged with governance concerning the scope and timing of the audit, etc.

During the audit, the auditor will need to communicate with the client on various matters. For example, making inquiries to help gather sufficient appropriate audit evidence.

There may be occasions when an issue is particularly sensitive and can only be communicated in a particular way. For example, if a fraud is discovered.

IMPORTANT POINT

Where an audit team member discovers a fraud, this issue should be communicated with the appropriate level of management, bearing in mind the auditor's obligations under anti-money laundering regulations and the tipping off rules. If the fraud involves management, it may be appropriate to discuss the issue with those charged with governance. In either case, it is important that such matters are communicated appropriately and quickly.

Communicating with those charged with governance

8.55   There are four objectives according to ISA (UK) 260 as follows:

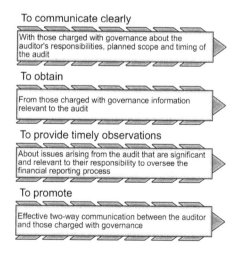

To communicate clearly
With those charged with governance about the auditor's responsibilities, planned scope and timing of the audit

To obtain
From those charged with governance information relevant to the audit

To provide timely observations
About issues arising from the audit that are significant and relevant to their responsibility to oversee the financial reporting process

To promote
Effective two-way communication between the auditor and those charged with governance

In terms of matters that need to be communicated to those charged with governance, these consist of the following:

- **The auditor's responsibilities in respect of the audit**

The auditor's responsibilities in respect of the audit will usually be included in the letter of engagement that is issued at the outset.

- **Planning, scope and timing of the audit**

The auditor must communicate the planning, scope and timing of the audit to those charged with governance. The purpose of doing this is to enable them to understand practical issues such as the timing of interim and final audit procedures. This also provides an opportunity for those charged with governance to ask any relevant questions about the planned audit approach.

It is important that the auditor does not give too much information away concerning the planned audit approach such that audit procedures are predictable. There is a possibility that management and/or those charged with governance will want to cover up issues such as a fraud so if the auditor goes into too much detail concerning their planned audit approach, this provides an opportunity for management and/or those charged with governance to cover their tracks.

Significant findings from the audit

8.56 Significant findings from the audit are communicated to those charged with governance usually at the end of the audit process when most of the audit evidence has been obtained. However, the auditor may still need to obtain some audit evidence from those charged with governance even at this stage in the audit – for example, details of significant subsequent events.

ISA (UK) 260 provides a list of the significant findings that the auditor must communicate to those charged with governance as follows

Significant findings	Other comments
The auditor's views about the qualitative aspects of the client's accounting practices which include: - accounting policies; - accounting estimates; and - disclosures in the financial statements.	This is especially relevant to issues such as: - use of professional judgement; - indicators of potential management bias; and - whether accounting estimates need to be revised.

Significant findings	Other comments
The auditor's views must also include any significant accounting practice that may be appropriate under the applicable financial reporting framework, but where the auditor considers them not to be appropriate in the client's particular circumstances.	
Significant difficulties (if any) that were encountered during the audit.	This may relate to un-cooperative staff members or an inability to obtain sufficient appropriate audit evidence in material areas (which may also impact on the audit opinion).
Significant matters that arose during the course of the audit that were discussed, or subject to correspondence with, management.	This could involve the discovery of material misstatements during the audit.
Written representations.	These must include the specific written representations contained in the Appendix to ISA (UK) 580 *Written Representations* as well as other client-specific representations that the auditor deems necessary.
Circumstances that affect the form and content of the auditor's report (if any).	This could include expected modifications to the auditor's opinion and Key Audit Matters that are to be communicated in accordance with ISA (UK) 701 *Communicating Key Audit Matters in the Independent Auditor's Report*.
Any other significant matters arising during the course of the audit.	These would involve any matters that, in the auditor's professional judgement, are relevant to the oversight of the client's financial reporting process.

The communication process

8.57   Communication must always be a two-way process. To that end, both the client and the auditor need to be aware of the following:

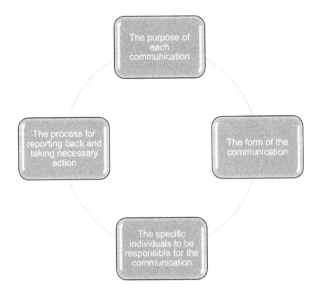

IMPORTANT POINT

In terms of the **form** of the communication, most audit firms prefer the communications to be in writing, although ISA (UK) 260 does not mandate this. Having said that, ISA (UK) 260 does acknowledge that oral communication is unlikely to be adequate when addressing significant findings from the audit.

When certain communications are made orally, it is important that they are subsequently documented within the audit working papers. This is so a contemporaneous record of the communications is on file. Such communications can also be confirmed by email as well.

Consideration of the effectiveness of two-way communication

8.58   ISA (UK) 260 requires the auditor to consider whether the two-way communication between the auditor and the client has been sufficiently adequate for the purposes of the audit. Where the auditor concludes the two-way communication has been insufficient, they must consider the impact (if any) on the auditor's assessment of the risks of material misstatement and whether they have been able to obtain sufficient appropriate audit evidence.

ISA (UK) 260 does not set out specific procedures to consider the effectiveness of the two-way communication process. In practice, it should be straightforward for the auditor to assess the effectiveness by considering how open management and, where applicable, those charged with governance of the entity, were in their dealings with the audit team and how easy difficult and/or contentious matters were resolved.

REPORTING DEFICIENCIES IN INTERNAL CONTROL

8.59   Back in the planning chapters (specifically **Chapters 5** and **6**) I examined internal controls a lot. When the auditor performs tests of controls (to assess the operating effectiveness of those controls), the results can contribute towards audit evidence.

ISA (UK) 265 *Communicating Deficiencies in Internal Control to Those Charged with Governance and Management* provides guidance to the auditor in reporting deficiencies in internal control. There are two types of deficiency we are concerned with here:

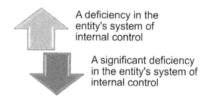

A deficiency in the entity's system of internal control

A significant deficiency in the entity's system of internal control

It should be clear to most that a **deficiency** in internal control is less serious (in terms of its overall impact on the financial statements) than a **significant** deficiency. However, ISA (UK) 265 sets out what it considers to be a deficiency as follows:

(a)   Where a control is designed, implemented or operated in such a way that it is unable to prevent, or detect and correct, misstatements in the financial statements in a timely manner.

(b)   A control which would be needed to prevent, or detect and correct, misstatements in the financial statements in a timely manner is missing.

In terms of a 'significant deficiency', ISA (UK) 265 recognises this to be:

•   A deficiency, or combination of deficiencies, in the client's system of internal control that (in the auditor's professional judgement) is of such importance that it merits the attention of those charged with governance.

All significant deficiencies must be notified to those charged with governance in writing because this will emphasise the importance of the matters and will also provide assistance to those charged with governance in fulfilling their oversight responsibilities. In practice, those charged with governance will also need to put measures in place to enable the entity to overcome those deficiencies.

So, as you can see, the difference between a 'deficiency' and a 'significant deficiency' is that the former simply merits the attention of management only; the latter merits the attention of those charged with governance.

ISA (UK) 265 provides guidance to auditors on examples of matters which the auditor would usually consider when determining whether a deficiency in internal controls is significant and includes:

(a)   The likelihood of the deficiencies leading to material misstatements in the financial statements.

(b)   The susceptibility of the entity to loss or fraud of the related asset or liability.

(c)   The subjectivity and complexity of determining estimated amounts (for example, fair value accounting estimates).

(d)   The financial statement amount(s) exposed to the deficiencies.

(e)   The volume of activity that has occurred, or could occur, in the account balance or class of transaction(s) exposed to the deficiency/ies.

(f)   The importance of the controls used in the financial reporting process, such as:

    (i)   general monitoring controls (such as oversight of management);

    (ii)   controls over the prevention and detection of fraud;

    (iii)   controls over the entity's selection and application of significant (material) accounting policies;

    (iv)   controls over significant transactions with related parties;

    (v)   controls over significant transactions which arise outside the entity's ordinary course of business; and

    (vi)   controls over the period-end financial reporting process (eg, controls over non-recurring journal entries).

(g)   The cause and frequency of exceptions detected due to the deficiencies in the system of internal control.

(h)   The interaction of the deficiency with other deficiencies found in the entity's system of internal control.

Example 8.8 – Deficiencies in a client's system of internal control

During the audit of the financial statements of Watson Enterprises Ltd for the year ended 31 July 2024, the auditor came across several deficiencies in the system of internal control in areas such as acquisitions of fixed assets, payroll, purchasing and taxation. In the client's payroll cycle, it was noted there were some missing controls such as review of the payroll prior to it being finalised.

The audit engagement partner has reviewed the audit evidence in these areas and has concluded that it is insufficient to enable an unmodified opinion to be expressed.

The auditor generally must have exhausted all options before expressing any type of modified opinion on the financial statements. Hence there are a few options still available to the auditor to try and avoid a modified opinion being expressed:

Extend controls testing

The audit engagement team could extend tests of controls in those cycles of the business where deficiencies have been identified. It may well be that the deficiencies are isolated ones and are not as bad as first thought; although any absent controls (especially in payroll) must be communicated to management.

Address the issue with those charged with governance

If the auditor has concluded that the deficiencies are significant deficiencies, the auditor should address the deficiencies with those charged with governance.

Carry out additional substantive testing

As substantive procedures aim to detect misstatements at the financial statement assertion level, the auditor could extend their sample sizes and carry out additional substantive procedures on the cycles where controls are deficient. In terms of the options available to the auditor at this stage in the audit, carrying out additional substantive procedures is usually the best option because they will help to quantify the extent of errors. In addition, additional substantive procedures can 'bridge the gap' where tests of controls have revealed deficiencies.

If the auditor is still unable to obtain sufficient appropriate audit evidence, they will have no alternative but to issue a modified opinion. The auditor must then assess the magnitude of the lack of audit evidence and it could well be the case that a disclaimer of opinion may be appropriate in the circumstances.

Communication via the letter of comment

8.60   A letter of comment (often referred to as a 'management letter') is a letter sent to management from the auditor at the end of the audit. ISA (UK) 265 requires certain issues to be communicated to management in respect of control deficiencies as follows:

(a)   A description of the deficiencies and an explanation of their potential effect(s).

(b)   Sufficient information to enable those charged with governance and management to understand the context of the communication. This means the auditor must explain that:

(i)   the purpose of the audit is for the auditor to express an opinion on the entity's financial statements;

(ii)   the audit included consideration of the entity's system of internal control relevant to the preparation of the financial statements in order to design audit procedures that are appropriate in the entity's circumstances (but not for the purpose of expressing an opinion on the financial statements); and

(iii)   the matters reported are limited to those deficiencies that have been identified during the audit and that the auditor has concluded that they are sufficient importance to merit the attention of those charged with governance.

In practice, the letter of comment may include a covering letter with the deficiencies noted in an appendix. This is illustrated as follows:

Deficiency	Implication	Recommendation
There is no segregation of duties in the purchasing department as to who approves expenditure below £10,000.	There is a risk that the company incurs additional costs that are unnecessary due to staff ordering goods below £10,000 that are not required. This is also a fraud risk factor.	All items of expenditure must be approved prior to the expenditure being committed. Approval limits could be set so that the purchasing manager authorises expenditure up to £10,000 and a more senior official approves expenditure over £10,000.
There are no checks carried out on the payroll prior to it being finalised and subsequently paid.	There is a risk that a 'ghost' employee could be created on the payroll and a fraud could arise. In addition, there is also the risk that errors are not spotted in a timely manner resulting in incorrect salaries being paid which can also result in a loss of employee goodwill.	The payroll should be reviewed by a senior official in the payroll department or by a member of the finance department.

CHAPTER ROUNDUP

- Auditors cannot be expected to be experts in every aspect of transactions and balances that make up the financial statements and hence the use of experts may be required in some situations.

- There are two types of experts which the auditor can consider: an auditor's expert and a management's expert.

- Many audit clients use service organisations and it is important that careful thought is given to the controls in operation at the service organisation as a weak control environment at the service organisation can impact on the relevance and reliability of the audit evidence.

- Extensive work will often need to be carried out on opening balances for a new audit client; whereas only limited procedures may be needed for a recurring engagement.

- The auditor must attend the stock count where stock (and work in progress) is material to the financial statements. If attendance is impracticable, there may be implications on the auditor's opinion.

- Litigation and claims are areas that could give rise to material misstatements in the financial statements and the auditor is required to devise specific procedures to address the risk of material misstatement where such litigation and claims are present.

- The auditor is required to obtain sufficient appropriate audit evidence concerning the presentation and disclosure of segment information which will usually go beyond checking disclosures against a disclosure checklist.

- External confirmations are a good source of audit evidence and are often used by the auditor because they are generated from a third party, but the auditor must remain alert to any contradictions that may be apparent with other audit evidence.

- The work of an internal audit function may be used by the external auditor (especially in respect of controls testing). However, in the UK, internal audit is prohibited from providing direct assistance to the external auditor.

- Accounting estimates can prove to be a tricky area to audit because of their subjectivity and the fact that they are never '100% accurate'. Specific risk assessment and audit procedures must be carried out by the auditor where material accounting estimates are concerned.

- The use of data analytics has increased over the last few years and they can even eliminate sampling risk because entire populations can be verified far quicker than a manual process. However, the auditor must bear in mind that data analytics will only provide a source of potential misstatement – they cannot be used to draw conclusions.

- Effective communication is crucial in an audit engagement and this is related to communication between management *and* those charged with governance.

- The auditor must communicate deficiencies and significant deficiencies in internal control to management and those charged with governance. This is usually followed up by a letter of comment (management letter).

PITFALLS TO AVOID

- Making reference to the use of experts in the auditor's report.

- Not obtaining a 'bridging letter/report' for a service organisation where the service organisation's balance sheet date is not coterminous with the client's year end.

- Failing to review the previous auditor's files for a new audit client.

- Failing to attend the stock count where stock and work in progress are material to the financial statements.

- Obtaining an external confirmation but not doing anything with it on receipt (ie, simply placing it on the audit file).

- Placing too much reliance on data analytics which cannot draw conclusions (they can only point to a potential source of misstatement).

APPENDIX: ILLUSTRATIVE SERVICE AUDITOR'S ASSURANCE REPORT

Independent service auditor's assurance report on controls at Professional Payroll Services Ltd (the 'Service Organisation')

To the directors of Professional Payroll Services Ltd

Scope

The directors of Professional Payroll Services Ltd have engaged us to report on the Service Organisation's internal controls in operation over related information technology services and to provide reasonable assurance over the suitability of design and operating effectiveness of those controls to achieve the related control objectives in Section III of the Service Organisation's controls report ('the Report') throughout the period 1 January 2025 to 31 December 2025. The controls and control objectives included in the Report are those that management of the Service Organisation believe are likely to be relevant to clients' internal controls over financial reporting.

Section II of the Report indicates that certain control objectives specified in Section III can be achieved only if complementary user entity controls assumed in the design of the Service Organisation's controls are suitably designed and operating effectively, along with related controls at the Service Organisation. We have not evaluated the suitability of the design or operating effectiveness of such complementary user entity controls.

While the controls and related control objectives may be informed by the Service Organisation's need to satisfy legal or regulatory requirements, our scope of work and our conclusions do not constitute assurance over compliance with those laws and regulations.

Our independence and quality management

In carrying out our work, we complied with the [relevant professional body] Code of Ethics, which includes independence and other requirements founded on fundamental principles of integrity, objectivity, professional competence and due care, confidentiality and professional behaviour, that are least as demanding as the applicable provisions in the IESBA Code of Ethics. We also apply International Standard on Quality Management (UK) 1 and accordingly maintain a comprehensive system of quality management including documented policies and procedures regarding compliance with ethical requirements, professional standards and applicable legal and regulatory requirements.

The Service Organisation's responsibilities

The Service Organisation is responsible for:

- preparing the Report, comprising the management statement in Section I, the description of the organisation and related information technology information provided to the Service Organisation's clients in Section II, the list of controls and related control objectives described in Section III, including the completeness, accuracy and method of presentation of the Report and the management statement and the responses provided in connection with the exceptions identified;

- identifying the appropriate control objectives in relation to the needs of clients;

- identifying the risks that threaten the control objectives; and

• designing, implementing and effectively operating controls to achieve the stated control objectives.

The control objectives stated in Section III are those specified by the Service Organisation. Management remains solely responsible for determining the suitability of the control objectives to address the needs of intended users.

Service auditor's responsibilities

Our responsibility is to express an opinion on the suitability of the design and operating effectiveness of the controls to achieve the related control objectives stated in Section III based on our procedures. We conducted our engagement in accordance with International Standard on Assurance Engagements 3000 (Revised) *Assurance Engagements other than Audits or Reviews of Historical Financial Information*. This standard and guidance requires that we plan and perform our procedures to obtain reasonable assurance about whether, in all material respects, the controls were suitably designed and operating effectively to achieve the related control objectives stated in Section III. An assurance engagement to report on the design and operating effectiveness of controls at a service organisation involves:

• performing procedures to obtain evidence about the suitability of the design and operating effectiveness of those controls to achieve the related control objectives stated in Section III of the Report;

• assessing the risks that the controls were not suitably designed or operating effectively to achieve the related control objectives stated in Section III of the Report; and

• testing the operating effectiveness of those controls we consider necessary to provide reasonable assurance that the related control objectives stated in Section III of the Report were achieved.

We believe that the evidence we have obtained is sufficient and appropriate to provide a basis for our qualified opinion.

Inherent limitations

The Service Organisation's Report is prepared to meet the common needs of a broad range of clients and their auditors and may not, therefore, include every aspect of the Service Organisation's internal controls in operation over related information technology services that each individual client may consider important in its own particular environment. Also, because of their nature, controls at a service organisation may not prevent or detect and correct all errors or omissions in processing or reporting transactions. Our opinion is based on historical information and the projection to future periods of any evaluation of the conclusions about the suitability of the design or operating effectiveness of the controls would be inappropriate.

Basis for qualified opinion

As stated in the Service Organisation's management statement in Section I, a control was not designed and placed into operation to review the performance of certain suppliers until 1 August 2025. Consequently, for the period 1 January 2025 to 1 August 2025, the following control objective was not achieved:

• Certain supplier activities are properly managed and monitored

Qualified opinion

In our opinion, in all material respects, except for the matters described in the 'Basis for qualified opinion' paragraph above, based on the criteria described in the Service Organisation's management statement in Section I:

• the controls related to control objectives stated in Section III of the Report were suitably designed to provide reasonable assurance that the specified control objectives would be achieved if the described controls operated effectively throughout the period 1 January 2025 to 31 December 2025 and the clients applied the complementary controls referred to in Section II; and

• the controls tested, which, together with the complementary user entity controls referred to in the scope paragraph of this assurance report, if operating effectively, were those necessary to provide reasonable assurance that the control objectives stated in Section III of the Report were achieved, operated effectively throughout the period 1 January 2025 to 31 December 2025.

Description of tests of controls

The specific controls tested and the nature, timing and results of those tests are detailed in Section II.

Other information

The information included in Sections II and III is presented by the Service Organisation to provide additional information about the Service Organisation's controls that may be relevant to its clients' internal control as it relates to an audit of financial statements. Such information has not been subjected to the procedures applied in the examination related to the internal controls in operation over related information technology services, and accordingly, we do not express an opinion on it.

Intended users and purpose

This report and the description of tests of controls and results thereof in Section III are intended solely for the user of the clients of the Service Organisation and solely for the purpose of reporting on the controls of the Service Organisation, in accordance with the terms of our engagement letter dated 10 November 2024.

Our report must not be recited or referred to in whole, or in part, in any circumstances, without our express prior written permission. To the fullest extent permitted by law, we do not accept or assume responsibility to anyone other than the Service Organisation for our work, for this report or for the opinions we have formed, save when terms have been agreed in writing.

Vizsla & Co LLP
Chartered Certified Accountants
Glasgow
31 March 2026

Chapter 9

Fraud, Laws and Regulations

CHAPTER TOPIC LIST

- Introduction (see **9.1**)
- Fraud versus error (see **9.2**)
- Responsibilities in relation to fraud (see **9.10**)
- Professional scepticism (see **9.18**)
- Closing the expectations gap (see **9.19**)
- Laws and regulations (see **9.23**)

INTRODUCTION

9.1   Fraud has unfortunately been in the headlines a lot over recent years and lots of press reports have been published about well-known companies where fraud has taken place. For example, in 2019, Patisserie Valerie (see **9.22** below) was the subject of fraud which forced the company into administration. This is one of many stories where fraud has taken place and the most well-known is, of course, Enron (an old one at that, but still well remembered and cited).

It is important to clearly understand the auditor's responsibility where fraud and compliance with laws and regulations is concerned, as well as management's responsibility and this chapter covers those responsibilities in detail. In this chapter, I will also examine appropriate responses to suspected or identified fraud and non-compliance with laws and regulations.

WHAT ARE WE TRYING TO ACHIEVE?

The auditor must consider the risk of material misstatement of the financial statements due to fraud (as well as error). To that end there are various actions that must be taken by the auditor to ensure compliance with the ISAs (UK) – in particular ISA (UK) 240 *The Auditor's Responsibilities Relating to Fraud in an Audit of Financial Statements*. Therefore, the auditor must obtain sufficient appropriate audit evidence that they have obtained **reasonable assurance** that the financial statements are free from material misstatement whether caused by fraud or error.

In addition, the auditor must also consider whether the client has complied with all laws and regulations applicable to it. Again, the auditor must obtain sufficient appropriate audit evidence in this respect.

Fraud committed by employees usually arises through the manipulation of weaknesses in the organisation's system of internal control. This can arise, for example, through a lack of segregation of duties or a lack of oversight by responsible individuals. This type of risk is assessed through the auditor's consideration of controls. Where a fraud risk factor comes to the attention of the auditor, they will tailor their procedures to address the issue.

Fraud is an issue that must be considered by the auditor at **all** stages of the audit. ISA (UK) 240 was last revised by the Financial Reporting Council[1] in May 2021 and the latest edition of the ISA (UK) saw some fairly wide enhancements to the auditor's responsibilities where fraud is concerned. This was off the back of the recommendations made by Sir Donald Brydon CBE who carried out an independent review of audit in 2019 and effectively concluded that the work carried out by auditors where fraud was concerned was weak.

There is, what is known in auditing, as an 'expectations gap'. This is the gap that exists between what the auditor is expected to do under auditing standards (ISAs (UK)) where fraud is concerned, and what the general public perceive the auditor should be doing. This expectations gap becomes clear when a large corporate collapse happens, because one of the first questions asked, particularly where fraud is concerned, is why did the auditors not spot it? There are high expectations that the auditor should find all frauds, but the reality is that they will only discover a minority. In this chapter I look at the expectations gap in some detail because it presents challenges for auditors, particularly how the expectations gap may be 'closed' (see **9.19** below).

Compliance with laws and regulations is also an important issue. Any non-compliance with laws and regulations can have a significant impact on the entity in terms of potential fines and penalties levied by legislating authorities. In serious cases this can bring into question the entity's ability to continue as a

---

1 The Financial Reporting Council (FRC) will eventually transition to the Audit, Reporting and Governance Authority.

going concern. Hence, it is important that we look at the requirements of ISA (UK) 250 Section A – *Consideration of Laws and Regulations in an Audit of Financial Statements.*

FRAUD VERSUS ERROR

9.2 At the outset it is important that the auditor clearly understands the difference between 'fraud' and a 'fraud risk factor' and 'error'. During the course of an audit, it is very likely that the auditor will discover some errors in the financial statements. These can range from simple differences on a prepayment calculation to more serious errors, such as cut-off errors resulting in a material misstatement.

IMPORTANT POINT

It is important to understand the difference between a fraud and an error because the two are very different. A misstatement in the financial statements arising from fraud is deliberate; whereas a misstatement arising from error is generally unintentional.

ISA (UK) 240 does not define the term 'error', but the key issue is that an error is a mistake, often a human error, and can arise at any stage in a process. For example:

- Posting purchase invoices to incorrect accounts in the nominal ledger.

- Misinterpreting or misunderstanding facts or the requirements of accounting standards.

- An incorrect manual calculation.

- Duplicating payments to a supplier, employee or other third-party unintentionally.

- Sending out incorrect quantities of goods to a customer.

This list is by no means exhaustive, but it provides examples of how errors can arise in everyday business.

As noted earlier in this chapter and in **Chapters 5** and **6**, during the planning stage of the audit, the auditor will assess the client's system of internal control to determine whether, or not, those controls are effective at preventing and detecting and correcting, on a timely basis, errors such as the ones listed above and test their operating effectiveness.

By evaluating the client's system of internal control, the auditor is also assessing the risk of both fraud **and** error.

Common reasons for errors arising in the financial statements, which the auditor may identify at the planning stage of the audit include:

- errors in gathering the relevant data and information from which the financial statements are drawn up;

- errors in applying the requirements of an accounting standard;

- misinterpretation of facts giving rise to an error in an accounting estimate; or

- incorrect classification in the financial statements.

In respect of a recurring audit, the auditor can draw on their previous experience of the client when considering such issues. For example, if the prior year's audit revealed a significant number of errors when processing financial information, then the risk of material misstatement is likely to be assessed as higher than if there had been no errors in the prior year.

For new clients the risk of material misstatement is likely to be high because the auditor does not have previous experience to draw upon. Hence, for a new audit client it would normally be the case that specific audit procedures are designed at the planning stage to address the risk of fraud and error. Generally, this involves a more substantive approach and less reliance on controls.

IMPORTANT POINT

For new clients, the usual protocol is to ask the predecessor audit firm for access to their audit working papers to obtain audit evidence over opening balances. This review is **not** a review of the quality of the audit. I examine client acceptance in more detail in **Chapter 4**.

Reviewing documents such as the management letter and schedule of unadjusted errors from the previous year can always offer an insight as to what to expect from the client in terms of the system of internal control. If the previous year's audit revealed a significant number of adjustments to correct the financial statements, it is likely that the system of internal control is weak.

In any first-year audit, it is likely that a more substantive approach will be taken because of a lack of experience of the client, its transactions, accounting system and accounting policies. While controls will be documented and operational effectiveness assessed, it would be unusual for

---

> the auditor to place full reliance on them as this would increase detection risk and audit risk beyond what would be normally be considered to be acceptable.

As I mentioned earlier in the chapter, all audits will generally reveal an error of some sort in the financial statements. While effective internal controls can help to prevent and detect errors, there is no system of internal control which is perfect, so it is not unusual to identify errors during an audit. As the audit progresses any errors will be carried forward to an 'audit error schedule' or 'schedule of unadjusted misstatements'. Typical errors discovered may include:

- Understated accruals due to goods and/or services being received up to the year end, but not accrued for.

- Depreciation charges calculated incorrectly.

- Directors' remuneration posted to staff salaries.

- Transactions denoted in a foreign currency translated at the wrong rate.

- Disclosure notes omitted or inadequate.

Some errors may be factual (ie, there is no doubt about them). Others may result from extrapolated differences on test differences. Once all the audit work is completed, the auditor must review the total errors and misstatements discovered which will help them form a conclusion as to the adequacy of the accounting records. The auditor must also compare the level of unadjusted errors against materiality levels to identify if any further work is needed, or if the financial statements contain a material misstatement. **Chapter 10** deals with the evaluation of misstatements in more detail (see **10.2**).

Errors and misstatements which the auditor discovers during the audit may have arisen because of a weakness in the accounting records, or deficiencies in the entity's system of internal control. These are issues which the auditor will need to discuss with management and/or those charged with governance.

Types of fraud

9.3   ISA (UK) 240 recognises two types of fraud which the auditor is concerned with:

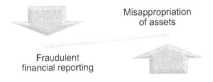

Misappropriation of assets

Fraudulent financial reporting

Misappropriation of assets

9.4   This type of fraud involves the theft of assets, such as theft of cash, high-value stock and computer equipment. In addition, using a company's assets for personal use is classified as misappropriation of assets – for example, if an employee uses a company vehicle for private use against company policy.

Fraudulent financial reporting

9.5   Fraudulent financial reporting refers to the deliberate manipulation of the financial statements so that they show a pre-determined outcome. This can include falsification of accounting records; omissions of transactions, balances or disclosures from the financial statements; or the deliberate misapplication of accounting standards. The objective of fraudulent financial reporting is to present the financial statements with a particular bias – for example, by concealing liabilities to improve the liquidity (and gearing) position of the entity – especially if the entity is trying to secure bank finance, or perhaps understating profits to reduce taxes. Fraudulent financial reporting is characterised by a deliberate breach of accounting standards.

Example 9.1 – Fraudulent financial reporting

The audit manager of Vizsla Audit Ltd has recently started planning the audit of a new client, Dalmatian Enterprises Ltd for the year ended 31 August 2023. The previous auditor resigned due to 'difficulties in agreeing the appropriateness of the client's accounting policies'.

Analytical review procedures have suggested profit before tax has remained consistent, although provisions for liabilities have reduced by some 20%. Revenue is also down on the previous year by approximately 18% while administrative expenses have also seen a significant decrease by 32%.

During the pre-planning meeting, the finance director made this startling revelation:

I need to emphasise the importance of us reporting a profit before tax of £1.3m. Under no circumstances can we have anything lower than this figure because this is what we have told the shareholders they can expect. The starting point for profit and loss is, therefore, what the shareholders want to see and we work up from there.

Further discussions concerning the provisions revealed the following admission by the finance director:

The provisions are made 'just in case' we have any claims brought against us. I suppose you could say they are a 'buffer' or a 'cushion' against any unexpected costs.

The analytical review carried out has already highlighted potential sources of misstatement with revenue, administrative expenses and provisions. It would appear that the provisions are not true provisions and when judged against the recognition criteria in FRS 102, Section 21 *Provisions and Contingencies*, they would fail to meet the recognition criteria.

It would be fair to conclude that the entity is committing the act of fraudulent financial reporting by deliberating manipulating the financial statements to achieve a pre-determined outcome for the shareholders. This is accentuated by the fact that profit before tax has remained consistent with the prior year, but revenue is significantly down.

Carefully planned audit procedures would need to be applied – particularly over the provisions for liabilities – given the reasons for their inclusion.

Why commit fraud?

9.6   Most people, thankfully, are honest individuals and the thought of committing fraud would never enter their heads. However, there are some unscrupulous people that do commit fraud and in some, rather sad, cases, fraud can be committed because the individual has found themselves in a situation that they are struggling to get out of (eg, financial distress, addiction or serious mental health difficulties).

The 'fraud triangle' is a behavioural model, developed by Donald Cressey,[2] which explains why individuals commit fraud.

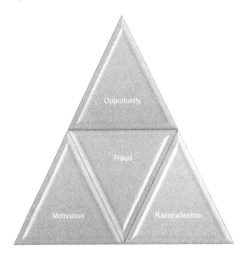

2 Donald R Cressey, *Other People's Money* (Montclair: Patterson Smith, 1973).

Opportunity

9.7   Opportunity must exist within an organisation for fraudulent activity to take place. This relates to both the means to commit a fraud and the ability to conceal it. This is why many frauds are committed by individuals who have access to the accounting system and the ability to override controls, ie, relatively senior members of the finance department are very well-placed to commit a fraud.

Rationalisation

9.8   It is typical that a fraudster believes that he, or she, is doing nothing wrong, although as a scheme escalates in complexity and value, this becomes less the case. Fraudsters often do not believe they are acting illegally or see themselves as criminals. For example, fraudulent financial reporting which hides liabilities or overstates profit is often rationalised by the perpetrator as an attempt to obtain more finance, appease investors and ultimately save a failing company. The fraudster essentially convinces themselves that they are a 'hero'.

Motivation

9.9   Most people commit fraud to make money. Financial pressure is often the root cause. It has been observed that during challenging economic times (eg, recession), there is an increase in occupational fraud, particularly asset misappropriation. Many fraudsters start off by stealing small amounts of cash (or other assets which may not necessarily be noticeable), but a fraud can quickly escalate. Greed is, of course, also a motivator – as is job dissatisfaction.

RESPONSIBILITIES IN RELATION TO FRAUD

9.10   Fraud, by its very nature, can be difficult to detect. In some cases it can be years before suspicions are roused. When a fraud is discovered, it can lead to tensions within the organisation and can be a very distressing time.

When a fraud has been going on for a long time, quite often the auditors are questioned as to why they did not spot it in prior year audits. Management may often try to blame the auditor. However, ISA (UK) 240 makes it very clear that the auditor does not bear the responsibility for the prevention and detection of fraud.

Management's responsibilities

9.11   ISA (UK) 240 states that the primary responsibility for the prevention and detection of fraud rests with those charged with governance and management of the entity. Hence, it is not the auditor's responsibility to prevent and detect fraud. If you think about it logically, the auditor is not present in the organisation for much of the year, so how could they possibly be responsible for the prevention and detection of fraud?

Establishing a sound system of internal control (which is also management's responsibility) will help to reduce the risk of fraud and error. An effective system of internal control will reduce the opportunities for fraud to arise and it will also increase the likelihood of fraud being discovered if it does arise. In addition, management should also create a culture of honesty, ethical behaviour and active oversight by those charged with governance.

Remember, no system of internal control will ever be so robust that it will entirely prevent a fraud or error. This is largely because of the risk of management override.

Example 9.2 – Internal controls relating to fraud

You are carrying out the audit of the payroll cycle for your audit client, Philbin Enterprises Ltd (Philbin) for the year ended 31 December 2023 and are reviewing the internal controls documentation. You have noted the following points:

● Philbin has a human resources (HR) function responsible for recruiting staff. However, the payroll department is responsible for completing joiner and leaver documentation and processing these within the payroll.

● The payroll is completed monthly and is prepared by the payroll clerk who processes the payroll, finalises it and prepares the bank transfer list that is sent to the finance director.

● The finance director reviews the total amount of the bank transfer listing for budgetary purposes and compares this to his cash flow forecast to ensure that the amount to be paid to the employees is reasonable.

● The bank transfer list is then signed by the finance director and sent back to the payroll clerk for processing.

The table below outlines the weaknesses in the payroll cycle of the business, together with suggested improvements to reduce the risk of fraud occurring within the payroll cycle:

Weakness and why it is a weakness	Suggested improvement
Philbin has a HR department which is responsible for recruiting staff. The payroll department completes the joiner and leaver documentation and processes these through the payroll. This provides an opportunity for the payroll department to complete a joiner form for a fictitious employee and process it as if it were a real person. This creates a fraud risk factor as it would be easy for a 'ghost employee' fraud to be set up.	The HR department should be responsible for completing all joiner and leaver documentation. These should be sent to the payroll department who should review them for completeness and then process the joiner forms in payroll. They should then be signed as completed and returned to HR.
The payroll clerk completes the payroll monthly, finalises it and prepares the bank transfer listing which is sent to the finance director. The payroll clerk has too much responsibility and there is a lack of segregation of duties. In addition to completing the joiner documentation (noted above), there is no evidence of a review of the payroll by a senior official. This not only creates a fraud risk factor in that ghost employees could be being paid via the payroll, but also friends and family of the payroll clerk could be receiving unauthorised payments via the payroll.	Once the payroll has been completed, it should be reviewed by a payroll supervisor or another payroll clerk. If such a person does not exist, the payroll should be reviewed by a senior member of the finance team. Once reviewed, the senior official should evidence their review by way of signature and inform the payroll clerk of any amendments or to finalise the payroll.
Only the total amount of the bank transfer listing is reviewed by the finance director for budgetary and cash flow purposes. No other reviews are carried out. Any deliberate changes to individual payments made will not be detected if a detailed review is not carried out.	The finance director should review the bank transfer listing in conjunction with the payroll reports produced by the payroll system to ensure that the amounts being paid to the employees are accurate and that only *bona fide* employees are being paid.

As you can see from this example, a weak system of internal control can easily create fraud risk factors. The example does not mention that any fraud has actually taken place, but it does highlight how fraud risk factors can increase the risk of a fraud. Management must be made aware of any weaknesses in the entity's system of internal control which create a fraud risk factor so they can implement measures to reduce the risk of fraud arising to an acceptable level. This will involve either implementing internal controls or strengthening existing ones.

Management should be aware of fraud risks within the business, and this should inform elements of their risk assessment and any corporate governance procedures they may have in place. Where the entity has an audit committee, this committee should review these procedures to ensure that they are in place and are working effectively. This will usually be done in conjunction with the internal audit function (if one exists).

For many companies, the internal audit function is a key element in the battle against fraud. The role of internal audit is to **review** systems of internal control; their role is not to implement such controls because otherwise they will be reviewing their own work. Management can request that internal audit carry out various tasks to reduce the risk of fraud arising, including:

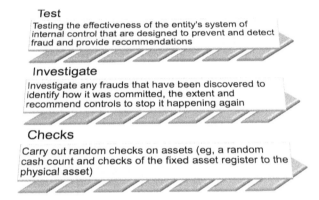

Test
Testing the effectiveness of the entity's system of internal control that are designed to prevent and detect fraud and provide recommendations

Investigate
Investigate any frauds that have been discovered to identify how it was committed, the extent and recommend controls to stop it happening again

Checks
Carry out random checks on assets (eg, a random cash count and checks of the fixed asset register to the physical asset)

The mere presence of an internal audit function can also act as a deterrent to fraud itself as there is more chance of a fraud being detected.

Auditor's responsibilities

9.12 The auditor's responsibility is set out clearly in ISA (UK) 240. The auditor is responsible for obtaining reasonable assurance (remember, it is not absolute assurance) about whether the financial statements **as a whole** are free from material misstatement because of fraud. This includes:

- identifying and assessing the risks of material misstatement of the financial statements due to fraud;

- obtaining sufficient appropriate audit evidence concerning the assessed risks of material misstatement due to fraud (this is done through designing and implementing appropriate auditor responses); and

- responding appropriately to fraud, or suspected fraud, identified during the audit.

Auditor's risk assessment procedures

9.13   We looked at the auditor's risk assessment procedures briefly in **Chapter 6**, but here I will expand on these procedures further. At the planning stage of the audit, the auditor must carry out risk assessment procedures aimed at identifying fraud risk factors. Remember, a 'fraud risk factor' does not mean that a fraud has been carried out; it is something that indicates there is a possibility that fraud could take place, perhaps due to weaknesses in the control environment.

There is no exhaustive list available to auditors that can provide definitive indicators that fraud is present. It is for this reason that the auditor must maintain professional scepticism throughout the audit (see **9.18** below). Maintaining an inquiring mind and not placing reliance on the past integrity and honesty of management and those charged with governance will help the auditor identify indicators of fraud.

Typical fraud risk factors may include:

- Aggressive management or aggressive responses from management and staff to the auditor's requests.

- Staff becoming nervous or anxious when asked certain questions.

- Dismissive attitude towards internal control and/or evidence of management override of the entity's internal controls.

- Inadequate accounting records or lack of explanations for certain transactions.

- Tolerance of petty theft and other minor breaches of laws and regulations or company policy.

- Staff members not taking holidays (for fear of the fraud being discovered during their absence).

- Large numbers of write-offs on control account reconciliations.

- Management and staff maintaining an expensive lifestyle when their wage or salary would not otherwise allow them to do so.

- Use of business assets for personal use.

IT-related fraud risk factors could include:

- A higher-than-average number of failed login attempts.

- Logins at unusual times of the day or at weekends or by a person who is on annual leave.

- System access controls being disabled.

REAL-LIFE FOCUS

Mr C was auditing a charity and was supplied with various supplier invoices from the client in PDF format via email. Mr C's suspicions were aroused because these invoices were all 'perfect' PDFs (ie, they had been created via a word-processing software rather than some of them being scanned in from original documents).

Mr C dug deeper and discovered that the PDFs had been created the night before as he had searched the 'File' | 'Properties' section of the PDF.

Mr C suspected that the trustees of the charity were committing fraud but could not discuss the issue in very much detail with the trustees because of his responsibilities under the Anti-Money Laundering Regulations (AMLR). AMLR makes it a criminal offence to 'tip off' the client about suspicious activity.

Mr C contacted his professional body who guided him through the process. Mr C had already decided that he was going to resign as auditor because he would otherwise have to express a disclaimer of opinion on the financial statements. Mr C was within his rights to resign as an auditor can resign at any time.

Mr C had to tread carefully not to mention to the trustees that a report to the firm's money laundering reporting officer was about to be made and he could not discuss the reasons for his resignation with the trustees or with anyone else. This included any potential incoming auditor who may enquire as to the reasons for his resignation.

The above case highlights the importance of not only carefully considering the requirements of ISA (UK) 240, but also other obligations imposed on the auditor (in this case, AMLR).

Conditions which may indicate that a document is not authentic

9.14   Indicators that a document may not be authentic (and hence may present a fraud risk factor) include the following:

- Serial numbers used are out of sequence or duplicated.

- Addresses and company logos are not as expected.

- A document style is different from what is 'normal' (such as a different font is used or a different format).

- Information that would be expected to be included is missing.

- Unusual terms of trade.

- Information appears implausible or inconsistent.

- The document is a copy rather than an original (and the original cannot be provided).

- Electronic documents have been edited after they have been prepared.

ISA (UK) 240 requires the audit engagement team hold a discussion that specifically focusses on fraud risk factors. It's important to remember that this discussion is not necessarily about whether a fraud has taken place (or whether a fraud is expected to be discovered), it is also to discuss **how** a fraud **could** arise (even if there has not been any past history of frauds).

In this respect, the auditor should specifically assess the risk of material misstatement due to fraud. The auditor must also consider how management responds to the risk of fraud. Discussions should also take place at the planning stage with management and/or those charged with governance concerning any specific fraud or fraud risk factors as well as business practices and how ethical behavioural matters are communicated to employees.

The auditor can undertake preliminary analytical review procedures (see **Chapter 6** at **6.8**) to identify any potential sources of a fraud. For example, if the company's operating profit margin suddenly reduces due to increased payroll costs, this could be due to a 'ghost' employee fraud.

The auditor's risk assessment at the planning stage requires a good level of understanding of the business. For example, if the business is experiencing financial difficulties, there may be pressure on management to present results which show the company is doing well (fraudulent financial reporting).

REAL-LIFE SCENARIO

Mr J is the audit engagement partner in a two-partner audit firm. They have three audit clients, two for whom the firm has acted for a number of years. For the two audit clients, hot and cold reviews are done on a cyclical basis to mitigate the long association threat (as the audit engagement partner has been the auditor in excess of ten years).

Mr J told me that he had sent one of the clients' files to an external training organisation for post-issuance (cold) file review. Feedback on this file following the review was mixed and the file was graded a D (the highest grade being an 'A'). Numerous deficiencies were found in key audit areas,

---

but the one issue that gave rise to the file being significantly downgraded was the fact that the audit engagement partner had written 'n/a' against fraud issues.

Mr J's response was that he had worked with the client for several years and had never encountered a fraud before, so why should he spend the time and effort looking for something that he knows is not there?

This response, unfortunately, is not an uncommon one. Audit firms are frequently criticised during file reviews because they have failed to demonstrate professional scepticism (ie, they have not maintained a questioning mind). In Mr J's case, he had relied on his past experience of the client and the honesty and integrity of the directors. What Mr J had, in fact, done is breach ISA (UK) 240, para 13 which requires Mr J to maintain professional scepticism throughout the audit, recognising the possibility that a material misstatement due to fraud could exist, regardless of the auditor's past experience of the honesty and integrity of the entity's management and those charged with governance.

Mr J told me that he thought these requirements were 'overkill' and 'completely unrealistic to apply in practice'.

While the responses by Mr J do indicate a lack of professional scepticism due to him placing reliance on his previous experience with the client, more worryingly is the perceived lack of independence. Mr J has worked with the client in excess of ten years, which is one of the main reasons why his file is subject to external review. It is clear in this instance that Mr J's independence and objectivity is impaired, and he should consider resigning as auditor, or asking his other partner to perhaps be the statutory auditor (if the other partner has an auditing practising certificate).

As noted above, in the case of Mr J, the response of 'we have never encountered fraud before, so why should we expect it now?' is a common one. Why should the auditor expect it now? Well, because the ISA (UK) says that effectively we must. If the auditor cannot demonstrate they have exercised professional scepticism, they will effectively be in breach of the ISAs (UK).

Fraud and revenue recognition

9.15   Revenue (turnover/sales, whatever you want to call it) is an element of the financial statements that is singled out by ISA (UK) 240. This is because it requires special consideration by the auditor. I mentioned this briefly in **Chapter 6** but I will look into it in more detail here.

The default presumption is that there is a risk of material misstatement due to fraud in respect of revenue. While this presumption can be rebutted (ie, the auditor can override that presumption), rebutting it can realistically only be done in very limited situations. Auditors have been criticised in the past for rebutting the presumption that fraud exists in respect of revenue recognition because it is either clear that the presumption should not have been rebutted, or the reasons for the rebuttal have not been clearly documented.

The problem with revenue is twofold. It can either be deliberately over or understated, depending on what management 'want' the figures to portray.

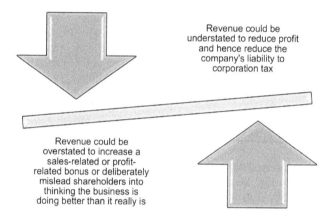

Revenue could be understated to reduce profit and hence reduce the company's liability to corporation tax

Revenue could be overstated to increase a sales-related or profit-related bonus or deliberately mislead shareholders into thinking the business is doing better than it really is

The auditor must ensure that they carefully consider revenue and the susceptibility of this figure to fraud and devise specific procedures which are responsive to the risks identified. It is reckless to simply rebut the presumption that fraud exists in respect of revenue simply because '… we have never found a fraud in the client's financial statements before.' This is where reviewers will be critical of an audit file and could result in the file failing an inspection. Rebutting the revenue fraud risk presumption inappropriately also increases audit risk.

IMPORTANT POINT

ISA (UK) 240 recognises that the risks of fraud in revenue recognition may be greater in some entities than in others. Cash-based businesses are particularly at risk of fraud where revenue is concerned. Later in this chapter I will look at a real-life scenario involving a large supermarket which deliberately inflated its revenue which articulates the risks involved for the auditor.

Some entities, particularly listed entities, may be under pressure to report a certain level of results, hence there may be an incentive by management to commit fraudulent financial reporting – especially where revenue is concerned.

When it comes to rebutting the presumption of fraud risk in respect of revenue, the ISA (UK) cites one example. This is where the auditor may conclude there is no risk of material misstatement due to fraud relating to revenue recognition where the entity has a single type of simple revenue transaction, such as leasehold revenue from a single unit rental property.

Where the auditor does rebut the presumption of fraud in relation to revenue recognition, they must ensure that the documentation in the audit file clearly outlines the reasons why that rebuttal is appropriate.

REAL-LIFE SCENARIO

Entity A was a company supplying do-it-yourself products with two stores in local towns. The company's year end was 31 January each year.

The company employed a full-time cash office clerk, Joan, whose primarily responsibility was running the accounting side of the business including posting purchase invoices, paying suppliers, performing credit control procedures for corporate customers and maintaining the pricing structure of the business.

Joan had been employed by the business for over 20 years and each year the audit firm would carry out the annual audit. Joan had dealt with the same audit firm for many years so knew what to expect when the auditors arrived on site.

During the audit of the year-end bank reconciliation, the audit junior noted that there were outstanding lodgements (cash paid in that had not cleared). As part of the audit of the bank reconciliation, the audit junior was to trace all unpresented items (including unpresented cheques and uncredited lodgements) to post-year-end bank statements to ensure they clear properly after the year end.

All items apart from the cash paid in cleared within one month of the year end.

The audit senior was informed of the issue and inquired of Joan what this cash related to. Joan informed the audit senior that she had recalled a 'system error' and that the cash was, in fact, the daily takings on 31 January that had 'doubled up' so the bank balance per the trial balance was, in fact, overstated (and so were sales).

While this happened a number of years ago, the accounting system itself was computerised using a well-known accounting system but the cash sales cycle was, in fact, manual. The till operatives would count their takings in their till at the end of each shift, fill out a cash record sheet, and do a 'Z' reading on the till to ensure the content of the till balanced with what they had taken during from customers during their shifts. The cash would then be transferred to the finance office where it would be counted again and subsequently banked.

The audit senior carried out further investigations and noted that the amounts recorded on the cash record sheets had been crossed out (by Joan as the amendments were in Joan's handwriting) and changed. All the amended amounts were less than the cash actually taken. The amended cash sheets then did not agree to the Z reading taken from the till.

What was, in fact, happening was a fraud. Joan had become disgruntled with one of the directors of the company whom she thought was being paid too much for his efforts in the business. She had also taken advantage of a weakness in the financial controls, which was a distinct lack of segregation of duties over the cash cycle as Joan had full autonomy over the cash once it had been passed to her from the till operatives. Joan had stolen cash from the business over a period of two years (in fact, records showed she had even stolen cash on the day the auditors were in).

Joan 'tripped up' because she had not amended the accounting system which recorded the gross amount of the cash taken on the 31 January purely by co-incidence (she had posted the cash sheets *before* amending them).

The fraud had been discovered because cash that was outstanding on the year-end bank reconciliation had not cleared and would never have cleared because it had not been paid into the bank. It had been 'pocketed' by Joan.

Investigations revealed that this fraud had been going on for a long time. Had the auditor queried the amended cash sheets in the prior year, there is a likelihood the fraud would have been discovered earlier.

Joan was immediately dismissed from her employment.

Following her dismissal, Jean was prosecuted and received a suspended prison sentence of two years'. At the time (this was pre year 2000) there was no Proceeds of Crime Act and so she was not required to repay the monies.

This situation highlights the importance of not incorrectly rebutting the presumption that fraud in respect of revenue recognition exists. A fraud had not been discovered in that business before, but one outstanding item on the bank reconciliation cost Joan her job and her integrity.

Reporting in the auditor's report

9.16   There is some interaction with ISA (UK) 700 *Forming an Opinion and Reporting on Financial Statements*. This is very much a UK-specific issue, but it could well be adopted by other jurisdictions. Under ISA (UK) 700, the auditor's report must include a section within the *Auditor's responsibilities for the financial statements* section as to how the audit was designed to detect irregularities, including fraud. This could include things like:

● Assessing compliance with laws and regulations.

● Assessing compliance with tax legislation.

● Reviewing correspondence (especially from lawyers) to identify any potential non-compliance with laws and regulations.

● Discussions with management and those charged with governance about any irregularities, including fraud.

Example 9.3 – Illustrative wording for the irregularities section of the auditor's report

Auditor's responsibilities for the audit of the financial statements

Our objectives are to obtain reasonable assurance about whether the financial statements as a whole are free from material misstatement, whether due to fraud or error, and to issue a report of the auditors that includes our opinion. Reasonable assurance is a high level of assurance, but is not a guarantee that an audit conducted in accordance with ISAs (UK) will always detect a material misstatement when it exists. Misstatements can arise from fraud or error and are considered material if, individually or in the aggregate, they could reasonably be expected to influence the economic decisions of users taken on the basis of these financial statements.

The extent to which our procedures are capable of detecting irregularities, including fraud is detailed below:

9.16 *Fraud, Laws and Regulations*

We gained an understanding of the legal and regulatory framework applicable to the company and the industry in which it operates, and considered the risks of acts by the company which were contrary to applicable laws and regulations, including fraud. We designed our audit procedures to respond to the assessed risks, recognising that the risk of not detecting a material misstatement due to fraud is higher than the risk of not detecting one resulting from error, as fraud may involve more sophisticated and deliberate concealment, such as through forgery or intentional misrepresentations or via collusion. We recognised fraud risks could arise from two sources:

- manipulation of weaknesses in the system of internal control; and

- management override of the system of internal control.

We focussed on laws and regulations which could give rise to a material misstatement in the financial statements, including (but not limited to), the CA 2006 and UK tax legislation as well as fire regulations and environmental pollution. Our tests included agreeing the financial statement disclosures to underlying supporting documentation, enquiries with management and reviews of correspondence. We paid particular attention to legal correspondence which may indicate a breach of laws and regulations.

There are inherent limitations in the audit procedures described above and, the further removed non-compliance with laws and regulations is from the events and transactions reflected in the financial statements, the less likely we would become aware of it.

During the course of our audit, we did not identify any key audit matters relating to irregularities, including fraud.

As in all our audits, we also addressed the risk of management override of internal controls (as noted above), including testing journals and evaluating whether there was evidence of bias by the directors which represented a risk of material misstatement due to fraud.

As part of an audit in accordance with ISAs (UK), we exercise professional judgement and maintain professional scepticism. We also:

- Identify and assess the risks of material misstatement of the financial statements, whether due to fraud or error, design and perform audit procedures responsive to those risks and obtain audit evidence that is sufficient and appropriate to provide a basis for our opinion. The risk of not detecting a material misstatement resulting from fraud is higher than for one resulting from error, as fraud may involve collusion, forgery, intentional omissions, misrepresentations, or the override of internal control.

- Obtain an understanding of internal control relevant to the audit in order to design audit procedures that are appropriate in the circumstances, but not for the purpose of expressing an opinion on the effectiveness of the company's internal control.

- Evaluate the appropriateness of accounting policies used and the reasonableness of accounting estimates and related disclosures made by the directors.

- Conclude on the appropriateness of the directors' use of the going concern basis of accounting and, based on the audit evidence obtained, whether a material uncertainty exists related to events or conditions that may cast significant doubt on the company's ability to continue as a going concern. If we conclude that a material uncertainty exists, we are required to draw attention in our report of the auditors to the related disclosures in the financial statements or, if such disclosures are inadequate, to modify our opinion. Our conclusions are based on the audit evidence obtained up to the date of our report of the auditors. However, future events or conditions may cause the company to cease to continue as a going concern.

- Evaluate the overall presentation, structure and content of the financial statements, including the disclosures, and whether the financial statements represent the underlying transactions and events in a manner that achieves a true and fair presentation.

We communicate with those charged with governance regarding, among other matters, the planned scope and timing of the audit and significant audit findings, including any significant deficiencies in internal control that we identify during our audit.

REAL-LIFE FOCUS

It is clear that the auditor is not responsible for preventing and detecting fraud. This responsibility rests with management and those charged with governance of the entity. However, in a high-profile corporate disaster in which fraud is present, the auditor is usually criticised for either not spotting the fraud, or not reporting it in the financial statements.

To a certain extent, the requirement for the auditor to describe *how* the audit was designed to detect irregularities, including fraud, does provide some information to the user on the issue of fraud and how the audit was designed to detect it. In addition, the current edition of ISA (UK) 240 does place a lot of responsibility for the auditor in the area of fraud, while recognising that the responsibility for the prevention and detection of fraud remains with management and those charged with governance.

Over the years, ISA (UK) 240 (along with other versions of the ISA) has received criticism which was largely due to the standard not being substantially changed since it was first adopted in 2004. Changes to ISA (UK) 240 were made to strengthen confidence in the auditing profession and reduce the expectations gap.

ISA (UK) 240 recognises that the risk of not detecting a material misstatement resulting from fraud may be higher than the risk of detecting one resulting from error. The ISA (UK) acknowledges that this does not diminish the auditor's responsibility to plan and perform the audit to obtain reasonable assurance about whether the financial statements are free from material misstatement due to fraud.

The current edition of ISA (UK) 240 requires the auditor to specifically look for fraud, which previous editions of the standard did not. Of course, this creates more work on the part of the auditor who will have to devise specific audit procedures which are designed to detect fraud risk factors could be extended to look specifically for fraud.

REAL-LIFE FOCUS

A company's principal activity is that of a food manufacturer with a 31 October year end. The auditor's opinion for the year ended 31 October 2021 was disclaimed on the grounds of insufficient evidence available to support the going concern presumption.

The same audit firm audited the financial statements for the year ended 31 October 2022. Again, this audit firm disclaimed the audit opinion on the grounds of insufficient evidence concerning the going concern presumption. In both years the financial statements had been prepared on a going concern basis.

Interestingly, the financial statements for the year ended 31 October 2022 showed a significant revaluation of an internally generated brand amounting to £500,000. The entries for this revalued brand were:

Dr Intangible assets additions

Cr Fair value adjustments in profit and loss

This had the effect of turning what would have been a reported loss into a small profit.

The financial reporting framework applied in these financial statements was FRS 102 *The Financial Reporting Standard applicable in the UK and Republic of Ireland*. FRS 102, para 18.8C(a) specifically prohibits internally generated brands being reported as an intangible asset on the balance sheet.

Not only was the internally generated brand inappropriately recognised on the balance sheet, but its revaluation was also inappropriate because there is no active market from which to derive a fair value. In addition, the credit to fair value adjustments in profit and loss was also incorrect because a revalued intangible asset is measured under the Alternative Accounting Rules in company law and hence the credit should have been presented within equity under the heading of 'Revaluation reserve' (if the revaluation had been permitted under FRS 102 in the first place).

These problems were further exacerbated by the fact that the same audit firm had disclaimed the audit opinion in the prior year. ISA (UK) 705 *Modifications to the Opinion in the Independent Auditor's Report*, para 13 would require the auditor to resign from the audit.

While this example demonstrates a lack of awareness of accounting standards by the audit client, it also demonstrates the way in which management may have a desire to manipulate the financial statements to achieve a desired outcome. Here, the company would have reported a loss had it not been for the inappropriate (and incorrect) revaluation of an internally generated brand. Auditors must therefore keep in mind the importance of applying professional scepticism throughout the audit and devise audit procedures that specifically respond to the risk of material misstatement due to fraud, particularly where the company is in financial distress.

Responding to suspected or identified fraud

9.17   Many people (particularly more junior members of staff) get 'excited' when a fraud, or a potential fraud, is discovered. They become curious to know what happens to the perpetrator and may inadvertently discuss issues outside of the audit team, which is strictly prohibited.

In reality, discovering a fraud is one of the most stressful and draining situations to be in (and I speak from experience when I say that).

When the auditor suspects or identifies fraud, they must tread very carefully. There are all sorts of obligations that the auditor is under where fraud is concerned. For example:

- Client confidentiality.

- Anti-Money Laundering Regulations.

- The requirements of ISA (UK) 240.

- Applicable regulatory issues (for example, potential reporting of a Matter of Material Significance in the case of a charity).

There are so many rules and regulations on the shoulder of an auditor that sometimes it is easy to fall into the many pitfalls. At the planning stage of the assignment, it is therefore vital that all members of the audit engagement team (including junior members) are fully briefed as to what should happen in the event that a fraud is discovered or suspected. Where any fraud is discovered, all members of the engagement team must be reminded of their duty of confidentiality and obligations under Anti-Money Laundering protocol.

The first thing to ascertain is whether the (suspected) fraud gives rise to a report to the audit firm's money laundering reporting officer (MLRO). All members of the audit team are required to observe the Anti-Money Laundering Regulations. If fraud is suspected, a Suspicious Activity Report may need to be lodged to the National Crime Agency by the audit firm's MLRO.

IMPORTANT POINT

Auditors must ensure they do not commit the act of 'tipping off'. Tipping off would arise if the auditor allows the perpetrator or client's management to think that the auditor has discovered the fraud and that they are going to take further action (such as making a money laundering report). Tipping off a client can happen very easily, even when the auditor may not think they have done anything wrong, so caution needs to be exercised to handle this issue carefully.

If a member of the audit team has discovered the fraud, they should report it in the first instance to the audit engagement partner who will then deal with the issue accordingly.

The audit engagement partner must then consider whether it is appropriate to report the actual or suspected fraud to an appropriate authority outside of the client (for example, a regulatory body). This may be required by law, regulation or ethical requirements. However, keep in mind that the auditor is bound by confidentiality, so they must only make disclosures outside of the client once confidentiality has been considered. Whether to disclose information about the fraudulent activity outside of the client is a complex and judgemental issue and the auditor would be well-advised to seek professional advice from their professional body to help devise a suitable course of action.

ISA (UK) 240 requires the auditor to communicate any fraud (or suspected fraud) on a timely basis to the appropriate level of management. The level of management to which the fraud is reported would usually be at least one level above the individual(s) involved in the fraud.

If the fraud involves management, the auditor must communicate the matter to those charged with governance. In situations when the auditor has concerns about the integrity of those charged with governance (for example, the auditor may suspect those charged with governance are involved with the fraud), the auditor should seek legal advice.

In exceptional situations, because of actual or suspected fraud, the auditor may consider that it is not possible to continue the audit engagement. If the auditor decides to discontinue the audit engagement, they should follow the appropriate regulatory and legal frameworks and should take legal advice (especially where the wording of the resignation statement and statement of circumstances is concerned). This is where professional bodies should be consulted to ensure the auditor follows correct protocol at all times.

REAL-LIFE SCENARIO

In 2015, the supermarket chain, Tesco, revealed that it had overstated profits by £263 million due to revenue recognition accounting irregularities. Effectively, Tesco had recognised supplier rebates in its financial statements that had not been received, nor was there any expectation that they would be received, because the rebates were based on targets that the supermarket was never going to achieve.

The impact of this was that profit and earnings per share were higher than they should have been meaning the shareholders were misled into thinking the company was performing better than it actually was.

This is an example of fraudulent financial reporting – deliberately misstating the financial statements to reflect fictitious transactions, events or conditions. An internal whistleblower raised concerns with the company's legal department, who in turn informed the chairman and CEO. The whistleblower was a member of the finance department who initially was concerned about the lack of documentation over revenue transactions.

The revenue rebates were based on estimates, hence their 'correctness' was not easy to 'prove'. The external auditor, PwC, had raised the issue as a 'Key Audit Matter' but Tesco's audit committee had said that it was not a problem. However, internal controls over revenue recognition were

---

either not robust enough or were overridden by management. The audit committee had dismissed the issue as a significant risk.

£263 million is a lot of money, it's fair to say! However, it was actually immaterial in individual years or cumulatively – the monetary amounts involved were less than 10% of the supermarket's profit before tax. However, the misstatement could be considered material by nature (ie, due to the risk of fraud and the level of subjectivity that is involved in arriving at the estimate).

Tesco was underperforming due to pressure from cut-price supermarkets, such as Lidl and Aldi. There was a perceived 'need' by management to improve results. Targets were not being met, which led to a motive to overstate revenue and profit. Bonuses were paid based on performance, so senior management had a personal incentive to maximise revenue and profit. Looking at the fraud triangle in **9.3** above, there was a lot of motive for overstating profit and senior management had the opportunity to override Tesco's system of internal control. This is what resulted in the fraudulent financial reporting.

This is just one example of how an entity's management may commit fraudulent financial reporting. In today's modern world (which is undeniably pressurised), management are under all sorts of pressure to deliver results. Such pressure can make people do things they may not otherwise do; hence other examples of fraudulent financial reporting include the following:

- Processing fictitious journals very close to, or at, the reporting date to deliberately manipulate the information presented in the financial statements.

- Advancing, or delaying, recognition of transactions and events in the financial statements.

- Failing to disclose facts which would affect the amounts recorded in the financial statements.

- Failing to disclose contingent liabilities or significant going concern difficulties.

- Inappropriately changing assumptions and judgements used in estimating account balances.

- Engaging in complex transactions which are deliberately engineered to provide a misleading picture in the balance sheet or profit and loss account.

PROFESSIONAL SCEPTICISM

9.18 So far in this chapter I have referred to professional scepticism several times. This is because it's a characteristic that is fundamental to the audit process. All too often we read about criticisms from regulators and professional bodies that auditors have not exercised enough professional scepticism. So what is it all about, and how do we do it?

Professional scepticism is something that cannot be taught. Adopting professional scepticism generally involves questioning everything and being alert for issues that just 'do not seem right'.

Consider this scenario that I'm sure everyone has experienced at some point in their lives.

You are in a restaurant with a group of friends. One of your friends has brought their friend along (who we will call Dave) who you have never met before. Your initial thoughts are that he has an outgoing personality and is a bit 'loud', but you can handle it.

Over the course of the next couple of hours, Dave tells you that he drives a Lamborghini, lives in a six-bedroomed detached house in a very expensive part of the borough, is best friends with a famous singer, is related to the prime minister and once won the lottery. You do not actually believe any of this and doubt whether anything that Dave says is true.

You are exercising scepticism! You are questioning the 'truth and fairness' of Dave's statements.

Turning to **professional** scepticism, training audit staff to exercise professional scepticism is a fine art. However, you can relate the Dave analogy above – all auditors need to do is to question the assertions made by management and challenge them. It's not necessarily the case that management will completely fabricate every element of the financial statements, but some areas of the financial statements could be subject to management bias. For example:

● Revenue could be overstated to achieve a bonus.

● Profit could be understated to reduce corporation tax.

● An accounting estimate could be misstated to hide a fraud.

● A provision for a liability may be understated to deliberately understate liabilities.

● Cut-off's may be incorrect to achieve accelerated or decelerated revenue and cost of sales.

419

ISA (UK) 200 *Overall Objectives of the Independent Auditor and the Conduct of an Audit in Accordance with International Standards on Auditing (UK)* says that professional scepticism is an attitude that includes a questioning mind, being alert to conditions which may indicate possible misstatement due to error and fraud, and a critical assessment of audit evidence.

The problem with professional scepticism (which I think is a perennial problem) is that there is no single way of demonstrating its application. It is essentially a mindset and one that can only be evidenced if it is properly documented in the working papers. Remember, the concept of professional scepticism is very closely related to the concepts of independence and objectivity – two traits that are fundamental ethical principles in auditing.

In my experience, professional scepticism can be exercised by being alert to audit evidence that may contradict other audit evidence. You can also exercise professional scepticism by questioning the reliability of documents (for example, scanned documents or copied documents) or responses to enquiries.

Example 9.4 – Demonstrating professional scepticism

The draft financial statements of McSharry Industries Ltd for the year ended 31 December 2024 show that management have increased the value of the freehold property by £100,000 in the year using an internal valuation carried out by the finance director. The revaluation has been accounted for correctly in accordance with FRS 102, Section 17, *Property, Plant and Equipment* with the deferred tax consequences also correctly recorded.

Jasmine, the audit senior has reviewed other similar properties in the area, and they appear to have increased in value as well. However, the increases are within the range of £25,000 to £40,000 depending on the square footage of the building. McSharry Industries' building is at the smaller end of the scale in terms of square footage and hence looking at the valuations on the internet, the valuation should have been in the region of £25,000.

The auditor has challenged management's valuation. While the accounting treatment for the revaluation gain appears to be correctly accounted for, the auditor is not satisfied that the valuation itself is reasonable.

In this situation, the auditor is concerned that the company is deliberately overstating its assets to present the company's financial position in a better light.

Jasmine could use an auditor's own expert to carry out a valuation of the building. If this valuation comes in showing an increase of some £25,000 then clearly the building is overvalued and should be written down to avoid fixed assets and equity being overstated.

Applying professional scepticism when reviewing audit evidence is also important. Remember, audit evidence must be both sufficient and appropriate and adequately cover the relevant assertions. The auditor can demonstrate professional scepticism by questioning the sufficiency and appropriateness of the audit evidence gathered in light of the entity's specific circumstances. Where the auditor has doubt concerning the reliability of information, or where audit evidence points to a potential fraud risk, the auditor must investigate further and determine what additional procedures should be applied to resolve the issue.

IMPORTANT POINT

The audit planning meeting is an opportunity to demonstrate professional scepticism at the outset. Remember, ISA (UK) 240 requires the audit engagement team to discuss the susceptibility of the financial statements to material misstatement whether caused by fraud or error. Discussing **how** the financial statements **could** be materially misstated due to fraud is the exercise of professional scepticism.

Simply stating that the audit engagement team has not encountered fraud (or discovered fraud risk factors) in the past is the opposite of demonstrating professional scepticism.

Also, keep in mind that as well as fraud issues, the audit engagement team must discuss how the financial statements could be materially misstated due to error. A sceptical mindset will approach the audit with an awareness that such misstatements could have happened during the year.

I also think that one of the most important areas where professional scepticism must be applied is when the auditor is addressing complex or significant areas of the financial statements, particularly those which contain a high degree of judgement on the part of management, for example:

- Accounting estimates (especially in respect of contract balances and revenue recognition in construction contracts) and ensuring that the auditor properly evaluates the reasonableness of the significant assumptions used in arriving at the estimates.

- Related party transactions and relationships and demonstrating that the auditor has remained alert during the audit for information which may indicate previously unidentified or undisclosed related party relationships or transactions.

- Significant transactions outside the ordinary course of business and evaluating whether the business rationale (or lack of) suggests the transactions have been entered into to engage in fraud.

- Consideration of laws and regulations (see **9.23** below) and being alert to instances of non-compliance which may have a material effect on the financial statements.

- Evaluating the going concern assumption and whether this is appropriate in the company's specific circumstances (such as evaluating management's plans for the future and whether those plans are realistic).

- Where significantly unusual or complex transactions arise, devising procedures to ensure these transactions have been correctly accounted for, and disclosed, in the financial statements.

Inherently, it can be difficult to demonstrate professional scepticism throughout the audit file but remember all it is (in a nutshell) is maintaining a questioning mind and not taking everything the client says, or states in the financial statements, as gospel. An auditor can simply demonstrate professional scepticism by documenting conversations they have had with management or those charged with governance. For example, it may be the case that the audit client has applied a certain accounting treatment which may be permissible under FRS 102, but which the auditor does not view as being appropriate to the company's circumstances. Challenging such practices and making sure the notes of any discussions are documented are key in demonstrating that professional scepticism has been applied.

CLOSING THE EXPECTATIONS GAP

9.19 So far in this chapter, I have looked at the issue of fraud and how it is 'immersed' in the expectations gap (being the difference between what the auditor is **required** to do under professional standards and what the auditor is **expected** to do by the general public). It's not just fraud which the expectations gap is concerned with, however, there are other elements which create such a gap.

In 2019, ACCA published a paper *Closing the expectation gap in audit*. This paper discusses the expectation gap as arising from three elements, including an additional component called the 'evolution gap'. These three elements are as follows:

The Knowledge Gap

The difference between what the public think auditors do and what they actually do

The Performance Gap

The difference between what auditors actually do and what auditors are supposed to do

The Evolution Gap

The difference between what auditors are supposed to do and what the public wants auditors to do, including how the audit process could evolve to add more value

Looking at each one of these in turn:

The Knowledge Gap

9.20   This arises from a misunderstanding about the role of an auditor and the requirements of professional standards such as the ISAs (UK). The belief here is that one of the auditor's objectives is to prevent and detect fraud (whereas this is actually a management duty).

The Performance Gap

9.21   This relates to auditors not following ISA (UK) requirements. Generally this indicates poor quality auditing such as the auditor not following the requirements of ISA (UK) 240 by rebutting the risk of material misstatement due to fraud in respect of revenue recognition incorrectly or not properly evaluating fraud risk indicators. In addition, the performance gap could indicate that the requirements of the ISAs (UK) are not clear or are open to misinterpretation. This was a reason I decided to write this book!

The Evolution Gap

9.22   This considers where auditing may need to change. Over recent years there has been a lot in the headlines about how this can be done. Specifically, the evolution gap looks at how audit should evolve to take account of the expectations of the users of the auditor's report. Audit can also evolve due to increasing use of technology, such as Audit Data Analytics and Artificial Intelligence.

ACCA's survey supports the view that the expectations gap exists. Only 25% of UK survey respondents could correctly identify the overall objective of an audit, which clearly indicates that a knowledge gap exists. Other evidence shows that a performance gap exists; for example, the reports from regulatory bodies such as the Financial Reporting Council issued each year which show the performance by the largest audit firms which do not meet the standards expected.

ACCA's paper asked a specific question concerning fraud, which placed focus on the evolution gap. This question asked respondents to select the statement which best reflects their expectations of the auditor's responsibility for fraud. Unsurprisingly, the responses showed that (generally) the public would like the auditor to have more responsibility, with 35% agreeing that *'I expect auditors to always detect and report any fraud.'*

ISA (UK) 240 was revised in 2021 and the revised version of this ISA (UK) does place more responsibility on the auditor to detect fraud. However, this cannot close the expectations gap completely because it is not, and cannot be, the auditor's responsibility to prevent and detect fraud at the organisation. This responsibility must rest with management and will rely on the controls they implement to prevent and detect fraudulent activity.

Notwithstanding the revisions to ISA (UK) 240 in 2021, paragraph 4 is clear that the primary responsibility for the prevention and detection of fraud rests with **both** those charged with governance and management. The auditor's responsibility is to obtain reasonable assurance that the financial statements **taken as a whole** are free from material misstatement, whether caused by fraud or error.

REAL-LIFE SCENARIO

The case of Patisserie Valerie has been well-publicised. In 2018, accounting irregularities were discovered at the café and sandwich shop chain. These irregularities came to light when HM Revenue and Customs took action against the company for an unpaid tax bill. It transpired that rather than having over £28 million in the bank, there was actually £10 million in two secret overdrafts which the directors did not know about. Further investigations revealed that the company's cash position was overstated by a staggering £54 million, liabilities understated by £17 million and other assets overvalued by £23 million. These are eye-watering amounts, and it is no surprise that jaws dropped when the irregularities came to light!

The auditors, Grant Thornton, had issued unmodified audit opinions on prior years' financial statements. Questions then started to be asked about why the fraud had not been discovered during the audit. David Dunckley, CEO of Grant Thornton, was called to the parliamentary Business Energy and Industrial Strategy Committee to discuss the audit. Under what would have been serious amounts of pressure, politicians angrily demanded to know why the fraud had not been discovered during the audit and, at one point, the expectations gap was discussed.

In response, David Dunckley commented:

> We are not doing what the market thinks. We are not looking for fraud and we are not looking at the future and we are not giving a statement that the accounts are correct. There is a clear expectations gap, and audit fundamentally gives a reasonable opinion on historic information and doesn't look for fraud. We're saying [the accounts] are reasonable, we are looking in the past and we are not set up to look for fraud.

Members of the parliamentary committee were far from impressed with this response. Their thought process appeared to be that Grant Thornton should have found the fraud.

Rachel Reeves MP added:

> Of course the audit company isn't committing a crime, in that case, but its fingerprints would be all over the crime scene. If an audit company isn't picking up on this type of behaviour, what is the point of audit in the first place?

On 27 September 2021, the Financial Reporting Council (FRC) imposed sanctions on Grant Thornton and David Newstead (the audit engagement partner).

Grant Thornton was fined £4 million (adjusted for aggravating and mitigating factors and discounted for admissions and early disposal to £2.34 million). In addition, there was a suite of non-financial sanctions, including reporting to the FRC annually for three years on the impact of the firm's remedial actions (including a root cause analysis) on audit quality; a review of the audit practice's culture relating to challenge; and additional monitoring in relation to bank and cash audit work. There was also a declaration that the statutory audit report for each of the three years did not satisfy the relevant requirements, together with a published statement in the form of a severe reprimand.

Mr Newstead received a financial sanction of £150,000 (adjusted for aggravating and mitigating factors and discounted for admissions and early disposal to £87,750). He also received a three-year ban from carrying out statutory audits and signing statutory auditor reports. He also received a declaration that the statutory audit report for each of the three years did not satisfy the relevant requirements, together with a published statement in the form of a severe reprimand.

Grant Thornton was also required to pay executive counsel's costs in respect of the investigation.

LAWS AND REGULATIONS

9.23   All entities have some laws and regulations that apply to them. For example, Health and Safety legislation, employment law and tax legislation. Some of the laws and regulations that are applicable to an audit client will have a 'direct' effect on the financial statements, in that they will affect the amounts and disclosures, such as tax legislation. Other laws and regulations will have an 'indirect' effect on the financial statements, such as Health and Safety legislation.

There are some sectors that are subject to more rigorous laws and regulations than others. For example, some entities operate in highly regulated industries such as banks and chemical companies. Others may be subject to non-industry specific laws and regulations which relate to the operating aspects of the business (eg, employment law).

Auditors must have an understanding of the provisions in ISA (UK) 250 – Section A *Consideration of Laws and Regulations in an Audit of Financial Statements*. In a nutshell, the auditor is concerned with any non-compliance with laws and regulations (NOCLAR) because this may result in fines and penalties being levied by the legislating authorities and could have a material effect on the financial statements. This is why it is important that the auditor considers all relevant laws and regulations which apply to the audit client.

IMPORTANT POINT

At the time of writing, ISA (UK) 250, Sections A and B were up for change. The proposals include removing the distinction between **direct** laws (that have a direct effect on the financial statements) and **other** laws (that have an indirect effect on the financial statements). Instead, the FRC are proposing to require the auditor to use a risk-based approach. This approach will direct the auditor's attention to identifying those laws and regulations where non-compliance may have a material impact on the financial statements. This will also enable the auditor to devise specific audit procedures to address the risk of material misstatement.

Using this risk-based approach will mean there will be more professional judgement needed on the part of the auditor. It is also likely to mean more work will need to be carried out by the auditor in identifying such laws and regulations. There will also be additional risk assessment procedures needed which will lead to an increased level of responses to those risks [of non-compliance with laws and regulations]. The FRC has established a number of additional risk assessment requirements, such as:

- Understanding those laws and regulations that relate to the applicable financial reporting framework or which arise from regulatory factors.

- Understanding management's process concerning compliance with laws and regulations and how those charged with governance oversee this.

- Determining whether there are any deficiencies in internal control relevant to non-compliance with laws and regulations.

- Making inquiries of management, those charged with governance and other individuals to obtain their views on which laws and regulations could have a material impact on the financial statements.

- Inspecting documentation for indications of non-compliance with laws and regulations.

The FRC is also proposing explicit requirements for the auditor to identify, assess and respond to the risks of material misstatement due to fraud or error relating to non-compliance with laws and regulations. It also proposes to introduce a requirement for the auditor to conclude whether non-compliance (or suspected non-compliance) with laws and regulations has resulted in a material misstatement of the financial statements.

ISA (UK) 250, Section B

In addition, ISA (UK) 250, Section B is expected to be withdrawn. The proposed amendments amount to pretty much a new ISA (UK) on the grounds that the current content is outdated and the FRC would like to introduce a more principles-based standard covering reporting and communicating to an appropriate authority. The numbering of the new ISA (UK) is expected to change and the title is expected to be *Special Considerations for Audits of Public Interest Entities – Communicating and Reporting to An Appropriate Authority Outside the Entity*.

There is a new definition proposed of 'reportable matters' which is information about which the auditor becomes aware during the audit that the auditor is either required to report to an appropriate authority or that the auditor determines should be reported to an appropriate authority outside the entity.

The structure of the revised ISA (UK) is likely to be in two parts:

- Requirements 11 to 13 will apply to audits of public interest entities.

- Requirements 14 to 21 will apply only if the auditor becomes aware of information that may relate to a reportable matter.

The scope of the new standard is public interest entities. However, the FRC has stated that it is intending that the new standard will apply to all entities caught by the new definition of 'public interest entity'.

Effective date

The effective date of the revisions to ISA (UK) 250, Section A and the replacement for ISA (UK) 250, Section B will be for audits of financial statements for periods commencing on or after 15 December 2024 (ie, 31 December 2025 year ends or short periods). Earlier adoption is expected to be permissible.

The remainder of this section examines the provisions of existing ISA (UK) 250, Section A and Section B.

Essentially, ISA (UK) 250 requires the auditor to:

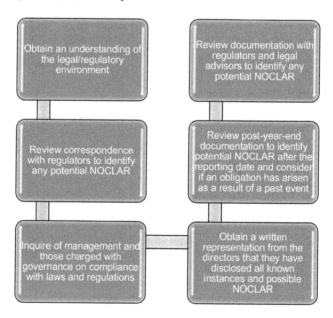

At the outset, it is important to understand the responsibilities where laws and regulations are concerned. What is set out clearly in ISA (UK) 250 is that the auditor is **not** responsible for preventing and detecting non-compliance with laws and regulations. It would be naïve to think that the auditor bears this responsibility because the auditors are only in attendance at the client's premises perhaps once a year (or maybe more than that if interim audits are carried out).

The table below sets out the responsibilities where laws and regulations are concerned:

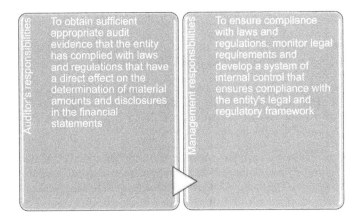

Auditor's responsibilities	Management responsibilities
To obtain sufficient appropriate audit evidence that the entity has complied with laws and regulations that have a direct effect on the determination of material amounts and disclosures in the financial statements	To ensure compliance with laws and regulations, monitor legal requirements and develop a system of internal control that ensures compliance with the entity's legal and regulatory framework

As I indicated above, the auditor is primarily concerned with NOCLAR because any NOCLAR can give rise to a fine or penalty which may need to be provided for in the financial statements. The risk of NOCLAR must be considered at a very early stage in the audit and procedures are devised through the audit plan to obtain the necessary audit evidence.

IMPORTANT POINT

The principal risk for the auditor where NOCLAR is concerned is that provisions for liabilities and expenses are understated, or the disclosure of a contingent liability is incomplete. In more serious cases NOCLAR can be a 'show-stopper' causing the business to fail.

If the auditor discovers any NOCLAR, this might give rise to the need for a provision for a liability (ie, a fine or penalty for non-compliance). The auditor would need to consider how material the NOCLAR is and also whether any NOCLAR leading to a fine or penalty means the recognition criteria for a provision in FRS 102 *The Financial Reporting Standard applicable in the UK and Republic of Ireland*, Section 21 *Provisions and Contingencies*, is met.

It may be the case that the client has complied with all laws and regulations applicable to it during the period under audit. In which case, the auditor must obtain sufficient appropriate audit evidence that the entity has complied with all laws and regulations that have a direct effect on the amounts and disclosures in the financial statements.

In respect of laws and regulations which have an indirect effect on the financial statements, the auditor has a limited responsibility to perform specific procedures to help identify any non-compliance.

Example 9.5 – Non-compliance with laws and regulations

Kirsty is the audit engagement partner in charge of the audit of Skiathos Enterprises Ltd. The draft financial statements for the year ended 31 December 2024 show a disclosure of a contingent liability in respect of a legal claim brought against the company on 28 October 2024.

The company was found to be in breach of a contract with a customer who is suing the company for damages of £25,000 for defective work, late delivery and a loss of earnings. The contingent liability disclosure states that the company is actively defending itself against the case and it is expected to win.

During the review of correspondence, Kirsty came across a letter from the solicitors dated 10 December 2024 which suggested that the company was, in fact, in breach of contract and that it could be proven. The solicitor's letter confirmed that if the case went to court, there is a more than 50% chance the company would be found guilty. The solicitor had also confirmed that damages in cases such as this one are in the region of £24,000 to £30,000.

In this scenario, the company has disclosed a contingent liability rather than recognised a provision for liabilities. A provision for liabilities would seem more appropriate given that the recognition criteria in FRS 102, Section 21 has been met in that:

(a)   the entity has an obligation at the reporting date of a past event: *the breach of the contract prior to the year end*;

(b)   it is probable (ie, more likely than not) that the entity will be required to transfer economic benefits in settlement: *the solicitors have confirmed it is more than likely that the company will be found liable*; and

(c)   the amount of the obligation can be estimated reliably: *the solicitor has confirmed that damages in cases such as this one are in the region of £24,000–£30,000.*

Consequently, a provision should be recognised in the financial statements for the year ended 31 December 2024 rather than disclosure of a contingent liability as the recognition criteria for a provision per FRS 102, para 21.4 has been met. The client may be reluctant to recognise a provision because they could argue that this is an admission of guilt, whereas disclosure of a contingent liability does not admit guilt and they are defending.

If the directors refuse to make a provision (when it can be demonstrated they should) and the provision is found to be material to the financial statements (both in isolation and in combination) the auditor must express a modified audit opinion.

Audit procedures to address NOCLAR

9.24 Identifying NOCLAR can be tricky for auditors, especially when it concerns fraud and/or money laundering. This is the main reason why auditors must exercise professional scepticism (see **9.18** above) and remain alert to the possibility that other audit procedures applied may bring instances of non-compliance (or suspected non-compliance) with laws and regulations to the attention of the auditor. Such procedures may include:

(a) reading minutes of board meetings;

(b) reviewing correspondence (paying particular attention to correspondence from lawyers);

(c) enquiring of management and/or legal advisers concerning litigation or claims brought against the entity; and

(d) undertaking substantive procedures on classes of transactions, account balances and disclosures.

Reporting identified or suspected NOCLAR

9.25 When the auditor discovers NOCLAR, they must first notify those charged with governance. However, this comes with a word of caution. If the auditor suspects that those charged with governance are involved with the identified or suspected NOCLAR, the auditor must communicate with the next highest level of authority (this could include the audit committee, if one is established). When a higher level of authority does not exist, the auditor must consider obtaining legal advice.

In addition, the auditor must also consider whether the NOCLAR has a material effect on the financial statements and, in turn, what sort of impact this has on the auditor's report.

9.25 *Fraud, Laws and Regulations*

In the UK, auditors can report specific instances of non-compliance in the public interest if the auditor does not have any confidence that management or those charged with governance will make any necessary disclosures to a regulator. This is a clear indicator of a lack of integrity because it implies that the client is attempting to hide non-compliance (perhaps to avoid regulatory inspection).

IMPORTANT POINT

The auditor must be extremely careful about making disclosure in the public interest because there is no clear definition of what is meant by 'public interest'. A situation where, for example, a non-compliance could endanger life would be in the public interest.

When faced with such situations, auditors are always advised to seek advice (including legal advice) to ensure their course of action is appropriate.

Remember, auditors are bound by rules on confidentiality. However, there may be occasions when the auditor's duty of confidentiality is overridden by law or statute. This will be the case when the auditor discovers acts of drug-trafficking or money laundering.

Example 9.6 – Reporting to a regulator

The Bright Light Foundation is a charity that works with vulnerable adults and people with additional learning requirements. The year end of the charity is 31 December 2024.

The objective of the charity is to enable its beneficiaries to have a better quality of life and enhance their independence.

During a review of compliance with laws and regulations, the audit senior discovers that the charity does not have a safeguarding policy in place. A review of the information held on its volunteers revealed that no Disclosure and Barring Services (DBS) checks have been carried out on its volunteers.

The matters are referred to the audit engagement partner who is unsure why the matter has been reported to him as the matters identified do not affect the amounts or disclosures reported in the charity's year-end financial statements.

The audit engagement partner is wrong to dismiss these issues. The UK charity regulators have issued guidance on *Matters of Material Significance*. There are nine reportable matters of material significance and one of those matters is 'risk to the charity's beneficiaries'.

As the matters discovered by the auditor effectively put the vulnerable adults and people with additional learning requirements at risk of abuse or mistreatment, the audit engagement partner must report the matter to the relevant charity regulator. The audit engagement partner's duty of confidentiality is overridden in this respect because a failure to report a matter of material significance to a charity regulator will result in the auditor committing a criminal offence.

The example above highlights a non-compliance issue that is specific to a particular sector (being a charity). Remember, the issue of laws and regulations is wide and there could be sector-specific reporting requirements which the auditor will need an awareness of to ensure their obligations are discharged properly.

CHAPTER ROUNDUP

- There is an expectations gap in auditing which is the difference between what the auditor is required to do under law and professional standards and what the general public perceive the auditor should do.

- It is important to distinguish between 'fraud' and 'error' as fraud is intentional, whereas error is not.

- Fraud can be difficult to detect because most frauds are sophisticated and are designed to be concealed to protect the perpetrators. Fraud typically consists of fraudulent financial reporting and misappropriation of assets.

- The auditor is not responsible for the prevention and detection of fraud. This responsibility rests with the management of the entity.

- The auditor is responsible for obtaining reasonable assurance about whether the financial statements as a whole are free from material misstatement due to fraud.

- Revenue is singled out by ISA (UK) 240 as needing special consideration by the auditor as fraud could exist where revenue recognition is concerned.

- ISA (UK) 700 *Forming an Opinion and Reporting on Financial Statements* requires the auditor to include a section in the auditor's report which describes how the audit was designed to detect irregularities, including fraud.

- The auditor must carefully consider laws and regulations and the entity's compliance with such.

- Non-compliance with laws and regulations can give rise to the need for a provision in the financial statements (for fines or penalties for the non-compliance) or the disclosure of a contingent liability.

- It is management's responsibility to ensure the entity complies with its laws and regulations. The auditor's responsibility is to obtain sufficient appropriate audit evidence that the entity has complied with its laws and regulations which have a direct effect on the amounts and disclosures in the financial statements.

- The auditor's duty of confidentiality may be overridden where breaches of laws or regulations are concerned, and they may be duty-bound to make a report to a regulator.

PITFALLS TO AVOID

- Incorrectly rebutting the presumption of fraud within revenue recognition.

- Assuming that fraud (or the risk of fraud) does not apply to the client because it has never been experienced in previous audits.

- Failing to properly discuss the susceptibility of the financial statements to material misstatement due to fraud (and error) at the planning stage of the audit (and properly documenting this discussion).

- Failing to discuss fraud in respect of transactions with related parties.

- Relying on previous experience of management's past integrity and honesty, thus failing to apply professional scepticism throughout the course of the audit.

- Placing too much reliance on a weak internal control system and not carrying out more substantive procedures.

- Not reporting acts of fraud or non-compliance with laws and regulations to the appropriate authorities in breach of the auditor's obligations.

Chapter 10

Audit Completion

CHAPTER TOPIC LIST

• Introduction (see **10.1**)

• Evaluation of misstatements (see **10.2**)

• Final analytical review (see **10.17**)

• Subsequent events (see **10.19**)

• Going concern (see **10.23**)

• Opening balances, comparative information and corresponding figures (see **10.34**)

INTRODUCTION

10.1   The completion side of the audit is probably *the* most critical aspect of the entire audit process and is often the reason a file 'fails' an audit inspection. It is at this point in the audit that the audit evidence is reviewed, misstatements identified during the audit are evaluated and the audit engagement partner begins to form their opinion on the financial statements as to whether they give a true and fair view (or present fairly, in all material respects).

Of course, there is a lot more to the completion side of the audit than just those tasks I have listed in the opening paragraph, but the important point to emphasise is that as the audit draws to a close, there are a number of the International Standards on Auditing (UK) (ISAs (UK)) that are triggered and there is a lot of overlap between the ISAs (UK) at this stage, which also means there is a lot that can go wrong (which we obviously want to avoid).

WHAT ARE WE TRYING TO ACHIEVE?

The completion side of the audit is the point at which the overall opinion on the financial statements begins to be developed. The audit engagement partner reviews all material areas of the file, paying particular attention to high-risk areas and those areas of the audit that proved difficult or contentious. The objective of the auditor at this stage in the audit process is to establish whether there is sufficient appropriate audit evidence to support an unmodified opinion or, if not, the type of modified opinion that is appropriate in the circumstances. The auditor will also need to establish whether any additional paragraphs are needed in the auditor's report, such as a Material Uncertainty Related to Going Concern paragraph or an Emphasis of Matter paragraph.

In addition, the auditor must also form their conclusion in accordance with the relevant ISAs (UK).

IMPORTANT POINT

An important point to emphasise is that the auditor's opinion is the sole responsibility of the audit engagement partner. None of this responsibility can be delegated to others on the audit engagement team; nor any third parties that may have been involved in some aspects of the audit, such as a management or auditor's expert.

Throughout the course of the audit, the audit evidence obtained should have been reviewed on an ongoing basis by a senior member of the audit engagement team. This review process is a fundamental component of a system of quality management and more emphasis is placed on supervision and review under ISQM (UK) 1 *Quality Management for Firms that Perform Audits or Reviews of Financial Statements, or Other Assurance or Related Services Engagements* and ISA (UK) 220 *Quality Management for an Audit of Financial Statements.*

Ongoing review of audit work throughout the audit process will enable any difficult or contentious matters to be dealt with swiftly. If the review process is weak, dealing with any difficult or contentious matters at a later stage not only has the potential to delay the audit, but it can also impact other areas of the audit which may then need to be reviewed again.

Final audit procedures will also need to be applied to opening balances and comparative information to ensure these have been correctly brought forward and reported in the financial statements. The auditor will also need to review 'other information' which is to be published within the entity's annual report to ensure it is consistent with the audited financial statements.

The ISAs (UK) which are particularly relevant to the completion phase of the audit are:

- ISA (UK) 450 *Evaluation of Misstatements Identified During the Audit*

- ISA (UK) 520 *Analytical Procedures*

- ISA (UK) 560 *Subsequent Events*

- ISA (UK) 570 *Going Concern*

- ISA (UK) 710 *Comparative Information – Corresponding Figures and Comparative Financial Statements*

- ISA (UK) 720 *The Auditor's Responsibilities Relating to Other Information*

EVALUATION OF MISSTATEMENTS

10.2 In practice, the volume of identified misstatements will depend on the state of the accounting records at the client. Some audits may prove to be very difficult due to errors made in the accounting records by the client or accountant, or a poor understanding of financial reporting by the client. In these sorts of audits, there may be a significant number of misstatements identified, most of which will need correcting to avoid a modified audit opinion. Problematic audits need to be discussed with management and/or those charged with governance with a view to significantly improving the accounting function of the business for future audits.

Other audits may go very smoothly and only a handful of misstatements may be identified (in some cases the auditor may not discover any misstatements, although this is quite rare in practice).

Misstatements in the financial statements can arise for a number of reasons, but primarily they arise due to:

Mathematical errors

Cut-off problems (eg, posting purchase invoices relating to the next financial year in the current year)

Discrepancies in the accounting system

Misunderstanding of accounting standards (eg, financial instruments and the amortised cost method)

Misposted invoices, such as recognising an item in fixed assets when it should be profit and loss expenditure

---

REAL-LIFE SCENARIO

Mr L is one of the audit engagement partners at a firm with approximately 22 audit clients. They had audited one of their former clients a number of years ago and during the audit of trade creditors, the audit senior noted a number of 'major' suppliers that either had a £nil or very low balance at the year end. Trade creditors, in fact, had seen a 27% reduction from the previous year, despite sales increasing by approximately 30%. This reduction was unexpected and so the audit senior began to investigate the reasons behind it.

During the investigation, it transpired that there were a number of purchase invoices that had not been accrued at the year end to the tune of some £175,000. Materiality on this audit was around £80,000 so this understatement was clearly material.

The improved sales performance had been noted, but the company's cash position had worsened. Analytical procedures performed at the planning stage had noted the company's overdraft had increased significantly from the prior year and the audit senior had also noted that the overdraft was, in fact, approaching its limit at the year end. Additional going concern procedures had been recommended by the audit engagement partner at the planning stage, as one would clearly expect.

Not only was this cut-off error going to need correcting to avoid any impact on the auditor's opinion, but it was also going to be the company's downfall.

The understatement had arisen because the purchase ledger clerk, who had only started part-way through the financial year, was posting purchase invoices on the actual day of receipt, rather than using the date of the invoice. The bank received monthly management accounts which also turned out to be wrong. The weak internal control environment over the purchase ledger meant that this problem had gone undetected by the client.

Once the trade creditors had been adjusted for the effect of the cut-off error, the reported profit turned into a loss. Not only that, net current liabilities increased significantly, the 'acid test' ratio went below 1 and the company was already experiencing cash flow difficulties.

A lot of fraught discussions were had about this situation and eventually the audit was signed off with an unmodified opinion.

The going concern basis of accounting was used at the time because the directors were confident the bank would continue to support the business.

Unfortunately, this did not happen and the company was eventually liquidated a year later.

This is an example of how a simple error in posting invoices on an incorrect date can cause cut-off errors which can have a significant impact on the financial statements. The draft financial statements showed an artificial profit, which the company had not made. Gross profit margins were higher than the company had actually achieved, and the directors had been misled into thinking that the company was doing better than it was.

However, audit procedures were responsive to the assessed risks. The audit firm had correctly identified an unusual correlation between increased sales volumes and significantly lower trade creditors but a bank overdraft that was nearing its limit. The analytical procedures had identified a source of misstatement, which was the artificially low trade creditor balance. Once the adjustment had been made in the financial statements, the audited accounts showed that gross margins had, in fact, declined to an unsustainable level.

The scenario above was serious and, thankfully, examples like this one are in the minority; however, they do highlight the severity of issues that an audit can reveal. It also reveals the importance of professional scepticism being maintained by the auditor as this enables a questioning mind.

ISA (UK) 450 provides guidance to the auditor on their responsibilities where misstatements are concerned. Essentially, there are two important factors the auditor must consider:

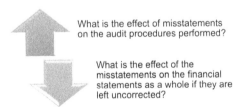

What is the effect of misstatements on the audit procedures performed?

What is the effect of the misstatements on the financial statements as a whole if they are left uncorrected?

In terms of the effect of misstatements on the audit procedures performed, the auditor must consider whether additional procedures should be carried out to identify if the misstatements are indicative of weaknesses in the relevant cycle. For example, if multiple misstatements are noted when carrying out substantive procedures over the year-end bank balances, this could be indicative of a wider problem in controls (eg, multiple write-offs to 'force' the bank reconciliation to agree). The auditor may need to increase sample sizes or carry out further audit procedures to address the risk of material misstatement.

In terms of the effect of misstatements on the financial statements as a whole, the auditor must consider whether the misstatements are material in isolation; or become material when aggregated.

IMPORTANT POINT

Remember, to consider materiality of misstatements in two ways: individually and in the aggregate. A number of individually immaterial misstatements may become material when they are aggregated.

If the effect of uncorrected misstatements is immaterial, the auditor can still express an unmodified opinion. However, if the effect of the uncorrected misstatements is material and the client does not rectify the situation, the auditor will need to express a modified opinion. The type of modified opinion to be expressed will depend on whether the uncorrected misstatements are material but not pervasive or material and pervasive.

IMPORTANT POINT

It is also important that the auditor considers any uncorrected misstatements from prior year audits to assess whether those become material. For example, if the client has failed to amortised an intangible asset, the **cumulative** value of amortisation should be considered as well as the charge for the year.

REAL-LIFE SCENARIO

Entity A is a chemical manufacturer with an accounting reference date of 31 December. The entity prepares its financial statements under FRS 102 *The Financial Reporting Standard applicable in the UK and Republic of Ireland.*

Prior to the UK's departure from the EU, the entity was required to obtain licences under the Registration, Evaluation, Authorisation and Restriction of Chemicals (REACH) regulations which allow the business to continue manufacturing certain chemicals.

The licences were capitalised as an intangible asset on the entity's balance sheet at a cost of some £100,000. While FRS 102 does not specifically cover REACH licences, this initial accounting treatment was deemed to be correct because the cost of the licences is known and the licences allow

---

the entity to continue to manufacture a product for resale (ie, the probable economic benefits criterion in the asset recognition rules is met).

The licences themselves do not contain an expiry date and the entity failed to recognise amortisation on the licences. The finance director suggested that the licences have an indefinite useful life because the chemicals to which they relate could be in production for years and years to come. The finance director refused to recognise amortisation on this basis.

Notwithstanding the fact that the chemicals to which the REACH licences relate could be produced indefinitely, FRS 102 does not allow indefinite useful lives to be assigned to intangible assets. Consequently, all intangible assets (including goodwill) must be amortised on a systematic basis over their useful economic lives.

There is a provision in FRS 102, para 18.20 which states that where the useful economic life of an intangible asset cannot be estimated reliably, the amortisation period cannot exceed ten years. It can be shorter than ten years, but it cannot be longer.

Remember, this ten-year 'cap' is only to be used in **exceptional cases** because invariably management should be capable of arriving at a reliable useful economic life.

In this situation, management should be amortising the REACH licences over a maximum of ten years, even though they consider that the chemicals to which the licences relate could be produced indefinitely.

When the auditor is judging the non-amortisation in terms of its materiality to the financial statements, they must do so having regard to the **accumulated** amortisation that would have been charged had the entity complied with FRS 102 and not just the charge for the year. The fact that the intangible asset has not been amortised means that it has an overstated carrying amount in the balance sheet and amortisation expense for the year is also understated. This is an example of how brought forward misstatements can have knock-on effects on the current year's audit.

Types of misstatements

10.3   At first glance, it might seem obvious that a misstatement is something clearly wrong in the financial statements. For example, an understated bank balance or an overstated depreciation charge. Well, this is **Chapter 10** and so, by now, you've probably guessed that as this is auditing, nothing is never quite as it seems …

ISA (UK) 450 recognises three types of misstatement that can arise:

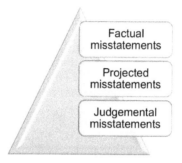

I have briefly referred to **factual misstatements** in the opening paragraph to this section when I mentioned '... that a misstatement is something clearly wrong in the financial statements.' By definition, a factual misstatement is a misstatement about which there is no doubt, such as a mathematical error of a value included in the financial statements.

Example 10.1 – Factual misstatement

During the audit of trade creditors of Ryland Industries Ltd for the year ended 31 March 2024, the audit senior noted that four purchase invoices relating to that year had not been accrued. The total value of these invoices amounted to £42,500 and all related to direct cost of sales.

In this example (ignoring any possible effect on stock), there is no doubt that trade creditors are understated, as are cost of sales. The factual misstatement is £42,500 (plus any associated VAT/other sales tax implications).

Projected misstatements involve the use of the auditor's 'best estimate'. They are the auditor's attempt at arriving at a value of a misstatement within a population where misstatements have been noted within a sample.

Example 10.2 – Projected misstatement

The draft financial statements of Rowan Industries for the year ended 31 March 2024 show trade debtors of £2,400,300. The audit senior has selected a sample of balances for a trade debtors' circularisation totalling £480,000. Errors were found in this sample amounting to £27,600.

Assuming the sample is representative of the population, the projected error would be £27,600 × £2,400,300/£480,000 = £138,017. The auditor would then have to decide if this is likely to be material and refer to performance materiality and tolerable error levels that were set at the planning stage. Alternatively, the sample could be extended (see below).

IMPORTANT POINT

Remember, in **Example 10.2** above, the misstatement could be projected across the population because the procedure was a **substantive** procedure. For a test of control, the auditor is not interested in monetary values. So, if the auditor found six invoices that had not been authorised in a sample of 60, the error rate is 10% – this is the projection of the error in that population.

In either case (substantive tests or tests of control), the auditor must compare this to materiality and tolerable misstatement. If it is not acceptable, the auditor will have to carry out more audit procedures. Where additional procedures are carried out and smaller or fewer errors are found in the additional samples, the significance of the sum of the errors becomes less.

If it is still not acceptable following the application of further audit procedures, the monetary amounts are included on the summary of unadjusted error schedule (or 'audit error schedule'). Management will not adjust the auditor's projected errors, but if they adjust actual errors, hopefully the remainder become immaterial in isolation and in the aggregate. If the remainder are material, the auditor considers the impact on the audit opinion.

In addition, for tests of control, the auditor will conclude that the control is not operating effectively and will carry out full substantive procedures (in other words, as no reliance is being placed on controls, substantive procedures cannot be reduced for reliance on those controls).

Judgemental misstatements are differences that arise from management's judgements (including those concerning recognition, measurement, presentation and disclosure in the financial statements) as well as the selection or application of accounting policies, which the auditor considers unreasonable or inappropriate.

Example 10.3 – Judgemental misstatement

During the audit of Fraya Enterprises Ltd for the year ended 31 March 2024, the audit senior discovered damaged stock with a cost price of £34,200 that appeared to be beyond repair. Management had written this stock down by £8,000 stating the difference is because they can sell the damaged stock for £26,200, hence it has been written down to estimated selling price.

The auditor is not convinced that the damaged stock can be sold as the production manager said it can only be scrapped as it cannot be used in any other products and, on its own, the stock is useless.

Here the value of the judgemental misstatement is £26,200 (£34,200 – £8,000). Management is claiming they can sell the damaged stock for £26,200 but the auditor has concluded this stock has a £nil value.

It should be noted that where the auditor discovers misstatements (whether factual, projected or judgemental), they are not required to classify them according to the terminology used in ISA (UK) 450. The idea behind this classification is to provide a useful framework for identifying and evaluating misstatements for subsequent discussion with management and/or those charged with governance.

Process of dealing with identified misstatements

10.4   The auditor does not correct misstatements they have identified as they go through the audit – the decision whether to correct errors is down to management. Remember, the auditor cannot make the adjustments to the financial statements because they must audit the relevant adjustments once processed to ensure they have been properly recorded in the accounting records. If the auditor were to do this, they would be effectively auditing their own work.

Instead the auditor applies the requirements of ISA (UK) 450 and carries out the following:

Record the misstatements

10.5   The auditor records all identified misstatements on an 'audit error schedule' or 'summary of unadjusted misstatements' schedule. The only exception to this rule would be where the error is deemed to be 'clearly trivial' (the level of triviality is set at the planning stage). A misstatement is classed as clearly trivial when it is clearly inconsequential (both individually and in the aggregate).

IMPORTANT POINT

It is worth noting that ISA (UK) 450 clarifies that 'clearly trivial' is not the same as 'not material'.

Consider whether other misstatements may exist in the financial statements

10.6   The auditor must consider whether the existence of a misstatement indicates that other misstatements may exist in the financial statements. For example, if the auditor discovers that the fair value gain on an investment property has been incorrectly credited to the revaluation reserve, this means there is a corresponding misstatement in profit or loss as the fair value gain should be recorded in profit or loss and not equity, and perhaps deferred tax is also incorrect.

Such other misstatements may then be aggregated with the identified misstatements which may then become material.

Effect on the audit strategy and audit plan

10.7   The identification of misstatements will usually mean the auditor must consider the effect on the audit strategy and resulting audit plan. In some cases, this may mean changes have to be made to both (eg, by extending sample sizes or increasing substantive testing in certain key areas rather than placing reliance on internal controls).

Assessing the materiality of identified misstatements

10.8   The auditor determines the impact of identified misstatements on the financial statements as to whether they are material or immaterial by looking at them both in isolation and in the aggregate. Remember, a misstatement may be immaterial on its own; but when it is aggregated with other identified misstatements, it could become material.

I examined materiality in a lot of detail in **Chapter 7**. It is important to bear in mind that materiality is not only a quantitative issue; it is also a qualitative issue, hence material disclosures are considered by the auditor as well.

Reporting to management

10.9   All identified misstatements must be reported to the appropriate level of management on a timely basis. Common sense prevails here. The auditor does not report to management every time they discover a misstatement because not only is this impractical, it would also get on management's nerves.

Instead, the audit error schedule (which accumulates all the identified misstatements) is discussed on a timely basis with management. In terms of the most 'appropriate' level of management, ISA (UK) 450 says that this is usually the one that has responsibility and authority to evaluate the misstatements and take the necessary action. In a lot of cases, this is likely to be the finance director.

Request that the misstatements are corrected

10.10   This can sometimes be a fraught discussion with clients, particularly if it involves reducing profits or making disclosures that management do not want to make, so the auditor must be prepared to 'stand their ground' here.

The auditor will want to ensure that all misstatements that are material (either in isolation or in the aggregate) are corrected. This is essentially to avoid modifying the audit opinion. If management are unwilling to correct material misstatements, the auditor has no choice but to modify the audit opinion accordingly depending on the materiality and pervasiveness of the misstatements.

If management correct all the material misstatements, a modified opinion can be avoided and everyone is happy. This is also the case if management correct the material misstatements and leave the immaterial ones uncorrected. Remember, though, that the unadjusted misstatements must be immaterial both in isolation and in the aggregate.

Management refusal to correct identified misstatements

10.11   If management refuse to correct all, or some, misstatements that have been picked up during the course of the audit, the auditor must consider the reasons for this refusal. In most cases, management are willing to make the adjustments necessary to avoid a modified audit opinion because they know that a modified audit opinion can have serious repercussions for the business.

However, in less common situations when management refuse to correct the identified misstatements, the auditor must take their reasoning into consideration when establishing whether, or not, the financial statements are materially misstated. Remember, this refusal could call into question the integrity of management who could be trying to manipulate the financial results.

REAL-LIFE SCENARIO

Ms R is the audit engagement partner in a three-partner firm and is responsible for three audits. One of her audit clients, Entity A, relies on an invoice discounting facility for its cash flow. At the time of the audit, the invoice discounter had notified the client that they were looking to renew the facility but wanted to see the audited financial statements for the year ended 31 October 2021.

Initially, the draft financial statements showed a profit before tax of some £1.2m which was a 20% reduction on the prior year. The client concerned had been suffering from cash flow difficulties following the COVID-19 pandemic, and the legacy of those difficulties was still being felt.

During the audit, the audit senior noted a number of misstatements in payroll postings including a holiday pay accrual not recorded correctly in the financial statements. Accrued income in the financial statements had, in fact, already been invoiced (hence the sales had been recognised twice in the financial statements).

Along with other identified misstatements, the £1.2m profit before tax would have dropped to some £0.1m once the misstatements had been corrected. The finance director was not happy.

Ms R explained that she had gone through the misstatements with the finance director who had suggested that they be corrected in the subsequent accounting period (ie, in the 2022 financial year). The client was desperate to show a healthy set of results (albeit at reduced levels from the prior year) and pleaded with the auditor to help them achieve this. At one point, the finance director offered the auditor the opportunity to increase their fee if they were to help them secure the borrowing facilities.

There are a number of problems that present themselves in this situation. The auditor would be compelled to express a modified audit opinion if the client did not adjust the financial statements, at least for the material misstatements. Regardless of the impact on the client's borrowing facilities, the auditor's judgement cannot be clouded by this. The auditor's position is clear – if the financial statements are adjusted so they **do not** contain material misstatement, the opinion can be unmodified; if they remain unadjusted such that they **do** contain material misstatement, the opinion is

---

modified. The ISAs (UK) do not make exceptions for businesses that may run into difficulties with their finance providers – this is not a concern of the auditor who must, at all times, remain independent and objective.

Next is the intimidation threat that arises. The Ethical Standard provisions would kick in where this is concerned. The finance director is pleading with the auditor to express an inappropriate audit opinion (ie, express an unmodified opinion when the financial statements contain material misstatements). This is clearly not a route any auditor wants to go down because it is reckless and can result in the auditor being struck off by their professional body if they give in to the client.

The final problem is the contingent fee offer. The finance director is proposing that the audit firm be given the opportunity of increasing their fee *if* they agree to 'help' the company succeed in renewing their borrowing facilities. The 'help' would, of course, be turning a blind eye to the misstatements such that the financial statements are misleading and contain material misstatement. Now, you do not have to know the ethical rules inside out to know that this is clearly wrong. One may argue that the contingent fee 'offer' is, in fact, a bribe.

In any event, contingent fees are a 'no no'. The audit fee must be based on the level of skill, time and resources needed to complete the work to the required professional standards.

So, what happened with this client?

It turned out that the auditor stood her ground (and rightly so). There were many fraught discussions before the financial statements were finally approved and an unmodified opinion was expressed because the client adjusted the financial statements such that they did not contain material misstatements. However, given the challenges the client had presented, Ms R resigned from the audit following the signing of the auditor's report.

You can see from the above real-life scenario that Ms R was right to resign. The client had suggested all sorts of unethical 'bribes' in an attempt to secure an unmodified audit opinion. Their integrity was clearly lacking and these are clients that no audit firm should have to deal with.

Uncorrected misstatements

10.12   As I mentioned earlier, most clients would want to correct misstatements to not only ensure their organisation's financial statements present a true and fair view, but also to ensure that the auditor's report is unmodified. There may be some misstatements, however, that remain uncorrected because management believe they are immaterial. Now, whether management believe the uncorrected misstatements are material and whether the auditor agrees with this belief may be two very different things. In many cases a suitable resolution can often be found.

Where the auditor agrees that the effect of uncorrected misstatements is immaterial, ISA (UK) 450 requires four steps to be taken by the auditor:

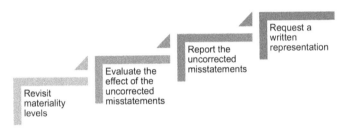

Revisit materiality levels

Evaluate the effect of the uncorrected misstatements

Report the uncorrected misstatements

Request a written representation

Revisit materiality levels

10.13   As I discuss in **Chapter 7**, materiality levels are not 'fixed' at the planning stage of the audit. They can change in response to findings throughout the course of the audit. Where uncorrected misstatements are concerned, the auditor must revisit the assessment of materiality to determine whether the levels remain appropriate in light of the facts and circumstances. This applies to **both** financial statement materiality and performance materiality.

Evaluate the effect of the uncorrected misstatements

10.14   The auditor must determine whether the uncorrected misstatements, both individually and in the aggregate, are material to the financial statements as a whole. This will require the auditor to consider the **size** and **nature** of the misstatements. Remember the qualitative and quantitative characteristics of materiality.

Report the uncorrected misstatements

10.15   The auditor must then report the uncorrected misstatements to those charged with governance. This may be the same body as individuals as the directors, but in some larger organisations this could be the shareholders or the audit committee. The auditor must explain the effect this may have on the auditor's opinion and is usually a discussion that is held with the audit engagement partner.

Request a written representation

10.16 The auditor must obtain a written representation from those charged with governance that they believe the effects of uncorrected misstatements are immaterial. If those charged with governance refuse to supply this representation, the auditor will invariably disclaim the opinion on the financial statements because it implies that those charged with governance are not taking responsibility for the financial statements prepared by management.

Example 10.4 – Evaluating the effect of identified misstatements

The draft financial statements of Olive Enterprises Ltd for the year ended 31 March 2024 show a profit before tax of £2.4m and total assets of £11.3m. The audit engagement partner has calculated a financial statement materiality level of £120,000 which is equivalent to 5% of profit before tax. This has been justified on the grounds that the pre-tax profit figure is the parameter most susceptible to change due to audit errors. The client prepares its financial statements under FRS 102 *The Financial Reporting Standard applicable in the UK and Republic of Ireland.*

During the course of the audit, the audit team discovered the following misstatements:

- Bauer Ltd, who is a customer of Olive Enterprises Ltd, went into liquidation on 10 April 2024 owing £72,000. The finance director has refused to write this off in the financial statements on the grounds that he considers the debt immaterial and that the client's liquidator only notified them in April 2024 which is after the year end. The finance director is insistent that this bad debt be recorded in next year's financial statements.

- On 7 April 2024, a batch of inventory costing £325,000 was sold for £220,000.

Trade debtor

As the customer has gone into liquidation shortly after the year end, FRS 102, Section 32 *Events after the End of the Reporting Period* will apply. FRS 102, Section 32 would regard this as an adjusting event and hence the finance director's argument that the debtor should be written off in next year's financial statements is incorrect. Olive Enterprises Ltd has already suffered a loss at the year end because Bauer Ltd was clearly not in a position to be able to pay its outstanding balance. If this adjustment is not made, trade debtors will be overstated and bad debt expense understated.

The trade debtor balance equates to 3% (£72,000 / £2.4m) of profit before tax and hence is immaterial in isolation (the bad debt also does not exceed financial statement materiality which is set at £120,000).

Sale of stock post-year end

FRS 102, Section 13 *Inventories* requires stock to be valued at the lower of cost and estimated selling price less costs to complete and sell. A batch of inventory costing £325,000 was sold for £220,000 shortly after the year end. In this case, estimated selling price is clearly less than cost and hence FRS 102, Section 13 would require a write-down to estimated selling price. If this adjustment is not made, stock will be overstated by £105,000 (£325,000 – £220,000). At 4.4% (£105,000 / £2.4m), the value of the write down is immaterial in isolation.

Considering the impact of the misstatements in the aggregate

Just because the two misstatements above are immaterial in isolation, this is not the end of the story. ISA (UK) 450 requires the auditor to consider the effect of the misstatements **in the aggregate as well**. Remember, that cumulatively misstatements have a bigger effect on the financial statements.

The total misstatements are £177,000 (£72,000 + £105,000). This aggregate amount represents 7.4% (£177,000 / £2.4m) of profit before tax and hence is considered material as materiality is 5% of profit before tax or £120,000. This means the misstatements now become material when aggregated.

Consequently, the two amounts will need to be adjusted in the financial statements to avoid a modified audit opinion.

FINAL ANALYTICAL REVIEW

10.17 Analytical review crops up a lot in audit. Remember, the auditor will carry out analytical review mandatorily at two stages of the audit: the planning stage (as risk assessment procedures under ISA (UK) 315 *Identifying and Assessing the Risks of Material Misstatement*) and at the final stage under ISA (UK) 520 *Analytical Procedures* to form an overall conclusion as to whether the financial statements are consistent with the auditor's knowledge and understanding of the client and the environment in which it operates. Analytical procedures may also be used during the audit as a substantive procedure under ISA (UK) 520 to obtain audit evidence, but this is not mandatory.

Towards the end of the audit, the auditor will carry out final analytical procedures to form an overall conclusion as to whether the financial statements are consistent with the auditor's knowledge and understanding of the entity as well as evaluating whether the financial statements are free from material misstatements. Remember, analytical procedures are a valuable tool for the auditor because they can identify sources of potential material misstatement.

I examine analytical procedures in a lot of detail in **Chapter 7** which includes comparison of current year figures with the prior year, calculation of ratios (such as gross profit margin, trade debtor days and the current ratio) and comparison of the client's figures with those of entities in the same industry. To all intents and purposes, the analytical procedures carried out at the final stage of the audit will not differ too greatly from those carried out at the planning stage.

IMPORTANT POINT

It is worth noting that while the analytical procedures carried out by the auditor at the final stage of the audit will not differ too much from those carried out at the planning phase, the principal difference is that at the completion stage, the auditor should have sufficient appropriate audit evidence available to explain the issues that have been flagged up by the analytical procedures and should, therefore, be in a position to conclude as to the overall reasonableness of the financial statements. For example, if the client's gross profit margin was expected to be similar to the prior year, but has, in fact, declined, the auditor should have sufficient appropriate audit evidence to explain the reason for the decline.

At the completion stage, if the auditor finds any previously unidentified risks of material misstatement, then further audit evidence will need to be obtained (ie, additional audit procedures will need to be carried out).

Example 10.5 – Final analytical procedures

The final draft financial statements for Revere Ltd for the year ended 31 March 2024 show the following:

	31.03.2024	31.03.2023
	£'000	**£'000**
Turnover	12,576	14,996
Cost of sales	(7,166)	(6,812)
Gross profit	5,410	8,184

At the planning stage of the audit, Jeanette, the audit senior, calculated the gross profit margins which are as follows:

2024:   £5,410 / £12,576 × 100 = 43%

2023:   £8,184 / £14,996 × 100 = 55%

The gross profit margin tells us that for every £1 Revere sold, Revere made 43p gross profit in 2024 and 55p in 2023. What this tells Jeanette is that something has happened in the current year which has resulted in gross profit margins declining. In a lot of entities, you would expect gross profit margins to remain relatively static, particularly as businesses generally try to remain competitive and the gross profit margin is usually a key performance indicator. In Revere's case, gross profit margins have declined, hence Jeanette must devise audit procedures at the planning stage that help ascertain the reasons why this has happened. Remember, management may be under the impression that gross margins have remained consistent, so Jeanette must 'arm' herself with the audit evidence to corroborate the decline in margins or identify any misstatements that have arisen which have brought margins down (eg, incorrect cut-off on stock, purchases or sales or an incorrect year-end closing stock figure).

Let's fast forward now to the evidence-gathering stage.

During the audit, Jeanette obtained evidence that six of the client's largest suppliers had increased their prices considerably due to inflation. While the client has tried, as far as it could, to pass price increases onto its customers, it has been unable to pass the entire price increases on because this would impact on the client's competitive advantage. Jeanette should ensure she has sufficient appropriate audit evidence to back up this reason and, assuming the evidence is sufficient and appropriate, the audit engagement partner can conclude that the decrease in Revere's gross profit margin is reasonable and is supported by the audit evidence obtained.

Now, consider if the gross profit margin had decreased because the year-end stock valuation was incorrect (let's assume there was some sort of discrepancy in the valuation method), and the client refuses to correct the error. In this case, assuming that the error is material, it is likely that the audit engagement partner will express a modified audit opinion because the financial statements contain a material misstatement.

You can see why carrying out analytical procedures towards the end of the audit is important. They help the auditor to justify any trends or relationships within the figures that may be beyond expectations. What they do is arm the auditor with explanations so that management can challenge the auditor during, say, the audit closing meeting, as to why certain figures are being reported.

Remember, some management members may only see financial information once a year in, say, a board meeting when the auditor is present, and hence may question certain figures or information in them. The auditor must be able to answer any such questions at the drop of a hat because otherwise they will more than likely look unprofessional.

Notes to the financial statements

10.18 While the focus of analytical procedures is clearly on numerical information presented in the financial statements, it must be borne in mind that it is not *just* about the numbers. The auditor must also look at the notes to the financial statements because these are also within the scope of the audit and contain crucial information concerning the figures in the primary financial statements as well as providing additional information that may not necessarily be presented (eg, a material non-adjusting event).

There are four primary reasons why the auditor must review the notes as part of their audit:

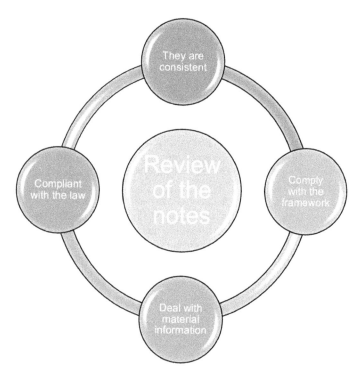

You can see from the above diagram that the auditor is required to:

(a) Ensure the notes are consistent with the financial statements themselves, for example, the disaggregation of turnover in the notes agrees to the turnover figure presented in the profit and loss account.

(b) Ensure the notes comply with the applicable financial reporting framework (eg, FRS 102) and they disclose everything that they are required to disclose, and no material information is missing or is obscure.

(c) Ensure the notes deal with material information that may not be presented in the primary financial statements (such as related party transactions or non-adjusting events).

(d) Ensure the notes comply with the requirements of applicable legislation, such as CA 2006.

REAL-LIFE SCENARIO

Mr L is an external audit file reviewer who has worked in many reputable training organisations over the years. Mr L explained to me that it is surprising just how many firms fail to ensure that they have an up-to-date disclosure checklist on their file.

Some years ago, Mr L had reviewed an audit file for a nine-partner firm and during the review had raised several deficiencies on the file. He explained that most of the deficiencies in the audit work were 'the norm', such as no documentation as to how the team had arrived at sample sizes, incorrect starting points for income completeness testing and some issues concerning a lack of testing of the recoverability of debtor balances. However, the main issue that resulted in the file essentially being a 'fail' was that the disclosure notes in the financial statements contained a lot of technical errors. For example, incomplete related party disclosure notes, no disaggregation of turnover, no disclosure of auditor's remuneration and a lot of 'boilerplate' accounting policies. For the record, this audit was in connection with a set of financial statements prepared under old UK GAAP.

Mr L explained that he was surprised that a nine-partner firm had not got an up-to-date disclosure checklist. The audit engagement partner informed Mr L that they relied on their accounts production software system to generate the financial statements and notes and were aware that other firms did the same.

The audit firm in question did not realise that 'presentation and disclosure' is, of course, a key financial statement assertion. The auditor covers this assertion through a careful check of the disclosure notes and this is usually evidenced by way of a disclosure checklist on the audit file.

> While it is not mandatory to complete a disclosure checklist every single year for the same audit client, the auditor must ensure that there is evidence on file that they have carried out procedures to check the presentation and disclosure of information in the financial statements. The reason the firm received a 'significant improvement required' outcome on their audit file was simply down to the fact that they had not adequately dealt with the presentation and disclosure assertion.

The key issue to bear in mind where narrative information is concerned is that materiality is also a **qualitative** issue, ie, it is not just about the numbers. Where certain disclosures, which are considered material, are inadequate the auditor will, of course, provide ample opportunity for the client to remedy the inadequacy. If the client fails to remedy the inadequacy, a modified audit opinion will follow.

SUBSEQUENT EVENTS

10.19   Life is anything but predictable and this certainly applies in the world of auditing. 'Stuff' happens between the client's balance sheet date and the date on which the financial statements are authorised for issue (approved) and the date of the auditor's report. Some of this stuff may need to be reflected in the financial statements to ensure the user of the accounts is fully informed of everything that has happened right up to the point at which the auditor signs their report.

To deal with these issues, ISA (UK) 560 *Subsequent Events* applies which deals with the requirements in respect of events which arise after the year end. I suppose you could say that ISA (UK) 560 is a 'companion' standard to FRS 102 *The Financial Reporting Standard applicable in the UK and Republic of Ireland*, Section 32 *Events after the End of the Reporting Period* because ISA (UK) 560 essentially requires the auditor to audit whether the client has correctly applied the provisions in FRS 102, Section 32.

ISA (UK) 560 states that 'subsequent events' are those events which occur between the balance sheet date and the date of the auditor's report. In addition, ISA (UK) 560 also discusses facts which become known to the auditor after signing the auditor's report. I'll examine some of these technical points further on in this section, but, for now, just bear in mind that to a certain extent, the auditor is relying on management being as open and as transparent as possible where subsequent events (often referred to as 'post balance sheet events') are concerned.

When you consider the timing of the audit, in most cases the bulk of the audit fieldwork takes place after the balance sheet date and it can be many months after the year end when the financial statements are approved and the auditor's report is signed – particularly if the audit has had difficulties or contentious issues to content with. Hence, there is often a long period of time after the year end when significant events can arise.

ISA (UK) 560 recognises that the auditor has two specific duties where subsequent events are concerned:

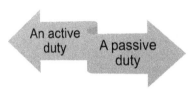

The auditor's **active duty** means that the auditor is required to obtain sufficient appropriate audit evidence that all subsequent events that require adjustment or disclosure in the financial statements have been identified. This duty applies between the client's balance sheet date and the date on which the auditor's report is signed.

The auditor's **passive duty** is where there is no specific requirement to perform audit procedures and will always apply after the auditor's report has been signed. This does not mean that the auditor can simply forget about subsequent events because if a fact becomes known to the auditor after they have signed their auditor's report which may have caused them to express a different opinion if that fact had been known at the time, the auditor must take appropriate action.

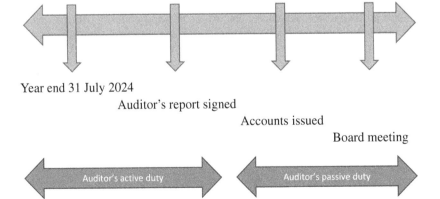

Year end 31 July 2024

Auditor's report signed

Accounts issued

Board meeting

IMPORTANT POINT

The auditor's letter of engagement will usually contain clauses whereby the client agrees to inform the auditor of all relevant subsequent events, including those that arise after the date of the auditor's report.

Adjusting and non-adjusting events

10.20 At the outset it is worth emphasising that standards such as ISA (UK) 560 and FRS 102, Section 32 only apply to those events that arise **after** the balance sheet date. In other words, they apply to events arising between the balance sheet date and the date the financial statements are authorised for issue and the date on which auditor signs their report.

FRS 102, Section 32 classifies events which occur after the balance sheet date as follows:

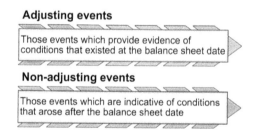

Adjusting events

Those events which provide evidence of conditions that existed at the balance sheet date

Non-adjusting events

Those events which are indicative of conditions that arose after the balance sheet date

Adjusting events are those events which arise after the balance sheet date which are then reflected in the year-end financial statements (ie, the financial statements are *adjusted* to reflect the event). This is because their conditions existed at the balance sheet date. The classic example of an adjusting event is a trade debtor that goes bankrupt shortly after the year end. This is evidence that the company had suffered a loss at the reporting date and hence the trade debtor is written off (ie, the circumstances leading to the bad debt – such as the customer's cash flow difficulties – were in existence at the year end).

Non-adjusting events are not reflected in the financial statements. Instead, they are disclosed where they are material. This is because their conditions did not exist at the reporting date, but they have arisen *between* the reporting date and the date on which the auditor signs their report. For example, a flood that occurs in a client's warehouse two months after the balance sheet date could damage a material amount of stock. This has nothing to do with a year-end condition and hence is a non-adjusting event.

The table below provides some non-exhaustive examples of adjusting and non-adjusting events:

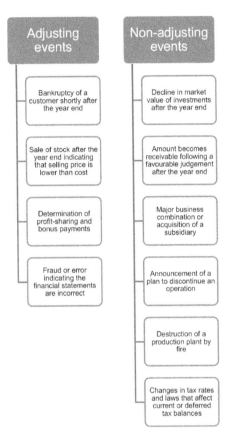

Example 10.6 – Non-adjusting event

The audit engagement team of Ryland Ltd have nearly completed the audit of the draft financial statements for the year ended 31 March 2024. The audit senior started the subsequent events review yesterday and noted a letter from Rowan & Co Employment Lawyers dated 16 April 2024 notifying Ryland Ltd of a legal action brought against the company by a former employee, Rita Morley, who was the firm's purchase ledger supervisor for six years. Ms Morley has claimed unfair dismissal on the grounds that she was summarily dismissed by the finance director without warning or going through proper employment law protocol. Ms Morley is claiming £75,000 which is considered to be material to the financial statements.

The audit senior held a discussion with the finance director who confirmed they believe they can successfully defend the legal action because Ms Morley was grossly incompetent at her job and had, in fact, been warned on several occasions. The finance director is unwilling to make any disclosures in connection with this case as he feels that readers of the financial statements will view the entity in an unfavourable light.

This is an example of a non-adjusting event. The claim was brought against the entity after the balance sheet date, but before the auditor's report has been signed and the financial statements authorised for issue. As the amount claimed by the former employee is considered to be material to the financial statements, the entity would be required to disclose:

(a) the nature of the event; and

(b) an estimate of its financial effect, or a statement that such an estimate cannot be made, in order to comply with FRS 102, Section 32.

If this non-adjusting event is not disclosed adequately, the auditor must modify their opinion accordingly due to the lack of disclosure on the basis that the issue is material.

Audit procedures where the auditor has an active duty

10.21 Remember, the auditor's active duty arises between the balance sheet date and the date on which the auditor signs their report. ISA (UK) 560 requires that the auditor performs audit procedures designed to obtain sufficient appropriate audit evidence that all subsequent events which require adjustment or disclosure in the financial statements are identified and properly recorded.

Such procedures may include:

● Inquiring of management if they are aware of any subsequent events that require adjustment in the financial statements.

● Reviewing accounting records such as budgets, forecasts and interim accounts (eg, post-year end management accounts) for evidence of any subsequent events.

● Inquiring of management's procedures for the identification of subsequent events.

● Reviewing minutes of directors' and shareholders' meetings.

● Reviewing correspondence with lawyers to identify any potential subsequent events.

- Inspecting post-year-end cash receipts from customers to identify any potential irrecoverable debtors which may need to be written off.

- Reviewing post-year-end sales invoices to identify any stock that may have been sold after the balance sheet date for less than cost price.

- Reviewing the entity's latest subsequent interim financial statements (if any are available).

- Requesting a written representation letter from management that they have identified all subsequent events that need adjustment or disclosure in the financial statements.

- Reviewing the disclosures in the financial statements to ensure they comply with the applicable financial reporting framework (eg, FRS 102 *The Financial Reporting Standard applicable in the UK and Republic of Ireland*).

Example 10.7 – Adjusting event

The audit of Philbin Enterprises Ltd for the year ended 31 March 2024 is nearing completion and the audit senior is carrying out audit procedures on subsequent events.

During the subsequent events review, the audit senior came across correspondence from Currie & Co Liquidators Ltd informing the client that a customer owing a material sum of money had gone into liquidation. The client has not written this debt off in the financial statements.

The client should be requested to write this debt off in the financial statements for the year ended 31 March 2024. More often than not, a customer's inability to pay/bankruptcy after the balance sheet date will be the culmination of a sequence of events that existed prior to the balance sheet date. For this reason, the bankruptcy of a customer shortly after the balance sheet date is generally an adjusting event.

Example 10.8 – Non-adjusting event

The audit of Carr Ltd for the year ended 31 March 2024 is nearing completion and the audit senior is carrying out audit procedures on subsequent events.

During the course of the subsequent events review, the audit senior came across correspondence from a customer, Burgess Enterprises Ltd, dated 4 May 2024 informing the client they were ceasing to trade with immediate effect and would be unable to pay their outstanding balance. It transpired that the reason the customer had ceased to trade with immediate effect was because of a mismanagement of large derivative contracts. The amount owed by Burgess Enterprises Ltd is material and the finance director has not written this amount off in the financial statements for the year ended 31 March 2024 on the grounds that the customer was in a position to pay their debt at the year end.

It is not impossible for bankruptcy to be triggered after the balance sheet date has passed. In this case, the mismanagement of large derivative contracts has brought about the customer's demise.

The auditor should request the client include a non-adjusting events disclosure note in the financial statements. The event itself is non-adjusting on the grounds that the customer was in a position to pay the balance at the year end and hence the conditions surrounding the bad debt did not exist at the balance sheet date.

Audit procedures where the auditor has a passive duty

10.22   The auditor's passive duty arises between the date of the auditor's report and the date on which the financial statements are authorised for issue. Hence, the auditor has signed the auditor's report and the audit for that particular year end is now complete.

Remember, the auditor does not have any obligation to perform audit procedures on the financial statements once they have issued their auditor's report. However, this does not mean the auditor can simply forget about them. If facts become known to the auditor between the date of the auditor's report and the date on which the financial statements are issued and those facts would have caused the auditor to express a modified opinion on the financial statements, the auditor must take the following action:

(a)   Discuss the issue with management and consider whether the financial statements require amendment.

(b)   Request that management amend the financial statements accordingly.

(c)   If management amend the financial statements, perform audit procedures on those amendments to ensure they have been recorded correctly.

(d)   Issue a new auditor's report.

(e)   If management does not intend to amend the financial statements and the auditor's report has not yet been issued to the entity, there is still time for the auditor to modify their opinion accordingly.

(f)   If the auditor's report has been issued to the entity, the auditor must notify management and those charged with governance *not* to issue the financial statements before the amendments are made.

(g)   If management issue the financial statements despite being requested not to do so by the auditor, the auditor must take action to prevent reliance being placed on the auditor's report. Normally, this will involve the auditor seeking legal advice.

Where the auditor becomes aware of a fact that would have caused them to express a modified opinion and the financial statements have already been issued, the auditor must take the following steps:

(a)   Discuss the issue with management to establish if the financial statements require amendment.

(b)   Request that management amend the financial statements where an amendment is required.

(c)   Request management take the steps necessary to ensure that anyone who is in receipt of the previous version of the financial statements is informed of the matter(s).

(d)   Perform audit procedures on any amendment made by management to ensure they have been recorded correctly.

(e)   Issue a new auditor's report on the financial statements which includes an Emphasis of Matter paragraph to draw attention to the fact that the financial statements and the auditor's report have been reissued.

(f)   If management refuse to recall the financial statements, the auditor must take action to prevent reliance on the auditor's report. This will usually involve the auditor seeking legal advice.

IMPORTANT POINT

I think it is worth emphasising that subsequent events can be difficult and contentious issues if a sound understanding of the accounting requirements (FRS 102, Section 32) and the auditing requirements (ISA (UK) 560) is not obtained. In some cases, the risk of material misstatement may be high, especially if the client has a high level of legal issues to contend with. Often, management are reluctant to disclose certain events in the financial statements in case the disclosure has a negative impact on the entity. Remember, financial reporting does not consider what management 'want' to report; it considers what information the user needs to be provided with to make informed decisions about the entity.

GOING CONCERN

10.23   Going concern is considered at all stages of the audit. At the planning stage, a preliminary assessment of going concern is carried out to identify risks that may affect the entity's ability to continue as a going concern and which could lead to the financial statements being prepared on a going concern basis when this basis is inappropriate. It is considered during the audit fieldwork stage as issues may be discovered by the auditor which may call into question the entity's ability to continue as a going concern. Finally, it is considered at the completion stage to assess whether the entity is a going concern, or, if there are uncertainties that are dependent on future outcomes which may call into question the entity's ability to continue as a going concern (or if the entity is a going concern at all).

The auditor's responsibilities in respect of going concern are outlined in ISA (UK) 570 *Going Concern*. The auditor will also have regard to the applicable financial reporting framework and how that deals with going concern. For the purposes of this section of the chapter, I am working on the assumption that clients will apply FRS 102 *The Financial Reporting Standard applicable in the UK and Republic of Ireland*.

To recap, FRS 102, para 3.8 states:

> When preparing financial statements, the management of an entity using this FRS shall make an assessment of the entity's ability to continue as a **going concern**. An entity is a going concern unless management either intends to liquidate the entity or to cease trading, or has no realistic alternative but to do so. In assessing whether the going concern assumption is appropriate, management takes into account all available information about the future, which is at least, but is not limited to, 12 months from the date when the financial statements are authorised for issue.

IMPORTANT POINT

As you can see from the above paragraph, the going concern assessment under UK and Ireland GAAP is 12 months **from the date the financial statements are authorised for issue**. Do not fall into a common pitfall and assume it is 12 months from the balance sheet date.

We then need to look to the provisions in FRS 102, para 3.9 which states:

> When management is aware, in making its assessment, of **material** uncertainties related to events or conditions that may cast significant doubt upon the entity's ability to continue as a going concern, the entity shall

disclose those uncertainties. When an entity does not prepare financial statements on a going concern basis, it shall disclose that fact, together with the basis on which it prepared the financial statements and the reason why the entity is not regarded as a going concern.

And if that's not enough to consider where FRS 102 is concerned, we then need to look at FRS 102, paras 32.7A and 32.7B which state:

> An entity shall not prepare its financial statements on a **going concern** basis if management determines after the reporting period either that it intends to liquidate the entity or to cease trading, or that it has no realistic alternative but to do so.

> Deterioration in operating results and **financial position** after the reporting period may indicate a need to consider whether the going concern assumption is still appropriate. If the going concern assumption is no longer appropriate, the effect is so pervasive that this section requires a fundamental change in the basis of accounting, rather than an adjustment to the amounts recognised within the original basis of accounting and therefore the disclosure requirements of paragraph 3.9 apply.

So, as you can see, there is an overlap between FRS 102, Section 3 *Financial Statement Presentation* and Section 32 *Events after the End of the Reporting Period* that need to be borne in mind both by management and the auditor.

IMPORTANT POINT

The term 'foreseeable future' is often cited where the concept of going concern is concerned. However, this is not a defined term in FRS 102. Under UK and Ireland GAAP, the 'foreseeable future' is deemed to be a period of 12 months from the date on which the financial statements are authorised for issue (ie, the date the financial statements are approved and the date on which the auditor's report is signed).

Responsibilities in respect of going concern

10.24 It is important to remember that it is **not** the auditor's responsibility to decide whether the entity is, or is not, a going concern. This responsibility rests with management. All too often is the auditor assumed to be giving a 'clean bill of health' if they express an unmodified audit opinion and this is part of the 'expectations gap'. I look at the expectations gap further in **10.33** below.

IMPORTANT POINT

The auditor's primary responsibility in respect of going concern is to obtain sufficient appropriate audit evidence that management's use of the going concern basis of accounting is appropriate and that management have complied with their responsibility under the applicable financial reporting framework (eg, FRS 102) to ensure that the period of management's assessment of going concern is correct. In addition, the auditor also has a responsibility in concluding on whether a material uncertainty exists about the entity's ability to continue as a going concern for the foreseeable future and to report in accordance with ISA (UK) 570.

Going concern is a forward-looking concept and this will clearly involve the use of judgement on the part of management. What the auditor must bear in mind is that the further into the future management go with their assessment of going concern, the more judgement will be needed.

Management can only carry out their assessment of going concern using information at their disposal at the time the going concern assessment is carried out. Management do not have a 'crystal ball' and so looking far into the future can be difficult. The important thing to bear in mind is that subsequent events can blow any judgements made by management out of the water (for example, if a fire destroys the client's premises or if a flood damages stock and the company subsequently finds out they are uninsured for such a catastrophe).

The period of assessment is something that has caused issues for file reviewers and audit firms over the years. Remember, UK and Ireland GAAP is more arduous than others, such as IFRS® Accounting Standards. Under standards such as FRS 102 and FRS 105 *The Financial Reporting Standard applicable to the Micro-entities Regime*, management must carry out a going concern assessment for a period of **at least** 12 months from the **date of approval** of the financial statements. It is not 12 months from the balance sheet date. If management have not covered this time period (ie, they have only done 12 months from the balance sheet date), the auditor must request that management extend their going concern assessment so they comply with UK and Ireland GAAP.

When management become aware of any material uncertainties which may cast doubt upon the entity's ability to continue as a going concern for the foreseeable future, the entity must disclose those uncertainties in the notes to the financial statements. Any inadequate or missing going concern disclosure notes will usually lead to the auditor issuing a modified audit opinion.

Factors which management should take into consideration are as follows (note, the list below is not comprehensive):

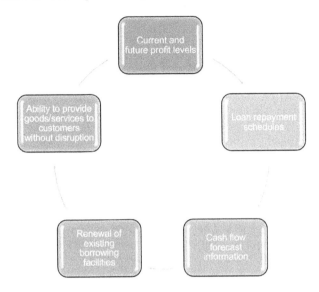

Management reporting on going concern

10.25 When management have carried out a going concern assessment, their conclusions are summarised as follows:

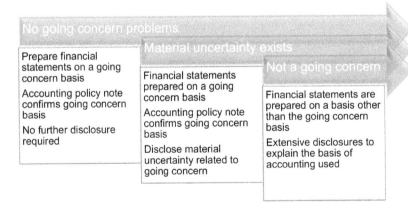

In practice, it is rare to see financial statements prepared on any basis other than the going concern basis. Another basis will generally only be used when the company is already in the hands of a liquidator or is about to be put into liquidation.

IMPORTANT POINT

Many accountants are familiar with the concept of the 'break-up' basis (a concept which has never been defined, nor is mentioned in UK and Ireland GAAP). Under this basis, assets are restated to recoverable amount and long-term liabilities are restated as current and provisions are made for unavoidable costs under onerous contracts and provisions for winding up costs. Therefore, the accruals basis of accounting becomes secondary because under the break-up basis, the financial statements reflect a forecast of future realisation rather than how the business has performed up to, and its financial position as at, the balance sheet date.

The break-up basis of accounting is inconsistent with the principles of UK and Ireland GAAP and hence would not be an appropriate basis under that framework, except in very rare circumstances. FRS 102 and FRS 105 both require the financial statements to reflect the transactions, events and conditions which have arisen up to, and exist as at, the balance sheet date.

Also, under the break-up basis, fixed assets are generally reclassified to current assets and long-term liabilities are reclassified as current liabilities. If the financial statements are prepared under, say, FRS 102, but on a basis other than the going concern basis, it would usually only be appropriate to reclassify fixed assets as current assets if their role within the ongoing business has changed. Long-term liabilities may need to be reclassified as current if, for example, there has been a breach in loan covenants which has triggered immediate repayment of borrowings.

Neither FRS 102 nor FRS 105 set out the basis on which the financial statements should be prepared in the event that the going concern basis of accounting is inappropriate. In any event, if the entity wishes to state compliance with FRS 102 or FRS 105, the financial statements must be prepared on a basis which is consistent with those standards, but amended to reflect the fact that the going concern basis of accounting is inappropriate.

Auditor's responsibilities relating to going concern

10.26   Back in **10.24**, I mentioned that it is not the auditor's responsibility to conclude on going concern as this is management's responsibility. So what exactly is the auditor's responsibility where the going concern assessment process is concerned?

ISA (UK) 570 clearly sets out the auditor's responsibilities, which are to conclude on:

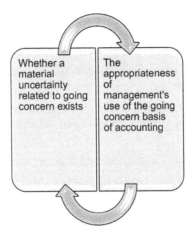

ISA (UK) 570 then goes on to clarify that these responsibilities apply even if the financial reporting framework used does not include an explicit requirement for management to make a specific assessment of the entity's ability to continue as a going concern. UK and Ireland GAAP does require management to carry out a specific assessment of the entity's ability to continue as a going concern.

Work on going concern must not be viewed as just a completion activity. In fact, the assessment of the entity's ability to adopt the going concern basis of accounting is considered by the auditor at the start of the audit during the planning phase. Remember, the auditor must obtain information about the entity and the environment in which it operates, including its risk assessment process, and specifically consider those risks which may impact on going concern. By starting the going concern assessment in the very early stages of the audit, the auditor can then direct appropriate audit effort to those areas which may threaten the entity's ability to continue as a going concern.

In addition to considering management's assessment of going concern, the auditor must also obtain sufficient appropriate audit evidence about:

(a)   Whether events or conditions exist which may cast significant doubt on the entity's ability to continue as a going concern.

(b)   Whether, or not, a material uncertainty related to going concern exists.

(c)   The appropriateness of management's use of the going concern basis of accounting when they were preparing the financial statements.

So, how does the auditor go about obtaining sufficient appropriate audit evidence in this respect? Well, there are a number of procedures outlined in ISA (UK) 570 which the auditor will need to carry out. However, keep in mind that the auditor may also need to devise additional tailored procedures in certain circumstances. The procedures outlined by ISA (UK) 570 are as follows:

- Evaluating management's method to assess going concern. This must include determining if:

    — the method selected is appropriate in the context of the applicable financial reporting framework and the auditor's understanding of the entity;

    — changes from the method used in prior years are appropriate; and

    — whether the calculations are applied in accordance with the method and are mathematically accurate.

- Evaluate the relevance and reliability of the underlying data used to make the assessment.

- Evaluating the assumptions on which management's assessment is based by determining whether there is adequate support for the assumptions underlying management's assessment. This must include determining:

    — whether the assumptions are appropriate in the context of the applicable financial reporting framework and, if applicable, changes from prior periods are appropriate; and

    — whether the assumptions are consistent with each other and with related assumptions used in other areas of the business, based on the auditor's knowledge obtained in the audit.

- Evaluating management's plans for future actions in relation to its going concern assessment, including determining whether the outcome of these plans is likely to improve the situation and whether management's plans are feasible in the circumstances.

- Considering whether any additional facts or information have become available since the date on which management carried out its going concern assessment.

- Requesting a written representation from management and, where appropriate, those charged with governance, concerning their plans for future actions and the feasibility of those plans.

The above procedures will enable the auditor to form their own view on the entity's ability to continue as a going concern because the auditor can compare their assessment to management's and judge how well management has performed their assessment.

Doubts exist about the entity's ability to continue as a going concern

10.27 When the auditor concludes there are doubts over the entity's ability to continue as a going concern, the auditor should devise specific procedures to obtain sufficient appropriate audit evidence that supports the auditor's conclusions. These procedures generally involve the following:

- Obtain a cash flow forecast (see **10.28** below) and other relevant budgets and forecasts and discuss these with management to understand the basis on which they have been prepared and consider the reliability of the data underpinning them.

- Obtain the latest available interim accounts (eg, management accounts) and assess whether these indicate going concern uncertainties.

- Review the terms of loan agreements and determine if they have been breached.

- Review/recalculate loan covenants and assess whether any breaches have arisen.

- Review correspondence from the bank for any indication that a loan or overdraft may be recalled.

- Read minutes of meetings of the shareholders and directors and remain alert to any issues concerning the entity's financing.

- With the client's permission, discuss any litigation claims with the entity's lawyers and assess the impact the outcome of these claims may have on cash flow.

- If borrowing facilities are not being renewed, discuss how the company will source alternative working capital requirements.

- Review the work done on subsequent events to identify any issues which may mitigate any going concern uncertainties or events which may create uncertainties in respect of going concern.

- Review correspondence with customers for evidence of any disputes which may threaten the recoverability of debtors.

- Look at dependence on individual customers and suppliers.

- Determine if the business is dependent on any external support (eg, the bank, directors' loans or group finance).

- Obtain a written representation from management regarding its plans for the future and how management's plans address the going concern problems.

Audit procedures over the cash flow forecast

10.28   Many companies maintain a cash flow forecast to keep a track of their cash position with the primary objective of making sure they don't run out of cash. They are vital tools in some businesses and are often maintained on a month-to-month basis, although some companies use a 12-month rolling forecast. Some companies even have forecasts going into longer periods, such as five years.

Cash flow forecasts can provide the auditor with comfort over an entity's going concern and liquidity status but this comes with a word of caution. The auditor cannot just take a copy of the cash flow forecast and put that on the file – they have to apply audit procedures over the cash flow forecast. It is not uncommon to see complaints from professional bodies in their published audit monitoring reports criticising audit firms for simply obtaining a copy of the cash flow forecast without doing any work on it.

The auditor is expected to carry out audit procedures over the cash flow forecast to make sure that the underlying data used in the forecast is reasonable. In addition, the auditor may also consider it necessary to test the controls over that data to ensure operating effectiveness.

So, what procedures should the auditor carry out over the cash flow forecast. The list below provides some 'typical' audit procedures that the auditor could perform, but the list is by no means exhaustive. Remember, the auditor may need to devise entity-specific audit procedures depending on their risk assessment.

- Agree the opening balance of the cash flow forecast to the closing balance of the cash book to ensure the starting position of the forecast is correct.

- Review prior years' audit procedures over the cash flow forecast to determine how accurate the entity's forecast has been in the past. If previous forecasts have proven to be reasonable, the auditor is likely to conclude that the current year forecast is reasonable.

- Determine the assumptions that have been used in the cash flow forecast. For example, if costs are increasing, there should be a corresponding increase in cash payments.

- Agree the timing of receipt of cash from debtors and payments of cash to creditors are in line with the company's credit period for debtors and creditors.

- Examine budgets and forecasts and assess whether the cash flow forecast is in line with these budgets and forecasts.

- Examine current year management accounts to determine whether the cash flow forecast is consistent with those management accounts.

- Agree cash outflows for fixed assets to supplier quotations.

- Consider the adequacy of increased working capital requirements and whether this has been accurately reflected in the cash flow forecast.

- Recalculate the cash flow forecast to verify arithmetical accuracy.

- Inspect board minutes for any other relevant issues that should be reflected in the cash flow forecast.

- Perform stress testing or reverse stress testing on the forecasts.

Reporting on going concern

10.29 I cover reporting on going concern briefly in **Chapter 11** but it's worth recapping the technical issues here while we are examining going concern because reporting on going concern tends to throw up some issues during engagement quality reviews. There are three types of situation that we need to cover where reporting is concerned:

The going concern basis of accounting is appropriate and there are no material uncertainties

10.30 In this case, management will confirm that they have carried out an assessment of going concern (which is often included in the notes to the financial statements). The auditor will issue a conclusion on going concern which is usually worded as follows:

Conclusions relating to going concern

In auditing the financial statements, we have concluded that the directors' use of the going concern basis of accounting in the preparation of the financial statements is appropriate.

Based on the work we have performed, we have not identified any material uncertainties relating to events or conditions that, individually or collectively, may cast significant doubt on the company's ability to continue as a going concern for a period of at least 12 months from when the financial statements are authorised for issue.

Our responsibilities and the responsibilities of the directors with respect to going concern are described in the relevant sections of this report.

The going concern basis of accounting is appropriate and there are material uncertainties

10.31 As I discuss in **Chapter 11**, where management conclude that the going concern basis of accounting is appropriate, but material uncertainties are present, the financial statements must disclose those material uncertainties to comply with the requirements of FRS 102, para 3.9.

The auditor must then review the adequacy of those disclosures and conclude whether those going concern disclosures are adequate or not. This conclusion is reached by the auditor considering whether the financial statements:

(a) Appropriately disclose the principal events or conditions that may cast significant doubt on the entity's ability to continue as a going concern for the foreseeable future as well as management's plans to deal with these events or conditions.

(b) Disclose clearly that there is a material uncertainty related to events or conditions that may cast significant doubt on the entity's ability to continue as a going concern. Therefore, there is a risk that the entity may be unable to realise its assets and discharge its liabilities during the ordinary course of business.

Where the auditor is satisfied that the disclosure is adequate, a Material Uncertainty Related to Going Concern paragraph is included in the auditor's report. An example of such a paragraph is shown below:

Example 10.9 – Illustrative Material Uncertainty Related to Going Concern paragraph

We draw your attention to note 29 in the financial statements which indicates that the effects of high inflation and challenging economic circumstances has had a detrimental impact on the company's operations and cash flows. In addition, the company's bank will not make any decisions about renewing the company's borrowing facilities until after the financial statements have been approved. As stated in note 29, these events or conditions, along with other matters as set forth in note 29, indicate that a material uncertainty exists that may cast significant doubt on the company's ability to continue as a going concern. Our opinion is not modified in respect of this matter.

Remember, the Material Uncertainty Related to Going Concern paragraph can only be used where management have adequately disclosed the going concern issues. If inadequate disclosure (or no disclosure) has been made, the auditor will modify their audit opinion accordingly. Also, do not forget to cross-refer to the relevant disclosure note number in the financial statements and clarify within the paragraph that the audit opinion is not modified in respect of the matter.

The going concern basis of accounting is not appropriate

10.32   There are some unfortunate situations where management will deem the going concern basis of accounting inappropriate. This is when management have decided to cease trading or liquidate the entity or have no realistic alternative but to do so.

When management make such a decision (which is obviously not taken lightly), they must prepare the financial statements on a basis other than the going concern basis. In addition, the directors must disclose the basis on which the financial statements have been prepared together with the reason(s) why the entity is not regarded as a going concern.

IMPORTANT POINT

Remember, this applies even if the directors conclude after the reporting date, but before the financial statements are authorised for issue, that the entity is no longer a going concern.

If the auditor agrees that the going concern basis is inappropriate and concludes that the disclosures made by management are adequate, an unmodified opinion is expressed and the auditor will include an Emphasis of Matter paragraph which will cross-reference to the relevant disclosure note and confirm that the auditor's opinion is not modified in this respect.

IMPORTANT POINT

A Material Uncertainty Related to Going Concern paragraph is not included in the auditor's report because the financial statements have not been prepared on a going concern basis.

Example 10.10 – Illustrative disclosure made by management

Basis of preparation of the financial statements

As explained in note 31 to the financial statements, the company will cease trading on 30 November 2024 and the financial statements have been prepared on a basis other than the going concern basis. This basis includes, where applicable, writing the company's assets down to net realisable value. Provisions have also been made in respect of contracts that have become onerous at the balance sheet date. No provision has been made for the future costs of terminating the business unless such costs were committed to at the reporting date.

In this situation, the auditor will consider the adequacy of the disclosure and if they conclude disclosure is adequate, a true and fair opinion will be expressed and an Emphasis of Matter paragraph is included in the auditor's report which cross-refers to note 31 and will confirm that their opinion is not modified in respect of the issue.

However, where the audit client has used the going concern basis of accounting, but the auditor has concluded this basis is inappropriate, and management refuse to change the basis of preparing the financial statements, the auditor expresses an adverse audit opinion.

IMPORTANT POINT

If the client uses the going concern basis of accounting inappropriately and refuses to change the basis, an adverse opinion must be expressed because the matter is both material and pervasive. An adverse opinion will state that the financial statements do not give a true and fair view. This means the users can place no reliance on the financial statements as a whole.

Going concern and the link to the expectations gap

10.33 The expectations gap has appeared lots of times in this book and the going concern concept illustrates how this can arise in practice. Remember, the expectations gap is the difference between what auditors do in accordance with professional standards, regulation and legislation and what the general public expect the auditors to do.

One way to think about the expectations gap and going concern is to consider what happens when a large corporate collapse happens and the media attention that follows suit. The audit firm is always one of the main focuses of attention and is often 'blamed' for not providing adequate warnings that the organisation is about to collapse. In really bad situations, the auditor may be perceived as contributing to the company's failure.

REAL-LIFE SCENARIO

Thomas Cook (the UK-based travel company) collapsed in September 2019, which sent shock waves around the UK. The UK government launched an inquiry shortly after the announcement where Rachel Reeves MP, chair of the Business, Energy and Industrial Strategy (BEIS) Committee stated:

> On the question of the role of the auditors, the committee has noted with concern various press reports surrounding the collapse of Thomas Cook and the role of its auditors, PwC and EY. The Times reported yesterday that the company's former chief executive revealed that the group had a balance sheet deficit in excess of £3.1bn, including £1.9bn of debt and guarantees. Despite this, the Daily Telegraph reported that Thomas Cook executives had awarded themselves more than £20m in bonuses over the past five years. The Times further reported that the company had used "aggressive accounting methods to flatter its financial performance." The Financial Times has drawn particular attention to the use of 'separately disclosed items' and 'exceptional one-off's' in its balance sheets and its treatment of goodwill. EY, in its 2018 audit of Thomas Cook's accounts noted that: "Separately disclosed items are not defined by IFRS and therefore considerable judgement is required in determining the appropriateness of such classification." The committee is dismayed that similar issues that we identified in the collapse of Carillion and BHS may have occurred at Thomas Cook, including the role of auditors in identifying and addressing problems. This latest collapse reinforces the need for urgent and meaningful reform of the audit industry.

The audit engagement partners from PwC (the Thomas Cook auditor until 2016) and EY (who took over in 2017) were called to the BEIS committee to answer questions. All the partners were challenged as to how they had audited going concern, as well as other areas of the financial statements (such as goodwill).

Rachel Reeves MP was scathing in her response to the audit partners, stating:

> I wonder how many more company failures, how many more egregious cases of accounting do we need? We've had BHS, we've had Carillion, we've had Patisserie Valerie and now we've had Thomas Cook. How many more do we need before your industry opens its ideas and recognises that you are complicit in all of this and that you need to reform? We can't rely on you to do the right thing and legislation is needed. We need tougher regulation because your industry is not willing

to make the changes needed. Reform is long overdue and the evidence today makes it clear that that moment has got to come soon otherwise we'll have more business failure and you will be complicit in those.

These are certainly stern words. Effectively, what Ms Reeves is suggesting is that auditors could be complicit in the failure of a company and goes much beyond criticising auditors for failing to highlight going concern problems. Some may argue that without any formal investigation, Ms Reeves could be out of line in her remarks.

At the time of writing, the Financial Reporting Council was still investigating the audits of Thomas Cook under the Audit Enforcement Procedure.

The case of Thomas Cook highlights the expectations gap once again. Sir Donald Brydon CBE conducted an independent review into the auditing profession. Brydon's final report recommends a 'resilience statement' (ie, how 'resilient' a company is to failure) and recommends:

- A resilience statement made by the board which incorporates, enhances and builds on going concern and viability statements.

- Auditors should report to the board of directors if they come across any information during their audit which leads to concerns about the resilience of the business which has not been reflected in the resilience statement. Where auditors consider the board has not done enough to address the concerns, the auditors should have an obligation to report to the regulatory body.

OPENING BALANCES, COMPARATIVE INFORMATION AND CORRESPONDING FIGURES

10.34 Clearly, opening balances are relevant to the accounts and ISA (UK) 510 *Initial Audit Engagements – Opening Balances* requires auditors to carry out audit procedures to confirm that opening balances have been brought forward from the prior year correctly. **Chapter 8** also covers opening in **8.14**.

IMPORTANT POINT

The title of ISA (UK) 510 refers to 'initial engagements' (ie, new engagements). However, for recurring engagements, the auditor is required to ensure that opening balances have been brought forward correctly into the current year.

The auditor must obtain sufficient appropriate audit evidence that opening balances that have been brought forward from the prior year do not contain material misstatement. In addition, the auditor also carries out procedures to ensure that the client's accounting policies have been consistently applied. To do this, the auditor will carry out the following procedures:

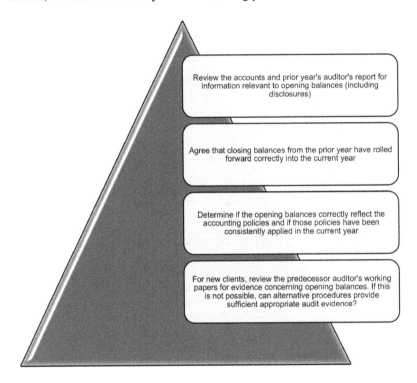

Review the accounts and prior year's auditor's report for information relevant to opening balances (including disclosures)

Agree that closing balances from the prior year have rolled forward correctly into the current year

Determine if the opening balances correctly reflect the accounting policies and if those policies have been consistently applied in the current year

For new clients, review the predecessor auditor's working papers for evidence concerning opening balances. If this is not possible, can alternative procedures provide sufficient appropriate audit evidence?

While there will always be some work carried out by the auditor on opening balances, the amount of this work will vary considerably from one audit engagement to the next. If the audit client is a recurring engagement, the amount of work may only be limited to ensuring that opening balances have been brought forward correctly (particularly if historically opening balances have always been brought forward correctly). For a new client, or where the risk of material misstatement due to opening balances is higher, more work will need to be carried out.

Example 10.11 – New auditors appointed after the balance sheet date

On 17 April 2024, Rowan & Co were appointed as auditors to Sunnie Enterprises Ltd to audit the financial statements for the year ended 31 March

2024. Sunnie Enterprises Ltd manufactures dyes that are used in the textile industry and has a material amount of finished goods in stock at the year end. A full stock count was undertaken by Sunnie Enterprises on 31 March 2024, but Rowan & Co did not attend this stock count as they were not appointed in time. The previous audit firm resigned on 31 January 2024 due to them no longer having sufficient resources in place to carry out this year's audit.

ISA (UK) 501 *Audit Evidence – Specific Considerations for Selected Items* requires the auditor to attend the stock count when stock is material to the financial statements. As Rowan & Co could not attend the stock count, there is an immediate problem because they have not obtained sufficient appropriate audit evidence concerning the existence, completeness and condition of stock at the balance sheet date. If the auditor cannot obtain this audit evidence via alternative audit procedures, the auditor will have to modify their audit opinion. In such a situation, any modification is likely to be a qualified 'except for' on the grounds of a limitation of audit scope.

The fact that Rowan & Co were appointed too late to attend the stock count as at 31 March 2024 can actually cause two issues: firstly, the impact that non-attendance at the stock count causes on the current year; and secondly that there will be a further modified audit opinion for the year ending 31 March 2025 as the opening stock brought forward will impact the profit and loss account.

Just because Rowan & Co did not attend the stock count at the year end, does not necessarily mean that the audit opinion is modified by default. The auditor could devise specific procedures to assess the existence, completeness and condition of inventory at the year end. Only if those alternative procedures fail to provide sufficient appropriate audit evidence will the auditor modify their opinion.

ISA (UK) 501 recognises that the nature and extent of audit procedures will vary from audit to audit and will depend on factors such as:

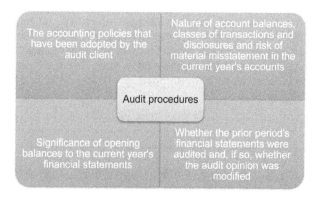

Comparative information and corresponding figures

10.35 Comparative information and corresponding figures are dealt with in ISA (UK) 710 *Comparative Information, Corresponding Figures and Comparative Financial Statements.*

When we think of the word 'comparative' we automatically think that it is a comparison against something. In the context of financial statements, that is exactly the case. 'Comparative' financial statements are those financial statements of the prior year or period that are presented in the current year's annual report.

Corresponding figures are also comparative information and include amounts and disclosures for the prior year that are considered to be an integral part of the current year's financial statements. However, they are only intended to be read in relation to the amounts relating to the current year (current year figures).

Comparative information

	31.03.2024 £'000	31.03.2023 £'000	
Turnover	9,245	10,650	
Cost of sales	(4,283)	(5,182)	
Gross profit	**4,962**	**5,468**	The figures in this box are the comparative financial statements
Distribution costs	(1,243)	(1,103)	
Administration expenses	(1,880)	(2,145)	
Operating profit	**1,839**	**2,220**	
Interest payable and similar expenses	(200)	(180)	
Profit before tax	**1,639**	**2,040**	
Tax on profit	(410)	(508)	
Profit after tax and profit for the year	**1,229**	**1,532**	

As you can see from the illustration above, when an entity prepares its financial statements, it will present the current year's figures (in the illustration above this is the 31 March 2024 information) and the previous year's (in the illustration above this is the 31 March 2023 information). The previous year's figures are known as 'comparative financial information' in order that the user can compare the current year's financial performance, financial position and cash flows against the prior year.

The auditor will need to confirm that the client's accounting policies have been consistently applied in the current year to satisfy themselves that there is no misstatement in the comparative year's financial statements.

Corresponding figures

Related party disclosures

During the year, the company received a loan at a below market rate of interest amounting to £150,000 (2023: £80,000) from a member of key management personnel. The loan is not covered by formal loan terms and is repayable on demand.

In this illustration, the corresponding figure is the 2023 comparative of £80,000.

Normally, the auditor will carry out far less work in respect of corresponding figures and the audit procedures will usually be limited to ensuring that corresponding figures have been correctly reported and appropriately classified. To do this, the auditor will:

- check that the client's accounting policies have been consistently applied; and

- check that corresponding figures agree to the prior year/period's financial statements and/or audit working papers file.

IMPORTANT POINT

The auditor must obtain sufficient appropriate audit evidence to ensure that comparative financial statements meet the requirements of the applicable financial reporting framework (eg, FRS 102). This will usually involve the auditor ensuring that the client's accounting policies have been consistently applied and that comparative figures agree to the prior year financial statements. Some of this work may be done during the audit of the opening balances (I examine opening balances in **Chapter 8**).

Prior period's financial statements not audited

10.36   If the prior period's financial statements were not audited (for example, because the company was able to claim audit exemption in the prior period), the auditor must state in an Other Matter paragraph that the comparative figures were not audited. Such a statement does not mean that the auditor does not have to obtain sufficient appropriate audit evidence that the opening balances do not contain misstatements which materially affect the current period's financial statements.

Example 10.12 – Prior year's financial statements not audited – reporting in the auditor's report

Other matters which we are required to address

Without qualifying our opinion, we draw attention to note 2 'Basis of preparing the financial statements' and the fact that the company's comparative financial statements were unaudited. For the year ended 31 December 2023, the company qualified as small and the directors took advantage of the exemption in CA 2006, s 477 and did not require the company to have its financial statements for the year then ended audited.

CHAPTER ROUNDUP

- The completion stage is the stage at which the audit engagement partner forms their opinion as to whether (or not) the financial statements give a true and fair view (or present fairly, in all material respects).

- Misstatements identified during the course of the audit are evaluated as to whether they are material or not both in isolation and in the aggregate in accordance with ISA (UK) 450.

- There are three types of misstatement that the auditor may deal with in an audit: factual misstatements, projected misstatements and judgemental misstatements.

- Final analytical procedures must be carried out at the completion phase of the audit in accordance with ISA (UK) 520. This is to ensure that the financial statements are consistent with the auditor's knowledge and understanding of the entity and the environment in which it operates.

- Subsequent events must be reviewed to ensure they have been adequately dealt with in the financial statements as adjusting or non-adjusting as appropriate.

- Where subsequent events are concerned, the auditor has both an active duty and a passive duty.

- Going concern is assessed at all stages during the course of the audit, but in particular at the completion phase. The auditor must ensure that management's period of assessment covers at least 12 months from the date of approval of the financial statements and the date of the auditor's report.

- The auditor must carry out audit procedures on opening balances and for new engagements this will invariably involve obtaining audit evidence from the predecessor auditor's working papers file. For recurring engagements, the auditor may simply ensure that the opening balances have been correctly brought forward from the prior year.

- Comparative information and corresponding figures must both be assessed by the auditor for adequacy and the auditor must obtain sufficient appropriate audit evidence that they meet the requirements of the applicable financial reporting framework.

PITFALLS TO AVOID

- Failing to consider uncorrected misstatements in the aggregate as well as in isolation (misstatements can become material when aggregated with other misstatements).

- Not carrying out a subsequent events review in accordance with ISA (UK) 560.

- Not ensuring that management have carried out a going concern assessment for a period of at least 12 months from the date of approval of the financial statements and auditor's report.

- Incorrectly using an Emphasis of Matter paragraph to highlight adequate disclosure in respect of a material uncertainty related to going concern.

Chapter 11

The Unmodified Auditor's Opinion

CHAPTER TOPIC LIST

- Introduction (see **11.1**)
- Content of the auditor's report (see **11.2**)
- The auditor's report (see **11.3**)
- Emphasis of Matter paragraphs (see **11.10**)
- Other Matter paragraphs (see **11.15**)
- Other information in the auditor's report (see **11.16**)
- Material Uncertainties Related to Going Concern (see **11.19**)
- Key Audit Matters (see **11.25**)
- Limiting the auditor's liability (see **11.29**)

INTRODUCTION

11.1   The culmination of the audit is the issuance of the auditor's report which contains the auditor's opinion. The report itself is addressed to the shareholders (also referred to as the 'members') and is included in the reporting entity's annual report which contains the financial statements. It is usually placed at the 'front end' of the annual report so that it is given the prominence that it deserves.

The reality is that the auditor's report is generally the only visible product of the audit hence it must contain all the information that the shareholders need. To that end, we need to consider the requirements of the specific International Standards on Auditing (UK) (ISAs (UK)) in the 700 series (which deal with reporting).

It's also important that the auditor 'steps back' from the actual regulations and considers whether the amount and type of information contained in the auditor's report is as relevant and useful to the users that it can be. Over the years, attempts have been made to amend the auditor's report to make it informative and concise, but even those attempts have, to a certain extent, failed in their efforts because users often complain that the language used in the auditor's report is unhelpful, confusing and technical.

WHAT ARE WE TRYING TO ACHIEVE?

The auditor must include an auditor's report with the financial statements and that report must comply with the requirements of the ISAs (UK) in the 700 series. The auditor must ensure that the auditor's report is appropriately worded and contains the required elements.

The 'unmodified' (or 'unqualified') audit opinion is one of the types of opinions the auditor expresses on the financial statements. An unmodified opinion is a 'clean' opinion and the auditor is confirming they have obtained **reasonable** assurance that the financial statements give a true and fair view, or present fairly, in all material respects. I've emboldened the word **reasonable** in this paragraph. Why? Well, throughout this book I have often highlighted the fact that the auditor can never express absolute, maximum or 100% assurance on the financial statements. Remember, an audit has its inherent limitations, such as the use of sampling, reliance on management representations and such like. Consequently, the auditor will never be in a position to state that the entity's financial statements are 100% accurate.

It's also worth recapping that because of the inherent limitations of an audit, even some material misstatements could go undetected. However, where the audit has been properly planned and executed, it is more likely than not that such material misstatements will not be present – especially with the increasing use of technology.

The focus of this chapter is the unmodified audit opinion. **Chapter 12** examines modified opinions and the reasons why a modified opinion may be expressed by the auditor. In this chapter I will examine a range of issues relating to the unmodified audit opinion, including additional paragraphs the auditor may include in the auditor's report to flag up important issues.

CONTENT OF THE AUDITOR'S REPORT

11.2 I think it's worthwhile flagging up the FRC Bulletin. A Bulletin is issued to provide auditors with timely guidance on new or emerging issues. Bulletins (and Practice Notes) are persuasive rather than prescriptive, but they are indicative of good practice. There is a Bulletin on the auditor's report called *Illustrative Auditor's Reports on United Kingdom Private Sector Financial Statements* which can be downloaded from this link: https://media.frc.org. uk/documents/BULLETIN_Illustrative_Auditors_Reports_On_United_ Kingdom_Private_Sector_Financial_Statements.pdf.

Before diving into the audit opinion, it's worthwhile just pausing for a moment and considering the actual content of the auditor's report to put the report into context. There are six ISAs (UK) in the 700 series of the standards which are relevant to auditor's reports as follows:

ISA (UK) 700 *Forming an Opinion and Reporting on Financial Statements*

ISA (UK) 701 *Communicating Key Audit Matters in the Independent Auditor's Report*

ISA (UK) 705 *Modifications to the Opinion in the Independent Auditor's Report*

ISA (UK) 706 *Emphasis of Matter Paragraphs and Other Matter Paragraphs in the Independent Auditor's Report*

ISA (UK) 710 *Comparative Information - Corresponding Figures and Comparative Financial Statements*

ISA (UK) 720 *The Auditor's Responsibilities Relating to Other Information*

In this chapter, I'll be looking specifically at the provisions in ISA (UK) 700, ISA (UK) 701 and ISA (UK) 706. **Chapter 10** examines 'other information' which is the subject of ISA (UK) 720 and comparative information which is ISA (UK) 710. **Chapter 12** examines ISA (UK) 705.

The auditor's report must be in writing and contain the following elements:

Element	Description
Title	The auditor's report must have a title that clearly indicates that it is the report of the independent auditor.
Addressee	The auditor's report must be addressed, as appropriate, based on the circumstances of the engagement (eg, to the shareholders or members of the entity for a company audited under CA 2006. Different addressees may be seen for other entities like charities depending on the nature of the appointment).

Element	Description
Auditor's opinion	This section contains the auditor's opinion on the financial statements and must also: • identify the entity whose financial statements have been audited; • state that the financial statements have been audited; • identify the title of each primary statement included in the financial statements; • refer to the notes, including the summary of significant (material) accounting policies; and • specify the date of, or period covered by each financial statement comprising the financial statements.
Basis for opinion	The basis for opinion paragraph must state that the audit was conducted in accordance with the ISAs (UK) and applicable law and refer to the section of the auditor's report which describes the auditor's responsibilities under the ISAs (UK). It must also include a statement that the auditor is independent of the entity in accordance with relevant ethical requirements and has fulfilled the auditor's other responsibilities in accordance with these requirements. The section must also state whether the auditor believes that the audit evidence is sufficient and appropriate to provide a basis for the auditor's opinion.
Going concern	The auditor must report in accordance with ISA (UK) 570 (Revised September 2019) *Going Concern* (see Chapter 10).
Key Audit Matters	For audits of **listed entities**, the auditor must communicate Key Audit Matters in the auditor's report in accordance with ISA (UK) 701. Unlisted entities are currently not required to include a Key Audit Matters section, although they can if they wish.
Other information	Where applicable, the auditor must report in accordance with ISA (UK) 720 (Revised November 2019).
Responsibilities for the financial statements	The auditor's report must include a section headed up 'Responsibilities of Management for the Financial Statements' (or equivalent according to the particular legal framework) which describes management's responsibility for: • preparing the financial statements in accordance with the applicable financial reporting framework and for such internal control as management determines is necessary to enable the preparation of financial statements that are free from material misstatement, whether due to fraud or error; and • assessing the entity's ability to continue as a going concern and whether the use of the going concern basis of accounting is appropriate as well as disclosing, where appropriate, matters relating to going concern. The explanation of management's responsibility for this assessment shall include a description of when the use of the going concern basis of accounting is appropriate.

Element	Description
Auditor's responsibilities for the audit of the financial statements	This section of the report clarifies that the auditor is responsible for expressing reasonable assurance as to whether the financial statements give a true and fair view (or present fairly, in all material respects) and to express that opinion in the auditor's report. The section also describes the auditor's responsibilities in respect of risk assessment, internal controls, going concern and accounting policies. The auditor's responsibilities section must also describe how the audit was designed to detect irregularities, including fraud. This section will be specific to the client and an auditor should avoid 'boilerplate' references. In the UK, the auditor is permitted to cross-refer to the applicable version of a 'Description of the Auditor's Responsibilities for the Audit of the Financial Statements' that is maintained on the website of an appropriate authority (eg, the Financial Reporting Council).
Other reporting responsibilities	This section of the report highlights additional reporting responsibilities, if applicable. This usually includes reporting on the adequacy of the accounting records, internal controls or other information published in the financial statements. Where the auditor is required to report by exception on certain matters, the auditor must describe the auditor's responsibilities for such matters and incorporate a suitable conclusion in respect of such matters.
Name of the audit engagement partner	The name of the audit engagement partner (for a company audited under CA 2006) must be included in the auditor's report unless, in rare circumstances, such disclosure is reasonably expected to lead to a significant personal security threat. In circumstances which the auditor intends not to include the name of the audit engagement partner in the auditor's report, the auditor must discuss this intention with those charged with governance to inform them of the auditor's assessment of the likelihood and severity of a significant personal security threat.
Signature of the auditor	The auditor's report must be signed. (Though only the client needs to receive a set signed in the auditor's own hand/name to protect against identity theft).
Auditor's address	The auditor's report must include the location in the jurisdiction where the auditor practises.
Date	The auditor's report must be dated no earlier than the date on which the auditor has obtained sufficient appropriate audit evidence on which to base their opinion. Any information which comes to light after this date will not have been considered by the auditor when forming their opinion.

THE AUDITOR'S REPORT

11.3   According to ISA (UK) 700, the objective of the auditor is to form an opinion on the financial statements based on an evaluation of their conclusions which have been drawn from the audit evidence obtained. The auditor must then clearly express that opinion via the auditor's report.

As I mentioned earlier in this chapter, there have been criticisms in the past about the auditor's report. There is a common theme when you look at these criticisms and it all seems to be about the wording of the report and the technical jargon that is used in the report. Often a layperson will not understand the information that the auditor's report is conveying and may miss (or misinterpret) some crucial content. Remember, the auditor's report is the only means of communication from the auditor to the users of the financial statements as some user groups will not be able to contact the auditor directly. Shareholders, for example, can communicate directly with the auditor where the auditor may exercise their right to be heard at an Annual General Meeting, but other stakeholders won't be afforded this luxury.

The availability of the auditor's report is driven by the requirements of legislation. In the UK, the auditor's report is attached in a legal sense to the financial statements. Therefore, if the financial statements are held on public record, so is the auditor's report. Listed companies in the UK are required to publish financial statements and the accompanying auditor's report on their website as are some specific sectors, such as academy schools.

In 2006, the International Auditing and Assurance Standards Board (IAASB), in conjunction with the American Institute of Certified Public Accountants (AICPA) began a project aimed at understanding more about how users perceive the auditor's report and how the auditor's report influences their decisions. Four research reports were commissioned to provide insights and to form a basis for the deliberations of the regulatory bodies. Usually, but not always, when the IAASB release an updated ISA, or a new ISA or International Standard on Quality Management (ISQM), countries such as the UK will adopt that standard and make tweaks to the ISA so that it is UK-specific (which is how it becomes an ISA (UK) or an ISQM (UK)).

The academic research carried out by the IAASB and AICPA resulted in a consultation paper being issued which identified several issues as follows:

- Users of financial statements and the auditor's report value the independent auditor's opinion.

- Other than the auditor's opinion, the content of the auditor's report was not viewed as very useful or informative.

- Users wanted to understand more about the reporting entity and the audit process and would value auditors' insight on a range of matters. The IAASB termed this issue the 'information gap'.

- Users thought the structure of the auditor's report could be changed to better convey useful information.[1]

The Appendix to this chapter contains an illustrative auditor's report with an unmodified opinion. You will note from the illustrative auditor's report that the Opinion paragraph is the first paragraph in an unmodified auditor's report. Remember, the auditor's opinion must be clearly expressed in the auditor's report to comply with ISA (UK) 700 and so the actual wording of the auditor's opinion should be expressed in one of the following ways:

> In our opinion, the accompanying financial statements present fairly, in all material respects, […] in accordance with [the applicable financial reporting framework];

or

> In our opinion, the accompanying financial statements give a true and fair view of […] in accordance with [the applicable financial reporting framework].[2]

IMPORTANT POINT

Keep in mind that the Opinion paragraph must clearly state that the financial statements give a true and fair view.

Whilst on the subject of a 'true and fair view' you may be surprised to learn that there is no statutory definition of 'true and fair', nor is the term defined in UK and Ireland GAAP. So how do auditors go about concluding on whether the financial statements give a true and fair view?

What is 'true'?

11.4 I think a good starting point would be to consider what true does **not** mean. Financial statements can never be said to be true because that implies they are 100% accurate or that they contain no errors whatsoever. This cannot be the case because an accounting estimate, for example, is exactly that – an estimate.

---

1 Enhancing the Value of Auditor Reporting: Exploring Options for Change, IAASB 2011.
2 ISA (UK) 700, para 25.

The idea of truth in financial reporting is that it implies a high (but not absolute) degree of technical accuracy and conformity with relevant legal or financial reporting requirements. It means that fundamental accounting concepts have been followed. True can also be interpreted as meaning that information is factual and conforms to reality and that the financial statements have been correctly extracted from the organisation's books and records.

What is 'fair'?

11.5   The 'fairness' aspect of the true and fair opinion is more about the judgements that have been used by management in preparing the financial statements. It implies that the financial statements are free from bias and have been as objectively prepared as they can be. The financial information presented in the annual report is presented in a balanced and fair way and reflects the commercial substance of the entity's underlying transactions.

So, as you can see, there are various facets to the true and fair concept that require careful consideration by the auditor. As financial statements will contain judgements and estimates (even relatively simple estimates such as depreciation), the auditor must consider whether the use of judgement is appropriate and free from bias. In addition, the auditor must also consider whether the entity's accounting policies are appropriate and conform with the relevant financial reporting framework. Remember, the entity must also disclose its material accounting policy information.

As a reminder, when the auditor expresses an unmodified audit opinion, they are stating that the financial statements are free from **material** misstatement. What the auditor is **not** stating is that the financial statements are completely free from misstatements. There could well be errors in the financial statements which remain uncorrected because management have concluded that they are immaterial. For the audit opinion to be unmodified, the misstatements must be below financial statement materiality both in isolation and when aggregated.

The Brydon review of the auditing profession and true and fair

11.6   In 2019, Sir Donald Brydon CBE issued his report following his independent review of the quality and effectiveness of audit. This report was

135 pages long and contained 65 recommendations to improve the auditing profession. Brydon's report made reference to the 'true and fair' concept and he was not supportive of it. His report suggests that the term contributes to the expectations gap (discussed further in **Chapter 9** and **11.9** below) stating that '... since the introduction of IFRS, the financial statements contain many estimates and assumptions (generally required to be set out in the notes to the accounts) that are dependent on judgements about the future. It does not need a philosopher to question how an opinion about judgments relating to the future can be "true"'.[3]

Brydon's report recommends that the term 'true and fair' be replaced with 'present fairly, in all material respects' explaining that, in his view, this wording strengthens the value of the audit opinion.

At the time of writing, the Financial Reporting Council (who will eventually transition to the Audit, Reporting and Governance Authority) had not fully implemented this change.

Reference to the applicable financial reporting framework

11.7   When the auditor expresses an unmodified opinion, the report must also confirm that the financial statements have been prepared in accordance with the applicable financial reporting framework (such as UK and Ireland GAAP including FRS 102) and relevant legislation and regulations.

Some entities may also be subject to additional requirements in the form of a Statement of Recommended Practice (SORP), such as a charity, housing association, pension fund or a limited liability partnership. A SORP interprets GAAP in the context of a particular sector and therefore the entity is required to comply with any applicable SORPs or explain why they have not complied. Any non-compliance with a SORP can mean the auditor expresses a modified opinion unless the reason for non-compliance is justifiable and the auditor agrees with the departure.

Reporting by exception

11.8   In the United Kingdom, the CA 2006 and the Listing Rules require auditors to 'report by exception' on certain issues. This usually means that the auditor's report simply has to state that nothing has come to the attention of the auditor in respect of these issues. You will note from the illustrative auditor's

---

3 Report of the Independent Review into the Quality and Effectiveness of Audit, 2019.

report in the Appendix to this chapter that the auditor expresses an opinion as to whether the information in the directors' report and the strategic report is consistent with the financial statements.

Example 11.1 – Reporting by exception

This is a typical disclosure in an auditor's report prepared under ISA (UK) 700 in respect of reporting under the Companies Act requirements:

Opinions on other matters prescribed by the CA 2006

In our opinion, based on the work undertaken in the course of the audit:

- the information given in the strategic report and the report of the directors for the financial year for which the financial statements are prepared is consistent with the financial statements; and

- the strategic report and the report of the directors have been prepared in accordance with the applicable legal requirements.

Matters on which we are required to report by exception

In the light of the knowledge and understanding of the company and its environment obtained in the course of the audit, we have not identified material misstatements in the strategic report or the report of the directors.

We have nothing to report in respect of the following matters where the CA 2006 requires us to report to you if, in our opinion:

- adequate accounting records have not been kept, or return adequate for our audit have not been received from branches not visited by us; or

- the financial statements are not in agreement with the accounting records and returns; or

- certain disclosures of directors' remuneration specified by law are not made; or

- we have not received all the information and explanations we require for our audit.

The expectations gap

11.9   The expectations gap is back again. As I mentioned in **Chapter 9**, there is an expectations gap between what members of the public think the auditor does versus what they are required to do under professional standards and regulation. One of the examples of the expectations gap is the fact that many users of the financial statements and auditor's report think that the opinion expressed is, in some way, certification that the financial statements are completely accurate and contain no errors. Another misconception relating to the auditor's report is that a clean audit opinion is guaranteeing the financial stability and longevity of the business.

I've mentioned the inherent limitations of an audit previously and I think it's a very important issue because the expectations gap where the audit opinion is concerned is potentially dangerous. Throughout the auditor's report you will see references to 'reasonable assurance'. Reasonable assurance is a high level of assurance, but it is not maximum assurance because of the inherent limitations of an audit. You can use the word 'fired' as an acronym to cite these inherent limitations:

● Financial statements include estimates and judgements which are usually subjective.

● Auditors will place some reliable on the entity's system of Internal control.

● Representations from management will be required for certain areas of the financial statements, and these representations may be the only source of audit evidence.

● Audit Evidence is persuasive rather than conclusive.

● Auditors Do not test all transactions and balances; instead they use sampling.

As I mentioned in **11.6** above, Sir Donald Brydon's report into the quality and effectiveness of audit suggests that references to a 'true and fair view' are misleading and hence contributes to the expectations gap.

EMPHASIS OF MATTER PARAGRAPHS

11.10   Emphasis of Matter (EOM) paragraphs are dealt with in ISA (UK) 706 *Emphasis of Matter Paragraphs and Other Matter Paragraphs in the Independent Auditor's Report.* The EOM paragraph has proven to be a somewhat 'thorny' issue for auditors. Why? Well, the main problem is that often an EOM paragraph is included in the auditor's report when there is no need for one; or, in more serious cases, the paragraph is used as a 'substitute' for modifying the auditor's opinion.

When an EOM paragraph is inappropriate

11.11   I think it's worth starting out with examining what an EOM is **NOT** used for. An EOM paragraph is not used as a means of 'protecting' the auditor against forming an incorrect opinion – the auditor reduces audit risk through the audit procedures they apply during the fieldwork stage and ensuring that sufficient and appropriate audit evidence is obtained. Having an EOM paragraph in the auditor's report as 'just in case' scenario is not going to help.

Next, the EOM paragraph can never be used as a substitute for modifying an audit opinion.

REAL-LIFE SCENARIO

Mr P had been a file reviewer for many years prior to his retirement. He explained that over the years he had come across several instances of an EOM paragraph being used as an attempt to modify the audit opinion. He cited one example to me of a firm that had been unable to obtain sufficient appropriate audit evidence in respect of related party transactions and just had a written representation from management stating that no related party transactions had been undertaken during the year under audit. While this case happened several years ago (in fact, pre-FRS 102 *The Financial Reporting Standard applicable in the UK and Republic of Ireland*) the outcome would still be the same.

The audit firm in question had expressed an unmodified opinion on the financial statements when the audit evidence for a material area (related parties) suggested this was inappropriate. If the audit firm could not obtain sufficient appropriate audit evidence to support management's assertion that there had been no related party transactions, a modified opinion should have been expressed due to a limitation in scope.

Instead, the audit firm had included an EOM paragraph stating that the firm had been unable to obtain audit evidence to support management's assertion, but as FRS 8 *Related party disclosures* (as it was then) was a disclosure standard, the amounts in the financial statements were unaffected. This is a major technical error and one which rendered the audit file significantly deficient. The audit opinion was, in fact, incorrect.

As you can see from the scenario above, the audit firm had tried to modify the audit opinion by using an EOM paragraph. Not only is this fundamentally incorrect, but it is also reckless.

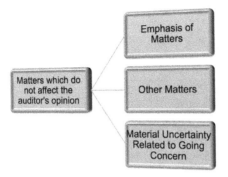

As you can see from the above diagram, an EOM paragraph can never affect the auditor's opinion because of the requirements of ISA (UK) 706. You can also see that an 'Other Matter' and 'Material Uncertainty Related to Going Concern' paragraph also do not affect the auditor's opinion. Other Matter and Material Uncertainty Related to Going Concern paragraphs are dealt with in **11.19** below.

When an EOM paragraph is appropriate

11.12   I think this is where we need to look at the definition of an 'Emphasis of Matter paragraph' as per the ISA (UK) 706. This states that an EOM paragraph is:

> A paragraph included in the auditor's report that refers to a <u>matter</u> <u>appropriately presented or disclosed</u> in the financial statements that, <u>in the</u> <u>auditor's judgment</u>, is of such importance that it is <u>fundamental to users'</u> <u>understanding of the financial statements</u>.[4]

I have underlined some of the 'key' terms in this definition which I think need to be elaborated upon as follows:

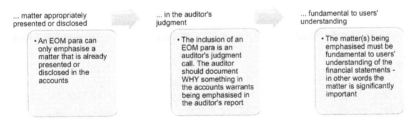

---

4 ISA (U) 706, para 7(a).

As you can see from the definition, an EOM paragraph should only be included to refer to a matter that is already appropriately presented or disclosed in the financial statements which, in the auditor's judgement, is fundamentally important to the users' understanding of the financial statements.

IMPORTANT POINT

There are certain procedures the auditor must follow when they determine that a matter is fundamentally important to users' understanding of the financial statements and hence warrants an EOM paragraph in the auditor's report as follows:

(a)   The heading of the EOM paragraph must include the term 'Emphasis of Matter'. Simply using this term as a heading will suffice.

(b)   There must be a **clear** reference to the matter being emphasised. The auditor must also cross-reference the user to the relevant disclosure that fully describes the matter so the user can then be directed to where in the financial statements further information concerning the matter can be found. ISA (UK) 706 requires that the paragraph must only refer to information presented or disclosed in the financial statements.

(c)   The paragraph **must** indicate that the auditor's opinion is not modified in respect of the matter being emphasised.

I think it is always worthwhile documenting the reasons on the audit file as to why the auditor views a matter as being so fundamental that it warrants an EOM paragraph. Remember, where the audit file is being reviewed for quality management purposes, the reviewer should be able to understand the 'story' behind the opinion in the auditor's report. Having the rationale for the EOM documented on the audit file will help a reviewer to form their conclusion on the appropriateness of the EOM paragraph as well.

Where a matter is considered to be fundamental to the users' understanding of the financial statements, but management have failed to adequately disclose it, an EOM paragraph will not be appropriate in the circumstances. If the inadequacy is not resolved satisfactorily, the auditor must modify their opinion.

Examples of matters which may give rise to an EOM paragraph include the following (note, the examples below are not comprehensive):

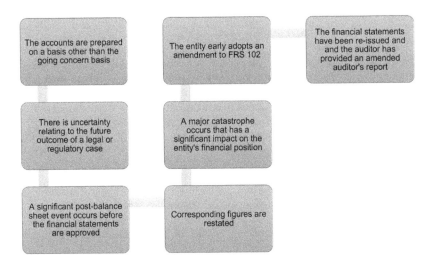

Example 11.2 – Incorrect use of an EOM paragraph (1)

The financial statements of Rowan Enterprises Ltd for the year ended 31 July 2024 contain a disclosure relating to a material uncertainty related to going concern. The auditor is satisfied that the going concern disclosure in the financial statements is adequate.

The audit engagement partner considers the going concern disclosure to be fundamental to the users' understanding of the financial statements and has included the following paragraph in the auditor's report:

Emphasis of Matter

We draw attention to note 20 in the financial statements which confirms the existence of a material uncertainty in respect of going concern. The directors are concerned about the ongoing inflationary issues and the impact of rising interest rates on the operations of the business. As stated in note 20, these events or conditions indicate that a material uncertainty exists that may cast significant doubt on the company's ability to continue as a going concern. Our opinion is not modified in this respect.

Under ISA (UK) 570 *Going Concern*, where an entity has **adequately** disclosed a material uncertainty related to going concern, the auditor must not use an EOM paragraph. Instead, they must comply with ISA (UK) 570, para 22 and include a 'Material Uncertainty Related to Going Concern' section in the auditor's report. This is examined further in **11.19** below.

Example 11.3 – Incorrect use of an EOM paragraph (2)

The audit of Arlo Industries Ltd for the year ended 31 July 2024 revealed a number of misstatements which the auditor has concluded as being immaterial both in isolation and in the aggregate. The directors decided not to adjust the financial statements on the grounds that the misstatements were immaterial.

The audit engagement partner has placed the following comment on the completion section of the audit file:

> To err on the side of caution, I deem an Emphasis of Matter paragraph to be appropriate here. When drafting the auditor's report, I suggest we refer to there being a number of unadjusted misstatements which are immaterial in isolation and in the aggregate and confirm that our opinion is not modified in respect of these misstatements. I think this just secures our position in case we are challenged.

There are four fundamentally flawed points to the partner's logic here:

(1)   An EOM paragraph can only be used when a matter has been adequately disclosed in the financial statements as the paragraph must cross-refer the user to the relevant disclosure note.

(2)   In this scenario, there is no disclosure note that can be cross-referred to as the company will not have made any disclosure concerning unadjusted errors that are immaterial.

(3)   There is no need to include an EOM paragraph in the auditor's report in respect of immaterial misstatements because the mere fact that they are immaterial means they do not warrant the attention of shareholders.

(4)   There would be no need to confirm that the audit opinion is not modified in respect of immaterial misstatements as an auditor's opinion would never be modified for misstatements that are immaterial in isolation and in the aggregate.

Example 11.4 – Post-balance sheet event

The audit of the financial statements of Robinson Renovators Ltd for the year ended 31 July 2024 has drawn to a close and the auditor's report is being drafted. During the audit, the audit senior discovered that one of the client's bonded warehouses had suffered a fire that had destroyed a large amount of the client's stock. The fire occurred in mid-August 2024 and hence the stock had not been written down to estimated selling price in the 31 July 2024 financial statements as the event is a non-adjusting post-balance sheet event. The auditor has concluded that adequate disclosure has been made in the financial statements concerning this event and the event is fundamental to the users' understanding.

In this scenario, an EOM paragraph may be appropriate and may be drafted as follows:

Emphasis of Matter

We draw attention to note 34 of the financial statements, which describes the effects of a fire at the premises of a third-party warehouse provider. Our opinion is not modified in respect of this matter.

REAL-LIFE SCENARIO

The financial statements of a company for the year ended 31 December 2018 shows the following EOM paragraph in the auditor's report:

Emphasis of matter

In our opinion, the information given in the Strategic Report and Directors' Report for the financial year for which the financial statements are prepared is consistent with the financial statements.

We have nothing to report in respect of the following matters where the CA 2006 requires us to report to you if, in our opinion:

- adequate accounting records have not been kept, or returns adequate for our audit have not been received from branches not visited by us; or

- the financial statements are not in agreement with the accounting records and returns; or

- certain disclosures of directors' remuneration specified by law are not made; or

- we have not received all the information and explanations we require for our audit.

The independent auditor's report then contains exactly the same text from the paragraph starting *'We have nothing to report ...'*.

This demonstrates a fundamental misunderstanding of how an EOM and Other Matters paragraph (see **11.15** below) works. The auditor cannot emphasise that the information given in the Strategic Report and Directors' Report is consistent with the financial statements because this is an issue that is dealt with in the 'Opinions on other matters prescribed by the Companies Act 2006' and not in an EOM paragraph (remember the EOM paragraph must cross-refer to a matter that is adequately presented or disclosed in the financial statements – consistence of the Strategic Report or Directors' Report is not 'presented' or 'disclosed' anywhere).

Secondly, the reporting by exception of other matters required by the CA 2006 in respect of adequate accounting records, agreement of the financial statements with those accounting records, directors' remuneration disclosures and receipt of information and explanations required for the are not matters that are dealt with in an EOM paragraph; they are matters which the auditor is specifically required to report by exception on in a separate heading.

The main 'issue' that springs to mind where this auditor's report is concerned is that the audit engagement partner has a lack of awareness of what an EOM paragraph is for and when one is appropriate.

Placement of the EOM paragraph in the auditor's report

11.13 So, you have concluded that a matter which has been adequately presented or disclosed in the financial statements is fundamental to the users' understanding of your client's financial statements and need to include an EOM paragraph in your auditor's report. The next question is *whereabouts* in the auditor's report do you place this paragraph?

ISA (UK) 706, para A16 states that the placement of an EOM paragraph will depend on the nature of the information to be communicated. It also clarifies that the auditor's judgement will need to be called upon in terms of the relative significance of such information compared to other elements which the auditor is required to report on in accordance with ISA (UK) 700 *Forming an Opinion and Reporting on Financial Statements*.

In practice, it is common to include an EOM paragraph immediately after the Opinion paragraph.

EOM paragraphs and Key Audit Matters (KAM)

11.14 KAM are dealt with in ISA (UK) 701 *Communicating Key Audit Matters in the Independent Auditor's Report*. KAM is also examined in **11.25**

below. ISA (UK) 701 is currently only mandatory for **listed entities**. However, this does not preclude the auditor of an unlisted entity including a KAM section in the auditor's report if they consider this appropriate. It is fair to say, however, that it is relatively uncommon to see a KAM section in the auditor's report of an unlisted client.

IMPORTANT POINT

Where a KAM section is included in the auditor's report, the use of an EOM paragraph is not a substitute for a description of individual KAMs.

It may be the case that the auditor concludes that some matters which are KAMs may also be fundamental to users' understanding of the financial statements. Therefore, a KAM can also satisfy the requirements of ISA (UK) 706 where an EOM paragraph may also be considered.

To do this, the auditor may consider highlighting or drawing further attention to its importance. This can be achieved by presenting the KAM more prominently (eg, as the first KAM, or by including additional information which indicates how fundamental the matter is to users' understanding of the financial statements).

Example 11.5 – Restructuring post-year end

The audit of the financial statements of Wrigley Enterprises PLC for the year ended 31 March 2024 is complete and the auditor's report is being drafted.

During the audit, the audit team were made aware of a significant restructuring that was communicated to staff members during the first week of April 2024. Disclosure of a non-adjusting post-balance sheet event has been adequately disclosed in the financial statements.

The restructuring did not require significant auditor effort and hence was not considered to be a KAM. However, in the engagement partner's opinion, the matter is fundamental to users' understanding of the financial statements.

In this example, an EOM paragraph would be appropriate, but it must be included in the auditor's report either directly before or after the KAMs section – it cannot be included within the KAMs section of the auditor's report. The placement of the paragraph would be based on the auditor's professional judgement as to the relative significance of the information included in the EOM paragraph.

OTHER MATTER PARAGRAPHS

11.15   ISA (UK) 706 *Emphasis of Matter Paragraphs and Other Matter Paragraphs in the Independent Auditor's Report* also deals with Other Matter paragraphs which can often lead to confusion by auditors as to what an 'Other Matter' actually is.

'Other Matter' paragraphs are included in the auditor's report when the auditor considers it necessary to communicate on matters which are not presented or disclosed in the financial statements and which, in the auditor's opinion, are relevant to an understanding of:

• the audit;

• the auditor's responsibilities; or

• the auditor's report.

IMPORTANT POINT

I mentioned in the last section ISA (UK) 710 which deals with Key Audit Matters. Remember a KAM section (see **11.25** below) is only required in the auditor's report for listed companies, but that does not necessarily preclude the auditor of a private company from including a KAM section in the auditor's report as well (although, in real-life, it's relatively uncommon for a KAM section to be seen in the auditor's report of a private company).

Where a KAM section is included in the auditor's report in accordance with ISA (UK) 701, an Other Matter paragraph cannot be used to discuss matters deemed to KAM as well.

Example 11.6 – Illustrative Other Matter paragraph

Other matter

Without qualifying our opinion, we draw attention to note 2 'Basis of preparing the financial statements' and the fact that the company's comparative financial statements were unaudited. For the year ended 31 December 2022, the company qualified as small and the directors took advantage of the exemption in CA 2006, s 477 and did not require the company to have its financial statements for the year then ended audited.

The above example illustrates the use of an Other Matter paragraph when the previous year's financial statements were not audited due to the company being small and being able to claim audit exemption. There are several matters which can be addressed in an Other Matter paragraph which listed below (note, the list below is not intended to be comprehensive):

- Communication of audit planning or scoping issues where law or regulation requires.

- Where law, regulation or UK and Ireland GAAP requires (or permits) the auditor to provide further explanations of their responsibilities.

- To explain why the auditor has not resigned when management have imposed a pervasive inability to obtain sufficient appropriate audit evidence (often referred to as a 'management-imposed scope limitation').

- Where there is a restriction on the distribution or use of the auditor's report, to communicate that the auditor's report is solely intended for the intended users and reliance cannot be placed by third parties.

OTHER INFORMATION IN THE AUDITOR'S REPORT

11.16   I've briefly flagged up other information in the auditor's report throughout this chapter and this issue is dealt with in a separate ISA (UK) being that of ISA (UK) 720 *The Auditor's Responsibilities Relating to Other Information.*

According to ISA (UK) 720 'other information' is information that relates to financial or non-financial information, but it does **not** relate to the financial statements and the auditor's report thereon, which is included within the company's annual report.

Nowadays, if you look at a set of audited financial statements (even for a smallish company), the report itself is long. When you look at the financial reports of organisations such as BT, Manchester United Football Club, Costa Coffee and such like, their financial statements span several hundred pages.

Financial statements will often contain lots of additional information which the organisation needs to include, not only because company law or regulation may dictate that such information must be included, but also because investors will need to have the information to hand to make investment-related decisions.

Examples of other information contained in the entity's annual report includes the following:

505

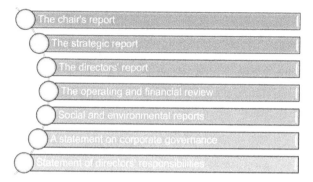

Now, not every audit client will have all those reports in their annual report. For example, a small or medium-sized entity is unlikely to include social and environmental reports (although nowadays companies are being encouraged to include these sorts of reports due to the impact of climate change). In addition, it is unlikely you'll see a statement on corporate governance in a medium-sized entity's financial statements as these are geared towards much larger organisations. However, you can 'get the drift' that the annual report of a company will contain other information **in addition to** the financial statements.

To sum up the overall objective of the auditor in the most basic of ways; the auditor sets out to form an opinion on the client's financial statements (ie, whether they give a true and fair view and have been properly prepared in accordance with applicable laws and regulations). So what has information that is considered to be 'outside' of the financial statements have to do with the auditor?

Well, ISA (UK) 720 requires the auditor to read the other information which the client has included in their annual report with a view to identifying any **material inconsistencies** in that other information when compared to the financial statements.

Example 11.7 – Inconsistency identified

Vivien is the audit senior working on the audit of Rowan Industries Ltd for the year ended 31 March 2024.

Vivien has reviewed the directors' report which states that the company's operating profit has increased by 25% from the prior year and that gross profit margins have remained consistent.

During Vivien's analytical review, she noted that the company's operating profit had, in fact, only increased by 6.2% and gross profit margins for the current year had declined by some 3% because of an increase in raw material prices which the client had been unable to pass onto customers.

This inconsistency between what the directors are reporting in the directors' report and what is being reported in the company's profit and loss account is likely to be materially inconsistent. It may be that the directors' report has been drafted some time ago and the financial statements may have been adjusted to take account of misstatements identified during the audit. However, if the directors do not correct this inconsistency, the auditor must make reference to it in their auditor's report.

IMPORTANT POINT

CA 2006, s 496 requires that the auditor must state whether, in his/her opinion, based on the work undertaken during the audit, the information provided in the strategic report (if any) and the directors' report for the financial year for which the accounts are prepared is consistent. In addition, the auditor must also consider whether the strategic report and the directors' report have been prepared in accordance with applicable legal requirements and if any material misstatements have been identified in those reports. Where material misstatements have been identified in the strategic report and directors' report, the auditor must provide an indication of the nature of each of the misstatements.

Remember, any material misstatements or inconsistencies in the other information are likely to undermine the credibility of the financial statements and the auditor's report.

In addition, the auditor cannot be associated with any information that is misleading. Hence, the requirement for the auditor to carefully consider the other information included in the annual report in terms of its accuracy and consistency with the financial statements. Any misstatement of the other information exists when the other information is incorrectly stated or otherwise misleading because it omits or obscures information which is necessary for a proper understanding of a matter.

Identifying a material inconsistency

11.17   Let us consider that the inconsistency noted by Vivien in **Example 11.7** above is a material inconsistency. What happens now?

Obviously, Vivien and/or the audit engagement partner will discuss the material inconsistency with management with a view to them correcting the misstatement (to avoid any impact on the auditor's report which may be viewed in a bad light). However, ISA (UK) 720 also requires the auditor to:

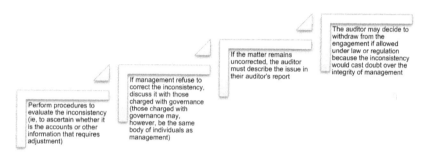

As you can see, it is not necessarily just a case of 'having a chat' with management about a material inconsistency and seeing if they will put it right. The auditor needs to 'go behind the scenes' to identify *how* the inconsistency arose in the first place. As I mentioned earlier, this may be as simple as the other information may have been drafted at an early stage in the audit process based on draft accounts; and those accounts may have been amended after the detailed audit fieldwork has been finished when the schedule of audit errors is being discussed with management (particularly material misstatements, so as to avoid a modified audit opinion).

In some other situations, there may be an attempt by management to deliberately mislead the users of the financial statements – especially if other issues that bring into question the integrity of management and/or those charged with governance have been identified during the audit. It may also be the case that the inconsistency identified is so serious that the auditor feels they have no alternative but to resign.

REAL-LIFE SCENARIO

Mr L was the audit engagement partner of a food delivery company which was primarily cash-based. The audit senior, at the time, had assessed the company's system of internal control as being quite weak in areas such as cash handling, payroll, purchasing and fixed assets. The client in question had an invoicing discounting arrangement in place which meant they were subjected to periodic 'audits' of their sales ledger by the invoicing discounter.

The directors' report and strategic report were both drafted by the external accountant who was appointed to prepare the statutory financial statements in preparation for the audit. The last three audits had previously revealed significant problems in the way that the financial statements had been prepared with significant balance sheet control account reconciliation write-offs and mistakes in the application of the company's accounting policies.

During the course of auditing the 2021 financial statements, the auditor discovered that the strategic report (which included an operating and financial review) was citing 'significant free cash flow', 'more than adequate distributable profit' and 'a high level of net current assets'. All these indicated that the company was in a sound financial position with (basically) nothing to worry about where the going concern basis was concerned.

Not only had the auditor discovered several misstatements during the course of the audit, there was also the question of where all this 'positive' information in the strategic report had come from given that:

- the company had no 'in hand' bank balances at the year end; all were overdrawn, and the company was wholly reliant on its invoice discounting arrangement;

- the balance sheet had net current liabilities of just over £1.1 million; and

- retained earnings were negative.

Interestingly, the client had not mentioned any of the above in the narrative reports and the external accountant and managing director stated their reluctance to amend the strategic report to present the facts as they were at the balance sheet date.

Given that the company's borrowing facilities were due to be renewed, it seemed that the directors were seeking to mislead the users (ie, the providers of the invoice discounting facility) into thinking the company was doing better than it actually was. The reality of the situation is that the invoice discounting facility would be looking at the primary financial statements and their credit committee would have benchmarks that would need to be met to renew the invoice discounting facility. It was also clear that if the invoice discounting facility was **not** renewed, the company would be facing closure.

The auditor told me that at this stage he had simply 'had enough' and resigned. There was clearly a deliberate manipulation of the figures, and he was not prepared to risk his professional standing. Lessons were clearly not being learned from previous audit findings and it was clear there was a blatant disregard as to the responsibilities of both management and the auditor.

Placement of the Other Information section

11.18   Ordinarily, the 'Other information' section is included after the 'Conclusions relating to going concern' section and before the 'Opinions on other matters prescribed by the Companies Act 2006' sections. It will confirm that the responsibility for the other information rests with the directors and that the auditor's opinion does not cover such information. Where the auditor does not identify any material misstatement of the other information, they are required to state this fact as can be seen in **Example 11.8** below.

Example 11.8 – Other Information section

Other information

The directors are responsible for the other information. The other information comprises the information in the Strategic Report, the Report of the Directors and the Statement of Directors' Responsibilities but does not include the financial statements and our Report of the Auditors thereon.

Our opinion on the financial statements does not cover the other information and, except to the extent otherwise explicitly stated in our report, we do not express any form of assurance conclusion thereon.

In connection with our audit of the financial statements, our responsibility is to read the other information and, in doing so, consider whether the other information is materially inconsistent with the financial statements or our knowledge obtained in the audit or otherwise appears to be materially misstated. If we identify such material inconsistencies or apparent material misstatements, we are required to determine whether this gives rise to a material misstatement in the financial statements themselves. If, based on the work we have performed, we conclude that there is a material misstatement of this other information, we are required to report that fact. We have nothing to report in this regard.

MATERIAL UNCERTAINTIES RELATED TO GOING CONCERN

11.19   I've interviewed many people from all backgrounds as research for my writing of this book and almost all of those interviewed who were involved in reviewing audit files for quality management purposes cited material uncertainties related to going concern as one of the main areas of the auditor's report deficiencies. I also drew on my experiences in speaking to delegates on audit update courses that either seemed unaware that there is a specific requirement for separate reporting of material uncertainties related to going concern within the auditor's report; or (more worryingly) did not know that they had to do anything with going concern issues in the auditor's report.

I looked at going concern a lot in **Chapter 10** where I mentioned that a clear understanding of the concept of going concern is crucial when it comes to financial reporting and audit. Over the last few years, there have been all sorts of challenges in business due to the COVID-19 pandemic, the subsequent war in Ukraine, high inflation, increasing interest rates and the economic uncertainty of the UK in recent years. All these uncertainties somehow feed into the operations of businesses and can create uncertainties for the business itself.

Going concern has always been a highly important issue for businesses. In auditing, it is a concept that has definitely moved up the ranks of importance over the last few years and is something that the auditor must ensure they have a sound understanding over.

There is a dedicated ISA (UK) for going concern, that of ISA (UK) 570 *Going Concern*. Now, I mentioned earlier in the chapter that auditor reporting is dealt with in the ISAs (UK) in the 700 series; but there is overlap with ISA (UK) 570 here where the concept of going concern is concerned. So, ISA (UK) 570 deals with the auditor's responsibilities for obtaining sufficient appropriate audit evidence over management's assessment that the business is a going concern; here we consider the reporting implications when the auditor concludes that:

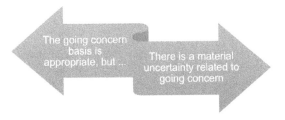

The going concern basis is appropriate, but ...

There is a material uncertainty related to going concern

We will also explore what happens when the entity has prepared its financial statements on a going concern basis, but the auditor concludes that basis is, in fact, inappropriate.

IMPORTANT POINT

It's important to remember that a **material uncertainty related to going concern** is an uncertainty which relates to events or conditions that, individually or collectively, could cast **significant doubt** on the entity's

---

> ability to continue as a going concern, and the **magnitude** of its potential
> impact and likelihood of occurrence is such that appropriate disclosure of
> the nature and implications of the uncertainty is necessary.
>
> So, essentially, the entity is stating two things:
>
> - the financial statements have been prepared on a going concern basis; but
>
> - there is a material uncertainty about that going concern basis because something might happen in the future that means the entity is not, in fact, a going concern.

Recap on financial reporting issues

11.20   I think, given that the issue of going concern can cause quite a bit of confusion for auditors, it is worthwhile revisiting the financial reporting requirements to 'set the scene'.

Most GAAPs (including FRS 102 *The Financial Reporting Standard applicable in the UK and Republic of Ireland*) cite only two reasons why an entity would not prepare its financial statements using the going concern basis of accounting: management either:

(a)   intends to liquidate the entity, or cease trading, or

(b)   has no realistic alternative but to do so.

As you can see, most entities will prepare their financial statements using the going concern basis of accounting, unless management intend to liquidate the entity or cease trading.

Consider a company that has serious cash flow difficulties, but management are actively trying to resolve them. Attempts are being made to refinance the business, but the bank will only consider its lending decision once it is in receipt of the audited financial statements and interim management accounts.

In this situation, despite the fact that the entity has serious cash flow difficulties, management is not intending to liquidate the business or cease trading. They are trying to save the business by refinancing it. Hence, the financial statements are prepared on a going concern basis, but management must include a disclosure in the financial statements that states that the going concern basis is in question.

REAL-LIFE SCENARIO

Most people (especially those, like me, that like travel) will be familiar with Thomas Cook Airlines. This company went into liquidation in 2019 following various economic challenges. The financial statements for Thomas Cook Airlines Ltd for the year ended 30 September 2018 showed the following going concern disclosure:

Going concern

The Directors believe that preparing the financial statements on the going concern basis is appropriate due to the continued financial support of the ultimate parent company Thomas Cook Group plc. The Directors have received confirmation that Thomas Cook Group plc intends to support the company for at least one year after these financial statements are signed.

However, the Directors note the publication on 16 May 2019 of the Thomas Cook Group plc condensed consolidated interim financial statements for the six months ended 31 March 2019 in which a material uncertainty related to going concern is disclosed.

As set out in those interim financial results the Group is facing challenging trading conditions and a strategic review of the Group Airline was announced on 7 February 2019. The Group prepared revised forecasts for the period to September 2021, recognising the continuing uncertain trading environment across the Group, which allowed the Group Directors to assess the level of liquidity and covenant headroom. This demonstrated a possible requirement for additional liquidity. These scenarios also assume the shareholders will approve, at or before the next AGM, the removal of Article 122(B) restricting the Group's borrowing limits.

The Group has agreed a mandate letter and a term sheet for a new £300 million secured bank financing facility with its lending banks. The availability of the new facility is principally dependent on progress in executing the new strategic review of the Group Airline. The strategic review of the Airline is progressing well, with a number of expressions of interest. The Group Directors recognise that there is uncertainty surrounding its timing and terms and the associated conditions in the new financing arrangement, which could impact the ability of the Group to access the required liquidity, and they have concluded that this matter represents a material uncertainty. This could cast significant doubt on the ability of the Group to continue as a going concern.

As a consequence, the Directors of the Company recognise there is a corresponding material uncertainty concerning the support provided by

Thomas Cook Group plc. This could cast significant doubt on the ability of the Company to continue as a going concern. Nevertheless, having considered the uncertainties described above and after making enquiries, the Directors have a reasonable expectation that the Company has adequate resources to continue in operational existence for the foreseeable future. For these reasons, they continue to adopt the going concern basis in preparing the Company financial statements. The preparation of financial statements in conformity with FRS 101 requires the use of certain critical accounting estimates. It also requires management to exercise its judgement in the process of applying the Company's accounting policies. The areas involving a higher degree of judgement or complexity, or areas where assumptions and estimates are significant to the financial statements are disclosed in note 2.

Putting aside the resulting outcome of Thomas Cook Airlines, the directors are saying that the financial statements are prepared on a going concern basis, but that basis is in question. The auditors also considered that this disclosure was adequate because they did not modify their opinion in respect of this disclosure (as you will see why next – so keep this real-life scenario in your mind for now).

Auditor reporting issues where there is a material uncertainty related to going concern

11.21 So, we know there is interaction between the requirements of ISA (UK) 570 and the way in which going concern is referred to in the auditor's report. The first thing the auditor must consider where there is a material uncertainty related to going concern is whether the client has **adequately** disclosed that/those uncertainty/uncertainties.

Where the auditor concludes that disclosure of a material uncertainty related to going concern is adequate, the auditor makes reference to this disclosure in the auditor's report.

IMPORTANT POINT

The auditor must make reference to an adequate disclosure of a material uncertainty related to going concern, but they do **not** do this through an Emphasis of Matter paragraph. Remember, I said there is interaction between ISA (UK) 570 and the reporting requirements of that ISA (UK).

Instead, the auditor makes reference to the material uncertainty related to going concern using a separate section headed up 'Material Uncertainty

---

Related to Going Concern' as this is a requirement of ISA (UK) 570, para 22.

We have now established, that the auditor refers to adequate disclosure of a material uncertainty related to going concern using a separate paragraph in the auditor's report which is clearly headed up as such. This separate paragraph must:

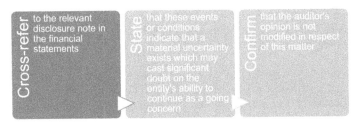

Cross-refer to the relevant disclosure note in the financial statements

State that these events or conditions indicate that a material uncertainty exists which may cast significant doubt on the entity's ability to continue as a going concern

Confirm that the auditor's opinion is not modified in respect of this matter

REAL-LIFE SCENARIO

I asked you earlier on to keep the Thomas Cook Airlines issue to hand. This is where you'll need to make sure you remember what management said in their going concern disclosure because we will now look at what the auditor had to say about it.

The auditor's report on Thomas Cook Airlines Ltd for the year ended 30 September 2018 included a 'Material Uncertainty Related to Going Concern' paragraph. This stated:

Material uncertainty related to going concern

We draw attention to note 1 (page 16) in the financial statements, which states there is a material uncertainty concerning the support provided by Thomas Cook Group plc. This may cast significant doubt on the ability of the company to continue as a going concern. Our opinion is not modified in respect of this matter.

Again, setting aside the unfortunate outcome of this organisation, the auditor was correct to include this paragraph in their auditor's report and will have carefully considered whether the disclosure made by management in the financial statements is adequate. The auditor concluded that the disclosure was adequate because the auditor confirms in the Material Uncertainty Related to Going Concern section of the auditor's report that *'Our opinion is not modified in respect of this matter.'* If the disclosure had

> been inadequate, the auditor would not have included such a paragraph in the auditor's report; they would have modified the auditor's opinion. We examine modified auditor's opinions in the next chapter, **Chapter 12**.

You can see from the real-life scenario that a Material Uncertainty Related to Going Concern paragraph acts in pretty much the same way as an Emphasis of Matter (EOM) paragraph. The auditor draws attention to the relevant disclosure in the financial statements (which they do when they include an EOM paragraph) and confirms that the opinion is not modified in respect of this matter (which they, again, do when they include an EOM paragraph). So, why not just use an EOM paragraph?

Firstly, ISA (UK) 570, para 22 specifically requires the use of a separate section of the auditor's report which deals solely with going concern issues that have been adequately disclosed in the financial statements.

Secondly, the auditing standard-setters believe that as going concern is such a fundamental issue in the preparation of financial statements, it warrants separate disclosure in the auditor's report so as to give it prominence.

For these reasons, an auditor can no longer include references to material uncertainties related to going concern in an EOM paragraph. Unfortunately, some auditor's reports do include references to going concern uncertainties in an EOM paragraph, which is technically incorrect and will render the auditor's report deficient during any quality management review or professional body monitoring review.

Placement of the Material Uncertainty Related to Going Concern paragraph

11.22   Neither ISA (UK) 570 nor ISA (UK) 700 specifies the location of the Material Uncertainty Related to Going Concern paragraph. However, *BULLETIN: Illustrative Auditor's Reports On United Kingdom Private Sector Financial Statements* suggests placing it after the Basis for Opinion paragraph and the Key Audit Matters paragraph (where applicable) (see Appendix 4 in the FRC Bulletin).

'Close calls' and links to Key Audit Matters (KAM)

11.23   Again, there is a link between the auditor's reporting requirements under ISA (UK) 570 and that of ISA (UK) 701 *Communicating Key Audit Matters in the Independent Auditor's Report*. Remember, ISA (UK) 701 is only mandatory for listed entities but that does not stop the auditor of a private entity including a KAM section in the auditor's report.

A 'close call' arises where the auditor has identified conditions which may cast doubt over the going concern status of the organisation, but the audit evidence confirms that no material uncertainty exists.

The auditor should disclose this close call as a KAM in line with ISA (UK) 701. This is because while the auditor may conclude that no material uncertainty exists, they may determine that one, or more, matters relating to this conclusion are KAM. The following table provides some examples of situations that may give rise to such close calls:

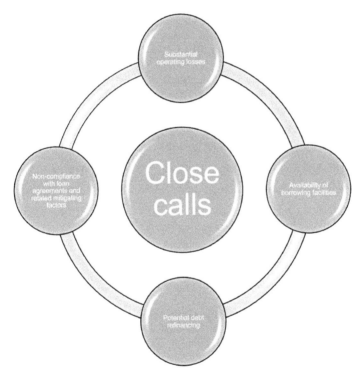

Inadequate disclosure of a material uncertainty related to going concern

11.24   If management have not provided adequate disclosure about a material uncertainty related to going concern and do not rectify the situation, the auditor will **not** use a Material Uncertainty Related to Going Concern paragraph. Instead, the auditor must modify their opinion instead. I examine modified audit opinions in the next chapter (**Chapter 12**).

KEY AUDIT MATTERS (KAM)

11.25 KAM has been mentioned a few times in this chapter and is an issue that I would say is 'relatively' new in terms of auditors' report requirements (although not *that* new). The Financial Reporting Council (FRC) introduced the concept of KAM in the auditor's report off the back of the International Auditing and Assurance Standards Board's (IAASB) changes that arose in 2015.

The IAASB are responsible for issuing International Standards on Auditing (ISAs). The UK then take those ISAs and then tweak them so they become UK-specific, ie we end up with an ISA (UK).

The IAASB carried out a lot of research as to what users (which includes investors) want from the auditor's report which resulted in the following conclusions:

- Enhanced communication between auditors and investors, as well as those charged with corporate governance.

- Increased user confidence in auditors' reports and financial statements.

- Increased transparency, audit quality, and enhanced information value.

- Increased attention by management and financial statement preparers to disclosures referencing the auditor's report.

- Renewed auditor focus on matters to be reported that could result in an increase in professional scepticism.

- Enhanced financial reporting in the public interest.[5]

Following the consultation and the issuance by the IAASB of ISA 701, the FRC followed suit and issued ISA (UK) 701 which became effective for audits of financial statements for periods commencing on or after 15 December 2019.

IMPORTANT POINT

ISA (UK) 701 is mandatory for listed entities, although auditors of private entities can include a KAM section in the auditor's report if they wish. The

---

5 The New Auditor's Report, IAASB, 2015.

reality is, however, that very few private entities choose to include a KAM section in the auditor's report.

So, what is a *Key Audit Matter*? Well, if you look to the definition of a KAM in ISA (UK) 701 it refers to matters that, in the auditor's professional judgement, were of most significance in the audit of the financial statements. KAMs are also selected from issues that are communicated with those charged with governance of the entity.

There are a multitude of matters which can arise during the audit process so the immediate challenge presented to the auditor is which matters should the auditor determine as being KAMs. This, of course, is down to professional judgement and there is no prescribed way of determining such in the ISA (UK). The auditor considers KAMs based on the nature of the client's business and environment as well as the facts and circumstances surrounding the engagement.

ISA (UK) 701 provides for three matters which the auditor must consider when determining KAMs:

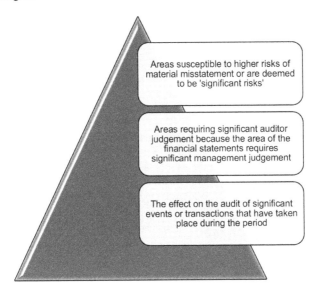

Areas susceptible to higher risks of material misstatement or are deemed to be 'significant risks'

Areas requiring significant auditor judgement because the area of the financial statements requires significant management judgement

The effect on the audit of significant events or transactions that have taken place during the period

IMPORTANT POINT

When it comes to deciding how many KAMs should be included, again there is no limit or specified quantity in the ISA (UK). The auditor must bear in mind that the volume of disclosure will be affected by the size and complexity of the audit client as well as the nature of its business and environment. However, auditors must strive to avoid including voluminous and lengthy descriptions of KAMs because this works against the idea of KAMS being those issues of **most** significance in the audit.

REAL-LIFE SCENARIO

A report produced by the ICAEW, including an analysis of listed company auditors' reports in the UK, found that the following matters were the most commonly reported as risks within KAM, each being reported in more than 10% of all auditor's reports:

● Revenue

● Carrying amount of goodwill and intangible assets

● Taxation

● Accounting for acquisitions

● Pensions

● Valuation of property

● Inventory

● Litigation and regulation

Of the matters listed above, revenue was (by far) the most reported KAM, being included in more than 60% of auditor's reports. In addition, the report found that most auditor's reports include two to four KAMS, but a small number included as many as nine KAMs.[6]

Communicating KAMs

11.26 Once the auditor has determined those matters that are to be included as a KAM, they must then ensure that each matter is appropriately described. ISA (UK) 701 requires the auditor to include a description of:

---

6 The start of a conversation - The Extended Audit Report (ICAEW, 2017).

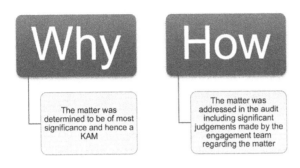

Presenting KAMs in the auditor's report

11.27   ISA (UK) 701 does not specify a location for KAMs, but does comment that placing it in close proximity of the auditor's opinion may give prominence to such information and acknowledge the perceived value of engagement-specific information to intended users. Again, though, the placement will all depend on the auditor's professional judgement, but in most cases, automated software will usually handle the placement aspects.

The order in which KAMs are presented is also an issue which the auditor should carefully consider. ISA (UK) 701 suggests that information be presented in order of relative importance. Again, this will be based on the auditor's professional judgement. Alternatively, it may correspond to the manner in which matters are disclosed in the financial statements.

One of the most important aspects to consider where KAMs are concerned is how the KAMs are described. They should be succinct and balanced to enable the users to understand why the matter was one of most significance in the audit and how the matter was subsequently addressed. Technical jargon should be avoided where possible.

REAL-LIFE SCENARIO

The financial statements of a retail chemists includes a disclosure of a provision for a liability which includes significant management estimation. The auditor has issued an unmodified opinion on the financial statements so there is no question as to whether the provision is materially misstated.

The provision is also the subject of a KAM in the auditor's report. This is understandable given that the provision required significant management estimation which, in turn, would have meant significant auditor attention is required in auditing that provision.

ISA (UK) 701 suggests that the description of a KAM should not be a duplicate of information that is already disclosed in the financial statements (ie, a 'copy and paste' exercise). However, the auditor should include a reference to any related disclosures to enable the users of the auditor's report to further understand how management has addressed the matter in preparing the financial statements.

There is no 'right or wrong' way of presenting KAMs and the amount of detail that the auditor includes in the KAM section will also be a matter of professional judgement. The following illustrates some of the issues the auditor may include when drafting the KAM section of the auditor's report:

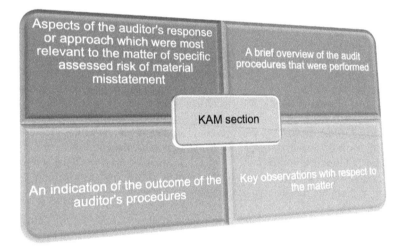

Ethical considerations

11.28 Ethical issues are at the forefront of the work of the auditor and must not be forgotten at any stage during the audit process. When the auditor concludes that an issue gives rise to a KAM, this will usually be the subject of lengthy discussions with management and/or those charged with governance. In some instances, pressure can be put on the auditor *not* to disclose a matter as a KAM which effectively gives rise to an intimidation threat.

Auditors are obliged to comply with the principles of integrity, objectivity, professional competence and due care and professional behaviour. Therefore, the auditor must not be tempted to exclude KAMs which would otherwise be included in the auditor's report for fear of being disengaged by the client, or other such reasons.

Example 11.9 – Illustrative KAM section

Key audit matter	How it was addressed in the audit
Provisions The industry in which the client operates is heavily regulated and the group is involved in a number of legal actions. At the year end 31 March 2024, the group had recognised provisions for liabilities amounting to £6.1m in respect of legal claims brought against the group.	We evaluated the design and tested the operating effectiveness of controls in respect of the recognition and measurement of provisions. We determined that we could rely on these controls for the purposes of our audit. We read correspondence with the group's legal advisers and, where appropriate, we examined correspondence connected with the cases. We considered management's judgements on the level of provisioning to be reasonable. We also evaluated the appropriateness of the disclosures in notes 34 and 39 which we considered appropriate.
Assessment of the recoverability of the carrying value of intangible assets The group has intangible assets totalling £11.1m. The carrying amount of intangible assets is contingent on future cash flows and there is a risk that the assets will be impaired if cash flows are not in line with expectations. The projections in management's impairment model contains a number of significant estimates including peak year and erosion sales curves, probability of technical and regulatory success factors and discounts rates. Changes in these assumptions may lead to an impairment to the carrying value of intangible assets. There have been concerns over the recoverability of the carrying value of specific assets in prior periods.	We evaluated the design and tested the operating effectiveness of controls in assessing the carrying value of intangible assets. We determined that we could rely on these controls for the purposes of our audit. For those assets tested we obtained the group's impairment analyses and: ● we tested the accuracy of the impairment models and agreed the cash flow forecasts used in the impairment models to the board approved 'Long Range Plan'; ● we tested the reasonableness of key assumptions including revenue and profit growth or decline, the expected loss of product exclusivity and the impact of the expiry of patents and licences including comparing certain assumptions to industry and economic forecasts; ● for higher risk assets, we performed sensitivity analysis focussing on which we consider to be reasonably possible changes in key assumptions; and ● we assessed the historical accuracy of forecasts to assess management's forecasting ability. We utilised our in-house valuation experts to assess the valuation techniques used, to independently corroborate the discount rate used by management by reference to market data and to assist with the evaluation of other key assumptions for higher risk assets. As a result of our work, we determined the net impairment charge of £4m was appropriate. We reviewed the disclosure in note 115 of the consolidated financial statements, including sensitivity analysis based on reasonably possible downsides. We are satisfied that these disclosures are appropriate.

LIMITING THE AUDITOR'S LIABILITY

11.29   One of the ways in which an auditor can attempt to limit their liability to third parties using the auditor's report is including a liability disclaimer paragraph, known as a 'Bannerman' paragraph in the auditor's report.

The name 'Bannerman' relates to the case of *Royal Bank of Scotland v Bannerman Johnstone Maclay & Others (2005)*. This case followed *Caparo Industries v Dickman & Others (1990)* where auditors have been liable for negligence to third parties provided that:

- the third party was known to the auditor at the time of signing the auditor's report to be relying on that report; and

- the reason for that reliance was known to the auditor.

In the Bannerman case, it was held that the company's bankers (who had extended the company's lending agreements) might not have done so if they had known about the misstatements in Bannerman's accounts (due to fraud) that had not been detected by the auditors.

The court held in favour of Royal Bank of Scotland on the basis that the auditors knew the identity of the third party, the use to which the information would be put and that the bank intended to rely on it for a known purpose. The court dismissed the defence's arguments that, for a duty of care to exist, there must be an express assumption of responsibility to the third party by the auditor.

More significantly, the judge commented that, having become aware of the details of the requirements of the lending agreement, the auditors could have disclaimed responsibility to the bank.

Hence, all of the bodies whose members are eligible to be auditors of UK companies (except ACCA), recommend that an extra paragraph with wording set out in **Example 11.10** below should be included in auditors' reports.

The Bannerman paragraph limits the audit firm's duty of care to third parties and are very common in auditor's reports as well as other reports issued by professional firms. Professional bodies such as ACCA do not favour the use of Bannerman paragraphs and their Technical Factsheet 84 *The Use of Disclaimers in Audit Reports* discourages member firms from including a Bannerman paragraph in the auditor's report. The Technical Factsheet states that if the audit firm has carried out audit work in accordance with the ISAs (UK), they would not need to include a Bannerman paragraph in their auditor's report and such paragraphs could devalue the auditor's report.

Example 11.10 – Bannerman paragraph wording

The wording of a Bannerman paragraph is as follows:

This report is made solely to the company's members, as a body, in accordance with the CA 2006, ss 495 and 496. Our audit work has been undertaken so that we might state to the company's members those matters we are required to state to them in an auditor's report and for no other purpose. To the fullest extent permitted by law, we do not accept or assume responsibility to anyone other than the company and the company's members as a body, for our audit work, for this report, or for the opinions we have formed.

It is common practice to include the Bannerman paragraph at the end of the auditor's report, directly before the auditor's signature. Some commentators have argued that placing it at the end of the auditor's report is inappropriate and it should be given more prominence towards the beginning of the report. The converse argument is that having the paragraph at the end of the auditor's report avoids the risk that any caveat is considered in the context of the auditor's opinion.

IMPORTANT POINT

It should be borne in mind that Bannerman paragraphs are a risk management tool developed by audit firms and the advice is that audit firms should think carefully about reservations they put on who the audit is undertaken for.

REAL-LIFE SCENARIO

The use of Bannerman paragraphs as a disclaimer was highlighted in the case of *Barclays Bank plc v Grant Thornton*. Grant Thornton (GT) prepared non-statutory audit reports on Von Essen Hotels Limited Group (VEH) and expressed unqualified opinions for both 2006 and 2007. Barclays Bank alleged that the financial statements had been manipulated to show that VEH was capable of meeting bank covenants on its loan facility when, in fact, it could not. Consequently, Barclays Bank suffered losses of some £45m when VEH went into administration in April 2011. The bank also stated that it relied on the unqualified opinions when making the loans to VEH.

Barclays claimed that GT owed a duty of care to them and that this duty of care was breached because the auditors failed to uncover the alleged fraud. Barclays also said that GT would have been aware that they would be placing reliance on the auditor's report. GT's auditor's report contained the Bannerman wording which sets out that they did not accept or assume responsibility in respect of the reports to anyone other than the company and its directors.

The judge accepted GT's argument and struck out the claim. The judge stated that Barclays Bank should have been aware of the Bannerman paragraph in the report – particularly as it was included in its first two paragraphs and, therefore, if Barclays Bank had not read it, they should have done.

The judge concluded that the Bannerman paragraph was reasonable having regard to the Unfair Contract Terms Act 1977.

CHAPTER ROUNDUP

- The format of the auditor's report is set out in ISA (UK) 700 and must contain certain elements.

- The purpose of the auditor's report is to express the auditor's opinion as to whether the financial statements give a true and fair view and have been properly prepared in all material respects. There is no statutory definition of 'true and fair'.

- An Emphasis of Matter paragraph is included in the auditor's report to flag up an issue that is adequately presented or disclosed that, in the auditor's professional judgement, is of fundamental importance to users' understanding of the entity's financial statements.

- Other Matter paragraphs are used in the auditor's report to communicate information on matters which are not presented or disclosed in the financial statements.

- Other information which is published with the annual report must be read by the auditor to identify any material inconsistencies in that other information when compared to the financial statements. Such inconsistencies, if unresolved, are referred to in the auditor's report.

- A Material Uncertainty Related to Going Concern paragraph is used by the auditor to cross-reference to an adequate disclosure concerning a material uncertainty relating to the entity's ability to continue as a going concern for the foreseeable future. If such disclosures are inadequate, a Material Uncertainty Related to Going Concern paragraph is not used as the auditor will modify their opinion instead (if the inadequacy is not resolved, of course).

- Key Audit Matters (KAM) are dealt with in ISA (UK) 701 which is only mandatory for listed entities. KAM are those matters which, in the auditor's professional judgement, were of most significance in the audit and are disclosed in a separate section of the auditor's report.

- Most auditor's reports contain a 'Bannerman paragraph' which is a means of limiting the auditor's liability to third parties.

PITFALLS TO AVOID

- Failing to produce an auditor's report which is consistent with the requirements of ISA (UK) 700.

- Including an Emphasis of Matter paragraph inappropriately.

- Using an Emphasis of Matter paragraph to cross-refer to an adequate going concern uncertainty disclosure.

- Not understanding the key provisions in ISA (UK) 701 where Key Audit Matters are concerned (especially overlaps with items giving rise to an Emphasis of Matter paragraph also).

APPENDIX: ILLUSTRATIVE UNMODIFIED AUDITOR'S REPORT

The following is an example of the wording of an unmodified auditor's report:

Independent auditor's report to the members of Sunnie Enterprises Ltd for the year ended 31 March 2024

Opinion

We have audited the financial statements of Sunnie Enterprises Ltd ('the company') for the year ended 31 March 2024 which comprise the Profit and Loss Account, Other Comprehensive Income, Balance Sheet, Statement of Changes in Equity, Cash Flow Statement and Notes to the Cash Flow Statement and Notes to the Financial Statements, including a summary of significant accounting policies. The financial reporting framework that has been applied in their preparation is applicable law and United Kingdom Accounting Standards, including Financial Reporting Standard 102 *The Financial Reporting Standard applicable in the UK and Republic of Ireland* (United Kingdom Generally Accepted Accounting Practice).

11.29   *The Unmodified Auditor's Opinion*

In our opinion the financial statements:

- give a true and fair view of the state of the financial position of the company and its performance and cash flows for the year ended 31 March 2024;

- have been properly prepared in accordance with United Kingdom Generally Accepted Accounting Practice; and

- have been prepared in accordance with the requirements of the CA 2006.

Basis for opinion

We conducted our audit in accordance with International Standards on Auditing (UK) (ISAs (UK)) and applicable law. Our responsibilities under those standards are further described in the Auditor's responsibilities for the audit of the financial statements section of our report. We are independent of the company in accordance with the ethical requirements that are relevant to our audit of the financial statements, including the FRC's Ethical Standard, and we have fulfilled our other ethical responsibilities in accordance with these requirements. We believe that the audit evidence we have obtained is sufficient and appropriate to provide a basis for our opinion.

Conclusions relating to going concern

In auditing the financial statements, we have concluded that the directors' use of the going concern basis of accounting in the preparation of the financial statements is appropriate.

Based on the work we have performed, we have not identified any material uncertainties relating to events or conditions that, individually or collectively, may cast significant doubt on the company's ability to continue as a going concern for a period of at least 12 months from when the financial statements are authorised for issue.

Our responsibilities and the responsibilities of the directors with respect to going concern are described in the relevant sections of this report.

Other information

The directors are responsible for the other information. The other information comprises the information in the Strategic Report, the Report of the Directors and the Statement of Directors' Responsibilities, but does not include the financial statements and our Report of the Auditors thereon.

Our opinion on the financial statements does not cover the other information and, except to the extent otherwise explicitly stated in our report, we do not express any form of assurance conclusion thereon.

In connection with our audit of the financial statements, our responsibility is to read the other information and, in doing so, consider whether the other information is materially inconsistent with the financial statements or our knowledge obtained in the audit or otherwise appears to be materially misstated. If we identify such material inconsistencies or apparent material misstatements, we are required to determine whether this gives rise to a material misstatement in the financial statements themselves. If, based on the work we have performed, we conclude that there is a material misstatement of this other information, we are required to report that fact. We have nothing to report in this regard.

Opinions on other matters prescribed by the Companies Act 2006

In our opinion, based on the work undertaken in the course of the audit:

- the information given in the Strategic Report and the Report of the Directors for the financial year for which the financial statements are prepared is consistent with the financial statements; and

- the Strategic Report and the Report of the Directors have been prepared in accordance with applicable legal requirements.

Matters on which we are required to report by exception

In the light of the knowledge and understanding of the company and its environment obtained in the course of the audit, we have not identified material misstatements in the Strategic Report or the Report of the Directors.

We have nothing to report in respect of the following matters where the CA 2006 requires us to report to you if, in our opinion:

- adequate accounting records have not been kept, or returns adequate for our audit have not been received from branches not visited by us; or

- the financial statements are not in agreement with the accounting records and returns; or

- certain disclosures of directors' remuneration specified by law are not made; or

- we have not received all the information and explanations we require for our audit.

Responsibilities of directors

As explained more fully in the Statement of Directors' Responsibilities set out on page five, the directors are responsible for the preparation of the financial statements and for being satisfied that they give a true and fair view, and for such internal control as the directors determine necessary to enable the preparation of financial statements that are free from material misstatement, whether due to fraud or error.

In preparing the financial statements, the directors are responsible for assessing the company's ability to continue as a going concern, disclosing, as applicable, matters related to going concern and using the going concern basis of accounting unless the directors either intend to liquidate the company or to cease operations, or have no realistic alternative but to do so.

Auditors' responsibilities for the audit of the financial statements

Our objectives are to obtain reasonable assurance about whether the financial statements as a whole are free from material misstatement, whether due to fraud or error, and to issue a Report of the Auditors that includes our opinion. Reasonable assurance is a high level of assurance, but is not a guarantee that an audit conducted in accordance with ISAs (UK) will always detect a material misstatement when it exists. Misstatements can arise from fraud or error and are considered material if, individually or in the aggregate, they could reasonably be expected to influence the economic decisions of users taken on the basis of these financial statements.

The extent to which our procedures are capable of detecting irregularities, including fraud, is detailed below:

We gained an understanding of the legal and regulatory framework applicable to the company and the industry in which it operates, and considered the risks of acts by the company which were contrary to applicable laws and regulations, including fraud. We designed our audit procedures to respond to the assessed risks, recognising that the risk of not detecting a material misstatement due to fraud is higher than the risk of not detecting one resulting from error, as fraud may involve more sophisticated and deliberate concealment, such as through forgery or intentional misrepresentations or via collusion. We recognised the risks arising from fraud could arise from two sources:

- manipulation of weaknesses in the system of internal control; and

- management override of the system of internal control.

We focussed on laws and regulations which could give rise to a material misstatement in the financial statements, including (but not limited to), the CA 2006 and UK tax legislation as well as fire regulations and Health and Safety. Our tests included agreeing the financial statement disclosures to underlying supporting documentation, enquiries with management and reviews of correspondence. We paid particular attention to legal correspondence which may indicate a breach of laws and regulations.

There are inherent limitations in the audit procedures described above and, the further removed non-compliance with laws and regulations is from the events and transactions reflected in the financial statements, the less likely we would become aware of it.

During the course of our audit, we did not identify any key audit matters relating to irregularities, including fraud.

As in all our audits, we also addressed the risk of management override of internal controls (as noted above), including testing journals and evaluating whether there was evidence of bias by the directors which represented a risk of material misstatement due to fraud.

As part of an audit in accordance with ISAs (UK), we exercise professional judgement and maintain professional scepticism throughout the audit. We also:

- Identify and assess the risks of material misstatement of the financial statements, whether due to fraud or error, design and perform audit procedures responsive to those risks, and obtain audit evidence that is sufficient and appropriate to provide a basis for our opinion. The risk of not detecting a material misstatement resulting from fraud is higher than for one resulting from error, as fraud may involve collusion, forgery, intentional omissions, misrepresentations, or the override of internal control.

- Obtain an understanding of internal control relevant to the audit in order to design audit procedures that are appropriate in the circumstances, but not for the purpose of expressing an opinion on the effectiveness of the company's internal control.

- Evaluate the appropriateness of accounting policies used and the reasonableness of accounting estimates and related disclosures made by the directors.

- Conclude on the appropriateness of the directors' use of the going concern basis of accounting and, based on the audit evidence obtained, whether a material uncertainty exists related to events or conditions that may cast significant doubt on the company's ability to continue as a going concern. If we conclude that a material uncertainty exists, we are required to draw attention in our Report of the Auditors to the related disclosures in the financial statements or, if such disclosures are inadequate, to modify our opinion. Our conclusions are based on the audit evidence obtained up to the date of our Report of the Auditors. However, future events or conditions may cause the company to cease to continue as a going concern.

- Evaluate the overall presentation, structure and content of the financial statements, including the disclosures, and whether the financial statements represent the underlying transactions and events in a manner that achieves fair presentation.

We communicate with those charged with governance regarding, among other matters, the planned scope and timing of the audit and significant audit findings, including any significant deficiencies in internal control that we identify during our audit.

Use of our report[7]

This report is made solely to the company's members, as a body, in accordance with Chapter 3 of Part 16 of the Companies Act 2006. Our audit work has been undertaken so that we might state to the company's members those matters we are required to state to them in a Report of the Auditors and for no other purpose. To the fullest extent permitted by law, we do not accept or assume responsibility to anyone other than the company and the company's members as a body, for our audit work, for this report, or for the opinions we have formed.

Mr J Smith FCA FCCA (Senior Statutory Auditor)

For and on behalf of ABC Chartered Certified Accountants and
Statutory Auditors
123 Long Lane
Anytown
AB1 2CD
16 June 2024

---

7 See **11.3** above.

Chapter 12

The Modified Auditor's Opinion

CHAPTER TOPIC LIST

- Introduction (see **12.1**)
- Modified audit opinion (see **12.2**)
- Material but not pervasive (see **12.8**)
- Material and pervasive (see **12.9**)
- Reporting a modified audit opinion (see **12.11**)
- Qualified 'except for' opinion (see **12.12**)
- Adverse opinion (see **12.14**)
- Disclaimer of opinion (see **12.15**)
- Going concern (see **12.17**)

INTRODUCTION

12.1   In **Chapter 11**, I looked at the unmodified (often referred to as 'unqualified') auditor's opinion which is where the auditor concludes that the financial statements are true and fair (or present fairly, in all material respects). This opinion is arrived at based on the audit evidence obtained throughout the audit. I have mentioned the 'story' that an audit file must tell – the story being the audit evidence; the conclusion being the audit opinion. In many cases, the audit client will 'live happily ever after' and receive an unmodified audit opinion; but in some cases, they don't live happily ever after and receive a modified opinion.

WHAT ARE WE TRYING TO ACHIEVE?

As I noted in **Chapter 11**, the auditor must attach an auditor's report to the financial statements. Where there is a material problem with the financial

> statements that remains unresolved, the auditor must express a modified audit opinion. The objective here is to ensure that the auditor arrives at the correct type of modified opinion based on the severity of the issue at hand.

As I examined in **Chapter 11**, the auditor may also include additional paragraphs in the auditor's report, such as an Emphasis of Matter paragraph, which highlights matters in the financial statements the auditor wants to bring to the user's attention. Such paragraphs (including Material Uncertainties Related to Going Concern paragraphs) do not affect the auditor's unmodified opinion. The unmodified opinion is basically a 'clean' opinion and is the best opinion that the auditor can express from the company's point of view.

I suppose you could look at this another way. The auditor is including additional paragraphs (eg, a Material Uncertainty Related to Going Concern paragraph) which does not modify the opinion, but modifies the standard unmodified auditor's report instead.

IMPORTANT POINT

Remember, that an unmodified opinion is only reasonable assurance. The auditor is not certifying that the financial statements are 100% correct or providing maximum or absolute assurance.

However, as is the case in life generally, 'stuff' happens, and situations may present themselves which mean that the auditor is unable to state that the financial statements give a true and fair view and/or have been prepared in accordance with the applicable financial reporting framework (such as FRS 102 *The Financial Reporting Standard applicable in the UK and Republic of Ireland*). There are two situations in which the auditor is unable to offer an unmodified opinion on the financial statements:

The auditor has obtained sufficient appropriate audit evidence that the financial statements do not give a true and fair view

The auditor has not been able to obtain sufficient appropriate audit evidence to reach a conclusion that the financial statements give a true and fair view

In either of these situations, the auditor will express a modified (often referred to as a 'qualified') auditor's opinion.

The type of modified audit opinion will depend on the severity of the matter(s) giving rise to the modification. To that end, the auditor must look to the provisions in ISA (UK) 705 *Modifications to the Opinion in the Independent Auditor's Report*. This chapter focuses on the issues that will generally arise leading to a modified auditor's opinion.

IMPORTANT POINT

Modified audit opinions are, in practice, quite rare but they do arise. The auditor will usually express a modified audit opinion as a last resort; in other words, where appropriate, the auditor will always give management and/or those charged with governance of an entity, the chance to remedy the situation that would potentially cause the auditor to modify their opinion. Often, the potential for a modified audit opinion will involve lengthy discussions with the client and attempts, where possible, by the auditor to get the client to remedy the matter(s) giving rise to the modified audit opinion.

Management will always want to avoid the auditor expressing a modified audit opinion. The implications of this can be very serious for an entity. For example, depending on the nature of the modification, they can cause suppliers to become nervous about the entity and perhaps withdraw credit facilities; banks may become 'jittery' about the entity's ability to meet obligations under loan agreements, and could 'call in' loans and overdrafts which could be catastrophic for the business; and insurers may increase insurance premiums if they perceive the modified auditor's opinion might mean the business becomes riskier. In addition, the company's credit-rating can (and often does) suffer as a result of a modified audit opinion. In more serious cases, a modified auditor's opinion can lead the shareholders to call for the director(s) to be removed from office. Therefore, it's in the business' best interests to avoid a modified audit opinion wherever possible.

Remember, the auditor will, wherever possible, always give ample opportunity for management and/or those charged with governance the opportunity to remedy the issue that is potentially going to cause the auditor to modify their opinion. If management and/or those charged with governance refuse to remedy the situation; or, if the steps taken by management and/or those charged with governance to remedy the issue are inadequate, the auditor will have no alternative but to express a modified audit opinion.

IMPORTANT POINT

The issues I will cover in this chapter build heavily on the audit completion issues examined in **Chapter 11** and **Chapter 10**. The issue of the modified auditor's opinion cannot be considered in isolation because the opinion is just one part of the overall auditor's report. Hence, arriving at the opinion involves the auditor considering many issues, such as going concern and subsequent events.

MODIFIED AUDIT OPINION

12.2   As I mentioned in the introductory section of this chapter, modified audit opinions are dealt with in ISA (UK) 705. When the auditor concludes that they have no alternative but to express a modified audit opinion, they must ensure that the appropriate modified opinion is clearly expressed in the auditor's report.

In the UK, an auditor's opinion is usually included in the first paragraph of the auditor's report and will be headed up 'Modified opinion' or 'Qualified opinion' accordingly. Both 'modified' and 'qualified' essentially mean the same thing – ie, something is wrong with the financial statements which is further discussed in the Basis for Qualified (Modified) Opinion section accordingly.

In the introduction to this chapter, I mentioned the two circumstances that generally give rise to a modified audit opinion: ie, the auditor concludes the financial statements contain a material misstatement; or the auditor is unable to obtain sufficient appropriate audit evidence on a material area or multiple material areas of the financial statements. It might also be the case that the auditor concludes that the financial statements do not comply with relevant legislation.

Qualified, adverse and disclaimers of opinion

12.3   There are three types of modified auditor's opinion, being a 'qualified' opinion, an 'adverse' opinion and a 'disclaimer' of opinion. ISA (UK) 705 states that the decision as to which type of modified opinion the auditor should express will depend on two specific issues:

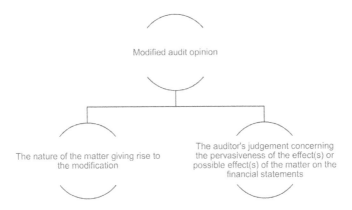

What the auditor must consider carefully in arriving at the most appropriate modified opinion is **why** the financial statements do not give a true and fair view. Once the 'why' part has been established, the auditor must then consider how **severe** the problem is. The severity of the problem effectively dictates the **pervasiveness** of the matter(s) as well. Ordinarily, this is not something that is arrived at lightly and will usually involve a lot of time in ensuring the appropriate modified opinion is arrived at correctly and may also involve consultation with others either within the firm, or through external consultations (such as with another experienced auditor or the technical advisory helpline of a professional body).

I also think that where there is potential for the auditor to express a modified audit opinion, the file should document (in the completion section) the rationale behind the opinion. This documentation can cross-reference to the relevant areas of the audit file that have been problematic and allows a file reviewer to see, at a glance, as to the reasons giving rise to the modified audit opinion.

It is fair to say that there is no one modified audit opinion that is ever 'ideal'. However, they can be 'ranked' in terms of severity as follows:

REAL-LIFE SCENARIO

Mr N has two audit clients and is a sole practitioner. He carried out the audit of one of his clients for the year ended 31 October 2022 and this resulted in the following discoveries:

- A fraud in respect of cash sales resulting in the recognition of a sundry debtor balance of £150,000. The auditor could not obtain sufficient appropriate audit evidence concerning the recoverability of this debtor balance.

- Revalued development costs, contrary to FRS 102, Section 18 *Intangible Assets other than Goodwill.*

- The recognition of a provision for liabilities when it was unclear that the recognition criteria in FRS 102, Section 21 *Provisions and Contingencies* had been met.

- Redeemable preference shares issued in the year had been recognised in equity as opposed to a financial liability because the client did not have discretion about when they became redeemable.

- Capitalisation of refurbishment expenditure in property, plant and equipment when this expenditure was of a revenue nature.

- Inconclusive income completeness testing because a corruption of the client's sales order processing module meant certain audit evidence could not be obtained.

In all cases, the client disagreed with the auditor concerning the correct accounting treatments and refused to make any amendments.

The impact of the above misstatements was judged by Mr N to be both material and pervasive. Consequently, the auditor disclaimed his opinion on the financial statements. The auditor entered into lengthy discussions with the client prior to issuing the disclaimer of opinion in an attempt to persuade the client to make the necessary adjustments, thus avoiding the need for a disclaimed opinion.

One could argue that the audit opinion should have been adverse rather than disclaimed on the grounds that audit evidence was available to suggest the financial statements contain material and pervasive misstatements. However, in the absence of any information to suggest otherwise, the auditor documented the rationale for his disclaimed opinion together with a conversation he had had with the technical advisory department of his professional body.

It would have also been advisable to consult ISA (UK) 705, para 13 which provides guidance on the course of action to be taken by the auditor when it comes to disclaiming an opinion. This paragraph states that if the auditor concludes that the possible effects on the financial statements of undetected misstatements (if any) could be material but not pervasive, a qualified opinion is expressed.

If the possible effects of undetected misstatements (if any) could be both material and pervasive, such that a qualified opinion is not severe enough, the auditor must withdraw from the engagement where practicable and possible under applicable law and regulation. If withdrawal is not possible prior to issuing the auditor's report, the opinion is disclaimed.

Essentially, where management are imposing scope limitations that would merit a disclaimed opinion, the auditor must consider withdrawing and only issue a disclaimer of opinion if withdrawal is not possible.

I will examine each of the above types of modified opinion in more detail as follows:

Qualified opinion

12.4   The auditor will express a qualified opinion where they disagree with an accounting treatment, adequacy of a disclosure note or other non-compliance in respect of a material item. Remember, the auditor is only concerned with **material** items so any **immaterial** non-compliance will not give rise to a modified audit opinion. The auditor will also express a qualified opinion when they have been unable to obtain sufficient appropriate audit evidence concerning a material item. Materiality is a wholly judgemental issue, and I examined this concept in detail in **Chapter 6**. As the issue of materiality is judgemental, any matters giving rise to a qualified opinion will also be judged in terms of materiality where the audit work is being reviewed.

A qualified opinion is usually referred to as an 'except for' opinion. This does seem a little strange at first glance, but a qualified opinion will generally include the words 'except for' indicating that 'except for' the matter giving rise to the modification, the rest of the financial statements present a true and fair view.

IMPORTANT POINT

The auditor must only express a qualified 'except for' opinion when the matter giving rise to the modification is **material** but not **pervasive**. I look at what is material and pervasive in **12.8** and **12.9** below.

Adverse

12.5   An adverse opinion is one which management of a company would never set out to get. They are very serious in terms of what the auditor is saying about the financial statements.

When the auditor expresses an adverse opinion on the financial statements, they are stating that the financial statements do not give a true and fair view and have not been properly prepared in accordance with legislation and the applicable financial reporting framework. This is essentially informing the user **not** to place reliance on the financial statements. In practice, adverse audit opinions are rare and are only expressed in instances of serious non-compliance with legislation, accounting standards or other relevant guidance.

IMPORTANT POINT

When the auditor expresses an adverse opinion, they are saying that the matter(s) giving rise to this type of modification are not only material; but they are material **and** pervasive. I'll examine what is, and what is not, 'pervasive' later in the chapter. The key point to emphasise here is that there are a number of things wrong with the entity's financial statements that have meant the auditor needs to ramp up the modified audit opinion to an adverse opinion because a qualified 'except for' does not warrant the severity of the issue(s).

Disclaimer of opinion

12.6   When the auditor expresses a disclaimer of opinion, they are doing exactly that. In other words, they cannot arrive at an appropriate opinion on the financial statements and hence are not expressing any opinion. Again, disclaimers of opinion are quite rare in practice, but do arise. The auditor will generally express a disclaimer of opinion when, for example, the accounting records have been destroyed and the auditor is unable to obtain sufficient appropriate audit evidence concerning the amounts and disclosures in the entity's financial statements.

IMPORTANT POINT

Again, the key issue where a disclaimer of opinion is concerned is the severity of the issue(s). The auditor expresses a disclaimer of opinion when they cannot reach a conclusion over a matter(s) which could be both material and pervasive.

Summary

12.7   To summarise the types of modified opinion, and to make it easier for you to identify 'at a glance' the types of modified audit opinion that may be necessary, I have brought it all together in the following table:

Auditor's overall conclusion	Auditor's conclusion as to the effect(s) of the matter(s) on the financial statements	
	Material but not pervasive	**Material and pervasive**
The financial statements contain a material misstatement	Qualified opinion 'except for' The auditor must include a 'Basis for Qualified Opinion' paragraph in the auditor's report	Adverse opinion The auditor must include a 'Basis for Adverse Opinion' paragraph in the auditor's report
The auditor is unable to obtain sufficient appropriate audit evidence	Qualified opinion 'except for' The auditor must include a 'Basis for Qualified Opinion' paragraph in the auditor's report	Disclaimer of opinion Do not express an opinion The auditor must include a 'Basis for Disclaimer of Opinion' paragraph in the auditor's report

From the table above, you can see the two situations that create the need for the auditor to express a modified auditor's opinion (those reasons essentially culminating in the fact that the financial statements do not give a true and fair view and/or the auditor has been unable to obtain sufficient appropriate audit evidence). In practice, the reasons for the modification will usually be clear.

For a matter to give rise to a modified auditor's opinion, it must be **material**. This could simply be one accounting treatment that the auditor disagrees with; or it could be because there are a number of immaterial misstatements that add up to becoming material. While the numbers in the financial statements are crucially important, it is also important to appreciate that there could be other reasons why the auditor determines it appropriate to express a modified audit opinion:

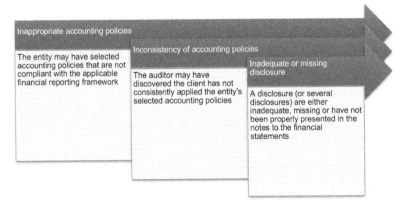

Inappropriate accounting policies

The entity may have selected accounting policies that are not compliant with the applicable financial reporting framework

Inconsistency of accounting policies

The auditor may have discovered the client has not consistently applied the entity's selected accounting policies

Inadequate or missing disclosure

A disclosure (or several disclosures) are either inadequate, missing or have not been properly presented in the notes to the financial statements

Example 12.1 – Irrecoverable debt

The draft financial statements of Sunnie Enterprises Ltd for the year ended 31 March 2024, prepared under FRS 102 *The Financial Reporting Standard applicable in the UK and Republic of Ireland* show the following:

	31.03.2024 **DRAFT** £'000	**31.03.2023** **AUDITED** £'000
Turnover	48,331	59,264
Profit before tax	2,886	4,130
Total assets	62,984	77,031

On 17 April 2024, the company received a letter from Bamber & Co Insolvency Services informing it that a customer, Hall Consultancy Services Ltd, had gone into liquidation. The liquidator confirmed in the letter that it is unlikely that unsecured creditors (of which Sunnie Enterprises is one) will receive any payment once the liquidation is complete.

The year-end trade debtors list shows that Hall Consultancy Services owes £347,000. The finance director, Kerry Morris, has informed the audit senior that she will not write this debt off in the financial statements for the year ended 31 March 2024 on the grounds that the company was not made aware of the bad debt until after the year end.

While Kerry is correct that the company was not made aware of their customer's inability to pay its invoices at the year end, it is an issue that must be considered in light of FRS 102, Section 32 *Events after the End of the Reporting Period*.

The bankruptcy of a customer so soon after the balance sheet date indicates that Sunnie Enterprises had incurred a loss by 31 March 2024. FRS 102, Section 32 would consider this to be an adjusting event, meaning that the financial statements for the 31 March 2024 year end should be adjusted to reflect the bankruptcy of Hall Consultancy Services.

Once the auditor has established the appropriate accounting treatment that should be applied to state compliance with FRS 102, the next step is to determine the materiality of the issue. Remember, the auditor is only interested in material items (or immaterial items that, when aggregated, become material) when deciding on the type of modified opinion to express, should the client not remedy the issue.

In this situation, the client's customer owes a balance of £347,000. If we assume that materiality is based on profit before tax (as this is the parameter that is most likely to be affected by the adjustment of misstatements), the bad debt is material at 12% (£347,000 / £2,886,000 × 100) of profit before tax but is not material to total assets at 0.5% (£347,000 / £62,984,000 × 100).

Hence, the bad debt is material to profit before tax and so should be written off in the 31 March 2024.

If the bad debt is not written off, the financial statements will not conform to FRS 102, Section 32 and therefore the auditor will be required to modify the auditor's opinion. As the matter is material, but not pervasive, the auditor will express a qualified 'except for' opinion. A Basis for Qualified Opinion paragraph will be included in the auditor's report which will explain the reason behind the qualified opinion.

IMPORTANT

As you have probably gathered by now, the auditor must use professional judgement in arriving at the most appropriate modified audit opinion. This will be based on the severity of the matter(s) giving rise to the potential modification and whether the severity is both material **and** pervasive or just material.

MATERIAL BUT NOT PERVASIVE

12.8   A matter is considered material, but not pervasive, when the issue only affects an isolated area of the financial statements. So, in **Example 12.1** above, the areas affected by the bad debt are current assets (trade debtors, which are overstated) and profit before tax (as expenses are understated); therefore, the issue giving rise to the modification only affects specific areas of the financial statements. Other examples of material, but not pervasive, issues include:

• Recognising research expenditure within intangible assets in contravention of FRS 102, Section 18 *Intangible Assets other than Goodwill*.

- Failing to adequately disclose a material related party transaction (particularly one which is has not been concluded under normal market conditions) in contravention of FRS 102, Section 33 *Related Party Disclosures.*

- Failing to disclose details of a material contingent liability in contravention of FRS 102, Section 21 *Provisions and Contingencies.*

The reason these examples are material, but not pervasive, is that the misstatement will only be confined to specific areas of the financial statements as opposed to several areas.

MATERIAL AND PERVASIVE

12.9   A material and pervasive issue is a serious one. When a matter is both material and pervasive, it means that the misstatement(s) affects several areas of the financial statements. The Oxford English Dictionary definition of 'pervasive' includes '… spreading widely throughout an area..'. In auditing terms, this means that the effect of a material misstatements affects multiple areas of the financial statements, such that they cannot be rendered reliable.

ISA (UK) 705 states that a misstatement has a pervasive effect on the financial statements if, in the auditor's judgement those effects:

- are not confined to specific elements, accounts or items of the financial statements;

- if so confined, represent or could represent a substantial proportion of the financial statements; or

- in relation to disclosures, are fundamental to users' understanding of the financial statements.[1]

Remember back in **Chapter 11** when I looked at Emphasis of Matter paragraphs and I said that such a matter must be **fundamental** to users' understanding of the financial statements; the concept of 'fundamentality' also applies to a pervasive issue. In other words, the issue must be *fundamental* to the financial statements to the extent that it renders the financial statements unreliable **as a whole**.

Examples of matters which may be material and pervasive include the following:

1   ISA (UK) 705, para 5.

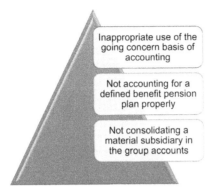

Inappropriate use of the going concern basis of accounting

Not accounting for a defined benefit pension plan properly

Not consolidating a material subsidiary in the group accounts

REAL-LIFE SCENARIO

Mr A is an audit file reviewer. He had carried out a review of an audit file for a firm's client that had an investment property on its balance sheet. The firm's client prepared its financial statements under FRS 102. Financial statement materiality had been set at £86,000 using profit before tax as the basis of this materiality calculation.

A review of the fixed assets section of the audit file indicated that the client had commissioned a firm of chartered surveyors to carry out a fair value exercise on the investment property at the client's year end. The investment property had increased in value by £125,000 due to enhancements of the property that had been carried out in the year.

The client had correctly increased the investment property (ie, the debit had been correctly posted). However, the client had recognised the fair value gain in a revaluation reserve rather than in profit and loss as required by FRS 102, para 16.7. This meant that profit was understated by a material amount.

Not only was the client unaware that the accounting treatment they had applied was incorrect, but the auditor had also concluded that the accounting treatment was correct too. The auditor was unaware that FRS 102, Section 16 *Investment Property* required fair value gains and losses to be recorded in profit or loss and not a revaluation reserve. Remember, FRS 102, Section 16 applies the Fair Value Accounting Rules in company law and not the Alternative Accounting Rules.

The upshot of this error was that the auditor had formed the incorrect opinion on the financial statements. Profit was materially understated, and the revaluation reserve was materially overstated.

Had the auditor challenged this accounting treatment, it may have been the case that the client would have been willing to change where the credit had been posted. However, had the client not been willing to correct the financial statements, the auditor should have expressed a qualified 'except for' opinion rather than an unmodified opinion.

The real-life scenario above illustrates the importance of a thorough understanding of the applicable financial reporting framework by the auditor. Not having this understanding means that audit risk is significantly increased.

Handling potential modifications to the auditor's opinion

12.10 Having concluded that a modified audit opinion is necessary, the auditor must discuss the issue with management and/or those charged with governance. As I mentioned earlier, a modified audit opinion can have drastic consequences for the business and invariably the audit client will not be happy about this. In some cases, the client may put pressure on the auditor not to express such an opinion.

Issuing a modified audit opinion is a last resort for the auditor and, wherever possible, the auditor will always try and give the client ample opportunity to remedy the matter giving rise to the potential modification. For example, it may be an accounting treatment that the auditor does not agree with and hence the auditor will request that the client corrects the issue to avoid expressing a modified audit opinion.

IMPORTANT POINT

The auditor must not give in to the client, no matter how much pressure is put on the auditor. Even if the client threatens to disengage the auditor, they must stick to their guns and proceed with a modified audit opinion where this is appropriate.

At all times, the auditor is required to comply with the ethical principles of integrity, objectivity, professional competence and due care and professional behaviour. Hence, the auditor cannot issue an unmodified opinion in circumstances where a reasonable third party would conclude that a modified opinion should be issued. This is reckless and will usually result in heavy sanctions being imposed on the audit firm (and the individual). In more serious cases, an auditor can lose their practising certificate and be excluded from membership of their professional body.

REPORTING A MODIFIED AUDIT OPINION

12.11 ISA (UK) 700 *Forming an Opinion and Reporting on Financial Statements* requires the auditor to include a Basis for Opinion paragraph in the auditor's report. Where the auditor has concluded that a modified opinion is necessary, this paragraph is titled according to the nature of the modification. The paragraph must also contain details of the issue giving rise to the modified opinion (including, where possible, quantifications).

ISA (UK) 705 requires the auditor to amend the standard 'Basis for Opinion' heading to 'Basis for Qualified Opinion', 'Basis for Adverse Opinion' or 'Basis for Disclaimer of Opinion' as appropriate.

Sometimes it may be the case that the issue giving rise to a modified audit opinion is disclosure related. For example, it may be the case that the client has not adequately disclosed a material related party transaction and refuses to remedy the issue. Where this is the case, the Basis for Qualified/Adverse/Disclaimer paragraph should explain how the disclosure(s) is/are misstated. Where necessary, the auditor should describe the omitted disclosures so that the user understands the problems.

QUALIFIED 'EXCEPT FOR' OPINION

12.12 As I mentioned earlier in this chapter, the auditor expresses a qualified 'except for' opinion when the matter giving rise to the modification is material but not pervasive. The Opinion paragraph will state that 'except for' the matter, the financial statements give a true and fair view and have otherwise been prepared in accordance with the applicable financial reporting framework. Hence, the auditor is saying that while the matter is material, it only affects a specific element of the financial statements and the remainder of the financial statements are unaffected.

The auditor must describe the reasons for the modification in the Basis for Qualified Opinion paragraph and quantify any monetary amounts where appropriate.

Example 12.2 – Auditor discovers a material issue in the financial statements

Philbin Ltd has prepared its draft financial statements for the year ended 31 March 2024. The draft financial statements show turnover of £22.6m, profit before tax of £4.1m and total assets of £12.3m. The financial statement materiality level is £205,000, being 5% of profit before tax.

12.12 *The Modified Auditor's Opinion*

During the audit, the audit senior discovered office refurbishment costs of £375,000 had been capitalised as fixtures and fittings. The audit senior disagrees with this accounting treatment and has held a discussion with the finance director who said:

> I do not agree that the refurbishment costs should be expensed to profit and loss. They should be capitalised as the board of directors approved that accounting treatment and based the dividend on the profit in the draft accounts.

The audit senior has concluded that the misstatement is material at 9.1% (£0.375 / £4.1m) of profit before tax and is, of course, higher than financial statement materiality of £205,000. As the finance director has refused to correct the issue, the auditor has no alternative but to issue a modified audit opinion as follows:

Qualified opinion

We have audited the financial statements of Philbin Ltd ...

In our opinion, except for the matter described in the Basis for Qualified Opinion section of our report, the accompanying financial statements:

- give a true and fair view of the state of the company's affairs as at 31 March 2024 and of its profit for the year then ended;

- have been properly prepared in accordance with United Kingdom Generally Accepted Accounting Practice; and

- have been prepared in accordance with the requirements of the CA 2006.

Basis for qualified opinion

The company has recognised an amount of £375,000 on the balance sheet as additions to fixtures and fittings which, in our opinion, does not meet the recognition criteria in FRS 102 *The Financial Reporting Standard applicable in the UK and Republic of Ireland*, Section 17 *Property, Plant and Equipment*. The company should have recognised these refurbishment costs in profit and loss for the year ended 31 March 2024 to comply with FRS 102. Accordingly, the company's tangible fixed assets should be reduced by an amount of £375,000 with a corresponding reduction in profit.

We conducted our audit in accordance with International Standards on Auditing (UK) (ISAs (UK)) and applicable law. Our responsibilities under those standards are further described in the Auditor's responsibilities for the audit of the financial statements section of our report. We are independent of the company in accordance with ethical requirements that are relevant to our audit of the financial statements in the UK, including the FRC's Ethical Standard, and we have fulfilled our other ethical responsibilities in accordance with those requirements. We believe that the audit evidence we have obtained is sufficient and appropriate to provide a basis for our qualified opinion.

As noted earlier in the chapter, it is not just material incorrect accounting treatments that can give rise to a qualified 'except for' opinion. Inadequate or missing disclosures that are considered material to the financial statements can also result in the auditor expressing such an opinion (even though the monetary amounts in the financial statements remain unchanged). In these situations, the auditor is required to make the relevant disclosure in their auditor's report, but will still express a qualified 'except for' opinion.

Example 12.3 – Lack of related party disclosures

During the year to 31 March 2024, Bauer Ltd entered into a number of material related party transactions with a company owned and controlled by the wife of the managing director.

The finance director has informed the audit engagement partner that the board have agreed not to include these related party disclosures on the basis that the board consider them to be commercially sensitive.

The auditor must still refer to these material related party disclosures *and* express a qualified 'except for' paragraph as follows:

Qualified opinion

We have audited the financial statements of Bauer Ltd …

In our opinion, except for the matter described in the Basis for Qualified Opinion section of our report, the accompanying financial statements:

- give a true and fair view of the state of the company's affairs as at 31 March 2024 and of its financial performance and cash flows for the year then ended;

- have been properly prepared in accordance with United Kingdom Generally Accepted Accounting Practice; and

- have been prepared in accordance with the requirements of the CA 2006.

Basis for qualified opinion

The company has entered into a number of material related party transactions during the year. The directors have failed to disclose the relationships or amounts of these transactions as required by FRS 102 *The Financial Reporting*

Standard applicable in the UK and Republic of Ireland, Section 33 *Related Party Disclosures*. The company bought goods and services from an entity controlled by the wife of the managing director at a significant discount. The total value of these goods and services was £200,000.

We conducted our audit in accordance with International Standards on Auditing (UK) (ISAs (UK)) and applicable law. Our responsibilities under those standards are further described in the Auditor's responsibilities for the audit of the financial statements section of our report. We are independent of the company in accordance with ethical requirements that are relevant to our audit of the financial statements in the UK, including the FRC's Ethical Standard, and we have fulfilled our other ethical responsibilities in accordance with those requirements. We believe that the audit evidence we have obtained is sufficient and appropriate to provide a basis for our qualified opinion.

In **Example 12.3** above, the monetary amounts in the financial statements are unaffected. It is the fact that management have not disclosed a material related party transaction which has given rise to the modified audit opinion. It is important to emphasise that materiality is not just confined to quantitative issues – the concept of materiality also has qualitative factors as well.

IMPORTANT POINT

A qualified 'except for' opinion could have an impact on other areas of the annual report. For example, if sales are misstated resulting in a qualified 'except for' opinion and the Key Performance Indicators disclosed in the strategic report include sales and gross profit related figures, then the qualified 'except for' opinion could also impact the strategic report.

Auditor appointed after the reporting date

12.13   If the auditor has been appointed after the reporting date, this can result in a modified audit opinion (limitation of scope) where the auditor has been unable to attend the year-end stocktake where stock is material to the financial statements. This is a common issue and so clients need to consider this carefully prior to changing audit firms because it may result in a modified audit opinion if the auditor cannot obtain sufficient appropriate audit evidence concerning the existence, completeness and the condition of stock at the reporting date.

Where an auditor has been unable to obtain sufficient appropriate audit evidence, it is also referred to as a limitation of scope.

It may not be the case that a modified audit opinion is expressed when the auditor does not attend the year-end stock count, if there are alternative audit procedures the auditor can adopt to obtain sufficient appropriate audit evidence concerning the existence, completeness and condition of stock at the reporting date.

Remember, though, that if the auditor does deem a qualified 'except for' opinion appropriate due to non-attendance at the year-end stock count, there will be a subsequent qualified 'except for' opinion in the next year as well because the closing stock figure becomes the opening stock figure in the next year.

ADVERSE OPINION

12.14   As I mentioned earlier in the chapter, an adverse opinion is expressed by the auditor when an issue is both material and pervasive. This means that the financial statements do not give a true and fair view and an adverse opinion essentially warns the user not to place reliance on the financial statements as they are misleading.

An adverse opinion is not only very serious in terms of the damage it can do to a company; but it also sends out a message to the users that management and those charged with governance of the entity are not acting ethically or appropriately.

Example 12.4 – Adverse opinion

Greaves Industries Ltd has prepared its financial statements for the year ended 31 March 2024 on a going concern basis. On 16 May 2024, the bank confirmed that it would not be renewing the entity's borrowing facilities as it had defaulted on its loan, breached its overdraft facility on several occasions and has failed to provide quarterly management accounts as required.

The company has experienced cash flow difficulties during the year as well and entered into a payment arrangement to pay a large sum of additional tax owing following an investigation into the company's affairs by HM Revenue and Customs (HMRC). The company has failed to comply with the payment terms agreed with HMRC and consequently the tax authority has threatened to issue winding up proceedings.

The directors have approached a number of other banks who have refused to help the company but the directors still remain confident they will secure the funding they need to ensure the company remains a going concern.

12.14 *The Modified Auditor's Opinion*

The auditor has concluded that the going concern basis of preparing the financial statements is inappropriate. The directors fundamentally disagree and have refused to change the basis of preparation to that of a basis other than the going concern basis. The reasons cited are they feel this will adversely influence the decision of any potential lender.

In this situation, the auditor must look to the provisions in ISA (UK) 570 *Going Concern*. This ISA (UK) states that when the financial statements have been prepared using the going concern basis of accounting, but the auditor disagrees that this basis is appropriate, the auditor must express an adverse opinion. This is because the effects of the inappropriate use of the going concern basis is both material and pervasive. The adverse opinion is worded as follows:

Adverse opinion

We have audited the financial statements of Greaves Industries Ltd ...

In our opinion, because of the significance of the matter discussed in the Basis for Adverse Opinion section of our report, the financial statements:

- do not give a true and fair view of the state of the company's affairs as at 31 March 2024 and of its loss for the year then ended;

- have not been properly prepared in accordance with United Kingdom Generally Accepted Accounting Practice; and

- have not been prepared in accordance with the requirements of the CA 2006.

Basis for adverse opinion

As explained in note 3 of the financial statements, the financial statements have been prepared on the going concern basis. However, in our opinion, due to the number and significance of the material uncertainties, the company is not a going concern in accordance with FRS 102 *The Financial Reporting Standard applicable in the UK and Republic of Ireland* and therefore the financial statements should not be prepared on the going concern basis.

Following a breach of the company's loan terms and overdraft facility, the company's bank has expressed their unwillingness to support the company and the directors have so far been unable to source financiers to continue to support the business. In addition, the terms of an arrangement to pay with HM Revenue and Customs in respect of additional tax arising following a tax investigation have also not been complied with.

We conducted our audit in accordance with International Standards on Auditing (UK) (ISAs (UK)) and applicable law. Our responsibilities under those standards are further described in the Auditor's responsibilities for the audit of the financial statements section of our report. We are independent of the company in accordance with ethical requirements that are relevant to our audit of the financial statements in the UK, including the FRC's Ethical Standard, and we have fulfilled our other ethical responsibilities in accordance with those requirements. We believe that the audit evidence we have obtained is sufficient and appropriate to provide a basis for our adverse opinion.

Where the auditor includes a Key Audit Matters (KAMs) section in the auditor's report in accordance with ISA (UK) 701 *Communicating Key Audit Matters in the Independent Auditor's Report*, the auditor is still required to include KAMs when the opinion is adverse. The matter giving rise to the adverse opinion is, by nature, a KAM. However, this is not described in detail as part of the KAM section of the auditor's report, and the auditor should refer in the KAM section of the report to the Basis for Adverse Opinion paragraph where the necessary details will be provided.

REAL-LIFE SCENARIO

Entity A Ltd is the manufacturer of chemicals that are used in the production of domestic cleaning products such as bleach, disinfectant and washing-up liquid. The company operates a defined benefit pension scheme for its employees that is closed to forward accrual.

For the year ended 31 December 2018, the company refused to commission a valuation of the defined benefit pension plan for the purposes of FRS 102 *The Financial Reporting Standard applicable in the UK and Republic of Ireland*, Section 28 *Employee Benefits*. The directors were unwilling to pay the costs to the actuarial firm to obtain the relevant information that would allow the accounting input and disclosure information to be produced in the financial statements in respect of this pension plan.

The auditor expressed an adverse opinion on the financial statements for the year ended 31 December 2018. This was on the grounds that not including the accounting input and disclosure information affected the profit and loss account, other comprehensive income, the balance sheet and the related notes to the financial statements. In other words, multiple areas of the financial statements were affected by the entity failing to obtain a valuation of the defined benefit pension plan for financial reporting purposes.

DISCLAIMER OF OPINION

12.15   A disclaimer of opinion is expressed when the auditor is unable to obtain sufficient appropriate audit evidence on which to base an opinion; hence they are 'disclaiming' an opinion. The auditor will also conclude that the possible effects of the issues giving rise to the disclaimer of opinion are both material and pervasive to the financial statements.

IMPORTANT POINT

Technically, a disclaimer of opinion is not an opinion. The auditor is essentially stating that they cannot form an opinion so are not providing one. When the auditor expresses a disclaimer of opinion, some users of the financial statements may incorrectly draw the conclusion that the financial statements have not been audited. To that end, the auditor must include confirmation in their auditor's report that *'the auditor was engaged to audit the financial statements'* rather than stating *'the financial statements have been audited'*.

There are usually two situations that could lead to the auditor disclaiming an audit opinion:

These two situations will result in the auditor expressing a disclaimer of opinion when they conclude that the possible effects are material and pervasive.

ISA (UK) 705 also requires the auditor to disclaim an opinion when there are multiple uncertainties and it is not possible to form an opinion on the financial statements due to the potential interaction of the uncertainties and their possible cumulative effect on the financial statements. This is despite the fact that the auditor may have obtained sufficient appropriate audit evidence concerning each of the individual uncertainties.

In practice, disclaimers of opinion are rare but they do crop up every now and again. When the auditor concludes that a disclaimer of opinion is appropriate in the circumstances, ISA (UK) 705 requires the auditor to:

(a)   State that the auditor does not express an opinion on the financial statements.

(b)   State that, because of the significance of the matter(s) described in the Basis for Disclaimer of Opinion section, the auditor has been unable to obtain sufficient appropriate audit evidence on which they can provide a basis for an audit opinion on the financial statements.

(c)   Amend the statement required by ISA (UK) 700, para 24(b) which indicates that the financial statements have been audited so as to state that the auditor was engaged to audit the financial statements (as I mentioned earlier in this section).

There are also other changes needed to the standard auditor's report when the auditor concludes a disclaimer of opinion is necessary as follows:

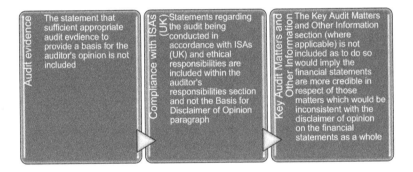

Example 12.5 – Disclaimer of opinion

Ratchford Ltd is a wholly-owned subsidiary of The Naylor Group Ltd and has prepared its financial statements on a going concern basis for the year ended 31 March 2024. Management have prepared the financial statements on a going concern basis on the grounds that the parent (Naylor Ltd) will provide support to the subsidiary. The parent has also expressed their willingness to provide a letter to the subsidiary's auditor confirming this support (often referred to as a 'comfort letter').

The auditor of the subsidiary has discussed the issue with the group auditor who has confirmed that the group has a significant level of overdue debt owed to it and, in the group auditor's opinion, the group, nor the parent, has been able to produce any detailed projections in the form of budgets or forecasts, which demonstrate the group's ability to continue as a going concern. The subsidiary is reliant on additional finance/investment which has not yet been secured.

The auditor of the subsidiary is unable to just rely on the comfort letter from the parent because this is internally generated and is a weak form of audit evidence to support the going concern status of the subsidiary. The auditor must try to obtain sufficient appropriate audit evidence from other sources to corroborate the financial ability of the parent to provide the subsidiary with support. In this example, the auditor has been unable to obtain this evidence.

Based on these facts the auditor has concluded that they are unable to form an opinion as to whether the going concern basis of accounting is appropriate and has expressed a disclaimer of opinion which is illustrated as follows:

Disclaimer of opinion

We were engaged to audit the financial statements of Ratchford Ltd ...

We do not express an opinion on the accompanying financial statements. Because of the significance of the matter described in the Basis for Disclaimer of Opinion section of our report, we have not been able to obtain sufficient appropriate evidence to provide a basis for an audit opinion on these financial statements.

Basis for Disclaimer of Opinion

The audit evidence available to us to confirm the appropriateness of management's use of the going concern basis of accounting was limited because the company is reliant on support from the group. The group has not been able to provide any corroboratory evidence that it is able to continue to trade for the foreseeable future as a going concern.

The group has significant levels of indebtedness and has not provided any financial projections which would indicate that it has the ability to continue to trade as a going concern for the foreseeable future.

As a result, we were unable to determine whether the going concern basis of accounting is appropriate in the company's circumstances.

Auditor's responsibilities for the audit of the financial statements

We conducted our audit in accordance with International Standards on Auditing (UK) and applicable law. Our responsibilities under those standards are further described in the Auditor's responsibilities for the audit of the financial statements section of our report. We are independent of the company in accordance with ethical requirements that are relevant to our audit of the financial statements in the UK, including the FRC's Ethical Standard, and we have fulfilled our other ethical responsibilities in accordance with these requirements.

Our objectives are to obtain reasonable assurance about whether the financial statements as a whole are free from material misstatement, whether due to fraud or error, and to issue an auditor's report that includes our opinion. However, because of the matter described in the Basis for Disclaimer of Opinion section of our report, we were not able to obtain sufficient appropriate evidence to provide a basis for an audit opinion on these financial statements.

Management-imposed limitations

12.16 There are exceptional situations that may present themselves during the course of an audit and management may impose a limitation which causes the auditor to be unable to obtain sufficient appropriate audit evidence. The classic case would be where management refuse to provide the auditor with written representations as required by ISA (UK) 580 *Written Representations*.

A refusal by management to provide written representations means that management are not accepting responsibility for the financial statements they have prepared. This is a serious issue. Management must be requested to remove the limitation and provide the auditor with the required written representations and if management continue to refuse, the auditor should escalate the issue to those charged with governance.

Where the auditor considers that it is not possible to obtain audit evidence from other alternative sources, the opinion is qualified where the management-imposed limitation is material but not pervasive.

However, if the issue is both material and pervasive (which is the case where management refuse to provide written representations required by the auditor), the auditor must not only conclude that a disclaimer of opinion would be necessary, but they must also consider withdrawing from the audit engagement. This is because when management impose a scope limitation on the ability of the auditor to obtain sufficient appropriate audit evidence, this is a serious matter. Indeed, ISA (UK) 705 states that where qualification of the opinion would be inadequate to communicate the gravity of the situation, the auditor must:

(a)   Withdraw from the audit, where practicable and possible under applicable law or regulation.

(b)   If withdrawal from the audit prior to issuing the auditor's report is not practicable or possible, express a disclaimer of opinion on the financial statements.

IMPORTANT POINT

Withdrawing from an audit is the last resort for an auditor. Where the issue is particularly sensitive, the withdrawal will need to be carefully handled. It does allow the auditor to remove themselves from a difficult situation provided they can do so in accordance with legal, regulatory or professional standards.

Where withdrawal is due to a management-imposed limitation of scope, the auditor will need to send a Statement of Circumstances to the shareholders and lodge a copy of this Statement with Companies House. There is strict protocol that must be complied with where this is concerned and I examine this protocol in **Chapter 1**.

GOING CONCERN

12.17   I looked at the concept of going concern in detail in **Chapter 10**. To recap, the specific ISA (UK) that applies is ISA (UK) 570 *Going Concern*. That ISA (UK) also covers the auditor's reporting responsibilities.

To recap on the definition of going concern, FRS 102 defines it as:

An entity is a going concern unless management either intend to liquidate the entity or to cease trading, or has no realistic alternative but to do so.[2]

I examine the concept of going concern in **Chapter 10** as well. The concept of going concern is that the entity will continue in business for the **foreseeable future**. Where the entity is considered to be a going concern, the going concern basis of accounting is applied.

IMPORTANT POINT

In UK and Ireland GAAP, the 'foreseeable future' is a period of at least 12 months from the **date of approval** of the financial statements. Remember, it is not 12 months from the balance sheet date.

---

2 FRS 102 Glossary **going concern**.

Going concern has always been a crucially important concept, but over the last few years has definitely moved up the ranks of importance. Following the COVID-19 pandemic, then the resulting Ukrainian war, high inflation and rising interest rates, going concern is an area in focus by many file reviewers and professional body inspectors, so it is important that a sound understanding of the reporting implications is obtained.

To recap on the auditor's responsibilities, ISA (UK) 570 requires the auditor to:

● Obtain sufficient appropriate audit evidence and conclude as to whether a material uncertainty related to going concern exists.

● Conclude on management's use of the going concern basis of accounting and whether it is appropriate.

● Report on going concern in accordance with ISA (UK) 570.

In **Chapter 11**, I flagged up the issue of reporting going concern in the auditor's report when a material uncertainty exists. To recap, the auditor includes a Material Uncertainty Related to Going Concern which flags the user to the relevant going concern disclosure in the financial statements. Such a paragraph does not, however, impact the auditor's opinion which is still unmodified.

However, there are two situations that may present themselves which will mean the auditor must express a modified opinion in respect of going concern:

● the auditor concludes the entity's use of the going concern basis of accounting is inappropriate; or

● there is inadequate disclosure in the financial statements about a material uncertainty related to going concern.

Going concern basis is inappropriate

12.18   The auditor may conclude that, based on the audit evidence obtained, the entity's use of the going concern basis of accounting is inappropriate in the circumstances. For example, it may be that the bank has confirmed it is unwilling to continue to support the business and management are struggling to find an alternative financier. There could also be an uninsured catastrophe that occurs which means the business is no longer a going concern, but the financial statements have still been prepared on a going concern basis.

When the auditor concludes that the going concern basis is inappropriate, it means that management have used an incorrect basis when preparing the entity's financial statements. This will give rise to a fundamental disagreement between management and the auditor (ie, the auditor does not agree that the entity is a going concern, but management do).

12.18 *The Modified Auditor's Opinion*

If management continue to insist the going concern basis of accounting is correct, the auditor must express an adverse audit opinion. It is not an option for the opinion to be qualified on the basis of material misstatement because using the going concern basis of accounting to prepare then financial statements when it is inappropriate to do so is **automatically** deemed to be material and pervasive. It should also be emphasised that this adverse opinion is expressed even if the client includes disclosures about going concern.

IMPORTANT POINT

FRS 102 *The Financial Reporting Standard applicable in the UK and Republic of Ireland* and other frameworks such as IAS® 1 *Presentation of Financial Statements* refer to going concern. FRS 102, paras 3.8 and 3.9 state:

> When preparing financial statements, the management of an entity using this FRS shall make an assessment of the entity's ability to continue as a **going concern**. An entity is a going concern unless management either intends to liquidate the entity or to cease trading, or has no realistic alternative but to do so. In assessing whether the going concern assumption is appropriate, management takes into account all available information about the future, which is at least, but is not limited to, 12 months from the date when the financial statements are authorised for issue.[3]

> When management is aware, in making its assessment, of **material** uncertainties related to events or conditions that cast significant doubt upon the entity's ability to continue as a going concern, the entity shall disclose those uncertainties. When an entity does not prepare financial statements on a going concern basis, it shall disclose that fact, together with the basis on which it prepared the financial statements and the reason why the entity is not regarded as a going concern.[4]

IAS 1 contains similar requirements to the paragraph cited above.

FRS 102 does not set out the basis that should be used when the entity is not regarded as a going concern. If an entity intends to cease trading, or is close to doing so, management need to select a basis 'other than the going concern basis'. FRS 102 does not set out what this 'other basis' is.

From an auditor's perspective, the fact that the financial statements are not prepared using the usual financial reporting framework does not necessarily

---

3 FRS 102, para 3.8.
4 FRS 102, para 3.9.

mean that the audit opinion should be modified. The auditor may be able to issue an unmodified audit opinion on the financial statements which have been prepared on a basis other than the going concern basis, provided they can obtain sufficient appropriate audit evidence. This is an unusual situation and one which is rarely seen in practice but it is a common misconception that the auditor would have to modify their audit opinion if the client has, or is about to, cease trading or bring the liquidator in.

While an unmodified audit opinion may be appropriate, the auditor would almost certainly have to flag up the issue in an Emphasis of Matter paragraph. Legal advice might also need to be sought because this would present as a high-risk situation.

Inadequate disclosure relating to going concern

12.19   When the auditor concludes that there is a material uncertainty relating to the entity's ability to continue as a going concern, the provisions in ISA (UK) 570 must be carefully considered.

The auditor must assess whether adequate disclosure of a material uncertainty related to going concern has been made in the financial statements. If it has, then the auditor includes a Material Uncertainty Related to Going Concern section in their auditor's report which cross-refers the user to that disclosure and confirms the auditor's opinion is not modified in respect of the uncertainty.

However, if the auditor concludes that the disclosure is either inadequate or missing, this can have implications on the auditor's report if the inadequacy or absent disclosure is not satisfactorily resolved.

In these situations, ISA (UK) 570 requires the auditor to:

(a)   Express a qualified or adverse opinion, as appropriate.

(b)   In the Basis for Qualified (Adverse) Opinion section of the auditor's report, state that a material uncertainty exists which may cast significant doubt upon the entity's ability to continue as a going concern and that the financial statements do not properly disclose this matter.

While the auditor is saying that the financial statements should contain a material uncertainty related to going concern disclosure, but they do not, this still means a qualified or adverse opinion is expressed. Remember, it is not the auditor's job to make the disclosure in the financial statements for the client.

When I looked at disclaimer of opinion in **12.15** above, I mentioned 'multiple uncertainties'. There may be multiple uncertainties relating to going concern, in which case the auditor might conclude that a disclaimer of opinion is warranted.

Deterioration in operating results after the balance sheet date

12.20   When a client's operating results deteriorate after the balance sheet date, management still have a responsibility to consider whether, or not, the going concern basis of accounting remains appropriate. FRS 102, para 32.7B reflects this requirement.

When management decide, after the balance sheet date, to close down an entity's operations, this is a strong indication that the going concern basis of accounting is not appropriate and the financial statements should be prepared on a basis other than the going concern basis.

FRS 102, para 32.7B states:

> If the going concern assumption is no longer appropriate, the effect is so pervasive that this section requires a fundamental change in the basis of accounting, rather than an adjustment to the amounts recognised within the original basis of accounting and therefore the disclosure requirements of paragraph 3.9 apply.[5]

As I mentioned in **12.18** above, FRS 102 does not elaborate as to what the alternative basis should be and in **very rare** situations, the 'break-up' basis of accounting will be applied.

IMPORTANT POINT

The break-up basis of accounting is inconsistent with the requirements of UK and Ireland GAAP. In practice, the basis to be applied when the going concern basis of accounting is not appropriate will not be too dissimilar to that of FRS 102 or FRS 105.

Many accountants are familiar with the concept of the break-up basis. Under this basis, assets are restated to recoverable amount (ie, net realisable value) and long-term liabilities are restated as current, with provisions being made for unavoidable costs under onerous contracts

---

5 FRS 102, para 32.7B.

and the costs of winding the business down. Hence, the accruals concept of accounting becomes secondary because under the break-up basis, the financial statements reflect a forecast of future realisation rather than how the business has performed up to, and its financial position as at, the balance sheet date.

The break-up basis of accounting must only be used in very rare situations because it is not compliant with UK and Ireland GAAP. FRS 102 and FRS 105 normally require the financial statements to reflect the transactions, events and conditions which have arisen up to, and exist as at, the balance sheet date. However, if management determines after the balance sheet date that it intends to liquidate the entity, or to cease trading, or it has no realistic alternative but to do so, it must not prepare those financial statements on a going concern basis.

In this way, what would normally be a non-adjusting event because it occurs after the balance sheet date, becomes an adjusting event if it means the entity is no longer a going concern. This is a necessary exception because the going concern concept is very much a forward-looking concept.

CHAPTER ROUNDUP

● The type of modified opinion expressed by the auditor will depend on whether the matter is material or material and pervasive. The severity of the matter(s) drives the level of modification.

● Modified audit opinions can have detrimental impacts on a business because they are essentially indicating that there is something wrong with the financial statements. This is likely to affect the client's credit-rating, insurance premiums and ability to secure finance.

● The three types of modified opinion are qualified, adverse and disclaimer of opinion.

● The Basis for Opinion paragraph is modified accordingly and will contain details of the issue(s) giving rise to the modified audit opinion.

● An issue is pervasive if it impacts several areas of the financial statements and can relate to the recognition of amounts in the financial statements as well as disclosures.

● Dealing with a situation that gives rise to a modified audit opinion must be done carefully as the discussions are likely to be fraught. At all times, the auditor must ensure they fully comply with ethical requirements.

- A qualified 'except for' opinion is expressed where a matter is material but not pervasive. The auditor is stating that 'except for' the issue(s), the financial statements otherwise give a true and fair view. An adverse opinion states that the financial statements do not give a true and fair view. A disclaimer of opinion is expressed by the auditor when they cannot form a conclusion on the financial statements.

- Management-imposed scope limitations that warrant a disclaimer of opinion (eg, a refusal by management to provide the auditor with written representations) may also result in the auditor withdrawing from the engagement.

- Where management intend to cease trading or liquidate the entity, or have no realistic alternative but to do so and this decision is reached after the balance sheet date, but before the financial statements are authorised for issue, the financial statements must not be prepared on a going concern basis.

PITFALLS TO AVOID

- Forming an incorrect audit opinion on the financial statements (eg, expressing a qualified 'except for' opinion when the opinion should realistically be adverse).

- Using an Emphasis of Matter paragraph as a substitute for modifying the audit opinion.

- Not considering the overlap with subsequent events as something might happen post-year end that gives rise to the entity no longer being a going concern, hence the basis of preparing the year-end financial statements is changed to a basis other than that of the going concern basis.

- Not preparing a modified auditor's report in accordance with the ISAs (UK). For example, not omitting certain headings and wording when disclaiming an audit opinion.

Chapter 13

Group Audits

CHAPTER TOPIC LIST

- Introduction (see **13.1**)
- Objectives of the group auditor (see **13.2**)
- Accepting a group audit (see **13.4**)
- Planning the group audit (see **13.5**)
- Relying on the work of component auditors (see **13.11**)
- Communication with the group auditor (see **13.12**)
- Auditing the consolidation (see **13.13**)
- Evaluating the sufficiency and appropriateness of the audit evidence (see **13.15**)
- Communicating deficiencies in internal control (see **13.17**)
- Expressing an opinion by the component auditor (see **13.18**)
- Communication with those charged with governance of the group (see **13.19**)
- Support letters (see **13.20**)
- International groups (see **13.21**)
- Transnational audits (see **13.22**)
- Documentation (see **13.23**)

INTRODUCTION

13.1   In this chapter I will look at the concept of a group audit. Group audits can be difficult assignments, especially when the group is large and complex. Therefore, it is especially important that a thorough programme of planning is carried out.

Group auditors are required to have a sound understanding of ISA (UK) 600 *Special Considerations – Audits of Group Financial Statements (Including the Work of Component Auditors)*. This ISA (UK) was revised by the Financial Reporting Council (FRC) in September 2022 and the revised edition applies to audits of consolidated financial statements for periods commencing on or after 15 December 2023 (ie, 31 December 2024 year ends or short accounting periods). I will examine the changes reflected in ISA (UK) 600 (Revised) throughout this chapter as relevant.

WHAT ARE WE TRYING TO ACHIEVE?

Group audits can involve several different entities and several different audit firms (especially in the case of a large group audit). The group audit engagement partner is ultimately responsible for the group audit opinion and this carries a lot of responsibility. It is imperative, therefore, that auditors have a sound awareness of the technical aspects applicable to a group audit to make sure it runs smoothly. We also need to make sure that other audit team members (including component auditors) know exactly what is expected of them during the course of the group audit.

In many cases, a group audit can be complex if a number of adjustments are necessary to the components' financial statements. When I refer to a 'component', I'm essentially referring to a subsidiary that has been consolidated in the group accounts. It follows that while the programme of planning for a group audit will be largely similar to that of a standalone entity, other areas must be considered such as group-wide controls as well as the consolidation process itself.

OBJECTIVES OF THE GROUP AUDITOR

13.2   There are two objectives set out in ISA (UK) 600 which are:

(a)   to determine whether to act as auditor of the group financial statements; and

(b)   if acting as auditor of the group financial statements:

   (i)   to communicate clearly with component auditors concerning the scope and timing of their work and their findings; and

   (ii)   to obtain sufficient appropriate audit evidence concerning the financial information of the components as well as the consolidation process. The primary aim here is to express an opinion on whether the group financial statements are prepared, in all material respects, in accordance with the applicable financial reporting framework (eg, FRS 102).

IMPORTANT POINT

It is important to mention that the objectives of the group auditor have changed in ISA (UK) 600 (Revised September 2022). There are four objectives in ISA (UK) 600 (Revised September 2022) which are to:

(a)   in respect of the acceptance and continuance of the group audit engagement, determine whether sufficient appropriate audit evidence can reasonably be expected to be obtained so the group auditor has a basis for forming an opinion on the group financial statements;

(b)   identify and assess the risks of material misstatement of the group financial statements (whether due to fraud or error) and plan and perform further audit procedures that respond to that risk assessment;

(c)   ensure the group auditor is sufficiently involved in the work of the component auditors throughout the group audit. This includes clearly communicating issues relating to the scope and timing of components' work and evaluating the results of that work; and

(d)   evaluate whether sufficient appropriate audit evidence has been obtained from the audit work (including components' audit work) as a basis for forming an opinion on the group financial statements.

The term 'component' is an unusual term and while it is defined in ISA (UK) 600 you can effectively view the term as meaning a subsidiary. For clarity, the term is defined in ISA (UK) 600 (Revised September 2022) as follows:

An entity, business unit, function or business activity, or some combination thereof, determined by the group auditor for purposes of planning and performing audit procedures in a group audit.[1]

This definition is different in the outgoing version of ISA (UK) 600 and hence it is important to understand these subtle differences when an ISA (UK) is revised.

Components and significant components

13.3   We know that a component is usually a subsidiary that is included in the consolidation. In the outgoing ISA (UK) 600, the standard included the term 'significant component' as well. This is a component that has been identified by the group engagement team as being significant to the group or, due to its specific nature or circumstances, is likely to include significant risks of material misstatement in the group financial statements.

---

1 ISA (UK) 600 (Revised September 2022), para 14(b).

13.4 *Group Audits*

ISA (UK) 600 (Revised September 2022) no longer differentiates between a component and a significant component; instead, the ISA (UK) just refers to components.

ACCEPTING A GROUP AUDIT

13.4 **Chapter 4** examines client acceptance in a lot of detail, and it should be emphasised that the same factors that are considered when accepting a standalone client will apply to the acceptance of appointment as group auditor. However, care must be taken to consider relationships and work done with all group companies by the audit firm as well as with any network firm. In other words, the group auditor must consider:

Ethical considerations

Such as whether any threats to independence and objectivity may arise due to accepting appointment as group auditor

Resources

Whether the audit firm has the necessary resources to carry out the group audit (especially if it is a large group with geographically spread subsidiaries including overseas subsidiaries)

The normal pre-acceptance factors will also be considered by the group auditor (eg, anti-money laundering protocol and whether the group audit will fit into the audit firm's risk boundaries). However, there are some additional issues which are specific to groups that the auditor must consider when deciding whether to accept or continue the group engagement:

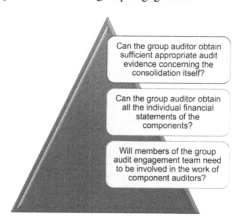

Can the group auditor obtain sufficient appropriate audit evidence concerning the consolidation itself?

Can the group auditor obtain all the individual financial statements of the components?

Will members of the group audit engagement team need to be involved in the work of component auditors?

IMPORTANT POINT

The group auditor will be unable to accept the group audit if they consider that it will not be possible to obtain sufficient appropriate audit evidence. This is because this will constitute a limitation on the scope of the auditor's work which is likely to result in a disclaimer of opinion.

Once all the pre-acceptance factors have been considered, the group auditor can then decide whether to accept the group engagement or not. In most cases, the group auditor can accept the engagement in which case the usual anti-money laundering protocol (identification checks and other appropriate checks) will be carried out, the client will be on-boarded and the engagement letter will be issued.

PLANNING THE GROUP AUDIT

13.5   As with a standalone client audit, a group audit will need to be carefully planned. There are additional factors that must be dealt with at the planning stage (such as planning how the consolidation itself will be audited).

ISA (UK) 600 requires the group audit engagement team to develop an overall group audit strategy and a group audit plan which complies with the requirements of ISA (UK) 300 *Planning an Audit of Financial Statements*. Remember, the responsibility for the entire group audit (including the planning) rests with the group audit engagement partner – none of this responsibility can be delegated to other members of the group audit engagement team or a component auditor.

It must also be emphasised that the planning aspects of a group audit will require more work than the planning for a standalone entity due to additional complexities that are present in a group audit and that must be addressed through specific audit procedures (eg, testing group-wide controls and whether reliance can (or will) be placed on such controls).

REAL-LIFE SCENARIO

Ms T is an audit file reviewer and she was asked to review an audit file for a group which consisted of a parent and three subsidiaries (one subsidiary had been acquired during the year and was wholly owned – the other two were majority owned hence there were non-controlling interests).

During the review, Ms T noted that the planning section of the group audit file simply consisted of a checklist. There were no background notes explaining the composition of the group and relative size of components, dates of acquisition, group-wide controls, systems notes etc. In addition, there was very little work devoted to the consolidation process itself. Ms T also noted that in respect of the mid-year acquisition, the subsidiary's profit and loss account had not been time-apportioned resulting in overstatement of group revenue and expenses.

Ms T also noted that the planning notes simply contained the names of the component auditors. They did not consider any aspects of the component auditors' competence or any group audit pack that had been issued to the components.

This group audit had been recklessly planned. The result of this group audit was that the incorrect audit opinion had been expressed (an unmodified opinion) and misstatements noted related to immaterial depreciation understatements and an incorrect accrual in one of the subsidiaries.

The above real-life scenario highlights the importance of not only a thorough degree of audit planning for a group audit, but also the need to have a sound understanding of ISA (UK) 600. Clearly, in this situation, the group auditor had no awareness of their obligations under ISA (UK) 600 and not only did the outcome of the file review demonstrate a significantly deficient audit had taken place, there were also significant technical knowledge gaps noted in terms of how the accounting treatment for a mid-year acquisition should occur. The conclusion here is that the group auditor is very likely to be 'out of their depth'.

Planning points to consider

13.6   It is very difficult to prescribe a definitive list of group audit planning points to consider – not only in a book like this, but for other products such as a group audit programme. The reason is that every group audit is different (in the same way that every standalone audit is different) and planning should be specifically tailored to the client and reflect the client's individual risk assessment.

I would say that 'typical' planning issues will normally consider the following:

- Determining the size of the group and its components as group audits in the UK will normally (but not always) be confined to medium-sized and large groups.

- Consideration of group-wide internal controls, such as:
  - the group's use of an internal audit function;
  - whether there is adequate segregation of duties (eg, in payroll);
  - the frequency of meetings between the group and component management;
  - risk assessment procedures;
  - whether there is a centralised financial reporting function; and
  - the existence of any group-wide fraud prevention strategies.
- Whether there are any issues that could give rise to a limitation of scope leading to a modified audit opinion.
- Whether components have their own finance function.
- Group accounting issues, such as:
  - the effectiveness of the process of eliminating intra-group transactions and balances;
  - uniformity of accounting policies or the need for adjustments where group entities adopt different accounting policies to those of the parent; and
  - uniformity of accounting reference dates.

Direct controls (which used to be called 'key controls') will also be documented by the group auditor at the planning stage. This documentation can take various guises – for example, flowcharts may be used whereby lines demonstrate the sequence of events and symbols are used to significant controls or documents. Due to the emphasis on **general IT controls** in ISA (UK) 315 *Identifying and Assessing the Risks of Material Misstatement*, the use of flowcharts appears to be on the increase.

For recurring group audits, direct controls may also be documented on the permanent audit file which is then updated on an annual basis.

The group audit engagement team should also consider the results of the previous year's audit and determine whether there were any problems encountered, such as inefficient internal controls or scope limitations. The group audit engagement team should also review the auditor's reports for individual components to establish whether the component auditor has encountered any difficulties during the previous year's audit which could have an impact on the current year.

REAL-LIFE SCENARIO

Mr H is a partner in a six-partner firm. A few years ago, the firm took on a new client which was a group consisting of a parent and two wholly owned subsidiaries. The group structure was not complex and the consolidation itself was prepared by another accountancy firm that did not have an auditing practising certificate. The audit firm was to be the auditor of the group and the two components.

During the early phase of the planning, it became apparent to Mr H that the consolidation itself contained fundamental errors. Notably:

- Share capital in the consolidated balance sheet included the share capital of all individual group members (rather than it being the parent's share capital only).

- A 'consolidation reserve' had been created in the equity section of the consolidated balance sheet which seemingly took all the imbalances due to the incorrect consolidation.

- An intra-group debtor and intra-group creditor had not been eliminated.

- Disclosures in the consolidated financial statements appeared to be incomplete or missing.

- The goodwill arising on acquisition of the subsidiaries had not been amortised.

Mr H contacted the accountancy firm and requested that the consolidation errors be amended so that the group financial statements comply with the requirements of FRS 102 *The Financial Reporting Standard applicable in the UK and Republic of Ireland*. The accountancy firm subsequently amended the financial statements but there was still a 'consolidation reserve' in the equity section of the consolidated balance sheet.

Mr H raised the risk of material misstatement to high – which was a correct response. There would be no point in relying on controls over the consolidation because it was clear that the accountancy firm preparing the consolidated financial statements lacked the required technical competence.

Material errors found during the audit were subsequently corrected by the client and the accountancy firm resigned from acting as group accountant shortly after the group auditor's report was signed.

The above real-life scenario demonstrates the need to have sound technical accounting knowledge of preparing consolidated financial statements. My discussions with Mr H seemed to indicate that the accountancy firm had prepared what they considered 'very draft' group accounts, and the group audit engagement team would then turn them into 'final draft' group accounts – which, of course, is not what the group audit engagement team is there to do.

When a group audit becomes problematic like the one which was dealt with by Mr H above, it can end up being a very time-consuming audit. Clearly, discussions with the client may be needed where additional work is required to correct fundamental errors, revise the risk assessment, reconsider group and component materiality levels, amend the group audit strategy and group audit plan and update the group-wide controls to reflect deficiencies. These problems can also roll-over into next year because if similar problems arise, the audit firm is back at square one. In Mr H's case, the accountancy firm did the right thing and resigned from acting as group accountant because their technical competence fell seriously short of the standards expected. However, other issues may arise with the new accountants that could cause similar problems in the next audit, and this is why it is important to consider difficulties encountered in the prior year.

Risk assessment

13.7   I would not like to even hazard a guess on how many times the phrase 'risk assessment' crops up in this book – but I reckon it's more than three figures. This is because the risk assessment stage is a fundamental stage in the planning of any audit. Risk assessments will essentially determine the level of substantive procedures necessary to execute the group audit.

Looking back to the real-life scenario above (Mr H), it would have been pointless to rely on any controls over the consolidation process because there weren't any to place reliance on. Hence, Mr H correctly devised more additional substantive procedures which aimed to detect misstatements at the financial statement assertion level.

Where the risk of material misstatement is judged to be high, the group auditor will usually place less reliance on internal controls and instead carry out a more detailed substantive approach using test of detail and, where appropriate, substantive analytical procedures. This does, of course, increase the time spent on the audit because it is likely to take longer to perform substantive procedures than it is to rely on the operating effectiveness of group-wide controls.

During the risk assessment process, there are some key factors that must be considered by the group audit engagement team:

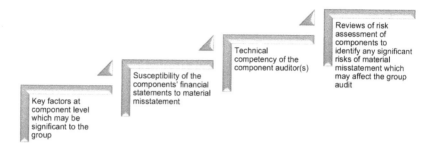

Remember, the group audit engagement team **must** carry out an assessment of the component auditors. This assessment is required to not only determine the technical competence of the component auditors (though this is clearly an important consideration); but it is also necessary in order to determine whether the component auditors understand (and will comply with) ethical requirements which are relevant to the group, including independence requirements. The group auditor must also consider whether the group audit engagement team will be involved in the work of the component auditor to the extent necessary that sufficient appropriate audit evidence will be obtained.

Risk-based approach under ISA (UK) 600 (Revised September 2022)

13.8   ISA (UK) 600 (Revised September 2022) introduces a pro-active risk-based approach to group audits. The focus is on the group audit engagement team's identification and assessment of the risk at the group financial statement level and emphasises the importance of designing and performing appropriate audit procedures to respond to those risks.

This new 'top-down' approach requires the group audit engagement team to perform a group-wide risk assessment. This means there is more focus on identifying and assessing the risks of material misstatement for the group **as a whole**, planning the approach to the group audit and performing audit procedures that respond to the group audit engagement team's risk assessment (wherever these risks are located in the group).

This new risk-based approach in ISA (UK) 600 (Revised September 2022) was brought in by the FRC to align the revised standard with ISA (UK) 315 (Revised). Hence, there is now a greater focus on obtaining sufficient appropriate audit evidence in response to the assessed risks. In response to this new requirement, the three questions that are now the key 'thrust' for group audits are:

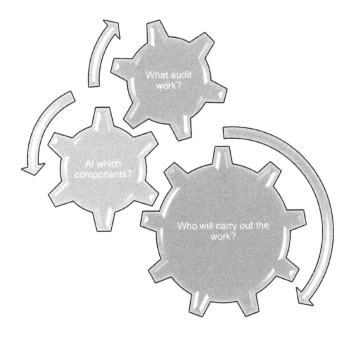

This means there is more focus at the group level on identifying and assessing the risks of material misstatement, planning the approach to the group audit and performing audit procedures at the appropriate locations that respond to the assessed risks.

Materiality

13.9   The group audit engagement team is required to determine a materiality level for the group financial statements as a whole when establishing the overall group audit strategy. In most cases, materiality for a component would be expected to be lower than group materiality. However, this is not always the case. For example, if group materiality is determined as a percentage of profit before tax and there are components that are both profitable and loss-making, it could be possible for the profit of an individual component to be higher than group profit. Where this is the case, the materiality level used for the component would need to be lower than group materiality – but not capped at group materiality. The question then arises as to how much lower, which is, of course, a matter of professional judgement.

Where a specific component has been assessed as being at a higher risk of material misstatement, particular attention must be paid to the areas of that component which are considered to be high risk. In this situation, appropriate substantive procedures will usually be applied to particular classes of transactions and balances which could be materially misstated.

There is overlap with ISA (UK) 320 *Materiality in Planning and Performing an Audit* and I looked in detail at materiality in **Chapter 7**. Remember, materiality is a wholly judgemental issue and there is absolutely no 'one-size-fits-all' where the concept of materiality is concerned (this also applies to performance materiality levels and triviality levels). As with a standalone audit, materiality levels for a group audit must be kept under constant review as they may need to be changed if problems arise (as they did in Mr H's group audit which we looked at earlier on this chapter).

IMPORTANT POINT

If it is concluded that materiality levels must change during the course of the audit, the reasons for changing them must be documented in the audit working papers (both the group audit working papers and, where necessary, the component auditor's working papers). This is so that the group audit engagement partner and any quality management reviewers can understand why materiality levels have changed and what they have changed to.

Materiality levels are driven by the group and component auditor's risk assessment. Factors which may give rise to a higher risk of material misstatement include the following:

- there are poor or inadequate internal controls;

- management take a poor attitude towards good corporate governance;

- the structure of the group is complex and frequently changes;

- there are unusual transactions with related parties;

- there is poor financial monitoring;

- there is a history of significant errors in the financial statements discovered by the group or component auditor;

- the group undertakes business in high-risk areas, such as those on the Financial Action Task Force's 'blacklist';

- accounting policies and accounting reference dates are not coterminous across the group for reasons other than necessity to comply with issues such as legislation;

- tax planning involves the use of aggressive tax avoidance schemes;

- there is a frequent change of auditor;

- there are significant problems in agreeing intra-group balances; and

- there are significant going concern and/or cash flow difficulties among components of the group.

I mentioned above the need to document any changes to materiality levels in the audit working papers. If the group or component auditor discovers an issue such as a significant accounting problem, not only will the materiality levels need to be revised, but the overall audit plan should also be revisited and changed where appropriate to reflect the new facts. As with a change in materiality levels, the reasons for changes to the audit plan must also be adequately documented in the audit working papers.

Materiality in ISA (UK) 600 (Revised September 2022)

13.10   If you look at the definition of 'component performance materiality' in ISA (UK) 600 (Revised September 2022), you will note that it refers to 'aggregation risk'. Aggregation risk is the probability that the aggregate of uncorrected and undetected misstatements exceeds materiality for the financial statements as a whole. ISA (UK) 600 (Revised September 2022), para A19 goes into more detail where this is concerned, specifically stating:

> Aggregation risk exists in all audits of financial statements, but is particularly important to understand and address in a group audit because there is a greater likelihood that audit procedures will be performed on classes of transactions, account balances or disclosures that are disaggregated across components. Generally, aggregation risk increases as the number of components increases at which audit procedures are performed separately, whether by component auditors or other members of the engagement team.[2]

It is my view that aggregation risk can increase for many other reasons (not just due to the number of components). For example, aggregation risk could also increase due to the extent of disaggregation of the financial information across components of the group as well as the nature, frequency and magnitude of misstatements in the component's financial statements. In practice, the auditor would respond to aggregation risk by reducing the component performance materiality to an appropriate level to enable audit procedures to be performed separately on the financial information of components across the group. Hence, I would say ISA (UK) 600, para A19 is somewhat limited in comparison to practical application so the auditor needs to bear this in mind.

---

2 ISA (UK) 600, para A19.

13.11 *Group Audits*

Specifically, though, ISA (UK) 600 (Revised September 2022) requires the group audit planning documentation to include the basis of how component materiality has been determined.

ISA (UK) 600 (Revised September 2022), para 35(a) requires the group auditor to determine component performance materiality for each of the components where audit procedures are performed on financial information that is disaggregated. Keep in mind that component performance materiality is likely to be different for each component. In addition, the component performance materiality for an individual component need not be an arithmetical portion of the group performance materiality. Consequently, the aggregate of component performance materiality amounts may exceed group performance materiality (although individual component performance materiality levels need to be lower than group performance materiality).

It is worth bearing in mind as well that ISA (UK) 600 (Revised September 2022) does not require component performance materiality to be determined for each class of transaction, account balance or disclosure for components at which audit procedures are performed. However, if, in the group's specific circumstances, there are one, or more, classes of transactions, account balances or disclosures for which misstatements of lesser amounts than materiality for the group financial statements as a whole could reasonably be expected to influence the decision-making process of the users, this should be considered by applying the principles in ISA (UK) 320.

RELYING ON THE WORK OF COMPONENT AUDITORS

13.11 It would be unbelievably straightforward if ISA (UK) 600 said that the group audit engagement team can rely on the work of component auditors. Of course, that may happen in a parallel universe, but it does not happen in the one you're reading this book in.

The group audit engagement team cannot rely solely on the work of the component auditors without having to carry out **at least** some evaluation work. This evaluation work must consider the standard of the work carried out by the component auditors, as well as considering the component auditors' compliance with ethical requirements.

IMPORTANT POINT

In ISA (UK) 600 (Revised September 2022), the FRC has included additional wording within para 25(b) to make clear that, in the UK, the group engagement partner must confirm with the component auditor that

---

578

they are able to comply with the FRC's Ethical Standard requirements that are relevant to the engagement.

The FRC's Ethical Standard is discussed in **Chapter 3** of this book. However, the requirements of the Ethical Standard relating to the use of other firms' work in audit engagements are not new and have been in place since 2019. The addition of the relevant paragraphs in ISA (UK) 600 (Revised September 2022) is to provide clarity to auditors.

It is down to the group auditor's professional judgement as to the determination of components at which to perform audit procedures. Matters which may influence the group auditor's decision to carry out additional audit procedures at components may include:

(a)   The nature of events or conditions that could result in a risk of material misstatement, such as:

    (i)   in-year acquisitions or newly formed entities;

    (ii)   subsidiaries in which significant changes have taken place;

    (iii) significant transactions with related parties;

    (iv) significant transactions have arisen that are outside the ordinary course of business; or

    (v)   abnormal fluctuations have been identified through analytical procedures performed at group level.

(b)   The disaggregation of significant transactions, account balances and disclosures in the group financial statements across components, considering the size and nature of assets, liabilities and transactions in the component relative to the group financial statements.

(c)   Whether sufficient appropriate audit evidence is expected to be obtained for all significant classes of transactions, account balances and disclosures in the group financial statements from audit work of identified components.

(d)   The nature and extent of misstatements or control deficiencies that have been noted in components in prior years.

(e)   The nature and extent of common controls across the group and whether the group centralises activities that are relevant to financial reporting.

Some group auditors have, in the past, asked why they cannot rely on the work of component auditors – especially when those component auditors are carrying out audit work to the same ISAs (UK). The reason is that the group audit engagement partner takes full responsibility for the group financial statements. If a component auditor has, for example, carried out deficient audit work that has failed to detect a material misstatement, the group auditor will be responsible as the component will be included in the group financial statements. This can, in practice, result in a negligence claim being brought against the group auditor as well as sanctions from the group auditor's professional body and/or the FRC.

IMPORTANT POINT

The group auditor has a responsibility for ensuring that component auditors:

(a)   are independent and objective in their work and have dealt with any threats to independence and objectivity properly (any such threats must be brought to the attention of the group audit engagement partner as soon as practicably possible);

(b)   the component audit team is professionally competent to carry out the work;

(c)   the group audit team can become involved in the work of the component auditors; and

(d)   the component auditors are regulated by an appropriate body which will ensure compliance with ethical standards and ISAs.

In practice, technical competence is not usually a major issue because audit firms are prohibited from taking on work which they are neither competent to carry out, or do not have adequate resources available to fulfil their obligations under ISAs (UK) and other applicable professional standards. The issues in a group audit which usually cause problems are:

●   the size of the component auditor and the materiality of the component to the group;

●   the availability of audit staff (especially in busy times); and

●   short deadlines imposed by the client.

Where short deadlines are concerned, it is important that the group auditor considers whether adequate audit procedures can be applied in the timescale given. Where the group auditor deems the time given to be insufficient, the group auditor must discuss the issue with management and/or those charged with governance and explain that the group audit must be carried out in compliance with ISAs (UK) and other professional standards and explain that inordinately short deadlines can give rise to a modified audit opinion on the basis of a limitation in audit scope.

In terms of time, it is also important that the group auditor ensures that procedures are implemented which allow adequate time to review the work of the component auditor. The primary purpose of this review is to ensure that sufficient appropriate audit evidence is obtained on which to base the group auditor's opinion.

IMPORTANT POINT

It is not uncommon for the group auditor to have a problem during a compliance visit if they have not reviewed the component auditor's working papers. Excuses such as distance (eg, for an overseas component) or a lack of time are not valid.

Where the group auditor has concerns about the quality of the work carried out by a component auditor, the group audit engagement team should carry out the work or request another component auditor to do it. In practice, this is rare due to rigorous pre-acceptance protocol that must be followed by audit firms prior to agreeing to carry out the group audit.

COMMUNICATION WITH THE GROUP AUDITOR

13.12   Timely communication in a group audit cannot be over-emphasised. If communication is lacking, the wheels are likely to fall off the group audit at a very early stage (and it is often difficult to put those wheels back on again and catch up).

Again, it is not possible to put together a definitive list of issues that must be communicated between the group audit engagement team and the component auditors. From a high-level perspective, such matters will usually include the work that is to be performed and how that work is going to be used as well as the form and content of the component auditor's communication with the group engagement team.

Moving into the more detailed communication maters, the group auditor should communicate the following to the components:

● A request that the component auditor will co-operate with the group engagement team.

● Ethical requirements that apply to the group audit.

● Component materiality, materiality levels for particular classes of transactions, account balances or disclosures and amounts above which misstatements are not to be regarded as clearly trivial to the group financial statements. Performance materiality levels must also be communicated.

- Significant risks of material misstatement of the group financial statements due to fraud or error which are relevant to the work of the component auditor.

- Related parties prepared by group management, together with any other related parties of which the group audit team is aware.

- A request that the component auditor communicates to the group audit team:

    — whether the component auditor has complied with ethical requirements relevant to the group audit; in particular independence issues and professional competence;

    — whether the component auditor has complied with the group engagement team's requirements;

    — identification of the financial information of the component on which the component auditor is reporting;

    — any non-compliance with laws and regulations which could give rise to a material misstatement in the group financial statements;

    — a schedule of uncorrected misstatements in the component auditor's financial statements;

    — indicators of potential management bias;

    — identified significant deficiencies in internal control of the component;

    — other significant matters which the component auditor has communicated, or expects to communicate, to those charged with governance of the component, including actual or suspected fraud;

    — any other matters which may be relevant to the group audit, or which the component auditor wishes to bring to the attention of the group audit engagement team, such as exceptions noted in written representations from management; and

    — the component auditor's overall findings, conclusions or opinion.

ISA (UK) 600 (Revised September 2022) requires the group auditor to consider matters related to communications with component auditors including any related to fraud, related parties or going concern. In addition, the group auditor must also consider matters relevant to the group auditor's conclusion concerning the group audit, including how the group auditor has addressed significant matters that were discussed with components, component management or group management.

AUDITING THE CONSOLIDATION

13.13   At the outset, the group audit engagement team must obtain an understanding of group-wide controls and the consolidation process and assess their effectiveness. This will then lead the group audit engagement team into testing those group-wide controls. In practice, the group audit engagement team will hope that group-wide controls are operating effectively as they can then place reliance on them, which, in turn, reduces the level of substantive procedures (or where substantive procedures alone would be incapable of providing sufficient appropriate audit evidence at the assertion level).

In practice, audit programmes will be used that contain comprehensive procedures that may be applied to appropriately respond to the assessed levels of risk of material misstatement arising from the consolidation process. Care must be taken, however, to ensure that such programmes are not used as a 'tick box' exercise and that procedures are tailored accordingly.

If group-wide controls have been assessed as being poor, this will create a higher risk of material misstatement than if they were operating effectively. To address this risk, the group engagement team would then apply more substantive procedures to the relevant controls and consolidation process rather than placing reliance on those controls.

The appendix to this chapter contains various audit procedures the group engagement team can perform. Again, I stress that these procedures are just illustrative and group audit procedures should be tailored to fit the nature, complexity and individual circumstances of the group audit.

During the audit of the consolidation process, the group auditor may test the operational effectiveness of controls as follows:

Group auditors can, in practice, expect to be provided with a consolidation schedule and this should be reviewed in detail by the group auditor to identify any omissions or misstatements. The auditor must also ensure that procedures are adopted over the audit trail from the component's financial statements into the consolidated financial statements. Reconciliations of various figures can be carried out to test this audit trail and to identify any omissions or errors.

IMPORTANT POINT

Sometimes the client will not have performed the consolidation and will engage the audit firm to prepare it on the client's behalf. In that case, it is essential that the group auditor considers independence issues and implements appropriate safeguards to address the threat to independence. The reasons **why** certain safeguards have been applied should also be documented on the file as well.

Use of analytical procedures

13.14 Remember, there are two **mandatory** stages when analytical procedures must be carried out and one stage where they can be used when it is appropriate:

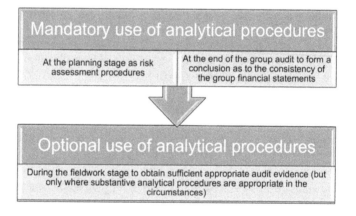

Mandatory use of analytical procedures

| At the planning stage as risk assessment procedures | At the end of the group audit to form a conclusion as to the consistency of the group financial statements |

Optional use of analytical procedures

During the fieldwork stage to obtain sufficient appropriate audit evidence (but only where substantive analytical procedures are appropriate in the circumstances)

EVALUATING THE SUFFICIENCY AND APPROPRIATENESS OF THE AUDIT EVIDENCE

13.15 In addition to evaluating the work of the component auditor, the group engagement team must also evaluate the component auditor's communication, including:

(a) discussing significant matters that have arisen from that evaluation with the component auditor, component management or group management, as appropriate; and

(b) determining whether a review of other relevant parts of the component auditor's audit documentation is required.

ISA (UK) 600 requires the group engagement team to carry out a review of the work performed by the component auditor. Usually, this will be done in conjunction with the group audit engagement partner because it is this person who is ultimately responsible for the auditor's report on the group financial statements.

IMPORTANT POINT

It would be reckless to form an opinion on the group financial statements without reviewing the work of the component auditors because issues may have arisen at individual component level that may impact on the opinion to be expressed in the group financial statements if those issues are not resolved satisfactorily.

Appropriate measures, such as outsourcing audit procedures or performing them directly, must be undertaken by the group engagement team in the event that they cannot secure the agreement to review the work of the component auditor. In practice, this is usually a rare occurrence because full co-operation will normally be granted by the component auditor to the group audit team at the outset.

Sufficiency and appropriateness of the audit evidence obtained

13.16 If the group engagement team conclude that the work of the component auditor is **insufficient** for the purposes of the group audit, the group engagement team must then establish what other audit procedures must be performed in order to resolve the situation. The group engagement team must also decide who is to perform those additional procedures; ie, whether it is the component auditor or whether the group engagement team will do the additional work.

If the group engagement team conclude that the reason for the insufficient and/ or inadequate audit work is due to the component auditor's inability or lack of knowledge, it would always be advisable for the group engagement team to carry out the relevant additional audit procedures. The objective here is to try, wherever possible, to avoid issuing a modified opinion on the group financial statements.

Remember, audit evidence must be sufficient **and** appropriate. To that end, the group engagement team must evaluate whether sufficient appropriate audit evidence has been obtained from the audit procedures performed on the consolidation process as well as the work performed by both the group engagement team and the component auditor.

It is the responsibility of the group engagement partner to evaluate uncorrected misstatements that have been identified during the course of the audit and to assess their impact on the auditor's report. Where there have also been limitations on the scope of the audit work (either the component auditor's work or the group engagement team's work), the group engagement partner must assess whether this inability to obtain sufficient appropriate audit evidence could give rise to a modification of the auditor's opinion on the group financial statements.

COMMUNICATING DEFICIENCIES IN INTERNAL CONTROL

13.17 Where the group engagement team have identified deficiencies in internal control, the group engagement team must determine which deficiencies are to be communicated to group management in accordance with ISA (UK) 260 *Communicating Deficiencies in Internal Control to Those Charged with Governance and Management*. In some instances, group management may wish to be notified of all deficiencies that have been identified during the audit process so that remedial action can be taken. However, in other cases, the auditor may only decide to notify group management of certain deficiencies and hence the group engagement team must consider:

(a) deficiencies in group-wide internal controls that have been identified by the group engagement team;

(b) deficiencies in internal control which the group engagement team have identified in internal controls at components; and

(c) deficiencies in internal control which the component auditors have brought to the attention of the group engagement team.

If fraud has been identified, or information acquired by either component auditors or the group engagement team, indicates that a fraud may exist, the group engagement team must discuss the issue with an appropriate level of group management on a timely basis.

IMPORTANT POINT

Remember, where fraud issues are concerned, the component auditor and group engagement team must exercise caution and ensure they comply fully with their obligations under the anti-money laundering regulations. It would be advisable to seek the advice of a professional body/other expert where such issues are concerned to ensure that a client is not 'tipped off' and that the team does not place themselves in a questionable position.

EXPRESSING AN OPINION BY THE COMPONENT AUDITOR

13.18 Component auditors may be required to express an audit opinion on the financial statements of the component. If this is the case, the group engagement team must ask group management to inform the component's management of any matter which the group engagement team becomes aware which may be significant to the component's financial statements. If group management refuse to discuss these issues with component management, the group engagement team must discuss the matter with those charged with governance. When the matter remains unresolved, the group engagement team, having regard to legal and professional confidentiality considerations, must consider whether it is appropriate to advise the component auditor **not** to issue the auditor's report on the financial statements of the component until the matter is resolved.

COMMUNICATION WITH THOSE CHARGED WITH GOVERNANCE OF THE GROUP

13.19 There are some matters that the group engagement team must communicate to those charged with governance of the group as follows:

(a) A general overview of the work to be performed on the financial information of components.

(b) Instances when the group auditor's review of the component's work raised concerns about the quality of that work and how the group auditor addressed that concern.

(c) Any limitations of scope on the group audit (eg, significant matters related to restrictions on access to people or information).

(d) Fraud, including suspected fraud, involving group management, component management, employees who have a significant role in group-wide controls or others where the fraud has resulted in a material misstatement in the group financial statements.

SUPPORT LETTERS

13.20 Sometimes, the group auditor may conclude it necessary to obtain a 'support letter' (often referred to as a 'comfort letter') from the parent where a subsidiary is perhaps in financial difficulty or there are other material uncertainties related to going concern which have been adequately disclosed. It could also be the case that the **subsidiary** is entirely dependent on the rest of the group (eg, when it is a UK subsidiary acting as a UK sales office and buying only from group companies) and so the subsidiary auditor may seek confirmation of group support.

The key thing the auditor must bear in mind is that such letters will rarely (if ever) serve as sufficient or appropriate audit evidence at group level.

Support letters are relevant for the subsidiary's individual financial statements. In practice, they are not generally useful to the component auditor unless they are received from an individual shareholder(s) and backed up with evidence of the ability of the company or shareholder to provide the relevant support.

REAL-LIFE SCENARIO

Mr P is a former audit file reviewer who has experience in carrying out audit file reviews for professional bodies. He told me that in one file review, the subsidiary had been making recurring losses for a couple of years. The subsidiary's net assets were very low and it was clear this particular subsidiary was in financial difficulty. A going concern disclosure note had been included in the subsidiary's financial statements stating that the directors were of the opinion the subsidiary was a going concern due to continued financial support from the parent.

Mr P stated that during his review of the going concern section of the audit file, the only sources of audit evidence obtained were a written representation from the directors confirming that the going concern basis of accounting was appropriate (in their view) and a letter of support from the parent stating that it was in a position to continue to support the subsidiary.

A review of the parent's financial statements indicated an even worse financial performance and position. The parent itself had been sustaining heavy losses and the balance sheet showed net liabilities (ie, the parent itself was technically insolvent). The parent's own financial statements also had a material uncertainty related to going concern note.

In this situation, obtaining a support letter is absolutely not a substitute for carrying out appropriate going concern procedures. Support letters are internally generated and are therefore designed to **complement** other forms of audit evidence.

The audit opinion on both the subsidiary's individual financial statements and the group financial statements was unmodified and included an Emphasis of Matter paragraph (this was technically correct at the time as it pre-dated the revised ISA (UK) 570 *Going Concern*).

> Mr P stated that based on the information available to him during his file review, he would conclude (as an auditor) that neither the parent nor the subsidiary was a going concern. This would result in either an adverse or a disclaimer of opinion being expressed where the financial statements are prepared on a going concern basis.

In the real-life scenario above, the problem arose because the auditor placed too much reliance on a letter of support. The auditor should not have accepted the support letter as definitive and should have evaluated the **overall** going concern ability of the parent and the subsidiary.

INTERNATIONAL GROUPS

13.21 A group may have a subsidiary (or multiple subsidiaries) located overseas, and this may cause the group auditor some logistical problems (especially where the group auditor is located in the UK). For example:

- the subsidiary may be located in a jurisdiction with no requirement to have an audit under ISAs. This may give rise to the need to request the component auditor to carry out (additional) substantive testing;

- if the financial statements of the subsidiary are prepared in a local currency, they will need to be translated into the currency of the group financial statements, and so additional audit tests will be needed on the consolidation process to ensure they have been translated correctly;

- where the auditor has significant doubts about the standard and quality of the financial information of the overseas subsidiary, or the audit of the subsidiary's financial statements, the group auditor may find it necessary to express a modified opinion; and

- language barriers may have a detrimental impact on the ability of the group auditor to obtain sufficient appropriate audit evidence. The audit engagement team will need to consider engaging a translator where language barriers arise.

In practice, where a parent entity has an overseas subsidiary which is material to the group, the group auditor must take into account all of these factors during the pre-acceptance process when determining whether, or not, to accept the audit engagement.

TRANSNATIONAL AUDITS

13.22 I am only covering transnational audits briefly, in terms of the issues to watch out for, because such audits are not primarily aimed at the target audience of this book.

13.23 *Group Audits*

A 'transnational' audit is an audit which may be relied upon in more than one country. This will cause issues in the UK because there will inevitably be some differences in company law and regulation of the audit profession in different countries. Issues primarily faced by auditors involved in transnational audits include:

Regulation and oversight of auditors

This may take different forms and the quality of the audit work may not be at the same standard as that in the UK giving rise to inconsistent audit practice

Corporate governance requirements

These will be different in other countries and will affect listed groups in the UK which have transnational audits, especially if corporate governance is weak in a specific country

Different accounting requirements

National GAAPs may give rise to different accounting treatments resulting in additional consolidation adjustments (eg, a US-based subsidiary whose parent is based in the UK)

Remember, the above issues are not comprehensive and if you are involved in a transnational audit, there will inevitably be some group- or entity-specific issues that you will need to consider carefully.

DOCUMENTATION

13.23 As you would expect, ISA (UK) 600 (including ISA (UK) 600 (Revised September 2022)) requires extensive documentation to be put onto the audit file. Again, I have to emphasise that I cannot put together a definitive list of documentation that a group audit working papers file should contain because that's just not realistic. However, a file reviewer would expect to see the following in the documentation as a minimum:

- A schedule analysing the components and the type of work performed on the financial information of the components.

- The nature, timing and extent of the group engagement team's involvement in the work carried out by component auditors on components including, where applicable, the group engagement team's review of relevant parts of the component auditors' audit documentation and the conclusions reached thereon.

● Written communications that have taken place between the group engagement team and the component auditors concerning the group engagement team's requirements.

IMPORTANT POINT

The group engagement team must retain sufficient and appropriate audit documentation to enable the competent authority (eg, FRC, ICAEW and ACCA) to review the work of the auditor of the group financial statements.

Not all audit firms are reviewed by the FRC, as the FRC usually confine their inspections to firms that carry out major audits as well as focussing on key industry sectors. However, where the group engagement team is subject to a quality assurance review or investigation concerning the group audit and the FRC are unable to obtain audit documentation of the work carried out by any component auditor from outside of the UK, the FRC can request delivery of any additional documentation of the work performed by that component auditor for the purpose of the group audit. To that end, the group engagement team must deliver such audit documentation and must:

(a)   retain copies of the documentation of the work carried out by the relevant component auditor for the purpose of the group audit; or

(b)   obtain the agreement of the relevant component auditor that the group engagement team can have unrestricted access to such documentation on request; or

(c)   retain documentation to show that the group engagement team has carried out the appropriate procedures in order to gain access to the audit documentation, together with supporting evidence in the event such access is prevented; or

(d)   take any other appropriate action.

ISA (UK) 600 (Revised September 2022) documentation matters

13.24   There are enhanced documentation requirements in ISA (UK) 600 (Revised September 2022) and this includes additional linkage material to the requirements in ISA (UK) 230 *Audit Documentation* as well as the documentation requirements in other ISAs (UK). The revised standard also clarifies what the group auditor may need to document in different situations, including when there are restrictions on access to component auditor audit documentation and cites the following as potential ways of overcoming the problem:

(a) Visiting the location of the component auditor, or meeting with the component auditor outside the location from where the component auditor is based to review the component auditor's audit documentation.

(b) Reviewing the relevant audit documentation remotely (when not prohibited by law or regulation).

(c) Requesting the component auditor prepare and provide a memorandum that addresses the relevant information and holding discussions with the component auditor to discuss the content of the memorandum.

(d) Holding discussions with the component auditor about the procedures performed, the evidence obtained and the conclusions drawn by the component auditor.

ISA (UK) 600 (Revised September 2022) also highlights the importance of the group auditor's review of component auditor audit documentation. The review of component auditor's documentation is directly related to, and influenced by, the group auditor's direction and supervision of the component auditor and the review of their work throughout the group audit.

Remember, ISA (UK) 230 states that the audit documentation must be sufficient to enable an experienced auditor (having no previous connection with the audit) to understand the nature, timing and extent of audit procedures performed, the evidence obtained, and the conclusions reached in respect of significant matters arising during the group audit.

The linkage to ISA (UK) 230 requires the following to be included in the audit documentation **as a minimum**:

(a) Significant matters related to restrictions on access to people or information within the group that were considered prior to accepting or continuing the engagement, or that arose subsequent to acceptance or continuance and how such matters were addressed.

(b) The basis for the group auditor's determination of components for the purposes of planning and performing the group audit.

(c) The basis for the determination of component performance materiality and the threshold for communicating misstatements in the component financial information to the group auditor.

(d) The basis for the group auditor's determination that component auditors have the appropriate competence and capabilities, including sufficient time, to perform the assigned audit procedures at the components.

(e) Key elements of the understanding of the group's system of internal control.

(f) The nature, timing and extent of the group auditor's direction and supervision of component auditors and the review of their work, including, as applicable, the group auditor's review of additional component auditor audit documentation.

(g) Matters related to communications with component auditors, including:

    (i) matters, if any, related to fraud, related parties or going concern; and

    (ii) matters relevant to the group auditor's conclusion concerning the group audit, including how the group auditor has addressed significant matters discussed with component auditors, component management or group management.

(h) The group auditor's evaluation of, and response to, findings or conclusions of the component auditors concerning matters that could have a material effect on the group financial statements.

IMPORTANT POINT

The FRC and professional bodies have also emphasised the need for the group auditor's documentation to include details concerning the nature, timing and extent of the work performed by the component auditor, including, where applicable, the group auditor's review of relevant parts of the component auditor's audit documentation, with a specific UK addition for this. They have also included specific requirements concerning the need for UK auditor documentation to be sufficient to enable a competent authority to review the work of the auditor of the group financial statements, along with further provisions where the group auditor is subject to a quality assurance review or an investigation concerning the group audit.

CHAPTER ROUNDUP

- Group audits can be very complex assignments and therefore a sound understanding of the provisions in ISA (UK) 600 and ISA (UK) 600 (Revised September 2022), the latter which effectively applies mandatorily from December 2024 year ends and short accounting periods, is required.

- The objectives of the group auditor have become more refined in ISA (UK) 600 (Revised September 2022).

- While many of the normal pre-acceptance procedures that would apply to a standalone audit equally apply to a group audit, there are additional considerations that must be taken into account prior to accepting a new engagement or continuing an existing group engagement.

- It is vital to thoroughly plan a group audit in pretty much the same way as a standalone entity audit, but there will be additional considerations such as group-wide internal controls and the consolidation process.

- Risk assessment procedures must be applied **across the group** by the group auditor, including reviewing component auditors' risk assessments for the individual components that are included in the consolidation.

- There is a new risk-based approach required under ISA (UK) 600 (Revised September 2022) which requires the auditor to consider what audit work is necessary, where this audit work is necessary and who will carry out the work.

- Complete reliance on component auditors' audit work cannot happen. The group auditor must carry out certain procedures to ensure the group auditor has a sound basis for the group audit opinion.

- Timely communication in a group audit is critical to avoid any misunderstanding or inappropriate/ineffective audit procedures being carried out.

- There are some 'typical' audit procedures that can be carried out over the consolidation process itself, but the auditor must consider the operating effectiveness of group-wide controls over the consolidation as there are many pitfalls that exist where a consolidation (especially a complex one) is concerned.

- The group auditor must evaluate the sufficiency and appropriateness of the audit evidence obtained in both the group audit and the component audit(s).

- The group auditor must communicate deficiencies in internal control to an appropriate level of group management or those charged with governance.

- In rare cases, the group audit engagement team may advise the component auditor to withhold expressing an opinion on a component's financial statements until certain matters are resolved.

- There are some matters the group auditor is required to communicate to those charged with governance as a minimum.

- Support letters must serve to complement other forms of audit evidence only and cannot be relied upon on their own as they are insufficient audit evidence and could give rise to an incorrect opinion being expressed on the group or component's financial statements.

- There are some specific issues that must be considered where international groups and transnational audits are concerned, particularly in respect of jurisdiction-specific matters.

- There are extensive documentation requirements for group audits and these have been extended in ISA (UK) 600 (Revised September 2022).

PITFALLS TO AVOID

- Placing too much reliance on component auditors' work and failing to carry out adequate procedures over their work (including evaluations of their technical competence) and failing to review component auditors' work.

- Using substantive analytical procedures inappropriately.

- Failing to understand the mechanics of a consolidation, thereby having an inability to detect errors in the consolidation (eg, failing to eliminate certain intra-group transactions and balances or failing to spot consolidated share capital in the group balance sheet).

- Carrying out the consolidation on behalf of a client without considering independence threats and appropriate safeguards.

- Failing to document changes to materiality levels, including performance materiality levels and resulting changes to the group audit strategy/audit plan.

- Failing to carry out a thorough programme of planning which essentially means the group audit engagement team 'goes in blind'.

- Omitting the minimum documentation that would be expected to be on file for a group audit.

- Placing too much reliance on written representations or support letters giving rise to increased audit risk (ie, the risk the group audit engagement partner forms an incorrect opinion on the group financial statements).

APPENDIX: AUDIT PROCEDURES ON GROUP FINANCIAL STATEMENTS

Typical procedures the auditor will perform at group level include the following:

- Obtain or prepare reconciliations of intra-group transactions and balances and ensure these have been appropriately eliminated in the group financial statements. Such transactions will often include:

  — intra-group sales and purchases, debtors and creditors;

  — fixed asset transfers;

- — interest charges and interest income and associated loan debtors and creditors;

- — management recharges; and

- — unrealised profits in stock.

- Obtain or prepare reconciliations of:

- — non-controlling interests;

- — goodwill arising on consolidation;

- — group tax including deferred tax;

- — reserves movements for the current accounting period; and

- — intra-group balances at the balance sheet date.

These reconciliations should be agreed to the group financial statements to ensure no material misstatement has arisen during the consolidation process.

Intra-group balances and transactions

Analytical procedures which may be carried out include:

- Reviewing the number and size of intra-group balances, comparing these to the prior year and investigating any significant variations. The group auditor can also use their knowledge and understanding of the group to assess current year expectations.

- If management charges have been levied across the group, compare the value of these in the current year to the prior year or against the auditor's knowledge of the group and investigate any significant fluctuations.

Audit procedures over the consolidation process

Audit procedures over the consolidation process may include the following:

- Where unrealised profits exist (eg, in stock), assess the values against prior years and/or the auditor's knowledge and expectations and investigate any significant variations.

- Perform a proof-in-total test on the amortisation[3] charge for goodwill and identify any misstatement between the auditor's **expected** charge

---

3 Amortisation is mandatory for goodwill under FRS 102, but not for group financial statements prepared under IFRS® Accounting Standards. IFRS Accounting Standards require goodwill to be tested annually for impairment.

and the **actual** charge per the group financial statements. In addition, consider whether the amortisation rate is reasonable and whether there is any indication of impairment.

- Review the level of non-controlling interest against expectations.

Substantive procedures on the group financial statements

The group engagement team must carry out substantive procedures which aim to detect material misstatement. Substantive procedures must be increased where the auditor concludes that the control environment is weak, or where the auditor discovers issues which give rise to either fraud risk factors or material misstatement.

Substantive procedures may include the following:

- Obtain intra-group balances (trade and sundry debtors and/or trade and sundry creditors) and agree these to the individual sales and purchase ledgers.

- If the group has intra-group loans among subsidiaries, agree these to any source documentation (eg, loan terms or agreements) and agree a sample of transactions.

- Obtain direct confirmation from group members concerning any intra-group balances; whether these arise from direct trading or from loan relationships.

- If considered appropriate, contact the component auditor directly and ask for confirmation of balances from components and discuss their knowledge of related party transactions to identify any undisclosed related parties.

- Where intra-group loans have been entered into, ensure that amounts included in the calculation of the closing balance comply with the financial reporting framework (eg, use of market rates for off-market rate loans, or if loan terms do not exist, that the loan is treated as current due to it being repayable on demand).

- Ensure that no netting-off has taken place between intra-group debtors and creditors.

- Where group balances have been outstanding for long periods of time, assess recoverability.

- Inquire of management of any security pledged for intra-group loans and review any associated disclosures in the financial statements for adequacy.

- If management charges are incurred, agree the terms of these and determine whether they are concluded under normal market conditions (ie, on an arm's length basis).

- Where there are any loss-making subsidiaries in the group, consider the carrying amount of the subsidiary in the parent's individual financial statements (cost of investment and any debtor balances) as the fact they are making losses may indicate the need for an impairment write-down.

- Where a subsidiary is loss-making, consider the need for a 'support letter'.

- For loss-making subsidiaries, ensure any support granted from a third party (eg, the parent) is realistic and that the supporter can provide the necessary support to enable the loss-making subsidiary to be regarded as a going concern.

- Review fair value adjustments carried out at the date of acquisition (eg, in respect of property, plant and equipment) and ensure that these have been correctly calculated and agree the fair values to supporting documentation.

Obtaining sufficient appropriate audit evidence

Depending on the size and complexity of the group, the group engagement team can carry out additional procedures to obtain sufficient appropriate audit evidence as follows:

- For any subsidiaries disposed of during the year, recalculate the profit and loss on disposal and agree to the financial statements. Agree disposal proceeds to supporting documentation and the accounting records (eg, cash book and an **original** bank statement) and ensure any related goodwill is removed.

- For acquisitions of further ownership interest in **existing** subsidiaries, ensure that such transactions are accounted for as transactions among equity holders (ie, the value of non-controlling interest is reduced and the parent's equity increased). No adjustment to goodwill is made for additional ownership interests where control had already been obtained.

- For disposals of interests where the parent **retains** control following the disposal, ensure the transaction is accounted for as a transaction among equity holders (ie, the value of non-controlling interest is increased and the parent's equity decreased). No gain or loss is included in group profit or loss.

- Reviewing questionnaires (internal control questionnaires: which contain a list of controls given to the client to say whether, or not, those controls are in place; or internal control evaluation questionnaires which ask the client what controls they have in place for a given control objective) and consider whether the responses give rise to potential risks of material misstatement at group level.

• Select a sample of subsidiaries' individual financial statements and review these against budgeted information for that particular subsidiary. Inquire of management and investigate any significant variations.

• Where there have been any deviations from group accounting policies, enquire as to the reasons and assess if this provides evidence of potential material misstatement.

• Obtain details of the group structure at the balance sheet date and consider whether all components have been consolidated. For any subsidiaries not included in the consolidation, inquire of management as to the reasons for not consolidating them and confirm this is acceptable (note, subsidiaries can **only** be excluded from consolidation if they meet the exceptions/ exemptions available in company law or accounting standards; or if they are immaterial to the group in combination as well as in isolation).

• Where individual components' financial statements are prepared on a different basis than the group (eg, different accounting reference dates and different accounting policies), ensure adequate consolidation adjustments have been made in the group financial statements.

• Obtain the working papers file for all components and ensure that the work is done in accordance with instructions from the group auditor and sufficient appropriate audit evidence has been obtained on which the auditor's opinion can be based.

• Ensure that all components in the group financial statements are being provided with an unmodified opinion. If this is not the case, assess the impact this will have on the group auditor's opinion in the group financial statements.

• Obtain the consolidation schedule and cast the schedule to confirm mathematical accuracy.

• Agree all eliminating journals and reconciliations in respect of intra-group trading and balances to ensure all intra-group items are eliminated from the group accounts. This will involve obtaining the consolidation schedule and agreeing the elimination process has been carried out correctly.

• Ensure the completeness and accuracy of current and deferred tax on consolidation adjustments is correct.

• Where contingent consideration has been discounted, ensure the rate used is appropriate.

- In respect of due diligence work for in-year acquisitions, assess the competency of those performing the due diligence work.

- Obtain written representations from the group that the consolidation process is complete and all applicable subsidiaries have been included in the consolidation.

- Perform subsequent events procedures to identify events at those components which occur between the balance sheet date and the date of the auditor's report on the group financial statements which may require adjustment or disclosure in the group financial statements. **This may necessitate extending the work done on the parent's own or subsidiaries' audit files, especially if there is a time lag between the signing off of the parent or subsidiaries' own auditor's reports and that of the group's.**

- Ensure the documentation in the group audit working papers file includes an analysis of components and the type of work performed on the financial information of those components, together with:

  — the nature, timing and extent of the group engagement team's involvement in the work performed by the component auditors; and

  — the group engagement team's review of relevant parts of the component auditors' audit documentation and conclusions.

- Ensure the group audit file contains documentation outlining the communications between the group engagement team and the component auditors concerning the group engagement team's requirements.

Chapter 14

Quality Management

CHAPTER TOPIC LIST

- Introduction (see **14.1**)
- Monitoring audit quality (see **14.2**)
- ISQM (UK) 1 (see **14.3**)
- ISQM (UK) 2 (see **14.14**)
- Quality management at the engagement level (see **14.20**)
- When the system of quality management fails (see **14.25**)

INTRODUCTION

14.1   The importance of a rigorous programme of quality management cannot be over-emphasised. When I refer to 'quality management' I am referring to two aspects – quality management at the firm level and quality management at the individual engagement level.

Recent high-profile corporate collapses have resulted in quality management being the focus of regulators. As I have mentioned in previous chapters, auditing is a regulated profession and regulators are keen to ensure that high standards of audit work are carried out. Where a regulator or a professional body find that a firm is falling short of the mark, sanctions can be imposed on the firm which may range from a follow-up visit to ensure that recommendations have been implemented to more serious sanctions such as expulsion from membership of a professional body and withdrawal of the individual's or firm's auditing practising certificate.

WHAT ARE WE TRYING TO ACHIEVE?

In this chapter, quality management is the focus. It looks at how firms can achieve high-quality audit work and the standards that have been issued by the Financial Reporting Council (FRC) to achieve this. It also looks at how the scalability provisions of the standards can be applied to ensure that a firm's system of quality management is proportionate to its size, nature, complexity and client base.

In this chapter, I will focus on three standards that are devoted to quality management:

- ISQM (UK) 1 *Quality Management for Firms that Perform Audits or Reviews of Financial Statements, or Other Assurance or Related Services Engagements.*

- ISQM (UK) 2 *Engagement Quality Reviews.*

- ISA (UK) 220 *Quality Management for an Audit of Financial Statements.*

At the outset it is important to understand how these standards work because while the focus of them all is on quality management, they do interact in different ways:

Putting this together in a table will enable an understanding of the more detailed aspects of the standards' interaction:

ISQM (UK)1	ISQM (UK) 2	ISA (UK) 220 (Revised July 2021)
ISQM (UK) 1 requires the firm to design, implement and operate a system of quality management to manage the quality of engagements carried out by the firm. The system of quality management creates an environment which enables and supports engagement teams in performing quality engagements.	Engagement quality reviews form part of the firm's system of quality management. ISQM (UK) 2 builds on ISQM (UK) 1 by including specific requirements for: • the appointment and eligibility of the engagement quality reviewer; • the performance of the engagement quality review; and • the documentation of the engagement quality review.	ISA (UK) 220 deals with the responsibilities of the auditor concerning quality management at the engagement level, and the related responsibilities of the engagement partner.

All audit firms are required to have a sound system of quality management in place. While this may seem obvious to many people, it is surprising just how many things can go wrong on an audit, resulting in professional bodies and regulators taking further action against the firm. In a lot of cases this is down to quality management processes (or a lack thereof). A poor system of quality management results in deficient audit work which then results in high audit risk (the risk that the auditor forms an incorrect opinion on the financial statements).

MONITORING AUDIT QUALITY

14.2   Audit quality is monitored by professional bodies and by the Financial Reporting Council (FRC). The FRC's inspections are generally confined to large public interest entities; whereas private entity audits are monitored by audit firms' professional bodies.

In the last few years there have been several high-profile corporate collapses which have resulted in investigations being carried out by the FRC. At the time of writing, the most recent high-profile case was that of Carillion.

REAL-LIFE SCENARIO

On 12 October 2023, the FRC announced that they had issued sanctions against KPMG LLP, KPMG Audit PLC and two former partners. These sanctions were in relation to the audit of Carillion PLC ('Carillion'), a company which collapsed and sent shock waves through the business community.

Carillion was a multinational construction and facilities management company based in Wolverhampton, in the UK. Over the years the company was very successful, and its logo was often seen hanging at the front of large construction sites. The company was not very old, despite its success, having been founded in 1999, so in total lasted some 18 years before its demise in January 2018.

The company's demise caused significant cost to not only the taxpayer, but also to investors, pension holders and employees. The FRC imposed record fines on KPMG due to significant failings in the audit work carried out on Carillion – a problem that seems to keep cropping up time and time again of late.

KPMG were the auditors of Carillion and its group companies for the financial years 2014, 2015 and 2016. In each of these years, KPMG expressed an unmodified (unqualified) audit opinion on those financial statements stating that the financial statements gave a true and fair view of the state of Carillion's affairs. KPMG's auditor's report for the financial year 2016 was dated 1 March 2017 and in July and September 2017, Carillion announced expected provisions totalling £1.045 billion. These losses primarily arose from expected losses on a number of its construction contracts and there was a goodwill impairment charge of £134 million. This was effectively the start of some colossal problems that would eventually lead to the collapse of the company.

The FRC stated that their investigation was '… exceptionally complex and required the analysis of a very substantial volume of information and documents.' During the investigation, the FRC noted an '… unusually large number of breaches of Relevant Requirements.'

In their investigation, the FRC concluded that the breaches found contributed to Carillion's eventual demise. The company was not subject to rigorous, comprehensive and reliable audits and in the 2016 audit, the work on going concern and Carillion's financial position was deemed to be 'seriously deficient'. Both KPMG and the audit partner, Mr Peter Meehan, failed to respond to numerous indicators that the company's core operations had become loss-making and that it was reliant on short-term and unsustainable measures to support its cash flow.

Other deficiencies in the audit work included:

- A failure to gather sufficient appropriate audit evidence to enable a conclusion to be formed that the financial statements gave a true and fair view.

- A failure to consider (adequately or at all) the implications for the audit evidence suggesting that Carillion's accounting may have been incorrect or unreliable.

- A failure to conduct its audit work with a suitable degree of professional scepticism.

- A failure to challenge management's judgements and estimates, even when those judgements and estimates appeared unreasonable and/or appeared to be inconsistent with accounting standards and might have suggested management bias.

- Other breaches were found in respect of Carillion's reported debt and its status as a going concern in 2016, including consideration of Carillion's use of a supply chain finance facility.

- A number of other discrete areas were found to contain deficiencies, such as in the 2016 pension liability and the testing for goodwill impairment.

During the investigation, it became apparent that Carillion was an important client for both KPMG and key members of the audit engagement team for the years in which the firm carried out the audit. This created an ethical threat to the firm's and the team's independence and objectivity. Such threats can result in the audit engagement team 'turning a blind eye' to transactions or events which may need further challenge or scrutiny. The FRC concluded that in a number of instances, both Mr Meehan and other members of the audit engagement team did not adopt a rigorous and robust approach. They simply accepted the information concerning the financial statements that was presented to them and which suited Carillion's management.

The FRC also found that in the 2016 audit, Mr Meehan and KPMG failed to ensure that the audit engagement was adequately managed and supervised. For example, audit procedures in a number of areas were not completed until more than six weeks **after** (yes, after!) the date the auditor's report had been signed. Records of the preparation and review of working papers were not only deemed to be unreliable, but, in some cases, misleading. This meant that Mr Meehan did not have a suitable basis to be satisfied that the audit opinion provided in the 2016 audit was, in fact, appropriate.

Issues in the 2013 audit

And then it goes on…

Another audit engagement partner, Darren Turner, was responsible for the audit of Carillion for the financial year ended 2013.

The FRC carried out a review of the audit work performed on the 2013 financial statements, in particular in respect of transactions entered into by Carillion in 2013 that involved changing its provider of outsourced IT services and business process services.

At the same time as finalising the contracts for those services, Carillion finalised other agreements with the same counterparty that involved the assignment of certain intellectual property rights in exchange for a significant sum plus 'exit fees' payable to the former outsourcing provider. These transactions were treated as being independent of each other in Carillion's financial statements, contributing to a significant increase in Carillion's reported profit for 2013.

The FRC noted that a key failing by KPMG and Mr Turner was that they failed to obtain sufficient appropriate audit evidence concerning the accounting treatment of these transactions (i.e. whether the accounting was correct). Both KPMG and Mr Turner:

- did not approach the audit of these transactions with a sufficient level of professional scepticism (i.e. challenging management's accounting treatment);

- failed to consider and respond to the risk of fraud;

- failed to obtain sufficient appropriate audit evidence concerning the accounting treatment adopted; and

- failed to identify that the disclosures in the 2013 financial statements about these transactions may be misleading.

It should be noted that the FRC also concluded that the breaches by KPMG Audit PLC and Mr Turner were not deemed to be intentional, dishonest, deliberate or reckless.

Sanctions

The FRC had two lots of sanctions to arrive at: one in respect of KPMG LLP and Mr Meehan and the second in respect of KPMG Audit PLC and Mr Turner.

Decision 1: KPMG LLP

The FRC imposed the following sanctions on KPMG LLP:

- A financial sanction of £26.5 million. This was reduced by 30% to £18.550 million on the grounds of the firm's co-operation and admissions. The firm also received a severe reprimand.

• A declaration that the auditor's reports signed on behalf of the firm did not satisfy the Relevant Requirements.

• An order requiring KPMG LLP to take remedial action to prevent these breaches reoccurring. This includes evaluating and reporting as to whether the measures taken by the firm since 2017 are sufficient in this respect.

Decision 1: Mr Meehan

The FRC imposed the following sanctions on Mr Meehan:

• A financial sanction of £500,000. This was reduced by 30% to £350,000 to reflect Mr Meehan's co-operation and admissions.

• A severe reprimand.

• Exclusion from membership of the ICAEW for ten years which runs concurrently with the period of exclusion already imposed in other proceedings.

Decision 2: KMPG Audit PLC

The FRC imposed the following sanctions on KPMG Audit PLC:

• A financial sanction of £3.5 million. This was reduced by 20% to £2.450 million on the grounds of the firm's co-operation and admissions.

• A severe reprimand.

• A declaration that the auditor's report signed on behalf of KPMG did not satisfy the Relevant Requirements.

Decision 2: Mr Turner

The FRC imposed the following sanctions on Mr Turner:

• A financial sanction of £100,000. This was reduced by 30% to £70,000 on the grounds of Mr Turner's co-operation and admissions.

• A severe reprimand.

It seems that most of the failures in the Carillion audits can be attributed to a serious lack of professional scepticism and management challenge. There also appeared to be an overlap of a self-interest threat as well that clouded the judgement of the audit team given that Carillion was such an important client to the firm and the team.

REAL-LIFE SCENARIO

Patisserie Valerie was another high-profile case that sent shockwaves through the business community. In their report, the FRC found that the audits for three consecutive years were deficient in relation to four areas:

- revenue;

- cash;

- journals; and

- fixed assets.

The FRC reported serious lapses in professional judgement, a failure to exercise professional scepticism, a failure to obtain sufficient appropriate audit evidence and/or prepare sufficient audit documentation. Consequently, the auditor, Grant Thornton, received the following sanctions:

- A £4 million fine which was reduced to £2.34 million for admissions and early settlement.

- A severe reprimand.

- A requirement for the firm to carry out root-cause analysis and to report their findings to the FRC.

- A review of the audit firm's culture.

- Additional monitoring of audit work.

In addition, the audit engagement partner received a fine of £150,000 (reduced to £87,750 for admissions and early settlement) and a three-year ban from carrying out audit work.

REAL-LIFE SCENARIOS

Other cases which highlight issues relating to quality management heard by the FRC are as follows:

Babcock International Group PLC (FY 2018 PwC)

- Per the FRC: '... numerous, serious breaches were admitted by the Respondents. Breaches were identified in respect of every audit investigated.'

- There was a general reluctance of the auditors to challenge management and a failure to review key documentations such as large contracts for revenue. One large contract was written in French but the audit engagement team did not have the document translated (nor was there anyone on the audit engagement team that was fluent in French).

- An aggravating factor was noted to be the sanctions imposed on PwC in relation to four other matters since 2019. However, it was noted that the levels of co-operation provided in some areas was 'exceptional' although they were criticised in other areas for errors and delays in the production of documents.

Luceco PLC (FY 2016 KPMG)

- The financial statements for the 2016 financial year included multiple material misstatements in relation to inventory and inter-company transactions and balances which resulted in a restatement in the 2017 financial year.

- There were failures relating to the design and performance of audit procedures, failures to adequately review and critically assess the audit evidence obtained, a failure to document the audit work and a failure to apply professional scepticism.

- Inventory had previously been identified by the audit team as requiring particular focus due to errors in the prior year.

Theworks.co.uk PLC (FY 202 KPMG)

- In respect of the existence of inventory, there was a failure to plan and perform and audit the inventory with a degree of professional scepticism. There was also a failure to prepare sufficient audit documentation and to design and perform audit procedures to obtain sufficient appropriate audit evidence, most notably:

  — the audit engagement team failed to respond to variances identified in stock counts and omitted these from the audit file so that the file provided a false degree of assurance;

  — the team used substantive procedures on the same sample as the stock counts but with the variances removed. The selection process was described on the file as 'random';

  — there was a failure to perform appropriate roll-forward and roll-back procedures; and

  — the audit engagement team accepted a third-party confirmation of inventory via the group's management rather than directly from the third-party itself.

Eddie Stobart Logistics PLC (FY 2018 PwC)

- Numerous failings were identified in respect of property transactions, notably:

  — a failure to identify the related revenue stream as a significant risk;

  — a failure by the audit engagement team to carry out a formal consultation on technical aspects of the accounting for these transactions;

  — a failure by the audit engagement team to challenge management's selection of accounting policies;

  — a lack of professional judgement in the audit team's work over these transactions; and

  — inadequate disclosures in the financial statements concerning property income which gave rise to the true and fair aspect being challenged (notably the financial statements would have shown a loss without them).

- On-boarding procedures in the first year of accepting the audit engagement were weak.

- Work over dilapidation provisions had not been carried out nor had the audit engagement team considered if these dilapidation provisions were, in fact, needed.

- A lack of work on the accounting applied to a subsidiary and a failure to consider if control existed.

- A failure to spot property lease accruals which did not account for planned rental increases.

Eddie Stobart Logistics PLC (FY 2017 KPMG)

- Failings were noted around property transactions (similar to those noted in the same case above).

- Work over dilapidation provisions had not been carried out nor had the audit engagement team considered if these dilapidation provisions were, in fact, needed.

- A lack of professional scepticism was noted over unsigned/undated lease documents.

A lack of work on the accounting applied to a subsidiary and a failure to consider if control existed.

When you think about the issues raised in these two cases, you can see that if quality management was sound, some of them are unlikely to have occurred. You can also appreciate why the FRC and professional bodies feel it necessary to instigate measures that increase the credibility of the auditing profession and restore trust in audit (something which is going to be a very slow process, I suspect).

ISQM (UK) 1

14.3 In July 2021, the FRC issued ISQM (UK) 1 which required a firm's system of quality management to be designed and implemented by 15 December 2022. An evaluation of the firm's system of quality management must have taken place by 15 December 2023.

When ISQM (UK) 1 was first introduced, many auditors thought that it may just be a new name for the predecessor, ISQC (UK) 1 *Quality Control for Firms that Perform Audits and Reviews of Financial Statements, and Other Assurance and Related Services Engagements*. This is not the case. While ISQC (UK) 1's focus was on quality **control**, ISQM (UK) 1's focus is on quality **management** and auditors must keep in mind that the firm's system of quality management creates an environment that enables and supports engagement teams in performing consistently high-quality engagements. This is something the FRC want to achieve across the board.

ISQM (UK) 1 changed the way in which a firm deals with quality management aspects, notably with the following characteristics:

- A more proactive and tailored approach to managing quality which is focussed on achieving quality objectives by identifying risks to those objectives and developing responses to those risks.

- Requirements to address the firm's governance and leadership, including increased leadership responsibilities.

- Requirements that modernise the standard and reflect factors that affect the firm's environment, including requirements to address technology, networks and the use of external service providers.

- Requirements that address information and communication, including communication with external parties.

- Requirements for monitoring and remediation to provide a more proactive monitoring of the firm's system of quality management as a whole and effective and timely remediation of deficiencies.

Establishing quality objectives

14.4   Going right back to basics, I think we can look at quality objectives as being the question 'how can the audit firm ensure its audit work is high quality?' This can then lead the firm into developing those objectives – for example:

- The firm's audit methodologies are appropriate in the individual client's circumstances.

- All audit staff will be technically up-to-date and competent.

- Audit clients must fit into the firm's risk profile and we will not take on clients for which we have no experience in dealing with.

- All audit work will be reviewed on a timely basis.

- Audit files will be fully assembled within prescribed timescales.

- The audit firm will require pre- and post-issuance reviews ('hot' and 'cold' reviews) to be carried out on a specific number of files each year.

These are just some examples of points to consider when the firm is establishing its quality objectives to give you an idea of the types of things to consider.

ISQM (UK) 1 tells us that the objective of the firm is to design, implement and operate a system of quality management for audits or reviews of financial statements (or other assurance or related services engagements carried out by the firm), which provides the firm with reasonable assurance that:

- the firm and its staff are carrying out their responsibilities according to professional standards and applicable legal and regulatory requirements; and

- the reports issued by the firm, or engagement partners, are appropriate in the circumstances.

It is worth bearing in mind that these objectives are very high-level ones. Consequently, ISQM (UK) 1 contains specific quality objectives for eight specific components of the system of quality management so that it is clear what outcomes must be achieved by the firm in order for it to have an effective system of quality management.

IMPORTANT POINT

The requirements in ISQM (UK) 1 are scalable. This means there is no 'one-size-fits-all' to establishing a sound system of quality management and the system itself is established by the nature and circumstances of the

---

firm, including how it is structured and organised. Effectively, a smaller firm's system of quality management will be very different in comparison with a large, multi-national audit firm.

Example 14.1 – A sole practitioner with two audit clients

Gil is a sole practitioner and has two audit clients which are standalone private companies. Gil is about to undergo a review of his system of quality management through an independent third party. He has read ISQM (UK) 1 in detail to identify any issues that he may encounter during this review and has noted the following requirement in ISQM (UK) 1, para 31(b):

> The firm shall establish the following quality objectives that address the performance of quality engagements:
>
> (b) The nature, timing and extent of direction and supervision of engagement teams and review of the work performed is appropriate based on the nature and circumstances of the engagements and the resources assigned or made available to the engagement teams, and the work performed by less experienced team members is directed, supervised and reviewed by more experienced engagement team members.

Gil is concerned that because he is a sole practitioner, he will not be able to fully comply with this requirement.

Remember, ISQM (UK) 1 takes a risk-based approach and is scalable. There are likely to be situations when a quality objective, or a part thereof, is irrelevant to an audit firm. In Gil's situation, ISQM (UK), para 31(b), 1 which addresses supervision and review is likely to be irrelevant to a sole practitioner. Reviews of the audit work can, however, be performed through a pre-issuance ('hot') or post-issuance ('cold') review by an external reviewer when this is considered necessary.

As a *very* high-level overview, the requirements of ISQM (UK) 1 are as follows:

As you can see from the above process, the first step is establishing quality objectives. ISQM (UK) 1 says that the audit firm's system of quality management is effective when those objectives have been met.

Now, there are **eight** components which make up a system of quality management:

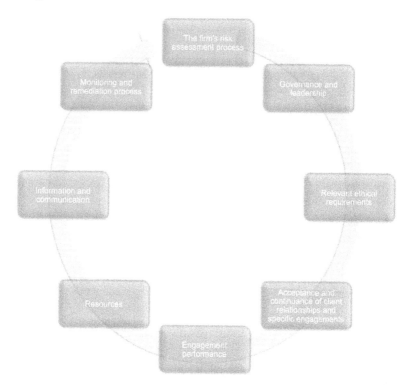

I'll discuss each of these in turn as follows:

1. The firm's risk assessment process

14.5   Auditing is now risk-based as we know. It follows, therefore, that ISQM (UK) 1 is also a risk-based quality management standard and the focus of the firm's risk assessment process should be the risks that might arise which prevent the firm from carrying out high-quality audit work.

There is absolutely no one-size-fits-all to this process and there is no definitive list of procedures the firm can apply that achieves this quality objective. It will all depend on the size of the firm, the complexity of the clients it deals with, the nature of technology involved and the use of external providers. You can expect a larger firm will need to carry out a more rigorous risk assessment process than, say, a smaller firm with maybe two or three audit clients that could perhaps carry out an annual risk assessment.

2. Governance and leadership

14.6   Effective governance and leadership are crucial to quality management at **both** the firm level and at the individual engagement level. When we talk about 'governance and leadership', we are referring to the way in which the audit firm embeds its culture and ethics as well as how it self-regulates by setting out requirements for the 'tone at the top'. This, in turn, can affect the public's perception of the firm and without effective governance and leadership, the firm does not operate in the public's interest.

The firm must be able to demonstrate a commitment to quality and ethics and this attitude should permeate throughout the audit firm.

3. Relevant ethical requirements

14.7   As we know, all auditors must comply with the requirements of the relevant ethical code (eg, ACCA's *Code of Ethics and Conduct* or ICAEW's *Code of Ethics*). This particular component of the system of quality management is concerned with ensuring personnel understand the regulatory ethical requirements and also any specific or additional requirements which have been set by the audit firm and how to fulfil those requirements.

ISQM (UK) 1 recognises that others who are external to the audit firm may be involved in the performance of engagements or various activities in the system of quality management. Consequently, the firm has a responsibility to address relevant ethical requirements that apply to others.

Keep in mind that the firm is only responsible for the relevant ethical requirements which apply to others **in the context of the firm and the firm's engagements**. Other professionals (eg, valuation agents) may be subject to other ethical requirements which do not relate to the firm. It is probably best to articulate this theory with an example:

Example 14.2 – Relevant ethical requirements

Toulouse & Co is a firm of chartered certified accountants based in the UK and is subject to ACCA's *Code of Ethics and Conduct*.

The firm is carrying out the audit of one of its clients, Carcassonne Investments Ltd and has engaged the services of an auditor's expert to carry out work to corroborate the valuation of certain complex financial instruments. The expert is provided access to highly sensitive information in order to carry out their work. In addition, the expert is regulated by their own professional body and is subject to their own ethical requirements.

- Toulouse & Co is not responsible for the expert's fulfilment of the ethical requirements of its own professional body. This is the responsibility of the expert themselves.

- Toulouse & Co is, however, responsible for ensuring that the auditor's expert understands the confidentiality provisions in ACCA's *Code of Ethics and Conduct*. The expert must treat the client's information as confidential.

It would be best practice for the firm to consider who is involved in the firm's engagements and carrying out activities for the firm's system of quality management. This will then lead the firm into considering how ethical requirements may affect them.

When considering responses to address others' fulfilment of relevant ethical requirements, the firm may find that the responses differ from the responses designed and implemented by the firm which address the firm's staff members' fulfilment of relevant ethical requirements. For example:

- staff members of the audit firm will be subject to regular training on relevant ethical requirements;

- in respect of service providers, the firm may include the specific relevant ethical requirements in the engagement teams; or

- when component auditors are involved (either inside or outside of the network), the relevant ethical requirements may be included in the group audit instructions. In some situations, however, the group auditor may determine it appropriate to provide additional training to component auditors.

4. Acceptance and continuance of client relationships and specific engagements

14.8   This component includes principles-based requirements to establish quality objectives that address the acceptance and continuance of client relationships and specific engagements. The overarching focus is on the firm's judgements in determining whether, or not, to accept or continue the client relationship or specific engagement.

Remember, ISQM (UK) 1 is scalable so smaller audit firms are expected to have a less complex system of quality management than a multi-national firm. In any event, a firm might provide the information which needs to be gathered relating to the nature and circumstances of the engagement. The firm may also provide details of the information needed to verify the integrity and ethical values of the client (which would include management and, where applicable, those charged with governance). ISQM (UK) 1 policies and procedures may also provide details as to the source of this information.

These policies and procedures may outline the type of engagements that the firm is willing to take on and those which it cannot (eg, many firms avoid cash-based businesses due to risk or charities due to the specialist nature).

When deciding whether, or not, to continue a client relationship, or accept a specific engagement, there is interaction with ISA (UK) 220 *Quality Management for an Audit of Financial Statements*. This ISA (UK) requires the audit engagement partner to consider whether the firm's policies and procedures have been followed and that the conclusions reached by the firm are appropriate. The audit engagement partner will need to document this process carefully on the audit file.

5. Engagement performance

14.9 First off, let us deal with the issues relating to smaller audits. Where an audit is being carried out by, say, a sole practitioner, it will be a case of the engagement team consists of 'me, myself and I'. Hence, as I already mentioned in the example above, the quality objectives that address direction, supervision and review are likely to be irrelevant. The firm's quality risks related to the engagement partner's responsibility for managing and achieving audit quality on the engagement as well as being appropriately involved throughout the entire audit may be assessed as being fairly low.

A small audit firm may not have internal personnel with the competence and capabilities to provide consultation (for example, on a complex tax matter or complex valuation techniques). The firm may, therefore, determine it appropriate to make the use of an external expert for the purposes of consulting on difficult or contentious matters.

There may also be challenges within the firm to have individuals who are responsible for resolving differences of opinion. The firm may determine it appropriate to use external service providers for the purposes of receiving and resolving differences of opinion.

Where engagement performance is concerned, ISQM (UK) 1 requires the firm to establish quality objectives which address the performance of quality engagements. Specifically:

14.9 *Quality Management*

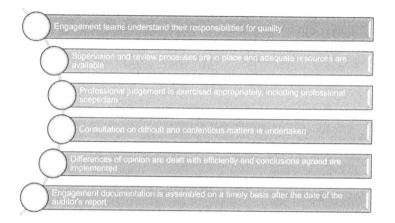

- Engagement teams understand their responsibilities for quality
- Supervision and review processes are in place and adequate resources are available
- Professional judgement is exercised appropriately, including professional scepticism
- Consultation on difficult and contentious matters is undertaken
- Differences of opinion are dealt with efficiently and conclusions agreed are implemented
- Engagement documentation is assembled on a timely basis after the date of the auditor's report

---

IMPORTANT POINT

The exercising of professional judgement and professional scepticism are two areas that can result in problems where audit files are concerned (primarily because they are either lacking or are used inappropriately). An audit firm may design and implement several responses to address professional judgement and professional scepticism which are then related to other quality objectives – for example, including responses which deal with direction, supervision and review and difference of opinion.

Examples of other aspects of the firm's system of quality management which may support engagement teams in exercising appropriate professional judgement and professional scepticism include:

- Embedding a culture that demonstrates the firm's commitment to quality.

- Members of the firm's leadership team taking responsibility and accountability for quality and demonstrating their commitment to quality through their actions and behaviours.

- Assigning appropriate resources to engagements, including HR, technological and financial resources.

- Developing appropriate intellectual resources, including creating alerts for engagement teams on circumstances giving rise to the need for professional judgement and professional scepticism and providing guidance for engagement teams in these circumstances.

- Managing the assignment of personnel to engagements and ensuring that they have the time required to carry out their work properly and fulfil their responsibilities.

- Making appropriate judgements concerning acceptance and continuance of engagements, such as considering whether the audit firm has appropriate resources to perform the engagement and whether the firm has the time to carry out the engagement given the firm's other commitments.

- Providing necessary training.

6. Resources

14.10   When we think of the term 'resources', a lot of auditors will automatically think 'people' (ie, engagement team members). If we look at ISQM (UK) 1, para 32, most will agree that the paragraph is quite lengthy and you will see that 'resources' encompasses more than just people. Of course, the people are important because without them the audit doesn't get completed, and it is important that the **right** people are engaged on the audit (ie, technically competent with the right skill set). Resources, in the context of ISQM (UK) 1 relate to the following:

- Human resources
- Technological resources
- Intellectual resources
- Service providers

Human resources

The term 'human resources' is wide and when it comes to ISQM (UK) 1 it covers individuals both inside and outside of the firm:

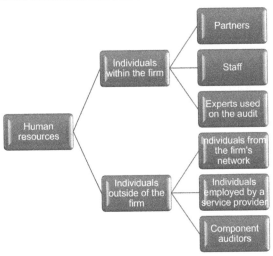

When the term 'personnel' is used in ISQM (UK) 1, it means individuals within the firm. When the term 'individual' or 'individuals' is used, it is intended to be interpreted in the context in which it is being used. So, it may refer to a specific individual, a group of specific individuals, or to all human resources involved in the firm's system of quality management or performance engagements. The table below illustrates how this may work in practice:

All individuals used in the system of quality management or performance of engagements	Only individuals within the firm	Only the individuals external to the firm who are used in the system of quality management or performance of engagements
The engagement team's responsibilities, direction, supervision and review of the engagement team and their work, exercising professional judgement and resolving differences of opinion.	Responsibility of personnel for quality relating to the performance of engagements or activities within the system of quality management and their expected behaviour.	Relevant ethical requirements in the context of others who are subject to the relevant ethical requirements to which the firm and the firm's engagements are subject.
Assigning engagement team members and individuals to perform activities within the system of quality management.	Relevant ethical requirements in the context of the firm and its personnel.	Obtaining individuals from external resources.
Exchanging information between the firm and engagement teams.	Hiring, developing and retaining personnel.	
Individuals who perform monitoring activities.	Personnel's commitment to quality.	
Communicating matters related to monitoring and remediation to engagement teams and other individuals assigned activities within the system of quality management.	Responsibility of personnel to exchange information.	
	Confirming compliance with independence requirements.	

Now, there is a link here to ISA (UK) 220 *Quality Management for an Audit of Financial Statements*. This ISA (UK) specifically outlines the audit engagement partner's responsibility in ensuring there are sufficient and appropriate resources available to perform the engagement in a timely manner. In the case of a group audit, for example, component auditors are part of the engagement team and hence the provisions of ISA (UK) 220 will also apply to them.

Technological resources

Not all technological resources that are used by the audit firm will fall in scope of ISQM (UK) 1. Keep in mind that technological resources may serve multiple purposes within the firm and hence some may be unrelated to the firm's system of quality management. The table below outlines how this may work in practice:

Examples of technological resources used in designing, implementing or operating the system of quality management	Examples of technological resources used by engagement teams in the performance of engagements	Examples of technological resources essential to enabling the effective operation of IT applications
IT applications for independence monitoring and client acceptance and continuance. IT applications used to monitor the system of quality management. IT applications for recording time and to track personnel's time off. IT applications to support training and for personnel's performance evaluations. IT applications for budgeting (planning and allocation of financial resources). IT applications for retraining and maintaining engagement documentation. IT applications for recording and tracking consultations.	IT applications used to prepare and compile engagement documentation. IT applications used for intellectual resources (eg, IT applications with policy manuals and methodologies). IT applications that are used as automated tools and techniques, including the use of Excel and macros in Excel.	The operating systems and databases supporting the IT applications used in operating the system of quality management or performance of engagements. The hardware to support the operation of the IT applications (eg, network systems and user hardware such as laptops). IT systems to manage access to the operating system and IT applications (ie, password applications).

There are also some quality **risks** which arise where technological resources are concerned, such as:

(a) engagement teams could place undue reliance on IT applications which may inaccurately process data, process inaccurate data, or both. This may give rise to quality risks related to engagement performance, especially with regards to exercising professional scepticism; and

(b) security breaches may lead to unauthorised access to client's data. This, in turn, may give rise to a quality risk related to relevant ethical requirements (eg, a breach of GDPR).

Intellectual resources

Intellectual resources include the information used by the firm to enable the operation of its system of quality management. They also promote consistency within the performance of engagements. Examples include:

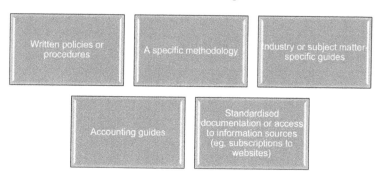

ISQM (UK) 1 requires the firm to establish policies or procedures concerning the use of the firm's technological and intellectual resources. For example:

- Certain engagements may require the use of specific IT applications or intellectual resources.

- Individuals may need specific qualifications to use the resource (eg, using an IT application which analyses data, the results of which require specialist skills to interpret).

- The engagement partner may have specific responsibilities concerning the use of technological and intellectual resources.

- Documentation may set out how technological or intellectual resources are to be used, including how individuals should interact with an IT application or how the intellectual resource should be applied.

Service providers

The reality is that not all audit firms will have the necessary resources available at their fingertips. Therefore, there may be a need to engage a service provider to assist in some elements of the system of quality management. Resources from a service provider can include technological, intellectual or human resources. Let us consider an example to bring this theory to life:

Example 14.3 – Outsourcing a system of quality management

Latte & Co are a firm of auditors who are looking at the possibility of outsourcing their system of quality management to a service provider to free up time for the partners to source new audit clients as they are keen to expand their audit department.

ISQM (UK) 1 does not allow the firm to outsource its system of quality management; nor the firm's responsibility for the system. Instead, the resources from service providers may assist the firm in fulfilling the requirements of ISQM (UK) 1. Hence, when using resources from service providers, the firm is responsible for ensuring that the resources are appropriate for use in its system of quality management or the performance of engagements.

Service providers may be engaged by the firm, the engagement team or a component auditor. In such cases, the firm's system of quality management must address the **appropriateness** of the service provider – even if the service provider has been engaged by the engagement team or another party.

As you would expect from a standard such as ISQM (UK) 1, there are several factors that must be taken into consideration which may affect the quality risks related to resources from service providers. These are outlined in the table below:

Example of factor	Examples of how the factor affects quality risks
The nature of the resource	When using a technological resource from a service provider, the quality risks may include: ● A lack of appropriate updates to the IT application, resulting in it becoming unreliable or unusable, and hence not appropriate for use in the firm's system of quality management or in performing engagements. ● Access to client data, particularly when the data is stored in a database managed and operated by the service provider, which could result in breaches of confidentiality. When using human resources from a service provider, the quality risks may include: ● A lack of appropriate competence and capabilities to perform the activity for which the human resource has been engaged, resulting in the resource not being appropriate for use in the firm's system of quality management or in performing engagements. ● Changes in the individuals assigned by the service provider (eg, due to reassignment) during the course of the activity for which they have been engaged, and new individuals assigned being inappropriate due to lack of continuity or experience related to the activity.

Example of factor	Examples of how the factor affects quality risks
The firm's responsibilities to take further actions in using the resource	• The firm uses an IT application from a service provider that is an off-the-shelf package. The IT application is maintained by the service provider. The service provider distributes updates automatically, and the firm receives an automated alert to accept the update. In this case, since the firm has relatively few responsibilities related to the IT application, the quality risks may relate to: — whether the IT application is appropriate for the purposes it will be used for; — whether the service provider provides the necessary updates; and — the risk that the firm does not accept the automated updates. • The firm uses an IT application from a service provider. Although the IT application is an off-the-shelf package and is maintained by the service provider, the firm builds on custom-developed applications that enable the firm to integrate the IT application with other IT applications. In addition, there are a number of responsibilities for the firm in using the IT application, including: — capturing firm-specific data into an underlying database, and maintaining the data; and — selecting various options related to the functionality of the IT application, which require a periodic review as the functionalities may change when the service provider updates the IT application. • In this case, in addition to the quality risks described concerning whether the IT application is appropriate for the purpose it will be used for, and the quality risks related to the updates, the firm may also identify quality risks related to: — the custom-developed applications not functioning correctly; — firm-specific data being incorrectly captured or not properly maintained; and — the selected functionality options being inappropriate.

Service provider statements should be obtained from the audit firm. In situations where the service provider does not provide the information required by the firm, and the firm is unable to obtain alternative information to satisfy themselves that the service provider is appropriate for use in the firm's system of quality management or performance of engagements, the firm may need to seek an alternative service provider. In some cases, the firm may be required to use the service provider, and if the firm is unable to satisfy themselves about the appropriateness of the resource, the firm may need to take other action to appropriately respond to the situation.

7. Information and communication

14.11   This part of ISQM (UK) 1 requires the audit firm to establish a quality objective which is related to the firm's information and communication system. Remember, an information system can include both manual and automated elements.

An audit firm will communicate and exchange information with a variety of parties, typically:

I have mentioned a couple of times in this chapter about the scalability aspect of ISQM (UK) 1 and this is relevant here. For a smaller, less complex audit firm, communication may be more informal and achieved through direct discussions with personnel and engagement teams. ISQM (UK) 1 does not require all communications to be documented, but the firm would need to document communication to the extent that it is deemed necessary to address the documentation requirements in ISQM (UK) 1, paras 57 to 60-1.

In terms of communicating with external parties, there are a variety of such parties. Communication related to a firm's system of quality management may, for example, include direct conversations with external parties, audit oversight bodies or management and those charged with governance.

There are four questions that are asked where communication requirements are concerned:

14.11 *Quality Management*

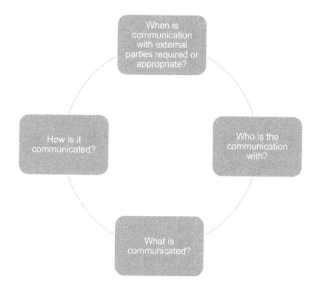

The answers to these questions can be summarised in the table below:

When is communication with external parties required or appropriate?	Who is the communication with?	What is communicated?	How is it communicated?
Law, regulation or professional standards require communication externally	Communicate with external parties specified by law, regulation or professional standards	Communicate information specified by law, regulation or professional standards	Nature, timing and extent specified by law, regulation or professional standards
Firm performs audits of financial statements of listed entities	Communicate with those charged with governance of the entity	Communicate how the system of quality management supports consistent performance of quality engagements	Nature, timing and extent determined by the firm
Communication is otherwise needed to support external parties' understanding of the system of quality management	Communicate with external party determined by the firm	Communicate information determined by the firm	Nature, timing and extent determined by the firm

For smaller firms, the firm may identify limited cases when communication with external parties is appropriate. For example, the firm may communicate with those charged with governance in circumstances where there are particular findings from an engagement.

8. Monitoring and remediation process

14.12   The monitoring and remediation process is the final part of the jigsaw in the audit firm's system of quality management. At the outset, it is worth noting that this is a **twofold** process:

ISQM (UK) 1 requires the firm to monitor the system of quality management so that it has relevant, reliable and timely information about the design, implementation and operation of the system itself.

The standard also requires the firm to respond to identified deficiencies such that these are corrected on a timely basis so that they do not reoccur.

The way in which a firm will do this is via four-step process:

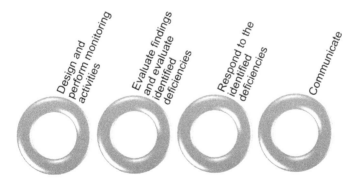

I think it is important to emphasise that the way in which a firm will carry out monitoring and remediation will all depend on the size, nature, complexity and the circumstances of the firm. It is also important to understand the firm is required to monitor the system of internal control **as a whole**, which could include monitoring:

- How responsibilities are assigned to leadership and whether the requirements of ISQM (UK) 1 have been met.

- The design and operation of the firm's risk assessment process, ie, how the firm establishes quality objectives, identifies and assesses quality risks, designing and implementing responses and identifying information related to changes in the nature and circumstances of the firm and the engagements it performs that may impact the quality objectives, quality risks or responses.

- The implementation and operation of the responses, including whether they operate according to how they have been designed and whether the responses effectively address the quality risks.

- Whether the firm's monitoring and remediation process is achieving its intended purpose.

- How the firm has addressed network requirements or network services and whether it complies with the requirements of ISQM (UK) 1.

- Leadership's evaluation of the system of quality management and whether it has met the requirements of ISQM (UK) 1.

Some of this may seem overwhelming to some firms of auditors, especially smaller firms. So, I think it's worth providing a useful analogy of what this part of the standard is looking for firms to do.

ILLUSTRATION

My first car was an old Mini Cooper which my parents bought for me for my 18th birthday (several years ago now). It is fair to say that the car broke down a few times in the years that I had it. Often, I didn't know when it was going to break down – the engine just stopped (writing this illustration reminds of the one time the car broke down in the middle of nowhere at night, which wasn't a pleasant experience, but that story is for another book). Various things were wrong with the car while I had it such as a faulty battery, then a faulty alternator and then something else and something else. The car had to be repaired each time something went wrong with it (ie, it was a 'reactive' process).

Fast forward to today. Modern cars now have all sorts of sophisticated computers on board that tell the driver when something has either gone wrong or is about to go wrong. The idea of this is to prevent the car from breaking down and potentially becoming expensive to repair.

Today's cars have a more rigorous 'monitoring' system in place that reacts when something is about to go wrong, or has gone wrong (eg, a warning

---

message appears on the dashboard when your tyre pressure becomes too low).

Apply this basic every day analogy to an audit firm's system of quality management. The system should alert the firm that there is something wrong (eg, the methodology applied on an audit is not appropriate) and the firm should then do something about it to prevent that something from having a systemic impact on audit quality across the firm. If something is not done about it, the problem will get worse (ie, if the tyres are not inflated to the correct pressure, there could be an accident or a 'blowout'). Hence, monitoring and remediation is meant to be a 'proactive' process.

Remember, ISQM (UK) 1 places more focus on monitoring **all** areas of the system of quality management as well as the types of monitoring activities that are carried out. To do this correctly, the firm will need to consider all eight component of the system. The overarching objective here is for the leadership team to conclude that the monitoring system is working as intended and can sufficiently identify deficiencies.

The nature, timing and extent of montoring activities will, of course, all depend on the size, complexity and geographical dispersion of the firm.

Pre- and post-issuance file reviews

Pre- and post-issuance file reviews (often referred to as 'hot' and 'cold' file reviews respectively) are a valuable source of information. Indeed, in my firm we have such reviews carried out externally to provide us with valuable feedback about what may need to improve on our files, but also what seems to be working well. Remember, it's all about assessing what the firm is doing **well** at rather than just using a glass half empty approach and focussing on what may be going wrong.

Firms will have been used to selecting audit files for review on a cyclical basis using, perhaps, the relevant audit engagement partner as a basis for selection. So, if a couple of audits have been reviewed and they haven't been assessed too well, it maybe that more of that audit engagement partner's files are selected as a means of trying to remedy the problem.

ISQM (UK) 1 takes a different approach to this and the selection of audit engagement partners can still be the basis on which files are selected, but generally it is tailored to the specific circumstances of the firm. Other factors may, of course, influence the selection of the engagement files for review, such as changes within the firm itself.

File reviews can also indicate whether the firm's system of quality management is working. For exmaple, if the results of file reviews highlight an increasing number of deficiencies, there may be a need to review the system of quality management and make necessary adjustments to it.

Evaluation of findings

Findings generally come from three sources:

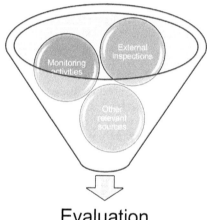

All three of these sources will identify if there are deficiencies in the firm's system of quality management. Remember, it is expected that monitoring activities will generate a lot of information concerning the system of quality management. However, it is not necessarily the case that every piece of information will need a response because not every piece of information will indicate a problem with the system. Hence, the firm will need to take the time to understand the information that has been gathered and analyse that information to ascertain whether any deficiencies have been uncovered within the system.

REAL-LIFE SCENARIO

Mr P is the audit engagement partner in a two-partner firm. The firm had three audits, all standalone limited companies with very little in the way of complexities. A file had been sent for post-issuance (cold) review and the feedback was mixed.

The reviewer highlighted a number of areas where the approach was inappropriate. For example, sample sizes across the board were 20 of everything, including sales invoices. The reviewer also noted that the firm

---

undertook sampling on a random basis on pretty much every material area of the audit and where sampling was from the nominal ledger, it always seemed to be transactions in the last month of the financial year which were selected.

The file was graded an E meaning significant improvement was required. Previous reviews had always been C, so things really had gone downhill when this particular file was reviewed.

Mr P acknowledged that the audit had been done in a rush due to the client requesting the audit be completed in less than two weeks (this is usually impracticable from start to finish) and so sample sizes were reduced across the board. The danger with doing this is that audit risk and detection risk both increase.

Mr P also told me that the reviewer had criticised the firm's supervision and review process in that the audit engagement partner had reviewed areas such as going concern and related parties (deemed to be high-risk areas of the audit) but there was no evidence of a partner review of other material areas of the financial statements.

These deficiencies can be attributed to the firm's system of quality management. Granted, the issues raised in this real-life scenario happened several years ago, pre ISQM (UK) 1, but if they had occurred recently, the firm would have needed to revisit its system of quality management and make appropriate amendments to it.

Responding to deficiencies

Let's face it – nobody likes to be told their work is deficient. However, let's also be realistic – it is almost impossible to produce a 100% perfect system of quality management (or even a 100% perfect audit file – believe me, I've tried, and it doesn't happen).

However, bad feedback happens (and so does good feedback, it has to be said). When you get a bad review, whether it's an individual audit file or criticisms about the firm's system of quality management, of course you will need to take on board the criticism (unless it is clearly and justifiably incorrect, of course) and the grading might not be great. The important thing is to think about how to turn the situation around. Don't dwell on the fact that a review hasn't gone entirely to plan, or that a file has got a grade D when last year it was B. Think about the criticism and how you go about changing the system of quality management such that the changes address the criticisms in the review. In other words, treat the review as a learning process.

Remember, monitoring activities are not confined to looking at what the firm may be doing wrong, or what isn't working well; it's also about looking at what is effective because the firm can then use these good areas on other files where the system that may not be working so well.

Root cause analysis has become very popular in recent years and is something the professional bodies would expect an audit firm to utilise because it forces the firm to ask three specific questions where deficiencies are concerned:

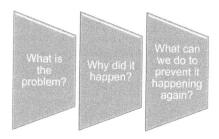

Where root cause analysis is concerned, the key thing to understand is that the firm should not necessarily be concerned about the 'symptoms' of the deficiency – instead the focus should be **getting to the root cause of it**. You may have to ask yourself 'why' several times until you get to the true 'root cause' of the problem.

REAL-LIFE SCENARIO

In a recent monitoring report, a professional body cited a case of deficiencies noted in a group audit. Various things had gone wrong in the audit of the group accounts and some procedures had not been carried out when specifically required by ISA (UK) 600 *Special Considerations – Audits of Group Financial Statements (Including the Work of Component Auditors)*.

A root cause analysis was carried out by the firm which identified a lack of training in auditing a group. Hence, the action the firm took to ensure these deficiencies did not happen again was to ensure that audit team members who are assigned to group audits have a sound understanding of the requirements of ISA (UK) 600.

Once deficiencies have been identified and root cause analysis performed, the firm must then design and implement remedial measures which respond directly to the results of the root cause analysis.

ISQM (UK) 1 requires the firm to evaluate the remedial actions for effectiveness and ensure that they are appropriately designed to address the identified deficiencies and their related root causes.

All identified deficiencies will need a response by the firm. As noted above, any deficiencies which are judged to be serious or pervasive ones must be addressed quickly. Where time is needed to address a serious deficiency, the firm would be advised to put in interim measures to ensure the risk of reoccurrence is reduced as far as possible.

FRC THEMATIC REVIEW ON ROOT CAUSE ANALYSIS

In 2016, the FRC published a Thematic Review on root cause analysis (RCA), which included the findings of an FRC review of how the large audit firms carry out RCA. The Thematic Review defines 'root cause analysis' as 'a process for identifying the causes of problems or events in order to prevent them from recurring. It is based on the idea that effective management requires more than putting out fires for problems that develop, but finding a way to prevent them. RCA can also be a means of identifying good practice as part of continuous improvement.'[1]

I have to say, I do like the reference to 'putting out fires for problems that develop...'. I think it articulates the definition very nicely. Anyway, moving on ...

Prior to the FRC's report, global bodies including the International Forum of Independent Auditors (IFIA) and the European Audit Inspection Group (EAIG) had also commented on the benefits of RCA for audit firms looking to identify and respond to issues with audit quality.

In their review of how audit firms carry out RCA, the FRC observed that practices varied greatly between firms, but that in all firms one feature of the RCA process was interviews with audit partners and sometimes audit managers. The FRC comments that interviews are a good source of information about audit quality, because the audit team members will be able to provide insight into what went wrong during an audit, and suggest the reasons. The FRC recommends that interviews should involve not just audit partners and managers; more junior members of the team should also be express opinions.

In addition, most firms use Audit Quality Measures (AQMs) to measure audit performance, for example an AQM can be used to measure the time spent by audit partners or managers on an audit.

1 Audit Quality Thematic Review – Root Cause Analysis (FRC, 2016).

The FRC found that most of the root causes for deficiencies in audit quality relate to:

- Audit team members' lack of knowledge or skill, eg, not understanding the client's business.

- Inappropriate behaviours of audit team members, eg, a lack of professional scepticism.

- Lack of care in audit work performed, eg, not preparing sufficiently detailed audit conclusions.

- Lack of direction by senior members of the audit team, eg, a lack of review of working papers.

- Problems with resourcing or managing the audit, eg, time pressure and too few staff.

- Lack of clarity in guidance, eg, relating to the firm's audit methodology.

In response to the root causes identified above, the firms provided more training to staff and issued better guidance and communications on audit methodology. Other responses included improving project (ie, audit) management, enhancing audit methodology, review of resourcing and providing better support to new members of the audit firm.

Documentation

14.13   Of course, ISQM (UK) 1 requires specific documentation concerning the firm's system of quality management. This must include documentation relating to the firm's:

- quality objectives;
- quality risks;
- evidence of monitoring activities;
- evaluation of findings;
- remedial actions; and
- communications.

While it is arduous documenting the firm's system of quality management, I think it is important to look at the reasons *why* documentation is important:

- It helps the audit staff to understand the firm's system of quality management and what is expected of them, so there can be no misunderstanding and none of *'well, I didn't know I had to do that.'*

- It enables the firm to create responses to assessed risks so that the system itself operates as the firm intends.

- It helps the firm retain knowledge about their firm (particularly useful in a large firm) as well as providing a basis as to why decisions relating to the system of quality management were made.

- It enables the firm to monitor the system of quality management and provides information to enable the firm's leadership to evaluate and conclude on the system.

- It creates a form of accountability for the firm in that there is evidence that the firm has designed, implemented and operated a system of quality management that complies with ISQM (UK) 1 as well as applicable legal and regulatory requirements.

- It enables external oversight authorities (eg, professional bodies) to fulfil their duties in inspecting the firm's system of quality management.

ISQM (UK) 2

14.14 ISQM (UK) 2 *Engagement Quality Reviews* was a new quality management standard issued by the FRC which became effective for audits and reviews of financial statements for periods commencing on or after 15 December 2022, and other assurance and related services engagements commencing on or after 15 December 2022.

Before we get into the 'nitty gritty' of ISQM (UK) 2, I think it's important to recap on what an *engagement quality review* actually is. According to the standard, it is an **objective evaluation** of the significant judgements made by the engagement team and the conclusions reached thereon. This is carried out by the engagement quality reviewer and is completed on or before the date of the auditor's report. ISQM (UK) 2 forms part of the firm's system of quality management and builds on the requirements of ISQM (UK) 1.

As you've probably gathered by now from reading this chapter, quality management is at the heart of any audit. It is often not enough to have one person just reviewing the audit work as the audit progresses with an engagement partner reviewing the working papers at the end. Sometimes it will be necessary to have an engagement quality reviewer carry out a review of the work, but more importantly, the **significant** judgements made together with the conclusions reached.

Despite ISQM (UK) 2 being a new quality management, the concepts covered by the standard are not new. It has always been a requirement for an audit firm to take steps to ensure that audit work is properly reviewed for two primary reasons:

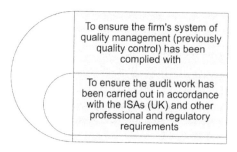

To ensure the firm's system of quality management (previously quality control) has been complied with

To ensure the audit work has been carried out in accordance with the ISAs (UK) and other professional and regulatory requirements

One of the most common types of quality management review is a pre-issuance ('hot') or post-issuance ('cold') review. A 'hot' review is a review of the audit work by a quality reviewer before the auditor's report has been signed; a 'cold' review is a review of the audit work by a quality reviewer after the auditor's report has been signed. These reviews can take place at the audit firm provided they are carried out by someone who has **not** been involved in the audit (because otherwise they will not be objective). In practice, a lot of firms tend to outsource this review to an external third-party. Having an external third-party carry out an independent review of the audit work has the significant benefit of a 'fresh pair of eyes' reviewing the audit work and making suggestions for improvement.

Like ISQM (UK) 1, ISQM (UK) 2 is scalable. It promotes a system which is tailored to the nature and circumstances of the audit firm and the audits which it carries out. ISQM (UK) 2 also deals with the appointment and eligibility of the engagement quality reviewer.

The overarching objective of ISQM (UK) 2 is for the firm to appoint an **eligible** engagement quality reviewer (EQR) that will carry out an **objective evaluation** of the significant judgements made by the engagement team and the conclusions that have been drawn on those judgements. For the purposes of ISQM (UK) 2, the EQR is:

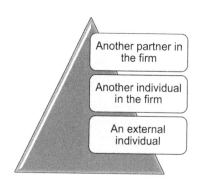

Another partner in the firm

Another individual in the firm

An external individual

Eligibility to be the EQR

14.15 The audit firm is required to set policies and procedures which outline the criteria that must be met in order to be an EQR. These criteria must ensure the EQR is sufficiently independent, competent, has the necessary time and has the seniority to perform the reviews.

IMPORTANT POINT

ISQM (UK) 2 is very specific that the EQR must **not** be a member of the audit engagement team. This rule is in place to ensure that the review is conducted in an objective and independent manner and to allow the reviewer to 'stand back' from the work performed and consider whether the audit engagement team has applied appropriate professional scepticism.

ISQM (UK) 2 also requires that the firm's policies and procedures on the eligibility of the EQR specifies a cooling-off period of two years (or longer if required by the FRC Ethical Standard) before the engagement partner can assume the role of EQR.

It goes without saying that the EQR must possess the competence and capabilities, including sufficient time and appropriate authority, to perform the review. An EQR who lacks appropriate experience may not have the ability (or even the confidence) to evaluate and, where appropriate, challenge, significant judgements including the exercise of professional scepticism by the engagement team on complex, industry-specific accounting or auditing issues.

When we talk about the EQR having 'sufficient seniority' or 'authority' it means that the reviewer's evaluation and conclusions are taken seriously.

Compliance with ethical requirements

14.16 Ethical requirements seep into every part of an audit and the EQR is no exception. All EQR's must comply with relevant ethical requirements, including in respect of threats to objectivity and independence. For example, the audit engagement partner should not create any intimidation threats to the EQR and the EQR must also comply with relevant laws or regulations, such as when involved in the review of entities operating in regulated industries.

Where the entity is a public interest entity, the audit firm must ensure that the review is carried out by an EQR who is eligible for appointment as a statutory auditor and is not involved in the performance of the audit to which the engagement review relates.

Audit firms should obtain a **service provider quality statement**. Such a statement contains various information, typically:

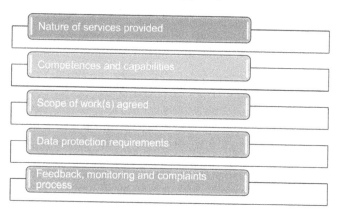

- Nature of services provided
- Competences and capabilities
- Scope of work(s) agreed
- Data protection requirements
- Feedback, monitoring and complaints process

The above list is not comprehensive.

Some firms have been known to ask for the CV of the person who may be appointed to carry out a review where the person is external to the entity (eg, a training provider). This can provide comfort to the audit firm that the reviewer has specific technical competences to carry out the review, particularly where the audit is specialist, such as with a pension fund.

What is NOT an engagement quality review?

14.17 I think this is a very important question where ISQM (UK) 2 is concerned and is one which is asked quite a lot. We know that an engagement quality review (EQR) is an **objective** evaluation of the significant judgements made by the audit team together with the conclusions reached thereon.

What must be borne in mind is that an EQR is not intended to be an evaluation of whether the entire engagement complies with professional standards and applicable legal and regulatory requirements, or even whether it complies entirely with the firm's policies or procedures.

We also know that the reviewer cannot, under any circumstances, be a member of the audit engagement team for obvious independence reasons. However, the fact that the firm is obtaining an EQR for the audit does not change the responsibilities of the audit engagement partner for managing and achieving quality on the engagement; nor does it change the partner's responsibilities for the direction and supervision of the members of the engagement team and the review of their work.

The EQR is not required to obtain audit evidence to support the audit opinion or conclusion on the engagement (this is not the job of the reviewer at all). However, a review such as a hot review will often give the audit engagement team more time to obtain further audit evidence in response to matters raised during the EQR. For example, the reviewer may have found insufficient audit evidence in a specific area once the review has been completed. As a hot review means the auditor's report has not yet been signed, there will still be time to obtain evidence such that it becomes sufficient (and appropriate as the case may be).

Requirements of the EQR

14.18 The EQR focuses on the significant judgements and significant matters which have arisen during the audit. The EQR is required to discuss these with the audit engagement partner, as well as other relevant members of the audit team, and review the audit documentation. The EQR is also required to evaluate how ethical requirements have been fulfilled.

In addition, ISQM (UK) 2 specifically requires the reviewer to:

(a) Read and obtain an understanding of information communicated by the audit engagement team concerning the nature and circumstances of the engagement and the entity as well as the firm and its monitoring and remediation process. In particular, identified deficiencies which may relate to, or affect, the areas that involve significant judgements made by the engagement team.

(b) Discuss with the audit engagement partner and, if applicable, other members of the engagement team, significant matters and significant judgements made in planning, performing and reporting on the engagement.

(c) Review selected audit documentation concerning the significant judgements made by the engagement team and evaluate the basis for making those judgements. This includes, where applicable, to the type of engagement, the exercise of professional scepticism by the team, and whether the engagement documentation supports the conclusions reached as well as whether those conclusions are appropriate.

(d) Evaluate the basis for the engagement partner's determination that relevant ethical requirements concerning independence have been fulfilled.

(e) Evaluate whether appropriate consultation has taken place on difficult or contentious matters (eg, a difficult tax matter) or matters involving differences of opinion and evaluate the conclusions arising therefrom.

(f) Evaluate the basis for the engagement partner's determination that their involvement in the assignment has been sufficient and appropriate throughout such that the engagement partner has a basis for determining that the significant judgements made, and the conclusions reached, are appropriate given the nature and circumstances of the engagement.

(g)   Review the financial statements and the auditor's report. This includes reviewing a description of Key Audit Matters, if appropriate.

(h)   For review engagements, review the financial statements or financial information and the engagement report thereon.

(i)   For other assurance engagements and related services engagements, review the engagement report and, where applicable, the subject matter information.

IMPORTANT POINT

In the UK, the FRC has included specific requirements in ISQM (UK) 2 that relate to public interest entities, including consideration of the independence of the firm from the entity, the significant risks that are relevant to the audit, and the measures taken to adequately manage those risks, the reasoning of the audit engagement partner, in particular with regard to the level of materiality and significant risks. There must also be consideration of the subjects discussed with the audit committee and management and/or supervisory bodies of the entity.

Documentation

14.19   ISQM (UK) 2 sets out a requirement that the audit firm must establish policies and procedures that require the EQR to take responsibility for documentation of the engagement quality review. That documentation must be included within the engagement documentation.

The EQR must also ensure that the review includes:

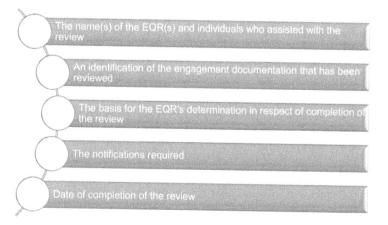

The name(s) of the EQR(s) and individuals who assisted with the review

An identification of the engagement documentation that has been reviewed

The basis for the EQR's determination in respect of completion of the review

The notifications required

Date of completion of the review

If the entity is a public interest entity, the UK has additional documentation requirements in respect of the oral and written information provided by the key audit partner to support the significant judgements and main findings. In addition, the conclusions drawn from those findings must also be documented as well as the key opinions of the key audit partner, as expressed in the draft of the reports required by ISA (UK) 260 *Communication with Those Charged with Governance* and ISA (UK) 700 *Forming an Opinion and Reporting on Financial Statements*.

QUALITY MANAGEMENT AT THE ENGAGEMENT LEVEL

14.20 So far in this chapter we have gone through the detailed requirements of ISQMs (UK) 1 and 2 which handle quality management at the firm level. Quality management does not stop there, and we must now look at the issue at the individual engagement level.

ISA (UK) 220 *Quality Management for an Audit of Financial Statements* deals with quality management at the engagement level. This is a crucial standard because compliance with the standard will result in a high-quality audit being carried out; but, equally, the firm's system of quality management must be designed in such a way that it complies with professional standards and the reports it generates are appropriate in the circumstances.

IMPORTANT POINT

ISA (UK) 220 contains a clear description of the audit engagement partner's responsibilities in addition to how the engagement team **as a whole** manages and achieves audit quality. It must be kept in mind that everyone on the engagement team is responsible for ensuring the audit is carried out to a high standard. However, ultimately, it is the audit engagement partner that is responsible for ensuring the work is done correctly.

To that end, ISA (UK) 220 requires the audit engagement partner to ensure that:

● all engagement team members take responsibility for contributing to the management and achievement of quality at the audit engagement level;

● the importance of professional ethics, values and attitudes are communicated to the team;

● there is an open and robust channel of communication within the team such that a team member can raise concerns without any fear of reprisal; and

---

- the importance of professional scepticism being applied throughout the duration of the entire audit is emphasised.

The standard also requires the audit engagement partner to:

- take responsibility in ensuring that other team members are aware of relevant ethical requirements, including the firm's related policies and/or procedures;

- remain alert throughout the audit (via observation and inquiry as necessary) for any breaches of ethical requirements or the firm's related policies and/or procedures by members of the team;

- take appropriate action where matters come to the engagement partner's attention through the system of quality management, or via other sources, which indicate that relevant ethical requirements have not been fulfilled; and

- prior to signing the auditor's report, the audit engagement partner must take responsibility for determining whether ethical requirements (including those related to independence) have been fulfilled.

Acceptance and continuance of an audit engagement

14.21   The audit engagement partner is required to carefully consider information obtained at the acceptance and continuance stage when planning and performing the audit engagement. In practice, this involves considering:

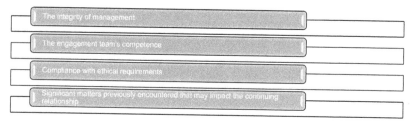

- The integrity of management
- The engagement team's competence
- Compliance with ethical requirements
- Significant matters previously encountered that may impact the continuing relationship

The audit engagement partner must also ensure that the engagement team has been provided with sufficient and appropriate resources to carry out the audit in a timely manner. This is not just a case of ensuring that there is a sufficient number of people on the engagement team (although that is clearly an important issue), but it is also about ensuring that any external experts are appointed in time to carry out the necessary work as well as ensuring they have the necessary skills and competence (this also includes internal audit, where one is in place at the audit client).

If the audit engagement partner concludes that resources are insufficient or inappropriate, they must take appropriate action.

Review of the performance including consultation and review

14.22 Remember, it is the audit engagement partner's ultimate responsibility to ensure adequate supervision and review processes are in place (this includes determining the nature, timing and extent of such review). Part of this is to consider matters such as providing on-the-job training (eg, training courses such as updates on ISAs (UK)) and assisting engagement team members in developing skills and competencies.

The review process is primarily concerned with the audit work and determining whether sufficient appropriate audit evidence has been obtained to form a conclusion. However, the audit engagement partner must also carry out a review of the financial statements (including a description of the Key Audit Matters, if applicable) and related documentation to ensure that the auditor's report to be issued on those financial statements is appropriate in the circumstances. This review must take place **before** the auditor's report is signed and dated.

In addition, the audit engagement partner is required to carry out a review of formal written communications (eg, the letter of comment) to management and/or those charged with governance before they are issued to, again, ensure they are appropriate in the circumstances.

Difficult or contentious matters and differences of opinion

14.23 No two audits are the same and it is likely that the engagement team may come across difficult and/or contentious matters. For example, if the audit client has a complex portfolio of financial instruments measured at fair value or there is a complex tax treatment. ISA (UK) 220 requires those difficult or contentious matters to be those which the firm's policies or procedures require consultation on as well as other matters which, in the auditor's professional judgement, also require consultation.

When we went through ISQM (UK) 2, I mentioned the importance of the audit engagement partner co-operating with the engagement quality reviewer and to ensure that other members of the audit engagement team are aware of their responsibilities to co-operate as well. Now, there could well be situations that present themselves where a difference of opinion may arise between the audit engagement partner and the engagement quality reviewer. It is therefore important that the audit firm has procedures in place to handle these differences of opinion.

REAL-LIFE SCENARIO

Ms T used to be a file reviewer working for a training organisation. During a review of a file for a four-partner firm, Ms T noted some intangible assets that had not been amortised in contravention of FRS 102 *The Financial Reporting Standard applicable in the UK and Republic of Ireland*, Section 18 *Intangible Assets other than Goodwill*. Under FRS 102, all intangible assets are deemed to have a finite useful life and must be amortised on a systematic basis over that useful life.

The audit firm had made a note on the file that the client had not amortised the intangible assets on the basis that the client considered them to have an indefinite useful life. On the audit error schedule (or 'schedule of unadjusted errors'), the auditor had included the charge for the year as an unadjusted error.

Ms T flagged up to the audit engagement partner that simply including the charge for the year was not the correct thing to do because it should be the accumulated amortisation charge that should be included (as previous years' amortisation has also been understated). The engagement partner disagreed with the reviewer and told the reviewer he would not be taking on board that recommendation.

The engagement quality reviewer was correct. On the audit error schedule, any uncorrected misstatements from prior years which affect the current year's financial statements should be included because the cumulative effect of them may become material in the current year. In addition, the audit engagement partner did not appear to challenge management's assertion that the intangible assets must be amortised under FRS 102 (there is no option under the standard to assign indefinite useful lives to intangible assets).

In this situation, the firm's system of quality management must have procedures in place that deal with such differences of opinion. While it is difficult to disagree with the reviewer's feedback in this particular case, there may be situations where an audit engagement partner could disagree with a subjective issue (ie, neither the reviewer nor the audit engagement partner is wrong – it is merely down to a matter of opinion or interpretation).

Where differences of opinion are concerned, the audit engagement partner must:

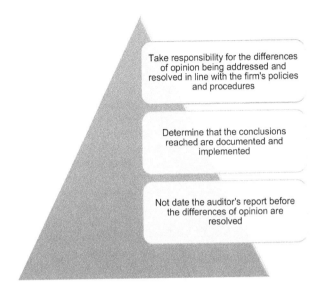

Take responsibility for the differences of opinion being addressed and resolved in line with the firm's policies and procedures

Determine that the conclusions reached are documented and implemented

Not date the auditor's report before the differences of opinion are resolved

If the conclusion drawn is that deficiencies are present, then remedial action must be taken as quickly as possible to prevent the deficiencies from recurring. This could involve additional staff training, making improvements to the system of quality management, arranging additional quality reviews or taking disciplinary action against those who are found not to be complying with the firm's system of quality management.

Managing and achieving audit quality

14.24 One of the main ways in which audit quality is achieved is to ensure there are adequate supervision and review processes in place (particularly where more junior members of the engagement team are concerned).

In terms of the audit documentation, it is important that this contains:

(a) A record of matters identified, relevant discussions with audit engagement team members and conclusions reached concerning:

  (i) fulfilment of responsibilities concerning ethical requirements (including those related to independence); and

  (ii) the acceptance and continuance of the client relationship and audit engagement.

(b) The nature and scope of consultations undertaken during the engagement, including the conclusions arising from those consultations and how those conclusions were implemented.

(c)   When the audit engagement is subject to a review, ensure that the review has been completed on or before the date of the auditor's report.

IMPORTANT POINT

In addition to the above, where the audit engagement partner has identified any significant threats to the firm's independence, the safeguards that have been applied to mitigate the threat to independence to an acceptable level must be documented together with the reasons why those safeguards are deemed appropriate in the circumstances. Evidence of communication to the client is also required.

WHEN THE SYSTEM OF QUALITY MANAGEMENT FAILS

14.25   There are no prizes for guessing what happens when a firm's system of quality management fails. The quality of audit work falls short of the mark and things can really spiral downhill very quickly if something isn't done about it very quickly.

As I mentioned before, no auditor ever sets out to do a bad job and no firm ever strives to be the one hung out to dry by a regulator for carrying out deficient audit work. However, the reality is that the role of an auditor has become extremely demanding in recent years. ISAs (UK) have become lengthier, expectations from the general public have become higher and professional body scrutiny has become more rigorous. It is therefore critical that the firm has systems and processes in place that can cope with these demands.

In the last few years, there have been some high-profile corporate collapses that have called into question the work carried out by auditors. I have mentioned some of these in earlier chapters. Another one in particular that springs to mind is British Home Stores (BHS).

REAL-LIFE SCENARIO

BHS collapsed in 2016 resulting in more than 11,000 people losing their jobs. Not only that, but the pension fund was also in deficit to the tune of some £570 million. PwC (the auditors of BHS) and the audit engagement partner were found guilty of misconduct following the investigation into the audit.

PwC admitted to 'serious shortcomings' in the quality of the audit work performed and stated that '… at its core this is not a failure in our audit methodology, the methodology simply was not followed.'

The FRC's investigation into the audit showed that the audit engagement partner had only recorded two hours of work on the audit during the completion phase. Most of the review had been delegated to a junior colleague who only had one year of post-qualified experience. This shortcoming was compounded by the fact that several high-risk areas (including revenue recognition and impairment) were not reviewed by the audit engagement partner.

The audit engagement partner was fined £350,000 and was banned from carrying out audit work for 15 years.

The BHS audit failures highlight the need for a sound system of quality management. If PwC had an effective system of quality management in place (which included timely supervision and review of work carried out, particularly in high-risk areas), and had followed it, it is likely that the problems would have been avoided. At the very least, the audit engagement partner would have been required to spend a sufficient amount of time on the review of the audit work and this sorry saga would not have happened.

So, as you can see, if a system of quality management is not effective (or is simply not put in place), the risk of audit failure is high. This can have catastrophic consequences, as can be seen in the BHS case, and can leave audit engagement partners (and team members) looking back and saying, 'if only…'.

In **Chapter 2** I discuss the role of regulators and professional bodies and some court cases of particular interest where audit failures are concerned. So, if you've not already had a look at **Chapter 2**, flick back to it as there are some very interesting real-life cases in there to have a look at.

CHAPTER ROUNDUP

- There are three standards that are devoted to quality management, being ISQM (UK) 1, ISQM (UK) 2 and ISA (UK) 220.

- Audit quality is monitored by the FRC and by the relevant professional bodies (who are referred to as 'Recognised Supervisory Bodies').

- ISQM (UK) 1 and ISQM (UK) 2 deal with quality management at the firm level.

- ISA (UK) 220 deals with quality management at the engagement level.

- There are eight components to a system of quality management.

- The engagement quality reviewer cannot be a member of the audit engagement team and must possess the seniority and technical competence to carry out the review.

- All audit engagement team members are responsible for achieving quality on an audit, but ultimately it is the audit engagement partner that retains overall responsibility for ensuring a high-quality audit is carried out.

- Weak or absent systems of quality management contribute to audit failure and this can result in catastrophic consequences, including the loss of jobs.

PITFALLS TO AVOID

- Failing to ensure a system of quality management is put in place (which is adequately documented and conforms to the requirements of ISQM (UK) 1).

- Not carrying out an evaluation of the system on a regular basis.

- Failing to ensure adequate supervision and review processes are in place.

- Not devoting enough time to high-risk areas of the audit when it comes to reviewing audit documentation.

Chapter 15

Other Types of Engagement

CHAPTER TOPIC LIST

● Introduction (see **15.1**)

● The framework for assurance engagements (see **15.2**)

● Review engagements (see **15.3**)

● Agreed-upon procedures (see **15.5**)

● Compilation engagements (see **15.6**)

● Due diligence engagements (see **15.7**)

● Social and environmental reporting (see **15.14**)

● Management commentary (see **15.16**)

● Providing assurance on historical financial information (see **15.17**)

● Providing assurance on prospective financial information (see **15.18**)

INTRODUCTION

15.1   Much (if not pretty much all) of this book has been devoted to audit – after all, the title is, of course, *An Auditor's Guide to Auditing Financial Statements in the UK*. However, it would be unfair of me to ignore non-audit engagements because these form a lot of a practitioner's work in real life professional practice so are worthy of coverage in this title. These types of engagements may be referred to as 'assurance engagements'.

An 'assurance engagement' is one whereby a practitioner is required to express a conclusion (not an opinion, as I will discuss in a moment) which is designed to enhance the degree of confidence of the intended user of the engagement report. Because a conclusion is being expressed, these sorts of engagements are often referred to as 'limited assurance engagements'.

WHAT ARE WE TRYING TO ACHIEVE?

An audit is just one type of assurance engagement that a practitioner may be asked to carry out for their client. Here, we need to gain an understanding of the other types of engagement (both assurance and non-assurance) that may be carried out by a firm. Some of these engagements provide minimal assurance; whereas others provide no assurance at all, and it is important to be able to distinguish between them so as to be able to advise clients correctly.

Remember, in an audit engagement, the auditor provides **reasonable assurance** on the financial statements. This is a high level of assurance but is not absolute assurance. A limited assurance engagement does not go into the same depth of detail as an audit which means the practitioner is unable to form an opinion; instead, they form a conclusion based on performing a limited range of procedures to obtain evidence.

I think it's worth noting that assurance can be provided on both financial and non-financial information. For example, there is currently an increasing demand for professional firms to provide assurance on sustainability reports and similar information published by companies. Firms can also be engaged to report on business issues such as a system of internal control or risk management. As you can see, assurance engagements can encompass many things and they don't necessarily have to be wholly financial in nature.

I'd say the 'bread and butter' type work that most accountancy firms offer is accounts preparation for a non-audit client. This type of service usually does not result in any conclusion being reached – the accountant's report merely states that the financial statements have been prepared from information and explanations provided to the practitioner from the client.

Other types of engagement which you could see being carried out in an accountancy practice include fact-finding exercises, such as due diligence work carried out on a target company which is being considered for acquisition by the client.

THE FRAMEWORK FOR ASSURANCE ENGAGEMENTS

15.2   There is a framework for assurance engagements which was first published by the International Auditing and Assurance Standards Board (IAASB) in 2004 and was subsequently updated in 2013. This framework sets out high-level principles that apply to all assurance engagements (including audit engagements).

There are **five** elements that must be present in an assurance engagement:

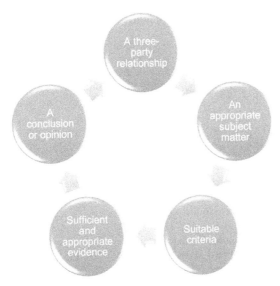

The **three-party relationship** involves a practitioner, a responsible party and intended users and the **conclusion or opinion** is expressed in a written report in a form that is appropriate to a reasonable assurance engagement (eg, an audit) or a limited assurance engagement (eg, a fact-finding exercise).

Example 15.1 – Ensuring the five elements of an assurance engagement are present

Philbin Enterprises Ltd wishes to raise finance and approaches its bank for a working capital loan. The relationship manager at the bank has considered the initial application and has said that the bank would like to see cash flow and profit forecasts which will then be evaluated as part of its lending decision. The bank have requested that some form of limited assurance be obtained by Philbin Enterprises Ltd on the cash flow and profit forecasts to enhance the credibility of the information. Philbin Enterprises Ltd has approached its external accountancy firm which has agreed to provide this limited assurance.

The elements of the engagement are as follows:

- The three-party relationship is between Philbin Enterprises Ltd (the responsible party), the bank (the intended user) and the external accountancy firm (the practitioner).

- The cash flow and profit forecasts are the subject matter.

- The suitable criteria are the benchmarks used by the practitioner to evaluate the forecasts (for example, the use of appropriate assumptions and whether appropriate accounting treatments have been applied).

- The evidence obtained by the practitioner will be obtained in pretty much the same way as the evidence obtained in an audit such as using materiality, identifying the risks of material misstatement in the financial information, carrying out specific procedures and reviewing the results to ensure that sufficient and appropriate evidence is obtained.

REVIEW ENGAGEMENTS

15.3   A review engagement is an example of a limited assurance engagement. Remember in a limited assurance engagement, the level of assurance is always **limited** or **moderate** and tends to be termed 'negative assurance'.

I think it's useful to compare a limited assurance engagement with an audit engagement because there is often confusion over the level of assurance the practitioner is giving when it comes to the two types of engagement:

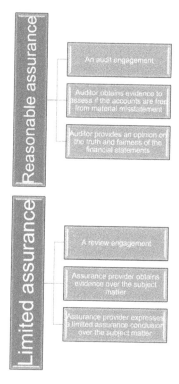

When carrying out a limited assurance engagement, the practitioner will:

- Obtain sufficient appropriate evidence to enable a conclusion to be drawn.

- Carry out fewer procedures than that of an audit and these procedures will usually be limited to inquiry and analytical procedures.

- Conclude that the subject matter is plausible in the circumstances, having regard to the identified criteria on which the conclusion is to be drawn.

- Provide a conclusion which is a **negative** conclusion.

Negative conclusion

At first, I think when you see the word 'negative' it implies something is wrong or unfavourable, but don't worry. When we talk about expressing a negative conclusion, all we are referring to is the type of wording that is being used. The table below highlights what we mean by a negative conclusion:

Audit assignment: Audit opinion	Limited assurance engagement: Practitioner's conclusion
In our opinion, the financial statements give a true and fair view.	Nothing has come to our attention that causes us to believe that the financial statements of Sunnie Ltd for the year ended 31 December 2024 are not prepared, in all material respects, in accordance with the applicable financial reporting framework.

As you can see from the comparison above, in an audit assignment the auditor is expressing a **positive** opinion stating that the financial statements give a true and fair view. In a limited assurance engagement, the practitioner's conclusion must be worded in the negative (ie, **nothing has come to our attention…**).

Summary of the types of engagement

15.4

Reasonable assurance engagement	Limited assurance engagement
Sufficient appropriate evidence is gathered to form an opinion	Sufficient appropriate evidence is gathered to form a conclusion
A conclusion is drawn that the subject matter complies in all material respects with identified suitable criteria	A conclusion is drawn that the subject matter is plausible in the circumstances and complies with identified suitable criteria

Reasonable assurance engagement	Limited assurance engagement
Rigorous procedures are carried out to obtain sufficient appropriate evidence such as tests of controls and substantive procedures	Significantly fewer procedures are carried out which mainly consist of inquiry and analytical procedures
A positively worded assurance opinion is expressed	A negatively worded assurance conclusion is expressed
A reasonable level of assurance is provided (this is a high level)	A lower level of assurance is provided

AGREED-UPON PROCEDURES

15.5   In an agreed-upon procedures assignment, the party which engages the practitioner or the intended user will establish the procedures that are to be carried out. The practitioner then provides a **report of factual findings** following the performance of those procedures.

IMPORTANT POINT

Where an agreed-upon procedures engagement is concerned, it is important to remember that this is **not** an assurance engagement and therefore no opinion or conclusion is expressed by the practitioner.

The guidance on agreed-upon procedures is contained in ISRS 4400 *Engagements to Perform Agreed-upon Procedures Regarding Financial Information*.

The process to adopt where an agreed-upon procedures engagement is concerned is as follows:

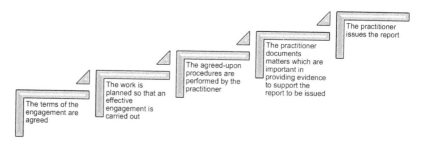

When the work has been completed, the report of factual findings will describe the agreed procedures but the report will generally not provide any assurance at all. However, this is not always the case and the practitioner may have been requested to provide some level of assurance. In this situation, the assignment becomes an assurance engagement and additional work must be carried out by the practitioner.

Example 15.2 – Illustrative report of factual findings

Olive Arts Ltd has agreed to provide a grant to Bauer Ltd on the basis that income and expenditure for the quarter ended 30 September 2024 is correct. Olive Arts has issued Bauer with a list of procedures that must be carried out by a qualified accountant and then certified by them in a report of factual findings. The procedures to be carried out are as follows:

(a)   Agree income for the quarter ended 30 September 2024 to source documents.

(b)   Agree income for the quarter ended 30 September 2024 to cash received.

(c)   Agree expenditure for the quarter ended 30 September 2024 to payments and purchase invoices.

(d)   Agree a sample of supplier balances as at 30 September 2024 to supplier statements.

The accountant has completed the above procedures and has concluded that everything is fine. The report of factual findings is issued as follows:

Report of factual findings

To Olive Arts Ltd

We have performed the procedures agreed with you and reviewed the income and expenditure of Bauer Ltd for the quarter ended 30 September 2024 which are set out in the accompanying schedules. Our engagement was carried out in accordance with International Standard on Related Services 4400 applicable to agreed-upon procedures. The procedures were performed solely to assist you in evaluating the validity of the income and expenditure and are summarised as follows:

(a)   We obtained and checked the income for the quarter ended 30 September 2024 to source documents, which comprised of sales invoices.

(b)   We compared the income to cash received. This involved tracing the sales invoices received to bank statements.

(c)   We agreed the expenditure for the quarter to purchase invoices and petty cash receipts.

(d)   We reviewed supplier statements to confirm balances owing at 30 September 2024. Some of these did not agree to the creditors' listing and we obtained reconciliations from Bauer Ltd. In respect of the reconciliations, we identified outstanding invoices, credit notes and outstanding payments. We obtained and examined such invoices and credit notes subsequently received and payments made after 30 September 2024 and concluded that they should have been included as outstanding as at 30 September 2024.

We report our findings as follows:

(a)   With respect to item 1, we found the income agreed to source documents.

(b)   With respect to item 2, we found the income agreed to cash received.

(c)   With respect to item 3, we confirmed that all expenditure for the quarter agreed to supporting documentation.

(d)   With respect to item 4, we found the amounts agreed, or in respect of amounts that did not agree, we found Bauer Ltd had prepared reconciliations which were in agreement, with the following exceptions:

[List the exceptions]

As the above procedures do not constitute an audit or a review made in accordance with International Standards on Auditing (UK), or International Standards on Review Engagement, we do not express any assurance on the income and expenditure of Bauer Ltd for the quarter ended 30 September 2024.

Had we performed additional procedures, or had we performed an audit or review of the income and expenditure in accordance with International Standards on Auditing (UK) or International Standards on Review Engagements, other matters may have come to our attention that would have been reported to you.

Our report is made solely for the purpose set forth in the first paragraph of this report and for your information and is not to be used for any other purpose or distributed to third parties without our express permission. This report relates only to the financial statements and items specified above and does not extend to any financial statements of Bauer Ltd, taken as a whole.

ABC Accounting Ltd

20 October 2024

COMPILATION ENGAGEMENTS

15.6   This is probably *the* most common type of engagement that a professional accountancy firm will be engaged to carry out. In a compilation engagement, the accountant will prepare financial statements, or other forms of financial information, from the accounting records provided by the client.

Guidance on these types of engagements is set out in ISRS 4410 *Engagements to Compile Financial Statements.* In addition, guidance is also set out in ICAEW guidance in the form of AAF 07/16 *Chartered Accountants' Reports on the Compilation of Financial Information of Incorporated Entities* and AAF 08/16 *Chartered Accountants' Reports on the Compilation of Historical Financial Information of Unincorporated Entities.*

In a compilation engagement, the process is as follows:

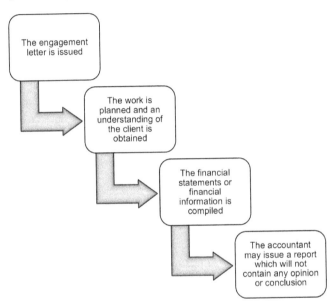

In practice, the financial statements or financial information may contain some form of accountant's report. Remember, unlike an auditor's report, an accountant's report is not legally required. Why? Well, because even when a business has engaged an external accountancy firm to prepare its financial statements, the client is legally responsible for the financial statements or financial information because it has been prepared from information and explanations provided to the practitioner from the client. In addition, it may well be the case that where the practitioner is a member of a professional body, that professional body may require an accountant's report to be included within the financial statements or financial information.

IMPORTANT POINT

The letter of engagement that is issued at the commencement of a professional relationship will make it clear that the accountant is not

---

carrying out any form of audit or assurance work and that management is responsible for the information produced. Where the work involves preparing statutory financial statements, these financial statements must be prepared using UK and Ireland Generally Accepted Accounting Practice or adopted IFRS® as well as applicable legislation, such as the CA 2006.

While much of the work in a compilation assignment involves the use of information and explanations provided to the practitioner from the client, there are some forms of analytical procedures the practitioner may use as well. For example, the calculation of gross profit margin in the current year and comparing this to the prior year to assess reasonableness and to identify if anything may be wrong in the trading account. In addition, analytical procedures can be used to identify any unusual increases or decreases in income and expenditure that may need further investigation. For example, if repairs and renewals expenditure has increased significantly in the current year when compared to the prior year, this may indicate that items of fixed assets have been incorrectly recorded in profit and loss rather than capitalised on the balance sheet and depreciated.

Remember, in a compilation engagement, while no opinion is being expressed, the professional accountant must carry out their work in accordance with professional standards and with a degree of diligence. Professional accountants who are members of a professional body cannot have their name associated with accounts which are misleading which is why the professional accountant must question any dubious transactions or information rather than simply relying on it.

Example 15.3 – Illustrative accountant's report on financial statements

Accountant's report to the directors of Greaves Industries Ltd for the year ended 31 October 2024

In order to assist you to fulfil your duties under the CA 2006, we have prepared for your approval the financial statements of Greaves Industries Ltd for the year ended 31 October 2024 as set out on pages 2 to 12 from the company's accounting records and from information and explanations you have provided to us.

As a member of [professional body], we are subject to its ethical and other professional requirements which are detailed at www.

This report is made solely to the board of directors of Greaves Industries Ltd, as a body, in accordance with the terms of our engagement letter dated 1 July 2024. Our work has been undertaken solely to prepare, for your approval, the financial statements of Greaves Industries Ltd and state those matters that we have agreed to state to the board of directors of Greaves Industries Ltd, as a body. To the fullest extent permitted by law, we do not accept or assume responsibility to anyone other than Greaves Industries Ltd and its board of directors as a body for our work or for this report.

It is your duty to ensure that Greaves Industries Ltd has kept adequate accounting records and to prepare statutory accounts that give a true and fair view of the assets, liabilities, financial position and profit or loss of Greaves Industries Ltd. You consider that Greaves Industries Ltd is exempt from the statutory audit requirement for the year ended 31 October 2024.

We have not been instructed to carry out an audit or a review of the financial statements of Greaves Industries Ltd. For this reason, we have not verified the accuracy or completeness of the accounting records or information and explanations you have given to us and we do not, therefore, express any opinion on the statutory accounts.

ABC Accounting Ltd

Address

Date

As you can see from this accountant's report, there are certain elements to it:

● The report refers to the fact that the financial statements are prepared on the basis of information and explanations provided by the client.

● It confirms that the client is responsible for the financial statements.

● It confirms that the client considers the entity is eligible to claim audit exemption.

● It confirms that the firm has not been instructed to carry out an audit or review of the financial statements, therefore no opinion is expressed. This is an important element because the user is aware that no assurance on the information in the financial statements is provided.

DUE DILIGENCE ENGAGEMENTS

15.7 In a due diligence engagement, the practitioner is requested to carry out inquiries into specific aspects of another entity's financial statements. Typically, these requests will arise because the practitioner's client is looking at buying the business or making a substantial investment into the business. The investor will want to know that they are buying into a viable business and hence information will be needed prior to the investment being made to make sure the investor has all the necessary facts and information to aid that decision-making process.

Due diligence is a way of obtaining this information. Again, a due diligence assignment is not an audit and there is no specific guidance from regulators on how to carry out a due diligence assignment (in some cases a due diligence assignment may not even be carried out by an accountant; they can be carried out by lawyers, surveyors, actuaries and other professionals who have experience in dealing with this area). In some cases, a due diligence assignment can even be carried out by the client themselves.

The actual scope of the due diligence assignment will be determined by the client and may typically include the following:

Organisational due diligence

15.8   This focuses on how the business is structured and its major shareholders. It also focuses on the types of governance arrangements in place and how risk is monitored and managed. An organisational due diligence assignment may also assess the effectiveness of the organisation's system of internal control.

Financial due diligence

15.9   This type of due diligence assignment focuses on the financial performance and position of the target company and looks into both historic and prospective financial information. Typically, the practitioner will carry out an evaluation of the quality of earnings, the asset base of the business, the level of debt and planned capital expenditure. During these sorts of due diligence assignments, it is not uncommon for the practitioner to uncover assets and liabilities that have not been included in the financial statements such as contingent assets and customer lists.

Operational due diligence

15.10   An operational due diligence assignment focuses on the commercial operations of a business. During such an assignment, there will be an evaluation of the organisation's business model, the resources which it uses, an assessment of relations with customers and suppliers as well as the company's overall strategy.

Legal due diligence

15.11   A legal due diligence assignment focuses on contracts and agreements such as those which relate to loans, leases or asset rental contracts. A legal due diligence assignment can also focus on contracts of employment, patents and copyrights as well as any legal claims that relate to the business.

People due diligence

15.12   The focus of a people due diligence assignment is on employees and directors of the company. Primarily the assignment will look at the skills and talent of the workforce, but there could be other characteristics or objectives to the assignment.

The above is not designed to be a comprehensive list as due diligence work can be varied. It is merely to highlight some of the more typical due diligence assignments that crop up in day-to-day business.

A due diligence assignment will always be looking into the future. This is because the acquirer will want to consider the business plan, cash flow and profit forecasts and projections and consider how realistic these are as well as evaluating how the acquiree could successfully integrate into the acquirer's business.

Due diligence report

15.13   Relevant (but not mandatory) guidance can be found in the form of ISRS 4400 *Engagements to Perform Agreed-upon Procedures Regarding Financial Information* and reporting on the results of agreed-upon procedures, which includes due diligence.

The due diligence report will be tailored to the client's specific requirements and will be a report of factual findings which should normally contain at least the following:

- Title and addressee which is usually the client who engaged the practitioner to carry out the agreed-upon procedures.

- Identification of specific financial or non-financial information to which the agreed-upon procedures have been applied.

- A statement that the procedures performed were those agreed with the recipient of the report.

- Identification of the purpose for which the agreed-upon procedures were carried out.

- A listing of the specific procedures carried out.

- A description of the factual findings, including sufficient details of errors and exceptions found.

- A statement that the procedures carried out do not constitute either an audit or a review and, consequently, no assurance is provided.

- A statement that the report is restricted to those parties that have agreed to the procedures carried out.

- A statement (when applicable) that the report relates only to elements, accounts, items or financial and non-financial information specified and that it does not extend to the entity's financial statements taken as a whole.

Example 15.4 – Due diligence assignment

Ratchford Enterprises Ltd is considering acquiring the entire share capital of Dwyer Industries Ltd. The directors of Ratchford Enterprises Ltd have approached their external accountants, Sienna & Co LLP to carry out due diligence on Dwyer Industries. Dwyer Industries has produced cash flow and profit forecasts for the next two years.

Sienna & Co discovered that Dwyer Industries Ltd has several customers, but one of their top five customers has a considerable overdue balance and their accounts are also late for filing at Companies House. The finance director of Dwyer Industries informed Sienna & Co that in his opinion, it is unlikely that the balance will be paid as rumours are circulating that the customer is about to go into liquidation. In addition, the customer list is worth a considerable amount of money.

Sienna & Co would need to assess the impact on revenue if the customer in question goes bankrupt. This is important because the cash flow and profit forecasts will more than likely include sales to the customer. As this customer is in the top five, the loss of revenue from this customer is likely to be an important factor and could significantly influence the investment decision. Procedures will need to be carried out to assess the going concern status of this customer and whether there are new customers in the pipeline (or which have already come on board) which could replace the lost revenue.

In connection with the customer list, Sienna & Co would need to carry out additional procedures. A key issue is that this customer list would need to be valued and this valuation exercise could be carried out by Sienna & Co provided they have the necessary expertise, or a third-party valuer would need to be engaged. A customer list is potentially a very valuable asset which could significantly influence the valuation of the business.

In the group financial statements, the customer list would be recognised at fair value and hence is an important consideration from both a commercial and a technical accounting perspective.

Sienna & Co will report their factual findings to the board of directors of Ratchford Ltd. It is then up to the management of Ratchford Ltd to evaluate the report and consider the findings of the report when deciding whether, or not, to go ahead with the acquisition.

SOCIAL AND ENVIRONMENTAL REPORTING

15.14 Many companies disclose information concerning climate change and sustainability within their annual report. Indeed, for larger companies, investors are increasingly calling for companies to provide specific disclosures on climate change and how they are contributing to reducing the impact of climate change. In 2015, The Task Force on Climate-related Financial Disclosures (TCFD) was founded with the objective of developing recommendations for voluntary climate-related disclosures.

Fast forward to June 2023 and the International Sustainability Standards Board issued two sustainability disclosure standards in the form of:

- IFRS S1 *General Requirements for Disclosure of Sustainability-related Financial Information*; and

- IFRS S2 *Climate-related Disclosures.*

Environmental reporting need not be in the annual report. Indeed, some companies have stand-alone reports which are dedicated to social and environmental reporting as well as having dedicated pages on their website. In some cases this can provide efficiencies and enable the annual report to be dedicated to the financial aspects of the business rather than having an extremely voluminous annual report.

Assurance can be obtained on non-financial information in order to enhance credibility. Indeed, the largest audit firms have specialist departments that can obtain the necessary evidence in order to provide this type of assurance.

A principal risk in respect of sustainability disclosures is the act of 'greenwashing'. This refers to the misleading practice of including disclosures that depict the company as environmentally friendly when, in reality, it is not. Greenwashing aims to attract investors and consumers whose focus is on entities that are environmentally friendly and have environmentally friendly products, processes and policies. Obtaining assurance on sustainability disclosures is a means of holding companies to account for such disclosures.

Guidance on Extended External Reporting (EER)

15.15   In April 2021, the International Auditing and Assurance Standards Board (IAASB) issued non-authoritative guidance on applying ISAE 3000 (Revised) *Assurance Engagements Other than Audits or Reviews of Historical Financial Information* to external assurance engagements. The IAASB recognised that there is an increasing number of companies that include integrated reports, sustainability repots and reports that focus on environmental, social and governance matters.

As part of this project, the IAASB considered a number of challenges that are often present when assurance providers are engaged to carry out this sort of work. Challenges such as applying materiality, identifying suitable criteria and evaluating information are just some of the key challenges as well as having to deal with information that is focussed on the future.

The IAASB's guidance suggests that the assurance provider obtains an understanding of:

As you would expect, the guidance is extensive and provides examples which are relevant to all stages of the EER. It is fair to say that performing this type of assurance engagement is a challenge and the work needs to be properly planned and executed to ensure the engagement is properly carried out. However, by applying the guidance the quality of the work performed will be enhanced and will result in a higher level of credibility.

MANAGEMENT COMMENTARY

15.16 Management commentary is also referred to as 'non-financial reporting' and has become an increasingly important focus for users of the financial statements over recent years. Such reporting includes information concerning:

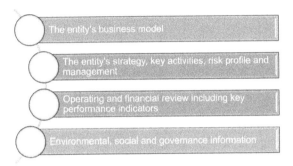

This is not an exhaustive list and the management commentary can include several other elements depending on the nature, size and complexity of the organisation.

The management commentary is often included in the front-end of the financial statements and depending on the jurisdiction in which the organisation is based, the management commentary may be required to comply with various regulations and guidance, such as:

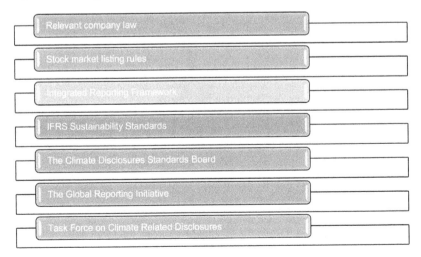

One way in which a company can provide management commentary is by the use of an Intergrated Report. Integrated reporting is a way that enables a business to present a holistic view of how its business model creates value over time. This approach is starting to become the 'norm' for many larger organisations and while obtaining assurance on this type of information is not usually mandatory, many companies do obtain independent assurance on at least part of the Integrated Report (such as on key performance indicators).

Assurance can be provided in several ways. For example, an entity's internal audit department are generally in a good place to provide input into evaluating existing systems and processes including the design and implementation of performance measures.

External assurance is also possible. An independent assurance provider (eg, a professional accountant) can be appointed to provide an unbiased conclusion and this can also be carried out by an auditor. However, it is important to keep in mind that the assurance provider can only ever provide limited assurance on such financial and non-financial information. Limited assurance can only be provided on information in a narrative report due to the subjective (and often hypothetical) nature of the information.

As I mentioned earlier, assurance may be obtained on just specific parts of the narrative report, such as the key performance indicators. In many cases, key performance indicators are subject to external scrutiny by auditors because these are quantified and hence more robust evidence can be obtained to confirm their validity. Hence, rather than providing assurance on the entire non-financial report, it is commonplace for assurance just to be sought on specific aspects of the report.

Example 15.5 – Illustrative assurance report on selected key performance indicators

To the Directors of Wolves Enterprises Ltd

Report on selected key performance indicators

We have undertaken a limited assurance engagement on selected key performance indicators (KPIs), as described below, and presented in the 2024 Sustainability Report of Wolves Enterprises Ltd (Wolves) for the year ended 31 December 2024.

Subject matter

We have been engaged to provide a limited assurance conclusion in our report on the following selected KPIs. The selected KPIs described below have been prepared in accordance with Wolves' reporting criteria that accompanies the sustainability information on the relevant pages of the report (the accompanying Wolves' reporting criteria).

Category	Selected KPIs	Scope of coverage
Environmental	• Total water usage (page 16) • Carbon footprint (page 20) • Waste generated (page 22) • Total energy usage (page 25)	Wolves' operations at all sites
Social	• Total trend spending (page 14) • Disabled employees in the business as a percentage of total employees (page 14) • Percentage of employees with additional needs as a percentage of total employees (page 15)	Wolves Enterprises Ltd
Health and Safety	• Lost time injury frequency rate (page 22) • Number of noise-induced hearing loss cases of more than 10% (page 23)	Wolves Enterprises Ltd

Directors' responsibilities

The directors are responsible for the selection, preparation and presentation of the selected KPIs in accordance with the accompanying Wolves reporting criteria. This responsibility includes the identification of stakeholders and stakeholder requirements, material issues, commitments with respect to sustainability performance and design, implementation and maintenance of internal controls relevant to the preparation of the report that is free from material misstatement, whether due to fraud or error. The directors are also responsible for determining the appropriateness of the measurement and reporting criteria in view of the intended users of the selected KPIs and for ensuring that those criteria are publicly available to the report users.

Inherent limitations

[Insert applicable text, if relevant]

Our independence and quality management

We have complied with the independence and all other ethical requirements of the FRC Ethical Standard and the Code of Ethics issued by our professional body [insert relevant professional body] which are founded on the fundamental principles of integrity, objectivity, professional competence and due care, confidentiality and professional behaviour.

ABC Accountants Ltd ('the firm') applies the International Standard on Quality Management (UK) 1, which requires the firm to design, implement and operate a system of quality management including policies or procedures regarding compliance with ethical requirements, professional standards and applicable legal and regulatory requirements.

Practitioner's responsibility

Our responsibility is to express a limited assurance conclusion on the selected KPIs based on the procedures we have performed and the evidence we have obtained. We conducted our assurance engagement in accordance with the International Standard on Assurance Engagements (ISAE) 3000 (Revised), *Assurance Engagements other than Audits or Reviews of Historical Financial Information*, issued by the International Auditing and Assurance Standards Board. That Standard requires that we plan and perform our engagement to obtain limited assurance about whether the selected KPIs are free from material misstatement.

A limited assurance engagement undertaken in accordance with ISAE 3000 (Revised) involves assessing the suitability in the circumstances of Wolves' use of its reporting criteria as the basis of preparation for the selected KPIs, assessing the risks of material misstatement of the selected KPIs whether due to fraud or error, responding to the assessed risks as necessary in the circumstances, and evaluating the overall presentation of the selected KPIs. A limited assurance engagement is substantially less in scope than a reasonable assurane engagement in relation to both risk assessment procedures, including an understanding of internal control, and the procedures performed in response to the assessed risks. The procedures we performed were based on our professional judgement and included inquiries, observation of processes followed, inspection of documents, analytical procedures, evaluating the appropriateness of quantification methods and reporting policies, and agreeing or reconciling with underlying records.

Given the circumstances of the engagement, in performing the procedures listed above we:

- Interviewed management and senior executives to obtain an understanding of the internal control environment, risk assessment process and information systems relevant to the sustainability reporting process.

- Inspected documentation to corroborate the statements of management and senior executives in our interviews.

- Tested the processes and systems to generate, collate, aggregate, monitor and report the selected KPIs.

- Performed a controls walk-through of identified key controls.

- Inspected supporting documentation on a sample basis and performed analytical procedures to evaluate the data generation and reporting processes against the reporting criteria.

- Evaluated the reasonableness and appropriateness of significant estimates and judgements made by the directors in the preparation of the selected KPIs.

- Evaluated whether the selected KPIs presented in the report are consistent with our overall knowledge and experience of sustainability management and performance at Wolves Ltd.

The procedures performed in a limited assurance engagement vary in nature and timing, and are less in extent than for a reasonable assurance engagement. As a result, the level of assurance obtained in a limited assurance engagement is substantially lower than the assurance that would have been obtained had we performed a reasonable assurance engagement. Accordingly, we do not express a reasonable assurance opinion about whether Wolves' selected KPIs have been prepared, in all material respects, in accordance with the accompanying Wolves' reporting criteria.

Limited assurance conclusion

Based on the procedures we have performed and the evidence we have obtained, [*and subject to the inherent limitations outlined elsewhere in this report*], nothing has come to our attention that causes us to believe that the selected KPIs as set out in the Subject Matter paragraph above for the year ended 31 December 2024 are not prepared, in all material respects, in accordance with the reporting criteria.

Other matters

No assurance procedures were performed on the previous sustainability report. The information relating to the prior reporting periods has not been subject to assurance procedures.

Our report includes the provision of limited assurance on [*name of the new selected KPIs for the year*]. We were previously not required to provide assurance on these selected KPIs.

The maintenance and integrity of the Wolves' website is the responsibility of Wolves' management. Our procedures did not involve consideration of these matters and, consequently, we accept no responsibility for any changes to either the information in the report or our independent limited assurance report that may have occurred since the initial date of its presentation on Wolves' website.

Limitation of liability

Our work has been undertaken to enable us to express a limited assurance conclusion on the selected KPIs to the directors of Wolves Ltd in accordance with the terms of our engagement, and for no other purpose. We do not accept or assume liability to any party other than Wolves Ltd, for our work, for this report, or for the conclusion we have reached.

Report on other legal and regulatory matters

[*The form and content of this section of the assurance report will vary depending on the nature of the practitioner's other reporting responsibilities.*]

Mrs Amanda Howard

Partner

ABC Accountants Ltd

22 February 2025

PROVIDING ASSURANCE ON HISTORICAL FINANCIAL INFORMATION

15.17 Some professional bodies actively promote limited assurance engagements on historical financial information as a basis of providing some form of assurance on a company's financial statements. These types of assignments are geared towards entities that can claim (and have claimed) audit exemption and are sometimes referred to as a 'mini audit'.

Again, when the practitioner provides assurance on historical financial information, they provide **negative assurance** (ie, ... *nothing has come to our attention to indicate that the accompanying financial statements contain material misstatement*).

There is guidance in the form of ISRE 2400 *Engagements to Review Historical Financial Statements* which deals with this type of engagement. ISRE 2400 clarifies that when carrying out such an engagement, the practitioner expresses a conclusion that is designed to enhance the degree of confidence of intended users concerning the preparation of an entity's financial statements in accordance with an applicable financial reporting framework (eg, FRS 102).

Remember, the practitioner's conclusion is based on the practitioner obtaining limited assurance (not reasonable assurance because this would constitute an audit and hence a positive opinion would be expressed).

When the practitioner carries out an assurance engagement on historical financial information, they will usually apply procedures such as analytical procedures and inquiry. Additional procedures will be carried out if the practitioner thinks there is a potential material misstatement. ISRE 2400 also requires that the assurance provider confirms that management is aware of its responsibilities for producing the financial statements (remember, this responsibility cannot be delegated).

IMPORTANT POINT

Unlike an auditor's report, which is generally addressed to the shareholders/ members of the company, the assurance report on historical financial information is usually issued to the company directors on the basis that it is the directors who have appointed the assurance provider to carry out the limited review.

PROVIDING ASSURANCE ON PROSPECTIVE FINANCIAL INFORMATION

15.18 Prospective financial information (PFI) involves financial information about the future (eg, cash flow forecasts or forecast profit and loss accounts). Often, assurance on prospective financial information will be asked for by a bank that is considering lending a company money and there is guidance in the form of ISAE 3400 *The Examination of Prospective Financial Information.*

ISAE 3400 identifies two types of PFI:

Forecast

A forecast is based on best-estimate assumptions (those which management expect to take place)

Projection

This is based on hypothetical assumptions (which are less certain than best-estimations)

Remember, PFI is based on events and actions that haven't yet happened (and may not happen). This means that work on PFI is highly subjective and the preparation of PFI requires a high degree of judgement.

As with any type of engagement, the practitioner must agree the terms of the assignment with management at the outset, as well as gaining an understanding of the business (without this understanding, how can one provide any sort of assurance?) A forecast usually covers a period of up to 12 months; whereas a projection can be up to five years (sometimes longer). These time conditions are not absolute and each entity will be different.

Written representations

15.19 ISAE 3400 requires management to provide written representations concerning:

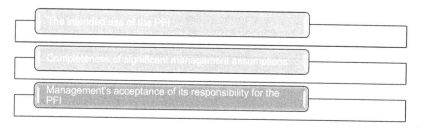

IMPORTANT POINT

The assurance report issued by the practitioner should make it clear that management is responsible for the PFI as well as the assumptions on which it is based.

Given the fact that PFI is based on 'ifs, buts and maybes', understandably an opinion cannot be expressed in the assurance report. The report will only contain negative assurance.

Obtaining evidence

15.20 ISAE 3400 sets out four specifications that the practitioner must ensure. Specifically, ISAE 3400 requires that the assurance provider obtains evidence as to whether:

Management's best-estimate assumptions on which the PFI is based are not unreasonable and, in the case of hypothetical assumptions, these are consistent with the purpose of the information

The PFI is properly prepared on the basis of the assumptions

The PFI is properly presented and all material assumptions are adequately disclosed including a clear indication as to whether they are best-estimate or hypothetical assumptions

The PFI is prepared on a consistent basis with historical financial statements, using appropriate accounting principles

Reporting

15.21 ISAE 3400 provides guidance on the content of an assurance report on PFI where the practitioner has examined forecasts or projections. To that end, the report should include:

(1) **Title and addressee** – This would be to the directors of the company.

(2) **Identification of the PFI** – This should be by reference to a page number in the PFI or to the titles of the statements that have been examined. There should also be a reference to the period that the PFI covers.

(3) **A reference to ISAE 3400 or other relevant regulations that apply to the examination of the PFI** – this adds an element of credibility to the report because it has been prepared in accordance with a recognised regulatory statement.

(4) **Management's responsibility** – This confirms that management is responsible for the PFI, including the assumptions on which it is based.

(5) **Where applicable, a reference to the purpose and/or restricted distribution of the PFI** – The report would reference the intended user (eg, the bank) and limit distribution of the report to the user for the objective of its decision (eg, whether to lend the company money or not).

(6) **A statement of negative assurance as to whether the assumptions provide a reasonable basis for the PFI** – This would contain the negative conclusion (ie, nothing has come to our attention which causes us to believe that the assumptions do not provide a reasonable basis for the projection …').

(7) **Basis of preparation of the PFI** – This would contain a statement as to whether the PFI is properly prepared on the basis of the assumptions and is presented in accordance with the applicable financial reporting framework.

(8) **Caveats** – This would contain caveats concerning the achievability of the results indicated by the PFI.

(9) **Signoffs** – This would contain the date, name of the practitioner and a signature.

CHAPTER ROUNDUP

- In addition to audit work, there are other types of assurance engagement that a practitioner may be requested to carry out for their clients.

- Some assurance engagements provide some limited assurance, whereas others provide no assurance.

- There are five elements that must be present in an assurance engagement.

- A reasonable assurance engagement (such as an audit) results in the expression of an opinion – ie, positive assurance.

- A limited assurance engagement results in the expression of a conclusion (usually a negative one).

- Various types of engagement can be requested, such as a 'review engagement', 'agreed-upon procedures engagement', 'compilation engagements', 'due diligence engagements', 'social and environmental reporting', 'reporting on management commentary' and reporting on historical and prospective financial information (although there are other types of such engagement that can be carried out).

- There is various guidance available to assist practitioners in carrying out different types of assurance engagement.

PITFALLS TO AVOID

- Carrying out engagements without the requisite skills and experience.

- Failing to ensure there is an agreement of term (eg, an engagement letter) in place prior to carrying out the work.

- Providing assurance on certain engagements (eg, compilation engagements) where no assurance is intended.

- Failing to understand the difference between a 'conclusion' and an 'opinion'.

Index

[All references are to paragraph number.]

A

access to books and records of company, 1.8

account balances and materiality, 6.3

accounting estimates, 8.38
  complexity, 8.41
  develop an auditor's point estimate, 8.46
  documentation, 8.50
  estimation uncertainty, 8.40
  evaluating and concluding on, 8.49
  interaction with audit planning and risk assessment, 8.43
  other audit procedures, 8.48
  responses to assessed risks, 8.44
  risk assessment processes, 8.39
  subjectivity, 8.42
  subsequent events, 8.45
  test how management has arrived at estimate, 8.47

adjusting events, 10.20

adverse auditor's opinion, 12.3, 12.5, 12.14

advertising, 4.5

advocacy threats, 3.3, 3.4

aggregation risk, 13.10

agreed-upon procedures assignment, 15.5

American Institute of Certified Public Accountants (AICPA), 11.3

appointment of auditor, 1.11

articles of association
  appointment of auditor, 1.11
  audit requirements, 1.2

assertion levels, 5.4, 5.23
  risks at assertion level, 7.4

Association of Chartered Certified Accountants (ACCA), 1.1
  advertising services, 4.5
  audit planning, 5.2
  Code of Ethics, 14.7
  continuing professional development, 2.12

Association of Chartered Certified Accountants (ACCA) – *contd*
  evolution gap, 9.22
  expectations gap, 9.19
  money laundering, 1.10
  non-PIEs and non-listed entities, 2.2
  regulation of auditors, 2.9, 2.10

Association of International Accountants (AIA), 1.1, 2.9

assurance engagements, 15.1
  elements of engagement, 15.2
  framework for, 15.2
  historical financial information, 15.17
  limited assurance engagements, 15.4
  negative assurance, 15.17
  prospective financial information, 15.18
  reasonable assurance, 15.1
  reasonable assurance engagements, 15.4
  three-party relationship, 15.2

attribute sampling, 7.30

audit completion
  comparative information, 10.35
  corresponding figures, 10.35
  evaluation of misstatements, 10.2
  final analytical review, 10.17
  notes to financial statements, 10.18
  going concern, 10.23
  audit procedures over cash flow forecast, 10.28
  auditor's responsibilities relating to, 10.26
  doubts exist about entity's ability to continue as, 10.27
  expectations gap, and, 10.33
  going concern basis of accounting appropriate, 10.30, 10.31
  going concern basis of accounting not appropriate, 10.32
  management reporting on, 10.25
  material uncertainties, 10.31

audit completion – *contd*
  going concern – *contd*
    no material uncertainties, 10.30
    reporting on, 10.29
    responsibilities in respect of, 10.24
  identified misstatements, 10.4–10.11
    audit plan, effect on, 10.7
    audit strategy, effect on, 10.7
    management refusal to correct,
      10.11
    materiality of, 10.8
    misstatements in financial
      statements, 10.6
    recording misstatements, 10.5
    reporting to management, 10.9
    request that misstatements are
      corrected, 10.10
  introduction, 10.1
  opening balances, 10.34
  prior period's financial statements not
    audited, 10.36
  subsequent events, 10.19
    adjusting and non-adjusting events,
      10.20
    procedure where auditor has active
      duty, 10.21
    procedure where auditor has passive
      duty, 10.22
  types of misstatements, 10.3
    identified misstatements, 10.4–10.11
    uncorrected misstatements, 10.12–
      10.16
  uncorrected misstatements, 10.12–10.16
    evaluating effect of uncorrected
      misstatements, 10.14
    reporting uncorrected
      misstatements, 10.15
    requesting written representation,
      10.16
    revisiting materiality levels, 10.13
audit evidence
  accounting estimates, 8.38
    complexity, 8.41
    develop an auditor's point estimate,
      8.46
    documentation, 8.50
    estimation uncertainty, 8.40
    evaluating and concluding on, 8.49
    interaction with audit planning and
      risk assessment, 8.43

audit evidence – *contd*
  accounting estimates– *contd*
    other audit procedures, 8.48
    responses to assessed risks, 8.44
    risk assessment processes, 8.39
    subjectivity, 8.42
    subsequent events, 8.45
    test how management has arrived at
      estimate, 8.47
  appropriate audit evidence, 7.5, 7.7
    relevance, 7.9
    reliability, 7.8
  audit sampling, 7.23
    attribute sampling, 7.30
    block selection, 7.28
    factors to consider when using
      sampling, 7.31
    haphazard selection, 7.28
    monetary unit sampling, 7.28, 7.32
    non-sampling risk, 7.26
    non-statistical sampling, 7.27
    random selection, 7.28
    sampling risk within substantive
      procedures, 7.25
    sampling risk within tests of
      controls, 7.24
    sampling techniques, 7.28
    statistical sampling, 7.27
    stratification, 7.29
    systematic selection, 7.28
  auditing opening balances, 8.14
    client requires audit for first time,
      8.16
    consistency of accounting policies,
      8.19
    current auditor audited previous
      year's financial statements,
      8.20
    key audit matters, 8.17
    opening balances contain
      misstatements, 8.18
    prior year auditor expressed
      modified audit opinion, 8.15
  communication with management, 8.54
    communicating with those charged
      with governance, 8.55
    communication process, 8.57
    effectiveness of two-way
      communication, 8.58
    significant findings from audit, 8.56

audit evidence – *contd*
corroboration, 7.20
data analytics, 8.51
advantages and challenges of, 8.52
use for audit sampling, 8.53
directional testing, 7.33
stock, 7.35
testing balance sheet in both
directions, 7.36
testing profit and loss account in
both directions, 7.37
use of, 7.34
experts, use of, 8.2
agreeing work to be performed, 8.6
assessing competency, capability
and objectivity of auditor's
expert, 8.5
carrying out evaluation of expert's
work, 8.7
determining need for auditor's
expert, 8.3
establishing audit procedures, 8.4
external confirmations, 8.30
carrying out confirmation request,
8.31
client refuses to agree to
confirmation request, 8.32
evaluating the results of, 8.33
group audits, 13.15–13.16
interim audit, 7.38
internal audit, considering work of,
8.34
documentation, 8.37
reviewing work of internal audit,
8.36
using work of internal audit, 8.35
introduction, 7.1, 8.1
litigation and claims, 8.26
management or lawyer refusal, 8.27
written representation, 8.28
obtaining audit evidence, 7.10–7.16
prior year evidence, 7.13
substantive procedures, 7.11, 7.15,
7.16
tests of controls, 7.11, 7.12, 7.14
professional judgement, applying, 7.21
reporting deficiencies in internal
controls, 8.59
communication via letter of
comment, 8.60

audit evidence – *contd*
responding to assessed risks, 7.2
risks at assertion level, 7.4
risks at financial statement level, 7.3
risk and, 7.22
segment information, 8.29
service organisations, use of, 8.8
fraud, 8.12
non-compliance with laws and
regulations, 8.12
responding to assessed risks, 8.11
service organisations and auditor's
report, 8.13
sources of information, 8.10
understanding nature and
significance of services
provided, 8.9
stock count, 8.21
attending stock count, 8.23
audit stock and work in progress
figure, 8.24
planning the count, 8.22
stock held at third parties, 8.25
sufficient audit evidence, 7.5, 7.6
tests of controls
evaluating the results of, 7.14
nature and extent of, 7.12
substantive procedures and, 7.11
types of audit procedures
analytical procedures, 7.17–7.19
data analytics, 7.19
external confirmation, 7.17
inquiry, 7.17
inspection of assets, 7.17
inspection of records and
documents, 7.17
observation, 7.17
recalculation, 7.17
reperformance, 7.17
audit exemption
statements, 1.5
thresholds, 1.3
audit failure versus business failure,
5.14
audit plan
changes to, 6.12
developing, 6.11
misstatements, 10.7
audit planning
audit fieldwork stage, 5.1

audit planning – *contd*
  audit risk, 5.11, 5.15, 6.1
    audit risk model and its
      components, 5.16
    control risk, 5.18–5.20
    detection risk, 5.11, 5.19
    inherent risk, 5.7, 5.11, 5.17, 5.20
  business failure versus audit failure,
    5.14
  business risk, 5.10, 5.13, 6.1
  client system and controls, evaluation
    of, 5.24
    general IT controls, 5.10
  disclosures, planning audit of, 6.13
  financial statements, 5.4
    assertion levels, 5.4, 5.23
    financial statement assertions, 5.21
    financial statement levels, 5.4,
      5.22
    risk of material misstatement, 5.10,
      5.20
  fraud, 6.18
    auditor's risk assessment
      procedures, 6.19
    related parties, 6.21
    responding to assessed risks of
      material misstatement due to
      fraud, 6.20
  group audits, 13.5–13.10
  International Standards on Auditing
    (UK), 5.1
  introduction, 5.1, 6.2
  materiality, 6.2
    account balances, 6.3
    audit risk, 6.6
    classes of transactions, 6.3
    disclosures, 6.3
    financial statement, 6.4
    performance, 6.5
    trivial error, 6.7
  objective, 5.2
  preliminary planning activities, 5.3
  reporting stage, 5.1
  risk assessment
    responses to assessed risks, 5.1,
      5.12, 6.1
    risk assessment phase, 5.1, 5.10,
      5.11
    substantive procedures, 5.12
    tests of controls, 5.12

audit planning – *contd*
  understanding the entity and its
    environment, 5.4
    economic challenges, 5.9
    regulatory factors, 5.8
    sources of information, 5.5
    understanding the entity itself, 5.6
    understanding the environment in
      which the client operates,
      5.7
audit procedures
  analytical procedures, 6.8, 7.17–7.19
    key ratios, 6.9
    substantive analytical procedures,
      6.17
  design of, 6.14
  substantive procedures, 6.16, 6.17
  tests of control, 6.15
  tests of detail, 6.16
Audit, Reporting and Governance
  Authority (ARGA), 2.3
audit risk, 5.11, 5.15
  audit risk model and its components,
    5.16
  control risk, 5.18–5.20
  detection risk, 5.11, 5.19
  inherent risk, 5.7, 5.11, 5.17, 5.20
  materiality, 6.6
audit sampling, 7.23
  attribute sampling, 7.30
  block selection, 7.28
  factors to consider when using
    sampling, 7.31
  haphazard selection, 7.28
  monetary unit sampling, 7.28, 7.32
  non-sampling risk, 7.26
  non-statistical sampling, 7.27
  random selection, 7.28
  sampling risk within substantive
    procedures, 7.25
  sampling risk within tests of controls,
    7.24
  sampling techniques, 7.28
  statistical sampling, 7.27
  stratification, 7.29
  systematic selection, 7.28
audit strategy
  changes to, 6.12
  developing, 6.10
  misstatements, 10.7

auditor's report (modified opinion)
adverse opinion, 12.3, 12.5, 12.14
disclaimers of opinion, 12.3, 12.6,
    12.15
management-imposed limitations,
    12.16
going concerns, 12.17
deterioration in operating results
    after balance sheet date, 12.20
going concern basis inappropriate,
    12.18
inadequate disclosure relating to,
    12.19
introduction, 12.1
material and pervasive matters, 12.9
handling potential modifications to
    auditor's opinion, 12.10
material but not pervasive matters,
    12.8
qualified opinion, 12.3, 12.4, 12.12
auditor appointed after reporting
    date, 12.13
reporting modified opinion, 12.11
scope of modified opinion, 12.2
summary, 12.7
auditor's report (unmodified opinion),
    11.3
address of auditor, 11.2
addressee, 11.2
audit engagement partner, 11.2
auditor's opinion, 11.2
availability, 11.3
Bannerman paragraphs, 11.29
basis for opinion, 11.2
Brydon review of auditing profession,
    11.6
content, 11.2
date of report, 11.2
emphasis of matter, 11.10–11.14
EOM paragraphs and key audit
    matters, 11.14
placement of EOM paragraph in
    report, 11.13
when EOM paragraph appropriate,
    11.12
when EOM paragraph inappropriate,
    11.11
expectations gap, 11.9
financial statements, responsibilities
    for, 11.2

auditor's report (unmodified opinion) –
contd
introduction, 11.1
key audit matters, 11.2, 11.25–11.28
communicating, 11.26
ethical considerations, 11.28
presenting in the auditor's report,
    11.27
limiting auditor's liability, 11.29
material inconsistencies, 11.16–11.17
material uncertainties relating to going
    concern, 11.19–11.24
auditor reporting issues, 11.21
'close calls', 11.23
financial reporting issues, 11.20
inadequate disclosure, 11.24
placement of paragraph within
    report, 11.22
other information, 11.16
material inconsistencies, 11.16–11.17
placement of within report, 11.18
other matter paragraphs, 11.15
reasonable assurance, 11.9
reference to applicable financial
    reporting framework, 11.7
reporting by exception, 11.8
signature of auditor, 11.2
true and fair view, 11.3–11.6
auditors
appointment, 1.11
objections to automatic
    reappointment, 1.11
duties, 1.9
responsibilities for fraud, 9.12–9.16
auditor's risk assessment
    procedures, 9.13
conditions which may indicate that
    document not authentic, 9.14
fraud and revenue recognition, 9.15
reporting in the auditor's report,
    9.16
resignation, 1.12–1.13
statement of reasons, 1.13
rights, 1.8

B
Bannerman paragraph, 11.29
block selection, 7.28
Brydon review of auditing profession,
    11.6

Bulletins (FRC), 2.7, 11.2
business failure versus audit failure, 5.14
business relationships and ethics, 3.9,
  3.13
business risk, 5.10, 5.13

C

classes of transactions and materiality,
  6.3
client acceptance
  agreeing terms of audit, 4.22
  anti-money laundering protocol, 4.20
  Anti-Money Laundering
      Regulations 2017, 4.21
  due diligence, 4.6
  ethics, 4.7
    fees, 4.12
    integrity, 4.9
    objectivity, 4.8
    reputation, 4.10
    resources, 4.11
    risk, 4.13
  fees, 4.12, 4.14
  initial contact
    advertising, 4.5
    direct approach, 4.3
    referrals, 4.2
    tendering, 4.4
  introduction, 4.1
  letter of engagement, 4.23
    continuing engagements, 4.25
    new engagements, 4.24
  professional handover, 4.15
    make contact with the outgoing
        firm, 4.17
    receive and consider information
        from outgoing auditor, 4.18
    request permission from client to
        communicate, 4.16
    review predecessor auditor's
        working papers, 4.19
client relationships, acceptance and
  continuance of, 14.8
client system and controls, evaluation
  of, 5.24
  general IT controls, 5.10
'close calls', 11.23
cold reviews, 14.14
communication
  quality management, 14.11

communication – *contd*
  with group auditor, 13.12
  with management, 8.54
    communication process, 8.57
    effectiveness of two-way
        communication, 8.58
    significant findings from audit, 8.56
    those charged with governance,
        8.55, 13.19
company books and records, access to,
  1.8
comparative information, 10.35
compilation engagements, 15.6
compliance factors, impact of, 5.13
component auditors
  expressing opinion by, 13.18
  relying on work of, 13.11
components, 13.3
computer-assisted audit techniques, 8.52
confidentiality, 3.2
consolidation, auditing, 13.13–13.14
consultation documents, 2.8
contentious matters, 14.23
continuing professional development,
  2.12
control risk, 5.18–5.20
corresponding figures, 10.35
corroboration, 7.20
credibility, 4.14
cut-off errors, 6.9

D

data analytics, 7.19, 8.51
  advantages and challenges of, 8.52
  use for audit sampling, 8.53
deferred tax assets, 5.9
deficiencies, responding to, 14.12
detection risk, 5.11, 5.19
differences of opinion, 14.23
directional testing, 7.33
  stock, 7.35
  testing balance sheet in both
      directions, 7.36
  testing profit and loss account in both
      directions, 7.37
  use of, 7.34
disclaimer of auditor's opinion, 12.3,
  12.6, 12.15
  management-imposed limitations,
      12.16

disclosure
  material uncertainties relating to going
    concern, 11.24
  materiality, 6.3
  planning audit of, 6.13
discussion papers, 2.8
documentation, 3.8
  group audits, 13.23–13.24
  quality management, 14.13
due care, 3.2
due diligence
  client acceptance, 4.6
  due diligence engagements, 15.7
  due diligence report, 15.13
  enhanced due diligence, 4.21
  financial due diligence, 15.9
  legal due diligence, 15.11
  operational due diligence, 15.10
  organisational due diligence, 15.8
  people due diligence, 15.12
duty of care, 2.13

E
economic factors, impact of, 5.13
efficiency, 6.9
emphasis of matter (EOM), 11.10–11.14
  key audit matters and, 11.14
  placement of paragraph in auditor's
    report, 11.13
  when paragraph appropriate, 11.12
  when paragraph inappropriate, 11.11
employees
  calculating average number of, 1.3
  screening, 4.21
employment relationships and ethics,
  3.14
  client staff joining audit firm, 3.16
  engagement team members joining an
    audit client, 3.15
  family member is employed by audit
    client, 3.17
  partners joining an audit client, 3.15
engagement quality reviewer, 14.14–
  14.15
engagement quality reviews, 14.1, 14.14
  documentation, 14.19
  engagement quality reviewer, 14.14–
    14.15
  ethical requirements, compliance with,
    14.16

engagement quality reviews – *contd*
  requirements, 14.18
  scope, 14.17
enhanced due diligence, 4.21
environmental reporting, 15.14
errors
  cut-off errors, 6.9
  fraud versus, 9.2
  posting errors, 6.9
  trivial error, 6.7
Ethical Standard, 2.8
  changes to, 3.34
    application of prohibitions to
      different categories of entity,
      3.38
    breach reporting, 3.36
    fees, 3.40
    financial interests of individuals,
      3.42
    non-audit and additional services,
      3.41
    objective, reasonable and informed
      third-party test, 3.37
    other entities of public interest
      (OEPI) category, 3.35
    partner staff and rotation, 3.39
  group audits, 13.11
ethics
  changes to Ethical Standard *see*
    Ethical Standard
  client acceptance, 4.7
    fees, 4.12
    integrity, 4.9
    objectivity, 4.8
    reputation, 4.10
    resources, 4.11
    risk, 4.13
  employment relationships, 3.14–
    3.17
    client staff joining audit firm, 3.16
    engagement team members joining
      an audit client, 3.15
    family member is employed by
      audit client, 3.17
    partners joining an audit client,
      3.15
  fees, 3.25
    client acceptance, 4.12
    fee dependency, 3.26
    overdue fees, 3.27

Index

ethics – *contd*
  financial, business, employment and
      personal relationships, 3.9
    business relationships, 3.13
    employment relationships, 3.14—
        3.17
    external consultants involved in
        audit engagement, 3.20
    family and other personal
        relationships, 3.19
    financial interest held by firm
        pension schemes, 3.11
    financial interests held as trustee,
        3.10
    governance roles, 3.18
    guarantees, 3.12
    loans, 3.12
  fundamental principles, 3.2
    advocacy threat, 3.3, 3.4
    confidentiality, 3.2
    documentation, 3.8
    documenting safeguards on audit
        file, 3.5
    due care, 3.2
    familiarity threat, 3.3, 3.4
    identifying ethical threats, 3.3
    inadvertent breaches, 3.5
    integrity, 3.2, 4.9
    intimidation threat, 3.3, 3.4
    management threat, 3.3, 3.4
    objectivity, 3.2, 4.8
    overall conclusion, 3.7
    professional behaviour, 3.2
    professional competence, 3.2
    responding to ethical threats, 3.3, 3.4
    self-interest threat, 3.3, 3.4
    self-review threat, 3.3, 3.4
    use of other firms in the
        engagement, 3.6
  gifts and hospitality, 3.29
  governance roles, 3.18
  introduction, 3.1
  litigation, 3.30
  long association with an audit client,
      3.21
    engagement quality reviews and
        other key partners involved in
        the audit, 3.22
    other partners and staff in senior
        positions, 3.23

ethics – *contd*
  long association with an audit client–
      contd
    public interest entities and long
        association, 3.24
  non-audit services, 3.31
    communication with those charged
        with governance, 3.32
    documentation, 3.33
  quality management, 14.7, 14.16
  remuneration and evaluation policies,
      3.28
  reputation, 4.10
  resources, 4.11
  risk, 4.13
  small entities
    advocacy threat – non-audit
        services, 3.48
    disclosure requirements, 3.50
    economic dependence, 3.44
    exemptions, 3.46
    management threat – non-audit
        services, 3.47
    non-audit services, 3.45
    persons approved as statutory
        auditor joining audited entity,
        3.49
    provisions available for audits of,
        3.43
evolution gap, 9.22
exemption statements, 1.5
exemption thresholds, 1.3
expectations gap
  auditor's report (unmodified opinion),
      11.9
  closing, 9.19
  evolution gap, 9.22
  going concern and, 10.33
  knowledge gap, 9.20
  performance gap, 9.21
experts, use of, 8.2
  agreeing work to be performed, 8.6
  assessing competency, capability and
      objectivity of auditor's expert,
      8.5
  carrying out evaluation of expert's
      work, 8.7
  determining need for auditor's expert,
      8.3
  establishing audit procedures, 8.4

extended external reporting, guidance on, 15.15
external confirmation, 7.17, 8.30
  carrying out confirmation request, 8.31
  client refuses to agree to confirmation request, 8.32
  evaluating the results of, 8.33
external consultants involved in audit engagement, 3.20

F
failure to report (money laundering), 4.20
fair value, 5.9
familiarity threat, 3.3, 3.4
family relationships and ethics, 3.9, 3.19
fees
  client acceptance, 4.12, 4.14
  ethics, and, 3.25, 4.12
    changes to Ethical Standard, 3.40
    fee dependency, 3.26
    overdue fees, 3.27
file reviews, pre- and post-issuance, 14.12
financial due diligence, 15.9
financial factors, impact of, 5.13
financial information
  historical financial information, providing assurance on, 15.17
  prospective financial information, providing assurance on, 15.18
  obtaining evidence, 15.20
  reporting, 15.21
  written representations, 15.19
financial reporting
  financial reporting standards, 5.6
  fraudulent, 9.5
  material uncertainties relating to going concern, 11.20
  reference to applicable financial reporting framework, 11.7
Financial Reporting Council (FRC), 1.1, 2.1
  audit planning, 5.2
  Audit, Reporting and Governance Authority, transition to, 2.3
  Bulletins, 2.7, 11.2
  competent authority, 2.2
  data analytics, 8.52
  Ethical Standard *see* Ethical Standard
  International Standards on Auditing, 2.2

Financial Reporting Council (FRC)– *contd*
  Key Audit Matters, 11.25
  Practice Notes, 2.7
  public interest entities, 1.1, 2.2
  publications, 2.8
  quality management, 14.2
  root cause analysis, 14.12
financial statements, 5.4
  assertion levels, 5.4, 5.23
  audit evidence, 7.3
  financial statement assertions, 5.21
  financial statement levels, 5.4, 5.22
  materiality, 6.4
  misstatements, 5.10, 5.20, 10.5, 10.6, 10.10
  notes to, 10.18
findings
  evaluation of, 14.12
  significant findings, 8.56
firm-wide risk assessment, 4.21
fraud
  audit planning, 6.18
    auditor's risk assessment procedures, 6.19
    related parties, 6.21
    responding to assessed risks of material misstatement due to fraud, 6.20
  auditor's responsibilities, 9.12–9.16
    auditor's risk assessment procedures, 9.13
    conditions which may indicate that document not authentic, 9.14
    fraud and revenue recognition, 9.15
    reporting in the auditor's report, 9.16
  audits as deterrent, 4.14
  closing expectations gap, 9.19
    evolution gap, 9.22
    knowledge gap, 9.20
    performance gap, 9.21
  error compared, 9.2
  introduction, 9.1
  laws and regulations, 9.23
  non-compliance with laws and regulations, 9.23
    audit procedures to address, 9.24
    reporting identified or suspected, 9.25

Index

fraud – *contd*
  professional scepticism, 9.18
  reasons for committing fraud, 9.6
    motivation, 9.9
    opportunity, 9.7
    rationalisation, 9.8
  responsibilities in relation to fraud,
    9.10
    auditor's responsibilities, 9.12–9.16
    management's responsibilities, 9.11
  responding to suspected or
    identified fraud, 9.17
  types of fraud, 9.3
    fraudulent financial reporting, 9.5
    misappropriation of assets, 9.4

G
gifts and ethics, 3.29
glossary of terms, 2.8
going concerns, 5.9, 10.23
  audit procedures over cash flow
    forecast, 10.28
  auditor's report (modified opinion),
    12.17
    deterioration in operating results
      after balance sheet date, 12.20
    going concern basis inappropriate,
      12.18
    inadequate disclosure relating to,
      12.19
  auditor's report (unmodified opinion),
    11.19–11.24
    auditor reporting issues, 11.21
    'close calls', 11.23
    financial reporting issues, 11.20
    inadequate disclosure, 11.24
    placement of paragraph within
      report, 11.22
  auditor's responsibilities relating to,
    10.26
  doubts exist about entity's ability to
    continue as, 10.27
  expectations gap, and, 10.33
  going concern basis of accounting
    appropriate, 10.30, 10.31
  going concern basis of accounting not
    appropriate, 10.32
  management reporting on, 10.25
  material uncertainties, 10.31
  no material uncertainties, 10.30

going concerns– *contd*
  reporting on, 10.29
  responsibilities in respect of, 10.24
governance and ethics *see* ethics
group auditors
  communication with, 13.12
  objectives of, 13.2
group audits
  accepting group audit, 13.4
  analytical procedures, 13.14
  audit evidence, evaluating sufficiency
    and appropriateness of, 13.15–
    13.16
  communication with those charged
    with governance of group, 13.19
  component auditors
    expressing opinion by, 13.18
    relying on work of, 13.11
  components, 13.3
  consolidation, auditing, 13.13–13.14
  documentation, 13.23–13.24
  internal controls, communicating
    deficiencies in, 13.17
  international groups, 13.21
  introduction, 13.1
  planning group audit, 13.5–13.10
  support letters, 13.20
  transnational audits, 13.22
groups of companies, 1.3
  Companies Act 2006 requirements, 1.3
guarantees, 3.12

H
handover, professional, 4.15
  make contact with the outgoing firm, 4.17
  receive and consider information from
    outgoing auditor, 4.18
  request permission from client to
    communicate, 4.16
  review predecessor auditor's working
    papers, 4.19
haphazard selection, 7.28
historical financial information,
    providing assurance on, 15.17
hospitality and ethics, 3.29
hot reviews, 14.14
human resources, 14.10

I
inadvertent breaches, 3.5

inconsistencies, material, 11.16–11.17
independent audit function within firm,
    4.21
information and communication, 14.11
inherent risk, 5.7, 5.11, 5.17, 5.20
inquiry, 7.17
inspections
    of assets, 7.17
    of records and documents, 7.17
Institute of Chartered Accountants in
    England and Wales (ICAEW), 1.1
    Code of Ethics, 14.7
    compilation engagements, 15.6
    continuing professional development,
        2.12
    money laundering, 1.10
    non-PIEs and non-listed entities, 2.2
    regulation of auditors, 2.9, 2.10
integrity, 3.2, 4.9
intellectual resources, 14.10
interest rates, increases in, 5.9
interim audits, 7.38
internal audits, 8.34
    documentation, 8.37
    reviewing work of internal audit, 8.36
    using work of internal audit, 8.35
internal controls, reporting deficiencies
    in, 8.59
    communication via letter of comment,
        8.60
    group audits, 13.17
International Auditing and Assurance
    Standards Board (IAASB), 1.1, 2.1,
    11.3, 15.15
International Ethics Standards Board for
    Accountants (IESBA), 2.1
International Federation of Accountants
    (IFAC), 1.1, 2.1
international groups, 13.21
International Standards on Auditing
    (ISAs), 1.1, 2.1, 2.2
    ISAs (UK)
        accounting estimates, 8.38, 8.39
        adoption of new standards, 11.3
        agreeing terms of audit engagement,
            4.22
        audit completion, 10.1
        audit planning, 5.1
        client acceptance, 4.1
        communications, 8.54, 8.58

International Standards on Auditing
    (ISAs)– *contd*
    ISAs (UK) – *contd*
        development of, 2.4, 2.6
        documentation, 13.24
        due diligence, 4.6
        going concerns, 11.19–11.23
        group audits, 13.1, 13.8
        key audit matters, 8.17
        letters of engagement, 4.23, 4.24
        materiality, 13.10
        modified audit opinion, 12.11
        quality management, 14.1, 14.20
        work of auditor's expert, 8.2
International Standards on Quality
    Management (ISQMs), 2.1
    adoption of new standards, 11.3
    development of ISQMs (UK), 2.4, 2.5
International Sustainability Standards
    Board
    sustainability disclosure standards,
        15.14
intimidation threat, 3.3, 3.4
Irish Auditing and Accounting
    Supervisory Authority (IAASA)
    continuing professional development,
        2.12

K
key audit matters (KAMs)
    auditor's report (unmodified opinion),
        11.25–11.28
    communicating KAMs, 11.26
    emphasis of matter (EOM), 11.10–
        11.14
    ethical considerations, 11.28
    presenting KAMs in auditor's
        report, 11.27
key performance indicators, 15.16
knowledge gap, 9.20

L
large companies, 1.3
    Companies Act 2006 requirements, 1.3
leadership, 14.6
legal due diligence, 15.11
legislation, impact of, 5.13
letter of engagement, 4.23
    continuing engagements, 4.25
    new engagements, 4.24

limited assurance engagements, 15.4
limiting auditor's liability, 11.29
liquidity ratios, 6.9
litigation, 3.30, 8.26
   management or lawyer refusal, 8.27
   written representation, 8.28
loans, 3.12
long association with audit client
   ethics, 3.21
      engagement quality reviews and
         other key partners involved in
         audit, 3.22
      other partners and staff in senior
         positions, 3.23
      public interest entities and long
         association, 3.24

M
management commentary, 15.16
management threat, 3.3, 3.4
management's responsibilities for fraud,
   9.11
market risk, 5.13
materiality, 6.2
   account balances, 6.3
   audit risk, 6.6
   auditor's report (modified opinion)
      material and pervasive matters,
         12.9, 12.10
      material but not pervasive matters,
         12.8
   auditor's report (unmodified opinion)
      material inconsistencies, 11.16–11.17
      material uncertainties relating to
         going concern, 11.19–11.24
   classes of transactions, 6.3
   disclosures, 6.3
   financial statement, 6.4
   group audits, 13.9–13.10
   misstatements, 10.8
   performance, 6.5
   trivial error, 6.7
medium-sized companies
   Companies Act 2006 requirements, 1.3
members' meetings, access to, 1.8
micro-entities
   audit exemption thresholds, 1.2, 1.3
   audit request by parent company, 1.5
   deeming provisions, 1.6
   voluntary audits, 1.5

misappropriation of assets, 9.4
misleading auditors, 1.8
misstatements
   evaluation of, 10.2
   identified misstatements, 10.4–10.11
      audit plan, effect on, 10.7
      audit strategy, effect on, 10.7
      management refusal to correct,
         10.11
      materiality of, 10.8
      misstatements in financial
         statements, 10.6
      recording misstatements, 10.5
      reporting to management, 10.9
      request that misstatements are
         corrected, 10.10
   types of misstatements, 10.3
   uncorrected misstatements, 10.12–
      10.16
      evaluating effect of uncorrected
         misstatements, 10.14
      reporting uncorrected
         misstatements, 10.15
      requesting written representation,
         10.16
      revisiting materiality levels, 10.13
monetary unit sampling, 7.28, 7.32
money laundering
   Anti-Money Laundering Regulations,
      1.10, 4.21
   client acceptance, 4.20
   Anti-Money Laundering
      Regulations 2017, 4.21
   suspicious activity reports, 1.10, 9.17
money laundering compliance principle
   (MLCP), 4.21
money laundering reporting officer, 1.1,
   4.20, 9.17
monitoring audit quality, 2.10, 14.2,
   14.12

N
negative assurance, 15.17
non-adjusting events, 10.20
non-audit services
   ethics, 3.31
      changes to Ethical Standard, 3.41
      communication with those charged
         with governance, 3.32
      documentation, 3.33

non-compliance with laws and
    regulations (NOCLAR), 2.13, 9.23
    audit procedures to address, 9.24
    reporting identified or suspected, 9.25
non-sampling risk, 5.19, 7.26
non-statistical sampling, 7.27

O
objective, reasonable and informed third-
    party test
    changes to Ethical Standard, 3.37
objectivity, 3.2, 4.8
observation, 7.17
opening balances, 8.14, 10.34
    client requires audit for first time, 8.16
    consistency of accounting policies,
      8.19
    current auditor audited previous year's
      financial statements, 8.20
    key audit matters, 8.17
    opening balances contain
      misstatements, 8.18
    prior year auditor expressed modified
      audit opinion, 8.15
operational due diligence, 15.10
opinion of auditor *see also* auditor's
    report (modified opinion); auditor's
    report (unmodified opinion), 1.9
    prior year auditor expressed modified
      opinion, 8.15
organisational due diligence, 15.8
other entities of public interest (OEPI)
    changes to Ethical Standard, 3.35
outsourcing quality management, 14.10

P
pension schemes
    financial interest held by, 3.11
people due diligence, 15.12
performance
    engagement performance, 14.9
    performance gap, 9.21
    performance materiality, 6.5
    performance reviews, 14.22
personal relationships and ethics, 3.9,
    3.19
physical factors, impact of, 5.13
planning audits *see* audit planning
political factors, impact of, 5.13
politically exposed persons, 4.21

posting errors, 6.9
practising certificate, 2.9
prior period's financial statements not
    audited, 10.36
prior year evidence, 7.13
private companies
    appointment of auditor, 1.11
proceeds of crime offences, 4.20
professional behaviour, 3.2
professional bodies
    qualification as member of, 2.10
    regulation by, 2.9
    role of, 1.1
professional competence, 3.2
professional indemnity insurance, 2.11
professional judgement, applying, 7.21
professional scepticism, 9.18
profitability, 6.9
prospective financial information,
    providing assurance on, 15.18
    obtaining evidence, 15.20
    reporting, 15.21
    written representations, 15.19
public companies
    appointment of auditor, 1.11
public interest entities
    letters of engagement, 4.25
    long association with audit client, 3.24
    monitoring of auditing firms, 1.1, 2.10
Practice Notes, 2.7

Q
qualified audit, 1.8
qualified auditor's opinion, 12.3, 12.4,
    12.12
    auditor appointed after reporting date,
      12.13
quality management
    cold reviews, 14.14
    engagement level, 14.20
      acceptance of audit engagement,
        14.21
      continuance of audit engagement,
        14.21
      differences of opinion, 14.23
      difficult or contentious matters,
        14.23
      managing and achieving audit
        quality, 14.24
      review of performance, 14.22

quality management – *contd*
  failure of quality management system,
    14.25
  hot reviews, 14.14
  introduction, 14.1
  ISQM (UK) 1 (quality management),
    14.1, 14.3
    client relationships, acceptance and
      continuance of, 14.8
    deficiencies, responding to, 14.12
    documentation, 14.13
    engagement performance, 14.9
    ethical requirements, 14.7
    evaluation of findings, 14.12
    file reviews, pre- and post-issuance,
      14.12
    governance, 14.6
    human resources, 14.10
    information and communication,
      14.11
    intellectual resources, 14.10
    leadership, 14.6
    monitoring, 14.12
    quality objectives, establishing, 14.4
    remediation process, 14.12
    resources, 14.10
    risk assessment process, 14.5
    root cause analysis, FRC thematic
      review on, 14.12
    service providers, 14.10
    specific engagements, acceptance
      and continuance of, 14.8
    technological resources, 14.10
  ISQM (UK) 2 (engagement quality
    reviews), 14.1, 14.14
    documentation, 14.19
    engagement quality reviewer,
      14.14–14.15
    ethical requirements, compliance
      with, 14.16
    requirements of review, 14.18
    scope of reviews, 14.17
  monitoring audit quality, 14.2

R
random selection, 7.28
ratio analysis, 6.8
reasonable assurance, 2.13, 11.1, 11.9, 15.1
  reasonable assurance engagements,
    15.4

reasonableness, 6.8
recalculation, 7.17
Recognised Qualifying Bodies (RQB),
  2.9
Recognised Supervisory Body (RSB),
  2.9, 2.10
referrals, 4.2
regulators, role of
  introduction, 2.1
regulatory framework
  Anti-Money Laundering Regulations,
    1.10
  auditors
    appointment, 1.11
    duties, 1.9
    resignation, 1.12–1.13
    rights, 1.8
  Companies Act 2006 requirements, 1.2
    audit exemption statement, 15
    audit exemption thresholds, 1.3
    calculating average number of
      employees, 1.3
    determining size of company, 1.4
    groups of companies, 1.3
    large companies, 1.3
    medium-sized companies, 1.3
    micro-entities, 1.2, 1.3, 1.5
    micro-entity audit, 1.6
    small entities, 1.2, 1.3, 1.5
    two out of three rule, 1.4
  introduction, 1.1
relevance of audit evidence, 7.9
reliability of audit evidence, 7.8
remediation process, 14.12
remuneration and evaluation policies,
  3.28
reperformance, 7.17
reporting by exception, 1.9, 11.8
reporting deficiencies in internal
  controls, 8.59
  communication via letter of comment,
    8.60
reputation, 4.10
resignation of auditor, 1.12
  statement of reasons, 1.13
resources
  adequacy of, 4.11
  quality management, 14.10
responsible individual, 2.9
return ratios, 6.9

revenue recognition and fraud, 9.15
review engagements, 15.3
  negative conclusions, 15.3
risk, 4.13
  accounting estimates, 8.39
  aggregation risk, 13.10
  audit evidence, 7.22
  firm-wide risk assessment, 4.21
  fraud, 9.13
  group audits, 13.7–13.8
  responses to assessed risks, 5.1, 5.12, 7.2–7.4, 8.44
  risk assessment phase, 5.1, 5.10, 5.11
  risk assessment process, 14.5
  substantive procedures, 5.12
  tests of controls, 5.12
root cause analysis, FRC thematic review on, 14.12

S
safeguards, documenting on audit file, 3.5
sampling risk, 5.19
Scope and Authority of Audit and Assurance Pronouncements, 2.8
search engines, 4.3
segment information, 8.29
self-interest threat, 3.3, 3.4
self-review threat, 3.3, 3.4
service organisations, use of, 8.8
  fraud, 8.12
  non-compliance with laws and regulations, 8.12
  responding to assessed risks, 8.11
  service organisations and auditor's report, 8.13
  sources of information, 8.10
  understanding nature and significance of services provided, 8.9
service providers, 14.10
  service provider quality statement, 14.16
shareholders
  removal of auditor from office, 1.12
  request for audit, 1.2
small companies
  audit exemption thresholds, 1.2–1.4
  audit request by parent company, 1.5
  voluntary audits, 1.5

small entities and ethics
  advocacy threat – non-audit services, 3.48
  disclosure requirements, 3.50
  economic dependence, 3.44
  exemptions, 3.46
  management threat – non-audit services, 3.47
  non-audit services, 3.45
  persons approved as statutory auditor joining audited entity, 3.49
  provisions available for audits of, 3.43
social reporting, 15.14
Staff Guidance Notes, 2.8
statement of reasons, 1.13
statements of recommended practice (SORP), 11.7
statistical sampling, 7.27
statutory auditors, 2.9
  qualification as, 2.10
stock
  directional testing, 7.35
  valuation, 6.9
stock count, 8.21
  attending stock count, 8.23
  audit stock and work in progress figure, 8.24
  planning the count, 8.22
  stock held at third parties, 8.25
stratification, 7.29
subsequent events
  audit completion, 10.19
  adjusting and non-adjusting events, 10.20
  procedure where auditor has active duty, 10.21
  procedure where auditor has passive duty, 10.22
substantive procedures, 7.11, 7.15, 7.16
  sampling risk, 7.25
support letters, 13.20
suspicious activity reports, 1.10, 9.17
systematic selection, 7.28

T
Task Force on Climate-related Financial Disclosures (TCFD), 15.14
technological resources, 14.10
technological risk, 5.13
tendering, 4.4

tests of control, 6.15, 7.11, 7.12, 7.14
  evaluating the results of, 7.14
  nature and extent of, 7.12
  sampling risk, 7.24
  substantive procedures and, 7.11
tests of detail, 6.16
tipping-off, 4.20
transnational audits, 13.22
trend analysis, 6.8
trivial errors, 6.7
true and fair view, 11.3–11.6
trustees, financial interests held as,
  3.10
two out of three rule, 1.4

U
understanding the entity and its
  environment, 5.4
  economic challenges, 5.9
  regulatory factors, 5.8
  sources of information, 5.5
  understanding the entity itself, 5.6
  understanding the environment in
    which the client operates, 5.7

V
voluntary audits, 1.5

W
withholding information, 1.8